THE SHAMEHOLD

By Jack R. Thornell

With

MAKESENSE

All come. Some go. Some stay. Go. Go where? To heaven some say. Heaven! If heaven, why do some stay?

While whying that Dear Reader, why this. Staying was not always my first choice... Butt-Butt! It was Makesense's. Always.

With that yet whying and with this, "I am not, I have never been, and I never expect to be... happy" stipulating you get me. A divorced me. A Mr. Negative plus me. And if you like negatarians, you'll love me. And you'll get my negative-isms, like 'em or not.

Like positively positive George, who does not. Who condemns, even hates, my nevers and nots. But, who does love my Wilma. Well actually, my used to be my, now his, Wilma. My, how I wish she was still standing next to me and standing ready to please me once more like no woman before my Wilma. Because, brother, I got the urge. The Saturday night urge. The urge most guys get most Saturday nights. Particularly, guys without partners. In particular, the guys with their hands planted, with their urges growing and with their pockets bulging between dances at the St. Clement of Rome single and single again social in Metairie, where the anxious come to find the overanxious, where again, I am again a "hands-in" guy.

Because wonderful Wilma isn't standing next to me, and that's because of me and my pushing her away and towards good friend George. For happiness sake, her's, I rationalized then. And for stupidity's sake, mine, later I realized. Because of desire, my then desire for the tall, the thin, and the splendidly-skinned Delphine.

And now with Delphine long shed of me, with me long without the pleasure and with my pockets-a-bulging, I find myself facing George and his Wilma, concealing my Saturday night urge and challenging George with my newest negative-ism.

Haphazardly found, happiness is rare, rarely held and when held, only held haphazardly. Really George, apart from you how many real happy people are there out there and how many are real?

"Jack! Oh, Jack! Your pessimism. Its persistence. It's showing. It's ruining you and you're letting it. Man! Look at you. You're good looking. Good with conversation. Good with money. And you're very good with the ladies. Man! You got the goodies, now get happy! Because if you don't, it's your own damn fault, because happiness comes from within."

But before I can respond to a good friend, a pretty lady breaks in, takes my hands and pulls me onto the floor. And before I can get in step with the music, a new depressing thought is already dancing... Oh George, if you only knew, knew of those comings from within...

Expelled from the womb with me to me it clung, inseparable, a parasite feeding to survive, before taking root and thriving to subdue—like Kudzu—covering, then smothering its host, but unlike the sun-crazed vine, it lives in darkness, feeding on the spoils of secrecy, the stored-up kind, the kind held down deep, deep at the root. And there it flourishes. Untouchable there, even unshakeable from there and by enjoying a vantage as yet unseen it rules from there and yet, by threatening to expose its secret vantage there, it enjoys its rule all the more.

What! Enjoying secrecy more by threatening secrecy more. What anomaly. What abnormal uses, can use such divisiveness. What kind?

The kind that: Enjoys lies, the choking kind. Enjoys confidence lost and incompetence found. Enjoys pessimism plus negativism. Enjoys proving happiness is priceless and misery free. Enjoys success spilled and spilled success. Enjoys asking, with success killing you, what will failure do? Enjoys overachievers, underachieving, perfectionists imperfecting, and undertakers overtaking. Enjoys harping all day, if nothing is ever good as a child, and then nothing is ever good. Enjoys lullabying all night, "Little Jackie Boy, 'tis true, 'tis true. The joy, the joy. The missing kind. 'Twas never meant for you."

What! Who is this? This beast! This anomaly! This thing! This Joyeater…SHAME! It's a shame! Shame of father! Shame of mother! Shame of home! It's ROOT SHAME! It's my SHAME. And it's SHAME'S HOLD!

The finale of life divided by shame has often been staged on my mind. The conclusion: in concrete. The equation: Life divided by shame equals silence beginning with a bang.

Butt-Butt... "Stop!" Hold that calculator. And make sense, now that Makesense is here. And that sounds crazy. Perhaps, you miscalculated. Perhaps, your equation is flawed.

Oh, dear reader, first let me introduce Makesense. Makesense is the voice I and only I, hear. Like the voice of reason, but more personal. Like one with staying status, like kin. And sounding I imagined like my, as close to me as can be and not be me, entirely me, live-in cousin would. The one dedicated to one's making sense and keeping one's head. Thus the personalization. Thus cousin "the voice" Makesense. Born talking during my—I'd rather not be, than be here—teen years. When exactly, I can't say. That date is a blur, blurred after decades of my trying to forget those then years. And strangely now, a date that Makesense never raises. But, now, when uncertainty rises and Makesense senses it, "the voice arises and butts in. And for some time now, Makesense has been raising and butting and raising and butting and more often than not, leaving me with more than a fair split of headaches.

But back to the question, the possibility of a flawed equation, "Sorry Makesense, but in chemistry and math I made A's. So butt out."

Butt-Butt... "Wait! Perhaps then, within shame lies a flaw, even a vulnerability." "Such as?" "Such as division. Try dividing shame as shame divides as shame makes unwhole." "But how?" "By examining it, by seeing if shame can be reduced to fractions by separating root shame—the smother—from earned shame—the gnaw—and once divided, make room for peace and perhaps, even for joy."

"Geesums, Loudmouth. Lower it, it's squeamish, even such thoughts provoke guilt gnaw, and prompt shame's smother. Geesums! It's gnawing and squeezing now. No! No! You're talking war. A gut-busting war, a spill-all war. Attack shame. Invade shame's space. Cut into shame. No! No! I can't. It's too late. I'm too old and too tired to fight, even to resist. God! And with a soul already spent, what else could I owe? Isn't enough, enough? Isn't choking on shame for half a century and never able to spit it out, choking enough?"

Butt-Butt... "Wait! Why not try? What's to lose, life. But, what's to gain, a life. And please remember, Makesense has a say in this too. Remember, if you go off the deep end, Makesense goes off the deep end too. And Makesense can't swim or fly. So, for a life's sake, try.

"But, Makesense, but how?" "By stabbing shame." "With what?" "The pen." "Geesums, now that sounds crazy, no, that is crazy. Stab shame with a pen, a puny pen. But suppose I did try, I'm so full of it, I'd be overrun in seconds and smothered." "Perhaps not, not if you STAB! WITHDRAW! SQUEEZE! EXPEL! EXPOSE! Try weakening shame that way. Yeah! That's how. Expel and expose. Expel and expose.

"Do this with a pen, a puny pen, you are crazy?" "No cousin, not with a puny pen, forget puny. But with a mighty pen, the one like a Lincoln wielded at Gettysburg that day, Aug 19, 1863? Some say "that" pen was mightier than the sword. The words penned then live on and on now, while the 28,000 casualties, both Blue and Grey are merely a passing footnote in history. So cousin, puny or mighty, the choice of weapons is yours."

"Okay! Okay! I heard and for this cause I take pause for... SEEKING A NEW SOLUTION THROUGH THE POWER OF THE PEN...

PUNCTURE THE SHAMEHOLD! Flood in marvelous light charging with comprehension, illuminating, then irradiating the malignant mass. Compressing it... Liquefying it. Feel it running... pursuing darkness... from the cranium... through the neck... over the shoulder... down the arm... to the hand... and into the chamber and of the pen. There, trapped and trying to escape the light and exposure. Help! Help it! Press down! Squeeze! Expel liquefied shame! Use it.

But beware, because it's cold, it's calculated, with its specialty, suffocation of the human spirit. And be aware, shame is no respecter of person. It salutes no one. It outranks status and achievement, often confiscating both and turning them and using them as weapons for administering mercy, it's kind... Silence beginning with a bang! For the indisputable proof, look at Vince Foster, friend and regular elbow rubber with President and First Lady Clinton or look at Admiral Jeremy Boorda, the Navy's top gun. Boorda notes, Foster doesn't, to his men, "I can't bear to bring dishonor to you." His shame, being seen wearing unearned combat devices on two ribbons, each measuring half the size of a postage stamp before going overboard and drowning in shame's irony, the irony is he thought he won 'em. Where is Foster and where is Boorda? Today, resting as great shame successes.

3

Or look at the joyless Elvis or joyless Marilyn, both idolized by millions and both fall prey to life's joyless excesses. At age 42, somewhere between deprivation and gluttony and despite wealth and notoriety shame strips a heavy, a sedated Elvis and smears him with chunky peanut butter with bananas and consumes him. And at age 36, poor over-medicated but still gorgeous Marilyn, shame strips, covers with depression and anxiety to abbreviate her life, despite the loving arms of many, including the great DiMaggio and President Kennedy. Where is Elvis and where is Marilyn? Today, enshrined in the Hall of Fame, Shame's! So, if ready, dispense the toxin. See it transformed into black on white. See it exposed for examination. See if the joy eater becomes impotent when stripped, when paraded and then held bare within the boundaries of white. But be cautious because a question remains unanswered. Can shame's venom be extracted through a pen point without evoking a fatal reaction to the holder?

With the question begging for an answer, I must ask…

Pen! Oh, pen! Can out come a paragraph apart from pain or a peace apart from shame, even a sentence's worth? Pen! Oh pen! Give me peace, the peace of a life. Or give me peace, the peace after-a-life. PEN! OH, PEN! Impale the beast! Draw its black gore. Transfuse its vile essence onto the purity of white. PEN! OH, PEN! MAKE YOUR MARK. MY HAND IS YOURS.

I have suspected for decades now that it is improbable, even impossible to be in a space of time and a state of mind again when I could consciously choose life over death. Now after squeezing the pen, the prospect of such shakes my spirit strong enough to dismiss my sleep, leaving me exhausted and alone but wide awake BEHIND A DOOR NAILED SHUT.

The contemplation of death ending my shame is long since a preoccupation, a self-defense mechanism, a loaded gun with its trigger inside my head, always at my disposal.

Cremate me! Recycle me as kitty litter, perhaps a less painful existence and for sure, a relief for some furry-purring creature. But now, can a new attitude come late? Can it be possible to live with a shame-filled self, emancipated? With mid-life crisis, conquered? With disintegration of family, accepted? Or with any possibility of enjoying a peaceful ride in the future without "the gnaw" and "the smother" accompanying me and playing bumper cars inside my head while never taking a break or giving a breather.

And yet, PEN, look at me. Tall, dark and handsome with a Pulitzer Prize on the wall. Still lucky with the ladies. Still left with money after the divorce split… and I even mingled with the King—Elvis Presley. So then, why must life be the downside—THE THREAT—and death be the upside—THE WELCOME?

However, in retrospect, during the time of youth, when although imprisoned by poverty and shame I pleaded life's case. Although not audibly, my cry only God could hear and my fear only I could feel, THE NIGHT DEATH WELCOMED…

It is past midnight in the summer of 1954 when sleep often falls prey to August heat. I am alone. Here, the room is stilled, not even the tiniest of fans is stirring. Here air conditioning is a dream yet experienced. The bare bulb, hanging from the ceiling head high, is cool, relieved hours before by illumination flowing in from a power pole and pouring across the bed. The precious light is a gift, a seen blessing, considering my dread of the dark. A dread so strong it

4

compels me to sleep backed down, with my eyes up, always set to spring. Something stirs! Shut eyes spring. Someone! Something! Is above me, towering above my bed. Geesums! It's Uncle John… Crazy Uncle John… his features, now reflecting the window light, are appearing. Now, I can see clearly. His sickly grin is growing. His arm is in motion, moving upward, then hesitating. There's something in his hand, glistening, Geesums! It's scissors. I see scissors. Thrusting downward towards my chest, racing my eyes shut… before the blow strikes… and before fear freezes over cold sweat, turning it and me into a solidified state and unable even to blink.

With seconds creeping, with thoughts streaking, with the possibility of another strike, of the sufficiency of the first, stiffened, I wait, I wait, I wait. Until finally, eternity gives way and I manage to crack my eyelids ever so slightly, then focus my gaze but five inches from my face. Geesums! There! There! The glistening scissors stood… protruding perfectly perpendicular from my chest… moving up … down… up and down… accompanying rapid heart beats… appearing to take life… with finger holds resembling plucked eye sockets facing me, as if choosing replacements.

Horror stricken, again my eyes slam shut, again demanding darkness, again the only defense. Unable to scream, even whisper, I manage a prayerful petition. "Please God! Let me live. Withdraw the blades. I'll be better. Do better. Let me grow up. I'll become a preacher man. Your preacher man. God! Please! Please! I PROMISE. I PROMISE. I PROMISE. Please, let me live."

After waiting and waiting for a reply and after there isn't one, with my eyes still shut and with my status still unsure, I force my hands up to my chest to feel for blades and to feel for blood, but found neither, nor is any pain felt. My eyes spring open and I find… an absence of scissors… and an absence of Crazy Uncle John. Only thick perspiration remains, covering an undernourished frame filled with fright now abounding within it. Above the bed, the suspended bare bulb swings to and fro, to and fro, telling of a past and a disturbed presence.

Finally, the disturbed swinging stops. And again the room is stilled. Except for two eyes straining to see… anyone or anything… a crazy man sneaking or a shadow creeping. Except for the two ears exerting to hear… anyone or anything… a door cracking or the floor creaking. Now backed down holding my must see from position, I feel and find the excrement of torridity an ally gluing me in place with thoughts exploding… am I dreaming now or was I dreaming then?

And then, movement! Hands reach down, grabbing the covers, pulling them and crushing them up against my chin. With arms following, folding and forming a cross above my chest. Perhaps now, the scissors if returned, won't, can't penetrate both wrists and bedding. With that the only comforting thought alive, comes the urgency to urinate. But I can't. I can't move, even budge. Fear holds me. To arise, to try, I fear to find the absence of blades but imagined. But, with the pressure of expanding kidneys comes relief. The growing pain I use to preserve consciousness and to hold back sleep until daylight comes to determine my fate.

"Jack! Jack!" The alarm sounds. It's not coming from heaven. Of this, I'm sure. Not now, not ever. This I know because I know that voice well, too well. Most times, with others present, the sounding of it causes me such embarrassment, even to shudder, while my mind tries to turn it off.

5

"Jack! For heaven sakes, get up! Hurry up! Come here!" But first, before my body can budge, my eyes move to make an examination, fixing on my chest and finding… no blades! No blood! "Jack! Jack!" "Mamma, I hear you. I'm coming." Although exhausted, I find energy enough to power myself up and out of bed. While still holding that urgent need, I answer the summons and enter the room, the one adjoining mine. And I find mother standing by the bed, the bed she shares with Crazy Uncle John. I stop short, about ten feet, but it's close enough to see the fear spreading across her face. "Come closer boy," she directs, moving me to her side. Now, with my full attention, she reaches down, takes hold of and raises the pillow. Crazy Uncle John's pillow. "Look here! See these," she points. Then I see, see the object of concern. Geesums! It's scissors! Long, shiny, silver sharpened scissors. The scissors I saw last night. My heart jumps to my throat, causing choking. My hands jump to my chest, covering and protecting. Without words, but while exchanging worried looks, we feel the floor giving. Crazy Uncle John is coming, coming in from the porch. Before he can enter and catch us there, mother drops the pillow, covering her discovery and backs away from the bed. Meanwhile my feet retreat, retaking the steps back into my room, where my hand takes hold of and shuts the door behind. God! For a lock, I'd give my soul. But then, that would be a waste because Crazy Uncle John abhors locks, forbids locks. Because when making rounds and gawking in the night, Crazy Uncle John finds locked doors disturbing, even insufferable. Now his voice is coming through the door, it's mumbling something to momma. Hearing his voice is torturous, but this I bear, but seeing his face, with his sickly grin, this I can't bear, not so soon, not now, not with his scissors so handy.

After, and about last night, not a word is ever spoken, not to mother, not to a living soul, not even whispered, even to God. Not of the thrust. Not of the fear. Not of the prayer. And not of the promise. Instead over the years THE NIGHTMARE and THE REALITY, mix and mix inside my head becoming inseparable, and finally, indistinguishable. With fear standing guard, commanding silence about that night—the night the scissors stood and death welcomed—until now, until released… THROUGH THE POWER OF THE PEN.

Many times over, over many years, I grew to regret the impetuous plea born of a pip-squeak unschooled in religion or on life. Often asking myself, "Why not let the scissors stand, cutting short those early years of poverty and shame and sparing these later years of the guilt of plenty, the joyless plenty."

With that life or death question still ruminating, the pen drops. Geesum cousin, that's a scary story, but it didn't kill you to spill it, did it? Just kind of eased out, didn't it. So, cousin, pick up the pen and give SHAME another STAB!" "Makesense your mouth never ceases to amaze. Hell! Easy! Easy for who? For you? But for me, the living of it then, and the reliving of it now, wasn't, isn't easy. And you should know, but for your absence there, where was your mouth then during those hungry days of biscuits, sugar syrup and less? I'll tell you. Shut tight, hiding out, not talking, not helping to make some sense of it. And now, with you and I knee deep in gravy… feeding at my expense… you scream… stab it again. Cousin, what kind of kinship is that? I'll tell that too. The missing kind."

"Oh dear cousin, you're right and the why of it, perhaps, that will be the subject of another story for another time. But Makesense is here now for this story. So please forgive for then."

"Oh Makesense, now your shame is showing. And you're playing dirty too. You know I'm a Christian now. And you know I must forgive every voice that asks, even yours. And, so cousin Makesense, I do. I forgive, so here, take my hanky and use it, since you use everything else of mine and dry those tears. But, as I pick up the pen, please tell me where to begin?"

"Cousin, most say that the beginning is a good place." "Well, then, I will. I'll pick up the pen and stab the joy eater, but remember… about my beginning… your beginning… our beginning… nothing was good."

Life, poverty and shame begin for me at Big Charity, exalted by Vicksburg as the last resort for the underprivileged. Here, hills are steep and steeper. Automobile brakes pedal life or death. Below the hospital and the hills the big Mississippi runs. Muddy, wide and deep, while its ferocious current churns, eating away the soil supporting the hills, and taking it away and with it and all too often, another poor soul, good swimmer or not.

Surrounding Big Charity, a sprawling 1300 acre park stretches, commemorating the fall of the Confederate stronghold. The ground is green and lush with vegetation springing up from the enriched compost, now the beneficiary of conflicting wills, bequeathing decay over dishonor. Above their contributions stand thousands upon thousands of plan gray markers and upon many is chiseled "unknown." A final testament to The Blue and The Gray buried here. Again united and together enriching Mother Earth—the clay and the sand—with their differences. But today the Civil War isn't an issue here. That war is over. Today I am. And my war is just beginning.

Inside Big Charity, Dr. Nathan B. Lewis, a big man with a gentle nature, bends down and feels the forehead of his patient, Myrtis. It's sweaty and it's obvious, by the moaning, the patient's in pain. "Now, now, Mrs. Thornell, hold on. It'll be getting better soon… be over soon," the good doctor reassures. But recoiling from the misery of the moment, she knows better. At 35, she ain't no fool, already feeling the pressure of another mouth to feed with few means for doing it. Thinking, God! Ain't things supposed to be letting up, even just a bit, instead of pressing down so hard, always pressing down. "God! It hurts so bad," she cries, "My God, my God."

"Calm… calm yourself Mrs. Thornell. Hold on… just a few minutes more." Lewis comforts, "It's almost time. It's almost here."

Minutes later with the labor done, Myrtis looks up to a healthy eight pound boy asking, "Boy! Where'd you get all that hair? So long… thick… black." And then she reaches for and recovers the two quarters from under her pillow, then squeezes them and secures them in her hand. Proof you don't get much poorer than us, least not so's one could detect. Any poorer and we'd be downright undetectable. "Doctor Lewis, this boy, all this hair. Ain't he a sight. Lord have mercy."

So, on August 29, 1939 at 11:40a.m., Jack Randolph Thornell became the third of three, but the first to see the inside of any medical facility. Coming out, like all before, kicking and screaming with present whereabouts unknown or future whereabouts as yet considered. And yet, if this very hairy baby boy had been blessed with a subliminal blink of an afternoon for winning a Pulitzer, an afternoon worse than most, an afternoon closer to self-destruction than most and if previewed with the agony accompanying failure yet realized or with the torture of waiting and watching for shame to come out and cut the heart out of joy, then the mighty Sampson would come out a loser in a tug-of-war to extract this very hairy boy from the womb whole. The Prize, the blessing: Avoidance. But then for the Thornells, prizes and blessings are far and away and… unreachable.

While making patient rounds and passing up the nursery, Dr. Lewis abruptly stops, turns about and walks back to and goes into the nursery. Despite his thick glasses, it was easy to pick out the crib holding the hairiest of babies. The one now screaming for recognition. Quickly, Lewis moves to the child, stops, then bending close and looking as if admiring his handiwork. Finished, he starts walking away, then stops, turns about and returns to the crib. Closer this time, bending closer, hesitating, and looking longer before leaving the room and perhaps, thinking himself alone with his somewhat peculiar behavior going unnoticed.

"It was an unusual occurrence, most unusual," the duty nurse observed during a conversation with Myrtis. "I have never seen Dr. Nathan B. Lewis drawn to a healthy child like that. Not for so long. And then leave, and then return, for a second look, perhaps, it was the hair, all that hair that attracted him. It must have been. Why, he was so captured by the child he didn't even notice me sitting there or admire my new permanent wave. Do you like my hairdo Mrs. Thornell?" "Yes ma'am, it's pretty, mighty pretty."

"With the evening, my first, comes my first encounter with brother Garnett—course I couldn't remember it 'till mamma told me later—who at 19 is already tall, dark and handsome— just like me later—and already a hit with the ladies, pretty or not, married or not, especially the one's hungry for fun and such. Between a greeting and a goodbye, it was at most five minutes, but it was time enough for those last two quarters to change hands. The one's he talked mamma outta, leaving us both, flat and broke with the Thornells entire net worth soon swallowed up for a beer and a song on a juke box in a little honky tonk just under the hill.

Garnett's ability to part people from their money grows with him. In his early twenties, he marries a country girl named Massey, Nell Massey she was, and then he embraces the insurance business. A smooth talker and so confident he was. Hell, under the guise of installing air conditioning, he could talk his way into Hell, collect a big down payment up front and then, without breaking a sweat talk his way back out, leaving with it still hot as blazes down there. Oh yes, a golden tongue was his alright. Like me, a high school dropout he was, but he was a head and shoulders smarter than those who weren't and he knew it. And when money come between'em, they soon knew it too. His regeneracy: Emerging from a falling down shack with some poor soul's last dollar pocketed, and bursting out with laughter without ever looking back and thinking aloud, "Damn! Ain't I good at this!" His degeneracy: Perfectionism, undying till age 55 when separated from family and from friends, he finds himself in ruins with a disability check his only support. Now, forced back to Vicksburg, forced into mother's decrepit house and forced to stay within reach of a mouth always catching him between constant criticism and annoying advice.

Time for Garnett has been costly, leaving his handsome face, disguised; his gray hair, flourishing and his last smile, inverted. This morning, shaving is finished. Teeth brushing, finished. Hair combing, finished. But Garnett isn't finished. Looking for perfection, he remains in front of the old, clouded, and cracked mirror. He picks up his favorite cowboy hat. He puts it on. He tilts it to his liking. He stares back into the mirror. He studies the face staring back.

And then… perfection shows. Calmly, from outside the mirror's periphery, a handgun reaches in and joins the reflection. Then, uses it. Takes aim. Makes steady. Then, a finger pulls. A trigger gives. A cylinder turns. A hammer hits. A shell explodes. A bullet strikes, shattering, scattering and spattering the bits and pieces of a once prized likeness across a clean kitchen floor.

Before beginning silence with a bang, the last words Garnett could hear came from mother's mouth, "Garnett! Please don't kill yourself," she pleaded while running from the house in fear, now with her own life a concern, after seeing a son with a gun at a mirror and looking more than suspicious.

Her plea, did it go unheard or was the sounding of her mouth the edge he needed? Unheard? Unheeded for sure, with Garnett's shame now, nothing more than a new stain on an old linoleum floor.

Garnett loved gardens, the vegetable kind. Loved homemade ice cream made from cranking a handle and he loved Nell and his family… but he couldn't tell 'em because Thornells never utter such nonsense. At the funeral in Monroe, up in North Louisiana, I put down five hundred dollars towards his exiting cost and, towards my guilt, while trying to say goodbye before ever saying hello. Alone with my thoughts in the funeral parlor, I relived his last visit to my Metairie home. Gaunt, looking as if shrunk by life and disappointments, he faces me with his eyes reaching into mine and observing, "You have it all, don't you? A lovely wife, two beautiful children, a nice home, a new car, a good job, and money in the bank. You have a wonderful life."

In Garnett's eyes my life, my everything, sparkled. Unaware, he couldn't see the things—The Shame Demons—like his, were also chasing me and gaining. To his observation, silence is my reply. What to say then, "Your inclination, mine." And what to say now, "Your own, sufficient."

About such, such deep things, such root things, we dare, not speak. Not the Thornells. How could we with shame always holding the microphone, always plugged into us, always deafening us with screams of, "You're nothing. Nothing, coming from nothings. Your equation: Mamma nothing plus Papa nothing equals baby nothing. You know that. You made A's in math." So, sorry brother! I wish I could have got to know you, to get close to you, to ask about your deep rooted pain, the pain we shared. And I would have, but for something standing between us, those demons. Shame's. And on many days and even more nights, I longed for Garnett's courage and the silence that begins with a bang.

Age seven is a time for saying goodbye to my deliverer. While sitting quietly and waiting patiently while mother is getting examined for a bladder infection, a too frequent occurrence, a presence is felt and I look up to find Dr. Lewis standing over me and gently patting my head. "What a fine, fine boy you have here," he said as mother enters the room, "so polite and so handsome. I'll take him Mrs. Thornell, any day, anytime." Enjoying the treatment, I send back a smile while withholding a secret wish, even call it a miracle wish if you wish, for Dr.

Nathan B. Lewis to be my father, to have some of him in me. For his second infinitesimal look at birth, the one I only heard about, and the gentle pat just registered, added up to more than I ever felt from my father. And if he ever put a quarter in my hand, I never felt it. Dr. Lewis' gentle touch now was my last contact with a kind man and a good doctor, who treated all his patients well, paying or not.

At forty, Benjamin O. Thornell, already the father of three and already divorced, is up to no good, tiptoeing, stretching and straining to see inside the Sunday school room. To say Sartaria is rural is an understatement. It's really rural and around here, the ground is flat, really flat and a true contradiction to a-high-fluting Vicksburg an hour to the south. To say it's poor here is an understatement, not the soil, cause the soil is rich, but the souls above it, a bending and scrapping over it, ain't. Here, they grow or go hungry. And the depression, the really big one, is still a good six years in the making. But here, they don't know it. Hell, they won't even see it coming, even recognize it when it comes. Hell, for these poor souls, it came already, already a gripping and already a choking.

Still tiptoeing with caution, Ben is being careful, extra careful, not to expose his intrusion while searching out a certain pair of eyes and praying to avoid those of a certain father, the Deacon Drayton Jones, a Bible teacher known for opening up certain passages—the ones filled with hell fire and brimstone—and using them to burn captive, impressionable and most importantly, still innocent, ears. The sought eyes belong to Myrtis, the pretty one, the young one in spotless white, the one trying to tune out the speaker. Finally, her gaze raises to the window. Eyes connect. Hearts leap. Smiles swap. Signals exchange. A voice vibrates. The room shakes. "Fornicators… I repeat… fornicators shall not… cannot… will not inherit the Kingdom of Heaven. Believe that! Bet your life on that! Do that and the fires of hell await!" With that vociferous vilification threatening, Ben is jarred back down to earth and heading for the cover of a nearby thicket, while Myrtis' brown eyes are jerked to the floor where she's holding 'em and hoping for an end to this lesson.

Sixteen, just. Pure, wholly. With a first kiss yet celebrated, Myrtis is anxious too, and most anxious to get on with life, her life and not the life Deacon Jones is ordering up. Chaperoned, always. A restriction rigidly enforced by parents dirt poor, but virtue rich. Except when tired eyes rest and desire awakens to overcome virtue.

"Shh… shush. Papa'll hear. And kill me. Just help me," cautioned Myrtis. Her room, without a door with only an old, tattered and faded sheet hanging there between 'em and papa's ears, quiet is of necessity. Maddie, a big sister by three years, helps by shoving Myrtis' few belongings into a washed-clean flour sack. "It's time to go. I love you. I'll miss you. You take care," Myrtis whispers without pausing for breath. "Oh Myrt, I'm not sure, sure I can stand it here with Papa and without you. Are you sure about this?" "I'm sure." Then with their hush, and with hands moving carefully and quietly the bedroom window raises. And with hugs and tears behind, Myrtis climbs through, stepping out into, then disappearing into a fading darkness, while heading towards an uncertain future.

The thought of an unseen moccasin isn't troubling. The thought of Papa awakening and interrupting a dream, is. She's TIRED, tired of… no… finished with damnation, and domination dished by a father who counts virtues more often than potatoes, even though potatoes are often so scarce. And now, figuring there's no turning back, she quickens her pace, figuring… how can longing for, even craving for something—to be held, to be kissed, to be loved—for so long, be so bad. God! Tell me... Just tell me.

Nervously, and carrying the experience of failed marriage and fatherhood, Ben paces under the big pecan, the rendezvous point. With his hands shoved down and held in the pockets of his trousers for covering the growing excitement inside. Of that pretty young thing! Of filling her need for the first time! Feeling alive, Ben plans to stay alive by planning to clear out before the deacon arises, fills his lungs with fresh morning air and after sniffing around, finds a bed half empty.

Myrtis is running now. Trying to keep up with a heart pounding for and speeding toward pleasure. And then she sees him, her Ben. And then, she's there taking to his arms, caressing and then, kissing. Hardly enough for a seasoned man but the rest will wait. But wait it must, with the daylight rushing, with the rooster soon perching and awaiting cue and with both a surety to stir the deacon up. So with the rest--womanhood and such--put to bed for now, the infatuated couple step into a skiff and use the swift current of the yellow Sunflower to carry them away before the daylight comes, before the rooster crows and before the consequences to follow.

Light breaks. Cock-a-doodle-do sounds, the deacon stirs, springs up and starts his nosing around. First, bed check, pulling back the sheet and peeking in on his beloved daughters. Only Maddie is there, but there is room to spare worry, thinking... shucks, Myrt's probably just outside and inside the privy. For a breath of fresh air, Drayton steps outside, starts pacing back and forth while, from over a shoulder, stealing looks from the direction of the privy. Ten more minutes drag by. His pacing stops and his running starts. At the privy, he nudges up against the door and shouts, "Myrt! Are you sick child?" Silence thickens. "Myrtis! Come'on outta there. Now!" With silence bursting, he grabs the door and yanks. But for a lingering smell, it's empty. Now, with a voice quivering, he cries out for his precious daughter. "Myrtis!...Myrtis!... where are you child... come to Papa." Silence. Then rushing back inside, he returns to the little room and faces down his first born. "Maddie! Maddie! Wake up." Slowly, Maddie pauses, knowing... there's going to be hell to pay and knowing... she's the only one left for the paying.

"Yes Papa." "Where's Myrtis?" Where's your baby sister? With a voice straining to speak and with tears, appearing, comes, "Oh Papa!" "Oh Papa! What? Where's Myrtis? Tell me girl. The truth. I want it. Now!" "Papa, she done run off." "What are you saying girl?" "Papa, I shoulda told. I know that now. Please don't whip me." "Settle down girl, make sense. Who did Myrtis run off with?" "With Ben." "Ben Thornell?" "That's right Papa." "Why Ben Thornell, why that son-of-a-bitch, why that no good child stealing bastard. Why, he's as old as me. Are you sure?" "Yes Papa. With Mr. Ben, Papa, I'm sure." Dazed, then pricked by a conscious caught between guilt and justification going head-to-head, he raises his voice. "Lord, forgive me for soiling these lips. You know that profanity and such like are contrary to my better nature, but Lord there just aren't any good damn words to use on him. Wouldn't it be more grievous to waste even one on this, this scoundrel Ben, who done took my darling daughter and run off with her? Lord! Lord! Forgive me but I can't help it..." Then, breaking his prayer, and running to the corner, the hard-shelled Baptist preacher reaches down for his shotgun and hoists it, swearing, "That Ben Thornell is an animal... to be hunted, forgive me Lord, but I'm gonna kill "em, that kidnapper... that no good... that Ben Thornell... so help me God."

After stepping into his boat and resting his shotgun within arm's reach, the Deacon Drayton Jones, now, two hours behind the fugitives, pushes off... paddling in pursuit... praying to rescue a still innocent daughter... and... planning to execute the sixth commandment by blowing that scoundrel Ben to Kingdom Come.

After two days and nights of pursuing and praying and still unable to find and save his foolish young daughter and unload his wrath and both barrels of buckshot into Ben, a godly man, a grieving man, and a feeling lost man, gives up the search, returning home and docking under the shade of a weeping willow, with its long whipping branches giving way to the summer breeze. Perhaps the handy switches were used too sparingly, he surmises... and now it's too late. Lord, too late, with two tired shoulders sagging and with a heavied head hugging the ground, the once proud papa maneuvers up the river's bank, not caring to notice a moccasin slithering past his feet, but forced to accept the damage done.

With forty years in the passing, Grandpa Jones checks out of Big Charity--my beginning's place---following a treatment for a condition of the heart. With a free doctor releasing him to go, he enters the hospital lobby with his thoughts on a faithful wife long departed, with his eyes searching for a missing daughter as yet to arrive, now worn down by life and by the things a man cannot change, even a good man now seventy five, he slumps his frail body down into a comfortable chair to await Myrtis' arrival and to rest before closing his eyes to life and opening his eyes for death where he is found alone again without his pride.

So, sorry Deacon Drayton Jones, Grandpa, I wish I could have known you, but you knew too well, that Thornell blood doesn't mix well, particularly with the Jones.

Except by sight, my father is a stranger. Even my official birth certificate shortens Benjamin to just Ben. Perhaps, indicating that good works, if any, came before me and are now well behind him. A failure at farming, at river boating, at fathering and everything else, except providing a pretty young wife and three young'uns with poverty-a-plenty.

Picking me up, holding and bouncing me on his knee, depositing two quarters in my hand or even delivering a well-deserved switching are non-experiences. Just undeveloped photographs of memories still missing. But, indelibly printed on my brain at age 13 is the image of a hoary, a bent and a disfigured body stepping, and stooping, and being forced to scrutinize the immense protuberance pressing out from his scrotum stretching his breeches to the limit and drawing attention to that said to be the result of a rupture from a fall. What a sight he was. My resembling him at any age, unthinkable and certainly, unbearable.

And just weeks before the death of that awful sight, now living in a small shed out back of Garnett's place at Redwood, just north of Vicksburg, he brings that awful sight to town and buys a ticket to embarrass me for one last time at the picture show. It's Wednesday night, a school night and a work night for me at the Joy Theatre where you can find me stationed at the ticket stand. There, I am a fixture for five nights and two afternoons a week.

Tonight business is as slow as it usually is at midweek. From behind the ticket stand I am shuffling my feet keeping the blood moving and I am stuffing my head with poetry required for English class. The verse is concealed under the movie schedule atop my stand, so other than someone seeing my lips move without the sound, then no one is the wiser, not even the movie manager. But tonight, poetry is soon to be forgotten. Tonight, I would have paid, perhaps my life, to be someplace else, anyplace, even hell. Then I look up. The heavy steel-framed door facing me is opening slowly. Someone is struggling, having difficulty getting in. Leaving my station, I rush over offering assistance. The man raises his head. His eyes meet up with mine. He says, "Hello son." Geesums! The poetry put to memory is erased. My heart surges and my lungs gasp. Only a whisper can be forced out. "Here, let me help you," I said with the sentence completing in my head... and get you inside and into the dark before someone else sees you up close, asks questions about you, about who you are, and then, connects you to me. At his pace, it takes forever to usher him in and have him swallowed up by the dark.

Back at my post, with my back to the concession stand, the voice from behind it, reaches out. "Jack! Jack! That man, that was your father!" Madge Evans asked in an exclamatory way. With eyes and ears fixed forward, silence is my reply. Then again, the question stabs and stabs at my back, "Jack! Turn around. I'm talking to you." Again, silence is reply. Then God steps in, sending customers craving popcorn and coke and getting Madge Evans and her questions off my back. Now, my brain spins... Did anyone else notice? Perhaps, he passed a remark at the ticket box; Perhaps he asked about me and called me by name. Oh God! Perhaps he introduced himself as my father. Although having gone unanswered, Madge's question is still spinning around in my head. Then, I reach down, pick up and fold up the poetry sheet and push it inside my pocket. With that question pounding, there is no way I can get anything else into my head. Not tonight. Not the last time I saw Father upright. Well, almost upright.

I wore a light-weight zip-up jacket. Father a suit of clothes, the ones put on him by the nice funeral parlor people. And nice enough to take them back off him after, figuring, on him, it just doesn't make good sense to waste a perfectly good suit of clothes. Not for such barrel-bottomed pricing.

After edging closer to the casket and peering inside, I take a long look, perhaps my longest and I take a close look, perhaps my closest. With his hideous lower extremity now covered, with his hair groomed and his face powdered and with his posture straightened, I couldn't help thinking... Father, in the horizontal, you sure looked better. I can't remember when I first became ashamed of you, and I can't remember when I wasn't. So, sorry father, I wish I could have got to know you, to get close to you, but the truth is, I couldn't stand the sight of you, until now. And then, backing away my hidden testimony betrays me by shaping and spilling tears onto my face. With some, filled with guilt. With most, filled with relief. Relieved that father's final mortification, now mine, is finally complete.

It's true, father never appears again at the picture show to humiliate me, but the images of his last appearance there and the one of his lying here appearing so comfortable in a borrowed suit, play on inside my head showing and sounding... IN LIFE AND IN DEATH, SHAME HOLDS FATHER OVER ME.

Those earliest of years, those ages one to five, are hazy. And from what I can remember, hazy ain't a bad term to describe'em and to leave'em, unless hazier comes to mind or unless you could forget'em. But one can't, not entirely, and that's because mother's mouth is always around and it's always moving. And eventually, everything shoots out, pretty or not. Barely, we exist outside of Rolling Fork. Not far from, but far bigger than Sartaria, population 125. Seen on more maps, Rolling Fork even offers a movie house and I could get in got free if I could get

13

there. But transportation is costly and anything costly is spared. One could say, we're more than cost conscious and one could see, out of necessity we go without. Isolated, our abode is a one-room shack with the toilet, the whole outback. It's electricity, free. Even running water is provided, pouring through holes in the roof that we sometimes catch in cans for drinking and for wasting on a bath. For food, on occasion there's a little squirrel meat, perhaps possum. In winter, between you and frozen feet are hot bricks put under the covers. And for entertainment, through wide cracks in the floor, there's... watching the progress of a chicken pecking. For Papa, there's one good thing, there's no need to get up and get off to work. There ain't none. And if there was, he wouldn't want it, not Papa. My calling Papa, Papa, is for a lack of a better name. Papa, most certainly, ain't a title earned. But then, what could less than a pip-squeak know about endearment, except what Mamma taught with those other names she uses on Papa, but those I don't know the full meaning yet. Although none were dear, I know they fit cause they got Papa's attention, often spinning him around for spinning off a few new names for Mamma and pronounced ever so loudly. And then at age five, comes city life with Mamma and Papa and Marshall--my middle brother, now age 11--and me moving to Vicksburg, the big metropolis to the south with a population of 28,000, near twenty times bigger than Rolling Fork. Our home is a cramped one room flat overlooking busy Washington Street near the corner of Clay and Crowley's Pool Hall, a convenience for Papa, to go for getting away from Mamma's name calling. Here, the toilet, though not out back, is down the hall. Here, between two beds swallowing the room, I survive the chicken pox, measles, and mumps. Sometimes Uncle John stays over, but only when brother Ben is away. Strange, but he sure gets comfortable after climbing into bed with Mamma, but a few feet over from Marshall and me. Strange, but still less than a pip-squeak, of such goings on, the meaning of 'em what could I know.

Outside the room, a dark stairway leads down to Washington Street to the sidewalk, and to the torture chamber next door. Unable to resist, it draws me there and then it pulls out my tongue, pressing it into glass and holding it there. And then, almost pulling my eyes out of socket, it stretches 'em, it focuses 'em, and it forces 'em to witness the execution of overindulgence stuffing victims with ice cream, sundaes, and shakes. Dear God! Wouldn't it have been better, more humane if you will, even heavenly if you will, not to have showed me the likes of such luxuries existed?

On Saturday afternoon everybody comes to town, even the colored, to congregate down on Washington Street. Today, even brother Garnett shows. Wearing washed and starched khaki pants and shirt to support his proud stance. Mighty handsome he is, most often the best looking man within arm's reach and often wearing a jealous reminder, a black eye for proving it. He's strolling near. I fall in and tag along behind him with pride ruling my face and with thought ruling my head and rising, "God, how I wish brother Garnett could be my father... perhaps someone passing us will mistake us for a father and a son on an outing... I hope so. Oh, there's the ice cream parlor, perhaps, he can't pass it up. Perhaps he'll see me and invite me in for a cone. Oh, he does and he doesn't. Then, he stops, turns back to me and stares down at the street. There his eyes find and fixate on my feet. Then my socks. My holey socks. The socks exposed by worn sandals. "Boy!" He reaches for and grabs my hand, then he yanks my arm and spins me around a yelling, "Look at you. Look at those holes. Boy! Get back home and take those God damn socks with you. Boy! You're an embarrassment. A God damn embarrassment." And the he encourages me with a push and a yell, "Get." I got, just as fast as a five-year-old's feet could carry and keep ahead of tears marking a trail behind me. Home, I put myself down halfway up the scary stairwell. This once, the darkness feels good falling around and concealing the shame at my feet. That afternoon, that yank and that yell, I never forgot and I never will. And till this day, I never again wished for brother Garnett to be my father. No, not ever since. Just thinking on it starts my stomach churning.

Twenty four years of papa and poverty changes childish infatuation into conflict and so Mamma casts off old Ben and beds Uncle John full-time. The siblings, long separated by hate, can't help sharing a common denominator: like taste in women. First, Ben marries Ada and along comes John. Ada divorces Ben and marries John. Later, Ben marries Myrtis. And along comes John, and now, with Uncle John becoming my stepfather, their embitterment broadens and their hate thickens. Is that what folks mean... about blood being thicker than water? So now, we got a new and a younger man in the family, but unfortunately for Mamma, Marshall and me, Uncle John too is afflicted with the Thornell malady, tired blood. And sooner and later, he teaches and teaches that his pitiful efforts can do little to change the pitiful conditions a chewing us up and a spitting us out. Hell, in my mind we ain't worth swallowing, not this poor white trash, not the Thornells.

And then comes good news, at least a mouthful, or so I reckoned when I heard it and then at age six, I find out what $18.00 a month will get you. Somehow Uncle John scrapes up $25.00 for a down payment and buys for Mamma, a wedding present. It's time to go see and open it.

Shocked! Out of my wits and stiffened without'em, I stand there looking up at it towering over me. A monstrosity! No! More! A shamehole! An eyesore beyond cure rising up down at the bottom of the hill, a very hazardous hill and I hear, for some, a dead end.

Geesums! I don't want to hear it, the scary story, I try to shut off my ears but fail, so the nosy neighbor forces it on me. History has it, the wickedly old house was erected by young carpenters whose lives got cut short by yankee artillery hammering down on'em back in 1863. Defaced, the house is devoid of paint with wide boards now dried to a decaying gray and still improving with every second's notice. Suitable for housing some uprooted spirits but certainly uninhabitable for the living, I think. At least this living, I shudder and I haven't yet seen inside.

The L-shaped porch, missing planks with others broken and falling, slants downhill reaching to a height of 12-feet on the west side with a missing rail offering a child's playful feet a way to injury, even death. This is home. This is horrible. We! I! Can't live here, I'm thinking aloud when I hear mother. "Jack, come in here. See your room." Forced inside, the ghastly AURA commands attention... From above, bare light bulb sockets with pull strings are dangling to arm's reach, just hanging to where a tall head could easily bump and send it into motion. Below 16-foot ceilings, now long stained by water--Geesums! Maybe not, I thought maybe with blood. Deteriorated wall paper, unglued and brittle, droops to uneven lengths towards an unlevel floor giving life to marbles dropped there.

Emanating from the kitchen is an odor so odious it draws attention and keeps refreshing it. There, a more than nasty wooden sink traps stagnated water and uses it to offend trespassers. Its puissance backs me off and into the bedroom dedicated to holding me. A ten-foot high window rises adjacent to a sealed-up fireplace, perhaps done so to keep something out or something in. It's fronted by a rusting, could be leaking, old space heater capable of putting someone like me to sleep for a long, long time.

And then I feel it... something... an unseen presence... some thing... reaching for me. Forth with, eyes are pulled over to the wall, raised, the stayed to a place halfway up. What's that, I wonder? A staircase. Geesums! An amputated staircase with its lower extremity, the part that's supposed to reach the floor, cut off. Geesums! It's been sawed off and removed. What's that... at the top? Geesums! There's a room up there. An upper room. It's unreachable! It's shut off! It's sealed!... BEHIND A DOOR NAILED SHUT.

Geesums! Geesums! What's up there? Ghosts and goblins? No, no... that's kid stuff. What? And then, answers besiege with imagination attacking and filling the space up there. Oh no! It's the carpenters... their spirits... restless spirits. The ones the neighbor blabbed about... the ones cut down too soon, way too soon, by the war... they musta been mortally wounded and maimed, felled by Grant's shrapnel... then, they musta dragged what's left of'em up there... but they musta stopped halfway up for sawing off the steps behind'em so nobody could follow and force'em to surrender honor, not to some low down trespassing yankee a trying to force some perverted morality on'em. Never! Before laying down before them, a bleeding, a starving, a dying, a pleasure. But now, the Blue Bellies can't get to'em and can't force'em, not now, not today, not ever, not with the stairs sawed off, there's no way to'em and for'em, there's no way out, not from behind a door nailed shut.

With the revelation and with all those misplaced souls stirring up there and up in my head, and just knowing that their full-time occupation is to get out, get down, and to occupy a sleeping young soul, I risk shaky legs and bolt into the yard and away from all those "UPS" and all those "THERES."

A week later with our scant possessions, Uncle and now stepfather John, Mamma, Marshall and me move into the house, the monstrosity, the eyesore beyond cure, the shamehole.

There, a presence rules and ruins my nights with its pore creeping down, finding and forcing my eyes up until fixing them on the mutilated stairs and then, taking them into... THE PEEPHOLE. With it surrendering an undeviating view to any bored or craving soul stationed on the other side. Stare wars commence. I stare up. The peephole stares down. The stares continue. My eye balls strain to outer limits. I see it! There it is, THE ODD EYE. Geesums! It's looking onto mine. I can't move, can't blink. With my fear running rampant, movement. I see it! Odd eye is bulging, penetrating the peephole... and a falling... and a pulling gosh awful remains behind it. And now, no longer just an odd eye a-peeping, but a Tom a-creeping and getting comfortable in bed beside me with what's left of 'em with a wanton look a-showing and a voice a-counting... a blessing. Me!

With first light comes a horrific urge to run and a need to. So, incorporating blurred focus with tunnel vision I do, leaping up and nearly trampling over feet—mine—one foot follows another, out the door, down three steps, into the yard, across unpaved Pearl, to the weed field and into the privy. It's the last of the neighborhood and most likely, the city. And it's ours. And it's my embarrassment. And inside, worse, with past accomplishments overwhelming, with breath holding a necessity and with giant, blood-thirsty blowflies a buzzing and a biting. The defense, the executing of 'em by the swinging of a folded up, old and unread by us newspaper, soon to be unfolded and turned into a more useful purpose. Even crumpled, its rough. The goings to and the coming from the two-holer is a dual humiliation. Sitting inside, one can feel the prying eyes pushing through wide cracks, invading and exposing. Stepping outside, my suspicions are confirmed by the condescending looks of noisy neighbors landing. During those moments, how I longed for days of constipation just for the avoiding of the humiliation of... the privy.

On some days you might get lucky and duck those reaching eyes but one sight you cannot duck when exiting the outhouse. From the front, it's a pushing backwards. From the back, the smell and the escaping blowflies are a-pushing forward. There sandwiched, an emptied soul a-wishing for a trap door—even a snake pit half full—would open up and swallow. Why? Outside, poised and awaiting, is a picture of unique ugliness overdeveloped with a three dementiable purpose: to hold, to marinate and to preserve its occupants with shame and then leave them jarred, like jam, unspoilable and spreadable over a lifetime. The picture is the house is the shamehole.

Even this side view across Pearl, takes you. Actually, the house faces Dabney Avenue, number 503. The last house at the dead end. Since Pearl is dirt and don't count as much of a street and since it don't go no place that counts. It's most definitely, a dead end, leaving the people living there, us, with no way out, except for and most likely, a one-way trip to the cemetery to be dropped off and into another hole at country expense. If the law would allow it, I figure, the neighbors would all get together, fire up a big bulldozer and push the house, the privy, and the Thornells plum down and into the gully below us, while a-cheering good riddance and a-thanking God that... the smell is gone.

Inside the house, meals consume little time with a small kitchen table oversized. Then, comes the invitation. "Jack! Come here boy. It's time to eat. There's biscuits and sugar syrup setting. No butter." "No butter" means no eggs, no bacon or sausage, no oatmeal, no juice and no nothing else. Just a little sugar combined with a lot of water, heated to a boil, and then poured over otherwise dry biscuits. Other times and often, there is goose liver a-waiting, thinly sliced and laid between two slices of bread, stale or not. Without refrigeration, the smell alone comes close to lifting a body a-holding it, let alone a swallowing it. I forced enough down to turn into a goose, but I didn't cause if I hadda, I wouldn't still be a-setting here a-eating it. I'd a-flown... away... way way away.

In late spring and summer, meals get better with the help of a garden growing across Pearl and supplying greens, beans, okra, tomatoes and such. Sometimes, hunger not craving perfection, we dine on a fried green tomato. On rare occasions, Christmas, Thanksgiving and the like, a chicken might show, but steak, roast, or pork chops are always next door or further. But missing, always absent, is the aroma of affection. There just ain't any aired here at any time of the year. If somehow, miraculously, affection appeared, the Thornells wouldn't recognize it and certainly couldn't stomach it, breakfast, lunch or dinner. Table talk usually concerns a next meal. Like, "Lord! Where's it a-coming from?" Mamma, when worried, usually prefaces "a need" with a Lord. "Lord! How we gonna pay the bills? The house note, $18, or all those utilities. And Lord! We just gotta have water." Table talk never gets around to me or plans for me like my schooling, college or such. Why should it? Shucks, a high school diploma for a Thornell is unheard of, much less, talked of. To our table, even though rodents and roaches have easy access, it ain't worth the coming in, because it's obvious, even to them, go next door or go hungry.

Uncle John—I call him cause I never got comfortable a calling him father or stepfather—works full-time at unemployment and part-time as a carpenter and a painter, skills rarely applied on the house, perhaps a feeling it beyond redemption with any attempt at improvement, futile. On lots of days, instead of working or looking for work, he flops on the porch and teaches me "set-back," a card game he masters, then in real life, practices to perfection.

This summer, without work for Uncle John and with a garden failing, victim of a dry spell, we uproot, go back to the flats north of Vicksburg, and integrate the cotton patch. By night we sleep on the dirty floor of a shack. By day, sunup to sunset, we bake at a 100 degrees plus between blacks better conditioned for such conditions. Them coloreds can pick, even the little ones, with their skilled hands out picking us, left and right. Uncle John calls 'em niggers. The word colored, unthinkable, cause he need his niggers. If he ever prays it's for the asking for God to keep on a making 'em, cause he just couldn't bare life without 'em. He plum needs a creature he can look down on as lower'n us and for him, that's a nigger.

Despite the blistering heat, Uncle John suffers more from the humiliation of those black hands outperforming ours, particularly at the end of the day when their's yields more cotton for ginning and more money for pocketing. This, to him, is a Goddamn shame, and after less than a week, we surrender the field to, when it comes to cotton picking, a superior race, and withdraw, retreating back to Vicksburg and back to the shamehole awaiting. Later, when on the verge of going hungry, and when faced with the choice of going back to the cotton patch, Uncle John swears, "Before I'd side up against those God damn niggers again, I'd starve first." What he meant was, we'd all starve first. And if the whole truth be sworn to, Uncle John wasn't and isn't prone to backbreaking work under any conditions, even when the job allowed for siding up against whites.

Inside the shamehole, there is a luxury of a week, a bath, in water drawn from a single-head faucet and hand poured into a round galvanized tub. While sitting down in it, Mamma scrubs me over with an overused wash rag and with it always comes the urge. Oops... There goes flowing relief. Then, all done, I step out and another body steps in to splash in the little tub of paradise with my wee contribution to the bath water, unnoticed.

Mamma stands a little bit over five-foot but at forty, from under the weight of lifelong poverty and with two boys yet growed, appears shorter. But per square inch, her mouth as loud and nasty as God ever created on a woman. For her, a powerful weapon. From her, a guided missile projecting a racket, till flooring opponents, then ricocheting up the walls, hitting the ceiling and echoing back down to exit and entertain the neighbors next door.

Her tongue, a curse freely spread, but her affection is reserved. The former Jones and the former church goer musta caught it from the Thornells. But patiently and tenderly she irons towels and sheets, but never bends to smooth my hair or whisper, "I love you son." Those strokes are limited to Jimmie the cat when nibbling at her ankles for a dropping of raw biscuit dough. Sometimes, I envy Jimmie.

For Mamma, heaven is a roof overhead and food on a table below, any roof, any food. Born August 2, 1907 without a pot her own, a deprivation, due to a weakened bladder condition, she remedied. And a showing it all too often with a prompt lifting of a skirt, a scurrying to and a squatting on the slop jar kept side her bed and a propelling me from the room cloaked with embarrassment.

If Mamma has any shame about her, all is for the showing and leaving little for the imagination. In summer, wearing overly thin dresses without the discomfort of undergarments and declaring, "It's just too damn hot for such nonsense." In the yard, she can be seen a stooping with her outside air a slowing men to a stop for taking notice of that which I cover with my mind. It's a real puzzlement though, why such things bother one so little so, but such things do. And like with Papa and long before I can remember exactly, but most certainly by now, age 10, Mamma is a walking talking squatting picture of shame a showering me, even on the sunniest of days.

On those sunny days she rains out bursts of profanity powerful enough to cause God and man to shudder. But when disturbed skies threaten, a foul-mouth is silenced but for the singing of hymns orchestrated by thunder. Them days or nights, she busies that mouth a praying for deliverance from lightning bolts dancing about while prowling the house like an agitated cat a going from window to door, then a pausing to look out before a resuming her march to the cadence of "Have mercy! Have mercy! Lord! Have mercy!"

The little woman is terrified of a storm.

When the weather worsens, no matter what hour, it could be 2 a.m., with fear a driving her, mamma, as if directed by divine guidance, storms into my room a hollering, "Jack! Jack! You better get up boy. We gonna get blowed away." Then, she'd grab my hand and start a dragging me out the bed, out the door, down the steps, across the yard and into... THE DITCH. By now, I am soaked through, wide awake and sure... I am not a victim of a dream. There, kneeling and grasping the rim of the culvert, half-in and half-out, with water rushing down the hill attempting to sweep us into that concrete coffin and while from above us lightning bolts streak attempting to ground a charge in us, we pray for an end to it. And, the amazing part of it, the going to the ditch, either threat—death by drowning or death by electrocution—are always more probable than "getting blowed away." Except that one time.

This afternoon turned dark, funnel-shaped clouds rotating like tops, spin up the Mississippi River before coming ashore and sucking up large pieces of historic Vicksburg. A city resurrected from civil war ruins and immortalized to suffer this day, another blow. Naturally, at 5:20p.m. this Saturday, Mamma and me are cowering in the ditch. Overhead and vehemently, storm clouds are swirling and are forming a monstrous megaphone, soon to be inverted, pointed down and used for intensifying a roar likened to a 100 locomotives harnessed in tandem and a plowing wide open and out of control. The pressure pops our ears and the sound deafens. Above the clamor, mother shouts, "God! Oh God! Save us." While I'm dividing my cleave between Mamma's hand and the culvert's mouth, the big chinaberry snaps, limbs fly, power poles tilt, transformers pop and sparks fly. Now, hugging the ditch, I am no longer demeaned by squatting in it, not while it withholds me and Mamma from a hungry wind. Nothing can withstand it. Surely, the house too will splinter, fall and free me of its haunt, I'm a thinking, a hoping and a praying.

Suddenly! While stretching my arm upward with hers, and as if summoned, Mamma straightens and fixes her gaze on the turbulence above us, then exclaims, "God! God! I see. I see." And then claiming to see behind the hostile elements, "A bright red cloud of fire encompassing The Almighty's chariot," and to hear, "An angry voice a perpetuating the storm with its sound and frenzy." And I take her word for it. Cause I can't look, not with my eyes stuck in the mud next to my feet at the bottom of the ditch. At least the rain is slackening, but the penalty for long time squatting—the leg cramps—aren't, they're killing.

Finally, the wind lets up and lets me up to join Mamma's trembling side. Until now, I've been facing west, not due west, but down west, so I turn up to the north and the direction of the house. Geesums! There! It's standing. It looks unscathed, like before, withstanding the bombardment of mighty Ulysses and now, this, this mighty blow. Geesums! Perhaps this means... that the neglect of time is damage sufficient and enough to prompt even a vengeful God to decree, "That further abuse to the house or dislodgment of those weary souls there, upstairs or down, ungodly, insufferable and unallowable."

Then, my attention is drawn back to Mamma, still leaning back, with her eyes still up in the clouds, with her observation, "This here storm ain't done. Not yet. She's a moving towards town. God! Have mercy on 'em there." Then, looking to the house, and seeing the silhouette of a man lurking inside, she goes quiet. Then Uncle John, who brags that he ain't scared of nothing, not a "fucking thing", not even God—and I reckoned that made sense cause if he had'a been scared of God, he wouldn'ta busied hisself with his brother's wife, so often, neither of 'em—pushes open the screen and moves to the edge of the porch where he waits to watch our ascension from the ditch. My eyes fix on his face. He looks pale, even shaken by that God he ain't a bit scared of. Then, trying to cover his fear, he stretches his grin and greets us with ridicule. "Why y'all as wet as swamp rats. And there ain't no swamp for near a hundred miles of here, " he snickered, before snickering on, "God damn it woman. I told you. This here storm, it weren't nothing to fret about. Just a lit'l blow. Just a fart'n the wind. That's all."

Downtown in the darkness of the Saenger Theatre they sit. Five year-old Carolyn Lorraine Thornell separates her twin sisters Brenda Kaye and Linda Faye, age 5, but shares popcorn with them. The occasion is a birthday outing for Stephanie, the daughter of Lillian and George Mitchell. Giggles fill the air with children often swapping seats and whispering secrets. There are sixteen in attendance. The movie, Botany Bay with Alan Ladd ends. The lights come on. The children empty their seats save for one. Holding onto it, she pleads, "Lets don't go. Let's stay. Just for the cartoon again." Before reply, a harmony of other little voices join, "Yes, oh yes, we need to see Bugs Bunny again. Please. Please. Let us." Overwhelmed, the chaperon gives in but reminds of the ice cream and cake awaiting. Seats are retaken. The film is rewinding. And then, lights go dim. The dark returns and surrounds them while happiness lights faces as Warner Brothers Presents fills the screen.

And then, before big and brightened eyes, the picture changes from delightful cartoon characters on the big screen to a larger reality... a horror show, not imagined. The twister twists down. Animation falters and freezes. House lights go out, back on, back out. In the blackness, eyes are drawn upward toward that dreadful noise, but eyes can't see clearly as delicate voices cry, "Mammaaa!" "Papaaa!" Outside, like a mega-ton dentist's tool, the twister bores down, twisting and drilling and splintering and turning the roof into kindling, now flying and filling the air.

The building explodes! The ceiling collapses, falling downward. The walls collapse, falling inward. And then converge, covering, blackening and burying angellic faces at mercy below.

On July 4, 1863, after a 47-day seige directed by General Ulysses S. Grant, Vickburg fell. On December 5, 1953, on an afternoon turned dark. It took seconds...............

Behind the rampart the cannons just stood, firing nary a shot. Just stood, silhouettes of bygone days. Just stood, show pieces on which tourists play. Just stood, muzzled and unable to sound a solitary salvo, even in salute of a superior power, uncontrollable and unconquerable, a blowing... Just stood!

The Vicksburg Hotel shook! The vibration lifts Lucille Thornell and pulls her to the window. Looking out, getting caught up in the storm's intensity and then disturbed by it, she senses danger and though weakened by uncertainty, moves back to her chair, bends close to a friend's ear and whispers louder than meant to, "My girls! My girls! I've got to go... to find... to get my girls."

Forsaking the meeting of Westinghouse workers, Lucille charges into the street and into the storm. The wind turns on her and assaults her with debris flying into, cutting through stockings, then into her legs and drawing blood. This pain and this blood goes unfelt and unnoticed with Lucille only feeling concern, concern for her girls. After seeing and passing overturned cars, Lucille sighs at the sight of her black 1941 Plymouth still there and with the feel of the storm easing up. Then, reaching for the door, something hits her. Something's wrong. This isn't the way the car was left. Then it dawns. "God, my car's been picked up, turned around, set back down and parked in the same space, except now it's facing north instead of south, the wrong way on Monroe, a one-way street." Driving away, amazement fills her, that her old reliable withstood the airlift without a new scratch showing. But again, only concern crowds in, filling her head with thoughts, some of hope racing ahead and framing pictures of happy faces alive with cheerful voices awaiting. Then, she's there. She's at the door. Her ringing, her pounding, her screaming is unanswered. Silence is reply. Her body goes limp and gives way to the stairs. Sitting, with her head bent and joining her lap, her eyes are finally drawn to her legs. Her stockings are shredded and saturated with blood. Now, with the waiting and the awful anticipating, Lucille feels the pain.

With dusk falling fast around us, Uncle John's grin fades even faster when we find John Jr., his son and my first cousin, just a pacing back and forth of what was his home. Now, it's shambles. Blown to pieces and piled. Subdued by loss and worry, John Jr. approaches us, stops and says, "Everything is gone. Wiped out, nothin's left. Lucille and the kids are gone," then after pausing with a voice breaking up and with tears breaking in, he continues, "Thank God! Cause if they'd been here, they couldn't survive under all this." As we walked away, John Jr. resumes his pacing, back and forth, past a lifetime of possessions at ruin at his feet, and as yet unaware of what fate has befallen his wife or his three precious daughters.

Back down in the black of the picture show, the girls remain. On a sunny afternoon the Saenger would be shaded by the towering Vicksburg hotel, the site of Lucille's union meeting, standing less than a short city block away. Under brick and mortar piled high, Brenda Kaye and baby sister Carolyn Lorraine are crushed together and held lifeless. Next to them, twin Linda

Faye is impaled by a spear of wood and pinned between the bottom cushion and the back of the seat, now serving as her shield. From under the rubble, little hands are reaching up, finding and holding onto other little hands. Then, little voices rise, uniting and wounding the air of horror about them, with Sunday school songs until their burden, the tons of, is lifted. Botany Bay, for five little ones, is to be their last picture show.

Mamma was right, after the storm spared us, she wasn't done. From the southwest, the tornado jumped the Mississippi River Bridge, tore through the Illinois Central Roadhouse on Levee Street, moved uphill. Along Veto to Washington, then crossing to damage St. Paul Catholic Church on Crawford before reaching down and tearing down the Saenger on Walnut. She left a path 200 yards wide and six miles long. She left 38 dead, 270 injured, 1200 homeless and property damage in the millions. No Mamma, she weren't, weren't done. Certainly not for Linda Faye. Sure, she was the lucky one, sure, she survived and sure, after months of painful physical therapy, she regained use of her leg. Except now, when there's a sudden flash of lightening or a loud burst of thunder she can start running and screaming, "Mamma! Papa! Hold me."

Literally, gone with the wind, the Saenger is bulldozed, never rebuilt, left an empty space in the 1200 block of Walnut, and, on a sunny afternoon, in the shadow of the Vicksburg Hotel. Years later, the final curtain is dropped on the tragedy, when the court condemns the tornado as "an act of God" thereby denying any earthly compensation for the little angels crushed there. Now, just victims of time and circumstance, by the space of a cartoon rerunning. On many more storm days and nights, I returned to Mamma's ditch, but gone forever are my complaints and Uncle John's comments. And, there's never a trace of his grin.

Below and toward the river railroad tracks support locomotives blowing their stacks and spewing cinders with some gliding and landing on wooden shingles. "The roof's on fire," Mamma hollers running next door to borrow the telephone after sending me across Dabney to wait. Backing away and looking up, I figure the house has finally met its match but twenty minutes later a fireman shouts, "We got it. It's out. Hell, I don't see any damage." First, Grant's cannon's fail, then God's whirlwinds fail and now, flames fail. Again the house shows and stands indestructible and inconsumable, a shamewell springing eternal.

For avoiding prying eyes trying to identify me with the house, its depravity, or with the people living in it, shame walks me home from school by the back way. Down Bomar Avenue, left on Oak, right onto an unnamed dirt road, then left on Pearl and to the house. The thought of inviting a friend from school there to play, is disgusting enough to make me throw up. Can't imagine what the putting of any such notion into words could do.

Beyond my shame of and my contempt for the house, there is all that contemptible talk coming from inside it. Mostly from Mamma's mouth. Today, Uncle John is out. I'm on the porch near a window. Aunt Maddie is inside visiting. Maddie, the quiet one, keeps her visiting short. Maybe that's cause cussing words ain't in her. It certainly ain't the talk the deacon taught. So mostly, Maddie just sits, drawing on a cigarette, listening and occasionally, nodding. Besides, when a wound-up Mamma takes the floor and lets loose, look out. If you can force a nod in, edgewise or otherwise, consider it an intrusion wasted. Cause listening ain't a virtue, not of Mamma, not when something's pressing up against her and forcing her mouth to open.

The voice reaches out to the porch and pulls back my ears. "What's so God damn wrong with fucking. Ben's a fucking. John's a fucking. Every swinging dick is a fucking. But if we're caught fucking, we're bitches and no God damn good." Maddie, holding her eyes hard to the linoleum floor, just nods as Mamma continues. "Those bastards, just cause they wear the britches, they figure they can look down on us, lording their things over us and telling us, we're whores. Just God damn whores." Today it's just Maddie ears and mine listening, but with strange company around, Mamma might dispense with a fuck word or two. But God damn, bastard or son-of-a-bitch, are to her lips like sugar syrup on biscuits, like on some days, all she had to offer. Sentences without cuss words, just incoherent or incomplete phrases that don't make sense. Even when no one's around to be entertained or detained by her verbs, she can't keep still or shut. Always a moving, a sweeping, a mopping, a wiping or a raking with her mouth in perpetual motion unloading the bothers. There's no debating or doubting it, Mamma's identity is her mouth.

About life Mamma never taught me much, reckoning I reckon, experience is enough. But about the crows, their calling and their reckoning, she educates. Trying to escape the afternoon heat of the house, we take a seat on the edge of the porch dangling our feet and trying to face up to a breeze. Side by side, we are about as close as we get, ever. Maybe, she's missing Jimmie. A couple of days ago we heard her screaming and saw her running up under the house to the shallow part where we couldn't get to her. She wouldn't come out. Mamma called and called. Tried enticing her with biscuit dough, but Jimmie wouldn't budge. A few days later, we started smelling something. Swelled up on poison, she'd gone and died on Mamma. Never seen Mamma cry like that. She went on and on. Said she'd kill the low-down murdering bastard quicker'n poison, if she could just lay hands on him. Mamma musta really missed Jimmie. Her nibbles, most mornings, about the most affection Mamma even felt.

Now, with Mamma sitting here beside me, I figure, she must be involved with some deep thinking cause she ain't talking, not at the moment. Then she see'd something. A worrisome look, no more like a fear, comes on her. She couldn't hide it. "What's a matter Mamma?" "Shush boy. Just sit quiet and watch." "Watch what Mamma?" "Crows." "What crows Mamma?" "Them crows, the ones up there on the power line, them." Turning and taking my eyes off her, I look up to where she pointed. "I see 'em. What about 'em?" With a fearsome look spreading she tells. "Boy! Three crows perching close like them means... wait! Listen boy... count 'em." Before I ask, count what, we hear 'em. The first, caw caw caw. The second, caw caw caw. And then the third, caw caw caw. I take my eyes off the power line and put 'em back on Mamma. Her fear looks tripled. "What is it? What's it mean... the cawing, the counting?" "Son it means... three bodies a dying, close together and close by." "Who Mamma! Who? Who's gonna die?" "Only them crows know boy and them that sent 'em" Despite the heat, Mamma looked chilled through when she stood up, looked back down, and says, "Come on back in the house boy, no sense tempting 'em" I did what she said, I always did, or risk a tongue lashing.

Getting up, something struck me as odd, Mamma hadn't launched a single cussword, not even a darn, while them black birds cawed. Two days later, Mrs. Finky, across and three houses up, is called on. And before the week is out two more neighbors pass on. Them crows, their cawing and their calling on, is a lesson never forgotten. And when I see 'em perching close like them three, I go quiet. I watch. I listen. I wonder. Who?

23

Back inside, by taking a seat in a squeaky old chair, I escape by rocking myself away to where... and to when... Christmas is not just another day. If Santa Claus exists, he never materializes around here. Perhaps the poverty perfected downstairs and the disturbed spirits up are just too much and just cause for Santa speeding his reindeer up. One year, the one and only present not under a tree—nothing to put on it and less to put under it, so a tree, a waste—is a wide-spaced black and red yoyo. The non-hesitating kind. The handicapped kind. The kind disabling me from performing, walk the dog, around the world or rock the cradle. It's just up and down, up and down, and boring. Another year my one and only is a dollar bill wrapped around an almondless Hershey bar from Nell and brother Garnett. After four bites and a movie, the Christmas memory soon passes. Another time, the most costly didn't come from Thornell money. The little red wagon, beautiful except it come from a truck with great big letters on it—Salvation Army. Bringing it, them were good people I'm sure, but I sure was glad for them to get gone and to take them great big letters with 'em. When the truck cleared the hill, I fell in love with my little red wagon, I couldn't before then, not with people hooking me and my wagon up to that Salvation Army truck and the shame it brung attached. But the best of the best come from saved-up box tops of Hadacol elixir finding their way into my possession. A blessing from a neighbor. Her name eludes me but she was old and didn't look like the remedy was fulfilling any of all those promises a listed on the label. She must to have believed in it though cause swallowing it could'na been too easy for her. Emptied, the bottles smelled worse'n spoiled goose liver. But I bore the smell, took the empties up to the Strand Theatre and traded them in for a brand new Daisy air rifle and a box of BB shot. The Daisy will enliven many long hours for me, but will deliver the end to many a critter resting above my aim.

Pow! Feathers fly. The blue jay recoils, unable to fly. Rapidly I re-cock, re-aim and fire a second shot. This one to the head. The blue jay drops dead. Pow! A sparrow falls. Pow! A Robin. Pow! A beautiful Cardinal. With the day nearing end, I gather my kill for the delivering. Big black eyes and big moist lips greet me. Belonging to the litt'l Sammy and his litt'l brothers a living in a house behind ours, just off dirty Pearl. To me, their house looks a heap better'n ours and moving in it would most assuredly be a step up. "Dem birds sure look good. Yes Suh. You some good hunting man Mister Jack," Sammy, about my age, about ten, offers for "dem birds." But the mister is mine causing he a black boy and me a white one. He a misses "a mister" and some white man, like Uncle John, stands ready to slam 'em down for it. One can almost hear the empty stomachs a growling as Sammy starts a plucking and ordering his lit'ler brothers to go and put on the cooking pot. "Mr. Jack, we got some good supper a coming. Wanna stay and eat some?" "No thanks Sammy. I got to get. Night is a falling." I can hear my stomach as I head to face the house and a goose liver sandwich or less, but thankful that the evidence of my carnage and a portion of my guilt will soon be swallowed up. No matter how hungry, I could never eat my kill, even the thought tastes awful.

With my Daisy, when the weather ain't storming cause when it is Mamma keeps me nearby and close to the ditch, I elude the house, its haunt, and the haunt of Mamma's mouth and Uncle John's grin by escaping to the ridge. Below, to the north and the south, but above the locomotive tracks, it runs for acres and acres. It's railroad property. There the underbush grows thick. There I lose myself. In the winter months, the tall blades of Johnson grass fall dry and often get set on fire from the spark of some hobo's fire. Every now and again, one will wander away from the tracks, up to the house, and knock or yell for something. Often, I wonder what could one suspect we got for 'em. But Mamma always talks to 'em, treat 'em good and usually to a mayonnaise sandwich. Goose liver, even if we got it, ain't for sparing, not usually. But this here one claims to be the uncle of a cowboy actor by the name of Bob Steele, and Mamma likes him, so she spares her precious goose liver. Wanted to impress him I figured, but I also figured the hobo out to be an imposter. Surely, his famous nephew can provide something more substantial. No, he was an imposter all right, but if imposting can get some hungry soul more'n mayonnaise, why not impost. Perhaps, Mamma knew too. Perhaps, she just liked his acting and awarded him "The goose liver."

Pearl street, going to the north past Sammy's place takes me away and into my hollow. The vegetation is more than thick. Until you pick your spot you got to watch your step or risk stepping on something. Snakes give me the willies, that and falling. Maybe that's because those theatre serials always end with Clyde Bailey a falling into a snake pit. He never gets bit though, always climbs out and then, walks and walks until next Saturday until falling into another one. Though he don't get bit, looks like, sooner or later, the fall would break a leg, if not a neck. My hollow is filled with trees and the trees with birds. It's here, I do my killing. It's here I do my thinking. Often the killing weighs heavier than my Daisy. But if murder is the price of escaping, then murder it'll be. The thought that death is only a trigger pull away strikes me. And that pull, I know I can deliver. Maybe God won't blame me. He can see, can't he? See this misery. See it smothering. Sometime, I put some blame on God for not reaching down, a giving me a hand and a lifting me out of this. God! This is killing me. God! I am only ten. Oh God! Why is this happening? Happening to me?

Now! My pen hand takes a rest stop but my mind doesn't. "Makesense! Oh Makesense! Where were you then? So alone, I could have stood a butt-in then. Were you too ashamed of my misery to ever raise?" "Butt-Butt... cousin, I already apologized for then. For now, there's nothing more for saying. Not now."

Grandpa Jones is visiting. Never calls first. Can't. Cause telephones cost, so we ain't got one, so he just shows up. Never stays long. Never the night. Maybe he ain't asked. Maybe he don't want to. The deacon tolerates Uncle John. Barely. That's cause he abhors divorce and adultery. With the good book, his divine guide, dictating to him, but one wife for life, with no ifs, ands, or butts between. But today, his condemnation ain't aimed at fornicators, it's aimed at me. Both barrels. And it's about murdering. My murdering ways.

"Boy! Can't you do something better than slaughter birds?" I stand mute. About five feet to my front, grandpa sits on the edge of the porch dipping and spitting snuff. A discharge lands three feet from my feet. I stiffen in place. Then, the full-time preacher and part-time shotgun toting scoundrel hunter continues his sermon. "Boy! This carnage. Can't you stop? Won't you? Birds are God's creatures too." He stops. He spits. This shot landing just two feet to my right. Still, I stand mute, holding my ground, "Can't you answer me boy?" I can't. He spits. It inches closer. True, my bare feet are already nasty dirty, plenty, but not so nasty dirty as liquidated snuff—something starting off as already nasty-dirty and getting nastier and dirtier per mouthful. "The birds, like you, like me, got purpose too. Entertaining. Ever hear a mockingbird sing? Such beauty, only God could'a fitted 'em with such sounds. Listen to 'em. Hear 'em imitating, to perfection, the voices of other song birds. Truly gifted. Mockingbirds are truly God's instruments." He spits. The discharge misses, just. I start backing and keep on backing. "Stop boy! Come back here. I ain't finished. Come close. Real close. Where I can reach you." His ordering draws me close, too close for spitting. With me not bowing to his rhetoric and

25

seeing an unrepentant soul, he reduces his demands. "If you can't stop all your killing, can you promise me one thing. To never kill a mockingbird, never again." Now, taking my arm, he starts a squeezing and a twisting for an answer. "Boy! Will you? Promise!" with his arm twisting, I start a hurting and my mouth starts a moving, "Yes! Yes! I promise! I promise! Never to kill a mockingbird, again."

With the declaration for taking my sights off of his consecrated songbird becoming music to his ears, grandpa lets go and lets me back away, way out of his reach and his stream.

Not long after, emptied of his preaching, grandpa picks up his old bones and starts negotiating the hill. For some unexplainable reason, I watch. To take the hill, takes him forever. After his lecturing, his spitting and his squeezing, I was more than glad to see him go and to disappear. Then a few weeks pass and I was sad. Sad about his going. Sad about his disappearing. This time for good when he sunk down in that big easy chair down in the lobby of Big Charity and started staring off into space. And with his lecturing, his spitting and his squeezing all done, let life go.

At grandpa's funeral, I am an absentee. No need, according to Mamma, for me to be there. Besides, the old shoes on me weren't fitting. But when staying home alone, but outside, cause I never stay inside, not alone, my thoughts are on grandpa and his departure. He never never had much, little or no money, but religion he had plenty of and he sure shared that. On some visits, not often, he'd put a quarter in my hand , "For show fare," he'd say with lips moistened from all his spittin. But, that last time, when he didn't, it registered in my head. I guess that's why I watched him walk up the hill, perhaps thinking he forgot my quarter, remember and would turn, come back down and give it to me. He didn't. And why would he. Why waste good money on bloodthirsty kin. On the likes of me.

In the solitude of the thicket, the warbling reaches. Instinctively, the Daisy raises, sights and "pow" interrupts the melody. Feathered friends fly. The songbird falls, silenced at my feet. Never took notice, not of its ashy-white breast, its ashy gray coat, or its darker wings and tail decorated with white markings. And then, stirred hands take over, hastily creating a small cavity under the leaves, hastily pushing the silenced one down and then hastily covering it. Hidden, under the dirt and the leaves, with the defused sun bleeding and the glistening tears streaming, mine, the consecrated warbler is the mockingbird. And underneath it all, is... the promise broken.

By day, the ridge and the hollow supply sanctuary, by night, it's flight on the wings of a dream. Unexplainably, my departures always originate from the ledge of a 10-story building. Grounded below and gathering, are the Shamebirds. The people watching ones. The ones loving splatter. Looking like, ones with duck-sized feet forced on a sparrow. Actually, human-sized and human-looking but for big beaks and those super-sized feet. Gawkers, I call 'em, cause Shamebirds are always gawking. Shamebirds can't fly and get satisfaction by watching people try. And fail. Off the ledge... I try. Beaks snap to attention. I fall. Gawkers gawk, I fall. Gawk! Gawk! Gawk! Five floors down with five to go, arms extend, take hold and away I soar. Below, Shamebirds looking sad and lowering beaks, waddle off swallowing disappointment, while having to go, go without their splatter.

On stormy flights, I often glide down to two-story level and take refuse by looking in uncovered windows. Inside, there's family life. Kids rolling on the floor. Undisturbed, a shaggy dog lazing up against a filled refrigerator door. Upstairs, behind a closed bedroom door a couple locks together. Suddenly, sensing the intrusion, the lovers look out and catch the encroacher. Exposing embarrassment sets me off, sending me to hide in a tall pine. There I perch, weighted with the guilt of stealing glimpses of things not meant for me. Things absent down at 503. Always.

With dawn comes awakening sounds. Geesums! It's mockingbirds! Congregating all around, raising voices and taking aim. Startled! Wounded by warbles, I fly back to bed, not waiting for or wanting to hear lyrics of condemnation for the one I slew joining their concerto.

"Makesense! Come talk." Butt-Butt... "Makesense is here." "Tell me. Why did those dreams always begin from a ten-story ledge, never from ground level, like with superman?" "Cousin, you ain't got to be a shrink with a flying license to figure that." "Figure what?" "Well cousin, if a body steps off a ten story ledge and if a body can't fly, there's but time for one mo-ge-ron-i-mo. No-mo. Just satisfied birds with beakfuls below. Filled with spatter." "Oh."

My first experience with silence beginning with a bang sounds close. Next door. Big Jack is tall and proper with his head always held high. His face, always properly clean shaven and lightly powdered as if a stand-in for the movies. In a fresh and stiffly starched uniform, he sits up proud and straight behind the wheel of a big city bus. Driving it up and down Washington street, stopping and picking up people who put their money into a little slot for the accommodation. For years, Big Jack, with five kids home, looks more than ready to leave for work each morning. Then, there's trouble. Big trouble for Big Jack. There's money missing. Then Big Jack loses his bus route to rumors of money not found. Then, early one morning, Big Jack straightens, raising up an unshaven face. Then, Big Jack raises up a hand, for putting an ending to the hearing of all that noisy and shameful talk keeping him awake, just killing him, and as with brother Garnett, his silence too... begins with a bang. Left, bearing his name, a housewife with a passion for creating homemade ravioli and children: Little Jack, Joe David, Anne, Louie and Marie, all under age 14. Before this morning, all envied by me for having a regular dad with a regular job for providing regular meals.

Soon, comes another close tragedy. This one, in most eyes, more terrible because choice ain't a consideration. This involves Harry Scott Jr. Three houses up on our side of Dabney, live his parents. Harry Jr. don't live with 'em now cause he got married and got a little boy. Before suppertime, Mamma comes rushing in. "God! Have mercy. Young Harry done gone and got a heart attack. Got rushed up to Mercy." Harry Jr., I always looked up to as someone special. That's cause he went off to college, and come back sensible. Inside his head he could figure things, things most folks never even thought to. His figuring shows, even in the hospital. Though just over 25 and though nobody told 'em about his body's most serious condition—touch and go—he pulls his wife close and whispers instructions for raising their little boy. Then, Harry Jr. let go. Never heard a bad word about him. From those closest, only good. A good son. A good husband. A good dad. Even, a good church goer. Geesums! The question keeps asking, why? Why would them crows call on someone so good... so young... so soon??? Why, oh why?

Little Jack, from next door, age 14 and three years older'n me, accompanies me to the ridge cause he wants to show me something. Having to do with man stuff, he says. So there in the heart of the dim thicket we stand, man to man. His showing begins with his hand disappearing, then reappearing with something growing in it. His something must'a itched something awful cause he tries and tries to soothe it. His trying is getting real vigorous when he cries out a name, Peggy... oh Peggy. He musta soothed it then, cause his trying ends with a sigh. Little Jack calls it manipulation, not exactly an itch, but like an itch that needs treatment more and more the older a man gets. Then Little Jack looks over and offers, "Okay now, let's treat yours." His offer sends me scurrying off and sets me thinking of a close encounter with a strange man who sits down beside me in the dark of the Strand Theatre down on Clay Street. Then, ever so politely, he offers me popcorn with one hand, while the other finds my little zipper, unzips it, reaches in and begins manipulating. That costly popcorn sure tasted good but I got scared, got up and run, just like today with neither his treatment nor his delicious popcorn enough to hold me there for long, not long enough for the full treatment. One night, alone in my room, I tried Little Jack's manipulation, but after it burned like hell, I adopted a "hands off" policy. Least for a while.

My first. Oh, I remember it well, although all doesn't end well, well, not exactly. But a first kiss is a first kiss. The setting is Bomar Elementary. More specifically, under the umbrage of the big Sycamore. There I stand a minding my particulars, when Betty Jo McCrary approaches. She doesn't say a word. Then, unexpectedly, she moves close, real close. Then I feel it. She kisses me. Backing away I don't find her slight hare lip objectionable, actually she's real pretty, but I find my thoughts are, even disturbing. What if Betty Jo ever set eyes on Mamma or Papa or Uncle John or ever set foot in the house and saw things. Would she or could she have stood getting that close, even for a second, much less, for the sparing of that kiss. Suddenly! Without warning, my rumination gets wrestled to the ground. On top of it and me is large Sherman Pharr. Evidently, he has eyes for Betty Jo and he must'a been watching her indiscretion being planted because he's surely making I pay. The price, a big black eye. My first.

Big Bertha Guidry, a bosom-heavy lady large on religion, arrives. She lives behind us in the little house with paint on it, just below litt'l Sammy. Finding me rocking and singing, she stops at the bottom of the steps, looks up to me and asks, "Is your mamma home?" Before a yes ma'am is out, Mamma pushes open the screen and invites her up. Big Bertha takes the steps. Porch planks give under her. I feel 'em from my should-be stilled rocker. Surprisingly, the old boards don't give in all the way. Polite palavering goes on between 'em for a few minutes, then, Big Bertha turns back and with the floor really giving, she points down at me and forcefully declares, "Myrtis! It's time. That there boy ought to be in church Sundays. Not here, just sitting and singing." Without so much as a second's hesitation or giving a notice to me, Mamma sheepishly says, "I know. I know. You're right." Right then and right there, Mamma turns my soul over to Big Bertha's care.

Sunday mornings in the pew down at Bomar Baptist, between Big Bertha and husband Joe, I'm squeezing low, covering ears and trying to tune out the preacher's roar. Geesums! How he goes on and on about lost souls getting stuck in hell and forever roasting. After though, things look up when Big Bertha and Joe stop at the ice cream shop for treating "such a good boy" to an ice cream cone. Me.

Next Sunday sinking lower in the same pew with my thoughts already going to the ice cream parlor, Big Bertha nudges me to start paying attention. I do. Then, sitting there, vilified, then, condemned to damnation tempered with hell fire and brimstone, the preacher's vociferously charged elocution jolts and jars me up and holds me standing at attention and recognized as a candidate for baptism and church membership. With, praise God pulsating, with hallelujahs reverberating and with me a shaking, the seemingly quite pleased moralizer shakes my hand and schedules my emersion as the main event for the evening services. It's called Baptism. On the way home, I'm rewarded with a scrumptious sundae, with all the fix'ens, my first. It's really something, something from heaven.

Big Bertha knocks. I'm not rocking nor singing, I'm hiding behind my bed. The wall butting the porch shields me from her unless she steps inside. Her voice reaches in. "Myrtis, oh Myrtis. It's church time. Jack's gotta get baptized." Mamma approaches the door, seeing me from the corner of her eyes, and stops, but don't say nothing. Berta sees her and says, "Is Jack ready?" "Bertha, I'm sorry. But Jack ain't a going. He's a feeling poorly," lied Mamma. "Myrtis, are you sure? Baptism is awaiting the boy." "No. He ain't a going." With her standing there so long, it seems like she suspects there's more, but she holds her Christian tongue and retreats from the porch. Mamma's a good liar, I thought, without making a sound for Big Bertha's ears to hear and prompt her return. Hours earlier, I'd been thinking of brother Garnett and his embarrassment of me down on Washington Street that Saturday, when I humiliated him with my presence and those socks. Now, my eyes go down to my lap and fix on my best pair of socks draped there, worn out and full of holes. To get baptized you got to take your shoes off, right in front of folks. No! No way! Would I expose that holey sight before the sanctified. Not to get my sins washed away. Not to get a free pass to glory. No! Not even for an eternity in heaven. There just ain't enough hell fire or ice cream in Vicksburg to make me… make me bare that shame.

A year later at age twelve, my first career opportunity opens up down at the Joy Theatre. The tornado passed over the Joy, spared it, and drove in its competition, the Saengar, not more than five blocks north. Actually, it started a little before, when I started passing out pamphlets of coming attractions. Putting 'em on car windshields. After six months, movie manager Edith Bounds put me in charge of rounding up the workers. I guess you could say she made me captain of it. The days I worked she'd give me a dollar and a free pass to the show. One night I was there and the ticket taker didn't show, so she put me at the stand. Standing, particularly in one spot, I find it tiresome. And the supposed to be one night stretches on. Perhaps, it's the patron's praise or just the hunger in my eyes that persuades Mrs. Bounds to let one so young stay on. She told me later she was surprised she did. "I never intended to keep you. Too young and with school and all. But the patrons praised you so. For your politeness and good manners. So, I decided to give you a try. Full-time." My thoughts go into motion… where in my world did politeness come from? At home, it certainly ain't on the menu. It's never considered. What could you put politeness under? The closest "P" entrée, Pellagra.

Right off, the first time I laid eyes on her, I wanted her. First, for my mother, then later, for my lover. Tall, attractive with sandy-blonde hair above glasses she wears over a sexy smile. But standing in the way of fantasy is a 6-foot-2 state trooper armed with a cocked look and a big gun. When her husband's eyes lock down on mine, I always feel suspect and wonder… what is he suspecting?

Thank goodness the giant is on duty chasing bad guys the night Mrs. Bounds, age 35, apprehends my hand between her thigh and the ice cream box. She presses hard. My passion spreads and grows. Then, abruptly she frees me while still engaging me with her smile. With that and with embraces only visualized, on my break, I rush off to the men's room and engage myself with one of those soothing manipulations. Like Little Jack showed me.

With my first paycheck comes destruction. Destroyed is a "free lunch card" handed out to the children of the destitute. At the expense of pride, it provides the noon meal. And to get the food you got to expose the card in front of the cashier and the kids in line with you. "What's that?" curious classmates would ask while readying their quarters. After the question, my appetite just up and left. After school, after that first payday, I rip to shreds that card and discard it along with the four free meals still entitled on it. Besides dignity, my twelve dollars a week buys all my clothes and my lunch and supper with any leftovers going to help feed Mamma. One Christmas, I used some of it to buy her a little cuckoo clock she'd been wanting and wanting. I learned then, when you save money up, you can buy things, like cuckoo clocks. It sure makes Mamma feel good and me, better. She sure is proud of it. When people are around and when the little bird sounds, she points to it and says, "Jack bought me that for Christmas." After it wore out and the little bird wouldn't pop out, that didn't matter to Mamma, cause she keeps on a keeping it and a pointing and a saying.

"Quo Vadis," it looks like, is going to be a blockbuster. It's 1 p.m. Sunday. The box office is readying. Behind the ticket stand, I wait. Outside, the line is long and growing longer down the block. Before unlocking the doors, Mrs. Bounds rushes up and pushes a camera into my hands. "Get outside and get a picture of that line. Today, we may break the record." Realizing the urgency but more the importance of her request, reluctance grips. "But Mrs. Bounds, I don't know about cameras. I've never taken a picture. Never. Please, you do it." "Don't be silly boy," she said, then directs, "Just look through this this. Then press this. That's all you got to do. Anybody, can. Now go." I go. I face the mob. I point. I press. Just like directed.

"Quo Vadis" is a smash, a bigger hit than Mrs. Bounds anticipated making my picture of more importance. Two days later Mrs. Bounds arrives, finds me in the lobby after school, "Jack, I just picked up the film. Come in the office. Lets see." Mrs. Bounds takes a seat at her desk. I stand looking over her shoulder, almost against it, as she flips through the prints. There's snaps of a house, her big husband, a dog, and a cat…but. Quickly she shuffles through them again. Then leaning away, she looks up buying her eyes into mine. "You picture is blank. It didn't turn out. Jesus! Point and press. That's all you had to do. Now, we don't have a picture to send Mr. Houck in New Orleans." Geesums, I think, Mr. Joy N. Houck is the big-shot owner of the Joy chain. It's more'n obvious that Mrs. Bounds is displeased with me. And I want to please her so. "I'm sorry Mrs. Bounds. Real sorry," is all I can get out except take my wounded body away. Almost through the door with my back exposed, a parting shot catches up. "Young man! A photographer you're not. No sir. A photographer you're not." Crushed, I disappear into the dark of the theatre, but that's not sufficient, now facing the more successful "Quo Vadis" without an ounce of pride left inside me, I feel like swapping places with those Christians up there. The ones being chased, caught, clawed, then chewed up by those hungry lions in breathtaking CinemaScope and beautiful Technicolor. Eaten up, a fitting end to me. But hopeless cause I ain't a Christian yet. Cause I ain't baptized yet. So redeemable, I'm not. Even fodder for the lions, I'm not. But, as a photographer, I am a record breaking flop.

Despite a good job putting money in my pocket and food in my mouth and despite good grades in school, life down at 503 is anything but rich, full, or good. Adolescence drags me down with a feeling of incompetence overtaking, taking over and growing. In the seventh grade I do get singled out though, when named most handsome. Mrs. Styles, one of my teachers, looks into my eyes with a look of more than regular homework on her mind, and tells me, "You're so good looking. You get to ride the school float down Washington Street in the Christmas parade." The catch is I need a cute sailor suit to wear to sit next to pretty Sue Sanders. What an ordeal. She musta thought the folks would run out and buy one. With what, I wonder. And Mamma, who ain't the best of sewers, scrounges up a real one and cuts it down to fit me. She works real hard on it, but her mouth works harder on me. "Why'd you go and get yourself in this shit for?" Mamma finally gets done, then the tornado comes to town and cancels the parade and my appearance. Instead, the school year book labels me, "Our popcorn boy who works at the Joy."

That work runs on for thirty five hours over five nights and two afternoons. On Saturday and Sunday after my shift at the stand, I walk home, draw up some water, take a bath, then what do I do? To escape the every-ies there, I re-take the hill and return to my Joy, take a seat in the dark and watch the picture for the umpteenth time. I hate it when blockbusters run on and on for weeks. Then, I concentrate on the credits. Heck, give me the name of a picture or a director's initials and I'll give you a name. Mamma wouldn't know one name from another. Not even Victor Fleming, although she should know him cause he's the director of "Gone With The Wind." And Mamma's mighty interested in things going with the wind. "Gonna Get Blowed Away," she titles it.

A normal day. Mine… up, 7a.m. School, 8:15 to 3:30. Walk to work, 3:30 to 3:45. Homework at the Joy, 3:45 to 5. Work, 5 to 10. Oh, supper. About 7:30, Mrs. Bounds relieves me at the stand. I walk to the corner, enter the Glass Kitchen and take up a stool at the counter. Before opening my mouth, a barbecue beef on a bun with sliced dill pickles and a coke appear in front of me. There's no need to order and the waitress ain't clairvoyant either, not exactly. It's just that for years now, for five nights a week my supper is, always is, a barbecue beef on a bun with sliced dill pickles and a coke. After five bites, supper is down but I keep on sitting, resting my feet, sipping my coke and admiring the pie on display there. Walk home, 10 to 10:45. On some nights the three mile walk escalates into a 3-mile run, especially, when "The Thing" is showing. Sensing the long strides of monster star James Arness—down off the screen and out for fresh blood—creeping up behind, walking ain't doable. Home, after looking under the bed at least three times, now with my back finally down, I start staring up at the peephole with little left to offer these upstairs demons. Some nights I wished they'd just come on down, get me and take me out of this. Finally, with an underdeveloped body pushed to the limit, restless sleep overtakes with the coming of tomorrow coming too early, and bringing on but an exhausting replay of yesterday.

Brother Marshall's been gone for some time now. He and Uncle John didn't get along at all, so at age 13, Uncle John tells 'em to get along. Living hand to mouth, sometimes he sneaks back here for a bite when Uncle John is gone. Mamma never has much to feed 'em, but spares all she can without Uncle John a missing and a suspicioning something a going or a coming.

31

With five years of schooling behind him, Marshall learns how to get in and out of trouble. Sometimes, he stays with Papa in a tent up on the side of the road at Redwood. He rides "his bike" there. Stolen for sure, some say, cause he sure ain't got money to buy it. From Vicksburg, it must be fifteen miles up there. That worries Mamma, thinking that in head-on traffic he'll get hisself killed for sure. Papa's tent with the dirt floor under it, I saw once, and once is plenty enough. Between Marshall and me, the only real brothering I recollect comes when Mamma and Uncle John leave us alone overnight without food in the house. She'll be back in the morning and bake up some biscuits, Mamma told us. So, ingenuity feeds us, by our crossing Pearl, finding and picking some green tomatoes. Marshall brings 'em up to the house, slice 'em up, rolls 'em in a little flour, drops 'em in hot grease and fries 'em up. Didn't like 'em much but hungry, I ate 'em up. And to make Marshall feel good, I kindly lied, saying they're good, even, I love 'em. I reckon most folks would say that Marshall's got it worse'n me, but to me that don't seem possible, but I reckon it just proves misery is measured different by people that ain't experiencing it.

Marshall's misery worsens when he gets caught in a motel room he ain't got a key to. In trouble, he goes to jail. And Mamma goes crazy, starts her pacings and ravings and her finding the idea of one of hers being incarcerated, being intolerable, "I don't give a good God damn what he done, he belongs to me and mine don't belong behind no bars, not while I'm a breathing." She'd gotta 'em out but she ain't got the twenty five dollar bail. So, she cusses everybody in or out of earshot, Uncle John, the neighbors "What the fuck y'all staring at. You low down bitches didn't drop nothing so God damn perfect neither, did ya! Finally, Marshall gets sprung when Mamma signs a waiver and at seventeen, gets signed over to the Navy and the aircraft carrier the USS Philippine Sea. Having already seen the worst of life, now he sees a clean bed, a roof overhead, and three squares a day, though, some sleeping and eating gets interrupted for refueling them planes for flying off and for dropping off them bombs over Korea.

After four years and three months Marshall gets a discharge, a general one and not a regular one, not the one called honorable. Something to do with behavior and getting three months in the brig for it. So, steada serving four years like he signed up for, it come to four years and three months with brig time not counting as time served. Then brother Marshall returns to historic Vicksburg. History sure acts funny around here. People flock here just to be near it, even pay to see it, even those endless rows of dead body markers. Funny though, people, like me, surrounded by it, pay it no notice and pray to one day be away from it. Way away. And let history be. Especially, the history holding me.

Now freed of deck duty, brother Marshall moves his base to the Joy Theatre, my Joy Theatre. His mission, the landing of ladies. He's real good looking, a lot shorter than Garnett, even me, but a bit taller than Mamma. He stays a few nights with us, with Uncle John being a little more tolerant with Marshall, the man, who if a mind too, could probably kick his butt. I'd a like to seen it, but Marshall is real reserved, ever passive when it comes to flexing his muscles, except when around a girl. He's quiet too, real quiet, never talking about much of nothing, certainly not of the past, not even of his ingenuity… frying up green tomatoes.

We Thornell brothers, Marshall, Garnett and me are more like distant cousins, separated by more than geography. Maybe it's history and the hard times doing it that keeps on keeping us apart. For sure, that history of ours is a hard subject, real hard, and not one for studying on, not together. Never.

It's Friday night and the last showing is about to start when two pretty girls come in and put their tickets in my hand. Jean, the prettier one and the younger one, smiles and smiles at me. They disappear inside, but a few minutes later Jean reappears to get a drink of water and smile some more. Then, she approaches the stand. "What time you get off?" "Any minute." "Good. Want to come inside and join us." Then, I mention that brother Marshall is already inside. "He can come too. But you, you're mine." Marshall convinces the girls to forget the show and take a ride, into Battlefield Park and park. While Marshall and his lady take a stroll amongst the corpses, I'm coming alive in the back seat with pretty Jean. Other than the peck from Betty Joe, any affiliation with girls has been non-existent. Until now. And now, I ain't resistant. Then, it becomes obvious to a more experienced smoocher that somethings a missing, so she stops kissing and starts giggling before asking, "Jack, how old are you." "Uh… Uh… fifteen, almost sixteen." "Oh, Jack! You're too young," she says overcoming laughter. "But I'm a good learner. You can teach me those things." "No. No. A shame though cause you're so cute," she adds between more giggles.

Well that was the beginning and the ending of my school-days-kissing days, except for those supplied by an aggressive imagination, one not checking i.d. cards. But before long, Marshall starts kissing Jean, then marries her, but never seems bothered about my kissing her first. In fact we never talk about that or about life or death or anything in between. Decidedly, in agreement about those things—our lives—as just too disgusting for discussing.

Hormones are troublesome and at 16, threaten my theatre career. That's cause I start talking like Mamma, not in front of the patrons, lord no, but in front of the girl working behind the concession stand. Actually, my talk is more suggestive than Mamma's. About sex and stuff, things about which I know nothing. But on slow nights, I'd turn around and act like I did. I'd even offer to show her. For a while, Madge makes concessions by turning her back on me and trying to ignore me. But I keep up my dirt talking until she turns on me, faces movie manager Bounds and tells on me.

The next afternoon after I show for work, a red-faced Mrs. Bounds faces me. "Jack! Come into my office. Now." I obey. "Sit!" I obey. "Jack! I can't believe what I'm hearing. This, this doesn't sound like you." Hesitating, her face grows tenser and redder. "Madge told me about your nasty mouth. What I heard. Well it's awful. It's unrepeatable and certainly intolerable. And you've always been so well-behaved, so well-mannered. What have you to say?" "Mrs. Bounds, I'm sorry, I'm done with it." "Boy, you'd better be. Boy! I thought about firing you, but you been here for four years now, so I'll give you another chance. But if it happens again." "Yes ma'am, yes ma'am, it won't, it won't." Going through the door, her last word catches me. "And remember young man, irreplaceable, you're not."

Getting set down like that. Getting belittled by the woman I love, it's more than humiliating and it liked to kill me, but it didn't, and it straightened me up. That and worry. Fired and without money, that free lunch card would be forced back on me and that would kill me for sure. Like Uncle John said about siding up against his niggers again, before enduring that lunchroom humiliation again, I'd starve.

Shouldn't a 16-hour day filled with school and work, be enough to knock any normal body out. Shouldn't sleep race the covers up and win. In other beds, in other places, probably, but not here and not for this body. Down here, sleep is always an uphill battle. With Oddeye trying to draw me up for another stare off. It must be 2 a.m. I'm stilled. Rest assured, I'm telling myself, cause there's no body or no thing under the bed. Cause by the fourth look I would have caught he, she or it by then. Or got caught trying. Just lying wide-eyed, backed down in my defensive position, covered, sweating and trying to keep my eyes out of that peephole up there. Thoughts occupy me. Dumb thoughts and smart thoughts. For instance why am I so smart, wouldn't it be for the better if I wasn't. Dumb sounds good, dumber better, cause smart notices things. Dumb just bumps into things. "Oh pardon me street post, I didn't notice." See, with dumb, bumps don't bother. Dumb just keeps on meandering until done bumping. I excel in chemistry and higher math. The hard stuff, harder for some rich kids than for me. How can that be? How can Papa be Papa and me be me? And me be so smart. If Papa's smart, or ever been, the little I saw of 'em, I never noticed. And that don't bother him none. He just keeps on a bumping. If tested, say I asked him about πr^2 (pie area square), what would he answer? Probably... Boy! What kinda dang fool question is that? Even idjiuts know, pie are round. Well, have to grade 'em above a zero, cause at least, he knows pie has to do with circles. For Papa, round pie is plenty good enough. And he probably wonders... where in the world did such a square head son come from. Oh God! To be more like Papa. To be just like Papa. Just a meandering. Just a bumping. Not noticing. God! Spare me.

The theatre is full. I guard the stand. Screams reach out. I rush in. More screams split the dark. Surrounded by 'em, I search... trying to identify the culprit causing the commotion. I look up. Towering over me, a hunk bigger'n life, a glowering down with hungry eyes over a twisted grin and with thick juicy lips a dripping Technicolor. Elvis! It's Elvis! In motion behind the plow and between the corn in, "Love Me Tender." It's Elvis' first film and my first look at "The King." Later on, real life will surprise me with a shake of his hand and still later, shakes me up with his internment at Graceland. On both occasions, the envy of Elvis covers me. First for his fame and fortune and then, for his peace now, found resting under a heavy monument for all eternity, beginning at age 42. Oh Elvis! Oh how I wanted to be you.

Sunday morning is about wasted with swinging on the porch, when a chauffeured car pulls up. The driver steps out, walks around and opens the back, as if for a celebrity. Uncle John emerges looking all glassy-eyed. Now, I recognize the driver, it's Uncle John's bossman. "John, you're home," he says. Then, Uncle John starts his starring, first up at the house, then up to me on the porch. His looking is more than scary. It gets me up on my feet. About then, Mamma pushes open the screen and comes out. The bossman says, "Mrs. Thornell, I brought John home. He couldn't remember where he lives. Not even his name. Don't know what happened to him. He ain't bleeding, hurt, or nothing. It's a shame. A real shame." The bossman leaves, leaving John a standing in the shadow of the house with his grin a spreading. What addled him, we never know, but we do know for a surety that somewhere in the darkness of the vast cotton compress warehouse, Uncle John, while making his rounds as a night watchman, loses his mind. And never again finds it.

So, with Uncle John turning crazy on us and with a last paycheck earned and spent, life down at 503, worsens. With school and work stretching my limits and with time and shame separating me from girls my age, the only relief for a growing libido is... sex with Mamma. Some nights, after Crazy Uncle John is done acting his craziest and slips into sleep, Mamma slips out of bed with him and slips into bed with me, just to get away from his reach. Fear pushes us closer than ever. Actually, sex with Mamma, whether real or imagined, it's impossible

34

to say now, lives on and keeps on disgusting. Sex with Mamma? How was that possible, when I couldn't stand the sound of her, much less the sight of her. Smothering shame doesn't air such things, real or imagined, while its gnawing kindred is constantly screaming its verdict, its real and guilty as suspected.

So, night after night for five years now, leaving home at 7 a.m. and getting home at 11 p.m., without time out for being a kid, I have crept into bed exhausted by life and the shame of it, and thinking, surely somewhere there's more than this. Just lying here, just staring up there, just waiting for the late show of demons to begin playing in my head. And down below, somewhere in the dark, Crazy Uncle John is stirring. God, if only I could uncross these arms, unprotect this chest, roll over on my belly and relax and rest the front side of me, how heavenly. But exposing my back, even for a second, with the thought of those scissors still planted, still alive in my memory, still standing perfectly perpendicular, now, that would be crazy.

After turning eighteen, though a skeleton of a man, some nights the boyish urge to scream out and let out this fear takes hold of me. But screaming, that could disturb Crazy Uncle John, stir him up and perhaps, bring out his worse. No, screaming ain't a possibility. Geesums! That could even pull those other elements down through the peephole and down on me. Fear, you can't show it, you got to hold it in, cause when fear gets loosed, it turns back on you, like hungry lions loosed on Christians, devouring.

So, these nights when fear can't be held quiet no longer, I wake up and call out, "Makesense." Butt-Butt… "Makesense is here." "Cousin, I'm scared. Tell these demons upstairs something." Makesense is silent. "Makesense! Tell 'em!" Oh, Makesense'll be out in the morning, a raising, a butting, and an encouraging me to hurry up, to get up and to get out of there. That awful privy, that's enough to raise most dead and Makesense's sensitivity, most certainly. Oh Makesense! I gotta get out of here. And away from here. Way away. If I want to live, I just gotta.

My senior year starts with the twisting on of a class ring purchased but unearned, with just two and a half credits needed for graduation. Last summer, to get away from the house and to get ahead, I took senior history. Then, when I tried to lighten my load and just take three subjects, Mr. Marshall, the principal said, "Sorry, you got to take four. It's the minimum. It's required. It don't matter you don't need the credit." If Mr. Marshall knew of all those things crowding my brain, he would'a broke the rule, I'm certain, but he didn't know and no way could I tell him. Not those things. The fear. The poverty. The shame. And the tire of all coupling and choking. Still, I'm only nine months away from becoming a modern day miracle. A Thornell with a high school diploma, but around here, success is still measured in goose liver, in ounces, not pounds and never in diplomas. If Papa or John ever finished grade one, they never bragged on it. Still, even with four subjects forced on me, it should be an easy year with algebra, geometry and chemistry, both one and two, mastered like someone preparing for college. But wise up, cause down at the bottom of the hill, down there to them, the term higher learning is but a faraway galaxy, unpronounceable. The far-fetched idea of my becoming a doctor, a lawyer or a man of the cloth is never put into words. Not with my family tree. Not with the roots of unworthiness strangling me. Of them and of the house, I'll never be free, with my epitaph reading… Born here. Died here. Without a life in between.

This morning, looking down and facing the trigonometry test, my brain up and leaves me. Skips. Cuts. Jumps. Vacations to wherever. Whatever. It's gone. It's off. It's not working. Digits twist and turn. Turning into distorted figures. Becoming unrecognizable. Everything freezes. Except for eyes freed, following and being tested by the dancing digits. For forty five minutes I sit, brain dead and motionless. Pencil never touches paper. Why did I do this? To myself? I didn't need to. I don't need trig. Trig is for college kids. Jack! You're so stupid. A's are for smart kids. Forget the honor roll. Kid! You're starring at a zero. You're getting just like Papa. But why is it killing you? You asked for it. You did, didn't you? Remember, smart notices. So stupid, turn in your paper. The bell sounds. So with nothing added to a zero, I pass the paper forward. Today, my only source for success and for pride, fails me. Today, shame follows me to school. And finds me.

Leaving school, walking to work, a fine misty rain finds, mixes with and dilutes my tears. Today however, work will be a second stop. First, a stop next door to the Joy. Outside, looking both ways, up and down Walnut, then over to and past the glassed-in box office. Mrs. Ramsey is looking away. Thank goodness, nobody sees me as I step inside the Army Recruiting Office. The polite sergeant looks up and asks, "Can I be of help?" "Yes sir. I want to join up." After a few questions, age and such, he pushes a stack of test papers at me. "You got forty-five minutes to complete them." That's good, I think, because it's 3:45 and I'm due on the stand at 5. There're be no time for homework. But if I pass this test, there won't be any more homework, not at Carr Central and not down at 503. It'll be finished. Finished.

Thank God, my brain is back. The test is a breeze. I finish early. "You got ten more minutes. Don't you want them." "No sir. No thank you, I'm finished." "Okay then, go sit over there for a few minutes." I do as ordered, focusing on the window and hoping that no one I know looks in and sees me. Through grading, he calls me back over, looks up, looking very sincere and says, "Young man. You'll be graduating soon. Why not wait? Come back then, then I'll gladly sign you up." Holding my reply, he looks back down at my score and adds, "I can see you're smart. Real smart. What's a few months?" An eternity I think, but respond, "I can't wait. I just can't. I must go. And now." With a conscious cleared, and smiling, the recruiter says, "Sign here," and adds another drop-out to his enlistment quota. Still smiling, he presses a bus ticket into my hand with instructions and says, "You'll be leaving day after tomorrow, at 10 a.m."

Hugging the wall for the few steps to the Joy, I enter undetected. After my five hour stand, I walk home in the lingering drizzle and fall into bed. Not having breathed a word of my escape plan to a soul. For the silence, I have my reasons. The shame of quitting school. But more. The fear of setting Crazy Uncle John into motion for perhaps, a final blow. And more. The fear of those demons dropping down, parading around my bed, and then, pulling me up and through the peephole for sharing their eternity up there... behind a door nailed shut.

"Jack! It's almost 7:30. You gonna be late for school. You best get up." With Mamma watching, I slide up, turn my back and slip into my breeches, then I turn back and face her. "Mamma, I'm not going to school. I'm catching the Greyhound." "What! What you mean?" "Mamma, I joined the army." "Jack oh Jack! What you gone and done? When?" "I just decided. All a sudden, it's done." With my announcement registering on her, Mamma starts her pacing, her crying and her crying out, "God oh God! What else can be done to me?" With my packing starting, Mamma continues crying and cutting her eyes over and into me. Finally, I can't stand it. "Mamma! Quiet yourself. Please. You'll draw John's attention." God! I shouldn't a mentioned John, crazy Uncle John. Our eyes meet up. Our fears join up. Then, our tears. "But Mamma, there'll be money for you. From me. Every month. You can count on it. Things'll ease up then."

Starting up the hill, carrying my little ditty bag, all the Army allows, I leave Mamma, still in a state of shock, standing at the edge of her ditch where we weathered many a stormy night. Reaching Oak Street, halfway up, I can still feel Mamma's eyes on my back. But I cannot look back. To take the hill a body must lean forward. And with this load of guilt. I can't straighten for looking back. No. Knowing what I'll be a seeing. Mamma a standing there. Alone. No. Knowing what I'm a doing. Leaving Mamma down there. Gripped by poverty by day and perhaps, some night by Crazy Uncle John. Mamma! I should have warned you about those demons upstairs. But I didn't want to scare you worse. Mamma! I'm sorry, so sorry Mamma. I shouted in my mind, before disappearing from her sight and her life. It's said… misery loves company, and my leaving just doubled Mamma's. I know, I'm good in math.

Just before topping Dabney and turning onto Washington, I pass up Principal Marshall's house elevated on my right. It's a simple shotgun, but it looks good to me cause its got paint on it. It'll be a few days before Mr. Marshall misses me and comes down looking. What will he think when he sees? Will he remember our conversation about lightening my load? I wonder. At least the Greyhound Bus Depot isn't next to the Joy like Trailways. That's good. Cause I don't want to see any familiar faces, even the custodian, and have to give any explanations or say any more good byes. Telling Mrs. Bounds last night was hard enough. "Jack! Have you lost your senses? You haven't graduated high school," she said, "Why didn't you come talk to me? Tell me what you're thinking?" She was upset. Partly, because my sudden departure puts her in a strain until she can find a replacement. Until then, she'll be forced to stand there tiring her feet for five hours. And to Mrs. Bounds, that's more than tiring, for a manager, that's degrading. Holding back my tears and the details behind my leaving, I start for the exit. Although she didn't say it out loud, I could hear and feel her parting shot at my back. "Young man! A graduate, you're not. Just like your parents. Just like your brothers. A dropout." With my own mind adding a final sentence… And, a modern day miracle, a Thornell with a high school diploma, you'll never be. You're so right Mrs. Bounds, now, I'm just like them. Exactly.

Behind me, the big bus door slams. My body takes a seat and slumps. My eyes squeeze shut, avoiding passing glances trying to get inside, spot me and try to stop me. A last look out isn't necessary, isn't wanted. Of Vicksburg, I've seen enough. My history here seems like two lifetime's worth, even at eighteen. And worse, with all of it shameful, nothing but miserable. And painful, nothing but. Up the road or down the road, there's got to be a kinder place for making history. There's gotta.

Kinderville, this ain't, is the reaction of this 129-pound body—the Army's bare minimum for a height of 5-foot-9 inches—stepping off the bus and facing a new kind of demon. Disturbed, pushing a finger in my face and screaming, "Boy! Your bony little ass belongs to me." With the chuckles of other recruits reaching his ears, he quickly turns on them. "Wipe those sissy-fucking Shirley Temple smiles off those faces. This ain't the movies." Returning his attention to me, he catches hands in my pockets and exacts punishment for the crime. "Boy! Pockets are forbidden territory. Get those hands out, drop down on 'em and give me ten."

Pushups, he's talking and I do, but without much upper body strength, barely. "Next time, it'll be fifteen." And we both know, I don't have fifteen in me.

Fort Chaffee, Arkansas is vast, spreading over 73,000 acres, eight miles southeast of Fort Smith in the Ozarks near the Oklahoma border. The chow is plentiful. The language is coarse, but nothing mother hasn't served up. Physicals, indoctrination and haircuts busy our first day. Shaving and showering every day gets to be routine but exposing private parts remains uncomfortable. But it sure beats drawing water twice a week and sitting on the rim of a tub grown too small. Here, behind guarded gates, I can sleep like a baby on his belly without fear. And during the day, I got drill Sergeant "Hawkeye" Wilson looking after me. "Drop down you wimpy little runt. Give me fifteen. Whenerya gonna learn?" Geesums! If only he knew, perhaps he'd look the other way and be more forgiving. Knew, for five hours a day for over five years, during lulls at the ticket stand, how I filled my pockets. With hands. Now trained, and going there. Automatically, unconsciously, like breathing. A practice, watchdog Wilson is hell-bent on breaking. That or a back. Mine.

Mamma's first letter reaches me recalling her conversation—a talent Mamma excels at— with Principal Marshall. "Oh Mrs. Thornell, all Jack had to do was show up and he would have graduated. What happened?" "Well Mr. Marshall, look around you," I told 'em. He didn't have to look far to see John a standing there, a looking back and a looking crazier by the second. "Mr. Marshall, you just don't know about all the goings on round here. Reckon Jack just couldn't stand it no longer. He was a good boy though. Never caused me no trouble." "He was good and smart too. I'm so sorry to hear this. So sorry." The most bothersome part of Mamma's news is Mr. Marshall's invitation to look around. Actually, it's more than bothersome. His seeing inside 503. His seeing where I come from each morning before his seeing me at school. It's punishing.

"For your information, this is a .30 caliber M-1. This is a weapon. This is not a gun. It was never a gun. It will never be a gun," shouts Sgt. Wilson, while hoisting the rifle aloft with his right hand, then grabbing his crotch with his left and shouting, "This is your gun. Used on the likes of Annie Oakley." Then, repeating the routine, yelling, "Have you horny morons got that straight yet. Kill with the long one. Love with the short one. Keep both clean and lubricated and you'll keep me and Miss Oakley both happy." Finally, he finishes the demonstration by cutting his eyes over to me and unloading, "Private Thornell. Ever fired your gun? I mean at a live target." I sit silent. "I didn't think so, " he responded.

For the next eight weeks my weapon gets preferential treatment. Firmly, I handle it. Closed eyed, I disassemble it. With oil, I massage it. Insuring longevity till time for feeling its recoil. On the other hand, my gun goes untreated. Unhandled and unmassaged, even neglected, with privacy hard to come by. In the john, the latrine, the toilet, the head or the privy, whatever you call it, there are no closed stalls, so any preferential treatment must wait. Oh! What a body would give for a Little Jack sigh.

"Lock and load. Ready on the left. Ready on the right. Ready on the firing lane," the range officers broadcasts, dividing his looks left and right. Prone, sweat attracts the dirt below me. I rub my eyes. Vision blurs. "Commence firing," sounds. A trigger jerks. A thumb jams into an eye. Paused by pain, half blinded, I look up. Looking down, watchdog Wilson barks, "Boy! I told you that would happen, tighten that sling." Shaking his head, he lifts his eyes and looks down range to check my score. A white flag sweeps back and forth behind my target.

"Maggies drawers," the scorekeeper hollers, confirming the humiliation of a target unpenetrated, still claiming virgin status. "Pucker up private. Unless you shoot better, instead of killing 'em, you'll be kissing 'em. The enemy," Wilson growls. Then, settling down and recanting my bird shooting days, I aim, squeeze and qualify as a marksman with a second black eye, a bonus.

The pin, I pull. I hurl. The grenade sticks to a sweaty palm and falls short. Too short and too close. Still standing and exposing my body above the bunker, Sgt. Wilson flies in. Pushing me down and covering my body with his. The explosion sounds. Dust and debris sail over. Wilson presses his face up against mine, but managing only a whisper, "Boy what you doing in the Army?"

"Watch your step! The hills are alive with the sounds of rattlers," our caretaker warns as we load up and move out to live out in the woods. War games, it's called. Out there, we pitch pup tents, dig foxholes and latrines. And turn friends into foes. But worry not, cause our guns don't got no live ammo. Really arm us. Get real. The Army keeps real bullets under lock and key. And out of the hands of qualified morons.

Dreams… of home… of demons descending… of a grinning man bending… catch me sleeping. Then something rescues me. A sound. Thank goodness I think, with my eyes widening. Then again it sounds, turning my head and drawing my eyes right. Beside me, coiled, a six-foot viper. Raising its head, finding, then sinking its eyes deep into mine. Now, ever so slightly, shifting its head side-to-side, as if in a mood and mode for penetrating a soul, even a dark soul like mine. Suddenly! As if stunned by the sight of a disturbed demon escaping a dream and rushing and brushing by, the snake goes limp. Collapses its spiral. Drops to the ground. Turns tail. Silenced. And slithers back to sanctuary, the woods. With only seconds elapsing, I'm up, dressed and outside the pup tent pacing, but watching my step and anxiously awaiting the sound of reveille.

"Ivy, LeDoux, Sanchez, Tho… T-h-o…n…no, make that a R… n-e-l-l, sorry, I can barely read it," the mail clerk announces. Geesums! Another letter from Mamma, but it must be addressed by her and not by a neighbor's hand. Seeing her scribble, feeling the attention, cringing, I back away and secure a secluded spot. There, guarding her spelling from eyes that might take delight in such ignorance and enjoy associating it with me. She's grateful for the $40 allotment. The Army turned down the matching amount. Cause she got a husband. And crazy don't matter. Plenty to feed her though and pay all the utilities. She's thankful the house is paid off and in her name. She's worried about me. Can I make it on $30 a –month. My experience replies. Mamma, you know we made do on nothing. Here, there's food, there's shelter and there's $30 for personals. Hell yes Mamma, I can make it. Make it fine. I can even close my eyes and sleep some. The other night, she finds Crazy Uncle John in my room, standing over and starring down at an empty bed and asking, "Where's Jack? What's happened to Jack?"

Surviving surprises me, undoubtedly the Army too, hallelujah brother, boot camp is over. With the taste of tear gas, the explosion of grenades, the recoil of M-ls, the alarm of rattlesnakes, all useful obstacles for clouding my thoughts of home. And don't forget those useful "How to's" learned. To turn on a dime without falling face down. To turn shoe toes into mirrors by spitting on 'em. To strengthen arms and shoulders by pushing hands into pockets. To swallow cream of chipped beef on toast for breakfast without instantly turning it into something worse looking.

While waiting for assignment, a lieutenant approaches me with news. "Private Thornell, you've been chosen to test for O.C.S." "What's O.C.S.," I inquire. "Officer's Candidate School," he said with a puzzled look before giving me the particulars of when and where to report. "Yes sir. Thank you sir," I said, then concluding with a salute. When learning the little gold bar recognized with sirs and salutes takes months of rigorous training to earn, my body sags. Geesums! I barely braved boot camp and almost blew up Sgt. Wilson. And myself. When it comes to the military, I don't know which end is up. If I know it, why don't the Army know it too? Then, facing the test, a strategy—missing every fourth question on purpose—takes over. So, with a score of 75, O.C.S. will be history and I'll still be graded slightly above moron. But honestly, at the bottom of my thinking are roots trailing back to 503. And knowing when the Army digs deeper, they'll uncover, they'll see and they'll correct a mistake by announcing… Private Thornell, after further evaluation, a candidate for officer and gentleman, you're not. A high school dropout you are and always will be.

It's sunny and cool as I stand at attention in the farewell formation. Sgt. "Watchdog" Wilson, with his golden hashmarks gleaming, is taking a final look. For twenty years now, his job has been shouting insults and getting best results from the boys they sent him. Soon, he'll be retiring and returning to civilian status and a quieter life. Hate him? I don't think so. No. But I sure hated his possessiveness. Boy! Your bony ass belongs to me. His assertiveness: Drop down and give me twenty. His suspicions. I suspect Private Thornell is yet to fire his gun at a live target. Oops! He's in my face. Going rigid, I take a deep breath and hold it. He takes my weapon, slides open the bolt, flips the butt into the air and glares down the barrel. Finished, he shoves the M-1 hard against me. And then, he turns human. With smiling eyes and a soft voice he offers, "Congratulations and good luck young man with whatever you do in life." Then, he resumes his inspection. But during our face to face, our eye to eye, and our heart to heart, I knew he knew. For me, the Army was not a choice, only a last resort. Perhaps, it was his too.

Unable to decide on a specialty school, the Army gets creative and decides for me. Radio repair. Figure that. In electronics my scores tested weak, weak, weak. Turn on, listen, and turn off is the sum total of my radio experience. The static accompanying the Grand Ole Opry on Saturday nights back home and sometimes drowning it, just a condition of listening. But complain about the Army's choice, there are no grounds. Other than, pass out pamphlets, tear tickets and stuff hands into pockets, I'm unskilled. Then, orders come. Next stop. Department of Specialty Training, Signal School, Fort Monmouth, New Jersey. But with the orders, there's leave. Geesums! My heart speeds, and my mind goes A.W.O.L. (Absent Without Leave). And orders are orders and must be obeyed. My bus ticket is routed through Vicksburg for a three-day stopover, then on to New Jersey. And I'm broke. Without money or anywhere else to go. Geesums! There's no escaping it. Even the mighty military surrenders to it. The past. With all its controlling devices still intact, still pulling my strings and still awaiting.

Dabney Avenue's incline forces my shoulders up and rigid as I resist the gravity trying to hurry my return. I pass the Scotts, the Finkeys, the Leafovers, the Lanes. Then, I stop. The house draws me. The dirty gray boards. The rusting tin roof. And the little attic window with the broken glass above my room and the amputated stairs. The house's umbrage reaches out and covers me. Under it and inside military garb worn by the conquerors of nations, I shrink. The door opens, Mamma looks out, sees me and starts running. Behind her, Crazy Uncle John grins. I swallow hard. With brief but still uncomfortable hugs concluded, my calling Mamma Mamma doesn't feel right, so then and there, Mamma becomes mother. A more standoffish and certainly, a more comfortable title, particularly, with me plagued by lingering doubt, did I or didn't I have sex with Mamma? With mother, it's unquestionably… I did not.

With her mouth unstopping, she pulls me inside, through the bedroom where my eyes avoid a challenge to look up and meet up with the peephole, before reaching the kitchen for a cup of hot tea with milk and sugar, her favorite beverage and a necessity for avoiding a headache. Plain tea will do her if that's all there is, but with my allotment check there's plenty for sugar and milk. After swallowing a mouthful of her tea, she begins. "Days ain't so bad, but Jack, the goddamn nights. I'm scared to close my eyes. Don't know how much longer I can stand it. Just don't." with her pausing, I look up and check to make sure Crazy Uncle John is still outside and out of earshot. Finding he is, I reply, "I know mother. But what about his children, Clifton and John Jr., can't they help?" "You're kidding, have a crazy around young'uns. They got more goddamn sense. And all we got to live on is your Army money. Without that, we'd be hungry.

The front screen door squeaks. Conversation stops. I feel a presence. Quickly standing, I ask, "Mother, where's the hammer?" "There," pointing she says, "In the bottom safe drawer." I reach in, pick up the hammer, then turn and face Crazy Uncle John standing in the kitchen doorway. After squeezing past him and moving over to the door separating my bedroom from his, I pause and reach into my pocket. Having stopped up at the Mississippi Hardware and making a purchase, I had come home prepared. My hammering begins and draws mother into the room. Neither spoke as I installed the latch on the door. Tonight there would be a lock between me and Crazy Uncle John. Grinning, he exits back onto the porch and collects himself in the swing. Mother, now seeing she can't escape into my room, moves back to the kitchen table and lifts the precious tea to her lips. I join her side. For the longest, we sit there, not speaking, with fear commanding silence. Even of the most powerful of mouths. Even of mother's.

Saturday night and a return to the Joy Theater and having to face familiar faces, is awkward. But I can't stay away, cause I can't stay home, that's worse, that's impossible. As before, the Joy is my ticket out. Mrs. Bounds, in place relieving the ticket taker, greets me. "You're two months late for work. You're fired." Then, smiling and admiring my uniform, presses me into service. When the regular worker returns, I move inside the theater, take a seat, close my eyes and feel my body relax. Now, I'm home.

With the walk behind, I enter the house, pull on the light string, move over to the door opening into Crazy Uncle John's room, pull it shut and push the latch into place. It's not much, just a hook, but snatching it loose should stir a light sleeper. Still in uniform, I go to my knees and do a search under the bed. Satisfied, I undress, pull off the light and get into bed. Like always, backed down, rigid and rushing my eyes to adjust to the dark. Like always, waiting for the peephole to find and take my eyes. Sometime before daylight, while listening for movement at the hooked door, a troubled sleep finds me.

The cold bites at my face as snow collects atop the dark green duffel supported by shoulders strengthened by pushups. Despite Sgt. Wilson's muscle building program, my upper body is still lacking. However, legs developed by years of standing and walking help in bearing the load. Facing me and rising into a gray December sky is a fancy, newly constructed mutlileveled dormitory. Appearing more than adequate to shield radio repair students from the worse nature has in the offering.

With my burden dropped near the door, and still shivering I face the duty sergeant. "Private Jack R. Thornell reporting to "A" Company for duty." After affording me a brief and expressionless look, the sergeant lowers his eyes back to the desk. He shuffles papers. Then reshuffles. Finally, scratching his head, he looks up and holds his eyes on me. "Private, that's Thorhill?" "No, it's Thornell… T-h-o-r-n-e-l-l." With an "Oh" out, he lowers his head and looks some more before looking back up. "Private Thornell, your name is not on the "A" Company roster. I tripled checked. It's not here." Seeing my shrug, he continues, "Wait a minute," then going into a desk drawer, he comes out with what appears to be a master list of names and starts moving his finger down it. "Aye," he sighs, "I found you. Private, you're in the wrong damn place. Your butt belongs to Company "O" on the old side of the post." Hastily drawing me a map, he pushes it into my hands and concludes, "Since your transport is gone, you'll have to walk. Watch your step, it's getting slippery out there."

With the weighty duffel pressing down on my shoulder and with a trail of snowy foot prints accumulating behind me, I trudge towards a new destination. After what seemed like miles, with a back killing and with a body just degrees from turning into a frozen likeness of Quisamoto, I chance stopping to get my bearings. Straightening enough to look ahead, survival hopes are raised by the sign of Company "O". Getting there, I see what the sarge meant by "the older side of the post." Facing me are single story super antiquated wood frame shells. Even the fresh coat of paint offers a chilling greeting.

Inside, after dropping the snow-covered bag, I turn, face the corporal and report in. "Private Thornell. Let's see. Yes, here's your name. You got any questions?" "When does radio repair school start?" "Radio Repair! What are you talking about? That's not taught here." "But that's my assignment, isn't it?" "Hell no private, you're going to still photography school." "What! But! But Corporal, there must be some mistake. A mixup. A clerical error. Something." Quickly looking back down at the documents, then back up, the company clerk responds, "Private Thornell, there is no mistake. You're going to photography school." Cutting off my argument with "The Army don't make mistakes," he points me toward the exit and says, "You're bunked two billets down." Stepping outside, the cold and the crush of the duffel goes unfelt, with anxiety going out of control, gripping and jerking me back to the Joy Theater, to the record crowd, to the camera, to the blank picture and to Mrs. Bounds admonition, "Young man! A photographer, you're not," stinging. Geesums! Geesums! Geesums! Blank! Blank! Blank!

Inside, Privates Robert Lally and John Feneran, both yanks and brothers of the Catholic Faith, greet me. Taking delight with my deep south accent, they pursue a conversation, often synchronizing their laughter. Naturally, at my expense. Lally, with his oversized nose overextending, inquiries, "Where y'all from?" "A Vicksburg, Mississippi." Apparently dying to draw out more of my drawl and looking down and seeing my class ring, asks, "Where'd y'all graduate from?" Without thinking and before I could stop, even slow my mouth, "A Carr Central High," escapes my lips. Immediately, shame rushes a ringed finger into a forbidden pocket for concealment and for beginning friendships punctuated by a lie. But why? I hadn't lied before. Not to grandpa about murder. Not to Mrs. Bounds about profanity. His shots and her arrows, I faced. But expose this. Before foreigners. I can't. Not with superior attitudes downing and degrading me. Not with their little bands of achievement being shoved under my nose and being held up there like them yankee schools bettered them. Not now, with the conversation continuing. "Ahh, a Vicksburg, A-Carr y'all say. How many A-Carr centrals and a-Vicksburgs y'all got down there?" Visibly grinning off Lally's "A" needling, my mind takes offense. Right then and there, it decides. I'm a done, a living, a talking, and a dying. That southern talk, that Mamma talk, it's finished.

Of the two, Lally is the outgoing one, the aggressor, neat neat, better looking with naturally wavy hair his best feature. Feneran is the quiet one, sloppy sloppy, average looking with a particularly peculiar way for holding a cigarette and tapping his thumb against the filter as if sending signals. After taking a deep draw of nicotine, Feneran exhales and explains his desertion from the seminary as "needing a break from the regimen." Give me a break, I think, swapping a frock, a bible and a regimen for a uniform, a weapon and a regiment. That's a crock and too far-fetched. But shyness orders my silence and my pretending to swallow his explanation for enlisting. And besides, my own lie is still fresh in my mouth, still being tasted. Lally breaks the pause. "Y'all sleeping up here. On top of Feneran. Y'all don't fall and hurt y'alls head." Looking up, he's right, if disturbed, if rolled over by a nightmare, it's a good drop to the floor. The three of us will become close, real close, but when disunity distances us, it's always the yanks against y'all. And over the next few months I try teaching them that "y'all" at the very least is plural, never singular. But their harmonized comeback is always, "Y'all don't say."

Settling in and with the physical rigors of boot camp behind, I'm more than ready to put down a weapon and pick up a book. But photography, that's Greek to me. I could keep complaining about the clerical error, but why, when I don't know a thing about radios either. So why make waves. But starring up at the ceiling, concerns press down. Can photography be learned? Or does it take a special talent, like painting or writing? Geesums! Soon enough I'll know and worse, the Army will know. And worse, Mrs. Bounds will say, "See young man, I told you. A photographer, you're not."

"Joseph Schiamone is my name. I am your civilian instructor. If successful, you will graduate with an M. O. S. (Military Occupational Specialty) of 841.1. Still photographers. Ready to cover anything from a bloody war to a boring tea party." Sitting there, I keep waiting for a tap on the shoulder and be told that I'm in the wrong damn place, but so far, no tap. "This class is very fortunate to have two graduates of Rochester Institute of Technology with degrees in photography. John Pichon. Frank Picket. Both draftees. Also, we have an experienced newspaper photographer. Harry Harris. With the trio standing and with the revelation of their credentials still echoing, I slip lower, trying to shrink, even go unnoticed for the next twelve weeks.

"This is a 4x5 Speed Graphic. Push the film holder in, like this. Cock the shutter, like so. Look through the viewfinder here, to compose. Then, to take the picture, push the shutter release, here." Then smiling he concludes, "But don't forget to pull the dark slide first, like this, or your picture will turn out blank," His "Blank" warning evokes my cringe. With that term summing up my experience, totally. And this Speed Graphic is big. And compared to Mrs. Bounds just point and push box Brownie, complicated. "The hyper focal distance is the space from the lens to the nearest point of acceptable sharpness when focused at infinity," Schiamone continued while moving to the blackboard to confirm his words with an equation. His chalk marks draw my smile. The math, I can do in the dark.

"Get the feel of the darkroom. See where everything is. Close your eyes and picture it. Now, feel the notches on the sheet of film with your right hand. Then, slide it into the film holder. The emulsion should be facing up with the notches in the lower right corner of the holder. With this done, carefully push in the dark slide and cover the film. With our eyes shut, but often stealing necessary peeks, we practice this again and again. Then, the lights are switched off. Working in the dark with the feel and by memory is challenging. Like going blind during sleep, awakening, getting up unruffled and cooking breakfast by remembering where everything is and feeling for it. If a blind man can do that, surely I can do this. After a few tries, I can. And handily. Perhaps, the practice of maneuvering down dark theater isles, of walking or running home in the dark, of starring up and into a dark peephole, gives me an edge, even an easiness for feeling things not seen.

The first victim of the dark is Sergeant First Class Dumas "Shorty" Delaney, a 20-year plus veteran, a retread, a career soldier who re-enlists for a new M.O.S., and who like me doesn't know a thing about photography. And with several weeks of darkroom training behind, he still fails to grasp in which tank to put the film first, the developer or the fix. Sharing a large darkroom the class loads film hangers with the weekly assignments. Then Pichon, the R.I.T> grad asks, "Is everybody loaded?" And after hearing affirmatives, says, "Okay men, drop film into the fix tank." Laughs fill the room as we ignore his directive and drop our film into the developer, save one, save "Shorty" who follows the orders of a lowly private. Within seconds, the fix—the wrong solution—eats away the undeveloped images, reducing his film to clear window panes. Blanks. Feeling degraded, even duped, the retread confers with instructor Schiamone about his future in photography. There isn't one, Schiamone concludes. With the Sergeant's desk sitting empty, I can't help but wonder… am I next?

For a beginner like me, still photography means taking pictures of still objects. Like a park bench, a parked car or a building. Cause with that big Speed Graphic, the one with a bellows large enough to swallow Mrs. Bounds' camera, takes time. To compose. To focus. To cock the shutter. And to trip the shutter and take the picture. Geesums! I forgot to trip the shutter and take the picture. Geesums! I forgot to pull the dark slide. Then, I do and repeat the steps. And my first attempt for the army isn't a blank, it's a snowbank, it's in focus, it's a miracle… it's a picture.

While my classmates are out getting drunk and getting girls, the kind you can turn your guns on, I'm staying in, staying up and studying. Even memorizing the Army handbook on photography. Even if my pictures stink, my answers, when put to paper, won't. But still, doubts hang heavy over my head, as the duty sergeant shouts "lights out" and flips the switch. But, even in the dark, my doubts linger… What can I learn in 12 weeks time and stand ready to compete with Pichon and Picket and their higher learning. Four years worth. At the Best. At R.I.T. "Makesense! If you're tuned in, pillow your head with that thought."

And then, in early 1958 it hit. The Cold War. The attack is relentless. Reminiscent of Grant's blitzkrieg of Vicksburg. But instead of cannon balls, it's sleet and snow crashing down. Tons of it. For days, for nights, forever, General January pounds Fort Monmouth. For it, everything stops. Automobiles and airplanes. Cats and dogs. People, electricity, telephones and running water. Even the postman stays home. Every-body but… the news photographer. Even getting out isn't easy. Snow barricades the door. The only exit. Through a window while ducking spears of ice pointed down. Outside, instead of a winter wonderland, I discover what I love about the South. Warmth! Down South at least, sweat is a relief. What this southern boy saw was an abomination. Hell frozen over. The assignment: Capture this record-breaking frost-biting foot-freezing phenomenon without overexposing the film. And me. Geesums! This excessively white weather beast affects everything. Even F-Stops, the size of the len's opening. And not only F-stops, but shutter speeds. To compensate for my shaking, I set the shutter to the highest, one five-hundredth of a second, point and pray. Snowdrifts head-high, buried cars, frozen creeks and a few shivering shoveling soldiers capture my eyes and the lens of the big speed graphic.

With the threat of the North—overexposure of the body and film—melting away the worse winter assault in decades, comes the unexpected, a smile. A Schiamone smile. Unrelated to the workings of the weather, instead to the workings of the classroom. Mr. Schiamone enters. He has papers in his hand. Test papers.

"The grades are in," Mr. Schiamone says in a louder than usual voice. "On your 12-week finals" and after putting on a pleasant smile, he points to me and says, "Private Thornell, please stand." Shyly I stood. As he continued, "You scored a 98, the best grade in the class, congratulations." Before I can retake my seat, he takes away his smile and replaces it with the face of indifference, as he turns and looks down on the seated R.I.T. boys, and adds, "Some of you didn't do as well as I expected, but everybody passed." With the revelation of my success still buzzing around the room, I couldn't help but notice the whiz-kids slumping, much like my slumping that first day, just after their formal introduction. The moment is uplifting but it soon passes with the realization… Pinchon and Pickett passed easily, and they never cracked a book, while Jack, the-drop-out-kid, studied days and nights.

And now, with the study of flash factors, converging meniscus of lens hyper-sensitizing, phenomena of the pinhole camera and syncro-sun completed, the world awaits to be seen through the lens of a camera, my camera. And up to now, in my short 18 years, I have only pictured a small world, a very small world. And most, if not all of it, bad.

My gloomy mood matches the gloomy gray sky collapsing around me and dulling the cold and the deserted stretch of Red Bank, New Jersey sand. After my classroom coup, I should be on a high. But I'm not. Highs, the few of my experience, are always short-lived, while the lows, the many, are always on the horizon, approaching, and crowding into my head. Today, I'm off. I'm not with the guys. It's just the beach, the sky, the sea, with all their gray and my crowded head. Weary of walking and wearied by the anticipation of travel orders to who knows where, abruptly I stop, and look back. I see footprints, a lone set of footprints, my footprints, coming from nowhere. And perhaps, no, most probably, going nowhere. The same destination as the destination of that ugly old man once identified as my father.

With that dread-filled thought, still hanging, still haunting, I turn back to face the sea. The Atlantic Ocean. The enormity of it. It's overpowering. It draws me nearer, then closer to its edge while rushing ashore to meet me and deliver an invitation to my feet. To join her. To become part of her enormity. Her pull is inviting, so inviting, knowing if embraced, so effortless she could dissolve all my pain. Swallow all my shame.

And then, as suddenly as it begins, her spell ends, with… Butt-Butt! "Makesense is here… careful cousin before you ruin the spit-shine on those dress shoes…, and remember…

Makesense can't swim. Or fly." "Oh Makesense, what's out there, for me? "Perhaps cousin, everything you've missed." And then, half crying, half laughing, I reply, "Hell Makesense, the truth is, if I could swim I would have joined the Navy."

Suddenly, I felt a craving for chili. Hot chili with crumbled-up crackers. "Come'on Makesense, let's take these army shoes back to the barracks." Abruptly, I executed an about face, turning my back on the sea and returning to my duty, while remembering... the oath taken and the promise given with my right hand raised high, the same hand raised to kill the last mockingbird of my youth.

Pandemonium breaks out with Lally running through the barracks in nothing but skivvies, and shouting, "Travel orders are being posted," before turning and running back to the bulletin board to be the first to scrutinize the list. Stilled, hung-over, sleepy-eyed bodies come alive, leaping from their bunks and joining the stampede.

Lally finds his name, then reads on before announcing, "Fineran...Thornell...you're going to Germany with me for beer and broads... Pinchon, Picket... you bright bastards, you're going to further your careers in Korea by living in tents surrounded by muddy ditches, and fuck'n slanty-eyed bitches," Lally gags, before being shoved out of position.

Still in my bunk, still digesting the news of the plum assignment while staring up at the ceiling, a question raises up... what fate awaits that would-have-been photographer who took my place at radio repair school... I saw him once... in the chow line... I heard him complaining to a friend... about the army fuck-up... I kept silent while keeping my eyes off his shirt while moving away... I didn't want to know his name. Now, his should-have-been graduation certificate is in my footlocker... with my name on it. Suddenly, the good news of Germany, of the plum-assignment, is spoiled. Spoiled by guilt. The guilt of a clerical error, the guilt of a career I stole.

The propellers roar. The big bird vibrates. This is a first, my flying. At least the first to originate from ground level and not with leaps from tall buildings as did all my past dream flights. In minutes, the roaring and the vibrating subsides as the big bird levels off. Soon, the whole east coast disappears from sight. Even the ocean hides its vastness under the cover of clouds. Sitting alone, my thoughts are trying to push Vicksburg even further away... Perhaps, the sea is sufficient to separate me from mother's mouth. From home. From shame. And it's hold.

So far, the army has taught two schools: The destruction of life with a weapon and the preservation of life with film. So far, my proficiency at either profession is untested, as is my ability to please a Miss Oakley.

The plane hits the ground hard and noisily. The accompaniment shakes me awake. Looking across the aisle, I see Lally, I see Fineran. Sitting, still unstirred, with their heads tilting together, almost touching, like lovers. Geesums! How I envy them, their closeness, their togetherness. Naturally, with only two seats together and one removed, y'all was removed. In a squeeze, y'all's succession is always mandatory, is always decree'd and decree'd by the twos. Perhaps here, here in Germany they'll let up on all that y'all crap. Surely, they'll tire. I have.

With our gear stowed on the back of the open deuce and a half, army lingo for a two-and-a-half ton truck, Lally and Fineran climb in and look down at me. Grinning, Lally extends a hand and says, "Y'all get on up here now, y'all here." As yet unwilling to share my southern accent with foreigners, even conquered one, I hold my peace, instead deciding to concentrate on the scenery. It's something. Like nothing I've seen. The buildings, their styles, look ancient yet still rise sparklingly proud as if knowing that it was built to last, built to stand and withstand. Immaculate cobble stone streets, looking freshly polished and buffed, lead us through residential sections. The houses are meticulously maintained. But the yards are overrun with garden plots. Not a bit of God's good earth is wasted. In one big garden, a rotund man, fitted with a harness, is substituting his body for a jackass and pulling a honey wagon. And dripping behind is the best of fertilizer known to a German man. That! That kind! Even the thought of that, shut my appetite down, but apparently not theirs. Despite the unpleasantries in the air and on the ground, the gardeners—mostly men—look hearty and healthy. And content, perhaps already anticipating their reward... sumptuous veggies. The best their human excrement can produce. "Holy Shit Makesense! This ain't India."

The ride ends on the outskirts of Frankfort, a place called Bonamese, with the transport pulling inside the walled compound of the Third Armored Division's 144th Signal Corps Battalion. The storied barracks seem sound, reflecting little change of status as a bright morning sun bounces off the stone-gray walls rising above us. Until 1945, the habitat for the procreators of the then-called "Master Race," now just a three-story hotel for horny, hung-over American G.I.'s occupying space.

After looking around, we collect our bedding and move inside, where a first relief on German soil is an experience. It's called, pissing against the wall. That over-sized back-stop, my first thought, labeled... ridiculous. But later, when standing there, tipsy, and swaying with an overfilled and now, an out of control bladder exploding... The floor to ceiling catch-all is mandatory. And it becomes clear, German genius, it's everywhere, even in their heads.

The first night, Lally, Fineran and I stay in and talk up strategy. How to arm ourselves with sexy frauleins, and then, at the most appropriate time, raise our guns and disarm them. After that, we'll get our fill of famous German beer, allegedly, the world's best.

With plans made, we turn in. And now, I suspect the twins are lying over there wide-eyed and full of can't wait expectations. While over here, I'm full of worry. Having to do with the strategy session, with information undivulged. And undivulged by me... Beer, I have never tasted. And, my gun is as yet, untested.

At 5:30 a.m. the reveille sounds, and we scramble for shower space. From under the spray, after washing the sleep and the soap away, my eyes focus on, then widen on that, that I see. A naked black man. A first for me. At Fort Chaffee, there were a few blacks on base, but never in the shower with me, and never naked. So, I can't help but to check him out. I start with his profile and work down. He's got pearly white teeth set-in and set-off by a black black face. He's short, about 5-foot-3. A little fucking black buck would have been Uncle John's characterization. And then he turns more head-on. And then, I looked down and I see. See more than God should ever allow on any one man. Even on a Paul Bunyon. Geesums! That's not a gun, that's a long, long rifle and without a doubt, capable of bringing down and pleasing the likes of any Miss Oakley. Demoralized and embarrassed, I reign in my gaze and lower it to the shower floor. Where I admire my 11-inch sized feet.

An hour later, while standing in the chow line, the now clothed little big man extends a hand. "Hi, I'm Anthony Black, my men friends call me "Little Anthony" but my lady friends, the ones I know well, really well, well they call me… "Big Anthony." Finishing his introduction off with a grin, I smile back, take his black hand into mine, shake it, and reply, "Thornell, Jack R., nice to see you with your clothes on." Laughing out, he says, "I thought that was you… in the shower." He found out, I was a photographer and I found out, he was a photo lab technician. We would be working shoulder to shoulder for many months to come. And Anthony Black would become my first Negro friend… with prejudice. And that prejudice part, that didn't originate with me. That was used. And then, that was put in me. And nurtured.

That putting, that nurturing, in light of my new association, takes my thoughts back and back to Mississippi, where my new association would be downright unacceptable, if not outright criminal. In Mississippi, there was no upside, not where niggers were concerned. If Crazy Uncle John could have seen me today, seen that handshake, white gripping black, he would have done the impossible. Gone crazier. Like he did that Saturday afternoon approaching my seventh year…

Mother, Uncle John—he wasn't crazy yet least not certifiable, certifiable came later—and I, were walking down Washington Street just a looking. Walking and looking is what you do Saturdays when you got no money for doing sump'em else. So, that's how we spend our every Saturday. Usually the quietest kid in town, but today, curiosity betters me. "Whats to matter with that black lady, the one coming there on crutches?" Uncle John goes crazy. Grabbing my arm and jerking me around—just like brother Garnett almost jerked me out of my sandals the day he spied them holey socks of mine—and then, he screams, "Goddamn it boy! Watch your mouth. What you saying. Don't ever let me hear that again." Shocked, scared, my little voice whispers back, "Say what Uncle John. Say what?" "Say 'lady' boy! That ain't no lady. That's a nigger. And a nigger ain't no lady. Never! Just a Goddamn nigger, and that's all. Do you understand that boy?" With his grip unrelenting, still crushing my arm, with me shaking and scared out of my wits, I cry back, "Yes Uncle John. Niggers ain't ladies. Yes. Yes. I understand."

At the time, at my age, Uncle John's zealous chastisement was to say the least, confusing and not clearly understood. But with years comes maturity and with maturity comes understanding. The understanding of his reasoning, back then, back in 1946 Mississippi, back when that used part got imparted on the young, got imparted on me. And now, fifty odd years later, my understanding is this… when you're dirt poor and white trash, like the Thornells then, the only comforting notion is… a nigger, any nigger, is lower down that you, no matter how low down you and your's gets. In essence, in niggers, the Thornells saw hope. Theirs.

Today is my first day as an army photographer. The photo department is located in the basement of our barracks. A convenience, I thought. A counter greets you and behind it and to the left is the portrait studio with lights on moveable stands. A beige curtain, the background, stretches across the wall. Still, to the left is a small room with camera lockers and chairs for sitting. Between assignments, I assume. In the opposite direction, just past the reception area, is a film developing room and a printing lab. Between the two, is a small work room with a large rotating print dryer. Lally and I chat with the photographers we're replacing while Fineran and Anthony visit the darkrooms. Anthony, I call Anthony, from day one—though from day one the army makes you a last name, and so first names are seldom heard and are soon forgotten—perhaps for personal reasons, perhaps born out of guilt, the guilt of my association with Uncle John and my acceptance of his not-so-sane tutoring. Or perhaps, born of fear. That just my contemplation of saying black-the-name, might just trigger nigger-the-name, just like taught.

After the introductions, our first assignment is the motor pool. There we kick the tires, raise the hoods, check the oil, then start and warm-up the engines on vehicles—a jeep and two trucks—assigned to the photo department. This is our first assignment six days a week, whether the vehicles have moved or not. It was here, I learned to drive in the three-quarter ton, with four unsynchronized gears on the floor. It took time, a lot of time, and a lot of scrapes, before I become licensed.

Back at the lab, Sergeant First Class John Scott issues me a Speed Graphic, film holders and a flash gun, while explaining that most of our assignments will be routine, portraits, socials, parades, aerials and presentations. At the time, neither of us expected the unusual, "The King" to become the routine.

With suds still clinging, the red-faced barkeep wipes his lips, puts on a smile and greets, Lally, Fineran and I, with a very loud "Yaah." "How much is a beer, the cheapest," I inquire. "Eine mark… a quarter, American," he responds. By the size of the enormous gut pushed against the bar in front of us, it's evident that he likes, if not loves, his product. We order up. Placing a bottle in front of me, securing the base with his left hand, then while squeezing the neck with his right, he presses his thumb hard forward against the wire fastener forcing it to slide upward until unseating the top with a loud pop. "Pop top," he explains, exploding with a grin and with the foam of my beer running down the bottle and over his hand. The beer sits. I look. The waiter, Lally and Fineran look, and hold their looks. On me. Finally, I raise the bottle and take in a mouthful, and immediately, I find it hard to swallow, but I do. With the twins in my face just waiting to raze me, I have to. I really wanted to spit it out, but I don't, not with pride upon the bar, so I hold it down while forcing up a smile, before encouraging my audience to step up and test the medicine. With another mouthful, I knew for sure, but never revealed, not publicly, that German Beer, tastes awful. Just awful. With money in short supply, with payday still a week away, we drink another and stagger back to the nearby barracks, laughing and airing strategy for a first expeditions to downtown Frankfort for the broadening of horizons. Ours. "Geesums Makesense! The frauleins, I hope I like better than, the beers."

With a stomach still stirring, still forcing the re-tasting of last night's challenge. And now, in the chow line, there is a new challenge to face. I can't. I look away from it. I speed past it. The steaming challenge. S.O.S. (shit on a shingle) it's called. But Makesense calls it D.E.I. (Don't eat it). And that's because Makesense don't speak no profanities, not once, not ever, not since his talking back to me started, sometime back in The Fifties, back when fear went to bed with me. And, you'da thought Makesense woulda learned it—That Talk—from me, just like Mother learned it to me. By amplification. Geesums Makesense, even the thought of it, chipped cream of beef on toast, sickens. And this morning, resembling something a nauseated cat deposits, then runs from, too gross, to even look at, let alone, sniff at. This morning, dry toast and orange juice, is more than sufficient, and all my stomach will allow.

Duty in Germany, compared to the states, is good. Although, about once a month, I do have to strap on a shoulder holster and fill it with a .45-caliber automatic for guard duty, and that, draws the ire of duty officers who question. "Private! Why are you carrying a handgun and not an M-1 like everyone else?" "Sir! I am a photographer. This is my official weapon. Sir!" They accept my explanation, but I can see they don't like it, probably because their weapon, a carbine, is heavier to pack around. However here, we are freed from K.P., kitchen police, and replaced by Germans, eager to scrub our pots and pans for a meager salary, bonused with self-fulfillment of the leftovers, all they can eat and carry home. And then too, there are those accursed alerts. Supposedly supposed to be a surprise to keep us on our toes, but they always sound approximately one hour before our scheduled wake-up call. Usually, about 4:30a.m., we hear the shouts of, "Alert! Alert! Everybody up! Get your weapons and get to your posts." Springing up, we get dressed, run to the armory, get our weapons, run to the motor pool, get into our vehicles and speed off to the alert positions around the city and the suburbs. Once there, we drop our weapons and our bodies onto the back of a flatbed truck and nurse hangovers deserving of a little more calm. The drill works well, until a wanna-be-brilliant general comes up with an oversized idea. Change the routine wake-up call to 1 a.m. The not so brilliant part. With curfew at midnight, only an hour earlier, most drinking men have barely found beds yet and none are nowhere near sober yet. And then comes the oversized part. In a blind rush, tipsy drivers cut corners, fail to negotiate those narrow turns, right and left, and crash trucks, jeeps, and tanks, through well-made German walls, exposing, then turning some pajama-clad krauts sour and up with arms and shouting, "Dumkoff! Dumkoff! Dumkoff!" Meaning, "Dumbass! Dumbass! Dumbass!" After the disaster, alerts return to the routine, about an hour before reveille, with the dumbass general's desk, still bleeding with letters of complaints and outrageous repair bills. No, those German streets were just too narrow for tipsy drivers, brilliant generals, and oversized ideas.

It's spring, it's sunny. It's pay day. A perfect day for manhood to bud. The price: Five dollars. With overnight passes in our pockets and with big plans in our heads we board the trolley and head downtown. Frankfort on the Main River. The city is big and bustling, with streets and parks swept clean and sparkling, as if prepared for our inspection. Men and women walk about wearing proud looks, and not the look of the conquered. When brushing shoulders with side-walk hogging soldiers on the prowl, proud looks are substituted for calculated smiles. They know why we're there. To occupy their daughters, their sisters, their mothers, even their grandmothers. Given enough beer. Given the opportunity.

While spending the afternoon on the river front and awaiting nightfall, a most curious question confronts me. Why do so many German men, supporting those enormous beer bellies on those tooth-pick legs, opt to wear those shorts and not, long britches? In the legs department, the German women seem to fair better, until a closer scrutiny shows hair, hair, hair, from heal to, to as far up as I can see. Geesums! After strolling the streets, riding a riverboat and scrutinizing the legs, we three sit down to a dinner of Vienna schnitzel, small potatoes and little green peas while anticipating our just desert, frauleins. And hopefully, ones without too hairy legs.

The neon lights are gaudy and glaring, and my nerves are pulsating as I try to fit in between Lally and Fineran, but can't, because their maneuvering, as always, keeps me the outsider, as we enter the Dolly Bar where girls and men are made. Famous for being filled with reasonable whores, the place is crammed, wall to wall. The space you're standing in is more than you're likely to get if you take another step towards the bar. G.I.'s are everywhere, some are falling down drunk, others are staggering around the dance floor and getting a little free grab ass while negotiating a price for more from frauleins eager to go to bed early and get to work. Finally, several finish their negotiating, grab their new loves and head for the door. With their exodus we press ahead, secure their bar stools and order up a beer to settle us down, and then, to face a competitive spirit, a sometimes aggressive spirit, serving up exploding bosoms as appetizers while pressing their offers of comfort by the hour. In short order, good Catholic Lally is wounded and woo-ed away by a very sexy blonde. And soon, his brother in the faith acquiesces with a bosomy brunette.

And that, leaves me. Alone, and in minutes, my shyness stands up and shouts... Run, run like hell, back to the barracks, behind those guarded gates. And then, practicality takes charge by asking... What about tomorrow's questions about tonight, about success under the sheets. What will you say? Geesums Makesense! Becoming a man, even here, for me, ain't that easy. For the moment, practicality is holding me down on that bar stool and pure will power is holding down that nauseating tasting beer. Three of 'em. Two more than necessary to render me more than tipsy. And perhaps, topsy.

And then, through the maze of aggressiveness, I see her. At a table. In the corner. Away from all the aggressiveness, at least, most of it. Sipping what could be a champagne cocktail. She's attractive. Mature looking, over 35 with great legs. Hair, on the head, short and light brown; the legs, if hairy, I can't tell from here. And then, it hits me. Geesums! She's the image of my former fantasy. She's the twin of theatre manager Edith Bounds. The woman I wanted to hold and to have ever since I was thirteen. But hold on Makesense, let me check my wallet. This is no five dollar girl. This, is a lady. There's a five and five ones left. Thinking, it's enough, I take my eyes back to the corner and I see that she's looking back at me. And smiling. And looking like she wants me to join her. That Mrs. Bounds look lifts me off the bar stool, like that gospel message lifted me back at Bomar Baptist, and catapults me over to her table. She is as beautiful as Mrs. Bounds was beautiful to me. And up close and hearing her voice, it is clear, a whore she is not. At worse, a proper, a very proper prostitute. "Young man, you look very handsome tonight. I am Gerta. Please join me." And after two very expensive champagne cocktails for her and another awful beer for me, and with the overnight arrangements consummated, Fraulein Gerta takes my hand and leads away from the Dolly Bar and towards her promised land for the comfort of her bosom, and with the baptism of the flesh scheduled to follow, immediately. How immediately, among other things, I didn't know. Yet.

At the top of the stairs, she stops at her door, and turns to collect the price of admission. "That'll be eight dollars please Private Jack. Nervous hands reach for and open the wallet. There's seven dollars. One dollar short. And I'll need money for the trolley tomorrow, I'm thinking. And when she sees my dilemma, she intercedes and says, "Give me six dollars now, and leave me something for collateral... for the other dollar." I offer my watch. Looking down at it, she sees my class ring and says, "Private Jack, you'll need your watch. Leave the ring." With the ring off and in her hand, she opens the door and invites me in. The apartment is roomy, neat, and nicely furnished. And affordable, with her making more in a night than a factory girl could in six days, I calculated. After setting my ring on the small table by the bed, she looks back to me, starts unbuttoning her blouse, and says, "Get undressed Private Jack and get under the covers." With Gerta looking away, I slid out of my uniform and under the covers, as ordered and thinking… when she joins me, there will, at least, be one virgin in bed.

Ignorant of my role, and not willing to show it or tell it, and after a round of kisses, a wrestling match ensues. And by now, it's more than obvious to this pro, that Private Jack, once in bed doesn't know the head from the toe, and then, a tiring Gerta maneuvers me over and on her, while directing a cocked gun to the target, where and when hardly there, it discharges prematurely, leaving me blushing and done. And making me, to be exact, a 30-second man. And then, a giggling Gerta brushes a hand over my flat-top while softly asking, "First time Private Jack?" With my whispered yes, she kisses me gently on my cheek, like a good mother would a son, before turning over to sleep, now satisfied that her night's work is done.

At daylight, not desiring to face Gerta again, I ease out of bed, quietly dress and tip-toe to the door. Half-in, half-out, I look back to the bed and to the little table beside it. Atop the vanity rests my class ring. The trophy unearned by me, is now… hers.

Outside, feeling the chill, a firm wind out of the west rakes across my face, fully awakening my senses, "Well Makesense, how does it feel to be a man?" Before cousin Makesene can butt-in, there is another voice, already airing in my head and sounding a lot like Mrs. Bounds; echoing… "Young Man! A lover, you're not."

Back on duty, over a cold engine and checking the dip stick, Sergeant Scott, the lab chief, interrupts, "Thornell! Get cleaned up and get over to the company commander's office… A.S.A.P." "Do you know what for Sarge?" "No Thornell, I don't. But put it in gear." Geesums Makesense, what's this about? Captains don't see, don't talk to privates, not often. While washing the grease off my hands, I feel the ring is gone and I can't help but start thinking… It's for the best… It was a risk… A Big Risk… Even a blind man with a hearing problem and a speech impediment could have detected my subterfuge and uncovered my lie… Simply… So Simply… Just by feeling, the embossment… The raised letters… 1958… A Class not scheduled to graduate… until next month. How could I explain that… to Lally… to Fineran… with another lie… No… A second wouldn't have stood… Not with the twins tripping over each other to take me down for something… for anything… No… Eventually they would have noted

the 1958… They would have caught me… They would have nailed my ass and this ring to the cross… For public humiliation… No… It's for the best… The ring is gone… And with it… THE WORRY.

"SIR! Private Jack R. Thornell reporting as ordered sir." I state, while saluting and standing at attention, before Capt. Warren R. Colville replies, "At ease Private Thornell. Stand at ease," before looking down at my personnel file. "Private, I see you send home an allotment, half your pay, to your mother back in Mississippi. Is that right?" "Yes sir!" "That's good private, even commendable. And I see that you failed to finish high school. Is that right?" "Yes sir!" "Well that's not good. But that can be corrected. Tomorrow, after motor pool, report to room 301 in the annex across from the parade grounds. See Sgt. Ridley for testing and grade placement. Private, you're going back to school. And graduate. Is that understood?" "Yes sir." "Very well then. Dismissed!"

Geesums Makesense! Whatta I do. My mouth said yes sir Capt. Colville sir, but my gnawing gut is screaming... No! Capt. Colville, you no good bastard, you son of a bitch, you mother fucker, what are you trying to do. Fuck me too. Yes Sir Capt. Colville sir, don't you know, going to class will expose me, and they'll know. Know I lied. I can already see those matched expressions mirroring... y'all a dropout—and—y'all a liar too.

After a breakfast untasted, just moved around on the plate and left, and after motor pool, I report to the guys that I am going on sick call. Instead, as ordered, I report to room 301. Sgt. Ridley, the instructor was pleasant enough and the testing, in English, science, history and math, was general enough and despite my nervous state the answers seemed to flow. After three hours, the testing ended with new instructions from Ridley. "Report back here after chow for grades and class assignments."

While eating across from Lally and Fineran, worry continues to fill my thoughts... What do I do? Confess? Tell 'em I lied. Tell 'em the truth? I didn't graduate. Oh Makesense, I can't, I just can't. They already think me inferior. And what would they think if they knew how. No Makesense, there's no telling.

Back in room 301, after looking around, I was at least thankful that no one there knew me and could report my presence to the photo department. Sgt. Ridley arrives and before making his announcements, he taps me on the shoulder and says, "You won't be attending class. It would be a waste of your time and our space. We can't teach you a thing. Congratulations! You passed. You just earned your G.E.D."

Outside, though silently, euphoria sounds inside of me. Not composed of achievement, nor of self-esteem, but of pride. Pride before peers. Pride I can keep. And to keep it, all that needs to be done, when that diploma comes, is... to see it buried... and deep... to keep other eyes from finding it... and... from feasting on it. Ever! Ever! Hallelujah brother! There is a God. He is alive. And today I know it. For today, I can keep my pride and the twins will never know... I lied.

Two weeks pass and it's Saturday and the sun is bright, with the company standing at attention, poised for inspection. After looking up one rank and down the other, checking weapons, uniforms and haircuts, Captain Warren R. Colville returns to face his men.

"Private Thornell, front and center," is his command. "Holy shit Makesense what have I done." Rattled, but without time for preponderating, I move front and center, face Colville, take the position of attention, salute and say, "Private Thornell, Sir!" "Private Thornell step closer." I stepped and stopped three feet in front of him. I could see something in his hand. "Private Thornell, you are hereby awarded your G.E.D., your high school Graduation Equivalency Diploma." Geesums! G.E.D.! Just the sounding of those abbreviated words sends me into shock well before the spelling out, Graduation Equivalency Diploma, reverberates up and down the ranks. Standing there, caught at attention, with my lie out and airing, with my back exposed to the men, all I can sense, all I can feel is... Eyes. Eyes! Eyes! By the pairs. Lally's eyes, seeing y'all the big liar. Fineran's eyes, blinking with agreement. Eyes! Eyes! Eyes! By the hundreds. Condemning eyes, tightening their focus. Executing eyes, visualizing the gallows all set for the hanging, and then, seeing to their duty. With the shame of a lie covering me from head to toe, I tune Colville's voice back in for more humiliation. "Men! Let this be an example to those of you who haven't finished high school yet. You can. Private Thornell did. And did it in a day." And then, with a somewhat subdued grin, said, "However for some, it might take longer. But men, it will be worth it. Well worth it. First Sergeant! Dismiss the men."

With "dismissed" echoing loud and clear, it is more than clear that "dismissed" does not mean me. Not today. Not with my lie still hanging, still airing. Dismissed? Not today and instead of death by humiliation my sentence is more severe. LIFE! Living with the knowledge of THE HOW and THE WHAT that I had become. The how: You mouth it. Chew it. Swallow it. Lie with it. Wallow in it. Sleep on it. Wake up with it. Put it on. Wear it. It becomes you. The what: A LIE.

Looking up I see more punishing coming. And running. In the forms of Lally and Fineran. Lally gets to me first. Puts me in a head-lock. Pulls me close. And yells into my ear, "Y'all sure some smart. Graduating and all. And all in one litt'o day." Now, unable to utter one word in self-defense, expeditiously, I escape his hold, his mouth and his eyes and retreat to the photo lab and into an empty darkroom. There, locked inside, I embrace the dark. And use it's darkness to hide my honor and my shame: A diploma for... the graduation of a lie.

Once back in the light, while waiting for those condemning eyes to lighten up, I busy myself with photography, especially portraiture. And soon, I become good at it. Using top-45 and Rembrandt lighting techniques. Top-45 delivers a fully-lit face, except for a small nose shadow. Rembrandt puts a small-lit triangle inside a half-shaded face. With Rembrandt, you can hide imperfections. With top-45, you can't. Today my test is the brigadier, the assistant division commander, with a face lined with deep trenches, encircled with acne bunkers and resembling a scared battleground. His command: A pleasing portrait, suitable for framing and displaying on walls throughout the command. With one look at General Frankenstein, the only thing working for me, besides my sweat is he isn't a major general yet. And the hope that, busting a Private E-2 back to an E-1, isn't worth the bother of all that paperwork. Geesums! His face is a disaster zone.

And then, the photographer begins. "Sir, please sit here. Sir. Please face me," then pausing to move the lights, I do, while thinking… Rembrandt, how I need you. "Sir, please face me. More. Lower your chin. Good sir. Moisten your lips. Eyes here. Hold that." And while the brigadier is holding, I slip the lens cap off and rotate it around the camera once before carefully placing it back on the lens. And then, without the sound of a shutter clicking, the norm, the general's face turns into a grimace. And he holds it, no doubt thinking that no one had seen the likes of that type of photography since the Civil War Era and Matthew Brady. And then he says just what I thought he was thinking, "Private! Don't you have modern day cameras, with shutters and such?" "Yes sir. We do. But this lens does not have a shutter sir. But it works well." With his body getting more rigid by the seconds he holds still for two more poses. Before taking to his feet and ordering, "That's enough Private," before leaving the impression, this kid just set photography back a hundred years. Or maybe, more.

With that maybe and with the knowledge of that Schneider-Kreuznach being as sharp as any lens can be, and dedicated to detailing every distinguishable mark, great or small, it sets me to thinking… perhaps, all the general's small imperfections will combine into a great one, and thereby, become indistinguishable. Believe, such a prayer is not far from my thoughts.

Since exposure is guesswork—ala Matthew Brady—I begin developing the film by the inspection method. This allows me to lift the hanger out of the developer, hold it up to a dim green safe light, and make a density check. That too is guesswork that only improves with practice. To call this private "nervous", would be a missed call, because generals petrify privates, so please, call me… petrified. And besides the guesswork, there's other worry. The general would only sit still for three exposures, instead of a planned ten. Alas, only three negatives. Only three choices.

In five minutes, one worry ends when I find the negatives to be exceptional, except for one exception. Every trench, even pit is there, perfectly detailed. Geesums! I'm done. Done with photography. Forced to join the late great Brady. With my history in photography… finished. Being demoted back to Private E-1 are the expectations preceding the conclusion: Private Thornell, turn-in your antiquated camera, roll up your sleeves, and report up to the motor pool. Forthwith! Screw-ups, everybody knew, always got shipped up to the motor pool. For good.

And then, I place my fate and the three negatives into the hands of Private Popoviski. A lab technician with a hidden talent, not taught by the army, but taught back home. Negative retouching. After placing a negative down on a light box, he presses his face down to six inches above the general's flawed image. And then, with a special pencil, tediously and patiently, he fills fox holes and trenches with varying shades of lead. Popoviski's handiwork takes hours, but finally, with the zits zapped and the craters covered, the enhanced image is slid into an enlarger, projected, printed, and then, delivered with his face on the 8x10 glossies showing up as smooth as a newborn's bottom would. And flawless. But, rather than being overjoyed, the negative side of me recalls the look in the general's eyes when he left me cold with, "That's enough Private!"

A week later I hear, "Private Thornell, report to the company commander." On the way there, my mind rushes ahead… Holy Shit! It's the general. The portrait. He hates it. He wants my ass. To bust it back to E-1. Shit! That'll cost me. Shit! Ten dollars-a-month. More than anxiously, I report and hear Captain Colville respond, "Be at ease private, be at ease." with my salute dropping and my feet parting, Colville continues, "Private Thornell, the general sends his compliments, and says this about the portrait, and I quote, 'It's the best damn picture taken of me in twenty years.'" While standing easier, I'm thinking… keep on calling me Photographer Thornell y'all… as the good captain closes his praising with, "Good work. Keep it up." And now, with my spirit soaring and carrying me back to the photo lab, I can't help but ask Makesense something. "Was it our good work, or, was it Popoviski's magic that made our day?" And Makesense replies, "All three, cousin. All three."

Later in the week, the lab chief drops a bombshell. And on me. Well, it looks like a bomb. And it comes in a shell, suitable for mounting on the wing strut of an L-19, a small single-engine airplane used mainly for reconnaissance missions. And, why is the Army's newest and the Army's heaviest aerial camera being dropped on me and not on the swelled-headed Lally? Who knows? The sarge didn't say. And who can figure the army's figuring anyways. But by now, I do know that privates don't ask sergeants, "Why me sarge?", without assuming the position. The push-ups position.

And so, already with overwhelming experience at that position, and without, even just a "Why me," I load up the camera and drive to the airstrip. After mounting the pod, I extend a very long cable release along and under the wing and into the cockpit where the pilot, Lt. J.J. Kidder, sits. "Sir, when you get over the target area, just press and hold this button for a few seconds. That will activate the camera." Grinning down at me, Kidder replies, "Private, I am the pilot. You are the photographer, so get in," he orders, while pushing the cable release back into my hands. "But sir, I don't have any aerial experience. Other than the flight over, I've never been in a plane." "Don't sweat it private. Strap yourself in the seat behind me. You'll be fine. But if you get sick, you will clean up your mess. Is that clear?" "Yes sir." Obeying his order, I climb into the cramped compartment directly behind him, and strap myself in as a new feeling sets in. Nausea.

After climbing to 2000 feet and after test firing the new camera, the lieutenant firms up his grip on the controls to show me just how Kidder gets his kicks. Geesums! It's with ups and downs. Sudden ups. Sudden downs. The plane responds. And I respond. On a sudden down, my breakfast starts up, and with his warning still fresh in my head, I grab my hat and catch the mess. And just in time. Now, with the Army's camera and my stomach emptied, the little plane lands, and I get out and I want to kiss the ground, but don't, because I don't feel that I can bend my head again without throwing up again. "Oh Makesense! Oh Thornell! Y'all some sick cats. And then, while approaching and seeing only a paled-face without a hat above it, the lieutenant's admonition reaches me first. "Soldier! You're out of uniform. Get that hat on." And now, at my side and finding a hat already filled, and while trying not to gag, the officer and gentleman, now mellowing, says, "Don't worry private, this flying, those sudden rushes, you'll get use to 'em. But meantime bring an extra hat." And this I discover, this I wouldn't wish on anybody, not even a body with a surplus of old hats, not even on a deserving body—like Lally's—not this, not this stuff. Air sickness.

With the under-the-cover charges at the Dolly Bar proving too costly, we of the photo staff transfer our pleasure over to the Mayer Gustyl. Where we seek true love, and free love. The big beer hall is busting to capacity. Filled with local Germans, with their families and friends, and with us—the American invaders—as their uninvited guests.

Down front, on the ground floor and on an elevated stage, a colorful and loud Bavarian Band plays. The musicians, all voluminous males, are all wearing loose fitting, suspender-supported short-britches, allowing plenty of room for expansion with the unlimited consumption of cognac and beer as the night wears on and long. And numb. And frequently—too frequently I think—the maestro steps down, goes out into the crowd, picks a patron, pushes a baton into his or her hand, then pulls the chosen one up and onto the stage to lead the band. And for the next five minutes, the libation filled guest conductor swings his baton and swishes his butt to enlist the roar of a now rambunctious crowd just loving to watch a fool in the making. And with the music stopping the fool is made, when the real maestro retrieves his baton and presents the guest with the check for seven beers for his band and a double cognac for him. Geesums Makesense! One trip to the stage and we'd be broke for the rest of the month.

Upstairs, on the balcony, and above the uproar, I lay eyes on her. Just sitting there, smiling and making points with her voluptuous breasts reaching out as if extending a very special and personal invitation. To me, I pray. And below those good points are flirting blue eyes below pretty, but dyed, blonde hair. Perhaps, in her late thirties, like Gerta, like Mrs. Bounds, I surmise. And then, with my eyes still on her, it happens, she invites Lally, Fineran and I over, introduces her roommate and girlfriend Anna, and now, broadening her smile and turning it to me, she looks deeply into my eyes and says, "Oh! My name is Wally… Wally," as if for the moment, forgetting her own presence, and seeing only mine. Accepting her invitation, we sit, with me getting the choice chair, the one next to Wally's, and leaving the twins with no choice but, to divide up their butts and sit with Anna between 'em.

"Would everyone like beer," I ask while motioning for a waiter. Everyone nods for beer. "Okay then, five beers it is." And when, I prepare to order, Wally leans close and suggests, "Just order one beer, to share." "One beer for everyone?" "Yes, one beer. Trust me." She says, smiling, and when the waiter arrives, she orders in German. In addition to the one beer, she orders raw hamburger on crackers. You can keep my share of that, I think, when I see it coming with the beer. It was some beer with its contents foaming over from a very large 5-liter mug and appearing very heavy to lift, if not unliftable. But little Wally—only 5-foot-2—lifts away for the first swallow, and then, passes the big beer on to me. I drink and pass it on, until it rounds the table. The raw meat, I pass on, and pass it to Lally. Naturally, to make me look like less of a man, he takes a mouthful, chews and swallows, then looking over at Wally, says, "Yum, yum, this is yummy," while licking his lips. Remembering that he picked out a blonde that night at Dolly Bar, I wonder… why is he making all that yummy with Wally? The soon to be, hopefully, my Wally.

With curfew approaching, and with Wally appearing to be very familiar with the comings and the goings of the men in olive green, proves it by leaning close and asking, "Jack, can you walk me home. It's not far." Three blocks away is the room. The room that Wally shares. The room is 8x12 feet, with a small single bed sleeping two pushed up against the wall in front of a coal stove next to a less than impressive dressing table, leaving little room for two people passing to go to or come from the shared bathroom down the hall. At most, the room is a wee little bit undersized, even for one, and much less for two. By comparison, proper prostitute Gerta abides in paradise. Feeling claustrophobia coming on, I look at my watch and say, "Wally, I got to go, or, I'll miss curfew." At the door, her arms pull me to her. And then from her lips comes, not a Betty Jo, nor a Gerta, not even a fantasized Edith, but a Wally. And now, with my body moving towards the trolley and with her kiss still resonating, my thoughts stay behind and on Wally… on her lips… on her breasts… and on the possibility that… she likes me. Me! Suddenly! Hands! Uncontrollable hands break military code by rushing into those forbidden pockets where they are put to better use… disguising a growing passion, and one left standing… for most of the long ride home.

With Wally's kiss still alive despite a week's worth of aging, I'm back at the big Mayer Gustyl looking for more Wallies. She's there, up on the balcony, with Anna. We, the twins and I, and three other members of the photo lab crew, join them and start the beer coming. After an hour of laughing and talking and drinking, and with Anna and the boys eyeing the floor show below, Wally leans close to my ear and whispers, "Let's slip away, go to my place, and be alone." "Okay, let's go." I whispered back.

Back in that tiny little room and on that tiny little bed, Wally turns possibility… into probability… into blessed assurance during the proving of… she likes me. Really likes me. And she will prove it again and again for weeks, even months. She must like me. Why else would she take such inexperience to her little bed and want to keep taking it there. Not for performance. Not mine. Not for sixty seconds and y'alls done. And certainly not for the cuddling that doesn't come after the loving. And that's because my body turns cold, wants to put its clothes back on and run. And not for money either. Because sex with Wally is the first not paid for in advance. And besides, there's not much left after mother's allotment deduction. To be exact. Thirty-five dollars. And that sum has to cover all personals, including my Wallies. No, Wally likes me. And it's not for sex or the love of money.

Well, according to Army figuring, private y'all is the aerial specialist designee. Hey! How can that figure? Aren't y'all plagued by that there propensity for that there air sickness? Yep. Didn't the Army count all those hat-fuls and account that to your favor? Nope. What then, did the Army do? Kept on selling me hats. What about the other photographers, and why couldn't they give flying a try. They tried. But they preferred keeping their feet attached to mother earth. And it showed. How? In blurry-ness. In fuzzi-ness. And when Lally and the rest saw the poor results, rather than disappointment, they showed contentment. In fact, Lally looked over at me, smiled and said, "Looks like y'all gonna do the flying. All the flying. So, y'all better stock-up on hats." And to achieve their purpose, I know what they did on purpose, but I can't prove it. They just propped that big Speed Graphic up there on the open window and let the not so good vibrations and a contrary wind work for them. Blurred images.

Instead of their shaky technique, I cradled and cushioned the camera in my hands while letting my arms serve as shock absorbers. And resulting in blur-and-fuzz-free photographs. So, that's the story of y'all becoming the department's fly-boy, according to the Army's figuring. And what about the selling and the filling of all those new hats? Well, just look at that as lagniappe… theirs and mine.

And today the story is for y'all to join up with Lt. Kidder again and get back up yonder and photograph those hills. Lots and lots of hills to be utilized in upcoming field maneuvers. And the assignment, if you're thinking about refusing it private, originated with the division commander. We're up there, and up there is taking hours. And while trying to contain that nausea, I hold the cable release in one hand and a map in the other while squished into that tiny little compartment behind Kidder. "Heads up," Kidder warns, "Check your map. This looks like a target area," as he noses the plane downward for a closer look-see. And with us this low, about 500 feet, the ground below really whizzes by us. I look out and down at the whizzing ground, then I look in and down at the map, re-focus my eyes, then, back out and down, then in and out comes another hatful. Finally, with the mission completed, Kidder lands the little plane, while on my lap, I balance the catch of the day.

Half-way down the runway, the little plane slows, then stops, well short of the hangar. About a hundred yards short. Now Lt. Kidder is getting out, leaving me perplexed and still strapped in. So I ask, "Sir, can't we taxi a little closer to the hangar. To my jeep. To load up." "No private we can't, not today." "Sir, may I ask why we can't." "Surely private, you may, and the why we can't, it's simple… we're out'ta gas," he answers while widening his smile to the far extremities of his face. He's laughing, but is he kidding, or what? And now with Kidder walking away from his plane and with me still inside, I knew that it was the "or what". The tank was dry. And my mouth was dry and getting dryer as I tried steadying myself on still weakening and yet wobbling knees. And as my body navigates its way to the jeep, my eyes take hold of, and won't let go of, the hills, the trees and all the rough terrain encircling the blacktop beneath my feet. "Oh Makesense! The Kidder wasn't kidding. And just look around us, and see just how close we were to becoming… splatter. Geesums! Splatter, Splatter, Splatter, Makesense, and not the dreamed of kind. The kind the shamebirds love to feast on after the fall. No

Makesense, this isn't the dreamed of kind, but the could have been for real kind. The could have been y'all kind.

The aerial film from the pod camera is large, so large, it doesn't have to be enlarged, just contact-printed on to an 8x10 sheet of paper. And the roll of film is long, so long we suspend it on a pipe running through much of the lab. But first, it has to be developed, and that's difficult, so I enlist lab tech Anthony, the Black, for help. While we're winding that long roll from one side of the developing tank to the other, always keeping it moving to keep it from sticking together and ruining, little Anthony unwinds. And his unwinding, his talking, it's about the South, his South and my South. And about the days and the nights he spent down there hopping cars at a-for-whites-only drive-up-to burger joint. And with the burgers, at least with some of the burgers, comes the dispensation of justice... Black's justice. His unwinding dialogue begins...

"Hey little nigger, what'ya gonna be if you grow up? A bigger nigger. That's all." The not-so polite but pure-white patronizer offers little Anthony with his order and with the back-up laughter of his good ole buddies spilling out of the car with his. "Boy! Bring me the large burger with mustard, onions and lots of pickles. And, hold that mayo. You got that boy?" And having grown accustomed to swallowing the pecker'ens of such red-necked peckerwoods (the generous name a black gives a white fouled-mouthed patronizer), and with my black eyes grounded to keep him from seeing into my thinking, and with my black ass stilled, but still just a puckering from his screwing over, my black mouth, ever so politely, just says, "Yes sir. A large burger with mustard, onions, and lots a pickles, and hold that mayo. Yes sir. I got it." "Well then Little Sambo, hop to it," he orders. And so, while turning and showing him my puckering black ass, I go inside and turn his order in. And when coming back outside and coming to that blind spot, the spot where those on the inside and them on the outside can't see me, I slow and ever so carefully, I lift the burger's lid, clear my throat, and redeposit all those forced-fed and swallowed pecker-ens. And then, with a big Little Black Sambo smile, I serve up one of the juiciest burgers in town.

With his burger delivery, his story telling breaks up with laughter, his. And now, after gagging on the imagined taste of those once chewed before me pecker'ens, my laughter joins his. And continues until he can finish his roaring with, "And to many a deserving fouled-mouthed red-necked patronizing peckerwood, I, respectfully, served up... COMEUPPANCE... mine, and for no extra charge."

With our laughing ending, and with us silently cranking the reels back and forth, my thoughts turn to those of thankfulness. Thankful for once that the Thornells were not only dirt poor, but car poor as well, and could never have been a patronize of, or, even a patron of, a black carhop serving up anything.

We whites of the photo lab, for the most part, treat Anthony with respect. We dine with him on base, go to the movies with him on base, and even horse around with him on base. And on base, we all call him friend. But off base, when we're off drinking, dining, movie going or chasing frauleins, friend Anthony is not to be seen. And that is to protect him and us, by not allowing his eyes to see our reaction to one predisposed of prejudice. A black and white one. And a unanimous one. And one often displayed when we see a black sergeant with lots of stripes and a beautiful fair-skinned blonde on his arm and strolling a downtown street. And after the sighting our heads turn and our stomachs fill with disgust, even the heads and the stomachs of the not-supposed-to-be-so-prejudiced yanks. And then, with our mouths relieving our eyes, the thoughts of what we just saw turns nasty. From black to Negro to nigger to who does that black bastard think he is, General Abraham Lincoln. "What could she see in that," someone asked. And someone answers, "A ticket to the states." And with that observation, the beautiful blonde is transformed into just another fucking whore without scruples.

And as my relationship with "friend" Anthony continued on base, the double standard, our double standard, my double standard, gnawed away with the asking of, are we more deserving of comeuppance than those red-necked peckerwoods? Who, at their very worse, were, at the very least, true to their colors. And then, the gnaw answers. Perhaps, we are more deserving. And perhaps, "friend" Anthony saw to it. Perhaps, on a night when we all shared pizza in the barracks, "friend" Anthony found a blind spot, and added an extra topping. And, for no extra charge.

Today, a letter from Mother arrived, and in it comes the news of the change down at 503. And for Crazy Uncle John, it's a change of address. Mother had him committed. Put him in a place called Whitfield, the state mental institution in Jackson, about forty-five miles east. And Clifton, the eldest son of Crazy Uncle John, the one he sired with Ada after he stole Ada away from brother Ben, is disturbed. "Now, he is disturbed," I thought. He sure as hell wasn't disturbed during any of those countless nights when the fear of him went to bed with Mother and me and held us there wide-eyed. Disturbed! Hell, I don't think so." Sorry but, he's a Thornell, ain't he, and Thornell men don't come around family often enough or even long enough to get disturbed. Hell! If a Thornell man even senses misery there, he stays clear of there. Figuring, hell, there's enough misery at home already, without going looking for more. And if they owned a wallet, they never showed it, not to any of us down at 503, not even when there wasn't even a single slice of gooseliver or green tomato to be seen. Put plainly, with the Thornell men, it was one for one and to hell with the for all. And Makesense, if your ears are on, and if you're harboring the possibility, even a remote possibility, of fielding even a duo of Thornell men for service in the musketeers, please, please inpale the possibility. So, a suddenly disturbed son speeds over to a Whitfield, signs out his suddenly beloved dad, and takes him home to live with his beloved family. Once there, all there discover that living with Crazy Uncle John is more than disturbing. It's crazy. And so now, son Clifton takes his once-to-be-beloved but now known-to-be crazy dad and checks him into a small room above downtown Washington street, like the place where mother, Ben, Marshall and me used to live. Where Crazy Uncle John used to visit mother after brother Ben was seen leaving. And now, because Clifton was disturbed, Crazy Uncle John is loose and free to roam the streets. And does. Mother says he comes back to the house, stands in the street, and shouts insults. Mother borrows a telephone and calls the police, but they can't or won't do nothing, not till after he's done killed her, or at least, tried. While scared and sleeping with one eye open, Mother files for divorce, gets it, and gets the house. Now suddenly, with mother without a husband to support her—as if she ever had a husband to support her—and now with the sudden loss of the support she never had, the Army figures that poor mother now qualifies as my dependent. And is now, entitled to a matching allotment. And mother just loves the Army's figuring. For now, at age 53, can open a first bank account. And, it's a savings account. With the allotment doubled to seventy, with the seven dollars a week she earns cleaning Mrs. Finkey's house, it comes to ninety eight dollars a month. And that is more money than mother has ever seen at once. And out of the ninety eight, she saves fifty dollars a month. Every month. And lives on forty eight. And the savings part, that part I appreciated.

With the reading finished, her letter, like always, is shredded and flushed. Before the likes of Lally or Fineran can put their eyes on it, see her near perfect illegibility, and while feasting on it, try reading of her new found eligibility. A handout. And then, associate all of it with me. Geesums Makesense! Will I ever be clear of the worry… of what other people might discover of me… of my roots… and then think their thoughts… those degrading thoughts.

Bad news greets Lally and me when we arrive at the photo lab, when the sergeant says, "From now on all assignments in the general's office will be handled by one of you. This is the word from Captain Mawn over at P.I.O. (Public Information Office)." "Is there a reason for this," Lally asked, while I stood silent but while knowing what he was thinking… assignments they were a bitch. Just to be in the general's presence we had to have on our dress uniform, with our brass highly polished and with our shoes spit-shined until capable of making any staring two-starred general squint. And squint. To be looked over by the general was like standing barefoot on broken glass while contemplating a wrong move coming. "Lally, after noon chow, get dressed and be outside the general's office, at 1400. And be sharp. And don't upset the old man like some of your co-workers have." "What's the assignment sarge." "Oh, some kind of presentation. Nothing special." Surprisingly, Lally takes the news and his selection with a smile while looking over at me with that look of his, that superior to me look, the one that says that he is number one on the general's list, while I am at best, a distant second.

In dress green, unwrinkled, and in shoes shined to the limit, the as sharp as can be Lally, with his chin and his nose out to their limits, shoves a big number 22—a bulb the size of a regular sized light bulb—into his flash gun, checks his focus, and stands at the ready. And then, with the presentation in progress, he triggers the shutter and the big bulb explodes. Like a gunshot. And sending shattered glass a-flying and a-flying towards a who was composed and onto a who now is forced to decompose and now general! Duck!

And suddenly, with just a pop and a duck, and to avoid such future humiliation and risk being labeled "General Duck," Lally was done and the glassy-eyed commander sees y'all as number one. And the only one allowed that close to a, God! A I-must-stay composed at-all-times division commander. And naturally, after his disgracing, Lally puts on a condescending smile and says, "Y'all can have the general, like y'all has all that flying and all that nausea." But, even with his saying otherwise, it's more than obvious to me that Lally's pride is pierced. He loved getting summoned by the general. Loved dressing up, shining up, and polishing up. And he really loved missing the dirty work details dumped on fatigues—every day work-in uniforms-wearing men. Like those dirty and greasy details at the motor pool. And now, on the days when assigned to grace the presence of the proud general, it would be the shame-filled and often nauseated y'all with the clean hands and not the pride-filled and now disgraced Lally.

And to avoid the possibility of firing off another cracked bulb and to have to face the repercussion like the one that felled Lally, I purchase a German-made explode-proof electronic flash. For using my own money, Lally says, "Y'all crazy." But with it hooked onto the big Speed Graphic, both the general and I stood easier.

Saturday morning after our weekly inspection, my eyes fixate on the overnight pass resting on top of my footlocker. Up until tonight, for Wally and me, it's been a quick blushing and done for me, and a quick good night salutation for her. But not tonight. For Wally has reserved a big hotel bed. For two. For all night. Geesums Makesense! My usual one-two, orgasm and exit, without a second thought for a second big "O", won't work. Not tonight. And that's got me nervous, really nervous.

Wally and I meet, embrace, exchange hellos and start the evening off slow and then, with dinner and a sub-titled movie behind us, we're off to bed. And there in the dimly lit room and after a few kisses are shared, Wally's head goes down and under the covers. What the hell, I wonder and now I know. She's kissing my chest and going lower. Geesums! She's kissing my belly-button and going lower. Geesums! Geesums! She's kissing my gun. That dirty thing. Geesums! And more. She's turning it into a lolly pop. And more. She's trying to swallow it. And more. All of it. And more. At once. And then, feeling her behavior as unbecoming a lady, I take her lolly pop away. Withdrawn, I lift my head and with a condemning voice, shout, "Wally~ What were you doing down there?" And she replies, "Pleasing you… I thought." "Well, you thought wrong. And who taught you such a thing?" And without pausing to deliberate, Wally answers, "My doctor taught me." And then comes the silence. And the doctor taught me story, well, I just swallow it. And without another word, another hug and most certainly without another kiss, I turn over and give Wally my back for the rest of the night. There would be no big "O" for me, and not even the possibility of a little "O" for Wally. Not tonight. Not after that, the it wants to make me throw up experience. And afterwards, Wally proves her patience by waiting two weeks for a next kiss. Two weeks of brushing, two weeks of flossings, and two weeks of gargling, was just what the doctor ordered. Well, at least, it was what a young and unlicensed practitioner prescribed.

Back at the base, the word is out. Promotions are due. And soon. And there's a problem. A big problem. The photo lab is being allocated one. Just one. And the rumor is, the choice is between Lally and me. Until now, Lally, Fineran and I have been promoted simultaneously. And now, we enjoy the rank of P.F.C. (Private First Class).

Lally and Fineran enter our sleeping quarters laughing. And probably laughing about me, I figure, while sitting on my footlocker, with my back to the door, sewing. Lally, while walking towards me, asks, "What y'all sewing." And when he gets to towering over me, he looks down and sees the specialist four stripe already sewed on my sleeve. And seconds later, after looking up, I find his stare still frozen there, as if he can't believe that the one and the only promotion to be had was had by a someone like me. And not a someone like him. A bona fide high school graduate. And with the remnants of his earlier laughter dispelled, he chokes out, "Well, congratu," and then, after choking some more, finishes, "Congratulations, y'all deserve it."

Out loud I say, "Thank you." But silently I'm saying, "Who's the liar now. With that you deserve it shit. Lally is. That's who." And after, he crosses the room, buries his head in his clothes locker and just stands there for the longest and all the while, he is talking to himself. I can't hear his words, but I can imagine them… That promotion, it had to be, and it couldn't be anything but… just another Army fuck-up, and, just the result of another clerical error.

With my stripes sewed on and hanging, and with everyone else's eyes having closed on the events of the day, I lie here with my thoughts keeping me awake and thinking… tonight of all nights, you should be happy. Shouldn't you? You got the promotion didn't you? And so now, you deserve to be happy. Don't you? And with the question pending, even shame encourages me to be happy. Happy? About devastating a friend, well, the closest thing to a friend ever known to me. Happy? About the urgent need to be recognized as something, as anything more than I have been seen as. Happy? About the shame in me just raring to rear an ugly head to pull rank on me? Happy? About never being asked, if you grow up little Jackie boy, what you gonna be? Even little Anthony got asked that, and by a nigger hating red-necked peckerwood. But that was never asked of me. By anyone. And certainly not by them down at 503 where the question of the day was and always was, how to survive one more night in hell. Happy? Happy, I have never been introduced to, and so happy, I couldn't recognize, even if happy was tattooed on my arm. "Okay Makesense, I sense your ears are up. And so to you dear cousin, I will confess to something. Yes, when I looked up and locked onto that frozen Lally stare, I did sense something. A tinge of something. But please, don't call it happy. If you must call it something. Call it… pleasing. And call it… comeuppance. And call it… Lally's."

Today, brings an unusual call, and unusual because, an orderly shouting, "Thornell telephone," is rarely heard here in Germany. It's Wally. With urgency, she says, "Jack, I need to see you and tonight. Can you come?" "Can't it wait till the weekend," I reply and she replies back, "No! This can't wait." And without further explanation I agree. Early that evening we greet each other and take a seat on a bench facing the river. And immediately, she starts crying. "Jack, I'm pregnant." Her revelation shocks me into a lifeless state, at least, for the next few seconds. And then, an aroused disbelief takes life and cries out, "Pregnant! But Wally, how can that be. You said that you couldn't get pregnant. That you have never been able to get pregnant. And now, and suddenly, you're pregnant." "I know, I know, and that's all true. Except that now, I am. And for two months." "But you can't be. You're too old. It's a lie. To trick me. To get to the states. On my arm. Isn't it?" "No Jack, it's not. You don't have to marry me. But you, we, have to do something. And soon." "Wally! I still don't believe you." "Just wait and soon you'll see the truth." "Wally! I want proof. Get me proof. Call me when you get the proof. And not before."

And with the sting of harsh words still being felt with the evening air, I stand, turn my back on Wally and walk away. And without even the whisper of a good night bid to soften a berating. Why waste words on good nights, when knowing, for Wally and me, good nights are done. But the words, "Jack, I do love you," follow after me as I retreat behind the tall gray walls of the Army compound. But even they couldn't keep these thoughts… like your father, like your mother, and just like you. Jack R. Thornell, this child will be… out of my head. "Will you marry me?" is not a question to be popped by me. Not now. Not ever. Not even to a pregnant Wally. A someone already well acquainted with poverty and, a someone quite accustomed to sharing her 8x12 foot cell. Oh Makesense, can you imagine the taking of a bride, even a conditioned one like Wally, home to meet mother. My mother. And have her see the house. That house? I have. And, just the imagining of it, is all the shame that I can bear, and live with. And with that disgusting picture still developing in my head, a new rationalization replaces it. Face it. This baby to be. Any baby to be. Would be better off not being, than being down at 503 or being upstairs in Wally's tiny prison cell. Wouldn't he? Wouldn't she? "Makesense, aren't you gonna butt-in?" "Only to say this cousin. About this rationalization, the one you're contemplating. Recognize this: YOU! If not the baby, will have to live with this… and live with this… and live." "Okay! Okay! I hear! I heard! Now butt out."

Three days later, Wally calls and says, "Jack, I got your proof. Please meet me."
Tonight the trolley ride into the city seems to take forever. And that growing urge that usually accompanies me is gone. Dead. Kaput. Sex with Wally isn't anticipated. Not tonight. Not ever

again. Tonight, my thoughts are on my predicament. Upstairs, I knock, and Wally opens the door. "Jack, please sit down. I sent Anna to the movies so we can be alone." Tonight, the tiny little room seems tinier and feels much more confining that usual. And tonight. I just want to get done with this, this business, and then, get up and get out of here. As usual. Just like I usually did after making love to Wally here on this tiny little bed. Hurriedly! And then, Wally sits down beside me and gets down to business. "Here is your proof," she said while handing me the letter. The greeting I can read but the rest of it, the proof part, I can't. It's written in German. And it might as well have been scrawled in Greek. "Wally! How the hell do I read this?" She takes the letter from my hand and says, "Here, let me read it to you." And as her translating begins, my suspicions begin. The letter, her letter and my supposed proof is from a doctor, she said. Which doctor? I thought. That cock-suck teaching doctor of yours. That doctor, my head said, but not out loud. And reading on, Wally says that the letter says that she is pregnant just like she said she was. With her translating completed, she pushes the letter back into my hands and looking down at it, I don't want to believe it. I don't want to believe Wally's translation of it. So, looking up, I ask, "How do I tell if the letter is for real. Authentic. Like you say?" "Take the letter. Take it with you. Get someone else to translate it. Then, you'll know." And finally, after considering her proposal, and deciding that I am not about to show that letter to another living soul, I ask, "What can we do? What can I do?" Cooly, calmly, Wally looks deep into my eyes as if seeing into my soul, and says, "You can give me two hundred dollars. And the doctor will take care of it. And the problem will go away." "How does it go away. Exactly how?" "Jack, they call it abortion. It's when they stop a could-become-a-baby from becoming a baby." "Okay! Okay! I get it. But it'll take a few days. I'll have to call home." And with the business finished, I stand to leave, but Wally reaches up from the bed, takes my hand and says, "Don't you want to stay for a few more minutes. And hold me?" "Oh Wally, I can't, I just can't. I got to go."

After leaving Wally, getting onto the trolley and taking a seat, I take off my hat and put it in my lap. Just in case. Geesums! I feel sick. Even sicker than sick. And with me well aware that this tiny little hat can't, can't possibly, hold all that sick. Nor can I. Not for much longer. Not with this unrelenting gnawing still growing in my gut.

With the streetcar emptying and with me not, the odds against my setting off a train-reaction of vomiting are improving. But now, the nauseating thoughts of having to call home and having to hear that mother's mouth again, are filling my head. And without this, this fucking predicament, I wouldn't be calling mother, not now, and maybe, not ever. But for that fucking money and the need for it. However, the asking for it, well, that's easy to justify. Fuck, if it wasn't for me and my marriage to the fucking Army there ain't no fucking money up there in that fucking First National. Fuck! Fuck! Fuck! Mother fucker!

Little Louie Lane answers my call and with my "Hurry up and go fetch mother," he runs next door. She's home. I know. Cause, where else can she be, but down there a watching the sun come up and a watching the sun go down. Day after day. Night after night. Year after year. Existing and just existing down there is it. And all mother expects. Where the only excitement is fear. Her fear, and the used-to-be-mine fear. And with the fear, no matter how hot the weather, when the sun disappears, mother shuts herself up. Except for that mouth. And God knows, that, that never shuts up. Because more often than not, God or the Holy Ghost, or the troubled souls trapped upstairs are her only choices for a victim.

Oh God! If she could just shut up like she shuts up the house. But God knows and I know. That ain't, just ain't possible. Because, the little woman with the big mouth, she don't demand much from this life of her'n, but to be heard. And that. She commands. By now I figure, mother's mouth will be on little Louie and soon on… "Hello mother, this is Jack." "Jack! Jack! Is that really you?" "Yes mother. It's me." "Your voice, it's so loud, so clear, from way over there." "Yours too mother." "How you been doing son?" "Pretty good mother, till lately." After an unusual pause, she continues, "Is somethump'n to matter?" "Mother, I got trouble. I got a girl in trouble. And to get her out, I need two hundred dollars." "Lordy lordy a-mercy Jack, what have you gone and done?" "Mother! If you don't send the money, she could go to the Army and report me. And maybe. Force me to marry her." And without a moment's hesitation, to think on my predicament or my solution she comes back with her answer. "Just as soon as I can climb the hill, I'll get down to the First National and get you your two hundred dollars." "Okay mother, that's good. Oh! One other thing. Take it to the Western Union and wire it. The mail wastes too much time and I got no time to waste." And with my need for money satisfied, and with mother's need to hear a distanced son's voice again, our conversation abruptly ends with two simple goodbyes and without a single "I love you." Those words, between Thornells, are never sounded. Even with a whisper. And not even oceans apart.

With the two hundred soon to be in my hands, then Wally's. And then into the cold hands of some abortionist, questions gnaw away. What did Wally see, really see, in me? Was it just a kid, a naive kid, lonely and lost, but with rich American roots. Was that it Wally?" Just a ticket to ride to the land of the rich. Isn't that what most frauleins see in all us American GI's? Rich. Give 'em a ride, then take 'em for a ride. Perhaps, like the ride you gave me. Oh Wally! Of the lonely and of the lost naive kid, you were dead-on. But of those rich American roots, the ones that you thought you saw, you were wrong. Dead-wrong. Oh dear Wally. If you could see those roots, or just see the pictures of 'em. Like the pictures I carry around in my head. The pictures not to be shared with another living soul. Not even to such a soul as poor as yours. See-em, and if by chance you're riding a crowded trolley when you see 'em, be prepared. For the odds of your setting off a nasty train-reaction, like I narrowly avoided the night I got your news, and then dear Wally, I'd say, the odds are fifty to one against you. But, if by chance you're hatless, up 'em to a hundred.

Two nights later, with ten new twenties in my pocket, I deliver on a promise. With the counting, Wally's eyes fix on the crisp bills. It's more than she can earn in six months time. It's more than I have even held in my hands. And now. It's going, going… gone. And gone for something never to be held or even beheld. By Wally or by me. And with the transfer completed, I look up and into Wally's eyes and catch her eyes looking back into mine, and the eyes say it. Wally! Jack! Your business together is finished. Over. And for good.

After the stairs are negotiated, the thoughts of the business transacted back up there pursue and catch me in the cool night air. And there, stirred up with my thoughts, I find a thread of hope to hang my guilt on. Perhaps this poor naive G.I. is faultless. And just the victim of a lie concocted for money and concocted between a cock-suck teaching doctor and his student-patient. Concocted to add to their pleasure after the lesson is over. Oh God! Let me be the victim. And not a contributor to something more. Like the slaying of someone's favored songbird. Like the one felled after the promise. And buried hurriedly at my feet. Before the punishing eyes of a grandpa could see and then, shout his condemnation at me. And of my crime. The killing of, another beloved mocking bird. And now back behind the walls at Bonamaze, and safe, my first relationship ends. In distress. In distrust. And perhaps. In death. And with that realization, a new promise is born… all future sex will be paid for. And in advance.

These nights, back in the barracks, with regular sex just a part of history, and besides a gnawing guilt, the only other thing to disrupt my sleep is, those dreams. And oh Geesums! Here comes another. And after scampering to the head at 0300 to clean up the mess, the question returns with me. Why is the orgasm of a dream so much more pleasurable than the real thing? Like sex with Gerta or with Wally. And then. too, there are those other kind of dreams. The regular ones. The recurring ones. In one I keep on returning to Vicksburg for disgusting sex with disgusting Mamma. And in the other, I'm up in the L-19 at 5000 feet and up without one J.J. Kidder. And licensed by a dream to fly solo. And to disappear in the clouds. And to not be seen. And to enjoy and to enjoy the experience. Until the fuel is spent and the little L-19 is forced to glide down and to land safely below where the Kidder is pacing to and pacing fro. And waiting to shout at me for putting his plane at risk. "That's my job Specialist Four. Not yours." And it is the most interesting to remember. That, during all that soloing. During all that enjoying, a negative thought never crashes into my head. Never. Not one. Like of a downer. And the likelihood of one such as I, becoming… splatter. And tonight it's one of those wet and messy ones that sits me up and then, sends me off scampering again. And on the way to the head, I note something unusual. Fineran is kneeling at a bunk not his own like he is praying over a body. And the body belongs to a transient, a cook, who had just re-upped and had returned from a furlough. And needed an empty bed for a few nights. On the return to mine, I notice that Fineran is back in his, and appearing as if he never left his. Good, I thought, because I didn't want to be confronted and asked about the reason for my scampering. And so, the night passes without any embarrassing questions arising. As to why Fineran or I, were up. And at that hour.

And then, three days later, the messy rumors start circulating and re-circulating. As to why the former seminarian was kneeling over that bunk. And it wasn't for praying, the cook told one Captain Warren R. Colville, it was for preying. And exactly what was Fineran doing? Just trying to please a stranger in a strange bed. And please him by employing the Wally method. The method her doctor loved teaching her. The method, when employed on me in some strange hotel bed, brought chastisement down on Wally's head.

And the strange part of the story is, the cook sleeps two more nights in a strange bunk before reporting the preying. When asked by Captain Colville, "Son, why didn't you report this sooner. Hell! Why didn't you just raise up and knock the crap out of him." The scolded cook responds, "Sir, I got to be honest. At the time. Then. It just felt so darn good, I just couldn't bring myself to stop it… him… stop him… sir!"

Before shipping out, the cook confronts me in the hall to razz me and does. "That's one queer roommate you got there pardner." And I razz back. "If you enjoyed it so fucking much partner, then, why in the hell did you tell?" And now hesitating, then scratching his head, and then putting on a sleazy-sleazy smile, he says, "Just call it a prick of conscious pardner… A prick of conscious," before breaking into laughter, before walking away, and before hearing the trailing whisper of mine… "And I hear tell pardner, a mighty small prick it is… mighty small."

So now, and well before the title of "gay" is ever pronounced ever so politely, Specialist-Four Fineran is titled to "Undesirable" by the Army. And his entitlement. A ticket back to civilian life, or if he prefers, another seminary. And now, with "The Fineran" gone, "The Lally" is a changed Lally. A different Lally. He appears shorter. Even his nose looks less offensive. His once seemingly proud and always appearing to be perfect posture seems less proud and certainly appears less perfect. Like gravity has become too much of a challenge. Even his urgency to put y'all down has left him. As if he fears a put-down of his own with questions. Troubling questions. Offensive questions. About his closest, his dearest but now, his discharged friend. A friend with one propensity which just ain't allowed here in this man's Army. Most definitely, "The New Lally's" recent posturing is less offensive and more defensive. But between us, there was no need. Because, to me he never defends Fineran. He never has to. Because, of him, of his new title or even of his entitlement, I never ask. Of him, we never, never speak. Nary a word. Between us. Fineran is gone. Just gone. And nothing more. As if, he never existed. And gone too is a need for calling me "y'all." Finally, with Fineran no longer at his side, the new Lally has learned something too. That... y'all is indeed plural.

"The King is coming," little Anthony shattered the afternoon calm with "The King is coming. And coming here," he clamored on. "Man! Oh man! Can't you see it. The pelvis just a showering with us. Just a shaking these buns. Man! Oh man! Elvis! Elvis! Elvis!"

And when the rest of the story catches up, I am more than pleased to learn that, he won't be shaking 'em here with us. Instead, he'll be shaking 'em out at one of the division's combat commands. A place where they keep the heavy artillery, and where a tank fitted for "A King" is awaiting to be mounted and wiggled into. Like one he trained in back at Ford Hood, Texas. This one is at Friedberg and a good drive from here. The good drive part pleases me too. There farther the better. For me. Why? When every other butt in the command wants to rub up against his'n . And literally. And so, why not your butt too? Pressure. More of it. Already there's the you must not shatter the general's confidence again, pressure. You must fly till you drop or till you fill your hat, pressure. And, you must take the most pleasing portrait ever taken, pressure. Pressure! Pressure! Pressure! And now, expect Presley pressure. And the question Specialist-Four, can you take more, is only being asked by me.

And when E.P. Day arrives, I get lucky. Well, if you call getting another opportunity to get nauseous again, lucky. And it comes in the form of an order. From the commanding general. He needs some very special aerials to be taken and to be taken today. E.P. Arrival Day. And while I'm up and getting nauseous, Lally is down getting the disembarking of "The King." And he's enjoying it. And most undoubtedly thinking… Kings are more important than generals. Much more. But he is overlooking something. My truth. And that is. Nauseousness is preferred over the expectant pressure accompanying Elvis. Even to stand in his shadow is perhaps, too close. With the spotlights of the best of the world press spilling over and onto those near him. Even an amateur like me. And if not on me, then perhaps on my work. My pictures. For professional scrutiny. And why would such professionals waste their time on me or my pictures. Of necessity. Because, after the arrival hubbubing, "The King" is disappearing. From all those who want a piece of him. Even autograph seekers. But especially those overzealous newshounds. Officially, Elvis is "off limits" to everybody. But mine. And Lally's. And even then, only occasionally will he be subject to us. And then, only selected photos will be fed to the hungry and the howling—because they can't get at him to get a piece of him—press.

This cloudy afternoon is one such occasion. And the occasion is mine. Shaking hands with "The King" was much like shaking hands with most mere mortals. But perhaps, briefer. Up close and facing me and even with his sultry scowl over scowling at me, he is some good-looking man. And now with close-cut hair and without movie make up, and looking better than when I first saw him in Cinemascope and Technicolor in "Love Me Tender" up on that big Joy Theatre screen. And now during a pause, other observations are being made. Beginning with the question. What is someone such as me doing here and standing in front of someone such as him? Isn't he accustomed to posing for the best? And only the best? And now, this stupid Army puts this stupid shamed faced kid in front of the most famous face in the world. And before I can answer myself, or even try, Elvis breaks into my thoughts with, "Okay specialist. I'm ready for you." The assignment was unspecific. Too unspecific. Just get some pictures of him in the field. Training and such. At least I outrank him by two stripes. But only on a sleeve. Because in my head, he's a star. And generals wear stars. And still waiting for a response, he freshens up his grimace, and continues, "Where do you want me?" Nervously and indecisively, I respond, sling your M-1 and crouch over there beside that big tree." And he responds. And I snap the picture using my electronic flash to brighten his image on this dull day. "What next?" he pressures. "Okay, hop up in your jeep and man that 30-calibre machine gun." And grimacingly, he does. "What now?" Geesums! He won't give me a break, I'm thinking, but respond, "Man the bazooka. Crouch over there." Apparently now, having tired of my directional debut or just plain tired of crouching, he picks up the armor piercing weapon with his scowl turning sinister, raises it, aims it straight at my head… and jerks the trigger. As his mouth explodes, "Boom." Just as if he'd been rehearsing the scene for hours. Fortunately, and most fortunately for my head, the big bazooka was without projectile. But by using it, Elvis had made his point. He had tired of breathing the same air as this unnerving and unnecessary idiot calling himself a photographer. And with his cue clearly heard and understood, and feeling lucky to have survived our first encounter, I dismiss him with, "That'll do. I got enough for today." And I wanted to add but didn't, and, "I know you have." And immediately, he put down the big bazooka. Picks up a small box of C-rations, takes out a dry soda cracker, and starts devouring it before offering me one. And then, it happens. Our eyes meet. I look deeply into his. He looks deeply into mine. And suddenly, and at that precise moment, I sense something more. An emptiness, not only mine. A sadness, not only his. And then, he takes his eyes away. And leading me to wonder… did he sense those things in me. Things men can't tell and still be men. And then, reality returns me to my senses with… you must be going looney. As looney as your Uncle John went when he began seeing things not there. And because you know as the world knows… Elvis is King. And got everything. A mansion named Graceland. A purple Cadillac. A pick of girls, girls, girls. A proud to be seen with papa. A cherished memory of a beloved mother. And a million dollars. And with all these things, he's got no room for those things. Emptiness. Sadness. Those things are mine. All mine. My inheritance. And can't, just can't, be his. And reality concludes with… no! Hell no Specialist Four! You're not going looney, cause you're already there. At Looneytown. No! No! Don't be ridiculous, lumping Elvis with me and my shame, it's not possible. Not now. Surely, with fame and fortune comes a little joy.

And with our first encounter over, Elvis jumps into his jeep and speeds away. Gone now is the opportunity for the picture of the day. The picture most wanted, even desperately, but secretly, desired. The picture that I couldn't ask Elvis to pose for. Just couldn't. Because in my mind, the question was already asked and answered. And shame had said no. Thereby: Censuring the picture. The picture of us. Elvis and me. Together.

And gone with him, at least for the day, is the fantasy of the day. Mine. That, Elvis will get to know me. And somehow, even if by miraculous intervention, will grow to like me. And like me best. And then say best pal Jack, when your Army hitch is up, forget going back to the hell down at 503 and come on up and live with me in beautiful Graceland. And there, for you, there'll be a brand new purple Cadillac awaiting. With a special plate on the front and the back and spelling out… Elvis' best pal Jack.

Hey Makesense, are you paying attention? Why isn't all this possible. Haven't you heard, with God, all things are possible. And today, I shook hands with Elvis. And I gazed into the eyes of "The King." And hell! Isn't that just about as close to a God as any poor soul is likely to get down here in this here life. Even if the worshipped one is just a walking talking grimacing god-like Elvis, but still, someone with the power to save a miserable soul, even one such as mine.

Okay! Okay Makesense. I know. I know. Fantasies are just fantasies. Unless you got another eight dollars to blow on a Bounds look-a-like. I know. I know. That's reality. And hell! Even things said. Hell! Even things officially stated do not always lead one to reality. Like the Department Of The Army's official statement concerning one Elvis Aron Presley. "he" will be treated just like any other G.I. "He" will be given a serial number just like any other G.I. "He" will have his hair cut just like any other G.I. And Makesense, just what did the Army do. Cut his hair. Numbered him. US53310761. But what about the first item stated? The treated "just like any other." That item. Let's explore.

"He" arrives. "He" moves into the barracks at Friedberg. Once rumored to have housed Hitler's elite SS troops during World War II. "He" wiggles his way out of wiggling into a tank every day, and instead, "He" jumps into a jeep and scouts on ahead of Company "C" while "He" enjoys the landscape and the fresh air. And when out of sight, "He" can scout up a peaceful place to pull over and rest a tired or perhaps, a hung over head. And now, with a clear and a rested one, "He" discovers a flaw in the Military Sponsoring Act. The one generally intended for career men and women with dependent children and with a need to live off post. And "He" moves his dependent dad and his dependent grandma over, rents a three-story villa on Goethestrasse in Bad Nauheim. And then, "he" moves in. And leaving behind, just a little more of that less elite space, just for all those "just like any other" G.I.'s to share. And Makesense, there's more to the just Elvis Aron Presley reality. Now, "He" must commute. And not, "just like any other." And how. By BMW. And, an awfully sporty white one. A convertible. And often driving up late, so late, the company is already standing at attention, and so what does "He" do? "He" slows, and then "He" flashes his famous grimace while "He" salutes the company commander from the most unusual, and usually, the totally unacceptable sitting position. Hell if any other one of the "just like any other" ever runs up late, even two seconds late, he assumes "the late" position. The one that I'm over-experienced at. The push-up position. But what's the commander of the usually combat ready, but now, minus one "He" of Company "C" gonna do? The only thing he can do. Return the salute. And then, just grimace and bear it. Because, "The He" is "The King." And Kings outrank Captains.

When not on duty, "The King" enjoys his villa. Where he finds comfort and takes pleasure. And according to his good, but talkative buddies, please put the emphasis on the pleasure. "The King's." And remember, his comes first. And so, while all pretty frauleins are arriving for all of "His" villa parties, all good buddies are to hug the walls. And just the walls.

And if necessary—which means good buddies if you can't control these urges—just sit down, cross those legs, and hold 'em down, just like an uneasy patient in a dentist's chair would. Cause good buddies, until "his host" examines all those pretty smiles and selects a winner, y'all is grounded.

But there was one occasion, call it an Act of God, or call it a general's order or call it both, when "his Host" loses the comfort of his villa. And call it, Grafenwöhr. A sprawling training area near the Czechoslovakian border. And call it freezing. And the general's order is, every swinging bun in this here command will be out there. And even "His Hosts" buns. And why? Because men, here we're situated smack-dab in the middle of the cold war. Hell men! The Russians are just over that there hill. And looking to come over here. And men, you must be combat ready at all times. Which means, no tops and no sides on those jeeps you drive. Geesums! Which doesn't make sense to me. Because, with the temperatures hanging around zero, how can a frozen stiff anything, including those frozen buns, be ready for anything. Even those beautiful but already rejected by "his presence" frauleins standing warmed-up and ready to be chosen by a lesser, but good buddy. But one with thawed and still responsive parts.

Out in Grafenwöhr, "His Presence" has to put his buns down and freez 'em just like any other G.I. In that snow and on that ice. And between "His Presence" and frostbite is hope. That a leaking air mattress won't let him down. Because frostbite of the buns could be devastating to anyone. And worse for the world's most revered shake, shake, shaking ones.

And so Makesense, by a general's decree, "His Presence" is just another G.I. out in the cold and facing the Russians for two solid and icy weeks. And then, after the thaw, it happens. A miracle. "He" could shake his buns again. And shake 'em like "He" shook 'em last summer. Baby! Perhaps, by an act of God. Or perhaps, by decree. A decree of "The King." And one unlike any other.

In the months ahead, "The King" and I will have occasion after occasion to come together as ordered. As the picture shows. The one taken with my big Speed Graphic after I focused, cocked the shutter, pulled the dark slide and, handed it over to another regular G.I. In that desperately desired "picture of the day," between The Elvis and the I, there's plenty of room to fit in a Lally. Even a fat Lally. Fatter. Even fatter. Oh Makesense! Just look at the picture.

Today, eighteen months after our first uneasy encounter, Elvis is leaving. And leaving as Sergeant Elvis Aron Presley. And leaving me just as "he" found me eighteen months before. Specialist Four, and one grade below sergeant. And leaving me feeling sore. Well actually, more than sore. More like raped. And why? History. The cockeyed kind. "He" arrives a private. I, a Specialist Four. "He" gets promoted to Private First Class. I, a Specialist Four. "He" gets promoted to a Specialist Four. I, a Specialist Four. And on January 20th, 1960, "He" gets promoted to sergeant. And in record time. And just in the nick of time. Two months before discharge time. And that too, is miraculous to behold. In anybody's eyes. And certainly in the eyes of all us "just like any other G.I.s" even an Audie Murphy serving in peace time would 'a died trying. Yep Makesense, there just ain't no doubt about it. It's another miracle. But this time… the fucking Army kind.

And the "Sergeant Elvis Aron Presley is leaving today" assignment is mine. This day is a dreary one. And that's a worry. That my fill strobe light will overfill and make a cloudy, dreary day look more like a cloudy, dreary night. And too much light on the subject will do just that. Turn the background black. And appropriately, today, it's drizzling. Just like in a movie funeral when it never pours, just drizzles. But today, the beloved is departing upright and by airplane with water beading up on the brim of his hat. Hell Makesense! "He" is halfway up the stairs. I got to get focused, get ready for his turn. And then, "He" stops, "He" turns, "He" smiles, and "He" waves. I fire. And as my flash lights up his face and his water-beaded hat, I want to shout, "Hey Elvis! Look here. Recognize me. Me! Your photographer. The one who wants to be standing in a pair of shoes next to yours. And going home with you. To live with you. At your beautiful Graceland. Oh Elvis! Your waves, your smiles are all directed around me and on to the crowd behind me. And before I can flip the film holder for a second shot, "He" steps on up and disappears inside the plane. And the Elvis is gone. And gone without imparting even the slightest of nods in my direction. And will I ever gaze into those Elvis eyes again? Only history, cockeyed history, will tell. "Hey Makesense! You got your ears up?" "Butt-Butt Makesense is here. With ears." "And what is the History lesson of the day?" "You say cousin, you say." "It is this. There's them are's. There's them ain'ts. Them that do the stepping on. Them that get stepped on. And again today cous', we is them ain'ts. And as history confirms, we Thornell's will always be the ain'ts."

With two years the longest the Army can keep one in Germany without one's permission, and with my time here nearing an end, the Army gives me a choice. Ship back to the states and finish up your last six months there or extend for another three months here, and get discharged three months early. And without any promise as to what I would be doing for those last six months there, and with K.P. a part of the stateside menu, I elect to stick here. Stuck at Specialist Four. Why? There aren't any slots left for new sergeants with an 841.1 M.O.S. And why? These fucking retreads again. Those, who at age 50, re-up and declare, now I wannabe be a photographer, then the director of photographers somewhere. Like 'Sergeant "Dumbass" at photo school. And like Sergeant "Moron." And the "Moron's" now and the somewhere is here, now, and with us. And here, he comes off as a man just dying to be liked. And dying for a laugh. And often, he pays too much attention to his joke telling and much too little as to what his hands are doing while, between punch lines, he's promising photographic miracles.

Like today, when a field commander, a captain by rank, arrives with a 4x5 negative, and facing our Moron says, "Sergeant, I need to get this printed. Possibly, for use in "The Spearhead", the division newspaper. And while taking the negative our Moron replies, "Yes sir. Can do sir." "Very good sergeant, but take a good look at it. It looks awfully, awfully fuzzy to me. See if it is usable." And after holding up the awfully, awfully fuzzy and past useless negative against the ceiling light and giving it his best squinty-eyed look, our Moron reassures the concerned captain. "Sir, don't worry. We'll just focus it on the enlarger." And as any moron, and particularly a Sergeant Moron, should know… that would take a miracle. Because fuzz is fuzz. And fuzz will always be fuzzy and unfocusable.

Two weeks later, in place of the captain a major stands. Meticulously attired, with his shoulders reared back and with his shoes spit-shined better than an enlisted man's. And on the counter in front of Sergeant Moron he places a film holder. And he explains that in that holder is one exposure. And not just any. But one to be turned into an 8x10 glossy. The one showing a pride-filled and meticulously dressed major standing next to the commanding general. And this precious film, he could not and he would not entrust to just anyone. And certainly not to a civilian lab. So, he entrusts it to… our Moron. Now, with the major standing rigidly in front of the counter, with the Moron standing uneasy behind it and facing the rigid major, and with the film holder still setting on the counter. Between 'em. Then the Moron determines that, now is the time to lighten up an uptight major with a joke. And with the telling, his nervous and unoccupied hands find the holder and commence to flipping and to turning it. Over and over. And around and around. And now, he's tapping it on the counter. And with the flipping, the turning and the tapping continuing, the major's eyes remain steadfastly focused on the holder. And before the punch line is out, the film is. Unconsciously, the moron had pulled the dark slide protecting the major's prized image. And there it lies, exposed before two pair of now saucer-sized eyes, and exposed long past ruination. Nothing now, but useless cream-colored and very very over exposed emulsion. Bullet proof, it's called after it's developed and examined. And so black, you can put a blowtorch to it, and until you burn a hole through it, you won't be able to see even a flicker of light coming through it. And his slide of hand was not only the ruination of a prized image but the ruination of a new career for an old retread. And one now working in the supply room, issuing blankets, and protecting fellow soldiers from exposure. And over exposure.

Lally is leaving today. And going home to his New Jersey. And as we say our goodbyes, we both know in our hearts, the goodbyes are for good. Home addresses or even phone numbers, are not exchanged. And by that, I am relieved. Geesums! His showing up down at 503 and saying, "Surprise! Surprise! Look y'all at who's down here." His seeing of everything—the dangling bare bulbs, the cracks in the walls, the collapsing floors, the kitchen where brother Garrett found his perfection in the mirror, the dreaded peephole up above my bed and then… mother. And his saying, "So this is what y'all come out of," would empty my stomach faster than any air sickness ever could, even the worst imaginable.

Geesums! Thank goodness, the Lally will never see any of "What y'all come out of." Or ever hear that mother's mouth. Not with 1200 state-side miles soon separating us. And here, even with the Fineran gone and long out of the picture, the Lally and I haven't come any closer. Not one inch. The gap was still there. Just like in the picture of Elvis—the gap—and me, the gap between us will always be there. Makesense! Being close ain't so easy is it? And if you've got things to hide? Things you could never, never share, it could become risky if you could be close, couldn't it? Never mind answering Makesense. When I know, and know too well, that those answers always are… yes! yes! And even so Makesense, not to worry, because "being close" ain't a condition likely to afflict a Thornell. With my time in Germany soon coming to an end, I come down with it. The fever. Car fever. And it draws me to a beige bug-eyed Austin Healy Sprite. A tiny two-seat convertible. Equipped with screw-off plastic windows. And equipped without radio, trunk, or door locks. And for a photographer with equipment to store, it's an impractical car. Totally. But for a fat man, it's an impossible car. Totally. Because big guy, you'll never fit into it. But despite all those impracticalities, even for a skinny man, Bug-eyes is still my dream car. And just what is separating a dream from a reality? Twelve hundred dollars. And that, I must separate from a mother. And again, just like it was for that it-could-have-been-for-an-abortion money, justification is siding with me. Because without me, that sixteen hundred dollars piled-up there in the First National wouldn't be piled-up there would it Makesense? But even with justification on my side, reality still sides with her. For, with my asking comes the hearing and the hearing and the hearing of her reality. That mouth!

"Hello mother. This is Jack." "Hello boy. How you doing?" "Oh fine. Fine mother. Nothings to matter. Except, I'll be getting out soon. And, I'll need a car." "A car?" "Yes, a car. And I got it picked out. I need you to send me $1200." "Boy! That's a heap of money. That took more'n two years to save up." "I know mother. I know." And then, that mouth surprises. "Jack, I'll get you your money. But you got to promise me somethump'n." "What? Promise what." "That you gonna come on home." "Mother, you know I'm coming home. Where else is there for me to go."

With two years worth of scrimping and saving and scrimping and saving, mothers, I buy my bug-eyed dream. And admiring it, I step back, and look at it head-on. And looking back are two headlights, setting high on the hood, perfectly rounded, and sticking out like two swollen eyes. Geesums Makesense, it's really a bug. But a dream bug. And ours cousin. Ours.

Sunday, the afternoon is beautiful. Sunny and warm. A perfect day to take the top down, throw a blanket in Bugeyes, just in case I get lucky and get a chance to spread it… and drive. I find myself following the streetcar tracks to downtown Frankfurt. And then, I find myself pulling over and parking outside Wally's building. And before I can find enough courage to get out and go up, she's coming out the door. And she sees me. And comes running. "Oh Jack! Is this cute little car yours?" "Yes, I just got it." "Oh, I love it. Take me for a ride."

And soon, we're admiring the countryside, when Wally reaches over, squeezes my arm and suggest something. "Oh, Jack, it's so beautiful here. Let's pull over and get out." And with the taking of my eyes off the road and the turning of them on her, comes, "Sure, Wally. That sounds good, real good." And with her hand still on me. But now, gently stroking my leg, I pull over, park, and we get out, but while I'm reaching back for that blanket, I'm thinking… Isn't this why I'm here with you Wally. To spread that blanket. And, get lucky. And for free. Hell, there's no other way. Not even down at the Dolly Bar. Not with my last five dollars already spent on gas for the car.

Fifty yards or so from the little traveled road, we stop next to a big tree, embrace and kiss. And after our kissing grows more and more passionate, suddenly, Wally pulls back her mouth, and says, "Oh Jack. I've missed you. Make love to me." There's no need to respond. Not verbally. Not with my response already being felt, and felt more so now, as I pull her even harder against me. And then, still standing, we disengage. I spread the blanket. We lie. Wally spreads. And we re-engage. Like before. Before that business between us. And like before, without Wally complaining. She just pulls me close and tries to hold me close. But she can't. For my desire to go untouched now is far too overwhelming for either of us to overcome. So, I pull free, pull her up, pick up the blanket, and hurriedly usher her back into the car.

The driving back into the city seems to be taking longer than the coming. And with Wally still next to me, seemingly much longer. But still, there are two things to be thankful for. The getting lucky. And the silence. Thank goodness she isn't pressing for small talk. But if you were Wally, what would it be about? Babies? Abortions? Or the aborting of something less, but still something more than a mockingbird. No! Don't want to talk about these things. Then, what about this? The cost of cocksucking lessons. Yours. No! She isn't pressing for small talk. Instead, she settles for silence. And hell, she's used to that. The silence that comes after the sex. That comes with my pulling away. With my turning away. And with my going from hot to cold. Posthaste. No Wally, no small talk today. So, just take off your bandanna. Lean your head

73

back. And let the wind take your hair wherever the wind wants. Just like I took you. And no Wally, no small talk from me either. There's no need now. Not with my getting lucky done. All done. And as far as I am concerned, the only things left for us to share is the silence, and the long ride home. So close your eyes dear Wally and doze. And we'll both feel more comfortable.

Finally, finally, we're back to where we started. And we get out, and I walk Wally to the door, the downstairs door, and once there she turns, reaches for and takes my face between her hands. And while still caressing, says, "Oh Jack. It was good, so good, to see you. Please come to see me for as long as you're here." Pulling back and out of her reach, I reply, "We'll see Wally. We'll see." With that said, I turn, dash to the car and without taking the time to open the door, I jump in and drive away. But even with my mouth repeating out-loud, "Don't look back. Don't look back," I find my eyes are already up and on the rearview mirror, focused, and stealing one last look at Wally. Still standing there. Just like I left her. And just like I left mother down at the bottom of the hill. Just standing there. With nowhere else to go. But back into a cell.

And now, while I'm speeding back to the barracks, guilt replaces the silence. And won't leave me alone. The guilt of using her and then, throwing her away like some disposable thing. Geesums! How could I have done that to her. To Wally. The first woman to want me and, and even to want me without five dollars in my pocket. And then, something pops into my head, something the great Confucius could have penned to ease such pricks and pangs of conscious. So, I recite it out loud… enlarged penis have very little conscience. But it that's funny, then why ain't I laughing? Because, my guilt freeing scenario, the one I wrote in my head, could be crumbling. The one that says… Wally was never pregnant. That says… that was just a lie. That says… I was just a victim. But now, I'm wondering… Do the facts of the day support that scenario. If Wally had lied then. If Wally had duped me then. Why would Wally want to take a ride with me now? And lie with me now? Makesense! Is it reasonable for Wally to lie to me then, and to lie with me now? Geesums! Its not, is it? Geesums Makesense! That getting lucky for free proves costly doesn't it? And most costly to a conscience on trial, by eliminating… reasonable doubt. All of it Wally. All of it. "With that deduction Makesense, wouldn't you agree?" "Makesense say, Jack son make good Charlie Chan. But, very bad Confucius."

Tomorrow, I will be leaving Germany, getting away from Wally, and heading back to the U.S. of A. And home. And home. And home. Just like promised. Just like promised. Just like promised. Geesums Makesense even thinking of H-O-M-E is haunting haunting haunting. And, reminding reminding reminding that the house is waiting waiting waiting to be filled with another poor lost soul. Me! Me! Me!

"Makesense! Talk to me. Should I re-enlist? And forget going home?" "Butt-Butt Makesense is here. And reminding you of a promise promise promise." "What promise promise promise?" "The one you made your momma momma momma. For that money money money. For bugeyes. Your come home promise cousin. Your come home prom…" "Okay! Okay Makesense! I hear! I hear! I heard!"

The going home party with the guys, the gals and the swallowing of all that awful tasting beer succeeds at taking me to inebriation and beyond. And even on to numbness and beyond. But fails at taking away those dread-filled previews of "The Homecoming Party." Still impending. And still playing on and on in my head. Geesums! There's Crazy Uncle John! Out and on the loose just like mother wrote. Under the street light and pacing as if he's trying to walk off a touch of over anxiousness, perhaps associated with his waiting for a certain presence to show. Inside, those troubled souls, usually unseen except for an occasional bulging eye, are now downstairs, smiling and setting the table for a coming home celebration. And now, adding to their delight is a preview of the menu to be served. First is, lie soup. Next, saute' sparrows. And then for dessert, Mockingbird Pie. And for entertainment, the running and rerunning a short film of my first sexual experience. Lasting just sixty seconds. Start to finish. Including fore-play and climax. And now, they're pointing to something. Something caked in dirt. And something looking like it could have been... oh Geesums... a baby. And then, with a rushed mouthful of beer refusing to be swallowed, I choke, cough, and expel the beer and the hallucination. And while I'm still trying to get my breath back, Frank Long, a replacement photographer, comes up, slaps me on the back, and beams. "A helleuvah party Thornell." "Yeah Long. A helleuvah party."

The voyage home isn't exactly swell. But, not for the lack of swells to be experienced, it's anything but. Rough and rougher, the sea is. And these days and nights, she is no lady. She's upset. She's full of anger. And she's persistent in taking it out. And who better to take it out of, than out of the bodies riding her. And most unfortunately, from most of the bodies she's taking it out of always seem to be riding her somewhere close to me. Oops, she just claimed a breakfast. And later, a dinner. But rarely does she claim a lunch. She doesn't have to because between meals, even the thought of food immediately brings up results. Oh Makesense! I never thought I would experience anything worse than air sickness. Until I experienced sea sickness. And then, experience it co-mingling with somebody else's. Oh Makesense! How I long for a return of air sickness, with limits of a hatful.

And finally, after days and nights of crossing and tossing, we disembark near Fort Dix. And after three days, with the Army's mustering out papers in my hand and with their re-enlistment pitch still fresh in my head, I press my body into Bugeyes, point its jutting headlights south and begin a new experience. And, a near death one. Highway driving. And while traveling down one of those all too narrow two-lane roads, with every passing of one of those roaring, road-hogging tractor-trailers comes a natural reaction. To cringe! And with every disturbing monster wake comes something else. The feeling of what a body pressed inside a Beetle (Volkswagen) must feel like. Beetle guts. And while facing one of those heavy-footed truckers, comes something else. Anticipation. Of something I'll soon get to know. Just how squashed beetle guts get made. Geesums Makesense! Without our cringing and our offer of less resistance, any one of those monster wakes could blow Bugeyes and us right off the road. Oh geesums Makesense! Here comes another. Cringe with me. Grip the wheel with me. And pray with me. That the oncoming squashing threat will safely pass.

Near Vicksburg, hills, giant hills, too numerous to be counted greet us. And tower over both sides of narrow Highway 80. And Bugeyes. And me. Just like I left them thirty three months ago. Still, like great pyramids. Still, the bury-ers of history. And a bloody blue and a bloody gray history it was too. As too many gray and decaying grave markers bear witness to. Geesums Makesense! Ain't they awesome. Looking up at 'em, one can't help but feel smaller. No, make that infinitesimal. Such hills. In most places, I reckon, people take their hills in stride, even for granted. But not here. Not by Vicksburgers. And not by General Ulysses S. Grant. As he proved in mid-May 1863. Attack in winter? Never! Because he knew, if the elements went against him and put down even a thin layer of sleet or snow, he'd never took Vicksburg. Cause:

He'd never took that first icy hill. Hell, he'd slide back into the river. And even with the elements backing the genius general, it still took 'em 47 days to take 'em.

Makesense, even the sun-crazed Kudzu can't conquer these monuments of time like it has some of the less challenging to the north around Yazoo city and to the south near peaceful Port Gibson. There, Kudzu—a perennial vine of the pea family, native to Japan and China, cultivated for its edible roots as a hay and ensilage, and sometimes used to curb erosion—grows. And grows uncontrollable. About a foot a day. Snaking in all directions. Seeking something to climb, to cover and then, to smother. And creepy too, is kudzu's bizarre behavior. Creeping around all those big roadside billboards. Like it knows something a thing shouldn't know. That billboards, but for boastful colors, aren't really alive. And therefore are, unsmotherable. And a waste of time and good vine. As to the Kudzu's appetite, call it insatiable. As to the many shrubs and plants in its path, call 'em mini appetizers. As to the great valleys accumulating its waves of vines, call 'em soon hidden and soon to be renamed... The Great Seas of Kudzu. And as to the trees. Even the big ones. Like the live oaks, the tall pines, and even the full and the Mississippi-favored magnolias standing in its foot-a-day expansion, call 'em soon spanned. And with the last ray of sunlight choked away, call 'em condemned. And with the buzzing sounds of a chain saw putting 'em down, call 'em, finally, at rest. Geesums Makesense, the slow smother, that's a hard way to be put down, even for a tree.

And just how did those Asian roots get a start here. The government experts brung 'em, planted 'em and saw 'em as an erosion slower. But, nothing more. But what those experts hadn't seen was, the effect the southern heat and humidity has on a particular perennial plant. And by the time they saw all that "nothing more" covering more and more and more. It was too late to do much about it. But study it. And one study found: Angora goats could eat Kudzu to a standstill. But what the study couldn't find: Enough Angora goats for so many Kudzu covered hills. And thus Makesense, the sun-crazed and the smothering Kudzu had its start and now, has its hold on so many Mississippi hills.

After passing through the archway on the east side of town, I keep Bugeyes pointing west, down Clay Street and towards the heart of town. Everything seems familiar and my thirty months away feeling like less than a day. Even at the corner of Clay and Cherry stands the same old sign. Sollie's Hot Tamales. Homemade and wrapped in shonough cornhusks, and reportedly delicious. And now with my mustering out pay still bulging in my pockets, I can afford to stop and find out just how delicious. But I don't. Not with my stomach already full and stirring with the dreaded anticipation of my coming home dinner awaiting.

"Makesense, some egghead probably once said, "The anxiety associated with the anticipating of something unpleasant is often much worse than the reality yet to come." Tell that to cousin Lucille after the "Big Blow" with her blood freely flowing through her shredded stockings as she awaited news of her three missing daughters. The anxiety. Last seen entering the movie. The reality, only one exists alive. Anxiety may be hell, but it sure ain't the hell of reality. Not in Lucille's case. And not in mine either, not knowing what I know... that shame is a silent greedy partner patiently waiting to steal away, then swallow up your next opportunity for joy before it can even materialize and Makesense, you know and I know, nothing good ever materialized down at 503."

After passing the Vicksburg Hotel, spared by the "Big Blow", I turn left toward and then, stop in front of the Joy. Here was my refuge. Here I survived my youth. Here I met two real movie actors. Hot rodder Robert Fuller and The Invisible Man Arthur Franz. And while shaking their hands imagining how great it would be to be an actor. To be able to change your name. To be able to become someone else. And so I tried it. Playing the part of a normal kid with normal parents living in a normal home where a normal kid can invite a friend over to play and to share a normal dinner of fried chicken with mashed potatoes, gravy, green beans, hot rolls and all the butter a body could ever crave for. But, and like all the good roles, they soon disappear as mine did every night as I exited the Joy and entered the reality awaiting.

"Oh Makesense, how great it would have been to be an actor. To be able to become someone else. Anyone else. Anyone but me."

From the Joy I follow my routine route home. Bugeyes will lessen the walking time of overtired legs after a remembered 15 hour day. Moving south on Washington, I pass the place, Bomar Baptist, where I was almost persuaded. Where all that stood between me and salvation was a pair of holey socks. A few blocks south the Dabney Avenue sign turns Bugeyes right toward the river and to a dead stop at the top of the hill.

"Geesums Makesense, do I, do we, really want to go there? To face Mother, to face the house. To face those demons. But why? Why must I come back? To renew the old pain? To regenerate old shame? Is it my lot? Is it my due? Must I surrender when the shamehold summons? Go or stay? Go or stay? Christ Makesense! Help me out here."

"Keep your promise cousin. Keep your promise. But for her. Her saving ways and her cashier's check for $1200, you'd, we'd still be walking and walking and walking. And Bugeyes, yet a dream."

"Okay! Okay! Makesense, I hear you. A promise is a promise. Particularly one bought and paid for."

Now, with history lessons rushing into my head and ruining any possible expectation that somehow, some way, conditions down there could have improved during my absence, I ease up on the brake pedal and let Bugeyes creep down the hill. And stop at the dead end. Still remaining in the car, and feeling like a fugitive about to be recaptured and re-incarcerated, I look for Mamma.

"Geesums Makesense, I'm doing it again. Calling Mother Mamma and we both know that is forbidden. And we both know why." And then, I see her. Over in the corner of the yard with her backside to me and the street and still wearing her see-through, see-all cottons. And without those most uncomfortable and most unnecessary undergarments—slip or panties— restricting her air flow. And what's most disgusting about this picture is... she is squatting and pruning an American Beauty rose.

"Makesense don't that just turn your stomach too, that picture?" But Makesense don't reply, because Makesense don't participate in dehumanizing. Not of anyone. Not even Mother.

And facing me is the house. Still the edifice of neglect. Still the eyesore of eyesores. Nailed to perfection.

Suddenly she turns, sees me, and starts running toward me, but her mouth reaches me first. "Son of a bitch! Son of a bitch! Boy! Is that you?" Our embrace is tenuous, terse, uneasy, unnatural and brief. Then she sees the car. "I'll be goddam, look at that little fucking car. I ain't never seen nothing like it. Can two people fit in there?"

After two walks around the car, she turns her gaze back to me, exclaiming, "Jack, I forgot to tell you. We're famous. Fucking famous. Go sit there in the swing and I'll show you." Now, relieved of entering the house, at least immediately, I sit and I wait, with my first impressions popping into my head and lingering there. One thing is for sure, Mother's mouth hasn't improved. Perhaps, it's worse. Sentences without shit and such in 'em still seem tasteless to her, and but a wasted attempt at communicating. Of course there's still hope. Hope for a stormy day when she still might let up with the profanity for a brief respite. At least until the thunder and lightning subsides. But as for first impressions, so far Makesense, so bad. So so bad. But what I wasn't dwelling on was her "fucking famous" remark. At least not till she returned to join me on the porch swing, and starts showing me. It's a newspaper article from the Vicksburg Evening Post. It's a story about Elvis and me. And next to it is a big picture of Mother sitting on my bed, and layed out next to her on my bed is a big 8x10 glossy of Elvis and me posing together. The one I mailed her from Germany.

And then more thoughts begin exploding in my head. Shame filled thoughts... Mother! Who the fuck appointed you, fucking illiterate you, my fucking press agent? How could you invite a goddamn newspaperman down here, show him this, all this, and then let him take a picture of it. And then, let him show the world where I came out of. Mother fucker! Mother fucker! Mother fucker! Mother, Mother, Mother, how fucking stupid can one be? And while fighting hard not to verbalize any of my thoughts, another explodes in my head. The car. The one of a kind. The only one in town. In the state. And it belongs to me. And anyone driving by will see it. See it parked outside the house and then connect the house to the car to the driver to me. Me! Me! Me! And though I loved Bugeyes, I can't help but ask, "Jack! Jack! Jack! How fucking stupid can one be?" And now with the what to do question stirring, I'm up, out of the swing, off the porch and rounding the west side of the house, the side adjacent to dirt Pearl, where little and often, no cars turn and take a look. Then, I drive Bugeyes between two brick pillars raising and supporting the porch. It fits perfectly underneath and out of sight of passing eyes. And with the threat of exposure reduced, Mother's voice beckons. "Jack, come on in the house and I'll fix us a cup of tea."

Still agitated with the combining of Mother's stupidity with mine, I pull back the screen door to enter the house and my room. The room I hungered in, smothered in, and died a thousand times in. Ducking around the bare bulb still dangling above my bed, and with my blood still hot with anger at Mother, and myself, I want to raise my eyes up and onto the dreaded peephole and issue my own invitation to. You fucking demons, you fucking whatevers up there behind a door nailed shut, come on down, I'm standing here, right here, waiting and more than qualified to face off with another troubled soul. But immediately, reservations set in. And cause me to wonder... Has the Army sent home a new and fearless man or just an older and more impulsive idiot? But it's still too early to tell. Cause those "whatevers" up there wouldn't have heard a word. Cause those "whatevers" are never up and stirring till dark sets in. So with sanity returning, I smother my would-be challenge, and keep my eyes on things below. To the bed offering little rest to a scared and undernourished kid starving for food and affection. To the slanted floor, now giving more life to dropped marbles than ever before. To the rusty space heater, still oxidizing in front of a fireplace still sealed tight. The only thing visible that pleases me is the cleanliness. There's not a dirty dish or a crumb to be found in the sink or on the floor. If nothing else, the little woman keeps a clean house.

While she's cooking chicken and dumplings, my coming home meal, she busies her mouth with her humming. Spiritual sounds like "Amazing Grace". Surprising it was that such sweet sounds could emerge from such a foul-mouth as hers. But, as we sit down to eat, the serenity ends.

"Jack, if you want to see that crazy bastard, you can find him at the corner of Clay and Washington. Outside Crowley's Pool Hall. Just standing there. And staring. Standing and staring, all day and half the night."

Just the mention of that crazy bastard, meaning Crazy Uncle John, stirs more than my interest. "Has he been back down the hill lately?" "No, he ain't but that don't mean he ain't. Cause if he hasn't lost the rest of his fucking mind, the little bit that was left, he'll be back." Oh what a pleasant thought, I thought... the demons inside, and Crazy Uncle John outside, just a-dying to join in. Geesums Makesense, it's not even bedtime yet, and already, the nightmare begins.

After supper, while sitting on the rim of the too familiar tin tub that's way too small for any man's body and while trying to remove the day's road grime, I find myself missing a pleasure of Army life... a hot shower. Outdoors, a rainbow is the reward of a shower. Indoors here a shower would be reward enough.

It's bedtime, and Army veteran Jack Randolph Thornell, conqueror of the great Atlantic—by air and by sea—a trained killer with bullets bayonets and bazookas, drops to his knees to look under the bed. Then, I take the position. Back down, face up, with my arms folding and forming a cross above my chest. Then, my eyes lock onto the peephole. And the waiting begins. Waiting for those upstairs demons to begin stirring from behind a door nailed shut.

Having survived a first night home, the second, the Joy beckons. It's a Wednesday night, an always slow night. Entering the lobby, Mrs. Bounds can be seen bending over the cooler re-stacking ice cream sandwiches and I can't help but recall that other slow night when she aroused me by sandwiching my hand between her body and the cooler, trapping and holding it there for the longest. Oh! How I wanted her then. More than a million ice cream bars. And how, I wanted her now. But before I can set a today's value on her, she turns, sees and greets me. "Well, welcome home Jack. It's been... what... about three years now?" "Thirty months to be exact," I reply as she invites me into her office to discuss my future. She'd love to have me back at the stand. Cause, I thought, it was hard to keep a body standing there for five hours a day, for seven days a week for less than $15.00. And with my body being there for nearly five years without missing a single day. No doubt, had saved her feet from filling in when a body would suddenly up and quit. Now, a body could do better just by re-enlisting, with three squares, shelter, and a signing bonus.

After reaching into a storage freezer, she selects an ice cream bar, one too imperfectly made for selling, hands it to me, begins smirking, shaking her head and saying, "News photography! Did you say... news photography?" "Yes ma'am... perhaps at a newspaper." Again she's shaking and saying, "Young man, you know that being an Army photographer, that's nothing like being a news photographer. That takes special skills. Skills like the Army never taught you. But good luck with that anyway."

And with her career critique still smothering my expectations I excuse myself, thank her for the treat while being grateful for the fact that she, at least, made no mention of my education, or the lack of it. And as I left her, that urge, that great urge to fuck her, to ride her for the limit, even a 60-second limit, was, at the moment, waning.

With unemployment high in the country and with only one newspaper in Vicksburg, The Evening Post, any possibilities here are limited. "Geesums Makesense! Thank goodness we got the Army to fall back on."

The next day, just my third day home, the Post editor is polite. Even likes my pictures. But as he is saying no, he is pushing 'em back at me while explaining, "I'm sorry. But we don't employ a photographer. Not full time. Our reporters take their own pictures to run with their stories." My portfolio is heavy with Elvis photos except for the two the Army honored with awards. One, a spectacular collision at home plate between a base runner and the umpire, stirring up a huge cloud of dust. The other, an artsy shot of a bugler, shrouded by fog, while blowing taps over misty grave markers on a Memorial Day. Disappointed, I left, but I wasn't disappointed by one thing... his not recalling "the picture", the one linking Elvis, Mother and me. Perhaps he was on vacation and missed seeing it. I certainly hoped so.

Now, with a job rejection now joining and fortifying Mrs. Bound's doubts, the next day, my fourth home, Bugeyes, with Makesense and me travel 35 miles to the east, to Jackson, the state capital. There, there are three dailies. First comes the "State-Times". There I find everyone is still out to lunch, so I walk a few blocks west to the "Jackson Daily News". Their newsroom is bare too, but I can hear the keys of a typewriter clicking away in a corner office. After slowly approaching it, I look in finding a man still pecking away, pausing, laughing out loud over his last sentence, before sensing my presence, turning and then asking, "Can I help you?" "Sir, I'm looking for someone to talk to about a photography job." "Come on in. Sit down. My name is Ward, James Ward, I'm the editor here." A racist, perhaps, but a devout segregationist for sure, he was, I would soon learn by reading his daily column, "Covering The Crossroads". The separation of the races--blacks from whites-- a birthright to be nurtured, even protected, down here in Mississippi. To him and many like him, more constitutional than the rigidly enforced separation of church and state regulation. Segregation for now and segregation for evermore might have been a more appropriate title for his column running daily down the left side of the front page.

After examining my pictures, he asks, "Can you type?" "Yes sir." "Do you have a car?" "Yes sir." "Good. But I can't hire you as a photographer as we only have one such position, and Norm Bergsma has it." Now, noticing my eyes meeting the floor, he quickly adds, "But I can put you to work on the news side. The job pays $70.00 a-week if you want it." "Yes sir! Yes sir! I want it." "Well then, report to state editor Bob Bloodsworth at six sharp on Monday morning." That night, back at the Joy, I report my job news to Mrs. Bounds adding, "Like here

80

in Vicksburg, reporters are required to take pictures too so that will keep my photography hopes alive." Less than ecstatic over my news, she says, "I guess you can give it a try. That reporter thing. But don't pin your dreams of ever becoming a news photographer, because Army photography and news photography are worlds apart."

Now, with my thoughts turning back to my Army experience, with the exception of aerial assignments and a few sporting events, most of all my subjects, whether receiving a citation or a certificate, turned into statues when I said, "Hold it." and remained such until I released them with, "Got it." So I guess what Mrs. Bounds is saying is... breaking news won't "Hold it", not for me, not for anyone. And now, after all that time... years, undoubtedly she hasn't forgotten my first photo fuckup and the should have been, but for being a blank snapshot, of that record-breaking "Quo Vadis" line. The one she wanted in her report to movie mogul Joy N. Houck as to how she single handedly, and so successfully produced all those sell-out crowds. As I'm leaving her presence, I imagine that she is now adding a new word to her earlier, bone crushing, ego crippling, "Young man! Young man! A photographer, you're not.", critique. And the word is... news.

It's Monday, it's 6am, with the sun just showing when my new career is born with news of the dead. Just minutes after my arrival and after brief introductions, boss Bloodsworth orders, "Take a seat, pick up line two, and take down this death notice." Immediately, I find myself one hand short. One for the phone and two for typing. Looking around the newsroom I see how the other reporters have mastered it. By pressing the phone between a tilted head and a raised shoulder and holding it there. That looks easy enough, so I try it but every time I tilt my head, raise my shoulder, hold the phone, and then trying to look down to find the keyboard, and begin typing while straining to hear the dictation, the phone drops and begins bouncing across the desk. Again and again it dropped, and again and again it bounced. And again and again I apologize to the caller with, "It's my first day and my first attempt at taking dictation." Finally, all that bounce-noise draws Bloodsworth's attention and a most quieting response, "Don't worry. By tomorrow you'll have a special holding bracket on your phone." After surviving the pressure of those hours of handling death notices, there's time to observe things. Immediately to my left is Bloodsworth's desk. It's completely covered with papers spread and piled high enough to cover a corpse, possibly two. And its top, if mahogany or metal would be, just a guess. Yet on deadline, though never rattled, he digs down deep into those buried news releases, pauses, then miraculously, pulls up the one worthy of resurrection. "Here Jack, give me five paragraphs on this. You got five minutes before deadline." And rewriting comes relatively easy, I find. All that is needed is for several paragraphs to be rearranged, perhaps shortened so as to not appear word for word as it would in other newspapers around the state. And thankfully, I had some experience shortening stories to a few sentences by writing captions to appear under published Army photographs. And here, in newspaper lingo, called cut-lines.

Across from Bloodsworth, just over his paper mountain, sits city editor Jack Fairley, a small, a meek-mannered man, with a voice hardly raised above a whisper. Until it comes to me. And in the days and the weeks ahead, it becomes clear that he wants a piece of me. Often demanding that after the state news deadlines passes, I should pass over to his control and finish out the day working on city news.

And with Bloodsworth's reluctance to completely let go, the pulling and the passing begins. Without having any experience covering the news, city or state, I couldn't figure out as to why either would want me working for them. And so I ask, "Makesense, why all the pulling over my incompetent ass?" "Pride and jealousy cousin, a lot of pride and a little jealousy. Bloodsworth now has an assistant and Fairley don't. Incompetence, don't matter."

To my right, over and just outside of editor Ward's office, with his desk catty-cornered and facing the newsroom, sits managing editor O.C. McDavid, who often removes his pipe to raise a voice of reasoning. As for the Bloodsworth-Fairley feud over control of me, with the wisdom of a King Solomon McDavid decrees... saw the sucker in half and share him equally. So from arrival to late morning I belong to Bloodsworth and thereafter to Fairley. Days the wisdom works well, but nights, my supposed to be off nights, it don't. And that's because Bloodsworth says, go here and Fairley says go there.

Next to McDavid sits police reporter W. C. Shoemaker, considered the staff's top gun, he knows just about every cop in town by his first name. Gifted with a nose for news, he often sniffs it out before the competition over at The State-Times. Although only separated from Shoemaker by a few desks, when it came to noses and know hows, I'm not even in the room yet. I like him though. And what I like most is his lack of a college degree. Education labels intimidate, even threaten me. Even with the thought of such a question as "Jack, where did you go to college?", I cringe. And cringe. And cringe. It's clear "The Educated" make me feel smaller than 5-foot-10.

To my back, occupying the opposite corner from McDavid's, is amusements editor Frank Hains. When Frank finds that I am commuting daily from Vicksburg, he offers me a ticket to a play he is directing and since the show will run late, he also offer me space on his fold-out sofa bed. But what he didn't offer was the revelation that his sofa bed would have to be shared. Shared with him. Because it's the only bed. With a man sleeping so close to my backside, the night and the bed are less than restful. Odd though that Frank didn't seem to mind, seeming to sleep just fine, even with my behind occasionally butting up against his. Soon the news of my sleepover would be uncovered by police reporter Shoemaker, and when it is, he approaches me with a broad smile and some personal advice, "Watch your back Jack. Friendly Frank prefers guys over girls." And despite many more overnight overtures, Frank never gets lucky, never gets more than friendly, and never gets to be more than a gentleman. But then I never gave him another chance, because all his future invitations, I quickly declined.

Anxious to cut my ties to Mother and to the house, I rent an apartment on Estelle Drive in north Jackson. Actually, the apartment isn't an apartment. It's one room. A converted single-car garage. With a refrigerator and a space heater. Not much to most eyes, but to mine, when comparing it to 503, it's a palace. Stairs lead up to a locked door letting in to the landlord's kitchen. And the keyhole adorning that locked door opens up trouble when I was caught looking through it and at the landlord's wife. His naked wife. And the saving grace, the grace that keeps me from eviction is my pictures. The pictures of their twin sons flying kites, eating watermelon, sledding in the snow, all showing on the front page of the Daily News. And since the landlord, the husband and the father, is in the insurance business, it's good for business having his name in the paper. And so, instead of an eviction notice, I get a chastisement. "Don't ever get caught doing that again." And to make sure, he tapes over his side of the keyhole. And how would I know that, discover that, that tape? Yep!

After surviving my first week of waking up with the dead, it was obvious to everyone there, that I had a lot to learn. Not only about the work, but about the drinking after. And so they take me to the basement bar of the old Robert E. Lee Hotel for, on the barstool training. The notion of surrendering it before the booze and beer stopped flowing at midnight by city ordinance, is never entertained. And neither is going home early and sober.

And the morning after such a drinking session, with a head a-pounding, with a telephone a-ringing and with typewriter keys a-clattering, I fulfill the dubious duty of laying the more fortunate souls to rest without being able to lift a finger to alleviate my own suffering.

With obituary writing down cold, editors Bloodsworth and Fairley decide to expand my education by sending me out of the building to Chamber of Commerce banquets, Kiwanis Club luncheons and beauty pageants to play reporter. Write the words, and take the picture. Well, writing it's not, not exactly. It's more like filling in the blanks. The daughter of _____ was chose Miss Brandon Saturday night. The lass, stands _____ tall, and attends the University of _____. Important the stories weren't. Sending me. More of a public relations ploy. But seeing my name above those stories and above those terrible line 'em up against the wall photos, though buried way inside the newspaper, provide a high never experienced before. Not by me. But over time and with more experience this aphrodisiac stops working. And a terrible photo with Jack R. Thornell under it, gnaws at me, long after the newspaper is discarded. Now, it takes a terrific picture, a front page picture to stimulate my pride.

After two years, it's clear to Editor Ward that writing is not my talent, but photography is, and with that discovery, comes good news. Chief photographer Bergsma resigns, leaving behind a wall of terrific pictures. The best shows a mother hound with a drowned pup held gently in her mouth and about to join four more already laid to rest atop a flooded doghouse. The pups, like Louise's girls, the victims of time and circumstance. But not without a mother's love. Bergsma was not liked much by the staff, who behind his back accused him of drowning the pups and standing by for such a great photo opt as this. Although I didn't like Bergsma much either, I don't buy their story. This picture was just too perfect to have been staged.

Naturally, I desire Bergsma's position as chief and only photographer. Not only to focus on photography, but because I was tired, so tired of being pulled between Bloodsworth and Fairley. Tired of working days and nights without any overtime pay or even a suggestion of compensating time off. Just the suggesting of either or could put a body at risk of being dismissed. And fast. That's just the way it is if you work for the Hederman brothers, Bob and Tom. Devout Christians and big contributors, who left their charity at the church door. And why would I say such a shameful thing. Because... besides not being compensated for those tons of extra working hours and compelled to use my car to cover in-town assignments without a whiff of gas money, I must not forget to pay for parking Bugeyes in the Hederman Brothers parking lot outback. And as for healthcare, life insurance or company retirement plans forget 'em, for there are none. As for raises, five-buck-a-week-a-year. Regardless of a body's degree of competency. And now, after two years, my weekly check is eighty dollars. "So Makesense, in another four years, I'll... we'll be earning a round 100 a week."

It's Monday morning and it's just between the State and the City deadline, when editor Ward approaches my desk and asks, "Jack you got a minute?" "Yes sir." "Mind stepping into my office?" Again, "Yes sir" is my response. "Jack you probably know by now that Bergsma is leaving. So his job is opening. And it's yours if you want it." "Yes sir! Yes sir! I want it." "Okay then, next Monday move over to the desk outside the darkroom. It's yours."

"Geesums Makesense, in just two years we graduate from incompetency class to this... the Chief Photographer's position. Isn't it grand?"

"Grand it is cousin, but it would be 'grandeur' if you had another body to chief over, besides your own."

On Monday morning, despite my new desk and despite my new title, I soon discover that... my body is not even my own to lord over. To Bloodsworth and Fairley, it's still theirs. And they keep on using and using it as before. So, nothing changed. Except coming in earlier, to process and print all the reporter's pictures before their pulling can begin.

And except for the view. Now, I can look directly into the glassed-in society department and onto the face of one Kay Haggerty, the new assistant ladies editor. Monday through Friday at 5pm, a guy can station himself at the corner of West and Capital, and for the next 10 minutes he can see some of the most beautiful girls in the world, certainly Mississippi's finest, leaving work. But here and now, from my vantage, I discover something. Not beauty. Not even pretty. Attractive, surely. And it's clear, I can't keep my eyes off of her. Tall with dark hair, with long lean legs and with years of college behind her. And with her eyes on me and with her lips addressing me in seductive tandem, she is, perhaps, the sexiest woman in the world. And in my world, for sure.

And with Kay, I would fall in love. For the first time and for the last time. And how could such a conclusion come so early for a man so young. Because of the depth and the density of the pain to come with the most and the worst of it, self-inflicted.

In the weeks and months ahead, we date, do dinners, movies, and bars. And we make love. And just when things seem to be going heavenly, a competition separates us. Not from another man, but from Mother Church. Her church. The Catholic Church. After we have sex, the good Catholic girl is afraid. Afraid to drive. Afraid to cross the street. Afraid her next bodily contact will be with a big Mack truck bound for hell and taking her with it. And so, the morning after, with her fear ruling her, and under a flag of caution, she rushes to Father Confessor for absolution. And then, and only then, is it safe to drive and dare cross a busy intersection. And as for sex, that comes only after less time at dinner and the movies and after more time at the bars. And thus, our on again, off again, relationship continues, especially when her religion is watered down by one too many beers. That is until Armageddon. And it starts with a good priest who keeps hearing and recognizing the same contrite voice repeating the same contrite confession. Sex with Jack R. Thornell. And undoubtedly, sensing the fear in her voice, lays down the law. "No more sex." And worse for her, "No more absolution" from him or any other priest on the face of the planet. The best thing for Kay, he suggests, is to keep a proper space between us, until after the proper "I do's." And marriage. Mine. To Kay, the love of my life, is not ever a consideration. Why? Because, eventually I would have to take her down to 503. To meet Mother. "And that, Makesense, ain't gonna happen. Not ever, not with anyone. Especially Kay."

With the effects of abstinence ruling my days and ruining my nights, whether cursed by a hex, or vexed by a virus, I catch it. It's unendurable. It's unending. It's untreatable. And it's always ready to erupt without warning. And it's about to erupt right now as I look up to see Sports Editor Lee Baker hovering over my Kay and laughing, while pressing his hands deep into his pockets, making fists and holding them there for the longest for hiding something. "Son of a bitch! That mother fucker has a hard on... and for my Kay," is my snap-second deduction. And with that blood-boiling green-eyed monster of disorder, the one called jealousy, erupting into rage, I rush into the darkroom slamming the door behind me before, exploding with "I bet she's fucking him. No! I know it! I know it! She's fucking Baker and not me."

And with my suspicions growing stronger and stronger, my relentless third degree begins. And tonight, sitting across from Kay at the Red Top Cafe in north Jackson where the ribs are good and cheap, I confront her with, "Baker sure is hanging around your desk a lot lately. What's he up to?" "Nothing. Just talking. Small talk. About his kids and stuff." "That's all?" "That's all." "And he wasn't making a pass?" "No Jack, he wasn't." "I don't believe that. He's trying to fuck you or he's already fucking you. Which is it Kay?" Her face reddening, yet still managing to keep her voice down, well below mine, she replies, "No Jack, he isn't and he hasn't. Believe me. There's nothing. Nothing between Lee Baker and me. And besides, I love you, and only you." And with the check comes our departure, but my rage isn't going anywhere. North State is icy and slick, but I don't care. I push Bugeyes' accelerator to the floor, and soon not only the wheels are spinning, but we are too. After a frightening 360, Bugeyes comes to a stop in a parking lot in front of a business sign reading "Dick X-Ray". For the rest of the ride to Kay's mother's home, neither of us say a word. But I was thinking, "Bugeyes, I almost smashed you up. And Kay and me and maybe that sign should have been all inclusive and should have read, "Dick X-Ray and Head X-Ray too." In past drive-bys the sign had always struck me as funny, until tonight, when we almost struck it.

During the short drive to my place, with my head still spinning and turning my thoughts to that something Kay said. That she loved me. "Gee Makesense, how can I know that, trust that, to be true. When I have never known love. Not in my 21-years. Not in Germany, even with Wally, and certainly not down at 503. And then, that knowing factor starts multiplying in my head... if Kay knew me, really knew me, knew where I came from, what I came out of, would she, could she, still say, she loves me? And I know that answer. No! No! No! How could she feel love, feel more than disgust and disdain for me. And at the very most, gratitude that 503 hadn't been her lot.

"Oh Makesense, why is the thought of taking someone down there so shame-filled and so pain-filled for me, and not for brother Marshall. Hell, he took women there, day or night. Even married two of them, Jean and Jerry, before moving 'em in to live in there with Mother. And Mother was as pleased as punch. One, company eased her fear of living alone. And second, there was another body to turn her mouth on. And we know the outcome of Marshall and Jerry's 10-year, rent-free, stay there. When they back up a rental truck to the front door, loaded it up and moved to Jackson early one evening, before telling Mother. And now, standing in the yard, shocked, with hysteria a-setting in because it was getting dark, and with fear a-setting in, she's forced back into the house with only hysteria a-keeping her company. And once inside, she visits Marshall and Jerry's side of the house to find two months of unpaid utility bills a-lying on the kitchen counter, even though she's handed them the money for a-paying. And now, another fear is a-gripping her... that the lights might go off and the house go dark at any moment. "Geesums Makesense, gratitude, that Thornell kind, for 10-years of rent-free living is something, something to experience.

Back at my desk, that once cherished view into the society office, is now turning my mind into a chamber for tormenting me. Besides Baker, and on a daily basis, I can catch Shoemaker, Crenshaw, Wallace, Ward and even gay and too-friendly Frank, all fixating on those too seductive eyes. But the guy raising my ire the most, wasn't even an employee. An Associated Press photographer named James A. Bourdier. He was dark and handsome, educated, an LSU grad with a degree in journalism, and he was in town quite often to cover the news. But quite often, by the time he got to town, the news, whether a demonstration, a sit-in or a killing would be long over. And where would he come to get the pictures he needed to rush out as AP wire photos. Yep! To me. And with his flirting behavior with Kay so fresh on my mind, I remind him that she was my girl, and that I had the power to cut his pictures off. At least until we had published them. But with powerful papers like The New York Times screaming for 'em for their morning edition, Bourdier know he would catch hell if he couldn't lay his hand on 'em right away. And being so smart, he backed away from my Kay, keeping his hands off her, at least, for the moment.

Between breakups with Kay, all resulting from my jealous and possessive behavior, time and circumstances directs my attention to, and focuses my cameras on the pain and suffering of others, the Black Man.

In late September of 1962, one such black man named James H. Meredith goes to register for college, not just any college, but to the revered University of Mississippi. And a bastion of enlightenment it was too, but limited to the lilly-white.

Despite his color, by being a Mississippi native, and more, by being a veteran of the U.S. Air Force, with the G.I. Bill backing him, his attitude is... Boy! I earned the right. But the general attitude of the white majority confronting him is... Boy! Get real. If you want to get into Ole Miss, fetch a broom, a mop and a bucket. The idea of setting your black ass down between white ones, even for the noble purpose of soaking up a little bit of higher learning, ain't gonna happen. Not down here in Mississippi, where even the thought of such... a sacrilege. And where the general consensus is... any idea for developing a smart nigger, a dumb one.

And today, with Meredith planning to put his attitude into actions, political reporter Bill Peart, a close chum of segregationist Gov. Ross Barnett, approaches me to deliver some "privileged" information. "Jack, you covering the Meredith doings?" "Yep." Then bending and bringing his mouth close to my ear, says, "I got a tip for you." "And what is it?" "Well... as soon as Meredith arrives outside the Woolfolk State Office Building to register, suddenly, all doors will be bolted, and all press, including cameramen, will be barred, with only Meredith and his entourage of government lawyers allowed to enter." "Damn Bill, if I wait outside to photograph the arrival, I'll miss a shot at any confrontation inside." "That's right Jack." "So what do you suggest Bill?" "Forgo the arrival. About noon, when most workers are out to lunch, with your camera concealed, meet me on the 5th floor outside the registrar's office." "Sure thing Bill." "And Jack, one other thing, keep this under your hat, because nobody else in the media knows... and I mean nobody."

Arriving two hours before Meredith is scheduled, hurriedly, avoiding the elevator where I could get recognized, I take the stairs. Fortunately, there wasn't a single member of the media, local or national, to be seen inside or out. While catching my breath and looking for an inconspicuous place to wait, I spot one, next to the water fountain. A small inset where I can just fit, just out of sight of eyes at either end of the long hallway. About 1 p.m., still an hour early, Bill shows and joins me. Another half-hour passes and then, the hall starts filling up with state troopers and curious workers. After employing Bill to find me a chair to stand on, he does and I step up, just six feet from the registrar's office for a vantage allowing me to see over a sea of heads, now packing the hall, wall to wall, like canned sardines but standing. And just like Bill said, not a single media head among them. Except ours. And I could smell a scoop, a big scoop coming. It's 2p.m., and right on schedule, and to my left, Meredith and his lawyers begin pushing their way through the crowd, ever so slowly, until stopping at the door. Finding it locked, Justice Department attorney John Doar reaches up and knocks. And it's time to expose my Leica M-3, the one I bought in Germany, and too late for any trooper to get to me and stop me, not through that throng. And besides, all eyes are on the door and Doar, who continues knocking. And then, the door cracks, opens about 12-inches and through it, the head of Governor Barnett, who has appointed his supremist segregationist self the acting registrar for the day, appears. Looking to Doar, a white man, with Meredith almost glued to his side, Barnett with his deep, gravelly, and serious sounding voice asks, "Which one of you two gentlemen is James Meredith?" With history in the making before my eyes, and with my flashes bouncing off the walls, I advance the film in my little Leica, shooting as fast as I possibly can. With Barnett now chuckling at his little off-colored joke, and with Doar not, Doar replies, "Let's get on with it." No longer grinning, Barnett obliges with, "Mr. Meredith, I do hear-by deny your admission to the University of Mississippi. And I do so politely." With the door slamming shut, the face-off is over, in just seconds, not even a minute, and history is recorded by me. And me alone.

Outside, undoubtedly feeling the chill of the missing of the events inside, the national and the local media await Meredith's departure and among them is a very disappointed Bourdier. And seeing me exiting the building behind Meredith, he knows or at least suspects that I had just scooped his Cajun ass. From little Opelousas, located half-way between New Orleans and the Texas border, he is one of the best news photographers in the country, and that, a known fact, because the Associated Press only hires "The Best". Even I admire his talent, but only his talent for covering the news, and not his talent for covering the ladies. And seeing him again, immediately, I suspect, inspite of my threat, he still desires to cover Kay. My Kay. But he won't today, because today he desires, even needs something more, and he lets me know it. "Hey Jack, did you just whip my ass upstairs?" My reply is a chuckle, a Ross Barnett kind. "Did you get it? Barnett, Meredith, together?" "Yep." "You lucky bastard. My walk-in, walk-out pictures are just shit. Let's go develop your film and see what you got." And then the sweating sets in, his, with my reply, "Gee Jim, I don't know. You know it's long past our deadline and we can't publish until tomorrow. And, if my picture shows up in a competing paper before then, it could mean my ass." "Okay, okay, I'll tell you what. Give me your second best frame and I'll give you an extra fifty bucks." Usually, just getting five dollars for pictures the AP uses, the fifty sounds too good to pass up, so I agree and say, "But you can't tell anyone where you got it, least not for a while." "You got it Jack."

My photograph, with Meredith and Barnett face-to-face, is quickly transmitted to newspapers and television stations around the world. The next morning, the New York Times, the bible of the industry, has it spread four columns above the fold, page one. Next, I see it on the front of the Memphis Commercial Appeal, our big competition in north Mississippi. "Oh shit Makesense, they beat us with our own picture." And then, my sweating begins, while hoping that editor Ward won't notice and ask any questions. Because, the next best frame is almost identical to all the frames. And that's because, it that crush, a body couldn't move, not even an inch. Thankfully, Ward don't notice and don't ask, and, after a day or so, the sweating subsides.

The next day, Meredith takes his "attitude" and lawyers, 150-miles north and to the campus of Ole Miss, near the family home of famous author William Faulkner. This day it would be Paul B. Johnson, Lieutenant Governor, standing in Meredith's way. This day there are lots of press, lots of camera, including Bourdier's, and more state troopers than before. This day, nobody gets scooped, because everybody gets pictures. Or, so I thought. Bourdier's pictures are fine. My pictures are fine. But this day "The Picture" belongs to Flip... Flip Schulke of Life Magazine. His low angle view blows everybody else's away. And Life likes it a double-trucks's—two pages wide—worth in their next edition. "Geesums Makesense, Schulke's picture jumps off the page, at you, don't it?"

In the months ahead, "The Picture" is copied and counterfeited by artists and plastered on billboards across the state. Although unauthorized by Life, the image is used by Johnson in his campaign for governor. With the caption reading, "I stood tall for you. Now stand up for me." And the slogan and "The Picture" are a little more than misleading. In the low-angle side view, it appears that Johnson is alone, all alone, with only his clinched and slightly-raised fist standing between Meredith, his U.S. marshal and enrollment. What isn't seen is the horde of very large and heavily-armored troopers backing his play, or and perhaps, more importantly, is the reaching out and the shaking of Meredith's hand. And who did the reaching and the shaking? None other than the new candidate and the next governor of Mississippi... Paul B. Johnson. "Makesense, never underestimate the power of "The Picture", especially like Flip's. The ones that live on forever, not only on the microfilm of libraries, but also, on the pages of history books. Geesums Makesense, you think we got it in us?" "What cousin?" "A picture like that... like Flip's."

Five days later Meredith achieves his purpose—enrollment at The University of Mississippi—but not before riots and death. Mid-afternoon of September 30, 1962, a task force of U.S. marshals, under the orders of U.S. Attorney General Bobby Kennedy, descends on Ole Miss to capture and surround, the Lyceum—The Administration Building—wearing bright orange vests garnished with gas grenades, white helmets over gas masks and brandishing short-barreled grenade launchers, the force looks more like invading Martians than marshals.

About dusk, I arrive, park Bugeyes, and approach the Lyceum. The campus is in chaos. The grove of giant trees fronting the building is ideal for cover. There the mob gathers. Rebel yells rise and reach me. Now within shooting distance, I raise my Leica, focus and shoot. The two quick flashes expose my position. Four rowdy youths surround me, start shoving me, while trying to tear my camera from my neck, and shouting, "What the fuck are you doing here?" Suddenly a fifth voice is heard, shouting, "Wait! Wait! Stop! I recognize him. He's one of us. With the Jackson Daily." After saving me and my precious Leica from a stomping, and as my attackers back off he appears and advises, "You'd better clear out of here. Cause if you take another picture, I won't be able to help you." Shaken, but still in one piece, and retreating back the way I came, I see a car overturned and burning. "Geesums Makesense, there's another. We'd better get Bugeyes out of here and to safety."

Until now, only verbal abuse—profanity, rebel yells, and heckles—had harassed the federal agents. Now it's dark. Now it's time for bricks and bottles. And now, the bombardment begins. The Feds retaliate with tear gas. The mob retreats, regroups and returns with Molotov cocktails, with acid, with chunks of concrete, and finally, with bullets.

Daylight exposes two bodies. One French reporter Paul Guilhard. The other, bystander Ray Gunter. Wounded is, Associated Press reporter Bill Crider. His back, peppered by shotgun pellets. Property damage including many more overturned and still smoldering cars, is heavy.

From the riot zone, I escape to the Ole Miss Motel where A.P. photo editor Jim Laxon is set up with a portable dark room. Laxon is anxious. New York has been calling and calling and pressing for a first photo. But Bourdier and several other staff photographers haven't dropped off any film yet. Laxon greets me with, "Jack! Give me your film. I got to have it." Without a way to get my pictures back to the Daily News, I strip my camera's film and hand it over to Laxon, who quickly disappears behind a black plastic curtain hanging over the bathroom door. Within twenty minutes my first picture is spinning around a 9x12 inch silver drum and into newspapers around the world. The second follows. Both, just showing the battle-ready marshals, are at best, just mediocre, but good enough to ease the anxiety of Laxon. This night great pictures escape me, and Bourdier and every other photographer present. Because this night, one more pop of a flash gun could cost you. Cost you your life.

Outside the Lyceum, with the smell of tear gas still potent, tired, teary, and thankful marshals rub their eyes, thankful the cavalry has arrived, not only the Mississippi National guardsmen, but members of the U.S. Army.

Inside, James H. Meredith—the Mississippian, the Air Force veteran, the college man, and The Black Man with an Attitude—takes a desk, and becomes the first "boy" to sit amongst the lilly-white at the great University of Mississippi. And now, with the rioting over, he looks at the carnage, confessing, "This is not a happy occasion."

Back in Jackson things are up and down, not only with my relationship with Kay, but with assignments too, and one in particular. With Managing Editor McDavid, removing his pipe, and motioning me over, asks, "Can you fly this afternoon?" "What time?" "Around two." "I got a noon tea party but I'll be free after." "Good, the Air National Guard has a vacant seat on its chopper." "What kind of pictures am I taking?" "Oh, just some new shots of the skyline." "Okay, I'll be at their hangar by two."

The helicopter is a small one, with two seats inside a glass bubble, called an H-13. With the pilot and I strapped in, we lift off and go up about a hundred feet. And then... the whirly-bird starts shaking, rattling, and rolling and then... dropping like a rock. On impact, the rotor rips, the bubble bursts and the camera cracks. With the chopper on its side and with the pilot on top of me, we manage to pull ourselves out. With the exception of a few bloody scratches, we're okay, but with only the paper's inexpensive Yashica beyond mend. After retrieving my Rolei from Bugeyes, and after returning to the crash site to take a photo, the pilot screams, "Oh my God, you're not going to put that picture in the paper, are you?" And we didn't, with McDavid, a man of integrity responding, "Jack, they did us a favor. Now let's do them one." And on leaving the office, looking into the sky, and saying to Makesense, "Today those gawk, gawk, gawking shame birds came close, close to enjoying their splatter, even closer than that day in Germany when the L-19 ran out of gas, still taxing down the runway.

This week, Kay having found a new and more forgiving Father Confessor, our on again, off again, relationship is on again. And this night we're right where I want to be. At my place. Doing what I want to do. Making love to Kay, my Kay. And with my mouth moving from her lips, down to her breasts, down to her waist, and still moving downward, gently she caresses my head stopping its downward motion and then, redirects it upward and back to her breasts. "Kay, oh Kay, don't you want me to... to?" "Yes, oh yes, I do. But let's wait. Let's save something for marriage."

An expert of oral sex, I wasn't, my only experience with it was with Wally. The night she performed it, only to get chastised for doing such a dirty-dirty thing. Perhaps, my motions and motives were selfish. Perhaps, a talent for the unnatural might make her tell her priest, any priest, to go to hell and stop judging what feels so good, good, good, as being so bad, bad, bad. "But you know Makesense, her stopping me probably saved her from something more." "What's that cousin?" "My vomit!"

But the parade of males, married or not, to her desk never stops. And neither do my jealous rages. Until finally she says, she's seen enough of them. And me. And with these words, "Jack! I won't. I can't. Give up my friends. Not for you. Not for anyone." Instead, she gives me up. And then, those Ray Charles lyrics... "Hit the road Jack... and don't come back... no more... no more... no more," start echoing in my head.

It's late, just past 2 a.m., and I am drunk, drunk out of my mind, and hurting, hurting like never before, when I stumble on to my bed, pick up the phone and dial the number. "Kay, you've got to come over. I've got to see you. I just got to." "Jack, I can't. It's too late and there's no point." "But Kay, I need you, I need you so bad." "We're waking up mother, I've got to hang up." "No! No! Wait! Without you Kay, I'm dying here, just dying." "I'm sorry, but I can't help you... goodbye." "Wait! Wait! Don't hang-up! Don't hang-up! Just listen. I'm getting up, I'm going over to the space heater, I'm turning it on, hear the gas escaping, I'm taking deep breaths now, can you hear, and then, with my coughing and my gasping, I hear, "Jack! Jack! Don't don't," just before the phone goes dead.

"Butt-Butt! Makesense is here. Turn off the gas. Open the windows." "What kept you?" "Couldn't get your attention cousin. And when, you're drinking, you know how impossible that is... getting your attention." With the gas off, with fresh winter air flowing in, and with the smell of rotten eggs dissipating, comes a knock at the door. "Jesus! It's Kay. Thank goodness," I'm thinking out loud, "come to save me." Instead of Kay, it's a policeman with a question, "Is everything okay in there... we got a call?" "Yes officer, everything's fine." "It is... it's freezing cold out here, and I notice that the window is open, open wide. Is that gas I smell?" "Probably, but just a little. It was a joke. Just a ploy to force my ex-girlfriend over to shut it off. But she didn't, so I did." "That was some joke, and dangerous." "I know, I know. You know I work with Shoemaker down at the Daily News?" "No, but I do know Shoemaker. He's a straight shooter." "Yes officer, he's the best." "Tell you what Mr. Thornell, if I don't get

90

called back here tonight, I'll forget about it." "You won't officer. You won't. And thank you, thank you very much."

Makesense, maybe just maybe, Kay still cares for me. Tonight, she cared enough to send a cop to save me. At least, she doesn't want me dead."

The next day comes with a second admonition from my landlord. He's upset but not yelling. He never yells. Even after he caught me spying on his naked wife, he didn't yell. Not even while he's following the possible path of the escaping gas, along the floor, up the stairs, under the door and into the kitchen to reach the stove's pilot light. "Hell Jack. You could have blown us all up. The house. The kids. The wife and me, and you too Jack." "I know. I'm sorry. It was stupid. And it won't happen again." And instead of an eviction notice, the power of "The Picture" comes into play again. The ones to come, of his boys, with the possibility of their faces, again gracing page one.

It's mid-December, and the Mississippi Power and Light party for the Daily News staff is in progress at the company lodge just north of Jackson. I'm there. Kay's there. But not together. Not tonight, and not since the policeman came knocking. And since I can't hold her, I hold a beer, then another and another. Just sitting there. Just drowning my sorrows, or trying to. As for anger and jealous rages, forget the trying because both are tireless swimmers, often noticed, then noted, for their amazing ability to grow stronger with each ensuing mouthful.

Drunk, oh yes, but not entirely blind, I can see enough. See how sexy Kay appears. See how she dances with man after man. And see, how permitted they are to press their bodies up against hers and hold them there. If asked, would Kay dance with me like that, permit me to hold her like that, in front of so many friends and colleagues? But, I'll never know. Because I'll never ask. And that's because, about dancing, about picking up the beat and moving my body to it, I haven't a clue. And after viewing any such attempt, Mrs. Bounds, most assuredly would judge, "Young man! A dancer, you're not."

After a quick bathroom run, I return to search the room for Kay. And soon, I find sports editor Baker, the guy who stirred-up more than my dandruff recently, just for standing and talking to her, is at it again. But this time, without a desk between 'em. "Thank goodness," it looks as though he's done talking, because he's turning away, but, "Son-of-a-bitch", he's not walking away. Instead, he's reaching back, taking her hand, and pulling her onto the dance floor, and then, closer and closer to him, until their bodies appear to be glued together. Forcing myself to look away, I find and force a smile on Jim and Nancy Cleveland while wishing that Kay and Baker could dance like them... with space between 'em. Jim, a graduate of Mississippi State, now sits at my old desk beside Bloodsworth. To get him there, they offered him the new title, "Assistant State Editor", while I was merely "The Assistant". He's a good writer and a good friend, both at the office and at home where Kay and I spent many evenings as guests.

With that diversion ended, I look for and find Kay in the far corner of the room and well away from the crowd, and dancing with someone, but I can't tell who. Because his back is to me. And he is not turning. And apparently he must be having trouble picking up the beat because his feet aren't moving. And then, it hits me, Son-of-a-bitch! He ain't dancing, or even interested in dancing, his only interest is having Kay in his arms and keeping her there. And before I can say, "Catman-don't", or give Makesense a chance to butt-in, a greeneyed monster growing inside of me all evening, and now, strengthened by more bourbon and less beer, grips me and takes me across the room and to the back of the, as of yet, unidentified ass, where I grab him, while screaming, "Get your fucking hands off her, you horny bastard," and before spinning him around to face me. And before I can complete son-of-a-, I see who it is. It's my boss... Editor Ward. While looking surprised and shocked, but staying silent, he turns and starts walking away with my whispered words following, "You got your fucking feet moving now, don't you."

Before I can turn around, Jim and Nancy are at my side saying, "Jack. Let's go. You're in no condition to drive. You're coming home with us. About 4 a.m., half-awake and half-asleep, with the reality of my actions weighing on me, I feel Nancy slipping in beside me offering her comfort. Naked, there's enough illumination spilling in from the kitchen light still on, to see just how thin and just how flat she is. Thinner and flatter than she appears by day with her clothes on. And while she's moving her head down past my waist, just like Wally, with these words coming out, "Jim just loves this," I respond, "Nancy, Nancy, you've got to stop. Jim might wake up and walk in. You'd better get back to your bed." And after demanding another minute of passionate kissing, she does, but without completing her Wally.

About an hour later, and still dark out, fate takes over, beginning with the blast of a telephone buzzer. It's Shoemaker with news, "There's been a flash flood over at Brandon. They're beginning to rescue victims with the National Guard's amphibious ducks. Jim, get over there and take Jack with you."

With Jim behind the wheel, there's time for anticipating the big headline of the day. News photographer Jack R. Thornell is fired for cussing out his boss.

With the pictures taken, I'm back in Bugeyes and driving in the direction of the paper, when the question, "Do I really want to go there?" slows me. And then comes, "Butt-butt, Makesense is here. Since you got the pictures, and some good ones, why not go in, get 'em out, and leave them as a going away present. And then you can go on a positive note." Okay, okay, Makesense, I hear."

It's still early, and too early for editor Ward's arrival, so I figure that I can get in, process and print, and get out, before he can find and fire me. But, when I come out of the darkroom to deliver the prints, I can see editor Ward closing his office door behind him. And as I'm considering making a run for it, Bloodsworth looks over and yells, "Jack take line one and take this story from Neshoba County." And as soon as I finish, he saddles me with another, then another, until it's mid-morning and editor Ward, has of yet, to emerge. Finally, it's lunch time, and Jim joins me with "Jack let's eat," and still, not a word out of a belligerent boss has reached my ears then, or when I leave for the day, while still pondering the big question. "Makesense, what about work tomorrow. Shall we show?" "Aren't you working on a color project?" "Yes." "And won't that keep you in the darkroom for most of the day?" "Yes." "And isn't the darkroom a perfect place to hide from the eyes of editor Ward and all those gawkers anxiously awaiting for the ax to fall." "Yes." "So why not show?" "That sounds sensible. Okay then, tomorrow, it's work as usual." And, after passing on the usual afterwork beers, and after pillowing a yet hungover head I couldn't arrest the thoughts of tomorrow and work as usual, because there isn't anything usual about it. Because tomorrow might be "the day" for the ax to fall, for a particular head to roll, and for those most patient shamebirds to finally, have their day... and their splatter.

Kay is leaving me for good, and the City of Jackson, at least temporarily, to take a position with a publishing house in New York City. "Makesense, is it true what they say about all good things coming to an end? What about the bad things, can't they come to an end too?" "Cousin, I can tell you the Good Book's answer... good things come to those who wait. And maybe cousin, it takes the next good thing to end the last bad thing." "Jesus Makesense! A bible scholar... when did you ever pick up a bible?" "Perhaps, you were too drunk to remember, but it was the one in a motel where there was nothing else to read... the one the Gideons left. And cousin, it also says... seek and you shall find the solution to all that ails you. So, if you wait and seek, for a little longer, perhaps you'll find the good." "Well, there's one good thing that strikes me." "What's that cousin?" "Kay's departure, it does take some pressure off." "What pressure?" "All her pressuring to go to Vicksburg, to see my home and to meet my mother... Geesums!" That sickening thought... Mother hugging Kay... sets my stomach to churning and turning out something worse than air and sea sickness combined could. "Hurry Makesense! Pass the hat, and make it a large one... very large."

With Kay gone, and with my testosterone levels soaring, I seek and find other skirts to lift. Some are light. Some are heavy with guilt. "Makesense, what's the worst thing a man can do to a best friend?" With Makesense silent, apparently preferring to hold his peace, I answer. "Yep! Fuck his wife. But what's a man to do, when a woman knocks on a door on a hot and lazy Sunday afternoon and bothers him. Her, with her skinny ass and him, with a fat hard-on. Yep! He lets her in to finish what she started that night on a best friend's sofa. And

undoubtedly, "The Finish" is less than expected. Even with Kay, as with Wally, getting in, getting off and getting gone is my one-two-three. As for cuddling and talking after... Never! Not with "The Cuddling" still an uncomfortable, even vulnerable position to lie in, knowing that "The Talking" could bring on questions of home and family. "Thank goodness that my army buddies rarely mentioned either, with "The Talk" usually directed toward the next opportunity for getting a beer, and then, getting laid. And, as for the act of adultery with a best friend's wife, if be chance, during her moment under me, she experiences an orgasm, it had to be a miracle. It had to be an act of God, and hardly a "qualified" sin to be held against her. Geesums Makesense, it's past 2 a.m. I guess my ramblings kept you up long enough." And finally comes a response, "Goodnight cousin." "Goodnight Makesense."

Today, the day after that knock-knock on my door, I'm having lunch with best friend Jim at the Elite Cafe, one block over and two blocks down from the newspaper office. Their fresh-baked and delicious dinner rolls, all you can eat, draws a hungry body in. And today, as usual, the topic for discussion is the State of affairs... Mississippi's, and that's because Mississippi is now, "The Hot Bed" for the Civil Rights Movement. With sit-ins on college campuses and sit-downs at "for white only" lunchroom counters, a large portion of the media's daily bread. But this day, it's impossible to stay my thoughts on Mississippi affairs, not with an over-friendly face smiling back at me, and certainly not with the state of my own "affairs" eating away at me. It was then and there, without moving my lips, I summoned Makesense to witness a promise... never, never again will I fuck a best friend's wife... for the guilt far outweighs the pleasure.

Weekdays, breakfast is usually cheese toast and coffee, over at Turner's Drug Store directly across from the newspaper. And this day, I see Clarion-Ledger photographer Perry Nations standing and talking to someone at a nearby table. And then, I see why... the great set of legs under it. She's blonde, with welcoming eyes over a lovely face above rather insignificant breasts, but forget that slight deficiency when she gets up, turns and shows a skirt filled with... a most significant... no... make that... terrific ass. "Damn it Makesense... dynamite."

With my eyes staying on her, she walks to the counter, leans over and signs a check for just tea and toast. Odd, I thought... charging such a small order, but neither my eyes or my thoughts, dwelled there for long, not with her walking away and putting into motion... one terrific body.

Over the next two mornings, with first edition pictures printed, I rush across the street, find a table near hers, sit down and wait for opportunity to knock. It doesn't. But on the third attempt, my eyes find hers, and hers, mine. I smile. She smiles back.

"That's a start Makesense. Maybe it's time to make my move?" But Makesense stays silent, as always when asked for advice on women, and, on best ways for bedding 'em, earlier, rather than later.

With a game plan in mind, and while whispering to Makesense, "Today is the day for a guy to get lucky," I rush across to Turner's for a fourth encounter. She's already sitting there with those lovely legs crossed and reaching out, rather than under the table. If it was her move, it worked, cause I couldn't pass her or her lovely legs up. Stopping, I say, "Morning, I'm Jack... Jack Thornell... from across the street." "Oh... hello... are you a newspaper man?" "Yes I am... I'm a photographer for the Jackson Daily." "The afternoon paper." "That's the one... and it comes with a picture of a pretty girl on it... and I wonder if you would consider posing?" "For you," she asked smilingly, "Or for the paper." "Oh, for the paper... for the paper." "Where and when, do you want me?" "How about here... noon tomorrow... and I'll take you up to the rooftop and use the skyline for a backdrop." "Okay then... I meet you here during my lunchbreak... noon tomorrow."

The picture idea, of her holding a divining rod—a forked stick—usually pointed downward to find water in a droughted Mother Earth, will be pointed upward into a cloudless sky. And why, there ain't no "Mother Earth" on top of the Mississippi Power and Light, better known as, "The electric building". And the picture turns out even cornier than the idea. Save for one thing. No. Make that two. Those lovely legs. Crossed and accentuated by a low, most low, camera angle. And where else could that view go, but on the Sunset—better known as the Sunsex—edition, naturally, above the fold, on page one, and with an even cornier caption overline under it... Devine Devining. And naturally, with a half dozen free copies delivered at Turner's the next morning, comes the phone number of the "not dating anyone special now" Carolyn Wilson.   After arranging a first date for dinner and the movies, I find she shares a near downtown half-double with best friend Betty Cunningham, who also comes from West Point, a two-cow town, and designated so, because of the Bryan Brothers, who garnered "Famous Son" status with their rather large meat packing plant there beginning to cut into the market share of their largest rival, Oscar Meyer. Betty is dating Sam Miley, a minor league ball player with hitting power, who at age 30, is still clinging to a dream and a management promise that he is next up to move up to the majors and put-on the pinstripes of the New York Yankees.

After picking Carolyn up, we drive to Dennery's, a very nice and rather expensive steak and seafood house, to begin our evening with food and conversation. "Carolyn, how did you end up in Jackson?" "Let's see... after graduating West Point High, I came here to attend secretarial school. And I liked it so much here, I decided to stay on." "Jackson is nice. I like it too." "But what about you Jack, where did you come from?" With that question, "come from", more than disquieting, I quickly answer, "Vicksburg, but I left at 18, joined the Army, got shipped to Germany where I served with Elvis." And my ploy—going from Vicksburg to Germany in one sentence—worked well, well enough to steer the conversation away from family and on to "The King". "Golly gee! You knew Elvis?" "Well, I took pictures of him for the Army. But, I was stationed in Frankfort, and he was stuck way out in the boonies, so we never got a chance to get close. But he did pose for a personal picture with me though." "Was he nice? Was he as good looking in person? Gee! I'd love to see your pictures." "You will... on our next date." With the "next date" proposal on the table, we finish dinner, skip the movie, go back to her place and recline on her sofa.

After a half-hour of passionate kissing accompanying the thought... Carolyn, just pretend this is Elvis' tongue in your mouth... with our bodies hard together, and with it obvious, I'm moving to have my way, suddenly, she interrupts my play. "Jack! Jack! We've got to stop. The timings wrong. I got my period." "Close but no Havana," I breathed to Makesense, as I am leaving the couch and Carolyn, "But next time I'll get past third base, don't you agree?" And since Makesense won't, I answer, "Yea! Yea! I know... when it comes to women cousin, you're on your own."

Meanwhile, back in my bed, after arresting my passion with "The manipulation" that "Little Jack Lane taught me, I'm thinking of the two things, besides those legs, that I really like about Carolyn. Number one: She's not Catholic, and thank goodness, because corrupting a Methodist has to come easier. Number two: without any college behind her, I can stand tall beside her, taller than I ever could have beside the educated Kay. And if not limited to a "top two", the third would be, her expensive clothes. She dresses, as those who see her say... like a million bucks. And how, I wonder, does she get all those bucks on a beginning secretary's pay? And how do I get all those bucks for dinners, for movies, and all that barroom drinking after? Hustling.

With my civil rights photos—like the just sitting down at the lunchroom counter negro, before becoming the pulled from the stool, the slammed to the floor, the kicked in the head and the never got to order lunch "Nigger"—catching the eyes of those northern editors, there is extra money flowing south. And those same, and mostly liberal editors, looking for more insight into the down in Mississippi situation, might ask... was that negro-pulling, negro-slamming, negro-stomping redneck arrested. No, no, naturally not. And was "That negro" arrested. No, no, naturally not, but "that Nigger" was... because this here boy! Is... down in Mississippi. So, those dating dollars came from pictures like "the kick", though already transmitted everywhere by AP wirephoto, if I expressed an original print to a particular magazine, it would often show with Jack R. Thornell, Jackson Daily News, under it. And more importantly, they expressed back a check for fifty bucks or so.

And with my pictures being printed in Time, Newsweek and U.S. News, my reputation as Jackson's "Action Jack" was growing. "Perhaps Makesense, it should have grown longer." "Longer cousin?" "The news photographer with more guts than brains." "Why cousin?"

"Because more than me, my personal cameras were subject to a stomping. And that $200 German Leica cost double over here."

After three nights of, just talking on the telephone, we begin date two with a night at the movies, followed by drinks at the Press Club Bar. And then, a return to that cozy couch to pick up where we left off on date one. And this time, without a "stop" order coming. And all that a part-time gentleman needs to say, is... get up Fidel and fire-up this Havana, cause this batter just hit one out'ta here. And with a strike to spare. And that Mr. Dictator, is because after three, I'm out'ta here and out'ta here for good, for after a third date without scoring, there's never a fourth. Honey, if you feel you deserve four, better date a football player.

With new girlfriend Carolyn, we socialize regularly with Bette and Sam, cooking out and dining in. Sam is most likable and it is apparent that he really likes Bette, but his real love is... golf. And when, he is not linking up with her, and with baseball season over, he has plenty of time to swing those clubs. And Bette doesn't seem to mind golf being the other mistress, or mind showing a hand with a missing fingertip. Some accident I supposed, but never confirmed with a question. It's clear though, that Bette fits Sam's easy-going, laid-back lifestyle to a tee.

As for me, with each passing day and date, I'm trying to keep any thoughts of Kay away, but still, I couldn't keep from thinking and hoping that perhaps, she took excess baggage with her. Perhaps, she took that green-eyed monster... all the way to New York City. The one with a single mission: To drive a particular ass crazy, then CRAZIER. "Geesums Makesense, I hope she took it, cause that last jealous rage almost got this particular and this crazier jackass fired."

Today is Monday and the morning for putting "hope" to the test. Carolyn, having finished her coffee, is leaving me at the table when girl-friendly photographer Perry Nations of The Clarion-Ledger shows, sits down, starts smiling and says, "I see you're dating Carolyn." "Yea, we've been out a few times." "Is it true what they say." "And what do they say Perry?" "How easy she is." "And where did you hear that horseshit?" "From the horse's mouth... a friend... a married one... who went with her for a while." With that news startling, and then, upsetting, it's clear... that green-eyed monster ain't gone nowhere. It's still here. Still inside of me and now, it's raising its ugly head and trying to explode but somehow, for the moment, I manage to muster enough pride to prevent an outburst. And before he can put that "easy question" to me again, I look at my watch, say, "Jesus! I got to go, I'll be late for my next assignment." And while I'm rushing out the door, Perry's "How easy?" "How easy?" "How easy?" keeps hitting me, again and again and again. "Christ Makesense, I know, I know, I know. For me, "how easy" was date two. And but for her period, probably date one. Oh Makesense! How many Tom, Dick, and Harrys have come before me? "But Makesense don't answer. "Okay! Okay." Makesense stay tuned out, but I'll be facing Carolyn tonight and I gotta have a game plan. What to do? What to do? Well... rushing in and raising hell won't do, not with Bette and Sam sitting there... what to do?... How and when do I hit her with Perry's, "How easy" news? I got it. I got to control it. Control my rage like with Perry at Turner's, and wait. And wait until everybody is in bed. And wait until, I've taken her "how easy" just once more. Just in case I dump her or she dumps and leaves me without the pleasure for days, for weeks or even, for months.

And now, with the aroma of our love making still filling my nostrils, but now, turning sour, and me with it, I hit her with, "Carolyn! You ever mess around with a married man?"

"Jack! Where did you hear that?" "From a friend... a friend of your married man." "Oh Jack! I did, but not for long." "How could you do that. Fuck around with a married man?" "Oh! I was so lonely and he was so nice to me." "And where the fuck is he now?" "He's gone." "And what about the others, how many have there been?" "Only Mike! Only Mike! And no more." "And who the fuck is Mike?" "He's a musician and a singer." "And where is that S.O.B. now?" "I don't know. He travels, and I haven't heard from him for a while." "And when you do, what then?" "If he calls, I'll remind him... it's over... we're over... and tell him, I'm seeing you." As I'm getting up, she reaches up, takes my arm and begins pulling me back towards her, while saying, "Jack don't go. Please don't go. I love you. I love you." And suddenly without explanation, that green-eyed monster relaxes its grip and allows me to fall back beside her. Apparently with neither of us quite ready to let go and end our relationship. The pain or the pleasure.

With the room dark and now quiet, ole green eyes isn't quite ready to pull up the covers just yet, and instead, starts with its own third degree... isn't it odd that Carolyn didn't press for the name of the tattletale friend... wouldn't she be dying to know, dying to confront him, and then, to slap his nosey face... but, she didn't even ask, did she... perhaps, because she didn't need to... because she already knows..., and perhaps the tattletale friend and THE MARRIED MAN are one and the same. "Son-of-a-bitch! Was that girl-friendly bastard, seen hovering over Carolyn the first day I saw her, just telling her half-truths and half-lies to get me out of the picture... his fucking picture? Jesus green eyes! Won't you ever let up, and let me put such thoughts to bed and let me get some rest?" And as I lay here, with my eyes opened wide and being deprived of my rest, a certain black man is being deprived of more, much more, by having his eyes shut for him and shut for good.

It's just past midnight, with the sweet-scent of honeysuckle filling the night air, when a sleepy-eyed Medgar Evers pulls up in his powder-blue 1962 Oldsmobile. It's a nice car, and "too nice for a nigger", some white folks say, "especially for a nigger working day and night at trying to be white by shoving civil rights down the throats of too many Mississippi mouths." Other white folks say, "Just shoot the black bastard and put him in his rightful place... out there at that nigger cemetery." It has been a long day, and Medgar is tired, too tired to notice even a hint of honeysuckle as he steps out of the car and onto his driveway. Inside, hearing the car pull in, faithful wife Merlie gets up and turns the carport light on for her beloved husband, the father of her three lovely children and the field secretary for the National Association for the Advancement of Colored People and usually, just called the N.A.A.C.P. To Medgar, there ain't no niggers down in Mississippi, just colored citizens with the same rights as white citizens get, like... living in a nice neighborhood, sending their kids to a nice school, and then, after working hard all week, be able to sit down with family or friends at a restaurant to their liking, and see food put on the table, rather than being yanked out of a chair, getting kicked in the head, and then, getting led off to jail, still hungry.

After reaching into the back seat and picking up a bundle of N.A.A.C.P. t-shirts, Evers straightens up, turns toward the house, and now, shows his back to Guynes Street. And for a second there, before he can put his tired legs into motion, he is perfectly still. And from in the honeysuckle vine under the sweet gum, it's a sweet-sweet sight. Especially to a nigger hater with a telescopic sight. And especially, with a target now perfectly silhouetted by a carport light. "Thank you Merlie. Awe, but from out here, in the dark, without ears to hear, just this once, let me address you as Mrs. Evers. Oh Honey, it's such a sweet-sweet shot, make that Lady Evers instead."

And then, without warning, the rifle explodes, discharging its load to dismiss the quiet with the disturbing crack of gunfire. Hitting its mark, the bullet tears into Evers back, rips through his body, and exits from his chest, before shattering window glass to find lodging in a kitchen wall inside the house.

Still standing, but staggering with his blood spilling and pooling at his feet, desperately, Evers slips and slides towards the kitchen door, marking his progress in blood on the concrete floor. Falling just short, he is met by Merlie, with the children running close on her heels and screaming, "Daddy! Daddy! Get up." But the husband, the World War II combat veteran, the civil rights leader, and the daddy, doesn't get up... ever.

Mr. Medgar Evers, at age 37, is pronounced dead at 1:14 a.m. on June 12, 1963. And now, only a statistic of shame, Mississippi's... for breeding, "Nigger Haters" and one in particular, with an old car, a vintage 1917 Enfield rifle, and enough hate for using it.

The telephone rings, Carolyn picks it up, passes it over to me, and Shoemaker in a low voice, almost a whisper, begins, "I thought I might find you there. There's been a shooting." "Who?" "Medgar Evers." "Holy shit! How bad is he hurt?" "He ain't. He's dead." "Jesus! I just shot a picture of him... just last week... with Lena Horne." "Better get over to his house... he was shot there... in his driveway... You know where it is." "Yea, been there a coupla times... the body, is it still there?" "No, no, it's already at the hospital... awaiting autopsy."

Driving there, I take it slow, giving the daylight more time to arrive, but my worry, my big worry, is already here... exposure. Dawn and dusk are bitches and the toughest time to figure the correct shutter speed and aperture settings. And without a light meter, I'm sweating exposure. And more than ever, because this baby is a big, big story. Usually, if I'm not sure, I fire off a flash, but flash will only light the foreground, and the light-starved background goes dark, even black. No! No! No flash, that'll ruin the picture. "Makesense, I got to get it right. Screwing up, isn't an option."

Arriving at the house, and after bringing Bugeyes to a stop, I see Evers' white Olds, and further up and under the carport, a black one. That must be Merlie's. But what I don't see is any sign of a police car. "Shit Makesense, we'd better sit tight... and wait. Being the first white face out and about could be dangerous. Dangerous hell, it could be deadly. With the possibility of photographer Jack R. Thornell making history, as the first white man ever lynched by black men... down in Mississippi. And they could add a little irony, even a chuckle too, by taking this white ass a coupla blocks over and set it swinging there... on Lynch Street. Then, a car pulls up and parks at the entrance to the driveway. Emerging are two plain clothed detectives with their badges showing. While they're walking over to Ever's car, I step, look down, and begin setting the Leica hanging from my neck. A 60th of a second, wide open at 2.8 seems right. One of the detectives is now standing next to Ever's car with both arms stretching out and lining up the trajectory from the bullet hole in the window... to Ever's car door... and the sweet gum across Guynes Street.

CLICK! CLICK! CLICK! Goes my Leica, before they can react and possibly back me up and away, and then, seal off the crime scene. But, they do neither. They seem oblivious to my presence, perhaps, one more white face lowers their odds of making history. So emboldened, I move closer to the house and up to the window where I focus on the bullet hole. CLICK! CLICK! CLICK! Hugging the house, I slip closer to the driveway and between the two cars, Medgar and Merlie's, parked about three car lengths apart. With the detectives directing their attention away and across the street, I move down the driveway while looking down and trying to avoid stepping on any evidence. And then, I see it, "Geesums", the evidence. A trail of dark dark blood looking more black than red. Carefully staying wide to the left, I follow the trail marking Evers desperate attempt to reach Merlie's arms before he could fall dead. CLICK! CLICK! CLICK! And the thick and gooey trail goes on and on, until stopping just short of the steps leading up to the kitchen door. "Oh Makesense, what a sickening sickening sight this is. A man's life, poured out... and soon to become nothing more than a fading stain on a concrete floor." And after turning back towards the street, I see one of the detectives is pointing back at me, motioning me over to his side, and says, "Better back off to the curb, you might contaminate the crime scene." But what he didn't know was... the crime scene had contaminated me.

A "negro lover", I wasn't, and I wasn't a "nigger hater" either, despite all of Uncle John's attempts—like the day I innocently called a black woman "a lady"--to jerk me into the "hater" category. Neutral was my position, until today. With seeing what I saw today—the ugliness of cold blooded murder at its finest. And with that picture playing in my head, I could feel the momentum shifting and driving me further and further away from the "hater" category.

Heading to the street as directed, I look at my watch, "Geesums Makesense, it's only 45-minutes to first edition deadline." But before I jump into Bugeyes, I count the pictures... the detective pointing... The closeup of the bullet hole... the blood trail. And it's the blood trail photo that bothers me. Because I hate "still life" photos, and so does the paper. Whenever possible I add the human element to give the picture scale and life. "Makesense, should I go back and try to position a detective by it? Before an answer comes, I'm already turning and moving into the yard when I hear, "Back off the curb... like I ordered." Perhaps, it's just as well, I thought, because I could have posed a hundred praying detectives, with their heads bowed low, without adding even a spark of humanity to that sickening "still life" photo.

After getting into Bugeyes, but before I go, I take one last look back at the bullet hole in the house where Mr. Medgar Evers had lived and I knew that... he left behind more than bits of broken glass on a kitchen floor... he left behind shattered lives... a widow's... and three children... now without "Daddy". "Makesense, this is shame, at its finest hour... down in Mississippi."

Back at the office, newsmen from the Associated Press and United Press, are standing at my desk, begging for first photos. "Just cool it," I advised, "First, I got to get prints out for our deadline, and then, you'll get yours."

With the ten minutes of processing—eight in the developer and two in the fixer—ending, my worry-worry—about that exposure and about that guess work—isn't done until the wet film is unrolled and I begin seeing images on it, and until, I erupt with, "Good guess... no... no... make that great guess Makesense... the negatives are perfectly exposed and will be easy to print."

The Daily News is printing the pointing detective on page one, but the blood trail photo is condemned as too much, and too likely to further stain a state's already tarnished image. And naturally, editor Ward would never play a part in that, not while he's still breathing air, not down in Mississippi.

After making prints for both wire services—AP and UPI—the real hustling begins. With four 11x14 prints--the three from today's shooting and a fourth of Evers escorting singer Lena Horne to a recent event--I rush them to the express mail office. The destination... Life Magazine... where it's every photographer's dream to be published. And that honor has eluded me during my three-year career here in Jackson. So, purely on speculation, I ship, cross my fingers and wait for next week's edition to hit the newsstand. Tuesday, when it does, anxiously, I flip through it... until I see it... "Geesums Makesense! Two full pages. The Horne-Evers picture... a full page on the right and on the left splashes that nasty blood trail in a deep vertical to share the page with the pointing detective and the bullet hole. Makesense! We made it... we made Life Magazine, but wait a minute there's no photo credit on these pages... Shit! They could have picked these up off the AP wire for nothing extra, and not even got my 11x14's... Geesums... which is it?" Frantically, I turn to the front of the magazine where photo credits are listed in tiny-tiny print. And there, Jack R. Thornell, Jackson Daily News, jumps out at me. "Wow Makesense! We really hit The Biggie. And, correct me if I'm wrong... aren't space rates $200-a page... and two pages makes $400... that's over a month's pay." And the next day, I get a call from former army specialist Zimmerman, the one who got busted in Germany for trying to peddle my Presley pictures. "Jack, congratulations, I just saw your great pictures in Life Magazine. I had already seen your name in the other news magazines... and now, in Life. Keep up the bloody good work buddy... and perhaps, I drop in on you some day." "Thanks Zimmerman, take care... and watch your Yankee mouth if you do visit the South. Cause there's a plenty of good ole boys more than ready to fit a southern fist into a Yankee mouth naturally, down here in good ole Mississippi.

"Jesus Makesense, for me... there's accolades and a big payday and for Evers... there's martyrdom and a grave marker at Arlington. And I suppose cousin, that's life and that's death in a nutshell." "You said it cousin, and you proofed and proved it." "Proofed and proved, I don't follow." "That cousin... life goes on, grass grows and needs attention. And you'll need that four hundred, because Bugeyes is dying too." "Oh Makesense! Don't remind me."

And Makesense was right on the money, and on Bugeyes too. For the past several months I had been overly generous with that thick and hard to pour engine treatment product, but by adding it, enough compression would build up to keep a sick engine running for a little while longer. But, I knew that any day now, the little engine would freeze up and Bugeyes would die. And so, two weeks later I parted company with Bugeyes and Life's most generous check. And as I drove away from the used car lot in my dark maroon Corvair Monza, I kept my eyes off the rear view mirror. I couldn't look back at Bugeyes, the way I looked back at Wally that afternoon in Germany, but I couldn't stop my mind from saying, "Goodbye dear Bugeyes, I really loved you."

Behind the body of Evers, the civil rights movement unifies, gains strength and picks up momentum. At a rally, the night after the slaying of her husband, Merlie Evers, drawn but composed, stands up and says, "Last Sunday Medgar talked of death and announced ... he was ready to go. He's gone now... and nothing can bring Medgar back... but the cause can live on."

And live on it did, spilling into the streets with marches and picketing and with indoor sit-ins often ending with demonstrations of police brutality.

And the living with it, and the covering of "The Movement" isn't easy, because, when the "Hey Nigger you can't sit there... Hey Nigger you can't eat here" sounds. I have got to be there with my cameras ready and waiting for another opportunity to make Life Magazine again.

So dastardly was that back shooting act, even some white leaders condemned it, even Governor Barnett did so. Jackson's Mayor Allen Thompson rushed back from vacation in Destin, Florida to call a press conference to declare he was "dreadfully shocked, humiliated, and sick at heart." He also posted a reward of $5,000 for information leading to the arrest and conviction of the cowards that done it. Even the Clarion-Ledger and Ward's Jackson Daily added $1,000 more.

A few days later, Byron De La Beckwith, a Greenwood fertilizer salesman, was picked up in California by the FBI. Seems he left more than a vintage rifle back in the honeysuckle thicket 150-feet across from the Evers house, he left his finger prints on it. And since he was arrested in California, it wasn't too much of a stretch for the Clarion-Ledger headline to read, "California man arrested in Ever's murder." Had he been caught sleeping in New York City, the headline could have read... New York Yankee arrested... and editor Ward could have had one terrific chuckle over it.

Since murder isn't a crime that can be prosecuted at the federal level, the FBI reluctantly handed Beckwith over to Mississippi authorities. And on July 2, 1963, he was indicted for murder in record time, just 21 days after the shooting. And that's where I get in and get the picture.

"Jack," Shoemaker says, "I just heard they're taking Beckwith over to the nuthouse at Whitfield to get his head examined." "When W.C.?" "In about an hour." "Thanks, I'd better get my ass in gear."

Driving there, "Nuthouse at Whitfield" rings a bell. "Hell Makesense, that's the place they took Crazy Uncle John to have his head looked into. And he passed the examination and was released. And there are only two possibilities for that outcome." "And what are they cousin?" "Well, either he forgot his scissors under the pillow, or the doctors didn't want such a crazy bastard lurking in their hallways at night."

After arriving and parking outside the administration building, I find that once again, I'm the only newsperson present. Ten minutes later, two detectives pull up, get out and escort Beckwith inside. CLICK, CLICK, CLICKING, I follow. They enter the building. I follow. They stop, ask for directions at the desk, and continue on down the hallway. I follow. Soon they turn right and into a small office and sit their charge down. I follow. And then, kneeling at his feet, I CLICK, CLICK, CLICK away, until two rolls of 36-exposure tri-X film is exhausted. And then, at my back I feel a tap on my shoulder and I turn to hear the man in the white coat ask, "Who are you?" "Oh, Doctor, I'm Thornell, Jack Thornell of the Jackson Daily." "Jesus Christ," he said while taking his eyes off me and putting 'em on the detectives, "You're not supposed to be in here. Pictures of patients are strictly forbidden." "Gees Doctor, I didn't know. I'll get out of here." And got out of there I did, before someone could think of a way to remedy my violation... like... the confiscation of two rolls of freshly exposed tri-X film. And back at the office, after dropping my prints off on the desk of front page editor Grady Crenshaw, he looks down at my pictures and then, looks up at me and asks, "How the hell did you get these. We only expected the usual walk-in, walk-out photos." "And Grady, that's just what you got. I just walked right in... I just knelt right down... and baby... I just walked right out... better change that to... ran right out." Now, grinning broadly, he offers, "And Baby, you just walked right in on page one, three columns above the fold."

After two trials and two hung juries, despite the finger print evidence, and despite the eye-witness testimony placing Beckwith near the scene at the shooting hour, on March 10, 1965, the indictment against Beckwith was nol prossed... abandoned.

Carolyn and I are moving along with our relationship, but not without an occasional eruption of ole green eyes coming between us. And this weekend, she's taking me to meet the parents. And though I accept the invitation, it comes with reservations, about what might come next... her pressing me to take her down to 503 to meet the family living there.

The Wilson house is out in the country, but only a short drive from downtown West Point. It's large, old and nothing fancy, but it has paint on it, and in my eyes, paint makes it a mansion. Her father Clifton grinds away days and some nights at a nasty and smelly rending facility to feed his wife Eloise and their three sons, Carter, Stephen and Richard. Mrs. Wilson, overweight with swollen ankles, proves herself as a cook by serving up fried chicken, creamed potatoes, gravy and great homemade biscuits. Ironically, it was the same dream dinner that I longed to enjoy and share with a guest anywhere but down at 503.

That afternoon, the family puts on a Sunday best and I lead them outside to pose in the shade of a cottonwood. The lighting there, without the harsh shadows the sun produces, is beautiful, and, so beautiful, I shoot a whole roll on my Rolei. And, after seeing the prints, Carolyn would come to treasure them, because Mr. Wilson, still in his forties, would suffer a massive heart attack and die. And from that day on, a social security check is the only means of support for Widow Wilson and her three growing boys.

Summers down in Mississippi with the heat and the humidity, are at times, murdering. And the summer of 1964 is like that. But for three young idealists it will take more than the heat and the humidity to slow them down. From New York State Michael Schwerner and Andrew Goodman, ages 24 and 20, come to reason out the why of things and to witness the way of things down in Mississippi. Sure, they've read things, and sure, they've seen things, but only in newspapers and on television screens. And as someone said... it takes the seeing for the believing... the up close and personal kind.

And today, June 21, 1964, and in the company of James Chaney, age 21, and the only black of the three, are seeing the still smoking kindling of the what used to be the Mount Zion United Methodist Church, allegedly set ablaze in the dead of the night, compliments of the KKK. "God! Why would the Ku Klux Klan burn down The House of God, when they too, bend their knees to pray at gathering places?", an inquiring New York man might ask. And with his praying done, a knee-jerking klan man might reason, "Them niggers go there to multiply, to unify, and to run out hell-bent on disrupting white people's lives and destroying all their great down in Mississippi traditions. With that Mr. New York man, comes the why: Burn all them nigger churches down and with no place to congregate, they'll grow weak and weaker until that civil rights movement dries up and dies. And, Mr. New York man, if that won't stop it, then perhaps, we'll have to waste a shotgun shell or two, or even three. And if them shotgun shells get too costly, we can line up them blackboys up, back to belly, back to belly, and back to belly, like the Germans did them Jew-Boys. And like them, save two shells. To execute this efficiency though, a body needs a high-powered rifle... like the one that shot clear through that high falutin nigger, Medgar Evers."

After surveying the ashes of Mount Zion, and seeing the way of things down in Mississippi, the three young men, who have dedicated their summer to the civil rights movement, get back into their 1963 dirty-white station wagon, a Ford Fairlane. Chaney wisely chose the backseat, while Schwerner and Goodman take the front. And Chaney's choice is wise because a Mississippi nigger sitting in the front seat next to a white man with another white man relegated to the back seat, could raise some eyebrows and even draw attention of the lawmen. And especially, Neshoba County Lawmen, who, if not all, fall into that "Nigger Hater" category. And especially, if a body wants to keep a-wearing that badge and a-toting that gun for High Sheriff Lawrence Rainey.

And one such body belongs to Deputy Sheriff Cecil "Chubby Cheeks" Price, who moonlights as an undercover agent for the KKK. And everybody, who knows Price, knows... whether on duty for the County by day or for the KKK by night, when confronted with life or death choices—whether to tear up a few agitating asses or to waste a shotgun shell or two—his loyalty lies with Imperial KKK Wizard Sam Bowers and not just with Sheriff Rainey. Almost immediately, the three civil rights workers are pulled over, allegedly, for speeding. And the reasoning authored by the KKK, for what was to follow is explained by the loyal deputy, something like this... Darlin' it don't matter none whose driving... all three of yah are outside agitators, ain't yah... all three of yah, are inside a speeding car, ain't yah... so all three of y'all are under arrest... for speeding, naturally.

After being locked up and held in the county jail at Philadelphia—a timber town with a population of 7000—until late that night and until, the "what was to follow" had been finalized by the Klan, are the three hungry and exhausted civil rights workers set free. As soon as they get back on the highway, a gang of Klansmen led by loyal deputy Price, give chase, catch up and finally stop them after they turned off the highway and onto a back road. There, in the blackness, they snatch them up, and after beating Chaney half to death, they take them to where an unmarked trail meets up with Rock Cut Road. And the choice... whether to kick or kill their agitating asses—comes alive. James Jordan, according to his own informing self, shoots the badly bleeding Chaney in the back and abdomen. Alton Wayne Roberts shoots Schwerner and Goodman, before turning back to finish off Chaney with a shot to the head. And then, the bodies, the dirty-white station wagon, and the pack of heartless killers are swallowed up by the darkness still lingering... still refusing to yield to the light... for the birth of a new day.

In the ensuing days ahead, headlines around the nation, keep reading... three civil rights workers still missing... down in Mississippi. The Philadelphia lawmen, the last to see them alive, reply to all the commotion stirring at their door as... Awe, them boys just took off for Chicago or somewhere, after we turned them out of jail all healthy and fed. They're probably reading and laughing, while making fools out'a y'all news and FBI men. Soon, they'll show and y'all can take them nosey asses back on out'a here. But, the FBI isn't laughing and swarms of G-men begin arriving and bringing with them hundreds of Navy Seabees to search the Klan country high and low, before putting on hip-huggers to wade through miles of waist deep swamp water in hopes of stepping on some clue. FBI man Joe Sullivan, one of J. Edgar Hoover's top executives and a friend to the news media, flies in to head the investigation with assistance from Roy Moore of the Jackson office. And following close behind are hordes of press people—newspaper, radio, and TV—with their cameras, microphones and notepads standing ready to cover the first break in the story. And it comes to the newsroom from a friendly voice, "We've found the car... in the woods near Philadelphia... it's been set afire."

Within minutes I'm in my unnamed Monza, and unnamed to avoid the pain of personal attachment, driving west towards Meridian before turning north on Highway 15. "Should take about an hour and a half Makesense... but how do we find the car... they've probably moved it by now." "Get lucky cousin, like usual." "So, we're riding on luck again." "Seems so cousin, seems so."

After passing the Welcome to Philadelphia sign, my eyes move ahead to the vehicle being towed just ahead, and... "Son-of-a bitch!" That's the dirty-white station wagon... see it all charred." But before I can say, "Lady Luck" the wrecker turns into a lot and immediately starts backing up, as I'm stopping, reaching for a camera and leaping from the car with only time to fire off one frame on my Rolei before the garage door lowers to shut away the car. "Makesense I'm learning the hard way. This camera operates too slow for fast moving targets. I got'a open the top, look down into the viewing glass, focus, trip the shutter and then, crank a handle 360 degrees to advance the film and cock the shutter for a second shot. Had my Leica been handier I could'a got off at least three frames. And that's got'a cost me money. Hustling money."

After arriving back at my darkroom, I find Bourdier already there and printing something. "Hey Jim, what you got?" And before he can answer, I'm looking over his shoulder and down at the image being projected, and it's an aerial view of the station wagon being towed with the country showing on both sides of the road. "Damn! That's a nice picture... and a lot better than mine... you got atmosphere and all I got is a closeup." "Thanks, can you wash and dry this print, while I go write a caption?" "Sure." But as I did, one thing comes to mind, "I hate getting beat...by anyone... even a good friend."

Still moody over getting topped I'm wide awake, but when the phone rings after 1 a.m., I close my eyes and pretend to be sleeping, when Carolyn picks up the phone, steps out of the bedroom into the hallway, and closes the door between us. I wait, counting the seconds. I wait, counting the minutes. And I wait until ole green eyes raises me up, out of bed and into the hallway to face Carolyn. "Who the hell you talking to at this hour?" With her hand over the mouthpiece, she turns her back and puts distance between us. But I follow, "Mother Fucker! It's musician Mike, ain't it?" Still shielding the phone, she doesn't respond. And by then, ole green eyes has assured me that indeed, it is none other than her former fucking boyfriend... Mike. After rushing back into the bedroom and jerking my pants on, I rush past her carrying my shirt and shoes, shouting, "Fuck you! Fuck marvelous Mike... cause Baby, I'm gone."

The next day, not wanting to see those lovely legs parked over at Turner's, I forgo the cheese toast and chocolate milk, but that night Carolyn calls, "Jack, are you alright? I'm sorry you got so upset last night... about Mike." "Son-of-a-bitch! I knew it... knew it was him." "When's he coming to see you?" "He's not. I told him he couldn't... because I'm seeing you now." "It took you a long fucking time just to say goodbye." "I know... I know... and I'm sorry... please forgive me." "Okay, okay, I'll let it go... this time... but the next time I catch you talking to marvelous Mike... I'll be gone for good."

After pillowing my head, my brain won't rest, so I try to engage Makesense with. "Have you got your ears up?" And since you won't give advice on my women matters, just listen." And as usual, Makesense don't answer, so I proceed. "If a man's easy, it's expected. It's just a guy thing. And it rates slaps on the back from other grinning guys. "But if a woman's easy with anybody but you, either before you or after you, she's nothing more than a low-down wallowing whore?" Again, silence is the reply. "Okay then, let me ask a personal question. When you gonna get mad, really mad, mad enough to violate that no cussing rule... and just let her rip?" And finally, comes a response. "No need cousin, cause there's enough foul coming out of your mouth to feed an army... a Chinese army... a million man army." Chuckling, all I can say is, "Goodnight Makesense." "Goodnight cousin."

After 43 days with the FBI staying busy by trying to infiltrate the KKK, and by offering bribe money for information leading to the bodies... payday comes on day 44. And the word is... it comes from a Judas goat choking on precise intelligence, but still money hungry enough to swallow his pride for 30 thousand pieces of silver... dollars.

After seven hours of digging in an earthen dam 540 feet long, 11 feet wide at the top and 83 feet thick at the base, located on the Old Jolly Farm owned by Olen Burrage, the FBI men are not only sweating from the extreme heat, but also over the possibility they'd been had, even worse, been ripped off with bad intelligence. And then, the big scoop stops and the crane operator hollers, "Hey! I think I hit paydirt." With the shout, the agents come running, then dropping to their knees, begin digging with their hands until... finding a hand... an arm... and then, the rest of a body. And with that stifling stench, comes up the lunches of several tough G-men.

Three fold on day forty four, Mississippi's shamehole is exposed. Uncovered are the decaying bodies of three young men senselessly slaughtered, with their bodies dropped into a 15 foot hole and packed down under heavy red clay to rot and rot and rot. While, shameless men, heartless men, and KKK men, just stood around telling jokes and laughing, and not ever breaking a sweat, while a bulldozer does the dirty work of covering up a shame so hideous, it'll live on in history books from here to eternity.

According to our FBI source, the area is sealed off so tight and the area so remote, the press won't be able to get within miles of the murder site. Before daylight on day 45, pulling a Bourdier, I'm taking off from the Jackson airport. "Makesense, it's going to be another one of those bitches... first light—only this time, the guessing will be done at 500 feet. And there's another hitch, I can't shoot at a slow shutter speed from a fast moving airplane. I'll need at least a 250th. Oh Makesense! Deliver us from light accompanying dusk and dawn."

The pilot takes his eyes from the ground and turns to me. "Doesn't that look like it... that red clay mound, while directing my eyes down to the ground streaking by faster and faster as we get lower and lower. "That sure looks like it... there's a huge crane... a lot of men... and this early... way out here... the FBI would be the only people stirring." Now, down to just 200-feet, the pilot jerks back on the controls in a maneuver reminiscent of Lt. J.J. Kidder, throwing our momentum from down to up and suddenly, I recognize something of more necessity than film exposure... "Oh shit Makesense! I forgot my hat."

After circling the dam site several times, the pilot points to all the other airplanes and helicopters beginning to fill the sky around us, he says, "That's it... it's too dang dangerous to make another pass." Once back at the office, I find Bourdier sitting at my desk and waiting to have a look at my film. The exposure was a good guess. But the dawn light was so flat, the negative had to be printed on contrastry number four paper. But on page one, the picture looked great.

The next night, Carolyn and I are at the picture show on Capitol Street, when over the soundtrack blasts, "Mr. Jack Thornell... CALL your office... it's an emergency." At night, "office" usually meant police reporter Shoemaker. "Hey W.C.... you looking for me?" "Yea... yea... they're bringing the bodies here... to University Hospital for autopsies... better hurry because they're on the way." "Thanks, I'm on my way." Carolyn's apartment is only half a block off my North State route, so I drop her off. "I'll come by later, if it's not too, too late," I tell Carolyn as I wait until she's safely inside due to a series of rapes still occurring at regular intervals. When I get to the hospital, I find the parking lot already crowded with media people, mostly reporters and a few photographers, but not Bourdier, because he headed back to New Orleans earlier in the day. A few minutes later I'm joined by Daily News reporter Perkins. "Hi John." "Hi Jack." "Will you do me a favor?" "What you need?" "For you to hold my slave unit." "I don't know... I need to be free to move." "I need you to move... with the action... just stay off to the side and point it... my flash will trigger the electronic eye." "Okay, I'll give it a try." "Great, I'll buy you a beer... make that two beers... after we get out'a here." The newside guys know I hustle, so they take the position that it's my duty to set a beer in front of them every now and then. And while we wait, I can't keep from grinning when I think of Bourdier. When he hears this news, he'll have to rush his Cajun ass right back up to Jackson. And having John holding a second flash unit is a luxury seldom tried on fast moving events.

"Hey John, get ready, here they come," I shouted as a convoy of police cars escorting three black hearses pull up, stop, and start unloading some fifty feet away from us. "Stand off to the right of the back door and hold that slave high," I shouted to John from the stampede of press people running to get closer. One after another the three black body bags are removed and rushed inside. Two are being carried by state troopers, but one is being handled by a deputy wearing a Neshoba County patch on his shoulder, so I focus on him. "Can I get your name." I shouted, while moving with him. Grinningly, he ignores my question, as I keep blinding him with exploding flashes until he disappears inside. "Damn John, that didn't take long. Look, I'm going in to process, and then I'll catch up with you at the press club in about an hour." "Okay, I'll just run a tab until you get there. Cause you're buying." "Yea, yea, I'm buying... just don't play chug-a-mug on me... take your time and enjoy every golden swallow." Both laughing, we part company.

An hour later, I join John, who introduces me to the two broadcasters sitting with him. One is Peter Jennings and the other, Tom Jariel, both I recognized from ABC's Nightly News. Perkins says, "This is Jack Thornell." Jennings replies, "The photographer". "Yea, for the Daily News." "I've seen your photo credit in some of the news magazines." "Yea, some of them," later, I thought, "Some hell, Mr. Jennings... all of 'em, including Life." But a self-esteem born down at 503, doesn't permit such self-adoration, not with a fear of failure and a return to poverty always knocking at my door. Later, I got to like Jennings more, when I discovered, that he too was a high school dropout, but with a doctor-father to boost his ego and to raise his feeling of self-worth. And it showed, whether in front of the camera or behind it. Soon, the bartender turns the conversation to the other talk of the town... the serial rapist. "Jack, your pretty girlfriend, has she got any protection?" "You mean like a gun?" "Yea, I got a sweet little two-shot derringer. It's perfect for her purse. I'll let you have it for ten dollars." "I'll take it, but keep it behind the bar until I leave, because the way John is chug-a-mugging, it might be too dangerous for him if you put a loaded gun in my hand." Laughing, with beer spilling freely from his mouth, John interrupts the conversation with, "Bartender, bring me another." "Jesus John! My hustling money will be long gone before it arrives."

At 6:30 a.m., I find a familiar body occupying my chair. It's Bourdier. "I need to look at your film." "Come on into the darkroom... it's processed but not printed yet." Quickly sliding his eyeball—magnifier—across the film, he stops, looks up into my eyes and says, "You have any idea what you got?" "You mean the unidentified deputy." "Unidentified hell, that's Deputy Sheriff Cecil Price, one of the suspects." "Are you sure?" "Sure, I'm sure, I saw him a coupla times at the jail." "Man, oh man." "And this has great lighting, how'd you manage that? "Just the work of a slave... a well-paid slave." The picture of a grinning "Chubby Cheeks" Price, facing the camera and carrying one of the young victims finds page one on hundreds of newspapers around the world.

"Makesense, how could he be smiling so broadly on the outside, while deep inside, his big gut has to be spilling over with worry, because if the FBI knew precisely where to dig for the bodies, what else might they know...?"

After turning back the covers and getting to bed, my own worries begin emerging... How long can newspapers reign as the kings of journalism? Although television news is still in its infancy, how long can it be relegated to the back seat, with the budding of such talents as Jennings and Jariel, now being given "The Time" and "The Money" to turn over every rock— just like the newspaperman—to uncover the story of the moment. And if their camera is rolling, "I got it," is heard a second later. But, one advantage is still ours, for as long as good people have got to glue their bottoms to a commode top and sit, sit, sit, newspapers will remain as, indisposable items.

With a smile fading, and after meeting the self-assured Jennings and Jariel, I can't help but ask, where's my self-assurance? I've been printed in every news magazine and every major newspaper in the world and still, a lasting joy, escapes me. Is it because that deep down at my root, I feel like nothing more than a short-lived anomaly? After all, doesn't ignorance and incompetence—without education in between—breed ignorance and incompetence? And soon, after turning in an inferior picture or two, won't the powers that be, see that too, and then, send me packing... and back to where I belong... back down at 503 with the ignorant and the incompetent? "Oh Makesense! With success killing me, what will failure do? What self-assuring advice can you offer?" "Only the same as before cousin... Keep on seeking... and perhaps, one day soon, you will find the joy... the joy that is missing." "Good night Makesense... and thank you." "Good night cousin... and you're welcome."

It's late July 1964, and the FBI is still in town and still searching for all of those KKK killers, mostly by conducting personal and very private interviews. And once behind closed doors, by attempting to corrupt a once loyal subject, by putting stacks and stacks of crisp green $100 bills down on the table between 'em, because they learned from an earlier experience... that money talks... even down here in Mississippi.

And once again, photographer Bourdier, is standing at my desk, but this time he's not asking for my negatives, he's just smiling. "Jack, you got time for lunch today... on me... no... make that, on the AP." "Sure, how does the Elite, with their chicken fried steak, french fries and salad, sound to you?" "Great, I'll be back around noon, and we can walk over together, there's something I need to tell you." "Great! I'll be here." As we indulge on another of those great rolls before us, Jim swallows and says, "Jack, I'm transferring." "What... to where?" "New York City." Stunned, while trying to control ole green eyes, I try not to over react to the news. But it ain't easy. Because, New York City is where my Kay is. And because, Jim knows and I know, that my Kay is on his fucking hit list. Regardless of his promise that she wasn't and because, I knew and he knew, that on many previous evenings, especially when Kay and I aren't talking, he would slip up and slip out with my Kay for dinner and dancing. And don't forget all those get-you-in-the-mood cocktails, just before bedtime. "Jesus Jim! Why transfer, when you got a great job down here?" "Yea, but its that... down here... that's getting to me. All those calls at all hours... hearing of another demonstration... another church burning... or... another killing. Shit Jack... all the violence is really getting to be a little much... Hell, all I got'a do to get this little Cajun ass kicked is... just show up in Philadelphia with a camera. When he said, Philadelphia, as in Mississippi, I couldn't help but break out laughing. When he asks, "What's so funny?" I turned around the early edition so he could read... Negros riot in Rochester, New York... the national guard called out, and, I respond. "I guess editor Ward is just pointing out to those uppety Yankees, that "this" is just what happens, when you don't control your niggers. Can't you hear editor Ward chuckling from daylight to dark, while writing his tomorrow's column?" And then, smiling back at me, Jim says, "I won't be covering this shit. I'll be sitting nice, cozy and safe behind a desk as a photo editor." "Shit Jim, now that's great... just great." But, what a great lie, because I know that the first woman that Jim will get to know there in the biblical sense—as Adam got to know Eve—is Kay... my lovely Kay. "And Jack, you want to know the other great news?" "Sure, but what can top that?" "My job is your job, if you want it." "Christ Jim, are you joking?" "No joke, I already recommended you... and highly. And the New York exec's want you. They know that your pictures have helped us clobber UPI over and over. What do you say? You want to work for the largest news agency in the U.S. of A, no... no... in the whole cotton-picking world?" "Oh Jim, I don't know... I've only been here for four years, and only two in photos. And you know, that unlike you, I'm not educated. All I got is a G.E.D., and even that's from the frigging Army... and that's it. And you're talking... THE ASSOCIATED PRESS—the biggest and the best." "You bet your ass baby... and they want yours. Forget about diplomas and bullshit. They've seen how you kicked my ass more than once. What about it... do you want the job?" "Jim, can you give me a little time to think about it?" "Okay, sure... but we'd need you in New Orleans by the end of August. And if you say yes, Chief of Bureau Sam Summerlin will need to stop by to chit-chat... but that's just a formality, because those Yankee bosses have already instructed me to... "hire his southern ass."

A few days later, editor Ward walks over to my desk and says, "Jack, mind stepping into my office, I want to talk to you." "Yes sir," is my answer, but the question rushing into my head is... is he just now getting around to firing my southern ass? Seeing my surprised, even pained expression, he quickly adds, "It's about that job offer. Sam called me... as a matter of courtesy."

After inviting me to take a seat and to relax, he continues, "Jack, there's a huge difference between working for a paper like ours, than working for the AP. We've got deadlines, but once those pass, we can relax until the next one. But with the AP there's never an end to them. Because every day and every hour around the world, there's always a new deadline approaching." "Yes sir, I know, and I've been thinking about that." "Well, think about this, you'd be the only AP photographer in Mississippi, Louisiana, Alabama, Arkansas and Kentucky. And you know what that means?" "No, not exactly." "It means that with all these racial stories popping at all hours, they'd be running your ass ragged. And why is Bourdier moving to a desk job in New York City, when even New Yorkers born and bred, hate living there? It's to get away from this racial climate, isn't it?" "Yes sir, he did say he was wearying of it." "Jack, you've got a good job here, with plenty of time for elbow bending after work, and the truth is... I just don't think that you can ever be happy with this job. You'd better think long and hard about that." "Yes sir, Mr. Ward, I will."

Makesense, what to do? Go? Stay? Go? Going would have one advantage... it would distance me from Carolyn and her marriage pressure. And her pressure to meet Mother. She says it's time. Time for both. And I can't bring myself to tell her that neither, meeting Mother or getting married, are in the cards, least not with this Thornell. Hell, she could load a six-shot revolver with six shots, spin the cylinder, cock the hammer, point and threaten to pull the trigger and all he'd hear is... I do not take this woman... before the shot sounds. Sorry honey, but the possibility of marriage to this Thornell is nothing more than an impossibility. Even my visits to Vicksburg have grown fewer and fewer. And when I do go, it's only for an hour, not even long enough to get my laundry done free of charge. And moving to New Orleans would put 200-miles between me and 503. And my infrequent visits could become, ever more infrequent.

Chief of Bureau Sam Summerlin is in town sitting across the table from me at Primo's and after our lunches are ordered, he puts his offer on the table. "Jack, I can credit you with all four years of your Daily News experience. And, at union scale, that would be $140-a-week to start... with annual raises... and after six months, health care, life insurance, and retirement benefits will kick in." "That really sounds good... really good... the pay... the benefits." "Well then, are you ready to start enjoying the fine dining down in New Orleans?" As the waitress sets the club steaks down in front of us, I ask, "Can I have a little more time to think on it." "You got till Friday, but then, I'll need an answer."

Carolyn and I are back at the Red Top for ribs, fries, and beer, when I break the news. "I'm taking the job with the Associated Press and I'm moving to New Orleans." "That's great... I think." "The pay and the benefits are just too good to pass up. A fifty dollar a-week raise. It would take another ten years here to earn as much. And as for the benefits, there are none here, nadda, zero, zippo." "When will you be leaving?" "Two weeks after I give notice." "And when will that be?" "Tomorrow." "What about us?" "We can still see each other. I'll be working and staying in Jackson some, and on free weekends, you can fly down and stay with me."

After failing to heed Editor Ward's final warning—you will be breaking your back by carrying around all that no-so-portable darkroom equipment from town to town and story to story—on Sunday August 29, 1964, my 25th birthday, I load up my maroon Monza and head south.

Three hours later, I arrive at Bourdier's old and now, my new apartment, and unload. An hour later, down at the Associated Press office on the fifth floor of The Times-Picayune building, I'm loading up and brother, emphasis "load". There's the transmitter, the power pack—two hernia's worth—the big enlarger case with the developing trays, the film tanks, the photographic paper grades one through four, the safe lights, the extension cords, the chemicals for film and paper, the changing bag, the film dryer, and the caption paper. And don't forget, the typewriter, the tripod, the cameras and all those lenses, the electronic flashes and rolls and rolls of film. Oops! Forget that giant roll of black plastic, and you're dead, because you can't turn a motel bathroom into a darkroom without it.

Now, sitting on the curb, with sweat dripping and dripping, and while trying to catch a breath or two, I must admit to you Editor Ward, that this job is indeed, a real "back breaker". But now, sitting here and contemplating my tomorrow, I feel your warning was way understated, because I know this job will be a real "brain bender" too. And why? Because I have never set up a portable darkroom or, ever operated one of those complicated looking wirephoto transmitters. And why sweat that, just wait till tomorrow and have an AP technician show you? So, stop with all that worry... and sleep on it. But, how can I sleep at all Editor Ward, when "tomorrow", my first day on the job, I'll be on the highway heading to Biloxi to cover a Mississippi elementary school desegregation, its first... and I'll be going it alone.

On this eventful day, mine and Mississippi's, even before arriving for my first assignment, I had realized two things. One, why Bourdier transferred last week... to miss this pressure, and two, new boss Summerlin is cheap, cheap, cheap... Because, the penny-pinching bastard has refused to send a reporter with me, because it might cost a little overtime, and that might cut into his annual bonus, for operating his office under budget. And, does it matter that this is the biggest story of the hour down in Mississippi? Apparently not, as I said, I was going it alone. And naturally, the possibility of violence and bloodshed isn't far from my thoughts.

After arriving at the school board office of this resort city of 60,000, I find major competition—two U.P.I. reporters and seasoned U.P.I. photographer Carey Womach, already there, and working the story. And my worry worsens, when I discover how closed-mouthed school officials are about specifics... like the name of any one of the elementary schools being integrated. Apparently, the official thinking is... if there's no press and no photographers present to witness and to record the taking of this nasty, force-fed dose of history in the making, then naturally, the easier is the swallowing, and the less humbling is this unholy integration experience.

After hanging around the building until the noon hour and hoping to overhear a slip of the tongue, I drive to the office of The Gulfport Daily Herald, walk in and ask for reporter-friend Jim Lund. He's at his desk polishing his integration story, and not hearing a "thank God" rising from under my breath. Because, if anyone knows the who, what, when, and where, it's this veteran ace. "Hello Jim." "Hi Jack... just let me proof my story and we can get some lunch. While I'm waiting, I'm thinking... All those mornings of taking Lund's stories over the phone and cultivating a friendship, may come in handy today. Over lunch, I pause, look Jim in the eye and say, "Man do I need your help today. Not only do I need a location, I need some information to phone in to the AP in New Orleans." "Hey! That's right, I heard you were going to work for them. When did you start?" "Today... and that's why this story is so important... I don't want to be the first staffer to get fired before he ever got to fill out a job application." Grinning broadly,

Jim says, "Hell Jack, how can they fire you, when officially you don't even work for 'em." "Jim, you know in this business, you've seen everything happen." "Amen brother, get your note pad out." Sighing with relief, I get my pen at ready as he begins. Your best bet is Gorenflo Elementary, where during recess, four negro kids held hands as they played a game of drop the handkerchief around a great pecan tree with their white classmates." "Jim that's great, Gorenflo it is. Anything else you can share?" "Let's see... all total... 16 black children, 12 girls and 4 boys integrated four previously all-white elementary schools without incident this morning. And without incident, because nobody can get within two square blocks of the schools and that nobody, in particular, means photographers. There's cops at every intersection stopping every car." "So, what are my chances of getting a picture when school lets out?" "Slimmer than none." "Damn Jim! Perhaps, after today, I won't be asked to fill in that application." While forcing my laughter to join his, I picked up the lunch check and thanked him for partially saving my ass. At least, I have a story to phone in, even if I can't get pictures.

Following Jim's directions, I find the barricade, pull over and stop well short of it. "Geesums Makesense, you can't even see the school from here. What to do? What to do? Every car is being stopped and turned around, until a Yellow Cab pulls up. The cabbie, rolls down his window, greets the policeman, who looks inside, checks out his passenger, removes the barricade, before waving the driver through. Immediately, I turn around, and start driving back to town, in search of another Yellow Cab. Finally, I find one, explain to the driver my plan, and surprisingly with a slight adjustment to his normal rate, he was game. I get in the backseat, put my camera bag on the floor, drape my jacket across the top of it, and say, "Let's go." Back at the roadblock, the policeman smiles, looks inside the car, and without saying a word, motions us through. "Keep driving around the school... slowly," I instruct. "It's almost time for classes to let out." And then, I notice another obstacle, a high chain length fence surrounding the school and obscuring my view. "Shit, what else," I thought, as I picked up a Nikon and put on a 300 mm lens. As soon as I looked back outside, I can see children exiting, and just as I'm instructing the driver to slow, there comes a blast over his radio. "Have you got a photographer in your car?" "Yes sir I do." "Son-of-a bitch! Get your ass and his'n out'a there... and I mean now." The startled driver steps on the gas, just as I see the image I was praying to see. Suddenly, with the car's momentum jerking me backwards, I point, focus and shoot. Within seconds, we're back at the barricade passing a pissed off policeman, who seems more pissed at the cabbie, than with me. Back at my car, and for our hasty retreat, the cabbie apologizes, "You understand, I got'a live down here." An extra twenty seems to calm him down, as I drive away to process my film and hopefully, have something to print. "Makesense, if the air condition is working, I'm not feeling it."

Later, with my eyeball against the negative, a smile develops, when I see that the telephoto lens, set at wide aperture, has cut right through the fence. And behind it, I see the image I prayed for... a little black boy between two little white ones, seemingly oblivious to all the goings on. The image, that no one down in Mississippi wanted recorded, much less seen, finds its way to page one of THE BIBLE... the New York Times... come morning.

For day two of my Associated Press career, there's another desegregation story awaiting 250 miles north of Biloxi. It's deep in Klan country. It's the birth county of "Roll with Ross" Barnett, who had played his role as Mississippi's chief civil rights "nemesis" well, during his four year reign as governor. And Carthage, the Leake County seat, is, but a hop, skip and a robe over from famous Philadelphia, where even the law rides with the Klan for the doing of murder and mayhem.

It's almost midnight, the night before, when I check into my motel, exhausted and feeling more than a little worrisome. But, at least here, I'm better prepared than I was down in Biloxi. Because here, local editor George Keith has secured me a place in a large storage shed directly across from the school. Because here, like in Biloxi, the press, and the photographers are even less welcome. And how does George secure the location information? That's because Brother George knows who is, and who ain't, under all them long white robes. And why does he share this top secret information with me? For doing my duty... by helping him lay all those fine Leake County folk so peacefully to rest, whether I was afflicted by the hangover of hangovers, or just a two-aspirin headache when he phoned me with those obituaries.

At 5:30 a.m., Mildred Dearman, a reporter who takes pictures, joins me and we enter a storage shed, check out the knot holes, until finding several large enough to shoot through. And then, we take a stool and wait and wait. At 8 a.m., a car pulls up, and out steps new student Deborah Lewis, who is accompanied by her mother Minnie Jordan, a negro N.A.A.C.P. attorney, and a number of local and twice as many state police. Until now, only their backs are showing, but as they turn, my Nikon starts sounding. "Damn it Mildred, I hope they don't hear us." "Shush honey! Or they'll hear your loud mouth." Within seconds everyone is inside, so I return to my stool and wait... and wait... and wait.

After a half hour, that seemed like an eternity, I tire of waiting and I whisper to Mildred, "I'm going to put my cameras back in my bag, slip out the side door, and try for my car." "Go ahead Honey but I think you're making a mistake," she warned. Before, she can say... wait, I'm outside creeping along the wall until I clear the shed, when suddenly, from my right and from my left, a half-dozen burly—looking like they have eaten a lot more beef than chicken—deputies come running and leaving me with only enough time for one comforting thought—they can't shoot, because, if they shoot and miss, they're likely to shoot each other—before they move in and surround me. Then, their spokesman says, "You're under arrest for trespassing." "But officer, I'm not... I have permission to be here... from the owner." But, before he can respond, he looks back to see local media darling Mildred being brought out of the shed. "Oh shit," he says, as he realizes his dilemma... arrest me and he'll have to arrest the town darling too. So while they're huddling, Mildred stands silent, but her eyes are saying... you stupid jackass... I told you to wait... didn't I? Finally, the deputy offers a compromise. "Hand over your cameras and your film... and you can go." "Officer I can't do that... give up my cameras." "If you refuse again, we'll take the cameras, the film, and your ass off to jail." Before I can reply, Mildred intervenes. "Here's mine... Jack... you'd better give up yours too... better let George sort this out later." But this time, I take Mildred's advice and avoid the handcuffs.

Early that afternoon, as George is handing me the cameras, minus the film, he says, "I was damn lucky to get these back... they're pissed, really pissed at me for helping you... you... you OUTSIDE AGITATOR you." "Hell George, Vicksburg is a lot further south than here." With our laughter ending, we shake hands and part company.

While driving back to New Orleans and nearing Jackson, I think of detouring over to Vicksburg, but that thought is immediately replaced with another… why would I want to visit the birthplace of so many failures… Mother Myrtis, Father Ben, Crazy Uncle John, shot-dead brother Garnett… and…

"No Makesense, after my failure today, I'll pass on Vicksburg." "Cousin, go easy on yourself. Yesterday, you made page one of The Bible. Today, you may have struck out, but remember too… you just got to the Big League." "Oh but Makesense, it's not the GETTING that worries me… IT'S THE STAYING."

So, instead of the hills of home, I visit The Daily News, find my old desk and greet Charlie Gerald, a good photographer who had worked for The Hattiesburg American before I highly recommended him to fill my vacancy.

"Hello Charlie." "Hey Jack. Good to see you. Hear you ran into a little trouble." "Yep, and I screwed up bigtime." "Did you get all your gear back?" "Yep, and with it, a get out'a town pronto card." "Least they didn't shoot you as an intruder," he laughed. "No, how's Shirley?" "Oh, she's fine. We're dating steady… and I want to thank you again for introducing us." "Has she rung your bell yet?" I asked in reference to her working in the public relations department over at the Bellhaven College. "No, not yet, but I promise you'll be the third to know." "How are you and Freddie getting along?" Fred Blackwell is the former copy boy, who, after learning photography from me, got promoted to a second full-time photographer slot. The one thing I didn't teach him though, was how to take dictation over the phone, and since he didn't type that well, Bloodsworth and Fairly couldn't ever start in their pulling match over him. After saying all my howdies, and then, my goodbyes, I resume the three hour drive south to the Big City… New Orleans.

Geesums Makesense, getting around the Crescent City, The Big Easy, or whatever you call it, is everything but… easy. But cousin, one thing is for certain, a body can't get lost here, because if a body keeps driving for an hour or so, a body comes right back to where a body started from. Might as well get out, get inebriated over in the French Quarter, get a good night's rest, then get up and have another go in the morning. Heck, I hear tell of tourists who ended up living out their days here, cause they couldn't find their way out'a here, not on all those going only one way and only back to here Crescent City streets. Yep Makesense, you must agree, that New Orleans is the ultimate… tourist trap.

But, even with all that driving around in circles, everybody just loves it here. For the red beans and rice. For the Mardi Gras. For all those French Quarter bars. And for the laid back way of life here, despite all that unbearable heat, heat, heat, and that high, high, high—drenched like a soggy towel—humidity making a body want to cry, "Lord if there's a place hotter than here, I don't want to experience it."

The land around New Orleans is Louisiana, the land of Parishes and not Counties. And it's the land of shady politics. But even so, one contented soul, who loves spicy red beans, almost as much as shady politics, airs out his true feelings… that Cajun Governor fellow has just got to be the finest dang crook ever produced by the State of Louisiana. And even he is honest enough to admit, that the only dreadful thing that can take him down in the eyes of his constituents, is, "Get caught in bed with a live boy or a dead woman."

And if you good ole boys are looking to celebrate the latest political upheavel, you might set yourselves down at to feast on a plate of dirty rice at a small diner near the intersection of where Desire comes together with Pleasure, before popping the question… just how many of our insurance commissioners did not pass go, but were sent straight to jail? Did somebody say three? Three in a row. And don't forget that governor, that attorney general, that judge, that legislator… THAT… "Jesus Makesense, this dirty politics disorder, malady, disease, ailment, affliction, or whatever you call it, is certainly… most infectious.

And, it just may be that from time to time, the almighty God tires of such shenanigans, and unleashes his wrath like a woman scorned. She's loud and foul. She's broad and strong. She's a killer. She's my weakness. And for me, she means disaster. It is because of Mother's fear, is it because of my rainy nights in the ditch, or is it because I can't swim a lick or even dog paddle despite one free lesson at the Y.M.C.A. that cost me dearly by leaving me with the pain of water on the lung… both of 'em. And needless to say… there was never a lesson two. And needless to say… that this God driven phenomenon is no lady, but she is… Hurricane Hilda. On October 4, 1964, as the red flags with the ominous black squares are being shredded by winds of 120 miles-per, approximately 150,000—remembering the 1957 Cameron howler that killed over 500—are already fleeing northward. When exhausted, Hilda has claimed 58 lives and left the sugar cane crop, estimated at $100 million, in ruins. And leaving me to survive on at best, very mediocre pictures. And lastly, leaving me with the realization that hurricanes, past or future, will spell more than disaster. For me, they all spell… Waterloo.

"Geesums Makesense! After 35-days on the job and still, without a complicated application, we've experienced… a whiplash in Biloxi… a jail threat in Carthage… a circling and circling in the Crescent City without getting anywhere… a nearly got blowed away by Hilda… and then…a left behind for drowning in the fish bowl holding New Orleans. And now Makesense, there's only one question left." "And what's the question cousin?" "What's coming next?" "Goodnight cousin." "Goodnight Makesense."

Well, a month later the "what" turns out to be a "who". And the news excited me. It'll complicate my life, and it could spell danger, even disaster for my relationship with Carolyn. And the "who" is none other than Kay… my special… special Kay. The New York job didn't last, and so, she's returning to Jackson and to her old desk. And the danger is that from time to time, I'll be returning to Jackson to share my old desk with Gerald, when I'm borrowing the use of his darkroom. So, it'll be impossible not to see her, not to talk to her and not to want her. And my wishful thinking is… now, that I'm filling Bourdier shoes, she'll see me in a new light and forget about ole green eyes and all those torturing third degree nights, and honey, don't forget that 50 per cent raise, for surely, that's a new and attractive incentive to look my way again. Oh dear Kay, it's not a matter of "what", it's a matter of "when" we're going to find our way back into each other's arms… again. And, Carolyn need not know every time that the work brings me back to Jackson, for opportunity after opportunity for Kay and I to happen.

And the opportunity knocked late Friday afternoon of December 2, 1964, sooner than expected, with a friendly FBI voice on the phone reporting some big happenings in the planning. For four months now, the Feds had grilled hundreds and hundreds of people in connection with the June murders of the three civil rights workers. And the government men had been catching hell from both sides—the black community and the army of KKK sympathizers. The Dr. Martin

Luther King, reflecting the outrage of negro leaders, condemned mightily the failing of the FBI for not bringing to justice even a single one of those murdering scoundrels.

And, on the other side, Neshoba Sheriff Rainey, tiring of the FBI traipsing all over his county and stepping on the toes of too many of his supporters, mouthed off openly about his sentiments on the matter. "If the FBI knows who killed 'em," he told an Associated Press reporter, "Why don't they make any arrests?"

Oh Sheriff Rainey, as some say, better be careful what you ask for, because, your tobacco chawing redneck ass—according to our informant—is at the top of the FBI's "To be arrested soon" wish list, you and your knight riding deputy "Chubby-Cheeks" Price.

Before daylight on December 4, I arrive at Philadelphia, and meet up with Jackson AP reporter Jim Bonney at the front door of The Neshoba Democrat awaiting the arrival of editor and friend Jack Tannehill. "Good morning Jack," Jim greets me as my thoughts take me back to one of my last talks with Bourdier, and what he said about Philadelphia… All I got to do to get my little Cajun ass kicked is show up in Philadelphia carrying a camera. "Morning Jim, but "good" remains a question mark. You know how this town feels about us agitating newshounds." "Yeh," he said above his laughter, "And don't get your feelings hurt if you don't see me anywhere near you and those cameras… Cause those Kodaks truly draw attention." "And I notice you're wearing a coat and tie under a white trench coat, and looking an awful lot like an FBI man." Knowing that I had blown his cover, he replies, "If it's a case of mistaken identity that saves my ass, then all I got to say is… Thank God for mistaken identities."

Jim was tall and very-very thin, but he had the heart the size of a watermelon. And if nice guys finish last, he's standing behind… behind… behind… that next to last fellow in line. That's the usual Jim, but today ain't usual, and this ain't Jackson, this is down in Mississippi's Philadelphia. And brotherly love doesn't reign here, the KKK does. "I think what you're telling me Jim… If I'm getting my ass kicked… you're going to standby just like the FBI does and… watch." "Hell Jack, you aught'a been a writer for exposing all those lying politicians, cause you sure can read minds." With the remains of my smile dissipating, and rapidly, he hits me with a less than comforting thought, "Heck Jack, look at it another way… if they only kick one ass… it'll only be half the pain."

A few minutes later, at 5:30 a.m. weekly editor Tannehill, arrives, greets us, unlocks the door and invites us inside. "Follow me and I'll show you the darkroom," Tannehill said. "Fine, but before we do that, can you give me a desk to set up my transmitter." "Sure." "I'll need power and a telephone to hook up to." "How about here," Tannehill says, as he leads me to a desk in the middle of the room. "That's perfect, now for the darkroom, where can I mix my chemicals." "Sure, follow me."

When I finish the mixing and the hooking, I turn to Jim and say, "It's almost 6:30, don't you think, we'd better go and get into position?" Agreeing, Jim gets into his car, I get into mine, and we drive around the corner and park facing the courthouse door. When, I look to my left to make eye contact with Jim, I find he has parked four spaces over, keeping his skinny ass away, and well out of harm's way. My way. My harm. Next, for the second time I check to make sure the door lock buttons are pushed down, even though there's no one stirring. And, now is the time to get my cameras ready. The Rolei, with my German strobe attached, I set at 1/250 of a second at F 16. With the poor light, the background will go dark, but at F 16, there will be enough depth of field to assure sharp images, even if the focus isn't exact. And the flash will eliminate the risk of guessing the exposure. I've taken hundreds of walk-in, walk-out, daylight or dark, photos this way, so, why am I worrying so? Next, I pick up my precious Leica, preset the focus at eight feet, set the shutter speed at 1/250 to stop the motion, and open the lens wide to 2.8, while I pray the arrest won't come until enough dawn light emerges to catch up with an over generous, and guessed exposure. Now, all there is to do is, sit tight… and wait… and watch. A glance to my left finds Jim is sitting tight too. From my vantage, it's well over a 100-feet up the steps to the courthouse door. On both sides, there are long, and thank God, empty benches. But before I can count my blessings, out walk two men, then four more, and they divide up, take a seat as if their assignment is, to guard the door. Now one takes out his pocket knife and begins his whittling.

Geesums! 7 a.m. is awfully early even for a good ole boy to set hisself down at the courthouse door to begin his day of whittling. Unless, the Klan knows that the FBI is coming, and coming early… I'm thinking. And with all twelve eyes zeroing in on me and my maroon Monza, a county car pulls up, parks, and out steps Sheriff Rainey. Alone he takes the steps and greets all those turning friendly eyes before disappearing inside.

Before The High Sheriff can get comfortable at his desk and take out his morning chaw, a white sedan, the kind the good guys drive, pulls up and parks about five spaces over and to my right. Two FBI men, dressed almost identical to Jim, take the steps while keeping their focus rigidly front and center to avoid making contact with all those turning very unfriendly eyes, both on their right and left.

"What to do! Makesense, what to do! I just can't sit here and miss "The Picture" of the day, hell no, the year. I've got to get out and get closer. I've got to have time and space to back pedal and to shoot at least a half dozen pictures. I know the whole wide world will be screaming for 'em, and at me, if I don't get 'em." And so, I look to my left and find Jim staying safe and snug inside his car. I look to my right in hope of seeing another media body, but the parking spaces and the sidewalks are empty. What to do? What to do? Then, the photographer in me takes over, lifts the Rolei up and around my neck, leaving it hanging chest high. The Leica is raised, hung over my right shoulder, leaving it dangling at my side just above the hip. After lifting the door locks, the photographer steps out, takes the steps and stops just short of the courthouse door, where he is greeted by the whittler. "Hey Boy! You got some fucking balls walking up here with them goddamn cameras. You'd better turn yo ass around and get 'em out'a here while they're still working and you're still walking." With his whittling getting faster and faster and with the chips dropping closer and closer—like Grandpa Jones' nasty snuff did the day he condemned me for killing all those birds—the photographer died, and Jack R. Thornell took over and said, "Okay! Okay! I'm going… I'm, not going to take any pictures." Knowing that if I raise a camera, it'll get busted along with a photographer's ass, and so I start back pedaling down the stairs. Then, the whittler lays his wood down, but keeping his knife handy, gets up, and follows, step for step, only to be reinforced by his five good buddies. Now, Sheriff Rainey is emerging through the courthouse door between two F.B.I. agents. Geesums! What to do? What to do? Shooting ten frames between here and the FBI car, would be as easy as shooting ducks from a blind just ten feet away. Except for the whittler, who is raising and pointing his knife, and now shouting, "Boy! Don't you touch that camera." All I can do is… keep on back pedaling. But once at the bottom step, instead of turning toward my car, I turn toward the FBI's, where I find another car has parked and formed an alley for me to retreat through. Once I reach the back of the car, I turn sideway facing my car and stop. Looking back I see my pursuers have stopped too, staying on the sidewalk and leaving the alley open for Rainey and his arresting officers to enter into. Just as the agent to Rainey's right, reaches to open the back door, I begin dragging the bottom of my right hand across the top of my Leica still dangling from my right shoulder… until finding and triggering the shutter button. CLICK! Sounds. The whittler sounds, "He took a fucking picture." "I didn't! I didn't. I didn't even lift a camera. You saw! You saw! I shouted back, while breaking into a run. Now, pursuing me into the street, they run head-on into CBS photographer Laurens Pierce, who had just jumped from his car left in the middle of the street. And with the attention off me, I glance back to see… Laurens is raising his camera… Oops! That's a no, no, Laurens. With his camera bouncing on concrete, while he is being gang tackled, I slip into my Monza and make my get-away. Looking into the rearview mirror, I can see Jim, safe and snug, inside his car.

After stepping inside the Neshoba Democrat, the first thing to greet me is the white sheet concealing my transmitter. White sheets are very popular with poor folks who can't afford the official Klan garments... I'm thinking... As editor Tannehill approaches with his explanation, "It's better for me if local folks don't know that I showed the outside press any southern hospitality." "Don't worry, I'll leave it covered, until and if, I have a picture to transmit." "Jesus Jack, I forgot... There's a call waiting... somebody from your New York office is holding," and pausing to look at his watch, "For at least ten minutes."

As I'm picking up the phone one thing rings true, the fear just as experienced during that run for my life, or my ass, doesn't compare to the fear I'm experiencing now, just with the sounding of those two foreign words... New York. But, both share a common factor—the kicking of, or the firing of—my ass. "Hello... Thornell here." "Resch here, Al Resch." "Yes sir." "When can we expect a first picture?" "Sir, I'm not sure I got a picture." Hesitating, possibly to suppress a growing dissatisfaction, then, he says, "Explain yourself Thornell." "Sir, I was there when Rainey was arrested, but I never raised a camera..." "What! You never what! Explain yourself." "Well, there were half a dozen rednecks there... and one of them was waving a knife... and threatening me if..." "hold it! Hold it! What did you mean... not sure if you got a picture... either you did or you didn't... Which is it?" "Oh, I mean... At the last second I turned and tripped the shutter on my Leica." "Well... that sounds better." "But Mr. Resch, the Leica was just hanging on my shoulder... I didn't... I couldn't... raise it... to frame a picture... and it's possible I could'a cut everybody's heads off... I just don't..." "Hold it! Go drop your film in the developer... I'll hold the phone."

"Son of a bitch! Son of a bitch! I shouted, after the darkroom door had shut behind me, and as I begin loading the reel, and thinking of the things that could still go wrong. Like loading the reel improperly and having the emulsions sticking together and pulling apart the images with the unwinding of it. Like dropping the film into the hypo instead of the developer like Sgt. Fuckup did up at Fort Monmouth... and then, all you get it window glass. "Oh shit,"... and before I tripped the shutter, when I loaded the camera, I may not have lined up the film notches with the camera sprocket to assure the proper advancement. "Oh shit!" Did I advance the film two frames to move the fogged leader over. "Oh shit!" And if I did all of that right, the film could have been damaged by X-ray machines... or... by the heat in the trunk of my car... "Shit!...

117

Shit... Shit...With the reel loaded, I feel for any bulges, and finding none, I feel for the developer tank... I find it... and feel for the tape around it... confirming that it is indeed the developer... and not the career ending hypo.

And with the film in the developer, with the timer set to five minutes and ticking, my thoughts turn to... my first conversation with "the man" in charge of all A.P. photographers worldwide. Al Resch. His voice sounded as cold and callous as I had heard it would. And, I had heard he was the chief of all no-nonsense executives with the power to fire a photographer quicker than a New Orleans Bureau Chief could say... jobless. And if, sweating bloody tears is what it takes to get "The Picture" particularly on "The Big Story", just consider those a bi-product of Al Resch's expectations. And if you ain't got "The Picture", why are you setting your worthless ass back down here in the office? Get back out there and get it, from a member photographer, from a freelancer, from an amateur with a box brownie, I don't care, just get it... "The Picture". And if you think an ass kicking or a little blood loss is excuse enough for missing "The Picture", Buster, you're dead wrong. And today, I'm Buster and "The Picture" is... a Klan connected sheriff being arrested by the FBI on charges of violating the civil rights of three young men by conspiring to kill 'em... down in Mississippi.

The timer sounds and I remove the film, drop it into the hypo, shake it up and down for a few seconds, and then, let it set for a minute or so to fix the image. And with the room temperature feeling like late August rather than early December, and with my sweat dropping and mixing with the wet chemicals below, I begin unrolling the film. Frame 36, unexposed and as clear as a just cleaned window pane. Frame 35... clear. Frame 34... clear. Frame 33... clear. Frame 32... clear. Frame 31... clear. Frame 30... clear. Frame 29... clear. Frame 28... clear. Frame 27... clear. Frame 26... clear. Frame 25... clear. Frame 24... clear. Frame 23... clear. Frame 22... clear. Frame 21... clear. Frame 20... clear. Frame 19... clear. Frame 18... clear. Frame 17... clear. Frame 16... clear. Frame 15... clear. Frame 14... clear. Frame 13... clear. Frame 12... clear. Frame 11... clear. Frame 10... clear. Frame 9... clear. Frame 8... clear. Frame 7... clear. Frame 6... clear. Frame 5... clear. Frame 4... clear. Frame 2... clear. And finally, with 54 inches of clear--blank if you prefer Mrs. Bounds--film dangling towards the floor, the magnifier with my right eye pressing against it, inches to the left to see Frame 1... "Oh my God! Oh my God! Thank you! Thank you!" It's "The Picture". Sheriff Rainey between two FBI men with the courthouse filling the background. And it's perfectly framed as if God had raised the camera for me.

Dropping the film back into the running water, I rush to the phone to tell Mr. Resch the good news, calmly and ever so a matter of factly, he replies, "Good, make a quick print and get it transmitted... The whole damn world is screaming for an arrest photo," before, finally letting go of the phone and letting me off the hook. As I'm returning to make my print, I see Jim walking through the door. "Hey Jim, you mind writing me a caption for Rainey being escorted to jail?" "God Jack, you got it... a picture. But I didn't see you raise a camera." I didn't... it's a hip shot... and you may want to include that the "Hip Shot" came after the AP photographer was threatened with a knife." "Did you really feel threatened out there Jack?" "Did you really feel threatened inside your car Jim?" "You bet your sweet ass, I did." "Then, there's your answer."

With "The Picture" spinning on the transmitter cylinder, I collapse into a chair only to be told there was another phone call for me. "Hello, this is Thornell." "Jack, this is Jim Laxon... Atlanta Photos... staff photographer Horace Cort will be arriving in Meridian before noon to help with the arraignment. You'd better pack up and get over there." "Okay Jim... as soon as the transmission stops." Nine minutes later, when the cylinder quit spinning, "The Picture" was available to newspapers and TV stations around the world. And our biggest competitor—United Press International—was leveled by "The Picture" much like Hiroshima was by "The Bomb".

Horace Cort was of medium height and wearing a big smile, when he reaches to shake my hand at the Holiday Inn where he is busy setting up a darkroom. A bowtie guy, and from his age, appears to be a long time survivor of ball busting assignments. And what he saw back was green, green, green and not as in money, but as in little green apples that had fallen too far from the tree. Jim said earlier that I was a "mind reader" and this mind is telling me the question that Cort is asking himself... How the hell did this kid get on with the AP, when the AP only hires THE BEST and THE MOST SEASONED. And so what, if he got lucky a time or two—like today—but blind luck does not an Associated Press photographer make. Not in the long term. He must have a rich uncle serving on the AP board of directors, because that's the only plausible answer for his working alongside the likes of me.

Together we drive to the Meridian Naval Air Station to cover the arraignment. There, we find a demure spinster by the name of Commissioner Ester Carter who practices law, and I mean practices, because she never spent a day in law school, sitting ready to preside over one of the most famous cases ever... down in Mississippi.

Besides arresting Rainey and Price at the courthouse, a horde of FBI men, coordinating precision timing, swooped down, arrested, handcuffed, and locked up nineteen others.

According to the complaint pending, ten of the men, "did threaten, assault, shoot and kill the three civil rights workers." The other eleven are facing conspiracy charges. The Feds used an obscure 1870 law titled, "Conspiring Against the Rights of Others." And, in this case, by "Taking away their rights to live." Specifically, the complaint states, "Deputy Price unlawfully arrested the three, held them in jail for six hours, before turning them out into the night and into the hands of The White Knights of the Ku Klux Klan, laying in wait." But, the best sentence the Feds can hope for is, ten years in prison. And that's because murder isn't a federal crime unless it is committed on government grounds. And any conviction may just be wishful thinking... because of the many voices declaring, "That Sheriff Rainey... he aught'a run for governor." And the playmaker from the arraignment is a close-up of Rainey having a chaw from his stash of Red Man tobacco. And was it the work product of the veteran ace? Well, let's just say... that when Horace was editing our film and that particular negative jumped out at him, he had the look of someone who had just taken a big bite from a very green and a very tart little green apple.

Back in New Orleans my major competition comes in the rather large form of Pete Fisher, the veteran UPI photographer with an ego the size of an elephant. If you want to know how great Pete art, just occupy a bar stool right next to him, shut up, and listen... Well Jack, you know, I'm a bureau manager, and I don't have to listen to some dumbass bureau chief like you do. You know, I almost won the Pulitzer for that picture of General Walker being arrested at bayonet point after allegedly leading a charge at the Ole Miss riots. And, you know... And I soon knew that Pete really loves the city, and in particular the French Quarter, where his office is located at WWL-TV, and where he loves sipping hurricanes down at Pat O'Brien's and turning up old fashions over at The Old Absinthe House. And the joy and the fulfillment of the moment often slows Pete's departures and delays his arrival for some major news events, when minutes, even seconds, can make the difference between success and a shellacking. Over the coming months, Pete's "over confidence" and my "insecurity" with my getting to the news scene earlier, and his arrival getting later and later, until finally, and despite his seniority, Pete starts catching hell from his bosses, both in Dallas and in New York. So proud Pete starts walking a tight rope, and hoping that his past successes will keep him from falling. And in the future, when we're competing, his successes will be my failures and vice versa. Naturally, my future depends on the vice versa. A consistent if not constant one.

Pete's lucky, pretty damn lucky in one area, not being responsible for all the upheavals down in Mississippi. His territory ends at the Louisiana state line, although he does cross over by invitation only to help cover a big story like the riots at Ole Miss. However, the Mississippi responsibility belongs to Cary Womach, who calls Montgomery home.

And, when I'm not up—and I mean up at all hours—in Mississippi, I'm down in Louisiana, where a 60-hour work week, like the ones in the cross hairs of Bloodsworth and Fairley, would be a heavenly, no, make that, a most heavenly experience. And a first day impression of C.O.B. Summerlin as being cheap, cheap, cheap, was wrong, wrong, wrong and a gross underestimation, because, he is cheaper than cheap. When denying my overtime, I get a look that's saying... This inexperienced and undereducated kid should be paying us for all of his exciting on the job training. And, finally one day after three months, he walks over to my desk, hands me a job application, and says, "Well... I guess it's time for you to fill this out." His reasoning for the long delay, I figured was... to keep me off-balance and insecure, and why? Because "The balanced" and "The secure" insist on getting paid for their work... all of it... particularly when there's a wire service union demanding it.

And when, you're cursed at, spat on, or threatened by press haters with something even worse, remember Jack, there are other stories to cover. Such as: Elections, legislative sessions, and the governor's travels, plane crashes, train and car wrecks, oil rig calamities, refinery explosions, fires with multiple fatalities and beauty pageants like Junior Miss and Miss Louisiana, mass murders, floods, tornados, and thank God hurricane season is over, and sports by the numbers, track meets, basketball and football, both high school and college and don't forget the Wide World Photos, the commercial arm of the AP that hires you out to do commercial crap like conventions and such. And when, you're free Jack, don't just set down that lazy ass in this air conditioned office, get out there, forget about that 100 degree heat and search the streets for an outstanding feature picture. And when you get back to the office, fill out all those stringer photo credits, cause if you want to keep their pictures turning on that transmitter cylinder, those boys got'a get their money.

And next Thursday, there's a new missile flying in my direction. And with the uncertainty of it hitting anywhere near its target, it's making me nervous, and it even has me practicing my ducking.

Good grief Makesense! What's a birdie? What's a bogey? What's a par? What's an eagle? Hallelujah brother, there's something I've heard of. Hell, nearly everybody has seen an eagle soar.

But beyond the knowledge of soaring eagles, dear gallery, this rookie doesn't have a clue as... How do you cover it? And that question dear gallery, puts me between the proverbial rock and the indubitable hard place. On one hand, the grand AP considers you as green as they come and doesn't want to pay you. But on the other, you're an AP photographer and you should know how to cover everything. So, how do you cover golf? Given no other choice, if you must learn, why not let Arnold Palmer and Jack Nicklaus teach you. I hear they're pretty good, and I know they're showing up for the lit'ole Cajun Classic staged over in Lafayette. The last tournament, and with a purse so small, all the big stars usually skip it. But not this time, because Palmer and Nicklaus are in a dead heat for the money title of the year.

Come Thursday, during that first round, I learn more about "How not to" cover golf than "How to". And if you think that facing a wielding knife is frightening, wait until you face one of those irate fellows yelling and wielding a long club with that big chunk of metal welded on it. And, all I did was... go CLICK! CLICK! CLICK! Somewhere between his back swing and the time his club connected with the ball. It seems, like the Rednecks at Philadelphia, he finds those clicks disturbing. And after I pick the very best camera position by lining up the golfer, the ball and the hole, and squat down to take the picture, the golfer delays his putting, looks over at me as if I had just laid an egg, and then, waves me up and away from my perfect position. Well, after getting lost over and over on acres and acres, while searching for the round's leader, and after laying a dozen eggs or more, I discover something of importance. And it's this: I hate covering golf, almost as much as I hate covering hurricanes.

This February afternoon, I'm driving up to Jackson to spend the night before covering a special session of the Mississippi legislature. Carolyn doesn't know that I'm coming, but Kay does. We have a date for dinner, drinks, and whatever follows. It's risky, with Carolyn likely to see my car on the street when she enters or exits the Electric Building. But, that can't happen until tomorrow, because this afternoon, I'm going straight to the Sun'n'Sand and check in.

While stretching out on the motel bed and trying to relax until date time, I find I can't. Instead, I find a feeling of uneasiness settling over me. Sure, there's always the possibility of Carolyn stumbling across our paths, but that's not my principal worry. No, it's the possibility, even the likelihood of Kay keeping me at arm's length until our date ends. And yet, she accepted my invitation without hesitation or reservation. So, I'm back to... whatever follows... follows.

After ringing the doorbell, instead of Kay, it's her mother that greets me. "Good evening Jack, won't you come in." "Thank you Mrs. Haggerty. How've you been?" "Oh... fine. Especially since Kay is back. I was afraid... with her up in New York... and all alone." "Yes ma'am... I know you're happy she's home." And before I can sit down, Kay brightens the room. "Hello Kay, don't you look nice." "Thank you Jack," she said, as she leans over to give her mother a peck on the cheek and says, "I won't be too late, but don't wait up." Kay looks delicious, dressed in a straight cut, but very sleek black dress covering her slender body most elegantly.

Once in the car, while putting the key in, then pausing, I look over to Kay to find her eyes meeting up with mine and then, she turns her sexy smile on, and keeps it on me for the longest as if she's saying... Dear Jack, it's been so long, I'm hungry for more than dinner... I'm hungry for you. "Oh God! I hope so," almost cracks from my lips.

After arriving at LeFleur's, a very nice, and a very upscale restaurant, we walk in with my eyes scanning the dining room. After not seeing Carolyn or any of our mutual friends, I sigh with relief as I pull back Kay's chair. After we're seated, our small talk begins. "How've you been Jack?" "Busy, busy, busy, with little time for anything but work." "I guess all this civil rights stuff keeps you hopping." "And a skipping and a jumping." With our mutual laughter joining, we continue like two old friends who have never had a cross word come between them. While waiting for the check, I suggest, "Why don't we go down to the Sun-n-Sand bar for a drink and a little piano music?" "That sounds good... real good." And "a drink" turns into another drink, then another, and when the bartender announces "Last call" we are very and very drunk. After ordering, two to go cups and whispering, "Not to worry, I'm not driving." And then, without saying another word, I take Kay's hand, and without even the slightest tug of resistance, I lead her across the parking lot and into my bed. She smells delicious. Her lips and mouth taste delicious. And with our bodies pressing hard together and trying desperately to become one, with my lips still devouring hers, and with my next intention to enter into the tunnel of love, the phone rings... "Shit! Who can that be, it's 2 a.m." I said, before turning idiot and picking up the phone. "Yea!" "Stan, New York Photos. You need to get going to Marion, Alabama. The Klan shot a demonstrator and NBC newsman Richard Valeriani got beat up bad... he's been hospitalized." Suddenly, the desire of the moment—to have my Kay—vanishes, because I know that you can't say no to a New York Photo editor and keep your job for long. After turning back to Kay and seeing the sheet pulled up and covering her small but firm breasts, I say, "I'm sorry Kay, but I got to get going." "Go where?" "To Marion, Alabama... there's been a shooting... a young black man." "But Jack, it's not safe for you to drive." "I know! I know! But when a New York voice says go... you go... and go now." It had been a long time since Kay and I had been between sheets together, and this time ended in disappointment—I hoped—for both of us. In order to keep awake and out of a ditch, I stopped the car every few miles, got out in the February cold without a coat, ran around the car a couple of times, got back in and continued the routine until I sobered up. And when I did, I couldn't keep from thinking... what a wasted opportunity. And asking myself... Why oh why didn't I enter the tunnel of love and delay my departure by another 60 seconds?

Today is March 1, 1965, and my six-month probation period ended at 5 a.m. But, the question still pending... is... this cause for celebration? Let's see. Let's review: Whiplash in Biloxi. Nearly arrested in Carthage. Almost blown away and left to drown by Hilda. Threatened personally by a jackknife in Philadelphia. A near clubbing at the Cajun Classic. And squeezed like a balloon ready to pop by the merciless pressure of east coast editors screaming for good LSU action pictures, long before the quarterback ever left the huddle. When Miami is playing LSU at a game starting at 8 p.m., it's already 9 p.m. in Florida. And by 8:30 p.m., The Miami Herald has already called three times yelling, "We're on deadline... where's the pictures?" And, where does the covering of night football rank on a list of hates? Somewhere between Gulf hurricanes and golf hazards.

But, the upside of staying on is, if I get gutted by a "Redneck" just dispensing his sense of Mississippi justice, or, if I get battered by an almost two-timed Carolyn, there's medical attention provided for without the pain of paying twice. And if by some miracle, this photographer can survive to age 50, he can take early retirement, provided he can get comfortable living in a pup tent for one, and eating something considerably less than three squares a day.

With probation behind me, I return to Jackson, pick up Kay and we return to the Sun'n'Sand for the completion of Act I, Scene I. And this time there's not even a remote possibility for a chilling call of death and despair to disturb and disengage us. And that's because, I not only took the phone off the hook, but I also dismissed that annoying buzzing sound by disconnecting the wire between the wall and the phone. And, if anyone desires to disturb Kay and I this night, be prepared to kick the door down, and better hope and pray I'm not packing Carolyn's double-barreled Derringer, because anyone can be tomorrow's headline.

And disturbed we weren't, but satisfied I was. And was Kay? I don't know. I never know, and I never ask because when I'm done, I'm done, as is the cuddling is always before. With Carolyn, with Wally, with a best friend's wife, or with all those one-nighters, it doesn't matter, when I climax my body turns its thermostat from hot to cold. Just lay there darling and don't touch anything... please. And if you must talk, keep with the declaratives and omit the questions, particularly, the personal-personal ones. Like... What's your mother like? And did you have a nice home life? Sometimes, starting a quick argument is a good diversion.

And Kay knows too well, that after sex, I'm a touchy guy, so we just lay there quietly at each other's side, undoubtedly contemplating what this night of pleasure means and what will its effect have on our tomorrows. Kay doesn't ask about Carolyn, our status, or our future, nor does she ask about us, and ours. And I was so relieved, she doesn't. What could I say... ditto the dilemma. Because Kay, I can't take you down to 503? Any more than I can take Carolyn. But, if I could overcome that shame-filled fear, there's little doubt as to which one of you would finally meet Mother... My dear and my lovely Kay.

After a dormant winter, the civil rights movement stirs, awakening the South, but this spring, the "Ain't gonna let no body turn me around," bodies are marching on Alabama, and praise the Lord, not on Mississippi. And more specifically, on Selma, Alabama. And it's because Dr. Martin Luther King Jr., a civil rights leader, the non-violent kind, has had his fill of discrimination at the ballot box and is wanting to focus the eyes of the nation on such going ons. He too is putting his marching boots on, for a 50-mile trek west to Montgomery. Why Selma? It's the capital of the Black Belt, so called for its dark rich earth. Its economy, poor. Its education and income, minimal. It's where only 325, out of potential 15,000 blacks, cast ballots. And why Montgomery? It's the birthplace of The Confederacy. It's where Dr. King's famed bus boycott began. And... it's where staunch segregationist George Wallace rules from the governor's throne.

With the sweet scent of yellow jasmine flavoring the spring air, the march is scheduled to begin. Meanwhile, in Montgomery, Gov. Wallace quickly issues a "No march order". "Such a disruption of a main traffic artery—The Jefferson Davis Highway—would be a menace to commerce and to public safety." To enforce the order, 100 state troopers race to Selma to augment Sheriff Jim Clark's mounted posse and the contingent of troopers already there.

Sheriff Clark, an unwavering champion of ole time traditions, is willing to do whatever it takes to keep 'em alive in his Dallas County where the privilege to vote belongs to the white man, and only to the white man. Sadly, in the neighboring counties of Wilcox and Lowndes, where the population is 79 percent black, not a single black soul is registered.

Clark, black leaders feel, is cut from the same cloth as famous Birmingham police commissioner Bull Connor who turned snarling attack dogs and powerful—knock you on your ass—fire hoses on demonstrators.

"Bull Connor gave us the civil rights bill," declared the Rev. Andrew Young, one of the King's aides, "And Jim Clark is going to give us the voting rights bill." And what is the response of the easily provoked Clark? Only a slight straightening of his lapel pin. The one inscribed... NEVER.

On March 7, 600 negroes and a handful of white supporters, march from Brown's Chapel, their rallying point, through the business district and onto Edmond Pettus Bridge leaving the city. Waiting on the other side is Clark, with his khaki-clad horseback mounted possemen. Flanking them is a line of state troopers wearing blue helmets, over those grotesque gas masks, and looking more like aliens from outer space than Alabama peace keepers. Some hold shotguns, other show tear gas grenades and billy clubs.

"You have two minutes to disperse," the trooper announced. With pulses quickening, the negroes halt, and drop to their knees. Then, the trooper shouts, "Move in." Tear gas grenades explode, and billy clubs swing. Forcing the crying, the moaning, and the defenseless marchers back on their feet and back across the bridge. Then, the mounted possemen give chase, yelling and prodding as they go. Yellow clouds hang over the area, replacing the last hint of Jasmine with a sharp stinging odor. Weeping and wailing, the negroes creep back to their starting point, Brown's Chapel, a mile away.

With the news, I couldn't help but to think... Thank God, not for the melee, Jesus no, but the fact that it happened over in Alabama, that's the Atlanta bureau's responsibility. And they're blessed with Photo Editors Laxon and Bill McGriff, along with photographers Cort and Charlie Kelly, not to forget Memphis' Bill Hudson who they call in regularly. Hudson has secured "Great News Photographer status" with his awesome photos of the Birmingham attacking dogs incident back in 1963. So, they can handle the Selma story just fine without having to involve me. And with everyone's eyes, off of Mississippi, and on Alabama, surely, I can find time to return to Jackson to cover more of the State Legislature, still in session. And naturally, to cover my lovely Kay once again. But, for fate and that fucking phone, Kelly and Hudson are already there, but they want my size eleven's planted firmly on that Alabama soil. This according to the young New York Photo editor knowing only... his way to the men's room, where to lunch at noon sharp despite breaking news, and most importantly, if he don't get to his subway stop by 5 p.m., he can't go home. And time with the family, you know, is so, so, so, beneficial.

With six long hours of driving still in front of me, my head is already in Selma, worrying and wondering what I'll be facing there. After pulling in at the motel and hooking up with Hudson and Kelly, I find things have simmered down, with little to cover, but those hot, steamy, and boiling over with rhetoric, nightly church rallies. Just put one more set of lungs in there, and the last breath of oxygen will be sucked right up. And don't worry about fainting and falling, because you're packed in there like standing sardines, so, how and to where, can one fall... and if you're not holding your camera high and above your head, and instead, left it dangling at your side, forget about taking the picture, because, raising the camera now, is a physical impossibility. Oh what I'd give for a chair.

Over the next few days, I find my way around Selma, and get to know Hudson and Kelly. Both are very likeable. Hudson is more like me in one sense... never, never volunteer your services for a "Big Story" just for a chance to make a "Big Name" for yourself, cause brother you never can tell, when something is going to go wrong, and instead of the hero, you end up the goat, like the one in Abraham's time, the one bearing the blame, the one turned out, the one called the... scapegoat.

Kelly is larger, particularly in the circumference, than Hudson, but has a jollier demeanor, except when he hears about management violating union rules, and about me being short-changed by the penny-pinching Summerlin. And when he does, out of the now frowning mouth of the union representative, comes, "Thornell, if you don't start filing your overtime pay... and if you do... and Summerlin won't approve it... I'm going to file a grievance on your behalf." "Okay! Okay! I hear you... but give me a little more time... I just passed probation... and I don't want to rock the boat... my boat... yet." "Okay... but make it soon... because I'll be watching."

After several uneventful days—except for including my weekend off—Atlanta releases me to go home. During that 6-hour drive, my mind is on one thing and one thing only, and this time, it's not Kay's, no, it's overtime pay. And with my next check, comes an extra $500. "Holy simollies," I exclaimed out loud and into the ears of technician Carl Mayo who was checking out my transmitter. "Hey Jack, what are you so excited about?" "Carl, I've been in the news business for four and a half years now, and this is my first cent of overtime." "How much is it?" "Five hundred bucks." "Hey, that's a lot of money... want some advice?" "Sure." "Open up a savings account over at the Whitney." "Thanks Carl, I will. I'll do exactly that." And that little green pass book with my name on it, with a $500 deposit recorded in it, becomes a source of pride, but more, a security blanket. And with every dollar added comes a hope that perhaps, just perhaps, there is a place to live, besides the place called—poverty. Like the place still alive down at 503 and still awaiting the return of another failure. Like big brother Garnett. Like middle brother Marshall. Like little brother...

With the little green passbook secure under my pillow, I call, "Makesense, are your ears up?" "Yes cousin." "Then let me ask you something." "Okay." "Are all poor southerners as dumb as the northern media perceives us to be?" "Sorry cousin but Makesense can't answer, because Makesense doesn't participate in dehumanizing. Whether black or white or yellow or north or south. But, you already know that. But still, a curiosity asks, why 'The Dumb' question?" "Okay then, I'll proceed with generalities." "Then, proceed cousin." "Why do some southerners like to do the things they do... like... murdering... beating... maiming... bombing... and... burning. When that's so dumb. And double dumb because it focuses all the world's eyes on the injustices still going on down in Mississippi, and now, over in Alabama. And for every dumb blow the KKK strikes, the fight for civil rights picks up momentum and advances ahead of schedule. So smarten up, and let 'Your Niggers' march and march in that hot summer sun without even turning a head to watch, and what have 'Your Niggers' got at the end of the day, but more blisters, and more worn shoe leather." "But perhaps cousin, all those shockingly evil doings are compounded by more than just the dumb factor, perhaps their fear plays a role." "Makesense, I'm talking dumb, simple dumb, and I'm hearing a compounded 'dumb fear'. Care to elaborate?" "Fear is a powerful motivator cousin. Like if 'Their Niggers' don't occupy the bottom rung of the social and economic ladder, then who will? Perhaps those, labeled as just poor white trash, and where can such trash go, save for 'Their Niggers', but down-down-down to the bottom of the heap. And perhaps cousin, just being one rung up above 'Their Niggers' can afford many a poor soul, trash or not, some degree of comfort. In short cousin, being one rung up, is better'n being one rung down and below every other body in Mississippi. And you know what's so dumb about that way of thinking?" "You got the floor Makesense... so tell me the dumb part?" "Well, if all they're eating is sugar syrup and biscuits, and after getting up and going out and maiming or killing a few of 'Their Niggers', what are they eating when they set back down to their supper table... sugar syrup and biscuits. And that is, dumb, dumb, dumb." And with Makesense's menu selection, I couldn't help but add, "Sugar syrup and biscuits, I know 'em well Makesense... I know 'em well... And perhaps, just perhaps, that's what moved me to murdering all those birds. But, enough of that murder, mayhem and sugar syrup and biscuits, I've had more than my fill... so goodnight Makesense." "Goodnight cousin, and so so sorry for digging up those bad ole days... the ones you'd rather keep buried and..." "And goodnight Rambling Rose!" "Oh! Goodnight cousin."

With thoughts of getting back up to Jackson and Kay dominating every part of me and one part especially, and just when it's arranged, once again fate steps in with another phone call. And another New York Photo editor. And one with a precious ass too-too precious to put out there in the line of fire, whether bullets, bottles or bricks. After all, what would his family do without his precious ass at home every day at 6 p.m. sharp, to discuss the events of the day over dinner. Jesus! I think I would shout hallelujah, if I got just one call from somebody who has been there and done that. And survived.

And what does the voice of inexperience want of me. He wants my big feet back in Alabama, because things are heating up over there. It seems, a white member of the clergy—the Rev. James J. Reeb—a Unitarian from Boston, just age 38, and a volunteer marcher, was clubbed to the ground and critically beaten by five white men shouting abuses at him after taking supper at a negro cafe. Despite an all-night prayer vigil for his recovery, the good reverend instead, passed away, with the restless souls remaining, now becoming even more restless in Selma.

Jesus, I thought, these dumb-dumb dummies are at it again. Not just killing one of 'Their Niggers' but killing a white minister, and a white minister from Boston. Jesus, don't any of you dumb bastards know that all the politically powerful Kennedy's call the Boston area home? And on their Cavalry, the Catholic Kennedys are going to want to raise five crosses, instead of just three. And do you know whose dumb asses?" "How about five guesses... each?"

With the death of Rev. Reeb increasing the determination to get the march going, in Washington on March 15, President Johnson is outlining his proposed "voting rights bill" to congressmen. The following day down in Montgomery, sheriff's deputies, and mounted state troopers wheeling wooden canes send some 500 demonstrators scattering.

Finally, President Johnson meets with Governor Wallace, orders him to back off and to stop all the bullying and beating, and let the march begin. After the meeting and after returning to his Texas ranch, at 1:30 a.m. the following day, President Johnson issues an executive order federalizing some units of the Alabama National Guard, and authorizes the use of the Regular Army units to support them.

With the march back on, I'm back driving those six hours to Selma with a lot of time for thinking this early Saturday morning. And if I was worried the last time I faced Selma, forget about it, for this time I am petrified. Not for the fear of personal injury, but for the fear of personnel. All the people I'll be working with are Yanks. The friendly faces of Hudson and Kelly won't be there to greet me. They claimed fatigue after being assigned there for weeks and weeks. And believe it or not, New York showed mercy by assigning a fresh team, who until now, had only read about or heard about, the down south culture. Calling the shots will be Bill Achatz, a former Marine Corps corporal, who prefers to be referred to now as... General Achatz. Occupying the photo editor's chair in Philadelphia, he often leaves it to go and cover the big stories of the hour wherever that may be. Although I haven't met him, I've heard that the first words out of the mouths of veteran photographers after learning that once again, they'll be working under Achatz is... Ah shit!

And the squad of photographers—besides y'all—are Baltimore's Bill Smith, Pittsburgh's J. Spencer Jones and Harrisburg's Paul Vathis. Vathis snapped, the still famous "Backview" of Presidents Kennedy and Eisenhower as they walked away from the press gallery at Camp David after the Bay of Pigs fiasco. The story goes that when Vathis gets back to the office, he looks for, but doesn't see his "Backview". He asks the editor, but his response is only a ho-hum gesture, so Vathis begins his own search after re-editing rolls and rolls of negatives without success, when he looks down and starts digging through the trash can when he finds where the ho-hum editor had filed it. He takes the negative, prints it, writes a caption, and then, transmits it to newspapers around the globe. And the rest, they say, is history... the trash-canned picture wins the Pulitzer Prize for 1962.

After checking in at the motel, I look into the dining room, see UPI photographer Cary Womack sitting a table full of his comrades, walk over, say hello, and ask if he knows if any of the AP crew is present. Cary smiles, points to a table across the room, and answers, "You see that little guy who's staring over here... that's Achatz." After turning, I see those staring eyes fixed on me, and staying fixed on me until reaching the table, where I said, "I'm Thornell... from New Orleans." Achatz, with his tight-skinned face getting redder and redder and pulling tighter and tighter, cracks, "Thornell! We do not... and I repeat... do not... fraternize with the enemy." Rather than trying to explain that I was only asking for directions, the only words that I could force out were, "Yes sir... yes sir." And then, he sits me down, introduces me to Smith, Jones and Vathis, before setting in on me again. "Thornell... How long you been with the AP... what is it... about six months now?" "Seven." "You hear that men... what we got here is a seven-monther... a premature baby." Above the laughter, again, all I can mouth is, "Yes sir." With his standing, I can see that if he ever wants to look an even five-feet tall, he'll need to tip-toe up to it. And then, looking back down at me, he continues with his belittling, "Kid, you're still wet behind the ears, and you don't have a lick of AP knowhow." "Yes sir." "And just so you know, I didn't ask for you, but New York wanted at least one southern boy on the crew, and that's how you got here." Again, "Yes sir." is all I can muster. Before dismissing me, he orders me to check out the church and take some preparation pictures. Again, "Yes sir." is my reply.

"Geesums Makesense, facing Achatz, I thought I was back in boot camp not knowing my weapon from my gun, and doesn't he remind me of another "Little Corporal" who promoted himself to dictator, instead of general. Well, doesn't he?" "Cousin, you know you know Makesense don't engage in dehumanizing, even of The Master Race." "Okay, okay, then, let me ask about my most puzzling predicament. If I'm such a know-nothing-nitwit, why did the Little General assign me the most important position... marching with the marchers?" "Don't know cousin, but I do know what a puzzling predicament is called." "And what's that?" "A conundrum." A what?" "A co-nun-drum." "Oh Makesense! You surprise me mentioning those things meant for use when you take the "nun" out of those good Catholic girls. And besides, I never use 'em." "Goodnight cousin." "Goodnight Makesense."

And so, from Brown's Chapel, early the afternoon of Sunday March 31, 1965, the great march begins. At its head is Dr. King. At his side, Dr. Ralph Bunche of the United Nations. And behind, is an overall-clad share cropper. Next, a nun, a rabbi, a priest and a lively coed, seemingly with little in common, except purpose: changing the "goings on" down in Alabama.

As the march begins, Smith, Jones, Vathis and I all shoot and ship our film with a motorcycle messenger being shared with UPI, which prompts my thinking... Gee General ain't that collaborating with the enemy? But, my sad story is, I need to have a better today than a worse than bad last night, when my close-ups of King firing up the crowd were—as Achatz pointed out—underexposed and except for two or three frames unprintable. After previewing the film with me, he pushed it towards me and asked, "Do you want it?" and with my barely audible "No sir." having reached his ears, he shows me his back, as he dropped my film directly into a nearby trash can, and concluded his critique with, "You're dismissed Thornell." As I left Achatz's presence, drained of the last ounce of confidence and pride, and headed toward my room, knowing that a good night's rest before the big day, isn't coming, not with Achatz's last choice words... You're dismissed Thornell... Echoing... Echoing... Echoing.

So naturally, once again, fear more than anxiety is driving me this day. And the first image catching my eye and capturing my film showed a little black boy riding the shoulders of a young white man as the march began. Without incident, 3200 marchers cover the first seven miles. No, make that 3201, with that additional one, of course, being the marching me. And not only do I have to keep up, but often I have to jog ahead with cameras bouncing, to get a hilltop vantage. And after they march by, I got to catch up and stay ahead of the leaders, and on and on the cycle goes. And when dusk comes, I drag my exhausted body back to the motel darkroom. And if Achatz, ah-shit, Little Corporal, Big General or Great Dictator announces... You're dismissed, and here is a bus ticket back to New Orleans... I'm gonna kneel right down and kiss his Holiness' feet, before announcing... as soon as I get back to the "Big Easy" I'm converting to Catholicism, because brother this marching is a killer.

But, back in the dark room, I find Achatz in a better frame of mind than the night before. Thus far our exchanges have been limited to his "chastisements" and my "Yes sirs." "Good job today Thornell... especially the shoulder riding boy... it's filling the front page of The New York Daily New's early edition." Finally, for the first time in his presence, a smile finds my face. And when he sees it, he quickly removes it with, "Don't rest on your laurels... because tomorrow there's another front page and be damned if we'll let UPI find it."

On day two, the number of marchers is reduced to a cadre of 300 according to a court agreement. The group is dwarfed by 1860 federalized Alabama National guardsmen, numerous U.S. marshals, about 250 FBI agents and two military police battalions from North Carolina and Texas. Helicopters buzz overhead, while soldiers guard crossroads, and demolition experts search under bridges lying ahead.

And today's first obvious picture is of a one-legged marcher trying to keep up on his crutches, and so I shoot a half a roll showing his determination. An hour or so and four or so rolls of film later, I meet up with the messenger at the same time UPI's Womack does. Hurriedly, we strip our cameras and our pockets to put our film into shipping envelopes when the messenger bends down, picks up a roll and asks, "Who dropped this?" Checking my envelope, I say, "I don't think it's mine." "So it must be mine," Womack claims as he snaps up the stray film and puts it in with his shipment.

The next morning as I check in at the darkroom before joining the marchers, I find Achatz on the phone, and he's saying, "Look! I've gone over every frame three times now...and I didn't miss it... it's just not here. We don't have it." It didn't seem possible that Achatz's drawn face could get any redder than the day he stared me down, but I discover today that I was wrong. But then today, he's firing from the defensive position, and not the offensive. After leaning close to the darkroom technician Bill Gory, I whisper, "What's going on?" "Oh Achatz is catching hell for not having a picture of a marcher on crutches... it seems UPI is in print everywhere with it."

With my heart skipping a beat, then two... three... four, my mind flashes back to the dropped roll of film and realizing that it had to be mine, all I can do, is check myself from shouting out... Ah shit! Ah shit! Ah shit!

A few minutes later, Smith, Jones and Vathis join us and we all stand facing a raving Achatz. "How the hell did all of you miss this picture?" With that question unsettled, and unsettling, because I know that Smith passed on taking "This Picture" when he saw me in position doing just that. Thankfully, he held his breath, as did Jones and Vathis. And the lesson I learned this day was when a photographer is facing a disgruntled photo editor, he or she never points the finger at a brother photographer, because tomorrow's finger may be pointing back at you, when your back's against the wall.

And so after day two, what General Achatz never knew... it was my picture of the man on crutches marching across the nation's front pages with the defining UPI logo under it. And where's my honor? Why didn't I be a man? Why didn't I step up and fess up? Apparently, I wasn't the nitwit perceived, because General, I was smart enough to know that after this—my second fuckup—became known, you would have put me against the wall and shout, "Thornell, you're fired."

Worried that day three may well be my last, I shoot pictures and pictures, moving and stationary... people shaving, cooking, eating, praying and foot rubbing, until the march gets underway. About a mile down the road, I look ahead to the next hill and see the possibility of a good picture, and perhaps, "The Picture". After running ahead, I take up a position behind the military police Jeep parked and facing the oncoming marchers. With a 200 mm lens on my Nikon, I frame the procession through the Jeep's windshield and wait, wait, wait until the CLICK, CLICK, CLICK sounds as the procession reaches the perfect place. Immediately after, I unload and carefully put the roll of film into an envelope and ship it. And then, I march on through a torrential downpour before ending day three 10-miles farther down the road.

On the fourth morning, the news from Achatz is good, and he even seems taller—maybe an even 5-foot—as he announces, "We swept the play today. The picture through the windshield is showing everywhere. The Daily News spread it across two pages." While he doesn't single me out as the shooter, he does throw me a rather pleasant look for all of two seconds. With the others rushing out to get breakfast, I lay back and face Achatz and ask, "You mind if I see the picture?" Looking over to lab tech Gory, he says, "Bill, show Thornell the print." And when he complies, I see it's not just a good picture, it is... "The Picture".

As I'm entering the dining room, UPI photo editor Gary Haines, out of Atlanta, grabs my arm and pulls me over. And as I am looking back to make sure Achatz isn't in sight, he says, "Jack, you've really been killing us. Would you consider coming to work for us?" "Oh, Gary, thanks for the stroking, but Achatz is right behind me and if he sees me talking to you, it's my ass." "That Achatz is something. Really something. But please consider it, because we'd love to put your ass to work for us." And what I didn't say was... "Gary, I did work for you, although anonymously, just the other day and didn't you notice how UPI swept the play?" And someday, after I'm long retired and if I ever write a book, then you and Achatz can read all about the day I scooped myself with my own picture on the famous Selma march.

Well, that over-burst of confidence lasted until I stepped back onto the highway, knowing that today, more than others, UPI will be gunning for me, and so naturally, fear and anxiety reoccupy those reserved spaces within me. Sixteen miles and rolls and rolls of exposed film later, the march is making camp on the outskirts of Montgomery, to rest up and to prepare for the finale on the steps of the State Capitol come morning.

And the following is the writing of the Associated Press' veteran reporter W.C. "Bill" Crider who was among the wounded at the Ole Miss riots...

The air was more Summer than Spring, with a threat of rain in the heavy air, as the colossal parade wound its way toward the Alabama Capitol. Overnight, the Army's ranks swelled up to 25,000. There was a glow of camaraderie about them as they stood before The Grand Ole Building, and a glow of accomplishment, as though the world were somehow better for their aching feet. After two hours of speeches and songs, the man they all came to hear finally arose. Martin Luther King did not disappoint them.

He called for more marches—on ballot boxes, segregated schools, poverty, "Until race baiters disappear from the political arena." He lifted the crowd to a peak with repeated promises that, "The hour of justice was not far off," and concluded in an oratorical crescendo:

"Glory Hallelujah! Glory Hallelujah! Glory Hallelujah! Glory Hallelujah!"

And the great march to Montgomery had ended. As night fell, a steady stream of cars moved along Route 80 carrying demonstrators back to Selma. One of the volunteer drivers was a 39-year-old Detroit housewife, Viola Gregg Liuzzo, the mother of five children. Mrs. Liuzzo took one carload to Selma, turned around and started back to Montgomery for more. With her was a 19-year-old negro barber from Selma, LeRoy Morton. Exhilarated by the day's events, neither was unduly concerned about the car they noticed following them. Together they joined in singing "We shall overcome".

As Mrs. Liuzzo rounded a slight curve on a lonely stretch of highway flanked by moss-hung trees, a car pulled alongside and the crack of gunfire split the night silence. The car lurched into a ditch. Mrs. Liuzzo slumped over, blood spurting from her temple. Morton, paralyzed with fear, hid on the floor of the car, then crept out and dashed down the highway toward Selma. He managed to hitchhike a ride, then blurted his story breathlessly to a Selma policeman. Sirens screamed back down the highway, but when they got there Mrs. Liuzzo was dead.

Mrs. Liuzzo was dead but her death did not blur, only more sharply defined, the symbolic victory sketched by a protest demonstration unmatched in the history of the negro revolution. Tens of thousands had taken part, three had died, and millions had watched its unfolding on television. The aim was to pry a federal voting rights bill from the conscience of America. In the aftermath of the great march, it did not seem possible this could be denied.

With the march ended, the FBI, the marshals, the military and the press disperses rapidly. And I mean rapidly. My northern counterparts, Smith, Jones and Vathis, along with Achatz, rush to the airport leaving me to transmit the last few pictures. Achatz had decreed that everybody could leave save one. And that one was southern boy me. Naturally, his thinking had to be... all these deep south "goings on" were because of dumb people just like me. And naturally, my say in the decision making isn't a consideration, unless you consider, "Yes sir." a say.

At first light, you will find me taking pictures of the death car, with its rearview mirror reflecting The Old Jefferson Davis Highway. A road just traveled, traveled with purpose: For life... For liberty... For justice. And for others, Mrs. Liuzzo surrenders all three.

And despite her noble death, an attitude of Alabama justification arises. From street corners... bar stools... and grocery store aisles, the justification usually begins with the question... What in damnation was a white woman doing down here alone in a car with a young black buck? What was she thinking? And we all know what the fuck that was. And, ain't she got a husband back up there in Detroit City? And, ain't she got five kids needing caring? So, what is that nigger loving bitch doing here in the first place, but getting what she asked for, getting what she deserved, from the decent folk of Alabama?

But, there were some southern born descent folk who strongly disagreed with that Alabama mentality. And among their leaders are none other than President Johnson, who on March 26, 1965, declared war on the Ku Klux Klan, after announcing the arrest of four Klansmen in the death of Mrs. Liuzzo.

The Selma story was the first time I had been part of a large team effort. Usually, I'm the Lone Ranger with a Tonto always on vacation, so the long drive back to New Orleans supplies me with time to reflect on the lessons learned. First: Never rat out on a fellow photographer because you could be next. Two: Learn the proper exposure for black people in a dark church. Three: Never stand by while your film is being put into a UPI envelope. Four: Don't complain about being the only one ordered to take every step of a 50-mile trek, unless you want to hear "double time". Five: And if you happen to crack three vertebra while double-timing to the perfect vantage with all that heavy gear bouncing, and bouncing, and bouncing, who's counting. Six: And if you ever work for a former corporal, salute as if he's a four-star general. No, better make that five.

In a nutshell, the Associated Press photographer is… just a means to an end to get "The Picture", and if the end comes while he's getting it, by all means roll over that body, secure and ship "The Picture", so those New York Photo execs can have something to celebrate during that two-martini lunch break.

No sooner than returning to New Orleans, I'm leaving for Bogalusa, a smelly paper-mill town, a KKK stronghold, and a place where black and white temperaments are at a crossroads. There, the negroes, who make up 35 percent of the population, are marching for better jobs and marching against public segregation. On April 9, jeering and cursing white youths attack a march by throwing a brick, striking, and seriously injuring a 19-year old negro. And come Saturday morning, the blacks are marching toward city hall. The KKK is marching away from city hall. A head-on calamity is imminent. But, at the last possible second, as if God is directing traffic, an intersecting parallel spur appears and the tommy-gun toting state troopers divert the Klan and avoid the collision.

And if that close call wasn't tumultuous enough, after Bogalusa's first black deputy named O'Neal Moore got his head blown off by a shotgun blast, the negro community decides to fight firepower with firepower, and calls in a group of negro vigilantes called the Deacons for Defense and Justice. And why more tumultuous? The Deacons got guns. The KKK got guns. The lawmen got guns. And the makings for a new calamity—a shootout—are in place and fermenting.

A white deputy, who was investigating the Moore murder, is shot at. Two shots ring out wounding a white man in the neck and chest after a marching negro girl is hit with a bottle. The Klan gets so bold as to stage a night rally, put Klan garments on their toddlers, and invite the press to take pictures. When the warring parties seem to be taking a time-out, I'd return to New Orleans, only to return at 2 a.m. the next morning when shots ring out in a black neighborhood.

This particular morning the blacks are picketing a shopping center, when a white barber interrupts a haircut, goes out to hose down his big window and a passing mustached white picketer after lathering him up with a bar of soap as his customers he-hawed him on in the background. That beauty rates another page in Life Magazine with Wide World Photos getting the credit and the money, and not Jack R. Thornell. It was never understandable why AP writers get their by-lines over mediocre stories and under great pictures the photographers get AP wirephoto or Wide World Photo credits. And doesn't that practice just about confirm the appraised value of the "means to an end" photographer. But of course, one must also consider the flip side of a coin. And that side says… Dear reader, if the photographer gets deprived of life while pursuing "The Picture", you can save your tears, cause you never heard of him.

Finally, back at my desk, I find the company's monthly newsletter, announcing the national non-cliché picture of the month… Selma marchers framed through a Jeep windshield. And naturally, with positive news, my mind always poses a counter-negative. For instance, did word of my fuck-up—the King close-ups—travel up to New York Photos. So, over in Selma, was I… the goat or the hero? But, that agonizing question doesn't need answering, because everybody knows from experience, that news of fuckups always travel faster and farther than success stories. And, are so much more enjoyable over two-martini lunches.

And from all that Alabama overtime pay, for all those 16, 17, 18-hour days, comes the cash purchase of a light green 1965 Chevelle Malibu Supersport with white bucket seats. And forget about those wearing me down four on the floor gear boxes, because this baby is automatic.

A week later, with Mrs. Liuzzo now resting in a Michigan cemetery, I get my final reward... a check of $100 for "The Picture" of the historic Selma march.

Bourdier, the photographer turned photo editor, is tiring of his 9 to 5, primarily because it never brings in a dime of overtime. And with alimony and child support to pay, he's finding it hard to pay his New York bills, and still go out to eat. And when a revolution flares up in the Dominican Republic, he volunteers to put his Cajun ass back into the line of fire.

While Bourdier is heading for Santo Domingo, I'm heading up to Jackson, not to see Kay, but to see Carolyn for a face to face. After calling last night, she said she has got to see me and see me right away. And after refusing to tell me why or even give me a clue, and when I started pressing her for more, she just hung up the phone in record time.

During the drive up, there aren't twenty questions popping into my head, only one. Has she found out about me seeing Kay? Carolyn knew Kay and Kay knew Carolyn. Both had exchanged pleasantries at parties. And the history of my dating both, they knew. But, what Carolyn didn't know was the depth and the intensity of my feelings for Kay. Had those been measured by the sheer volume of my—defined by me as love perpetuated—jealous rages, and had they compared notes, then Carolyn would have Kay to be ahead by four to one in abuse— defined by me as love—points alone. Oh Makesense, I'd prefer two conundrums to this one unnerving uncertainty.

After arriving at the apartment, Carolyn meets me at the door. I could tell she'd been crying, and when I leaned in to give her a hug, instead of hearing, "We're history," I hear history in the making. "Oh Jack, I'm pregnant... What are we going to do?" And with her tears comes my never to be said ever words, "I guess we'll have to get married." With Carolyn's body going limp in my arms, and with me going into a state of shock, the second guessing begins... Why did I say those "get married" words so hastily... Was it just a slip of the tongue... Wasn't there another alternative??? And immediately, my mind takes me back to Germany... to Wally... to the abortion... and to the guilt. Then, I had my answer... never again. "How soon can we get married?" Carolyn asked. "How far along are you?" "Over two months now." "Where do we get hitched?" "Back home in West Point." "Okay, then, call your mother, get her to arrange for a church and a preacher." And with those words spoken, Carolyn squeezes me tightly, straightens her sagging body, and says, "Oh Jack, you've made me happy... so happy."

With our state of affairs seemingly settled, Carolyn's state of happy doesn't last long, not when ole green eyes raises its head, and some disturbing questions. "Jesus Carolyn! What was I thinking... Maybe I jumped the gun... because you know I didn't ask the critical question." "And what is that?" "Are you sure... absolutely sure... this is my baby?" "Yes Jack... I'm sure... absolutely sure... it's your baby." "Yea! But you're saying it don't make it so... Hell... marvelous Mike could've been right here on this sofa the nights I'm over in Selma." "No Jack, he hasn't... I haven't seen him." "Bet he called though, didn't he?" And with her slight hesitation, I already knew her answer. "He did call... but just to say hello... we only talked a few minutes." "Son of a bitch! Son of a bitch! I knew that bastard wasn't done with you... or you with him... He just won't let go... will he?" "Jack! Jack! I've told you and told you it's over between Mike and me." "Yea baby... you're saying it... but is the fat lady singing? I'm not so sure." And with that unsettling conclusion coming just short of neutralizing my proposal, with Carolyn crying, with my, "I'll call you in a day or so," and with three hours of a self-directed, grueling and most torturous third degree still facing me, I drive away and back towards New Orleans.

"Makesense! Makesense! Your ears up?" "Up Cousin." "I know you don't discuss women things… but this is a marriage thing… and there's troubling, troubling, troubling questions." "Question on Cousin." "Where did that spontaneous marriage proposal come from? Was I out of my skull or what?" "Perhaps Cousin, the best way to give the right answer to a most difficult question is to do it spontaneously." "And why so?" "Because Cousin, the more you think on it, the more likely you'll come up with the justification for the wrong answer. Right is right dear Cousin, and right will always be right no matter how long you think on it." "Oh Makesense, but what do I know about fatherhood? What did I learn from always gone Daddy Ben or Crazy Uncle John, except the Thornell philosophy… let somebody else get off the porch, get a job, make some money, and feed those hungry kids, because setback's my game. So Makesense, with that fatherhood history, what words of wisdom can you impart on me?" "The same as before Cousin. Life goes on, grass grows and needs attention." "Jesus Makesense! I'm now facing the burdensome responsibility of feeding, clothing, and housing a wife and feeding, clothing and raising a child, and all you can impart on me is that some'o, same'o grass roots philosophy?"

"Yep, and instead of goodnight Cousin, let me say, keep those eyes open and on the highway." "Well finally, there's some advice worth taking."

Early the next morning, having come to terms with my responsibility and knowing that another abortion is not, not, not, a consideration, I ease Carolyn's mind with a call instructing her to get on with the wedding plans.

Now, with the probability of a wedding announcement coming in a few days, a matter of more urgency overtakes and overcomes me. And it's Kay! Kay! Kay! I've got to see her. I've got to be with her. I've got to fuck her one more time. So, I call her, set up a date, pick her up, wine and dine her and take her to my bed like the two times before. And where is my conscious? The same place as hers. And certainly not in the bed between us. And when our lovemaking's done, do I come clean? Most certainly not. Why ruin a wonderful climax to a long and past rocky romance? And after dropping her off at her mother's door, I drive away thinking… Dear Kay, tonight I really stuck it to you… in more ways than that enjoyable one… and guess what… sorry, I'm not.

Two days later, Carolyn exits the Electric Building, walks across the street, enters the newspaper, takes the stairs and enters the society department. There, she faces Kay. And the immaculately dressed and groomed Carolyn says, "I have a wedding announcement." And Kay's reaction? Is it shattering? Is it devastating? I can only imagine, because I certainly couldn't quiz Carolyn, but I surmised, that during their encounter both ladies acted like ladies. And the date set for the blessed, but past due, event is June 4, 1965.

Meanwhile, down in the Dominican Republic, Cajun Bourdier is reborn, not just with "The Picture" but with "The Pictures". The first shows a dressed for school teenage boy bending double with the nervous soldier who shot him still pointing the rifle. The second, an older demonstrator lifting the bloodied arm of the fallen lad. The third, other demonstrators hoisting and carrying the body away from the Presidential Palace. And with the sound of a single shot, Buddy Bourdier has had his day, his month, and his career.

And while hero Bourdier is basking in glory and thinking… Pulitzer, I'm wallowing in worry and thinking… After I'm singled out as goat, goat, goat, and fired, then all roads lead back to Mother's mouth and 503. And what will the first words out of baby's mouth be? Dada? Mama? Not likely. With Mother's profanity penetrating every wall, most likely, the choice words will be… Mother fucker. But then, that scenario is contingent on Carolyn ever spending the first night down there, and not running back up to West Point screaming to family and friends… You'll never believe where Jack took me to live.

And with that worrisome scenario playing over and over in my head, it's reminiscent of some old warning about worrying your way into something worse, and sure enough, the worse came with, "Thornell, pick up line two." "Hello." "Jack, this is Pat McDonald, New York Photos." "Yes sir." "I need you down in Santo Domingo." "I thought Bourdier was there." "He is, but I'm pulling him back to San Juan, Puerto Rico, to handle the daily transmissions because phone lines back there are terrible and almost impossible to get." With my phone hand shaking, with my nerves pulsating to Morse code levels, with the deputy News Photo director holding, and with the patented answer expected is, "Yes sir and how soon," instead my answer is, "Mr. McDonald I got a problem." "And what problem is that?" "I'm getting married." "When?" "In just two weeks." "Then there's no problem." "And why is that?" "It's pretty rough down there and we'll be rotating photographers in and out every week, so get your gear together." "Yes sir, but let me tell you the other problem." "And what is that?" "My girlfriend's three-months pregnant and we can't delay the wedding… not any longer." "Don't sweat it. I'll get you back in time… plenty of time." "And what do I take besides film and cameras?" "Complete darkroom, transmitter… everything." "Okay then, I'll get started with reservations." "When you confirm them, let me know so I can advise Bourdier." "Yes sir."

After hanging up the phone, I realize the question begging to be asked before sending somebody to a war zone is… Jack, just how much Spanish do you understand? And Mr. McDonald, my patented answer would have been… Si… Tequila… Siesta. And now Mr. McDonald, I have a question or two, like how do I respond to a nervous soldier pointing his rifle at me and saying in Spanish, "Stop Gringo, put your hands up, or I will shoot." When the only word I understood was "Gringo". And, haven't you seen Bourdier's great pictures of the teenage kid being gunned down, despite being fluent in Spanish? And what about Carolyn's worry? If daddy gets killed, who's left holding an illegitimate baby? Just Carolyn. And let's make the last question more personal, if you were getting married in two weeks, would you care to squeeze in a bloody revolution between week one and week two? And why didn't I ask Mr. Deputy Newsphoto Director any one of those most pertinent questions? Because as unwavering as he was, with his decision to send me and just me, I knew he would have considered any such second guessing from a just past probation green horn as totally impertinent. And, wasn't it decided early on—a nitwit—I wasn't.

After making the flight reservations, I call Carolyn with the news. "Jack! You're covering what! A war! With our wedding just two weeks off, couldn't you just say no?" "Hey! I know this is upsetting, but when New York calls it's just like God calling. And you don't say no unless you want to risk getting swallowed up, so, what can I do, but go." "But aren't people getting killed?" "Yes Baby, but just the natives. Don't worry. I'll be okay. I'll be working with

Bourdier." "Oh Jack, be careful." "I will. And I'll be back in plenty of time… Mr. McDonald promises."

With just two weeks until Carolyn and I are to begin our married lives, and with five very large—so large you need to be a weight lifter to lift 'em—cases, I'm off to cover my first revolution moving at a slow snail's pace. And what I'll be facing is not just one, but two coups d'état already in motion. And, with President Johnson having declared, "American lives are in danger," waiting to greet me are the 24,000 troops, including Marines and the 82nd Airborne.

After landing the first hurdle is customs. Try keeping up with the line while moving five pieces with only two hands, because porters aren't allowed inside the custom's zone. And when finally, you face the luggage inspector, and he tries to open everything, it's difficult to say no, you'll ruin the light sensitive photographic paper. Particularly, with his contingent of mean ass nervous looking machine gun toting soldiers standing by and eyeing my every move. And with the transmitter, with all its dials, switches and spinning drum, out of its case, with them looking down at it and then back up at me, it was obvious their initial thinking is… Gringo spy. "Prenza Associata! Prenze Associata! Associated Press! Associated Press!" I repeated in a friendly, but firm voice until finally they motioned me through. After, apparently concluding… even a stupid Gringo spy wouldn't be so backbreakingly obvious. And my conclusion is… if I can survive customs, I can survive a revolution.

In the lobby, Bourdier greets and introduces me to the taxi driver Bienvinito, hired to shuttle around the writer out of Mexico City, who of course, is Spanish speaking. After filling the trunk and the whole back seat with all of my cases and after noticing how low the back of his aging American car is sitting, he says, "Mr. Jim, all this weight not good for Bienvinito's rear end." And with a smile forming, I add, "Nor for mine… Bienvinito… Nor for mine."

During the ride to the hotel, Bourdier fills me in on the dos and don'ts of the revolution. "Jack, you can shoot a lot of good features of the American military near the hotel. But, when you venture out, make sure Bienvinito is driving you. He knows the safe from the unsafe neighborhoods. You can get shot by snipers from any one of three sides." "Geesums! This sounds like Bogalusa and the crossfires of the Klan, the Black Deacons and the police." Now laughing, he adds, "After a day or two here, you'll probably prefer the madness of Bogalusa." "Yea, and there at least, I could understand the language." "Oh, and one more thing, you'll have to put your film on a daily 2 p.m. shuttle to San Juan." "Hey, if you're not in San Juan now, who is?" "Achatz." "Ah shit!" "Oh that's right, you worked under him on The Big March." "Yea, I worked under him, way under, that's for sure."

The El Continental, a sprawling eight story hotel, is surrounded by thousands of American GI's, dug in and manning howitzer and machine gun positions. Part of LBJ's force to protect the Americans staying here, I surmised. Once checked in, and with all my cases stowed, I turn to Bourdier and ask, "How much film do you have for the 2 o'clock flight?" "None… I've been busy picking you up." "Ah shit! Knowing Achatz and with Achatz knowing I'm here, he'll blame me for not having pictures." "Screw Achatz." "That's easy for you to say, because you're still in the hero category. Why don't I run down and shoot a couple of rolls and get 'em on that flight?" "Go ahead. I'll be having lunch, and then we can hookup and make a run to the airport." "Okay, fine."

Apparently there had been showers for the past several days, because the encampment is littered with large mud puddles. My first picture catches a GI, with his mess kit in hand, jumping a puddle with his reflection in the water. It's a beauty. And when I identify the soldier as being from Philadelphia, it becomes more beautiful because that's General Achatz's hometown. And there's nothing that pleases him more than pleasing his Pennsylvania newspapers with pictures of hometown boys. After exposing two rolls, Bourdier and I reunite, rush to the airport and ship my film. And the picture of the puddle jumping GI splashes across many front pages.

The next day, I'm up early shooting so Bourdier can take my film with him on the afternoon shuttle. I'm nervous about being left here alone, but I'm relieved that Achatz is leaving. There's this fear I can't shake, and that is, the Little General would love firing my ass more than he loves eating southern fried chicken. As for Bourdier, he's more photographer than editor, and at least he's been on the firing lane, while the generals like Achatz and those in New York always keep those precious asses back at the rear where the risk of it becoming a sniper's target isn't even imagined. Now, for Bourdier, like with Achatz, the only risk in San Juan is falling asleep on one of those beautiful sand beaches and getting a sunburn. And what would I love more than all the fried chicken in the world? Jesus! Just to be more like Bourdier. Because, after living through a horrendous day, and after a hot shower, he can go out and enjoy dinner and wine, with or without the women. And with tomorrow's worries, only tomorrow's worries, and never tonight's. Yea! Bourdier! If you're faking it, you've got a backup career waiting for you back in New Orleans… playing the Brando role in Street Car.

With day one down, and with only six to go to finish out my week here, I shoot and ship, shoot and ship. Pictures of our soldiers pointing rifles. Their soldiers pointing rifles. The civilians pointing rifles. On day two, much of the same. Then, on day three, comes… Action. A heavily armed military force from the OAS—Organization of American States—moves in to take control of the sniper laden heart of the city. Behind them, with every raised head a potential target, I move firing my Nikons at will. When they drop, I drop. When they move on, I move on. And then, I see a good picture, but I must move and put myself between the OAS and the sniper position. And the only thing moving me forward is fear. Because with me, since going to work for the Associated Press, the fear of missing "The Picture" always trumps the fear of getting killed. And soon now, when the only person standing between a wife and a child and poverty is me, the question is… Will that fear be tripled??? Especially when the choice of a sniper's bullet or a return to 503 isn't a choice… Not for me.

After shooting the desired picture, I freeze in place as the OAS troops rush past me and into the nearby buildings. After securing them one by one, it's reported that the snipers fled through rear exits, rather than fire a single shot at their Latino brothers coming from Brazil, Costa Rica, Honduras, Nicaragua, and Paraguay. And was the desired picture of the advancing troops waving a large OAS flag and taking up a defensive position in front of a bullet riddled building worth the exposure. Newspapers coast to coast thought so, according to a note from Bourdier.

Days four, five, six and seven pass with my shooting and shipping continuing on and on. And still, there's no sign of a replacement. Attempting to get a call through to New York or even San Juan, is a waste of time. And if I could get Mr. McDonald on the line, what could I say except… You're a lying bastard. Because, there's no way he can just say… Sorry, Jack… I forgot about the wedding. Not after all the nitty-gritty I laid on him… The stuff great gossip is made of… The stuff you pass around the office… The stuff you don't forget… after a week, a month, a year… Ever.

And so, what to do? What to do? And what do I do but keep on shooting and shipping, with the wedding date getting closer and closer and with pressure of both growing and growing, until relief is a must. And then I remember what Bourdier had said… Anything you need, just ask Bienvinito. And on the morning of day twelve, I approach him and say, "Amigo, I need a senorita." "What kind you like Mr. Jack?" "Pretty, young, clean." "When you need?" "Tonight… about nine." "I send her up." As I handed him a twenty, I jokingly ask, "Bienvinito, if my girlfriend calls with me still in bed with the senorita, and asks, what are you doing? What do I say?" "The truth Mr. Jack." "Tell her I'm doing a pretty senorita? Are you crazy!" "No, no, she'll laugh. Think you make joke, because you not so crazy." However, as I weighed his crazy, but funny answer, I know any such call is not only unlikely, it's most likely, impossible, with every phone in the country fucked up. "Okay Bienvinito, take me for a ride, so I can shoot and ship."

That evening, while anxiously anticipating a knock at my door, I stretch out on the bed and try to relax, while rereading a Today's note from Bourdier. It said… Keep the film coming. We're sweeping the play. And New York is pleased, very pleased. And with my body tensing, I'm thinking… Bourdier, instead of this bouquet of pleases, why haven't you sent over my replacement? You too knew of my wedding date. So why haven't you prodded New York? Hell, as the reigning hero of the hour, surely they'll listen to you and send in a fresh warm body, and let this tired and stressed ass go home.

And before completing my not so pleasing tirade against buddy Bourdier, comes a knock knock at my door. And before my feet can hit the floor, I realize that I'm already up and ready to meet up with my whore.

A senorita she is. But pretty, she's not. Beautiful, with skin lighter than dark, she is, as I offer her a cold beer. With her "Si" and after a few swallows, I discover she speaks a little English, but very little. And that's good, I thought, because conversation isn't an issue. Only relief, and more specifically, my relief. So with our beers down, I take her hand and lead her over to bed, just like the obedient Kay did those nights back at the Sun'N'Sand. And as usual, I'm barely in her, before I'm out of her and done. And within seconds, not minutes, my state of horny is replaced with a state of relief. And what's most unusual is, when she moves to get up I reach over, take her hand, and surprisingly say, "Stay… not go," as I point down at the bed, and then to the pillow while saying, "You sleep here… with me. All night." And with her beautiful smile growing until it sounded into laughter, she pulls me close, until I could feel her head nodding against my breasts… Yes, yes, yes. And I knew I could fuck her again, or not, and in the morning her smile would return just as beautiful, without judgment and more important, without questions of family or home. Because her only interest lies with that beautiful money. Unable to sleep, just lying there with my hands joining under my head, I'm thinking… Everybody in the world gets fucked… the senorita by me… Me by New York… And you my dearest Carolyn, by both.

After looking over at my sleeping beauty, after checking my watch, and finding it's almost 3 a.m., and still unable to shut my brain down, I summon Makesense. "Your ears up

138

Cousin?" "Up Cousin." "You've witnessed most all of my years of stress and worry, haven't you?" "Most all Cousin." "Okay, then, the other day when I stood up out there in no man's land and put my butt in jeopardy, was that mental stress or physical stress?" "Makesense felt both, a lot of both." "And was I trying to go get "The Picture"… get shot… or both?" And before Makesense can respond, a most unusual sound—the ringing of a telephone—draws my hand to the receiver.

"Hello" "Oh Jack, is that you?" "It's me." "Oh! I've been so worried. I've been calling and calling for days, but I couldn't get through." "Yea! The phones have been out." "Oh Jack! Why aren't you back?" "Looks like New York forgot about me… on purpose." "And what about the wedding?" "Well, it's already Friday, and there is no way I can get there by tomorrow." "Oh Jack! What are we going to do?" "Postpone until next Saturday. And I'll be there, with or without this job… I promise." And with my declaration of intent calming her, she asks, "What are you doing?" "You mean right now?" "Yes." "Sleeping with a beautiful senorita… what else?" And with the sounds of her nervous laughter reaching my ears, just as Bienvinito had predicted, I quickly add, "Carolyn! It's 3 a.m… I'm in bed… trying to get some sleep." And with me thinking… and that's the truth, the whole truth, and nothing but, including the truth of this beautiful butt beside me… The phone goes dead.

With my Saturday shipment to Bourdier, I included my SOS: I missed my own wedding today. It is rescheduled for next Saturday. I must be present. Please notify New York.

And on Tuesday, my replacement arrives. And it's Bourdier. Hell, no wonder—I'm thinking—he didn't go to bat for me for fear that his Cajun ass might be put back into the line of fire. Actually though, things are easing up after the OAS collected weapons and the warring parties agreed to a meditation. The US Marines began pulling out on June 6. And all that was left for Bourdier is to shoot a few mop up photos, before he too will be heading home. And that now is Miami.

On the way to the airport for my return, the state of poverty of this so-called banana republic, reaches in the car and grabs me. It's everywhere. It's overwhelming. And it's worrisome. Because earlier, while facing my own seemly overwhelming situation, I was too absorbed by it to even notice what was staring back at me. And shouldn't that be unforgiveable for someone like me, an expert on poverty and its accompaniment of shame that continuously plays on and on even after the poverty is gone. My war here ended today, but theirs continues… It's called the war for survival—food and water and shelter. And it's one hell of a motivator for the killing to continue and continue and continue and…

On the plane, flying back to the land of plenty, where the poorest, like Mother, can draw food stamps now. And she's not too proud to get 'em or to use 'em, no matter who may be looking. But, that who won't be me. Because, if she asks me to take her to the grocery, I disappear before she presents them to the checkout person. I suppose though, during those sugar, syrup and biscuits and less years, had we had 'em, I would have grown up liking 'em. But I didn't and now, even the thought of using a single one of them food stamps turns my stomach upside down, quicker than air sickness.

"Geesums Makesense!" "Yes Cousin." "At 30,000 feet hadn't I better shut up about air sickness?" "Unless Cousin, you want to witness an embarrassment more sickening than the thought of food stamps brings up." "Right on… so… let's take a nap and give poverty… killing… and the thought of air sickness a rest." "Nap on Cousin… nap on."

After another back breaking getting thorough customs experience, I take all the equipment back to the office, check in, and Chief of Bureau Summerlin gives me the weekend off. And at first, I chalked it off to him just being in a generous mood, even though he owed me for hundreds of unpaid hours. And there, I thought, his generosity is the result of a surge of sympathy running through his bones. After all, he had experienced all the complications of wedlock. And then, I looked at the posted work schedule, and saw that I was already scheduled the weekend off. And so, what else is there to think about such a cheap C.O.B. except, drop the "C" and add an "S" once again.

And the first order of business is for me to purchase a first class suit of clothes. I had owned one sport coat during my army years, but before that, only zipper jackets. Like the one I wore to my—and oh how I hate to call him—my father's funeral. And I find a nice dark blue inexpensive one, because after I'm married it'll just hang in the closet, because dark blue suits can get ruined on one dirty assignment.

On Thursday morning, there was a note waiting for me to call Mr. McDonald in New York Photos. And so, I pick up the phone and dial. "Hello, this is Thornell." "Oh, Hello Jack, I'm glad you're back. I'm sorry I forgot all about the wedding. But let me say that you did a great job down there. So go and enjoy your wedding." "Thank you sir." And after he hung up with that "I forgot" lie still hot on his tongue, I have a question still sizzling on the tip of mine. And it is this… If I had gotten killed during my second week there Mr. McDonald, the week I was supposed to be back home getting married Mr. McDonald, would you have expressed your regrets to: A not quite bride, a not quite widow, or a still quite pregnant Carolyn.

Thursday evening on my way to West Point, I stop off in Jackson to meet with William Peart, the political reporter and my best man. After he answers the door, I greet him with, "Hello Mr. Pert." And immediately, before even saying hello, he corrects me with. "Peart… P-E-A-R-T." And I follow up with, "Bill, I did some research and found out why being called Pert is so offensive to you." "And why is that Mr. Cornball?" "Because Pert means impudent and sounds like impotent and with your prematurely all-gray hair, you're so damn worried that someone may confuse the two. You can't stand it and thus, your automatic correction, "That's bull Thornell, hell, you named me the best man didn't you?" And with our laughter getting louder, we're joined by his new wife Joanne. And Bill quickly adds, "If you're still confused about the two, just ask Joanne, and she'll straighten you out. Impudent maybe, but impotent, never."

While I'm trying to apologize for tying up a second weekend, Bill stops me, asks me to turn around, and says, "I don't see any bullet holes so I suppose it's okay to get married… that is… if you used the proper protection down there in the land of inexpensive senoritas. No telling what a careless fellow can catch." And before, having to lie about or having to confess to being a careless and condom free fellow, Joanne returns to the room with coffee and cookies to free me from answering. After coffee and after discussing the wedding timetable, I excuse myself to continue on to West Point.

Once in the car and heading northeast, Makesense butts in. "Cousin, aren't you driving over to Vicksburg to pick up your mother?" "Makesense, you know I'm not. And you know that she doesn't even know there is a wedding." "And what about Marshall, Garnett and the rest of the family… aren't they invited?" "No! No! and No!" "So you will be the only Thornell present?" "Yes! And count that as a blessing… you want me to be humiliated by Mother's mouth… no thank you Makesense." "And when will you introduce your new wife to the family?" "Later, much later, when I'm forced to Makesense, when I'm forced to."

Mrs. Wilson has moved her boys into a white-shingled house in town. And to get to it, I must drive past the sprawling Bryan Meat Packing plant. And with it coming up on my right, I can't help but connect it to something Peart said. And yes, had I been a careful fellow and had I been packaged properly, Carolyn wouldn't be pregnant and I wouldn't be getting married Saturday. And perhaps, never. But, because of a night late and a condom short, a lifetime of responsibility, is about to be laid on me. "And Makesense, if that's the least bit funny, why don't I feel like smiling, instead of crying?"

Carolyn wore a white two-piece suit and I wore my new dark blue, as we stood in front of the Methodist minister. And with every word—love, honor, cherish, obey, faithful—we agree to without blinking. But what we're there for, what we're really agreeing to is… having a name waiting for a child coming in December. And apparently, any name will do, even one of unknown origin like… Thornell.

Besides the Pearts, the only friends of mine in attendance are Bette and Sam. And after I had spent a few minutes with them at the small reception, Mrs. Wilson corners me for a heart to heart. "Jack, we need to agree on a story." "A story, what story?" "About the baby being premature." "What!" "People will talk, you know that." "Hell, let 'em talk. I'm not concocting any story. Hell, I already told my New York boss the whole story." "But Jack, this is West Point, not New York." "Mrs. Wilson tell any story you want. We'll be in New Orleans when the baby comes. And if anyone confronts me and starts counting months, and if they stop at six, I'll drop 'em for a 10-count." And instead of showing a slight smile over my punch line, she shows a smirk, the enduring kind, until finally, I turn away, knowing that a new mother-in-law is very disappointed in a new son-in-law. And what else was there to say in my behalf, except Mrs. Wilson, if you're disappointed in me, wait till you meet the rest of the family, and get a whiff of some most unpleasant history. There's a dead father I didn't know, not even a quarter's worth… A mother so fluent in profanity, it's her preferred language… A brother, and a swindler of the poorest of the poor…, a brother, and a jailbird in and out of uniform… An uncle, turned crazy stepfather who'd rather stab a sleeping body than look at it. And then Mrs. Wilson, there's me… the father to be, a high school dropout who got a master's degree for lying about it so convincingly, and so repeatedly. And there's a big question still looming. When Carolyn meets the Thornells, will she be shocked or sorry or both. And then Mrs. Wilson, will she come running home and then, with no other choice, but to turn Catholic and get an annulment on the grounds that I had been hiding something from her… the family tree.

With the reception over, I drive to Biloxi for a two night, one day, honeymoon, while feeling the pressure of a pregnant wife, now a lifelong passenger, sitting beside me. While we're checking in, a picture of a trio performing in the hotel lounge catches my attention, and then Carolyn's. From her, "Oh my God!" expression, I know it's marvelous Mike's Trio. And so to confirm it, I ask, "Isn't this Mike's group?" "Yes I think it is." "Isn't this him in the picture?" "Yes, it is." "Good then, after dinner, we'll take in the show." "Are you sure you want to do that?" "Why not. You and Mike are over. We're married. So what's the problem?" "So long as you promise not to make a scene." "No scene… I promise." "Okay then."

After I down two quick cocktails, with a look of disapproval growing on Carolyn's face, the show begins. And boy, am I disappointed. Marvelous Mike sings great, plays great and looks great. And after his set is over, he plays the role of perfect gentleman by marching over to our table and saying, "Hello Jack, Hello Carolyn, congratulations." And boy, does that start my wheels to spinning and spinning. But as promised, I held my peace, but back at the room Ole Green Eyes comes alive. "How the hell did your Mike know that we got married today? And how the hell do I know that he is not this baby's father?" And despite her denial, denial, and more denials, finally I tune her out, turn over and give her my back for the rest of the night. Sex with Carolyn, now that it is most appropriate on this our wedding night, isn't even a remote possibility. Not even if I wake up with a massive hard on.

And while we're driving to Metairie to occupy a very small one-bedroom furnished apartment, what better way to add to the stress and strain of a rocky and sexless honeymoon, than to bring up the subject of finances. "Carolyn F.Y.I., my bills are paid. The car is free and clear. I don't owe a dime. And I have over $500 in a savings account. So, tell me your status." "I only have one debt." Relaxing, I ask, "And how much is that?" "$1100" "You don't have a car, a TV, or furniture, and you owe $1100?" "Yes." "And to who?" "The Emporium." "The clothing store?" "Yes, that's right." "Son-of-a-bitch, haven't you ever heard of pay before you wear?" "Don't worry, as soon as I have the baby, I'll get a job and pay you back." And with silence coming between us, I think back to the first time I admired her legs and her ass, and I noted she was charging a cup of coffee, and that, I now know, should have set off bells and whistles. And for those pretty shoes on the store mannequins' feet, she'd probably hock her soul… and mine. And now, the bill for all those beautiful clothes, the ones she freely took off for Mike and other men, is handed over to me for payment due. The following week, when I'm up in Jackson, I arrange a payment schedule with the Emporium. With finance charges it comes to $70-a-month for 18 months, and it takes a large piece of my $600-a-month before taxes pay check.

Now, back in New Orleans, besides a new wife, I have a new boss to contend with. And why do I feel I have to prove my worth all over again just to keep the job I already have. And some bosses love to capitalize on that fear. And he soon proves himself to be a more proficient blood sucker that his prede-sucker. With this rallying cry… Cover the story… Feel proud… And forget the overtime… Isn't working for the great AP reward enough? His name, James Mangan.

Civil rights demonstrations in Jackson, Natchez, Fayette, Bogalusa and elsewhere keep me out of town and leave Carolyn alone in a tiny apartment and in a town too large, especially without the company of friends. And when I return, despite having Carolyn at home waiting for me, she doesn't fill the emptiness I feel, and have felt for as long as I can remember. She tries to fill it, but how can she, when she doesn't know what's missing. And neither do I. And if I did, I couldn't tell. Because every man knows a man can't show any such feelings tonight, and still be looked on as a man in the morning. And besides I know, with all certainty, that if I even show the slightest sign of weakness I'll crumble. And crumble. And crumble. And never to be made whole again, even for the sake of appearances.

And besides the emptiness, there's a state of uneasiness that always accompanies me home. Always reminding me that at any second the phone can ring, as it often does, and I'll be up and off again to experience the reality of all that awful anticipation. And the overriding reality is, to work for the Associated Press and to continue working for the Associated Press, day in and day out, I must be the best and I must continue being the best until… I crumble.

And so, with Carolyn caught between my emptiness and my uneasiness, with her belly growing more and more uncomfortable, we dine on cans and cans of Dinty Moore beef stew while sharing a homemade hell produced and directed by yours truly.

In September, the heaven belong to Betsy, but the closet belongs to Carolyn as the hurricane pounds against the door. With the 125 M.P.H. winds howling, with the transformers popping like fireworks and with the lights flashing off and on until finally off, Carolyn, now six-months pregnant, cowers in the dark closet until daylight. And keeping her company is the wife of AP reporter Ed McCuster.

And Ed and I aren't looking after our wives, because we're down in Plaquemine's Parish covering a twister that struck LaRose community. And there the light is not good, poor at best, and I'm back guessing exposures. And more troubling is veteran UPI photographer Pete Fisher is there shooting pictures. After finding a hotel room at Houma, I set up a darkroom and start processing film. When the clock sounds, I find the lid is stuck on the developer can, and I can't get it off. And with the air conditioner not working, the temperature is soaring and compounding the overdeveloping woes. Finally, the film is out, but way-way-way over developed and almost impossible to print. The print exposure time, rather than five-to-ten seconds is several minutes. And naturally, the quality suffers. But I do manage to get a couple of prints transmitted before the power goes out.

When the story winds down a week later, and with the power still off at our apartment, Betsy goes in the record book as the most destructive hurricane in history. Estimates start at $1 billion. And it took its toll on both Carolyn and I. "Never again will I stay here with a hurricane coming," she vowed. And with the baby soon to join us, I agreed. As for me, it was my second Waterloo, in just a few days past my one year anniversary. First, the Hilda Beast, and now, heaven forbid Betsy. And again the pictures stink… stank… stunk. And though the AP didn't keep reminding me of "How bad", I knew "How bad", with that torturous reminder always keyed up and ready to be played over again in my head, particularly when a new storm is approaching the Gulf with the unanswered question pending… How many more hurricanes can I survive before "The Stink" of "The how bad" claims me?

December 1965 is here and thank God hurricane season is over, but pressing news is… Carolyn is due. At 11:38 a.m. on Thursday December 23, at age 26, I reluctantly become what I knew absolutely nothing about… being a father.

Carolyn is fine. The baby girl we named Candice is fine. But fine, I'm not. Not with that ugly question rising and asking, "Is my daughter really my daughter?" Even Carolyn's good doctor, at Carolyn's insistence, tries to pinpoint the date of conception and naturally his figuring and Carolyn's figuring points to me. But with that past experience or that conspiracy, whichever or both, of Wally and her abortion doctor replaying in my head, convinced I'm not. But then, minutes later when I raise my Nikon with a 105 mm lens to take a close-up through the viewing window, and I focus in on her lying there, in the incubator, on her side, so delicate, so helpless, facing me, and oh so innocent of any past experience or conspiracy, more than a shutter clicked. My daughter, she's precious.

Before I can get back to Carolyn's bedside, a nurse summons me to the phone. "Hello Jack, this is Mangan, I hear you had a baby." "Yes sir." "Boy or girl?" "A girl, a beautiful baby girl." And with the Chief of Bureau's congratulations summed up with "That's great," he reveals the reason for his phone call. "Well Jack, with that accomplished, I need for you to get up to Fayette, Mississippi." "Why Fayette?" "The Blacks are boycotting the white merchants. They're staging a Christmas Eve march through town. And with the Klan so active in that neck of the woods, there could be trouble." "What time is it?" "Noon tomorrow/" "Okay, then, I'll be there." "Great, and again congratulations… and Merry Christmas."

Merry hell, I think, with Mangan's marching orders being relayed to Carolyn who finds it hard to swallow knowing that she will be left totally without the support of family or friends. "Why didn't you tell him no. Tell him you couldn't desert your wife, and child. Tell him to send somebody else." "Carolyn, you know I can't, no more than I could refuse to go to Santo Domingo on the eve of our wedding. No is not an acceptable answer. Not if I want to keep this job. And now, with a child to raise, not just I, but we, need this job more than ever."

And with that "need" ruling, I pack up and head up to Fayette at 5 a.m. on Christmas Eve leaving family responsibilities in a distant second place.

At noon, over 500 negroes march down Main Street without incident. And without incident means that there were not any worthwhile pictures to be taken, which means that my 15-hour day was a waste of time and might qualify as a civil rights violation, and if not mine, certainly Carolyn's.

Christmas time, for me is the worst time of the year, with memories of Christmas' Past, always ruining the day. And it's true and I know it's true, know from experience, that if you never experience the joy of Christmas as a child, you can never experience the joy of Christmas as a man. Not fully. Not ever.

And instead of joy I get the ball-busting annual Sugar Bowl event. There's tennis, there's track, there's basketball, and there's football to cover day and night, leaving me exhausted, both day and night. And even if by a miracle, I could have learned to fit a little joy into a Christmas new, there wouldn't have been time for it, nor room for it, not with event after event to be covered, nor with the pressure on to capture The Best Picture.

Even when the pressure of the Sugar Bowl ends on January 1, with that "what next" question foremost on my mind, fun is never fun for me. Even on "Fat Tuesday", a day known as the "Fun Day" of the year. And a day better known to the world as "Mardi Gras". A day when anything and everything goes. When guys go as gals and gals guys, when the best dressed gays get a prize. When marching bands strut, colorful floats roll and bare asses, breasts, and penises of all sizes greet the public and the police down on Bourbon Street. And it's all called fun. But for me, Mardi Gras is trying. Trying to get here. Trying to get there. Trying to maneuver through the crowd and survive the crush while searching for The Good Picture when there are thousands of good pictures everywhere. For a million people every year, "Fat Tuesday" is fun, but for me it is everything but.

With late spring comes the worse day and the best day of a career. It's the same day, the same place and the same story. But the time between expected failure and unexpected success is an eternity. And almost insufferable. The day is the sixth of June. The year, 1966.

The day before in Memphis, Tennessee, a subject from the past crosses my path again. His name is James H. Meredith, the negro who integrated Ole Miss and sparked a riot. And what's his mission now after moving to New York, attending Columbia Law School, and then disappearing on the continent of Africa before returning home to his racist Mississippi? His plan, a 225-mile hike down Highway 51 through the heart of rural Mississippi and onto the steps of the State Capitol in Jackson.

"There are two purposes of this trip," Meredith said, "First we want to tear down the fear that grips negroes in Mississippi… and we want to encourage the 450,000 negroes remaining unregistered to register."

By "tearing down fear", I surmised he meant… The most hated living Nigger in Mississippi history could swagger though open Klan country without getting shot. Unlike Medgar Evers, the Klan's number one target in 1963, who was shot down in his own driveway inside a black neighborhood.

Even without the backing of the local black community, who considered "The Loner" way too uppity and absolutely devoid of charisma—the ingredient most necessary to move black feet down a hot highway—and despite the quiet snickering of national black leaders at his idea as "the silliest ever heard of", Meredith will not be swayed, feeling a "divine responsibility" to face fear head-on. But what Meredith doesn't know is that just down the road, just one afternoon away, fear wins the day, with Meredith screaming its bloody triumph.

Sunday at 2 p.m., after his press conference, Meredith strides away from the famous Peabody Hotel—where ducks waddle through the lobby daily to the delight of tourists--with his ebony and ivory swagger stick, a gift from a Sudan tribal chief, and heads south. Joining Meredith for the first twelve miles to the Mississippi State Line are Robert Weeks, an Episcopal priest from Monroe, New York and Sherwood Ross, his press coordinator. Joining me is AP photographer Bill Hudson who I worked with in Selma and who is now stationed at Memphis, and young AP reporter Ronald Alford. But starting tomorrow, Hudson will be gone and in the hospital having elbow surgery. "Don't you just love the timing?", Hudson ribs, "Sorry I won't be available to walk those other 213 miles with you." And reporter Alford will be gone. And why? Both my boss Mangan and New York managing editor Sam Blackmon, agree with Meredith's black critics that his "silly march" isn't newsworthy, and certainly isn't worth the time of a reporter or a second photographer. So their solution? Let Thornell do it. And do it alone. Let him phone in a few paragraphs daily for a brief update. And let him take a few pictures. So, to me, their plan is clear. Let Thornell bake his brain from daylight to dusk and at the end of the day's trek, now exhausted, hungry, and still on foot, trek 15 to 20 miles back to where his car is parked so he can drive to the nearest motel, check-in and set up his not so portable darkroom for a processing and transmitting.

Just contemplating this scenario is enough to give a non-worrier a nervous breakdown. And as Mrs. Bounds might quickly point out, "Young man, a non-worrier, you're not." Of course I could elect to pull off early in the afternoon, go in and get a picture out while Meredith is still marching. But, nobody told me I could and nobody told me I couldn't. And what happens if something happens, and I'm back at the darkroom, or heaven forbid, having lunch? Whose lunch gets chewed up and spit out now? Mine... The Scapegoat's.

On day two, Meredith arms himself with a bible, crosses the state line into Mississippi and pauses for a roadside prayer with his handful of followers. Shortly after resuming the march, Meredith and his companions overhear, "I don't think he'll make it to Jackson," echoing through the open window of a pickup truck occupied by three white men. And there's more bad news from one Charles Sterrett who joins the march and brings with him the warning of a white man waiting down the road hell bent on shooting Meredith. But with local, state, and federal agents patrolling the road, the threat is shrugged off as just poppycock.

Since U.P.I. has two men, reporter Ken Cazalas and photographer Sam Parrish working the story, I'm disadvantaged. With two bodies, one can walk, take pictures or report while the other follows with a car. And since I can't walk and drive, I made a deal with Sammy. "Look, Hernando, the first town is just ahead. There could be trouble there. Why don't we drive ahead, park one car south of town, drive back with the other, rejoin the march on foot and walk through town with Meredith?" Sammy agrees and I'm relieved because he and his reporter could have done it without me. My car ends up in town, and his, south of town.

In Hernando, Meredith stops, gives a pep talk to a few blacks standing around, and without incident, moves on south.

Among the press entourage this afternoon is Tom Jarriel of ABC with cameraman Chuck Farris, Vernon Merritt III on assignment for Life Magazine, and a reporter with a camera from the Memphis Commercial Appeal.

When Sammy and I reach his car, we get in and start leapfrogging ahead while keeping Meredith and his marchers in view. While we're stopped Life photographer Merritt pulls up, parks behind, approaches and says, "Man oh man, is it hot. An ice cold coke sure would taste good." "Would it," Sammy responds, while moving his tongue along his dry lips. After I concur, Merritt offers, "I'll buy if one of you goes back to Hernando and gets 'em, as he bends lower to make eye contact with me, the junior photographer present. "Sorry Vernon but I can't leave and leave Sammy back here with Meredith. And besides, I ain't got no wheels. Mine are back in Hernando." Then, he turns his gaze back to Sammy who says, "Sorry, Vern, but I can't leave either." "Well hell then," the thirsty Merritt retorts, "I'll go get 'em and buy 'em too. I'll be right back."

With Merritt disappearing back up the highway, I turn to Sammy and say, "Hell, he can afford to buy. He's making $150 a-day, plus expenses and plus space rates. I'm making $150 a-week, and sometimes that's a 7-day, a hundred-hour week. What's that, a $1.50 an hour. And for that, we risk getting our teeth kicked in or worse." "Yea! Life sure ain't fair unless you're lucky enough to be working for 'em." "Amen Brother, amen."

While Sammy keeps his eyes on the rearview mirror and the procession, I rest mine while leaning back and anticipating that coke.

It's 4:15 p.m. and the cokes have yet to arrive, but now blessed shade is beginning to cover part of the hot pavement. Both sides of the two-lane highway are tree lined and brush filled. The march is progressing toward Sammy's parked Mustang but on the opposite side of the highway facing traffic. Suddenly, from the vegetation a white face pops up, points his shotgun and shouts, "James Meredith! I only want James Meredith!"

Boom! The shotgun sounds with the warning, Meredith's comrades cut and run, leaving him to stand alone, while Sammy and I exit and take cover behind the car.

Boom! The shotgun sounds again. The pellets tear into Meredith's back, spinning him around to face his attacker while sending his pit helmet flying and bouncing off the pavement and him sprawling onto it.

Click! Click! Click! Sounds my Nikon. "Shit! I'm under-lensed." I complain under my breath while shooting away with a 105-mm anyway, knowing that if I stopped to change to a needed 200mm, the incident could end while my lens was off and "THE PICTURE" could be missed. And missing is not something to live with, not in this business.

Meanwhile, Meredith, still sprawling, still clutching his precious swagger stick, turns away from the direction of the gunfire and starts crawling towards Sammy and me, putting us directly in the line of fire.

Boom! A third shot sounds. Meredith grimaces. My Nikon clicks. I duck. The shooting stops.

Having reached our side of the road, he relaxes his grip and his swagger stick shakes free. Lying motionless now, with blood oozing through the back of his shirt, his missing comrades return to his side. Then, the press gathers, circling his body like vultures sharing the carrion. Still belly down and back up, he manages to raise his head enough to plead, "Will somebody help me… will somebody get me an ambulance?" We respond by pressing microphones and camera lenses ever closer.

Finally a shaken Merritt runs up, but without the cokes. He's sick. He's missed the feast. With only leftovers remaining, still he squeezes in, joins the circle, firing his cameras at rapid speed, still hoping it's not too late to claim a cover of Life of Meredith bleeding at his feet.

And now, bad news reaches my ears as I hear U.P.I. reporter Cazalas shouting to Sammy, "I'm leaving to phone in. You stay put."

Geesums… I'm thinking… with UPI's news flash soon to be broadcast around the world, what am I to do? With Sammy still here, still clicking away, I can't leave. Better yet, with my car still back in Hernando, how can I leave? So you bosses in New Orleans and New York will just have to wait for that daily progress phone call that you put on this photographer's back because you were too cheap to send a reporter. And soon, for this monumental blunder, somebody must pay. I pray it won't be the body of this former obituary writer.

With that dilemma resolved in my mind, I check my cameras. One is empty. The other, down to the last two frames. As I'm about to reload, somebody yells, "Look! Down the road!" I look. I see a state trooper emerging from the woods carrying a shot-gun and holding on to the arm of a white man. Immediately, the circle around Meredith collapses as we stampede off to photograph the suspect before he is sped away.

After two exposures, I stop, reload and return to Meredith's side to photograph him being loaded into an ambulance. As the door closes, Sammy turns to me and asks, "Did you see the guy in the bushes?" "Yea, I saw him when they brought him out." "No, I mean during the shooting." "No Sammy, I didn't." "I did, and I think I got him in the picture." "During the shooting?" "Yep, during the shooting."

As I'm visualizing Sammy's picture, the ambulance speeding away with its siren screaming isn't the only screaming sounding in my head. If I'm not done in by the story fuck-up, I will be over the photo fuck-up. With UPI's one-two, I'm down and done.

As I stand stunned, still processing Sammy's—it's killing me—news, he jumps in his Mustang and speeds away, but without his passenger. Now, I'm left stranded with my state of shock deepening, until ABC's Ferris rushes past me towards his car, then stopping and turning back to ask, "Jack… you okay?" "Sure Chuck, but I sure could use a ride back to my car in Hernando." "Come on, I'm going that way."

Heading back towards Memphis and the darkroom at the Commercial Appeal, I stop at the first available phone and call New Orleans. News editor Gavin Scott answers with, "Jack! Where have you been? UPI is running with the shooting… and New York is screaming bloody murder." "Gavin! Gavin! Shut up and listen. Meredith has been shot… from ambush… he's wounded… but he's alive… He asked for an ambulance." "Okay, okay, got that. What else?" "A white man in a white shirt was arrested. That's it. I gotta go." "Wait! Wait! Don't hang up. I need more…" "Sorry Gavin, but no more time," I replied before hanging up on my number two boss. And what I didn't take time to tell was that the UPI photographer was well up the road—at least ten minutes and ten miles ahead—and well on his way to burying me with an even bigger scoop… THE PICTURE.

Now, I'm back behind the wheel with my thoughts going crazy. Sammy's got the picture. I don't. I got a wife. I got a child. I got a mother waiting to welcome us down to 503 to live with her. Like Garnett. Like Marshall. Oh God! What to do? What to do? With my heart pounding, with my foot pressing the accelerator, I see the solution. It's coming up fast. It's a bridge abutment. Chicken shit! You missed it. Wait! There's a gulley ahead…

"Butt-Butt, Makesense is here. Calm down Cousin." "Oh Makesense, why are you butting in. You know there's nothing ahead but ruin… my ruin… and even worse… poverty again." "But are you sure… absolutely sure?" "Sure, I'm sure. You heard the glee in Sammy's voice of his expectation." "Yes Cousin, but as you well know, expectations aren't set in concrete. Let me remind you of another day and your expectation." "What day?" "When they arrested the sheriff in Philadelphia. When you could only get off a hip shot. When you were sure you faced ruin for letting the sheriff walk right past you without you raising a camera. You remember?" "Sure! Sure! I remember, but that was luck… Just luck." "And perhaps you'll get lucky again today." "Not likely." "But how can you know, know for sure unless you develop the film and take a look, like at Philadelphia." "and remember one more thing." "What thing?" "If you crash and burn now, Makesense crashes and burns too." "Okay! Okay! Makesense. I'll go back. I'll get my pictures out. I'll take my beating, but when the morning papers confirm it, I'll not wait to get fired, I'll resign."

After arriving at the office, newsman Alford sees me, points to the phone next to the darkroom and says, "New York is holding for you." Son-of-a-bitch! I'm thinking, just like in Philadelphia when Boss Resch was holding, but this time instead of moving toward the phone I move to Alford, put my index finger across my lips and whisper, "I'm not back yet," before disappearing into the darkroom.

With every minute counting and I'm about to start loading the film reels, I stop and think. This developer has been sitting here all day in an unlocked darkroom, and if some scoundrel poured a little hypo solution in with the developer then my film is ruined. "Son-of-a-bitch," I scream, remembering Bergsma back in Jackson, my suspicions, and the blank film, before I quickly dump the developer, open a new can and begin mixing. There's powder to dissolve and that takes warm water. And now overheated, it has to be cooled. And that takes ice water. And to get the developer back to the desired 70 degree temperature takes time. At least five minutes worth. So now, I'm running at least fifteen minutes behind Sammy who is working just one floor above.

Finally, with my three rolls developing, I emerge from the darkroom, pick up the phone, breathe heavy as if I just rushed in and hear, "This is Al Resch. Develop your film, but don't waste time editing. The first good picture you see, stop, print it and get it on the wire. We're right on first edition deadlines in New York. And F.Y.I., Newside really screwed up. They killed Meredith. And there's going to be hell to pay. Now, get going.

Killed Meredith? I'm wondering, as I hang up only to hear Alford's cry, "Jack, another call on line two. It's New Orleans and Chief of Bureau Mangan. He wants more story info." Ignoring Alford, I slip back into the darkroom, sliding the door behind me and leaving my boss hanging.

After squeegeeing the wet film between my fingers, I hang up two rolls and hold up the third—the shooting roll—to the light for a quick look. There, near the end, one frame jumps out... Meredith crawling... towards me... looking into my lens... and screaming.

Carefully, I put the still wet negative into the enlarger, print it, blot it off with a towel and twist it around the transmitter cylinder when I hear, "Memphis, come in. Memphis, come in please." "New York, this is Memphis." "How long before a first picture is ready?" "As soon as I write a caption." "Write." As I'm typing, I hear the monitor announcing, "All points, standby, we're holding the network open for the first picture of the Meredith shooting."

With a two sentence caption on the print, I pick up the network phone and announce, "Memphis is ready." "Go ahead final Memphis." On his command, I start the transmission. The cylinder spins, the exciter lamp scans and the beep beep beep sounds as I rush back inside the darkroom to take a closer look at my film, knowing that in only nine minutes, I'll need a second image printed and captioned.

This time I pick up my eyeball to magnify the negatives and start scanning frame by frame, but this time stopping to scrutinize each and every image. "Shit! Shit! Shit!" I shout, seeing that I was under lensed, way under lensed on the early shooting frames, leaving the subjects too small for an acceptable print. And then, as I move to the next frame, from the bushes, a face pops up.

Not believing my eyes and before taking a second look, my mind flashes back to my youth and the night the scissors stood. They were there. Standing on my chest. I saw them. And then, after my plea, they were gone.

And now, with the precious seconds ticking away, my voice reaches upward again. "Please! Please God, help me. Only today, let the image I saw be real and not imagined."

Immediately, I look back to the negative and I see… Meredith sprawling in the foreground. I see… the gunman's face in the background. Oh my God! I see… Sammy's picture. The picture he described right after the shooting. And the picture I never saw… until now.

In minutes, "THE PICTURE" of Meredith and the gunman facing off is on the transmitter and spinning into newspapers around the world.

After transmitting three more pictures, Chief of Bureau Mangan manages to get me on the phone. "Jack! Why didn't you take my call… talk to me… damn it… I needed more information." "Sorry sir, but Mr. Resch ordered me into the darkroom immediately."

After feeding Mangan more details, I look across the room and see reporter Alford sitting motionless, even trance-like. He looks sick, really sick. And then, I find out why. He killed James Meredith. What? How? He wasn't even there. And what's worse? He killed him live on Walter Cronkites evening news. "James Meredith is dead," Cronkite airs, "This just in from the Associated Press."

Only, it isn't so. After Cronkite airs, the hospital issues a statement contradicting the Associated Press exclusive. Meredith is "not" dead, only wounded, and breathing just fine.

After being dead for 35 minutes on AP wires, Meredith is resurrected, Cronkite eats his words, actually Alford's and doesn't like the taste of it. And the only thing left is for cub reporter Alford, only 24, to be chewed up and spit out.

How does the largest, the most respected, and usually, the most reliable news agency in the world blunder so? Here's how. First, UPI scores big with the first news of the shooting, beating my call to New Orleans by fifteen minutes. Meanwhile in Memphis, already shook up by the screams of New York trying to play catch-up, young Alford rushes into the big and noisy newsroom of the Commercial Appeal. There, he listens in on a call from their reporter still at the scene. The reporter says, "Meredith was shot in the head," but anxious Alford mishears, "Meredith was shot dead." And without verification, runs with the "shot dead" bulletin. Meanwhile, UPI hears the "shot dead" report, figure they are now scooped, and pressure reporter Cazalas to kill off Meredith too. Cazalas says, "Sorry! But I can't confirm it. So I can't report it." And he doesn't. And after the dust settles, Cazalas emerges as an even bigger hero.

The Associated Press saves a reporter's pay, but loses face, while choking on the biggest blunder of the ERA, and while UPI promotes itself with the slogan... Fast and accurate.

The next morning, competitive newspapers everywhere use the UPI story with AP pictures. Even the Memphis Commercial Appeal, owned by UPI's parent company Scripts-Howards, and usually preferring the UPI product, use mine. Spreading Meredith and the gunman across eight columns of page one. Below it, a grimacing Meredith. And next to it, the arrested suspect. And under each, AP photo by Jack R. Thornell.

Sammy gets crushed. I feel for him, really feel for him. Because I know how he feels. I felt it all the way from Hernando to Memphis.

Today, I don't get fired, although Alford does. Today, I don't resign. Because yesterday was MIRACLE DAY—my MIRACLE DAY.

Meredith survives with suffering Mississippi diehards complaining... what a waste of birdshot, when with buckshot the dead nigger would have stayed as dead as reported. From Meredith's head, back and shoulders, doctors dig out 90 to 200 small pellets. The wounds are not serious.

The shooter, Aubrey James Norvell, age 41, unemployed, balding and overweight, is described by neighbors as a "quiet Christian man." After posting a $25,000 bond on charges of "assault with intent to kill", Norvell is sprung and goes home to sleep in his own Memphis bed. But with that bothersome question still gnawing at some Mississippi guts... Why didn't he load up with buckshot and blow that meddlesome head clear off?

Meanwhile a media circus is coming to town. Arriving hourly. Reporters and photographers from all over. Even now, the AP has dispatched its crack team. Knowing another major blunder must be avoided, regardless of the cost. And on their heels competing civil rights groups, including the same black leaders who snickered just days before, fly in to fill Meredith's shoes. And of course, CASH in on his bloody publicity. For Meredith's "silly" little march is now... headline news. Among them are Dr. Martin Luther King Jr. of the Southern Christian Leadership Conference, Floyd B. McKissick of the Congress of Racial Equality and the young and violative Stokely Carmichael of the Student Non-Violent Coordinating Committee. Although they're putting their feet together on the same hot pavement to continue the march without Meredith, motives separate their movements.

And on the evening of June 7, the night after the shooting, Carmichael proves it, preaching, "The Negro is going to take what he deserves from the white man." Then, ten days later, while emerging from a Mississippi jail with a fist raised high above his head, he shouts, "Black Power", a new phrase, soon to be the cry for a new phase... civil disobedience.

The march into Mississippi, without Meredith's presence, resumes with its leadership split. Dr. King, in disagreement with Carmichael over the use of violence, gets pushed around by state police but isn't injured or arrested. With the heat more stifling with each new day, salt tablets are dispersed but still, one marcher collapses and succumbs. Meredith had left Memphis with only a handful of followers, but today at Batesville, 600 pairs of feet feel the heat, held and raised by the pavement. And naturally, mine are among them.

Tonight, I'm having dinner at the Monte Christo Motel, Grenada's finest, and celebrating. The reason, the march is halfway to Jackson. Joining me are photographers Sammy Parrish and Joe Holloway of UPI, Life's "I hate cokes" Merritt, and AP's Charlie Kelly and photo editor Lou Garcia. Since the county is dry, which means alcohol cannot be sold—legally—we're drinking ice tea with a lemon twist, talking and laughing when the tall skinny blonde waitress, with a voice loud and reaching, butts into our conversation. Hey! Y'all boys are newspaper men ain't ya?" We nod. "Well, I got a hot tip for ya." "Yes ma'am, Holloway respectfully responded. "That God damn Meredith shooting… it was a put up deal… all a set up… all arranged." "Arranged by who?" Holloway inquired. "By Life Magazine." "And how do you know?" Holloway asked, "Y'all saw them pictures in there. They hired the gunman. They told him when and where to shoot him. No doubt about it. It was a put up deal."

With her revelation, laughter rocks the table and then, cruelty personified is imparted. Holloway, a very short man, but very long on jokes, leans over, wraps his arm around Life's Merritt, pulls him close and cackles, "Vern, too bad those dumb asses up at Life didn't tell you about the when and the where, so you could have passed up that coke run." Laughter loud and cruel rises. Hidden in it is Merritt's pain. I feel it. Mixing in with mine. Left over from that day. Still disturbing. It's a terrible feeling. One not talked about. One not laughed about. Never! Not in a lifetime. The picture the waitress identified as exhibit one was mine. The Meredith-Norvell face-off is a double-truck—two pages wide. Exhibit two: The grimacing Meredith, a half-page. And while I should be on cloud nine enjoying the high of highs, particularly after Commercial Appeal photographer Bob Williams approached me holding up his paper's front page filled with my pictures and saying, "Jack, you're looking at the next Pulitzer." But, I'm not, I'm still down on earth facing humiliation,

What humiliation? The humiliation associated with the story fiasco. The humiliation that comes when the mass media, still laughing at the AP blunder, start making assumptions. They had a photographer there, we know from the pictures. And we know they didn't have a reporter there. So, the photographer had to be the one to call in the "shot dead" story. And the talk circulating about is, "Their photographer got some great pictures but he sure fucked up the story, didn't he?" When actually, every word of my report—wounded but alive—was accurate to the letter. And it's not until the June 17, issue of Time, with its step-by-step report of the foul-up crucifying Alford and exonerating me, do I feel somewhat relieved. But how do you take back humiliation already portioned out, already suffered.

As we're preparing to move the darkroom from the Monte Christo to a motel farther down the highway, photo editor Garcia directs, "Jack, get in your car, go home, see the wife, get laid, play with Candy, then rest and relax." "What?" "You deserve a few days off. I cleared it with New York." "What about the march?" "Don't worry, with three photographers left, we've got it covered."

While driving towards New Orleans, I'm planning on following Garcia's instructions, except for the relax part. With the past reaching forward and with the anticipation of the future reaching backward to find and ruin the present, how can I? Relax Mr. Garcia? No, that I cannot do.

In New Orleans, back at the AP office and the adjoining Times-Picayune newsroom, the back slapping begins, while I'm thinking…gently, not so hard, or you might crack the hollow

152

shell encasing your hero. At home, Candy, now six months old, is crawling, climbing and exploring every inch of our tiny apartment. And a pleasant distraction from my daily parade of thoughts. But after looking into her big and beautiful blue eyes, worthy enough to grace any Gerber bottle, I can't help but feel a twinge of guilt for wishing that her carefree thoughts were mine, instead of mine being mine, knowing that in a few days I must return to Mississippi.

Rejoining the march, I sense a mood swing. Perhaps it's the tear gassing and the clubbing two nights before in Canton, just for pitching tents on forbidden public school property. Perhaps it's the aggressive oratory of an eager new voice still echoing those two arousing words, "Black Power." Or perhaps it's just time for a change of attitudes. But Charles Evers, who leads the march for a day, and hears, "Hey! Hey! Whatta ya know. White folks must go," doesn't agree. In fact, the brother of the slain Medgar and like Dr. King, an advocate of non-violence, warns, "If we are marching these roads for black supremacy, we are doomed."

The march finale, staged on the Capitol steps, is nothing more or nothing less than anticlimactic. Despite a crowd of 16,000. And despite the return of Meredith. The noticeable difference between the successful Selma march and this one is... the absence of white faces.

The grueling trek covered 250 miles over 22 days. It earned television time and newspaper headlines, but it splinters the Negro movement. Different voices with different directions cause dissension and cloud objectives. Even the docile and less than articulate Meredith has misgivings about the march, concluding, "I think something is wrong... some shenanigans are going on that I don't like."

And on that sour note, and with swollen feet, eyes and heads, from walking, gassing, and clubbing their only trophies, Meredith's marchers head home. As do I.

On the long drive back, I summon Makesense, "Your ears up." "Up, Cousin." "Do you believe in prayer?" "Like your darkroom plea?" "Yea, like that." "Well Cousin, it certainly didn't hurt, did it? And with that second look, you went from goat to hero in an instant, didn't you?" "No it didn't Makesense, and yes I did... yes I did."

Back home with Carolyn and Candy, and with the morning paper in hand, I read, "Richard Speck sadistically butchers eight Chicago student nurses." That's big news, I think. And good news. Those headlines will take the heat off the south... and me. It's a bloody heartless thought, I know, but what I didn't know is, I'll soon be paying for it and paying for it back up at Grenada.

The town hasn't been the same, not since those Meredith marchers tramped through, and certainly not since they desecrated the statue of the honorable Jefferson Davis. The nerve of "them niggers" planting an American flag between his toes. Right there, right in the middle of town square. And that's something to be reckoned with, is the attitude of many whites, including one Constable Grady Carroll. Especially with the "local niggers" now stirred up, now forgetting their place and marching around that sacred statue day and night. And when there's marching to be done, count my feet in. And on this trip, those of veteran AP reporter Bill Crider.

Tonight, as the march nears the square, cherry bombs begin flying through the air, with their lite fuses streaking, before exploding about head high. Now, a whizzing passes my ear, and close. "What the hell was that?" I wonder. And then, I see a teenage girl lying on the ground. I move closer. She's bleeding profusely. And as I focus my camera, I see why. Jesus! Her nose has been torn off. And with more whizzings and explosions rattling me, Crider approaches and warns, "Watch out for that whizzing sound." "Why, what is it?" "Steel ball bearings and chain lengths cut in half and sharpened." "What?" "Yea! Those crazy redneck bastards are using sling shots, better known in these parts as nigger shooters." "Son-of-a-bitch, son-of-a-bitch," I respond as I feel my body trying to compress, trying to shrink smaller, for what better target is there than the guy recording such madness.

Later, back at the church and safety, I recognize one of the marchers. It's Andrew Young, the handsome light-skinned protégé of Dr. King. He wasn't hit, but he still looks shaken. Perhaps, like me, he's still under the influence of fear, the hard to shake off kind. The kind that keeps on gripping and gripping long after it first grabbed hold. I thought of moving closer to Young and saying something, but what could I say, except share my plea… Please God, instead of another night like this, deliver me with a speeding bullet.

But even after a night like that, the black folks keep on marching and the white folks keep on getting more and more fed up, when from a Main Street diner, out steps Constable Grady Carroll. It's just past noon, and a crowd of Carroll's kind of folks are standing around. And with a readymade audience, Carroll can't contain himself and starts shooting off his mouth, and loudly. "Boys, we're gon'na fix those black bastards. We're bringing in a truckload of murderers from Parchman… black murderers," Carroll chuckles, "With nothing but time on their hands and nothing to lose. They gon'na surround and protect Ole Jeff Davis… and bust some nigger heads. Yes sir! We gon'na have some fun tonight." But while Carroll is holding court and disclosing privileged information, reporter Crider has blended in with "his kind of folks" and is taking it all in, and down, just like Carroll says it. And then, phones it in.

At 5 p.m. Crider's story is all over television news shows. An hour later, there's a loud bang on the motel door, so I crack it. Pushing past me and into the room is Constable Carroll. "I'm looking for Bill Crider," he shouts, "You him?" "No sir, I'm not. He's not here." "Are you sure?" "Yes sir." "That lying bastard got me into trouble… big trouble… with the governor… he just finished chewing on my ass," he roars while moving towards the bathroom for a looksee. "He's gon'na take back those lies or eat 'em." The rip-roaring mad Carroll continues from the bathroom. He doesn't see Crider there but what he does see is a new fifth of Jack Daniels standing on the counter next to the ice bucket. "Boy! There's whiskey here. This is a dry county. It's illegal. Boy! I'm gon'na lock your ass up." "But wait! I thought you wanted Crider." "I do, I do, but he ain't here, so you have to do." "Wait! Would it help if you knew where he is?" "Where is that lying cocksucker." "If you leave right now, you can catch him at the church." "Alright! Alright! But if I don't find him there, I'm coming right back here." As Carroll storms off, I rush into the bathroom, grab the whiskey—Crider's whiskey—break the seal, pour it into the toilet, flush, and dispose of the bottle outdoors.

Now, knowing Carroll's armed, and in his crazed state, dangerous, I rush to warn Crider of the impending danger coming his way. Standing over six-feet, Crider is a very good looking man with a nature as easy going as one comes. In explosive situations, he likes standing in background, well away from the media horde, puffing on his pipe, observing and staying out of harm's way. Except that riotous night at Ole Miss, when those buckshot found his back. Now wounded, Crider continues on with his reporting. Thank goodness Bill isn't easily rattled, I'm thinking and hoping to single him out of the crowd before Carroll can.

After I arrive, I see and shout, "Shit! I'm too late," as Carroll has Crider cornered. He's in Crider's face, shouting, "Man! You got to take back that story… about them convicts." Undaunted, Bill draws on his pipe, expels the smoke and calmly explains, "Constable, I was there. I heard what you said. And said loudly. The story is true. The story stands." Now, with more and more blacks—not exactly the Constable's kind of audience—gathering and pressing closer to the pair, the getting more and more uncomfortable Carroll backs away from Crider while lowering his voice to a whisper, "This ain't the last of it."

With Carroll gone, I ask, "Bill, you okay?" Smiling, he says, "Sure. I'm just fine." "Good…and I'm sorry about ratting you out." "What are you talking about?" "Well, back at the motel that crazy idiot was threatening to arrest me until I fingered you and your whereabouts." "Aaah forget about it. Let's go back to the room and have a drink." "Oops, that poses a problem." "Why?" "I flushed your fifth." "You what!" "Hell Bill, after Carroll busted in and spotted the booze, what else could I do? Hell, he threatened to come back if he couldn't find you." "Jesus! You used my sipping whiskey for drain cleaner, knowing there's not another drop for fifty miles?" "I did Bill and I'm sorry." "Jesus Jack! That hurts… hurts… hurts." As for my turning Judas, Bill graciously forgives, but as for my flushing good whiskey, his, well that's another story. That's an unpardonable sin. And one not to be forgotten. Ever.

Even without a libation, Bill is a pleasure to work with, and a professional. After the navy, he gets a job with the Chattanooga News-Free Press by lying about having writing experience. He didn't, but before long he does. And he proves good at it. So good, the Associated Press hires him despite the fact that he, like me, is a high school dropout. But unlike me, that fact doesn't seem to bother him.

And for a big story, when New York calls New Orleans with marching orders, they don't say, "Send somebody." They say, "Send Crider." And when the lights go off, Bill switches off, and is soon fast asleep. While lying in the bed next to his and listening to his snoring, I wonder if he has fears like mine? Insecurities like mine? Questions I can't ask, not out loud, not without the possibility of exposing myself, and my own weaknesses. And if he does, he never shows it. No matter how big, how intense the story, his pulse rate never seems to fluctuate, not even when facing tougher mugs than Constable Carroll's. Sure, to get a job, Bill lied about having writing experience, but not about being a writer and not just a writer, but the finest.

Finally the marching slows long enough for a brief respite, but with September comes my return to Grenada for more schooling.

During the integration at Horn Elementary and John Rundel High, a boy is knocked to the ground, kicked and beaten. "That'll teach you nigger. Don't come back," his white educator shouts. The youngster cries, "I didn't want to come. My momma made me."

Righard Sigh, age 12, runs a gauntlet of axe handles, pipe lengths and tire chains before escaping with a broken leg and a bloodied body, while local police with their hands pocketed, just watch. Meanwhile, Federal District Judge Claude Clayton, not liking what he's seeing in the newspapers, orders in helmeted Mississippi State Policemen. Forming their own gauntlet, this one, with shotguns raised, integration proceeds, with agitated whites keeping their distance, and raising only their voices of disapproval.

On the way home, at Jackson, instead of keeping south, I force a turn west to Vicksburg and then, down to 503. There brother Marshall, his wife Debra, and daughter Debra Jean, are living with Mother. Still keeping his navy flattop, he, like Mother is short, but unlike her, is quiet-natured and anything but a constant talker. He's older, but there's more distance than the six years between us. The past we never talk about. Hell! He's still living it. I know he loves free rent, but how does he stand it? Living here. In this. And so close to Mother's never ceasing mouth. Even with her grandchild standing there, she never cleans up her language. Mother hates living alone. So much so that when Marshall or Garnett aren't living there, she'll take in free loaders just to have a warm body and a captive pair of ears near. And about her fears, her insecurities, I don't have to ask, because I know. It's the loss of 503. And not having a roof overhead. A roof she can share with her boys whenever they get down on their luck and get put out on the street. That's her dream, to be there, right down at 503, for forever, for her and her boys. And her dream is my continuous nightmare. That like Garnett, like Marshall, I too will be down and out, and will be pulled back here and held behind a door nailed shut.

As I'm walking up to the house, I think back to Grenada, to the whizzing of ball bearings and to my effort to shrink, I ask myself, why didn't I just picture this in my mind, because every time I see it, I feel smaller.

"Hello Mother." "Hello Son. When you bringing Carolyn and the baby to see me? Shit! She'll be walking soon, won't she?" "Soon, Mother soon." Carolyn was well into her pregnancy, when I announced that her youngest was married. Was she hurt by my snubbing? She never let on. For what's a little more hurt added on to a lifetime of it? After a very short visit, and while I'm driving away, an old dread is revived. The dread of that day. The day Carolyn meets Mother.

And that day is here. In the yard Mother greets us, hugs Carolyn and reaches for Candy. "Goddamn! Look at that child. She's a pretty thing, ain't she." I try closing my ears. "Y'all come on in." I try shutting my eyes. But my thoughts race on. What will Carolyn think? Think of her? Think of this… the shamehold? And then, think of me? Oh God! How I'd rather not be, than be here. Oh God! What did I do, what could I do, to deserve this? This humiliation. The humiliation of humiliations.

On the road home, Carolyn is quiet and Candy is sleeping while my mind is still being bombarded by the same questions. What did she think of my mother? What did she think of my home? She didn't say. She didn't have to because I already knew her shocked but silent reaction had to be… That's your mother! That's where you escaped from! It's no small wonder that you've been hiding this. What fool wouldn't. I'm so sorry, sorry I had to see… see this… this part of you… your roots.

These days civil rights stories keep me hopping from one hellhole to another, often for weeks at a time. When I do return home, my presence is felt, with my perfectionism setting a double standard. And baby, before I step foot in the door there are things I want. I want them toys picked up. I want them floors, vacuumed and mopped, needing it or not. Honey! Just assume they need it. And as far as money goes, and her spending of it, I examine those receipts with a magnifier while never letting her forget that Emporium debt, the one I'm still paying on. God's hell could only be an upgrade from mine, as I, perhaps subconsciously, try to relieve my own pressures by expanding hers. With my bad news—such as get back to Bogalusa—being her good news. For with my absence comes some semblance of relief. Hers. Mine comes with the next good picture.

And it's a haymaker. It's thrown by Carlos Marcello, the reputed Mafia boss of Louisiana. The chin belongs to the FBI's Patrick Collins. Days before delivery at the New Orleans airport, there's a special luncheon being attended in New York City at LaStella in the affluent Forrest Hills of Queens. The diners, besides Marcello and brother Joseph, are Joseph Colombo, Carlo Gambino, Michele Miranda, and seven others. With their before dinner drinks being lifted, the police burst in, then, just like in the movies comes… hold your cannolis, don't you good fella's know it's a crime to dine with brothers in crime for the furtherance of "the family" business? So the twelve reputed underworld chieftains were cuffed and led out. The charge: Consorting with known criminals. In this case, each other. THE CHECK: $100,000 each. The accommodations: overnight in jail.

Marcello is perhaps a tad over or a tad under five-feet. Nobody knows which and nobody's about to ask. But over being arrested, over spending his first night in jail in over twenty years and being publicly humiliated by having his picture put in the paper, the little man's outrage is huge.

It's Friday night, the night after Marcello's arrest. I'm home, and I'm supposed to be off, when the phone rings. "Hello Jack, this is McCusker." "Yea." "We just got a tip." About Marcello's return. He's coming in on a 9 p.m. flight." And so, I'm up and off.

With a quick look around the terminal I see that the AP was not the only beneficiary of the FBI tipoff. There's plenty of other media present. But my nemesis, Pete Fisher of UPI isn't. Probably figuring that a routine picture of "The Little Man" walking through the terminal isn't worthy of his precious time. And he's probably right. And then, I see something unusual, most unusual. Two FBI agents are mingling in with the media. Both are dressed casually, instead of their usual coat and tie attire. And one is carrying a movie camera. And that I note, isn't the norm. Usually, they stay well in the background, observe, and never carry a camera.

Finally, Marcello emerges. We hound him. We blind him with flashes. We press microphones to his mouth as "The Little Man's" obvious outrage grows. As he exits the terminal, the real press drops back with the imposters—the FBI agents—hound on, staying on his heels. As he's reaching his waiting Cadillac, Marcello undoubtedly thinking that his two hounders are but lowly members of the Fourth Estate, stops, turns back, faces the pair, and explodes, "Are you looking for some fucking trouble?" Agent Collins, who stands over six-feet, retorts, "I can handle trouble." Marcello shouts back, "I'm the boss around here." And then, he swings. Collins ducks. My flash explodes. And freezes the motion and the moment. It happened so fast, my colleagues got caught with their camera down. WWL-TV reporter Bill Elder, who was doubling as a photo stringer for UPI's Fisher, exclaims, "Damn it! I missed the picture." Liking the sound of that, I rush to the phone, call McCusker and report the story. "Jack are you sure that this was a G-Man he swung at?" "Absolutely." "How?" "I asked him and he confirmed it. Although he declined to give his name. The other, the one with the camera, I knew was an FBI agent from an earlier outing." "Good then. Great story. And thanks Jack."

An hour later, the phone on my desk rings. It's UPI's Fisher. "Jack, you were at the airport?" "That I was Pete." "Did you get it… the punch?" "Well Pete, you know he had left the terminal… it was pitch black out… I had dropped back… he was a good distance away." "Come'on Jack! Did you get the damn picture or not?" "Yes Pete, I nailed it." "Good for you…good for you," he said ever so softly before slamming the phone down ever so loudly. With that abrupt disconnect, I summon Makesense and ask, "Was that good for you, two lies or one?" "Well Cousin, you know that what is good for you is bad for him. And after seeing your picture it looks bad for him… real bad."

The next morning, Marcello sees "The Picture" on page one of the Times-Picayune and after reading the caption, he learns that he socked-it to a G-man and not a newsman. So, what's the difference? It could add up to several years in a federal pen. And before breakfast is digested, "The Boss" is arrested for assaulting a federal agent, and goes to jail for the second time in three days.

My punch picture flattens Big Pete. It's page one everywhere, including New York where our bosses see it first with their morning coffee. And even though Pete wasn't there, he should have been and it counts against him as a big loss in the career column.

Now, the court sparring begins, with Marcello pulling back his punch and calling it "a gesture". But with Collins still saying, "A haymaker", that puts me smackdab in the middle with my picture and my future testimony as the guts of the government's case. Before the trial date, the "Black Hand" appears and re-appears. Daily on my typewriter. Face up. A stark black imprint of a mysterious hand. My colleagues deny the handiwork as theirs. But when my worried look appears, they don't deny their laughter. One suggests, "Jack, play it safe, shut your eyes before starting your car." Boom! My thoughts explode… will my demise dismiss my picture… its use… from the evidence pool? Shit! Why are these guys laughing so, is Marcello just a lit'ole tomato salesman from Jefferson Parish, as he claims, just a Godfather to nieces and nephews, or is he the… Capo di Tutti Capi? And if the latter, if the strong arm of the mob as the FBI claims, then doesn't he have the power to plant whomever he chooses under his tomatoes?

The "Black Hand", the "Bomb" and the "Tomato Fertilizer", may well be the products of jokesters and an over active imagination. But guess what fellows… I'm not laughing. And particularly, not this morning. Not with the appearance of a fresh "Black Hand". Not after the FBI appeared here yesterday, with a fresh subpoena ordering me to testify. And all the government wants fellows, is for me to hold up "The Picture", to point to that "Little Man" and to say, "He did it."

As I get on the flight to Laredo, the thought of bombs in the cargo hold, cross my mind, as does the question, why Laredo. Why did the government seek and get a change of venue to a distant Texas border town? Is it because that "Little Man" has too much power and influence back in Louisiana even for the "Big Government", to contend with?

At the trial, Marcello's eyes fix on me on the witness stand, and then, follow me over to the jury box where I pass around "The Picture" for their scrutiny. Even Marcello's attorney Sam Wassaman, while trying to reduce a haymaker to a gesture and while holding up the front page of the New York Daily News showing this little man standing his ground against this government Goliath, smiles and says, "This indeed is a good picture. A very good picture."

Despite "The Picture" and the independent eyewitness testimony of WWL reporter Bill Elder, the jury hangs 11 to 1 for guilty. And with a unanimous verdict necessary to convict, a mistrial is called with the word on the street pointing to the possibility of jury tampering.

For the re-trial in Houston, this time the jury is sequestered and guarded. This time it will be impossible for anyone to get close. This time the Tomato Salesman or the Capo-di-Tutti Capi—which ever or both—is convicted and sentenced to two years in a federal penitentiary.

And without a doubt, it was my picture that delivered the kiss of death. And with the trial over, still I wonder… will my name remain active in Marcello's account ledger? Will a Capo di Tutti Capi forgive and forget so easily? Will I continue shutting my eyes every time I turn the ignition key?

With the need for more space for a growing Candy, we move to a two-bedroom double on Tugie Street, just a few blocks away. It has a carport and a little fenced-in-backyard where we can turn Candy loose. In the rear apartment resides Kenneth and Fern Milstead, with daughter Stacey, who is Candy's age. And soon, we become the best of friends. While the children play, we play hearts. Fern, like Carolyn, is a housewife. They spend hours together talking and drinking coffee. Kenneth's 9 to 5 at State Farm, I envy, because when I sit down with them, I can't be sure I'll get to play the cards I'm holding before I'm rousted and sent running.

Tonight, it's dinner with competitor Pete and his gorgeous wife Georgia. Pete talks incessantly. "Jack you know, I almost won the Pulitzer… Jack you know, I'm my own boss… Jack you know, I make more money than you." Until finally, I've had my fill of his putdowns. "Pete you know, I made over fifteen thousand last year." With widening eyes, Georgia interrupts with, "Gosh Pete, you didn't make nearly that much." To ease Pete's humiliation, I add, "That's only because I get overtime pay and Pete doesn't." Pete, turns up his old fashion, and responds, "Come on, let's play cards." Several games, and one too many highballs later, Pete confesses, "Jack, you really busted my ass with that Marcello picture."

A few days later, Pete is made an offer he couldn't refuse. Take severance pay or take a transfer to Dallas. Pete takes the transfer. And now Pete, the once UPI heavyweight is back in the lightweight division with me. And like me, under the thumb of a boss, with the power to push his buttons both day and night. Even on Christmas Eve.

With Pete's abrupt departure messing with my head and keeping me awake late, I summon Makesense for a reality check and ask, "That's kinda scary isn't it… what happened to Pete… and after he came so close to winning a Pulitzer." "Not so scary so much as it is… reality." "What you mean?" "Like I said before, life goes on, grass grows and needs attention. And what can you do when your yardman sits in the shade drinking lemonade all day and never gets behind the lawn mower except…?" "Yea I know… fire him… and that's what scares me… because I now know, that you're only as secure as your next picture is good… and forget about yesterday's accolades… because today, they won't save your ass." "Anything else Cousin?" "Yea, let me lighten the subject a little and ask, did you ever tell a lie?" "No Cousin, never have, never will." "Well, let me ask you this… Have I ever told a lie?" "Well Cousin, Makesense must refuse to answer… because that answer Cousin, will definitely incriminate you." "Good night Makesense." "Good night Cousin."

A few weeks later Pete's replacement arrives, his name is John Frair. He's young and eager to make a name for himself. So, that'll take blood… mine.

Today is November 21, 1966, and it finds reporter Crider and I flying up to Memphis to cover the trial of James Norvell. He's the man charged with the shooting of Meredith. And the alleged man raising his head in my now famous picture. After landing we rent a car, load up, turn the radio on and start driving toward downtown when a news bulletin sounds… Norvell pleads guilty to the shooting of Meredith… his plea change comes one day before his trial to begin… he was sentenced to two years in jail.

After making a U-turn and start heading back to the airport, I find many questions are following… Was the shooting an act of impulse? If not, it was planned. But planned by who? Norvell? The Klan? Then, why birdshot and not the deadly buckshot? And without a trial, the questions never get answered. My conclusion: Birdshot indicates impulse. Unless of course, a publicity seeker contracts a wounding and not a killing. But since Norvell shot for the head and not the legs, that's about as likely as what the Grenada waitress claimed… Life Magazine did it.

Another Christmas comes with Candy turning one. Perhaps, her big smile and her big blue eyes can cheer me up for a change. But down deep, I know that's not likely. Hell, nobody and nothing has been able to lift the depression that grips me at this time of year. Carolyn wants a tree and we get one. At age 27, it's my first. If I could only pretend to enjoy Christmas, if only for Carolyn's and Candy's sakes. But with those Sugar Bowl pressures starting and rising day and night, there's no time to pretend. And nor is this a time for pretending. Not with UPI's new gun in town. And knowing he's looking for a kill shot. And if that distressing concern isn't depressing enough, there's the reality of Vietnam and the headline… Our plane drops our bombs on our troops killing 16 marines and wounding 11 more. God! How I hate this time of the year.

In January 1967, Lurleen Wallace keeps husband George in power by becoming Alabama's first lady governor. As she takes the oath, you can find me standing back on the same steps the Selma March ended on just two Springs back. And have things changed here? And for the answer, just look up and see the flag of the proud Confederacy yet flying, yet signaling the status quo.

On Saturday afternoon of February 18, the phone rings. "Hello Jack, this is Ed." "Yea Ed." "You need to meet Crider over at the courthouse." "Why, what for?" "To play catch-up… We missed a big news conference." "Whose?" "District Attorney Jim Garrison's. The one announcing his investigation of the Kennedy assassination." "What!" "Yep, according to UPI, he claimed the plot was hatched here, right here in New Orleans. And New York is bitching and wanting us to match it." "Okay Ed, I'm rolling."

Driving there, I'm wondering, how do we match it if the news conference is long over and everybody is long gone. Gees New York, it is Saturday afternoon. After hooking up with Crider, we rush up to Garrison's office and we find the foyer deserted. No media. No secretary. No warm bodies, not even a janitor's. "Looks like we're screwed Bill." But the cool, the calm and the persistent Crider walks over to the D.A.'s closed door and knocks. And who answers? And who invites us in? None other than the 6-foot-6 pistol packing D.A. himself. "So you AP fellows, missed my news conference? Take a seat. Let me try to make it up to you." And not only does he rehash the stale meat and potatoes, but he pours on a little gravy, fresh gravy.

"Since you fellows gave up your Saturday afternoon, I'll give you something extra. Something I didn't announce earlier." Bill and I sit still and silent, as Garrison pauses to take a draw off his pipe before continuing. "I will make an arrest… and soon… and I will get a conviction."

The Punctual Press missed this, served only to us latecomers, and we end up scooping everybody. UPI is baffled. They think we made it up. They know we weren't even there. This should have been their scoop, not ours. Now, their New York office is screaming at them, "Match this… And fast." After talking with us, "Big Jim" compounds their misery by losing himself for the weekend. And UPI, nor anyone else, ever catches up, with him, or with us.

As "Big Jim" keeps his word with the arrest of business executive Clay Shaw on March 1, and charges him with conspiring to kill President Kennedy. If there's truth to it, it's a big story. If it's a lie, it's a big story. Either way, the world's top reporters converge on New Orleans, bringing their investigative tools and trying to dig up the truth. At least, the media circus, playing on and on, keeps me in town. But sometimes, that just seems to bring the bad news home.

On March 30, on their final night in New Orleans, the 32 high school seniors from Juda, Wisconsin, a hillside hamlet of only 300, are concluding their poolside dance and starting back to their rooms at the Airport Hilton for a 1 a.m. curfew. Above, a Delta DC-8, on a routine training flight, is circling. And then, at 12:51, the airplane while making a steep banking maneuver, falls from the sky, crashes into the rear of the Hilton, explodes, and brings me running.

Over there! A priest gives the last rites. My flash explodes. There! A fireman hoses an engine. Flash! There! The tail section against the Hilton. FLASH! And then I step on something. It feels like a body. And when I direct my flashlight down, I see it… Geesums!... It's not a body… It's a hand.

After rushing back to the office and expediting the night views, I return to the scene at daylight. It's sealed off. The FAA—Federal Aviation Authority—has secured the area. The press is prohibited. And from the street, you can't see a bloody thing. So I defy authority, flank the police, and go in. The tail section, I see is still the best picture. Click! Click! And then, I see the burnt-out engine blocking the doors of two rooms. After moving closer, I look inside and I see the rooms turned to charcoal. Every inch, the walls, the ceilings, the floors, blackened and burned. And I see where just hours earlier, the horror of horrors unfolds… Finding their escape blocked, the eight Juda girls retreat, take refuse in the shower and turn the water on. There, clinging together. There, praying together. There, screaming together. And finally, there… cremated together.

Consumed by thought, I stand there, motionless, yet drifting, until a loud voice snaps me back together. "Hey! You're not supposed to be here," the deputy snaps, "This area is off limits. Come with me."

In all, 18, including nine Juda classmates perished. One, Linda Williams, age 17, had a premonition about the trip. Before leaving, she told her minister that, "Something serious was going to happen." And yet, she went. And perhaps, dispelling her fear with the rationale… What is life without your friends.

And for me, their horror of horrows ends as… Just a picture… Just an 8x10 glossy… Just a story… Just a beat or a humiliating defeat. For such is the nature of the beast—The news business. "Damn it to hell, Makesense, without a hard shell, this business crushes you." "That it can Cousin, THAT IT CAN."

In Nashville in April, Stokely Carmichael clamors "Black Power" again, and three days and nights or riots follow at Fisk University. In Peorio, Richard Speck is convicted for his heinous crime. For eight lives, he gets life. Late in the month, I fly to Houston where Cassius Clay refuses to fight, not in the ring, but in the Army. For ducking induction, Clay is stripped of his championship belt.

Between rounds of the Garrison-Shaw-Kennedy conspiracy theory goings on, on May 1, I happen to be at home with the afternoon off. And that's because Chief of Bureau Mangan sent me home at noon, so I could return that night to cover a boxing match and naturally, without any overtime cost to him. Carolyn is out, and I'm on the floor with Candy when that dreaded sound disturbs our play. Oh hell! What now, I'm thinking, as I pick up the phone. "Hello Jack, this is Gavin. Guess what?" "There's a bloody riot somewhere and it started without me." "No Jack, that's not it." "What then?" "You just won the Pulitzer." "What!" "That's right." "Jesus! Are you sure?" "Sure I'm sure, it just came over the wire."

Still, in my mind, I'm not so sure, so I summon Makesense. "Are your ears up and were they up for the call?" "Are and were Cousin." "Any chance this is another clerical error, like the Army's, the one that put me in photography?" "Not a chance Cousin, Makesense heard what you heard." "Then you believe?" "Yes! Yes! Yes! And cousin, and if there was ever a moment for joy, it is now. So enjoy the moment." "And therein lies the problem Makesense. It's only a moment. And the very next moment, the call is indeed about a bloody riot, and I'm up and off and the joyeater is back and gobbling."

After Carolyn comes home, after I shock her with the news she gives me a big hug and her, "Congratulations Jack, you deserved it."

What does the Pulitzer Prize mean for Carolyn? More money. More clothes. A big home. Probably, all of the above. And for me… more pressure. The rationale. If you're so great Jack, you have to continue being great. And Jack, you're only 27, the youngest to ever win Journalism's highest award, but remember, there are many, many, many more riots, revolutions and hurricanes ahead. And soon, the greatness is reduced to a paragraph in "Who's who", the monster of a book, and who reads it? Hell! Who can pick it up?

And in person, I don't pick up my Pulitzer, even though Carolyn and I are extended an all-expense paid trip to New York for the ceremony by Columbia University. Instead, on May 12, I'm presented with a riot in Jackson. It's night and I'm looking down on Lynch Street from the second floor office of the N.A.A.C.P., just across from Jackson State, an all-black college. Downstairs, rocks and bottles are flying at passing cars. During a lull in traffic, the students turn their attention to a parked luxury car, obviously the property of a white, turn it over and then, set a torch to it. With the car in full flame, I yell to AP reporter John Pearce, "Hey John! Come take a look." After rushing to the window, and looking down, he exclaims, "Christ-a-mighty! That's my car… my brand new car."

With my thoughts stirred and disturbed by the glow of John's car, with the rioting intensifying and with the national guard enroute, I start asking myself... why the fuck am I here and not in New York, eating my filet mignon, sipping my champagne, hearing my name amplified and taking my bow? I could have insisted on going. Chief of Bureau Managan could have insisted. New York could have insisted. But nobody insisted. So, I'm here. Boom! The gas tank explodes. The guard is pulling up. And I realize... It's time to cut the crap... It's time to face up... It's time to get down stairs... It's my livelihood... It's Carolyn's livelihood... so fuck danger Jack... Get the picture.

Back home, while at the grocery store shopping with Carolyn, I pick up a magazine. "Look Carolyn, here's a picture of Priscilla Beaulieu." "Who?" "The under-age teen Elvis groomed to be his bride... the one he met while serving in Germany with me." "Gosh! She's beautiful and he's so handsome." "See the date of the wedding... May 1... Does that ring a bell?" "It sure does. That's the same day you were awarded the Pulitzer Prize." "Yep, and after seeing Priscilla all grown up, it looks like he topped me in the prize department." "You think Elvis saw your picture in the paper and remembered you from Germany?" "Not a chance Carolyn... Not a chance."

A few days later, my prize arrives in a big brown envelope. It's nothing special to look at. Just a white certificate, only the size of an 8x10 photo, with bold black letters saying... The trustees of Columbia University in the City of New York make known to all men that Jack R. Thornell has been awarded the Pulitzer Prize in Journalism for News Photography. Holding it up to Carolyn, she exclaims, "That's it?" "Yep, that's it."

And with it, comes news more than disappointing. Call it unbelievable. Call it upsetting. "He's gon'na do what? Damn it! Not again," is my response to the caller. "Yes, again. In late June and early July." "Mother Fuck-errr! Forget the goddamn sniper. The heat'll kill him... and me."

James H. Meredith looks at me, half smiles, and shakes his head as if I owe him money. Obviously, he's thinking that this poor white boy got rich off his black ass. Well, he's wrong. After the certificate came a check for $1,000, which the AP matched. So, rich! No Mr. Meredith, dead or alive, your black ass was only worth two grand to me. What about a merit raise... surely? Sorry, not a dime Mr. Meredith. I'm still making union scale, the same pay the worst of the worse AP photographers make.

This time for Meredith's encore march, I put my foot down and complained to New York, "There's no way I can cover this alone and be with Meredith every step of the way." They agree and bring in Bourdier from Miami to join me.

Along the way, we share a motel room and conversation. And finally, one night with Jim stretched out on his bed and me mine, and after the sharing of a few beers, I bring the conversation around to someone else we may have shared. "Jim, tell me about New York and your time there." "About New York... or about Kay?" "About Kay." "Well Jack, I knew how you felt about her, so I'm reluctant to say anything." "Hell Jim! I'm married. And I'm long over Kay," I lied. "You sure?" "Absolutely Jim, absolutely," I lied again knowing that I would never be over "My Kay", not absolutely. "Okay then. I took her out for dinner and drinks. After I took her home, she invited me in. Naturally, I accepted. And then, she disappears into the bedroom. Minutes later she reappears wearing a short and sexy negligee. And you know the drill, so, the rest, I'll spare you." I imagined the rest. And it hurt. Absolutely.

Several days later, we're staying at the Monte Christo, Bourdier's first and my third time there, when at 4 a.m. the phone stirs us. Bourdier picks it up, answers, and mouths to me, "It's New York Photos." When he hangs up, I ask, "What did they want?" "They want you to get back to New Orleans… and pronto." "Why?" "Jane Mansfield just died there." "Shit! How?" "In a car crash."

After driving to Jackson, boarding a plane, and now sitting there at 30,000 feet, my head is pounding with questions. With the big one being… Will anyone have pictures I can get my hands on… and pronto?

When arriving at the Times-Picayune building, I bypass my office, and rush right in to the newspaper's darkroom. There, I sigh with some relief when I find the film of photographers G.E. Arnold and Terry Friedman. Both have police scanners at home. And both rushed to the crash scene without knowing that one of the victims was the blonde Bomb Shell. "Geesums! What luck for them… and for me." I'm thinking as I slide my eyeball from frame to frame, until I freeze, "Jesus she's been decapitated!" I relate to Makesense as I see long blonde locks trailing off the dashboard. And then, Arnold joins me in the darkroom. "Gerry, is this Jayne's head… on the dash?" Smiling he replies, "No Jack, it's one of her famous wigs. Apparently it was dislodged when her head shattered the windshield." In the next frame, on the pavement she lies, covered, but for her favorite cowboy boots reaching out from under the bleak white sheet. "Gerry, did you uncover her boots?" "Now why would I do that?" "Hell yes you would… you know you would."

After the pictures are transmitted around the globe, UPI suffers a monumental shellacking. Fisher is undoubtedly elated that he's not in New Orleans to take the heat. And his replacement, Frair, isn't here either. He lasted only eight months. So who is? Well, there's a new gun in town, the one gunning for me, is Bernard Cleary. From Austin, Texas, he has a wife named Laura, and they have seven children. And was "The gun" at the scene? Not before the bodies of Mansfield, her lawyer-lover Samuel Brody, and her chauffer Ronnie Harrison had been removed. Not before her injured children had been rushed to the hospital. And not before the wrecked car had been towed. And unable to get his hands on the Times-Picayune photos, thus the shellacking.

On July 4, Meredith finishes his second "March Against Fear" without incident and without marchers. Instead of ending at the Capitol, it ended at Canton. Instead of 2500, only a handful showed. And without birdshot and blood, most of the media dropped out miles before. Even Bourdier, leaving me alone for the finale, and Meredith, with only sore feet and an aching back for his effort. And why so fruitless? I call it the Meredith Malady. And liken him to slow peaches. Late to bloom. Never ripening. And never enjoyed. And nothing a pinch of Dr. Martin Luther King's charisma wouldn't have cured. Had he had it, with his history, he could have become "THE KING" of the civil rights movement. Instead, he remained, the wounded loner.

Later in the month, a national "Black Power" conference calls for a "Black Revolution". It suggests splitting the U.S. into two equal parts. A black half… and a white half. Within four

164

days, Detroit riots leave 44 dead, 1000 injured and another 2600 arrested. The dollar cost: 200 million.

This violent change in the civil rights movement forces change on me. The change is called swapping sides. During earlier demonstrations, fearing the Rednecks, even the police, I stood with the non-violent blacks and behind their lines. Now, fearing the Blacks more, I stand behind police lines. The difference, a brick or a billy. And, with Dr. King's non-violent notion still mudding the water, my dilemma is compounded. Changing sides, changing colors, continues on. Today, white. Tomorrow, black. "Oh, Makesense, how I long for the days of sepia tone."

While thousands, coast to coast, protest the Vietnam War, I stand outside the federal courthouse in Meridian. Inside, a preliminary hearing for the men charged in the slaying of the three civil rights workers is underway. Outside with me, the cameramen congregate, and Laurens Pierce of CBS—the photographer waylayed at Philadelphia in my place—is holding court. "Damn it I'm tired of getting roughed-up by Rednecks… and today I'm prepared," he declares. "Here take a look at my invention," and then, he holds up a heavy duty hammer handle. It's been modified to screw on the bottom of his camera. But it ain't attached to his camera. It's attached to his wrist, secured by a rawhide loop. And then, after swinging it back and forth through the air violently, he stops, laughs and states, "Camera extender or ass protector. Today, I feel… ass protector."

The hearing concludes. The defendants scatter. One, Alton Wayne Roberts, an ex-night club bouncer confronts hammer-handled Pierce who swings away, but missing his target, until Roberts secures the handle and Pierce's wrist, locking both between his left arm and body. "Look out Laurens!" someone shouts, "Here comes his right." And with Laurens' body unable to give an inch, his chin takes on full force of the blow as my Nikon clicks. And today the photographer is "THE PICTURE" and front page news, with New York Photos declaring, "We don't get this kind of picture at boxing matches… even 15 rounders."

With October comes the main event: The KKK—versus—The FBI. The trial for Sheriff Rainey, Deputy Price and twelve others, and the trial of the decade down in Mississippi, is about to commence. Friday night, three days before, I'm home in Metairie drinking beer, when Carolyn says, "It's for you." And hands me the phone. It's Terry Keeter, a former colleague and drinking buddy, from my Daily News days, and now the court reporter for the Meridian Star. "Hey buddy, when you coming up?" "Sunday night." "Well, that's too late. Get here by noon and no later." "Sorry pal, but I'd have to get up with the roosters to get there by then." "Jack! Just get here. Pick me up at the paper. We got someplace to be at 1 p.m." "AAAH Terry, what are you doing to me?" "Sorry, I can't tell you more, but trust me, it'll be worth the lost sleep," the mysterious Keeter concludes. After I agree to get there, and after the hangup, my suspicions abound. He just wants me there early to begin buying the beer early. And if that's it, I'm going to be pissed, really pissed.

After picking up Keeter in Meridian, the mystery leads up to the home of the Rev. Delmar Dennis. He's a circuit preacher. But more importantly, he's a titan of the Ku Klux Klan. And most importantly, he's seen the light and turned FBI informant. After failing to coax him into his KKK robe for my picture, I convince him to just hold it up to the camera. With the picture taken, the Rev. Dennis returns the garment to his closet, after straightening it neatly on a hangar.

And now, Keeter wants his beer. I oblige, and after the first gulp, I ask, "Why the urgency? Why couldn't I have taken the picture tomorrow?" After emptying his glass, and bursting into laughter, he reports, "Because tonight, the good Reverend vanishes." "Vanishes, why?" "He's a SECRET witness at the trial. And until he testifies, he'll be in protective custody. The FBI's." And then, while putting his arm around me and pulling me close, he orders another round, chuckles and says, "Thornell, for this scoop, you're getting off cheap… cheap… cheap."

The picture is printed and held until the preacher has his day. That day, the Rev. Dennis, still under wraps, is slipped into the courthouse, unseen by the cameras, even mine. On the stand, after confessing to the error of his ways and after admitting to getting tax dollars for his testimony, he provides information linking the Klan to the killings of the three civil rights workers.

During the afternoon break, two FBI men pass me, stop at a newspaper rack, look down at the front page, and see their secret witness with his Klan robe, spreading across four columns with AP photo by Jack Thornell under it. Seeming shocked and perhaps, pissed, the duo do an about face, approach me and one asks, "You're Thornell aren't you?" "Yes, that's right." "How the hell did you get that picture? We've had him hidden away." "I got it for a six-pack. And I got it cheap, cheap, cheap," is my smiling and only reply. Shaking their heads, walking away and undoubtedly still pondering the how of the picture, they can be certain of one thing. They too had been sold out. And cheap, cheap, cheap. For less than the price of a newspaper.

Another witness, James E. Jordan, gives the gristly details of the deadly night. In his monotone voice, telling all… Deputy Price springs the three… chases them down… catches up… stops them… and delivers them to his KKK pals. Then, they take them down a desolate dirt road in the dead of night… and shoot them one by one. "I was just a sentry down the road. I didn't see the shootings. I only heard the shot," Jordan swears. "A liar! A murdering liar. A nigger murdering liar," one defendant calls Jordan.

The trial climaxes with U.S. Attorney John Doar reading the confession of one defendant, Horace Doyle Barnett. "Jordan comes running up after Schwerner and Goodman are shot, yelling… Save one for me… and shoots Chaney as he backs across the road. "At least I killed me a nigger," Doar quotes Barnett quoting Jordan saying.

Down in Mississippi, it's been three long years now, since the brutal and senseless murders of Mihael Schwerner, 24, Andrew Goodman, 20, and James Chaney, 21. And now the all-white jury is deadlocked. That is, until Judge Harold Cox, delivers the "dynamite charge" jolting them back into deliberations. On the morning of October 20, 1967, a reporter comes running out of the courthouse shouting, "The verdict's in! The verdict's in!"

Among the convicted are Deputy Price, Slugger Roberts, and five others. Acquitted are Sheriff Rainey and seven others. On three the jury stayed deadlocked. Photographer Pierce, with his black eye not forgotten, is delighted, as is one of the most liberal newspapers in the state. Greenville's Delta Democrat Times sees the outcome as "Lightening the moral burden which has been crushing our state for generations." Even Jimmy Ward's Daily News, perhaps the most conservative in the state, prints, "The guilty findings will also discourage those bent on violence from future activities of that sort in Mississippi."

"Makesense. Your ears up?" "Up." "Does the time fit the crime? That sort: A hate crime. A triple murder?" "And what is the time Cousin?" "For violating those boys civil rights by murdering them, it's a maximum of ten years." "Yeeps! That seems a bit short of justice doesn't it?" "No Makesense, awfully short."

With the trial over, the thought of going home feels good, with the sight of Carolyn and Candy inviting. "Makesense, life sure has its twists and turns doesn't it?" "How so Cousin?" "Well before Candy was born, I didn't want her… the responsibility… and now, I can't imagine being without her." "Like I said before Cousin, life goes on, grass grows and needs…" "Yea! Yea! I know the rest. And I'll attend the backyard ASAP."

With December comes the first successful transplant of a human heart. In Cape Town, South Africa, 55-year-old Louis Washkansky takes the heart of a young woman killed in an auto accident, lives another 18 days, and dies. And the question I ask and answer, would I? To live another day, or two, or three? No! No! No! Not even for a million more.

Despite a Pulitzer adorning my living room wall, 1967 ends, leaving me tired, tired, and tired. And with last year still wearing on me, 1968 begins with that same old and tiring question continually asking… What next?

While famous baby doctor Benjamin Spock is facing the pain of a federal indictment over his "How To Avoid The Draft" book, I'm facing my own. Back pain. Lower back pain. Dr. Stuart Phillips, an orthopedist, points to the X-ray, says, "Disc problems. See right here." And prescribes "light duty." For me I explain, "Light duty is three Nikons and a camera bag bouncing up and down on my neck and shoulders." An amateur photographer himself, he says, "Those cameras can get heavy." Agreeing, I add, "Let me tell you about my heavy duty," I add, "It's lugging a transmitter, a power pack, a complete darkroom etc." "You mean enlarger trays, tanks, photo paper and such?" "Yep, and just the "such" is another large case full." "Wow! That's some heavy lifting." "Heavy enough to give Superman a hernia." Dr. Phillips gets the picture, places me on light duty, and warns, "With lifting comes pain and possibly surgery." And suggests I keep my driving to a minimum until my back mends. While leaving Dr. Phillips' office, I reflect back and to another warning, Editor Ward's, "Take that job and it'll bust your balls and break your back." And now Editor Ward is right on both predictions.

Despite my "light duty" assignment, Chief of Bureau Mangan dispatches me to Jackson to cover the swearing in of the first negro legislator ever elected down in Mississippi. It's a momentous occasion, especially for me. After an uncomfortable three hour drive, I slowly and carefully get out of the car, lug the transmitter up a flight of stairs, set it up, and then, I go to the Capitol building and cover the story. With my picture spinning on the transmitter, pain strikes and sends me spinning. It's a sharp pain, a repeating pain, a pain like I'd never suffered before, excruciating, and so excruciating a body would die to stop… and soon. It sends me sprawling across my old desk at the Daily News and sets me to screaming and crying like a newborn. And I can't help myself, even though my Kay is watching me helplessly from her desk. Until finally, the stretcher, and the trip to the hospital with the screaming sounds of the ambulance's siren joining and muffling mine. A first shot of Demerol has no effect and I beg for another. And with it, relief. Without it, give me cyanide and fast. Jim Bonney, the reporter who covered the arrest of Sheriff Rainey with me, places me on the backseat of my car and drives me back to New Orleans with me holding tightly to my bottle of Demerol. Hospitalized, with traction, I get better and avoid surgery, but with Dr. Phillips reminding, "The knife is swinging above your spine like a pendulum. From now on, it's a constant threat."

In March, a salt mine collapses at Calumet, LA. There the families wait. There I wait. There their trapped loved ones numbering 21 are found, not alive. There, with my camera, I invade their cries.

Sunday night late, Atlanta Photo Editor Garcia calls and says, "Jack, somebody screwed up. We don't have a photographer in Memphis and we need you there." "When and for what?" "Tomorrow morning… for a King march." "What time?" "It's scheduled for 10 a.m. but you know the Blacks operate on C.P.T." "And colored people's time means an hour or two later." "Yea, but to be safe, be there early." So, before daylight on March 28, 1968, I'm on a Delta flight to Memphis wondering… why me? Atlanta has two staff photographers. So why not one of them? Isn't Tennessee their responsibility? Why must I get screwed over someone else's screw-up? "Hey Makesense! Wake-up." "Up." "Tell me, why me?" "You know why Cousin." "And what do I know?" "That you're afraid to say no… because you feel that no is not an acceptable answer, not if you want to keep this job." "And ain't that one hell of a conundrum Makesense?" "And how so Cousin?" "A job I'd die to get out of… A job I can't live without."

The march, in support of the striking garbage men, is gathering. The press, including myself, is waiting. Strange I don't see Sammy, I think, because this is his territory, and he should be here. Knowing that UPI's shooter is missing, allows me to relax a little. Finally, Dr. King and his entourage arrive. After shaking a few hands, Dr. King, with the Rev. Ralph Abernathy—his right hand man—at his side, takes the lead and steps off. Sending me into motion, back pedaling, facing the march and firing my Nikon. After three or four shots, I turn about, move to the side, and continue marching.

After turning onto famous Beale Street—the origin of the Blues—a segment of youths break ranks with 6000 marchers and begin breaking windows and looting stores. King, seeing his lifelong advocacy for non-violence being desecrated, flees. I follow the rioters. Police rush in with billy clubs swinging and tear gas streaming. A policemen passes me, grabs hold of a looter, and raises his club. As it starts downward, my camera clicks. In the store window, another looter… I see… as my Nikon sounds catching him in mid-air jumping overturned furniture and carrying a new suit coat. Then, more looting and more clicks, until I back off and into the middle of the street. Then, I look up and see a barrage of bricks and bottles raining down on me. Too late to run, I freeze in place as the missiles crash against the street, just missing me by inches. Then, a tear gas canister explodes. Its fumes find me. Crying and coughing, I retreat and rush to the darkroom with two rolls of film and without a scratch. And then, in the supposed safety of the darkroom, I get hit. Quickly switching on the light, I see a yellow jacket buzzing about after swooping down and burying its stinger in my right temple. "Damn it! That hurt," I say to photographer Bob Williams as I emerge and find him standing there. He pulls out the stinger, applies ointment, and I survive, avoiding the humiliation of a lifetime with the headline… Pulitzer Prize winner survives riot, but succumbs to WASP bite… as my laughable epitaph.

Photo editor Garcia and photographer Kelly, who, like me, must have been off Sunday night, fly in that afternoon to assist with coverage. Sammy finally shows, but well after the riot, claiming his flight was late. And for Sammy, a friend about to get stepped on, about to get hurt, I feel for, because I can feel myself standing in his shoes one day soon, helpless, and anticipating a decimation coming. And when the morning edition of the New York Times—the bible of journalism—hits the street with four of my pictures—two on page one and two inside—appear with my by-line, it's evident that I not only stepped on Sammy, and hurt Sammy, I crushed him. And completely. Now, the two best showings—the Meredith shooting and the riot—of my short career have come in Memphis. And at Sammy's expense.

The rioting ended with 16-year-old Larry Pain shot to death, with over 50 injured including police, and with over 4000 National Guardsmen patrolling the streets.

On the flight home, I summon Makesense. "What about these riots, in the North, in the South, in the East, and in the West." "Don't know Cousin, don't know." "Want to know the cause and the remedy?" "According to who?" "President Johnson's national advisory commission on civil disorders… so says this article." "Read on Cousin." "White racism is essentially responsible for the explosive mixture which has been accumulating in our cities since World War II," said the commission, adding that "Racism and riots would split the nation into two societies, one black, one white—separate and unequal—unless massive and costly remedies are begun at once." "Why unequal and not equal?" "Cause the white majority has got the economic power and the gun powder for keeping it that way. Did you see any black faces in the ranks of those Tennessee guardsmen standing there, at ready, with their bayonets fixed?" "Not a one Cousin, but Makesense saw one great picture there." "Which one?" The one you took of the little black boy running his finger up and down the blade of that bayonet, feeling its sharpness." "Yep. And at his early age he learned something else. Call it a fact of life… that too many white folks still need a body to look down on… a black one."

In Memphis, a week later, it's storming out. Lightning flashes. Thunder bursts. Wind whips. Rain batters. And the windows of the Masonic Temple rattle. Inside, striking sanitation workers sit, pondering their plight. For their messenger is still upset. Upset about the rioting… Upset about the looting. Upset about a boy's death. Violence is not his way. His Nobel Peace Prize proves it. Violence is the white man's way. As the messenger makes his way through the throng, the sound of applause overcomes the noisy elements still beating down.

Dr. Martin Luther King Jr., takes the pulpit. Four thousand eyes look up and bear witness to his prophetic words, now rising above the turbulence, occasionally punctuated by thunder.

"I just want to do God's will. And he's allowed me to go up to the mountain, and I've looked over and I've seen the Promised Land. I may not get there with you. But I want you to know tonight that we, as a people, will get to the Promised Land," proclaimed Dr. King, whose passion and his preaching is, and always was, one for non-violence. And yet ironically, it was violence that brought him back to Memphis this April Wednesday. And it will be violence that will not allow him to depart.

The next afternoon at 3 o'clock, a neatly dressed white man rents a room at 422 ½ South Main. A bathroom window down the hall offers a clear view of the Lorraine Motel. After renting the room and checking the view, the man registering as John Williard, disappears, keeping to himself and out of sight.

Across a weedy, debris-strewn lot, just 205-feet away, in room 306, a light conversation is unfolding. "Hey Doc! You're getting fat," preacher Samuel Kyle jokes, ribbing his idol Dr. King, a guest at the Lorraine, who is dressing for dinner, grins back as he struggles to button his shirt collar. Through dressing and needing a breath of fresh air, Dr. King steps out onto the second floor balcony where he is soon joined by associate Jesse Jackson, who introduces Ben Branch, a member of the "Breadbasket Band". A smiling King requests, "Ben, tonight I want you to do Precious Lord". But before an answer, his smile shatters... his tie severs... his neck... his jaw separates and the mighty champion of non-violence, is slammed back against the wall before falling to the floor with blood from a ghastly fist-sized wound gushing, and gushing, with the echoing sound of a rifle shot ending.

At St. Joseph's Hospital, just past 7 p.m., the spirit of a preacher, a prophet, a poet and a King... passes.

And perhaps, someplace, someone is shouting... Look up and see him and hear him... crossing the Jordan... over into The Land of Milk and Honey... over to a place even the great Moses couldn't go... A place where everyone is sepia tone... There! Duty free... Free to loosen his collar... Free to taste the sweet evening breeze... Free to embrace a peace so perfected... There! A place, a peace like never before. There! The Promised Land... There! Home! And with the realization of his faith becoming sight, the voice of the preacher man echoing across the heavens... "Free at last, free at last, thank God Almighty, I'm free at last."

A news bulletin breaks into the program, "Dr. Martin Luther King Jr. is dead... Assassinated at a Memphis motel," stirring me up and off the couch and setting me to pacing like an agitated cat, just like Mother when a storm was disturbing her peace. My first thought... Thank God I'm here and not still there. My second... Does Kelly have pictures? God if he doesn't, I wouldn't want to be in his shoes. And my third... Shit! They'll be calling any minute and sending me back... to fry... because the blacks are gonn'a burn Memphis down. The phone rings. "Carolyn! Don't answer that... I've got to think." She obeys. The ringing stops. Then seconds later the ringing begins again. "God damn it! Let it ring... Let me think." When the ringing ends, I pick up the phone, call the airport, and find the last flight for Memphis at 10 p.m." As soon as I hang-up, the ringing resumes. "Carolyn, we're not answering until 10 o'clock." The ringing continues as does the intensity of my pacing. At 10:05 the phone rings for what must have been the hundredth time and I pick it up and get my marching orders from photo editor Garcia. As soon as I hang up Carolyn asks, "Are you going to Memphis in the morning?" "No, I'm going to Atlanta this weekend for the funeral." "What about Memphis?" "It's already flooded with staff photographers." "Had they tried to call you earlier?" "That I don't know and hopefully I'll never know." Relieved for the moment of not having to face the music in Memphis, I wasn't relieved of the guilt I was feeling for not answering the phone. I had never ducked an assignment before, I had always answered the call... until tonight.

But, ugly violence answered. And although Memphis isn't burned to the ground, bricks and bottles are hurled at cars there, in Jackson and elsewhere. Travis Crow Jr., age 19 and white, is the first to die, a victim of a fire bombing at Tallahassee, Florida. Memphis police shoot and kill a negro man. In Detroit, two policemen are wounded by gunfire. In Boston, a crowd of negroes stone police cruisers while in New York's Harlem, looters roam 125ᵗʰ Street. Washington was the worst with negro mobs looting stores and burning buildings within two miles of the Whitehouse where a white man was dragged from his car and stabbed to death. With the dawn's early light, an aerial photograph—showing smoke still billowing from buildings in the foreground and the spared Washington monument still towering in the background—is recorded for history lessons. When the smoke clears, 46 are dead amid property damage in over 100 cities.

Sunday is declared a day of mourning, "In our churches, in our homes and in our private hearts," by President Johnson who orders the American flag to be lowered to half-staff on all federal facilities throughout the world. For a Negro, it is the first time such an honor has been bestowed.

Saturday, on the flight to Atlanta, I'm thinking of my photographer friend Kelly and feeling his pain. He wasn't there for the shooting and the local newspapers weren't there either. Nor was UPI. So, seemingly, there's nowhere to turn for "THE PICTURE". What Kelly must have gone through with New York's screamings, constant and clear… get "the picture"… draw it if you must… but get it. The pressure he must have felt until… the pressure got worse. Not having "the picture" is bad, but if nobody else has it either, especially UPI, it's not as bad. And the getting worse begins when an AP photographer flown in from Chicago lets the only person who does have "the picture" get off the phone without successfully bargaining for his film. And worse, he lets him hang up without getting his name or his phone number. And when New York Photos say, "Call him back and offer him the moon," he can't.

"The picture" by student photo-journalist, Joseph Louw appears exclusively in the next issue of Life Magazine showing a collapsed King, with a towel over his bloodied neck and head, and with his comrades pointing in the direction of the shooter. The bargained price: $10,000. And that turned out to be some bargain for Life, who then sold the picture around the world. And to the Associated Press for a rather large capital gain.

Saturday around noon, I arrive in Atlanta, rent a car and drive to the bureau. There's turmoil there. Photographer Horace Cort is in the darkroom. He has abandoned his vigil at King's casket. We're unprotected at the scene. On duty photo editor Phil Oramous sees me walk in and shouts, "Jack! Get to Spellman College… Mrs. King… the kids are on their way to view the body." "Shit! Where is Spellman College?" A black photo stringer hears and says, "Come, I'll drive you there." Now! I'm in turmoil. With my thoughts driving ahead… What if I'm too late… What if Mrs. King has come and gone… And what if all that New York hears is that Thornell missed "The Picture"?, when it's Cort's ass that should be taking the kicking. Pulling up to Sisters Chapel, I shout, "Oh Shit!" As I see two empty limos already parked out front. "Oh shit!" The security guard stands at the door, blocking my way. "Sorry sir, but no one else gets in until the King family comes out." Ignoring his order, I push past him and start running down the aisle, while setting F-stops and shutter speed and while seeing the King procession stepping onto the stage. Hurriedly, I cut in between pews, step up on one and seeing that I'm still too far, I start high stepping pew to pew like a hurdler at a track meet and turning mournful heads… until I reach the row where the UPI photographers sit. There, I stop, focus and shoot, as someone lifts King's young daughter Bernice, age 5, up for a better view of "Daddy", as Mrs. King looks on. It's over in a flash. And then, UPI's Pete Fisher, my old New Orleans nemesis, looks over, shakes his head and whispers, "You lucky bastard… We've been sitting here all day for that."

With my heart pounding like a jack hammer, and with my sweat pouring, "lucky" I only feel all those mournful eyes turning to outrage, hundreds of them, and turning on me and fixating on me and condemning me, for my outrageous and disrespectful behavior. With my eyes on the floor, in a state of humiliation—much like the day I was publicly awarded that illegitimate high school diploma so proudly by Capt. Colville—I withdraw from the chapel… But not without "The Picture".

Outside the Ebenezer Baptist Church, the crowd is gathering early. It's Palm Sunday. Thousands are finding it difficult to find two square feet of space to stand in. For the services inside, 1300 are seated. Outside, some 50,000 stand. Make that 50,000 and 1, since my feet are among them. And after yesterday's embarrassment, I'm grateful and perhaps lucky to be here, to be lost among the masses even though my body is being squeezed like a dry lemon. Senator Robert Kennedy is here. So are Vice President Hubert Humphrey, Senator Eugene McCarthy and New York Governor Nelson Rockefeller, to name a few. On this day of national mourning, Kennedy is unaware that his own twilight is drawing near, and that in just two short months, he too—like Dr. King and like Brother John—will be lying in his own pool of blood, gunned down by an assassin. Before these eyes of the elite, and those of the world press, King's coffin is placed on a plain farm wagon drawn by two scruffy mules, a symbol for and his parting gesture to his beloved poor.

The five-mile procession winds through Atlanta, with the powerful and the wealthy uniting their voices with the powerless and the poor to sing, "We Shall Overcome". At Moorehouse College, King's Alma Mater, I'm thankful to be positioned on a raised platform above a sea of humanty, estimated at 150,000. The photographer next to me places one of his Nikons down on the platform between his feet. And when he reaches back for it a few minutes later, it's gone. As is the champion of the civil rights movement. Etched in Georgia marble above his resting place, the epitaph reads… Free at last, free at last, thank God Almighty, I'm free at last.

So long Dr. King. We've shared some scary times together, haven't we? And what was the scariest? Was it the Memphis riot, the time you ran? Was it the Meredith march, the time you got pushed around? Was it at Money, Mississippi, the time the white madman approached your podium yelling obscenities? Was it somewhere between Selma and Montgomery, the time you sensed a sniper's scope. Or, was it at Philadelphia, Miss., the time you, Brother Abernathy, and I walked into the sheriff's office unnanounced? Remember you were marching nearby, when something moved you there. The place the three civil rights workers were last seen alive. And you were so scared, as was I. I could see it on your face. I could see it in your eyes. And I could feel it in my every fiber. Yes Dr. King, we were some scared that day, scared enough to unite and form "fear incorporated" and yes, God walked with us that day, because Sheriff Rainey, Deputy Price, and the Klan Killers were out and didn't see our comings or our goings. So long Dr. King, I'll keep you alive, alive in my memories, particularly… the scary ones.

Upon my arrival home, little Candy comes running to the door screaming, "Daddy! Daddy! Daddy!", and jumping into my arms. With a successful assignment behind me and with her hugging arms drawing tighter, the load of my responsibility seems to lighten, but ever so slightly and only temporarily. Because within a day or two, that little high will drop faster that "Little Boy" fell on Hiroshima. And my demand for perfectionism—Carolyn's—explode again and again. "Goddam it Carolyn! Why can't you get the fucking work done before I get home?" "Jack, I try." "Try hell! Try drinking less fucking coffee with Fern." "Jack! Jack! Candy will hear."

Immediately, I walk into the back yard and start the lawnmower, but, instead of its roar slowing my thoughts, it propels them... From you Carolyn dear I only demand small things... and... from me, the AP demands great things. Can't you see, can't you realize I can't keep doing this... the job... not until I'm 65... Either I'll get killed at a riot... or... I'll be forced to begin silence with a bang... So Carolyn dear, why can't you try harder... Why can't you please me? And why don't I tell her these things, so perhaps then, I won't feel so lost, so alone and so much a prisoner still of 503? It's the same old story that I know so well, that with even a whisper of my inner going on's, I'd weaken and I'd crumble until my crumbling is complete.

"Makesense! Makesense! Your ears up?" "Up Cousin." "That's a beaut of a twister isn't it?" "How so Cousin?" "My outer strength lies and lives by the keeping of my inner weakness—my shame—secret." "You mean like the mighty Sampson?" "Exactly... and what happened when he exposed himself?" "He crumbled Cousin, he crumbled." "Exactly." "But Cousin, Caroyln saw your home and met your mother." "I know! I know! And her knowing just doubles the humiliation and the shame I feel. And that, those thoughts I can't tell... ever tell... without crumbling."

And so, the remedy for relieving the burden of my guilt for verbally battering Carolyn for and with my insecurities, I believe will come with the hoisting of a few with the boys after work. And those daily hoisting stops, get longer and longer and later and later. But instead of turning into a happy drunk, when Carolyn greets me with, "Where have you been?" I turn into a meaner man. And naturally, Carolyn feels the pain. So what's the solution for me, the job and Carolyn? Money! Money! Money! And the accumulation of it, I figure. And with it, the power to retire by age 50. And perhaps, sooner rather than later, so I can say, take this paycheck and shove it, and let my life begin. And with gold as the goal, I tell Carolyn that we must start spending less and saving more for retirement. And what did she say? A better question, what could she say? Not a goddam thing. Because, she knows all too well, that around here Honey, the words of Jack R. Thornell ARE THE LAW.

"We will have a bad summer," said President Lyndon Johnson, "And we will have several bad summers before the deficiencies of centuries are erased." Richard Nixon, a Republican party candidate for president predicted war in the streets. Black Nationalists warned of guerrilla warfare in the brick canyons of American cities. The U.S. army sets up seven task forces totaling 15,000 men, "Specifically earmarked and available for civil disturbances." National, guardsmen practice anti-riot techniques. Cities assemble stocks of riot control armaments and send policemen to special mob control schools. And there are stories circulating of vigilantes organizing, of housewives taking target practice, and of blacks and whites alike urging their friends to get guns. The pessimistic forecast is reinforced by the wave of violence sweeping across America since the King assassination. With more than 100 cities torn by riots, with 46 people killed, and with more than 3500 injured, one might ask, if this could happen in April, what will the heat of July and August bring?

"Makesense, your ears up?" "Up Cousin." "Reading these AP reports, it sure looks like a long, hot and violent summer ahead." "That it does." "What does Makesense think about it?" "That Makesense goest where thou goest." "And hopefully, thou and Makesense comest home together. And in one piece."

In May, racial violence flares in Salisbury, Maryland after a deaf mute negro is shot dead by a white cop when he failed to stop for questioning. And black militant H. Rap Brown is found guilty of the federal firearms act for bringing his automatic rifle aboard a passenger plane in his carry-on bag.

On June 5, moments after making his victory speech in the California presidential primary, Sen. Robert F. Kennedy is fatally wounded by an assassin's bullet. A 24-year-old Jordanian named Sirhan Bishara Shirhan, soon to be known as just Sirhan Shirhan, is arrested.

If Bobby had to die, I'm thinking, I'm sure glad he did it way out west. And not closer, like Memphis, Atlanta or Miami where I might have gotten stirred into the mix. Most young and eager photographers want to draw the big stories, to get "The Picture" and to make a name for themselves, but not me, because the bigger the story, the more I want to be somewhere else. But unfortunately, "The Big Story" often seeks me out, and even comes to my door.

Carolyn interrupts my thoughts as she returns from a doctor's visit and finds me sitting on the sofa. "Jack, I've got some news." "And what is it?" "I'm pregnant." "You're what?" "You heard, I'm pregnant." "How pregnant?" "Two months… the baby is due in January." And surprisingly, the news is less alarming than it was when she announced Candy's coming that fateful day in Jackson. And before I can digest her news, she interrupts my thoughts again. "And I've got more good news." "Jesus Carolyn, I'm not sure I can handle any more good news right now… Don't tell me it's twins." "No, no, not that." "What then?" "I've found us a house." "A house!" "Yes, I've been looking for a while… and now, with another child, we'll need another bedroom." "And where is this house?" "Come get up and I'll show you." "Okay, I'll look, but I'm not promising anything."

The house is on Utica Street, about a mile from where we live. It's very nice, carpeted, with three bedrooms, two baths, living and dining rooms and a very large paneled den with a wet bar. Compared to 503, it's a palace fit for kings. I can see that Carolyn appears to be standing in heaven, but when I look over the back fence and see grading equipment, I see something else. I envision a noisy hell coming on wheels. "Carolyn, we can't, I won't buy the house." "But why, it's beautiful." "Hell! Within a year, maybe less, Interstate 10 will be roaring past our back door." With Carolyn, shrugging and not seeming to care where her dream house stands, I try shaking her up. "Damn it, have you ever seen the crater left by a dynamite truck that crashed and exploded. I have. It's huge. And this is ground zero."

Carolyn keeps house hunting but keeps bringing me back to ground zero. Or the money, she finally convinces me to forget about dynamite trucks, gasoline trucks, nuclear waste trucks and such. And so, for four thousand down, we purchase 5236 Utica for twenty-six thousand. That withdrawal weakened our savings account and me, because now, with only two thousand left, my dream for an early retirement is disturbed… and even worse, delayed.

In late August we move in and the very next day, I depart for the National Democratic Convention, leaving Carolyn behind four months pregnant and with a house to put in order.

Chicago! Chicago! I find, is not my kind of town. And forget the heat and the humidity. And forget the taxi, the bus, and the telephone strikes. And forget the hippies, the yippies, the disenchanted liberals, the far out radicals and the impassioned college kids, who one and all want to stop the war… the Vietnam War… And to do so, are willing to wage disorder despite the billies, the bayonets, the gas and the guns, awaiting.

But don't forget that Al Resch—in the flesh and not on the phone—is here and waiting. The man with the ax, the man every AP photographer fears after a major fuck-up. And even if he doesn't drop the ax, he most assuredly will be breathing down every neck, hot and heavy, while simultaneously airing his demand… "Boys! This is the story…" now get "The Picture".

Rather than being in Resch's presence, I'd take a gassing, and the first night there I do. Common sense should have dictated that two Chicago photographers, both knowing their way around, and more importantly, having cars to get around, should have been dispatched to cover the anti-war demonstration. But instead, the less than sensible editor dispatches an older—never covered a riot before—New York photographer to accompany me to the park. And to get there, because of the strike, we find it hard, but finally do, hail a taxi. About two blocks from the park, the driver stops and says, "This is as far as I go fellows." After leaving the cab, I find this is as far as my comrade in cameras is going. Standing on the curb and pointing to the dark park ahead, he says, "I'm not going in there." "But how can we get pictures if the shit hits the fan?" "Fuck the pictures." "Are you kidding?" "Hell no! And if you go, you must be crazy." But what the fearful photographer couldn't comprehend was… that it is the fear of missing the picture, the thought of it, that drives me crazy and on into the darkness ahead.

At 10 p.m., police with megaphones order the mass of protestors "to leave or be arrested." The protestors budge not, but the police do. And wade in. And, like in Memphis, I duck the bottles and the billies, but not the tear gas. It got me. But not before two rolls of film get exposed.

At the staff dinner, the night before the convention starts, my buddy Bourdier is table hopping until he stops, faces boss Resch and offers some advice, "Hey Al, remember Miami, the Republican Convention?" "Yes." "Remember how the Miami staff covered the rioting?" "Yes." "Well, we're in Chicago now, so, let the locals cover it." Resch smiles and says, "Jim, you really think so?" "Hell yes." "Well, we'll see."

Later in the evening, Bourdier gets a call from the Chicago photo desk. "Jim, you've been assigned to riot coverage." "What! Who says?" "Al Resch says. He just called." And worse, I get assigned to the convention floor. And this frightens me more, at least with riots, I'm experienced. Hells bells, Mr. Resch, I don't even vote.

The first night, crushed between wall to wall delegates and pushy, but experienced, press members, I feel so misplaced, with my pictures and the lack of a good one showing. Yet, night after night, the stubborn Resch keeps sending me back, with Bourdier dying to be in here with the media stars, and me dying to be out there ducking billies and whiffing gas. But after three hectic-hectic-hectic nights and after thousands of pictures had been taken by a dozen AP photographers, two stand out. One is mine. Showing Chicago Mayor Richard "The Boss", Daley raising an ugly and contorted face showing his disgust with Senator Abe Ribicoff's blistering attack on the "Gestapo street tactics" deployed by Daley's street cops. Back at the hotel, I pass Bourdier in the hallway. "Hey Jim, I see you survived. How was the war?" "A bitch, a real bitch, and that Resch is a son-of-a-bitch, a real son-of-a-bitch."

Happy to be leaving, even happier to be airborne and high on success, while laying my head back, closing my eyes, trying to relax, while trying to think of tomorrow's news and how it might affect me. And now, unreachable at 36,000 feet, I try enjoying a peaceful flight home. An hour later, a clap of thunder rocks the plane and shakes me wide awake. Lightning flashes and cuts inside. The plane shakes and shakes. And I shake and shake. Still early afternoon, after forcing a look out, I see the sky is BLACK-BLACK. The thunder, the lightning, the shaking worsens as does the fright collecting on faces. As silent prayers accompany the loud and violent sounds of the storm, a shaken voice—the pilot's—comes over the intercom advising, "The storm is worsening… we're changing course… flying east, then south… we'll approach New Orleans from the Gulf… we hope to be out of this shortly." Shortly hadn't come soon enough when I ask, "Makesense, your ears up?" "Up! Up! Up, Cousin. And as your Army idol Elvis might sing… All shook up and then some."

After landing an hour late, more heat and humidity greets me as does a pregnant wife. As does the thoughts of more responsibilities, more stories, and more pressures awaiting. And not even to the car yet, with a new mortgage to pay and soon a new mouth to feed, I'm already feeling the pressure and thinking… Nothing ever gets better for me, just worse, and just possibly, even before tomorrow's sun comes up, because the news never sleeps.

After surviving another draining Sugar Bowl and a most depressing Christmas, I'm presented a son—Jay Randolph Thornell—on January 9, 1969. United with Carolyn and with Candy under the sign of Capricorn, leaving me the lone Virgo, the outsider. The perfectionist, and asking… Stars, you look down, measured my roots, you see my emptiness, my incompleteness. Stars, how can one born into such imperfection, such incompleteness such as I, expect, even demand perfection from anyone under the stars? And yet, oh stars, do I.

After two years of tall talking about his Kennedy assassination theory, D.A. Garrison is doing some more. This time before a jury trying to hear evidence and not just "tall talk" against the charged Clay Shaw. "Conviction", he said, "would be the best way to communicate to the government that we do not accept fraud… The government murders truth… and if it can murder truth… it can murder freedom." After 34 days of hearing "evidence" or "tall talk", the jury is only out for an hour. At 1 a.m. on March 1, the foreman reads, "We find the defendant not guilty." And their decision for acquittal comes after just one vote. One, David I. Powe, reports the thinking. "Garrison had a right to his opinion about the government and the Warren Commission, but I just don't feel his 'opinion' is enough to convict a man." My close-up of a beaming Clay Shaw behind a "not guilty" headline indicates "the fraud" was Garrison's and not the government's. And the man charged with conspiring to murder President Kennedy is free, but financially ruined, all for a whim… Big Jim's.

One day later, I'm up and off to Memphis to cover another trial, James Earl Ray's. The man who allegedly used a .30-06 Reminton Gamemaster with 2370 pounds of knockdown power—enough to drop an elephant—to kill Dr. King. Just as the jury is selected, Ray, surprisingly, changes his plea to guilty. And instead of facing trial and endless questions as to the how of it, like in the Meredith shooting, those questions never get asked or answered. Yet, how could an escape from the Missouri State Penitentiary, who had been less than sensational as a burglar and a robber, under the alias of Eric Starvo Galt, plan and kill King, get a false passport, pay for travel, and live, until his capture at a London airport?

And yet, with the plea, I'm more than a little delighted, because a trial would have lasted weeks, maybe months, and days and days of my having to chase lawyers, run down witnesses and fight for position when inches could mean a mile of difference in getting the best picture.

In May, a milestone is set when a black man is elected mayor of a bi-racial—two thirds black—community down in Mississippi. Charles Evers the brother of the slain Medgar, is the one going to head city government at Fayette, and he's the one who picked up the phone right after Dr. King was shot and heard, "We just killed that black S.O.B. Martin Luther King—and you're next." Does the unseating of R.J. Allen, a white man who'd held the office for the past 20 years, make him an even higher priority target—or—are things a-changing, even looking up down in Mississippi. Maybe. Maybe not. But since 15 of 16 white city hall workers resign before inauguration day, suggesting they'd rather be jobless than working for "that Nigger", so, just maybe "THE MAYBE NOT" deserves the capitalization,

"That's one small step for a man, one giant leap for Mankind," Astronaut Neil Armstrong broadcasts as he puts a foot down on the moon. It's 10:56 p.m. EDT, Sunday July 20, 1969, and I'm there, not on the Moon, but in Houston following the footsteps of the Moon-man's wife. And sharing a room with me is another Pulitzer Prize winner. His picture of a Viet Cong prisoner being shot in the head by a South Vietnamese general is world famous, as is Eddie Adams, considered by many as the best of the best, and certainly so, by his employer, the Associated Press. After getting up this morning, I find Adams is anxious. "New York orders me here and expects me to come up with a picture." "Of what?" I ask. "Something different, something spectacular, I don't know." "Now, his worry is worrying me even more. If the best of the best is feeling pressure, how much more should I be feeling?" Geesums, I'm ready to explode, and not only because of New York's expectations but because Philadelphia Photo editor Achatz—general ash-shitz—is here and in command.

That afternoon, Adams and I take our worries to the Armstrong house. Finally,Mrs. Armstrong emerges with the children. The press rushes her, jocking for position, and I win the middle ground. After a light-hearted question, with an uncontrollable burst of laughter, with her head bending back, and with her mouth stretching wide, my shutter snaps and freezes the moment. Back at the darkroom at the Space Center, I approach Achatz and ask, "I get anything decent?" Without breaking his stern expression, or his rigid jaws, he merely points to a print on his desk. And though a staff photographer from the New York Daily News was there, next to me, my picture captures the front page of his paper. And, that day, I beat 'em all, even the grat Eddie Adams. AND IT WAS only a MATTER of inches.

After returning to Metairie, I surprised myself and Carolyn by driving up to Vicksburg, picking up Mother, and returning her for a visit. Her first. When she steps out of the car and sees our new house, her eyes widen in amazement, perhaps shocked to find a Thornell, any Thornell, living in such a fine house. Air conditioned, with two baths, and with carpet on the floor instead of the worn and stained linoleum found down at 503. Hell, in all her sixty-two years, she'd never lived under a roof that didn't look to be on the verge of collapsing on her head. And when she sees the Pulitzer on the wall proclaiming the Thornell name to "ALL MEN", is she proud? If she is, she never says "Congratulations!" How to say it, even how to spell it. Isn't in a Thornell head. Hell, the only thing she'd known about the Thornell name was, it only brung poverty and pain. And from Brothers Ben, then John, she'd got plenty of both. With her every "Goddamn", Carolyn cringes as I warn, "Mother watch your mouth… The children." "Shit Son, I don't mean nothing." After three days of warnings, Mother is ready to return to 503. And I'm ready, more than ready, to take her back to where she belongs… At the bottom of that hill.

And after I return, I become ever more careless with my mouth, particularly after stopping off for a few too many with the boys over at Beau Louie's. And why does a wife have to stir up those ugly-ugly words and pull 'em out of me by starting in on me at the door with, "Where have you been? You know what time it is? Your supper's cold." Instead, why can't she greet me with, "Welcome home Dear, your supper's on the stove. Come, I'll warm it up for you." Instead, I get the spaghetti and the sauce, warm it up and start to eat when she starts in again, "Jack! You're drunk. You got a wife. You got kids. You got…" And before she can continue that list of my responsibilities. I let her have it. With a lift and a jerk of the plate, I send it flying across the table with the perfect aim to hit the target… her face. Now, heavy with sauce, just the way I like it—my spaghetti. "Goddamn it woman! Shut the fuck up!" I shout as she flees to the bedroom trailing noodles and tears. Fuck the dinner, I'll just have another beer, I decide, while asking myself… Do I have a drinking problem? Fuck naw! Carolyn's mouth… that's the problem.

Brother Marshall, on his second wife Jerry, still lives with Mother and with their three kids, Marcie, Kenny and step-son Roger. Marshall, I don't understand. And his apparent state of contentment there, even now, with a bathtub, and hot and cold running water, and a window air conditioner for his and Jerry's bedroom. And as for the rest of it and the apparent state of decay inside and out, he doesn't flinch or express an ounce of disappointment of shame. And that, I'll never understand.

As for brother Garrett, he's still living, but not for long, in a little frame house in Monroe with wife Nell and their children Jimmy, George, Ronnie, and Judy. In comparison, my Metairie home swallows theirs, with plenty of room leftover. In the backyard Garrett keeps a garden and a swing, where he sits alone for his thinking. Despite the lack of an education, he's got quite a brain, not only for numbers, but for mechanical things. And when I visit and join him on his swing, sitting that close seems to make him uncomfortable. And before he finds excuse to move away, what do we talk about. Not much. For Thornell men, sharing isn't a family tradition. Brothers by blood, I reckon, but the gene for getting close to anyone, except for sex, is sorely missing. And as for not getting close, that is a family tradition.

Outside winds are pounding, rain is pouring, transformers are sparking and popping, while inside, windows are breaking and children are screaming as these words echo, "I think, and pray the building will stand up." Those less than comforting words coming from a civil defense spokesman about his sturdy, several stories high, brick and concrete headquarters. Outside Hurricane Camille is playing hell. Hell with Gulfport and hell with the entire Mississippi Gulf Coast. Inside, reporter Guy Coates and I are huddling on the floor with several families taking shelter there. Outside, Hurricane Camille is blowing and blowing its way into history books with its 200 mph-plus winds breaking gauges and making it a, "Storm of the century."

Earlier that afternoon I'm on a beach at a nearby Biloxi trying to find storm preparation pictures, but since the storm is predicted to hit the Florida panhandle farther to the east, I find sunbathers and a few people boarding up windows, but certainly nothing breath taking. After checking in with the office, I'm told that Bureau Chief Mangan wants a word. "Jack, call your mother right away." "What for?" "She's been giving me hell for sending you there. And she keeps calling and calling and wanting to talk to you." "I'm sorry about that. I'll call her right now." When she got to the phone over at Mrs. Lane's house, she gets hysterical. "Jack! Jack! You got to get out of there… This storm's gon'na be a goddamn monster." "Mother! Mother! Simmer down, it's supposed to hit east of here. It'll be safe." "Safe shit! If so fucking safe, why ain't your boss's ass a setting over there instead of your'n." "It's my job Mother, I can't leave." "Son, this here Camille is gon'na be bad, I can feel it in my bones. And bones don't lie." "Mother, I got to go, get back on the job." "What good's the fucking job to ya' if ya' get blowed away."

Late that evening the storm doesn't turn east, but instead keeps churning north, and toward me as if I have a big bulls eye painted on my back. And with every report, getting stronger and stronger. Before dawn, just like Mother felt in her bones, a monster tidal wave twenty feet high breaks ashore. The six-story Hancock Bank building disappears. Only its unopened vault is left behind to find. "The wind is blowing rocks," a Gulfport deputy reports, "There's a boat out in the parking lot and we're three blocks from the harbor." Dozens of tornados spawn, and twist down shredding structures. Large ships are beached. The resort towns of Waveland and Pass Christian, a few miles to the west, all but vanish. In Pascagoula, snakes! "There are hundreds, and I mean hundreds of black water moccasins and cotton mouths in Mother's back yard," a shaken Anne Mansfield states.

With the winds still howling, I' still sitting here and waiting for first light, the kind I hate, so I can venture out and photograph the damage done. And while waiting, I'm filled with fear, not of getting "blowed away" as Mother feared, but of getting blown away by the competition… UPI. And with the history of Betsy and Hilda still alive in my head and reminding me constantly that covering hurricanes is my weakness, my Waterloo, getting "blown away" seems likely, mighty likely.

And but for the support of Bourdier, Hudson and Phil Sandlin out of Miami, "mighty likely" it would have been, because after being kept up all night by the storm and being worn down to a frazzle by anxiety and anticipation, I am not in the best condition to take great or even good pictures. Putting it bluntly, I'm a wreck in need of a tow. And when I finally step outside, I feel totaled, because I see wreckage everywhere. And like Mardi Gras, it's difficult to single out a good picture from so many possibilities. And when I get to my company car, a little four door Ford Falcon, I shout, "Thank God," and "Thank God," because the giant oak fell south, rather than north. Otherwise, my wheels would have been crushed, and I would have been stranded. Highway 90, the main coast road, I find has been ripped up, littering the beach with huge chunks of concrete. The big Bay ST. Louis bridge is covered with a sea of debris as if a designated dump site. Over 200 are dead and the damage is estimated at over a billion dollars. And the Mississippi Gulf Coast, likened to Hiroshima after the atomic bomb exploded, is my stomping grounds for weeks and weeks. In the end, I'm lucky, because I'm neither blowed or blown away.

After things have calmed in Mississippi I'm back in Metairie, and back at Beau Louie's with another storm brewing. With my laughter with the boys and the barmaid exhausted, and with a six pack downed on an empty stomach, politely, I bid goodnight. And somewhere between inebriation and home, rage overtakes me. Pulls me over, and the monster gets in. And when the monster opens the front door, a smart mouth, wide and loud, greets it. "You're drunk again. You can't keep doing this… to me… to the kids." "So fucking what? Ain't I entitled? Who makes the money? Who pays the bills? Who fills the plates? So just get the fuck out of my face." "No! No! I'm not. I'm not putting up with this… I can't… Not any more." "What fucking more you want woman… an ass whipping?" And before she can reply, she feels the sting of the monster's hand slapping across her face. And next she feels the weight of the monster's body straddling her's down on the floor. And with the monster's hand raised and readying to strike again, a little voice rushes in screaming, "Daddy! Daddy! You're hurting Mommy." Looking up and seeing those beautiful eyes of blue streaming down a contorted face of four, shame subdues the monster, and Daddy gets off Mommy.

The next morning, hung over, ashamed and alone in the kitchen, I ask myself… Will the picture of Daddy hurting Mommy be forever etched in those beautiful eyes of blue? And will sweet Candy ever again come running and screaming, "Daddy! Daddy! Jump into his arms, hug his neck, and feel safe and secure, knowing that inside Daddy, a monster lives.

And if little Candy, in search of understanding, could put pen to paper, perhaps she'd write in her diary something like this… Entitled two silly questions.

Mommy! Daddy! Can trees talk?

Mommy say can. Daddy say can't.

Can! Can't! Can't! Can!

They fuss. They fight. I cry.

Mommy! Daddy! Do we need trees?

Mommy say do. Daddy say don't.

Do! Don't! Don't! Do!

They fuss. They fight. I cry.

Mommy! Daddy! Do you love me?

And do I apologize for being that monster, before leaving for work? Apologize? And break a Thornell tradition. Now that's a silly question. But before I reach the car, I hear a voice from the past, Mrs. Bounds' ringing ever so loudly, "Young man! Young man! A husband, a father, you're not."

Driving to the office, I consult Makesense. "That monster wasn't so bad… only one slap." "Cousin, it might as well have been a thousand." "A thousand? How so?" "Now every time you raise your hand… even your voice… slap or not… she'll feel it… and it counts against you."

The next day, with the umbrellaa of evidence escaping around Carolyn's dark glasses, the monster sees… the monster learns… ass whippings are out, are word whippings are in… without an ugly eye starting back, and condemning the monster within.

Today, awful anticipation is riding with me to Baton Rouge and driving my thoughts… Will the riot be over?…Will I get killed in the morning papers? The getting there consumes me, even suggesting that slight turn of the wheel to the left or to the right will end this awful anticipation. But when I get there the riot isn't over, and I spring into action. The deputy levels his shotgun, it blasts, and its muzzle smokes, as my camera clicks. With it, a good picture, my worry weakens. Today, it's the campus of Southern University, where eight students are wounded during their clash with police protecting firemen fighting a blaze. And with order restored and that awful anticipating ended, that same disturbing question keeps arising and asking… With success killing you, what will failure do?

On November 10th, there is rioting in Memphis again, and again I'm back. Here, police, armed with riot guns, battle 400 negro youths hurling rocks and bottles. The melee began after police arrested 53 demonstrators demanding an end to white resistance to racial equality. Memphis, like New Orleans, is a river town, but instead of red beans and rice, the aroma of barbeque ribs cooking, escapes into the alley and pulls people into the Rendezvous to dine at tables covered with red and white checkered clothes. Unfortunately, it ain't the great ribs, that keeps bringing me back. A few months ago, it was confessed King killer James Earl Ray. But, ain't he serving a 99-year sentence for his evil deed? He is. But now, he wants to take back his guilty plea and stand trial, but the judge says no and his sentence stands. And all he gets for his trouble is a chance to set me on my ass, and at that, he succeeds.

In handcuffs, on his way back to jail between two deputies, he enters the garage of the courthouse and finds Sammy and I in his face, back pedaling and shooting. But, he has his head down, way down, making it difficult, if not impossible, to photograph his face. So I keep lowering my camera, back pedaling, and shooting unaware there's an ankle high concrete barrier rising behind me. When I hit it, my legs stop, but my butt comes crashing down and the impact sets the Nikon over each shoulder to bouncing off the pavement. And then, as Ray reacts by raising his head in laughter, comes THE PICTURE. And I miss it. And I miss it because my hands are still glued to the pavement from catching my fall, and I can't get 'em back to the third Nikon still around my neck. And I'm helpless, armed only with my thinking power… Laugh you murdering bastard… Laugh for the next 99 years.

Sammy gives me a hand up and asks, "You okay Jack?" "Oh, I'm fine, but I'm not sure about my cameras." "Well then, I'll see you." "Yea Sammy, thanks, see ya," I say as I depart hoping and praying… that this is the last I'll ever see of James Earl Ray. At least, in this lifetime.

In January, 1970, a first Superbowl hits New Orleans, and I find the covering of it to be a bitch, a real bitch, and equal to the record setting pressure of Hurricane Camille. There're workouts. There're press conferences, and with two teams, the Minnesota Vikings and the Kansas City Chiefs, double that. And while special requests from dozens of newspapers for a picture of this player, then that player, smothering me, even interfering with the coverage I must supply the AP, while thousands of fans are pouring in, filling the French Quarter, swallowing raw oysters by the dozens, peeping through doorways at near-naked ladies, and then, mellowing out by tuning in some soulful jazz or by turning up Pat O'Brien's famous Hurricanes from dusk till dawn. Essentially, everybody but me, is having a good time. Even the band of AP photographers, the best of sports shooters, find time to enjoy the town. For them, covering a Superbowl is a reward. They dine, they dance, they tell old war stories and laugh their asses off while I'm working and worrying off mine.

Bourdier is here. Chasing skirts and trying to score. And appearing to be at the top of his game without a worrisome thought crossing his mind. How do you do it, shut it off, I want to ask, but couldn't. But when we're alone, I do ask, "Jim, I know I owe this job to you. But do me one more favor." "And what's that Jack?" "When you need help covering your next riot, your next revolution, be a friend, and don't ask for me. Ask for somebody else." Jim doesn't pry as to the why of my request, he only breaks out into a laugh, perhaps, he just assumes I'm joking, because when he gets in a next hot spot he continues calling New York and asking for me. Perhaps he figures, that with me at his side, I'll do the worrying for two. And he's right, so, so right.

And speaking of worrying, with a new boss, a third already, here I go again. Having to prove myself again. Having to please new eyes again. And feeling a fresh demand… Thornell! Your past performance has upped the stock of my predecessors… Now! Get out there and up mine. His name is Ed Tunstall. A native son, a Tulane grad returning to his roots. And actually, I find him a blessing when compared to his two penny-pinching predecessors—Summerlin and Mangan. His attitude—cover the story and screw the cost—I find most refreshing, and even better, more rewarding. And the opportunity to up his stock value and mine, is soon at hand.

Some say dead. A victim of a bomb blast. Others say alive and living in a foreign land. The FBI says fugitive… A "ten most wanted" in America. And Stokely "Black Power" Carmichael says of his successor as chairman of the student non-violent coordinating committee, "You'll be happy to have me back when you hear from him—He's a baaad man." And of this 1971 night, everybody hears. This night, in a Westside New York bar, twenty-five black patrons lie face-down on the floor under the gun. As four robbers flee, they run into police outside. A gun battle ensues. Two officers and one suspect are shot. The tall, thin black male, nursing a stomach wound, says little, except that his name is Roy Williams. Fingerprints say H. "Rap" Brown, a federal fugitive for the past seventeen months. His birth name—Hubert Geroid Brown—hardly an engaging one, soon changes when rallying black militants calling for "armed action" to get them social justice, began shouting at their new leader, "Rap it to 'em baby." And thus, "Rap" is born.

In New York, nobody gets pictures of his capture or his bedside arraignment or his leaving the hospital for jail, and everybody wants 'em. And wants 'em bad. And unfortunately, that's where I come in. A few weeks later, news editor Prince calls me over to his desk and says,

"Guess what Jack?" "What?" "H. "Rap" Brown is coming to town." "What!... What for?" "To face charges for carrying that carbine on a plane... the ones he skipped out on." "Shit! Shit! And more shit," I exclaim while thinking and asking... "Why does the heavy stuff always fall on me?"

With hundreds of Big Apple photographers... newspaper, AP, UPI, and free lancers still unable to lock a lens on "Rap Baby", day by day, the demand is growing and the pressure is building. Meanwhile, his hearing is scheduled at the federal court building in the French Quarter. Just across from the famous Brennan's restaurant. The time is set for 10 a.m., but for security reasons his travel plans, both his departure from New York, and his arrival in New Orleans, are kept under wraps. And all the media knows, and all that I know, is that "Rap Baby", is supposed to be seated in that courthouse by 10 a.m. Wednesday. And I also know, that the federal marshals are not going to parade him past, or have to push him through a herd of pushy reporters and photographers. And when I decide what I'm going to do, the day before the hearing, I approach the news editor Prince and ask, "You mind if I leave a little early today?" "What for?" "Because I'm coming in real early tomorrow." "For the Brown thing?" "Yep." "How early?" "2 a.m." "Are you kidding?" "I wish I was." "Take off, there's nothing going on."

At 2 a.m. Thursday, I'm pacing up and down Chartres Street, near the back door of the courthouse, and passing wine-o's sleeping in the shallow green space just off the sidewalk. After watching the sunrise, and with my legs long past weary, the familiar face of a U.S. marshal, arriving for work at 8 a.m., approaches me, and asks, "You here for Brown's appearance?" "Yes, I am... since 2 a.m." With his smile widening, he responds, "Well that's postponed until tomorrow."

And tomorrow, having lost a little enthusiasm and a lot of sleep, I'm back at 4 a.m., pacing and wanting to trade places with the drunks all curled and sleeping. At 5 a.m., a sedan races up and stops near the back entrance. With my flash charged and ready, with my 35 mm lens pre-focused at six feet, I approach the car. Four men get out. One, I see, is Brown. Quickly the agents surround him, rush him past me and through the door, but not before I get two quick flashes off and capture the face that has escaped so many cameras before. It's 5:01 and but for those sleeping souls, I'm back alone, but, within minutes I'm back at the bureau and alone with "THE PICTURE" most wanted in America... "Rap Baby" in cuffs.

At 9 a.m. as I'm returning to Chartres Street to await Brown's departure, a WDSU-TV cameraman sees me coming, looks down at his watch, then, back up at me, obviously thinking that he is seeing something unusual—catching me tardy—announces to the already assembled media mass ever so loudly, "Hail! Hail! Mr. Jack Thornell is here. So let the news begin." Laughing with him and at him, I announce, "Hello! Hello! Mr. Mike Lala. I'm not late... because I was 27 hours early." And finally, at ten to ten, the competitor clearly of UPI shows, and sets me to thinking... if I had seven kids to support, I would have arrived earlier than ten minutes before a ten o'clock hearing, a lot earlier. Perhaps, 27 hours. And from his New York bosses, Mr. Bernard clearly, instead of hearing, "Hail! Hail! He catches, "Hell! Hell!"

183

With my big-time score. In Boss Tunstall's eyes, my net worth reaches a new high, so high, he puts out a special promotion to state newspapers saying something like... While you're sleeping... not to worry... because Pulitzer Prize winner Jack R. Thornell is not... He's there.

Unfortunately that high, again as usual, doesn't fly for long, before it is shot down by that awful anticipation. The only high I can keep up is the thought of retiring, and like Dr. King, be free to loosen my collar. And be free to go or stay, whenever the call comes.

And when I'm not covering big stories I'm covering little ones. And when I'm not out and about, I'm behind my desk hiring and paying stringers, ordering supplies, getting cameras repaired, begging member photographers to transmit pictures in Shreveport, Baton Rouge, Alexandria, New Iberia, Hattiesburg, Jackson and Gulfport, and dealing with Wide World Photos, the commercial arm of the Associated Press, that wants me to cover conventions and such or, if I must, hire a stringer for a laughable sum. And when I feel I'm catching up with paper work, and get caught resting my eyes, I hear... Perhaps Jack, this would be a good time to get out there and come back with a real good feature picture or two. Jokingly, I ask good friend Hudson, if he'd like to swap positions. Mine in New Orleans, for his in Miami where he is now assigned. His reply, "Jack, you must be crazy. Work there in that slaughterhouse. No thank you. Because then, I would be crazy, because your job is a killer, a real killer." And what I wanted to reply, but didn't, was... It's too goddamn bad the bosses that be can't see that too. That carrying this load is killing me. Either they don't, or they don't care, because they keep on piling it on and sending me back out there and beyond my Mississippi-Louisiana border of responsibility, which is job enough. When people, whether on the street or in a journalism class, ask, "What is your favorite assignment?" "Time off," I reply while faking laughter. Then smiling back the questioner offers, "Man! You got a great job...being there when stuff happens." Great, yea I think, it grates on and on around the clock without stop whether on vacation or not, and unending until...

Bullets hit! The cockpit cracks. The rhythm of the rotor blades break. The helicopter spins, and spins out of control until dropping into the dense Laotian jungle. Lying dead in this God forsaken land are: Renowned news photographer Larry Burrows of Life, Henri Huet of the AP, Ken Potter of UPI, and Keisaburo Shimamoto of Pan Asia. Three months later, three more plunge and perish in the English Channel covering Atlantic Alliance war games. The AP's Dennis Royale is one. And leaving me wondering the why of it...

All come. Some go. Some stay.

Go! Go where? To heaven some say.

Heaven! If heaven, why do some stay?

"Makesense, your ears up?" "Up Cousin." "Why do I stay?" "Perhaps to find your purpose Cousin." "Jesus Makesense! Purpose smerf-fuss, you're back to that seek and you shall find your joy bull." "Could be Cousin, could be." "Get real Makesense, when do I have time to seek anything... even a moment's peace?"

In January 1972, another Superbowl between Dallas and Miami, is staged in New Orleans. The Cowboys beat the Dolphins 24-3, but I take a bigger beating. And that's because, just after picture day—the only day we get to film the athletes—ends. And when I'm back in the darkroom and up to my elbows in film, mine and Kelly's, who flew in to assist me with early coverage, comes a knock and a shout at the darkroom door. "Thornell! You got to get up to McComb A tornado just leveled a shopping center," shouts news editor Prince. Now, I have to drop everything, and pick up a transmitter, a complete darkroom, load up, and drive ninety miles north with a double dose of that anticipation accompanying me, knowing that today, I can take a beating in two places. New Orleans and McComb. After shooting pictures I find the Enterprize journal is without power, but I find a marine recruiter still manning his office, but more important, still with electricity. He allows me to set up my darkroom and transmitter there. After I'm done, about 10 p.m., I pack up the heavy gear, and drive back to New Orleans to face and to feel the continually building pressure of Superbowl week. Who won, who lost, I didn't care. I just wanted the Cowboys, the Dolphins and the pressure gone.

Paralysis is one man's price, for another, a prize and glory. "Hey George! Aren't you going to shake my hand?" Calls a voice from the crowd. Hearing the request, Alabama Gov. George Wallace turns, extends his arm, and finds a hand, just two feet away, filled with a snub-nose revolver. Five shots, in rapid succession, explode. The presidential hopeful goes down. Secret service and police converge, subdue and arrest 24-year-old Arthur Herman Bremer. On the pavement, down on all fours, in shock, Mrs. Wallace hovers over her husband, using her shadow to shield his eyes from the glaring afternoon sun. Five bullets leave seven wounds—his stomach, right forearm, upper right arm, right shoulder, chest, left shoulder blade and his spinal column.

Following the action all the way is a camera. It's in good hands. It's in seasoned hands. It's in the hands of my friend Laurens Pierce of CBS. This day, from shot one, the pictures belong to Laurens. This day, he doesn't take it on the chin. This day, the glory is his… all his.

When I hear the news and see the film, I sigh, thankful of being absent from Lauren's side in Laurel, Maryland. We've been close. Close in crowded Negro churches. Close in courthouse chases. Close in civil rights marches, even close with the same woman. Well, I remember the day he told me about her at the Federal Building in Jackson. "Jack, guess what?" "What Laurens?" "I'm engaged." "Who is she?" "Here, let me show you a picture," Laurens says, while reaching in his wallet. When he shows me, I say, "Oh! Pat Penniger. She's pretty." With his smile dissolving and his demeanor tensing, he quickly asks, "How do you know Pat?" "I dated her." Seeing his look of concern, and knowing the question—How well—he is dying to know the answer to, I quickly add, "Congratulations! Pat is very-very nice. I only dated her twice. And I never got to first base." It was good to see a look of relief spreading across a good friend's face and find his smile returning. My jaw breaking picture, an 11x14, of Laurens taking the blow, hangs on his den wall in Atlanta.

On the day after the shooting, Wallace wins the Maryland and Michigan presidential primaries by wide margins. The next day, May 17, Dr. J. Garber Galbraith, a professor of neurosurgery at the University of Alabama, reports that Gov. Wallace has less than a 50-50 chance of regaining the use of his paralyzed legs. But the career segregationist, rather than getting lucky, rolls snake-eyes and a wheelchair for the rest of his years.

"Hey Makesense! Want some advice?" "Shoot Cousin." "Well if you're a contractor, never live where you build. As ours did, right next door. And he's moving." "Why Cousin?" "He finds himself too close to complainants." "Like who?" "Like us. We knocked three times. Once for missing attic insulation. A second time for re-painting. And a third to replace warped wall paneling. And when they pulled the paneling back, I said look, there's no insulation under there. We need that too." "So where is he moving?" "I dunno, he won't say."

Our new neighbors are Bill and Billie Swart. They're from Texas. Bill, a warehouse foreman for General Motors, shows a beer gut rivaling Germany's best. Billie, I find, is a desirable, most desirable housewife. With two daughters, Linda and Darla, they are ten years our senior, but we bridge the gap by playing Hearts most Friday and Saturday nights, primarily when football is out of season and when the AP isn't running my balls off to someplace else. And before long, Billie is leading Carolyn and the children to her religion and the Hickory Knoll Church of Christ every Sunday. Although not a member of the flock, on occasion Bill accompanies Billie to the gathering of Saints, especially when a big fellowship meal is in the offering after services. A real food lover, for it, he'll stomach a sermon and a few amens, to get to the meat and potatoes. And the salad. And the vegetables. And the bread and butter. And for a taste of the six kinds of dessert. Sometimes on Sunday, after watching football and downing a six-pack of beer, he'll get angry about something, engage his wife and then, stomp off and down on the accelerator, screeching tires and disturbing the peaceful neighborhood. And perhaps, it's that common denominator—anger—we share and show that brings us closer, and more like brothers, than just neighbors.

This Sunday for me, it's the New Orleans Saints playing arch-rival, the Atlanta Falcons. For kickoff, UPI's Cleary is not ten minutes early, he's five minutes late. When he arrives he kneels down beside me on the already burning my knees synthetic turf at Tulane Stadium. After getting off a few frames, he turns my way and asks, "Have I missed anything?" "Nothing but Archie Manning getting flipped over the back of a Falcon." At first, feeling I'm pulling his chain for being tardy, he continues following the action. During a lull, he looks back and asks Times-Picayune photographer Robert Steiner, "He is kidding isn't he?" "No Bernie, he kids you not. It was a hell'euva shot." And when I processed the film, I found that it is indeed a "Hell-euva shot." The shot of the game, and perhaps, the season.

Remember where you were and what you were doing when something astounding happens. Like when President Kennedy was shot. Just about everybody does. But news photographers remember where they wasn't.

It's the afternoon of November 29, 1972, and I'm standing at a urinal in the fine new Times-Picayune facility at 3800 Howard Avenue, when Managing Editor Fritz Harsdorff, comes in and interrupts my flow. "Jack, you don't know?" "Know what Fritz?" "About the big fire downtown… at the Rault Center… there's people trapped." "No I didn't… thanks for telling me… I'm out'a here."

186

When I arrive, I see and shoot dark black smoke billowing from the top of the 17-story building. Then, I try entering the main lobby. As I'm being turned back by fire officials I meet Picayune photographer Arnold head-on. With his police-fire radios blaring in his car by day, and by night, in his home, he's the best in the city for getting to breaking news. And getting there first. At this moment though, he's not wearing the look "Scoop accomplished." Instead he looks troubled. And then, I hear why. "Jack! I hear some people just jumped." "Shit! Jumped where?" "Off the back of the building." "Oh shit Gerry! We're on the wrong side." Now, running and circling the block to get to the back, my head is being hammered with the unthinkable… I missed it! I missed it! I fucking missed it. Perhaps, the next Pulitzer and perhaps, Cleary wasn't tardy. But when I turn the corner, what I don't miss is the sight of the UPI stringer. The tall, lanky and hippie looking Bob Coleman is standing there, and gazing upward from the neutral ground. While sensing my worst nightmare scenario is taking life, I approach him and nervously ask, "Bob, did you get the jumpers?" No Jack, I was seconds late… but I did get a great picture." "Of what?" "People who did see it, kneeing and praying." "Want to sell it?" "How much you offering?" "Fifty bucks, sight unseen." "Man! That's a lot more than I'd ever get out of UPI." "A deal then?" "Deal." And as he's stripping his camera to hand me his film, he pauses, looks up at me and says, "Promise me something." "What Bob?" "You won't tell Bernie where you got it." "That I can do. I promise."

Meanwhile, back at the office C.O.B. Tunstall is arriving, back from a business trip to Greenville. Noting the office is abuzz, he hurries over to teletype operator Ralph McConnell, hovers over him as he is transmitting and asks, "What's going on?" Pausing, he replies, "Ed, there's a big fire at the Rault Center… people are trapped." Immediately turning his attention to news editor Prince across the room, he shouts, "We covered on this?" "Yea Ed, Thornell, Crider and McCusker are there." "Good, good, he echoes back before taking his eyes back to the copy McConnell is still typing. A minute later, after his typing is done, he looks back up and says, "Ed, there's something else." "What Ralph?" "My daughter Jacqueline is up there… on the 16th floor… getting her hair done." "Oh Ralph, no." "And Ed, there's something else… she's pregnant." "Jesus Ralph! Let's pray the firemen get to her in time."

And back at the Rault Center, the firemen tired, and franticly so. But, nets for jumps over four-stories are worthless. But, the ladder truck's reach is three stories short. But, the rope guns keeps hitting wide of the window where Mrs. Jacqueline Maillho, Mrs. Norris Farley, Mrs. Jannas McBeth, Mrs. Charles Michel and Mrs. Natalie Smith, are huddled, feeling the heat, gasping for air, and between breaths, screaming for help. Temperatures in the Lamplighter Beauty Salon are already well over 300 degrees, with flames advancing until finding the perfect mixture of gases to ignite and achieve flash over, which immediately explodes the room into wall to wall flames, now soaring to 1800 degrees. Pushed by the unbearable, the unendurable, one by one, they jump. And one by one, their bodies come crashing down. Of the five, Natalie Smith is the lucky one. If you call—nearly two months in a coma… six months in a body cast… four months in a wheel chair… and body weight dropping to 80 pounds—lucky.

Sam Katz saw it all. When he hears of the fire, he rushes to the rooftop of his 11-story 2-3-4 Loyola building abutting the Rault Center. "I want to tell you, I'll never forget those faces," he said. "They were begging for help, pleading for their lives. You just can't imagine the desperation. These women knew they were going to die. The expressions. The pleading. I have never been so close to anyone getting ready to die."

Having missed "The Picture" and having five shots at getting one, upset is the best and the worse way to describe me. But later, I return to the office and hear the horrendous McConnell story. My co-worker is best described as a quiet man, a gentle man, but his daughter isn't the lucky one. She's dead. As is his unborn grandchild. And that news too, is upsetting. But which is more upsetting, I ask myself, missing "The Picture", or hearing the McConnell story? Now, that's a cruel question Jack. And one that I'm ashamed to answer. Too ashamed.

And yet, again today, I'm lucky. With Coleman's great picture of the pray-ers, with an amateur's box-brownie shots of the women falling, and my burning building pictures, the Associated Press sweeps the play. And again, I survive the fall.

That Wednesday night, after pillowing my head, and with Carolyn soundly sleeping at my side, I summon Makesense. "It's been some day, hasn't it?" "It has Cousin, and a day for getting even." "Getting even?" "Today you got a roll of UPI film. In Selma, you gave UPI a roll of AP film… yours." "Oh yea, that's right. And I didn't even get a dime for it." "No, but today, you got a great picture. And it should have been UPI's." "Okay then Makesense, let's call it even." "No Cousin, call it more than even." "Goodnight Makesense." "Goodnight Cousin."

Today a Godfather is out burying his mother after pulling a two-year stretch in a federal pen. A pen that I put him in. It's about 10 a.m. when news editor Prince learns of the 11 a.m. services, and immediately, he calls me over. "Jack! Get to the church and get some pictures of Marcello attending." "Kent! I don't think so." "What-a-yah-mean?" "Who's the last guy you want to see at your mother's funeral… the guy who buried your ass in prison with a photograph." Prince disappears into the office of Chief of Bureau Tunstall. They talk. Prince leaves and I'm summoned in. "Am I hearing this right… you're refusing an assignment?" An angry, red-faced Tunstall shouts. Trying to explain my position, he interrupts and repeats, "You're refusing an assignment?" And all that I could say is, "No sir, I'm not." After leaving his office, I approach Prince and ask, "If this is such a fucking story, why aren't you sending a reporter?" Now, turning red-faced, he calls to reporter David Steinberg, "Go with Thornell."

Outside the church, with my telephoto lens attached to my Nikon I stand, when two six-foot plus goons approach me, stare down at me and forcefully say, "You'd better get your ass and that camera out'a here while you can." After they go inside, I turn to Steinberg and say, "It probably would have been my ass, right then and there, but for you, a witness standing there." "Thornell, since I saved yours, kiss mine." And I understand why he sounds annoyed. Hell, what's he going to write, a two sentence story. Marcello goes to Mother's funeral? AP photographer gets his asked kicked. Now, that's breaking news. When Marcello emerges behind his dear mother's casket, I focus on his face through the telephoto lens. I can see his eyes focusing back on me, as I engage the camera's noisy motor drive.

Back at the office I process, print, and transmit the excellent quality photograph. I even deliver an original print to the Times-Picayune photo desk, but with the morning paper I find that nobody uses the picture. Not the Times-Picayune, not even the Baton Rouge Advocate, which has a New Orleans edition and almost always prints every picture I transmit. And I am delighted. So much so, I write Tunstall a note saying… It looks like nobody, and I mean nobody thought the funeral was newsworthy, except you and Prince. Tunstall shoots back with his written reply. And the replying continues on for days, until he calls me in. "Jack, let's drop this nonsense. Why don't I pull our exchanges out of the file and throw them away?" "Yes sir, that's fine with me," I replied.

The battle with the boss is over, I assumed, until new and nonsensical notes, unworthy of paper, start showing on my desk. When I'm in town, and when I can, I take lunch with Picayune managing editor Frtiz Harsdoff, City Editor Vince Randazzo and chief photographer Phil Guarisco. The lunches are usually at Bozo's, where the menu of the day is catfish and beer. It's good public relation, I figure, and worthy of an hour of mine and the AP's time. But, I figured wrong, because every time I'm late—longer than my allotted half hour—another nonsensical note appears stamped with the date and time.

Friday, about 11:30, Guarisco approached me at my desk and says, "Jack, we're going to Bozo's. Come join us." "Phil, I can't." "Why not, you got an assignment?" "No, what I got is a bastard of a boss building a file on me… about long lunches." "Son-of-a-bitch, the bastard," the little but feisty Italian fires back. "To hell with him. Come on." "Sorry Phil, but I can't, just can't." Now, cutting his eyes to Tunstall's office, with his anger still growing, he asks, "Why do you, how can you, work for that prick… that asshole?" "It has to do with timing Phil…Bad timing… enjoy that catfish and beer."

And 1972 ends with the heart breaking news that Life Magazine is ceasing publication with its December 29th issue. And with me doomed to dine daily on cafeteria food downstairs, featuring the dreaded liver and onions every Wednesday.

Unexpected, like lightening from a blue sky it comes, striking, then paralyzing the city for twenty-four hours. For me, it's a ruined Sunday, for others, their last. But for everyone, January 7, 1973 is the Day of the Sniper.

On the eleventh floor of the Downtown Howard Johnson's motor lodge, Dr. Robert V. Stegall and his bride of seven months, Elizabeth, are on their second honeymoon and on their way to lunch. He is 28, and she, 25. While waiting for the elevator, they witness a crazed man ripping a phone book and kindling fires with its pages. Dr. Stegall confronts and tries to stop the thin young Black. For his heroic effort the young physician gets shot in his chest and falls to the floor fatally wounded. With the crazed gunman fleeing down the hall, Elizabeth rushes to her husband's side. Kneeling she lifts his head, cradling it in her loving arms, while allowing his blood to stain her dress. The gunman suddenly stops, looks back and sees the grieving wife and apparently decides… I got time… time for this… and calmly walks back to the couple on the floor. There, he raises his powerful .44 magnum rifle, presses its muzzle against the back of Elizabeth's head, and pulls the trigger, exploding the round and sending its sound echoing through the building. Executed, she slumps, burying the remains of her head on her dying husband's bloodied chest. Beside their bodies, a black, red and green "black liberation" flag is dropped before the rampage continues.

The next to die is hotel assistant manager Frank Schneider, who is rushing to check out a report of somebody running about with a rifle and setting fires. When he doesn't promptly return to the lobby desk, manager Walter Collins is the next to go. Only, to get gunned down on the tenth floor. On the street below, firemen and policemen are arriving, unrolling hoses and pointing weapons. And that turns the gunman into a sniper. And a most effective one. Patrolman Paul Persigo, taking cover behind his car, raises his head and his rifle. A shot sounds, and patrolman Persigo falls dead. Another shot, this one from the eight floor, sounds and officer Phil Coleman drops.

At home, the music stops and the radio blares... "Shots are being fired at the Downtown Howard Johnson's... Police are pursuing a sniper... Please avoid the area." "Carolyn! Did you hear?" "Christ, I did." "Call the office. Make sure they know. Tell them, I'm on my way."

With crossfire sounding and filling the afternoon air, I take cover behind a car in front of City Hall, and take pictures of other people taking cover. Off in the distance and well out of camera range, on Loyola Drive in front of the hotel, I see two medics putting a wounded policeman into their ambulance, when bullets start ricocheting at their feet. And behind their patient, they dive inside.

After a half hour, stilled penned down, with a block of "No Man's Land" between me and the hotel, and knowing that New York is already screaming for pictures, I cautiously back away, and rush to the office. And after expediting several of my photos, I check the Picayune's darkroom. And the first on the scene Arnold is back and printing. Watching the images appearing in the developing tray, I shout, "Holy shit Gerry! These are fantastic pictures." In one, Patrolman Coleman, lying mortally wounded, is having his pulse checked by his grieving partner. In another, a wounded officer propped up against a tree trunk, is getting attention. As soon as he finishes, I grab his film and rush back down the hall to my darkroom to print and transmit his images. When that's done, I return his negatives and find other staff photographers are back. Rather than rushing back to the scene, I turn photo editor and continue printing and transmitting their pictures. And while these great pictures are being delivered to newspapers everywhere, competitor Cleary is still down at the scene, still waiting, still hoping for an early end to the story.

Meanwhile, the sniper is still running floor to floor, setting fires and stopping long enough to pick a target on the street below. In the stairwell Deputy Chief Louis Sirgo, leading a rescue team to officers trapped in an elevator, reaches the landing on the 16th floor. Bang! A rifle sounds. Its bullets cut into Sirgo's back, severing his spine, and knocking him back down the stairs and into the arms of comrades trying to break his fall. With the electricity off, out of the darkness, a voice sounds, screaming, "Oh my God! I'm dying. Oh God! Help me." Frantically, doing all he can -- to comfort the Chief, stop the blood—Sergeant Bernard Flint presses hard against the wound and feels half his fist sink in. And it's obvious, his "hands on" boss is a goner.

Above, his killer reaches the top floor, the 17th, and opens a steel door leading into a small room on the roof. Made of reinforced concrete, made like a bunker, it offers protection. In there, the "racist pigs" can't shoot him. In there, they can't gas him. In there, they can't touch him. A "racist pig" just tried. And he almost died. Gut shot opening the door. The only way in from below. A "racist pig" the sniper's sixth victim was anything but. Deputy Chief Sirgo, addressing, a police fraternity, once said that poverty breeds crime and that the status of Blacks was, "The greatest sin of American society."

The police, not only frantic but furious over their fallen comrades, keep trying to get to their killer. They even place their own snipers on rooftops, taller than the Howard Johnson's. There, they perch waiting for a kill shot. One to the head will do it. Below, life is at a standstill. A 50-block radius is sealed off. And seven people lie dead or dying. Sixteen others are nursing wounds.

Police Chief Glarence Giarrusso, an ex-marine, is frustrated, about as frustrated a man can be and still keep his wits about him. With shots still sounding, he calls on the Marines. And in flies a big "Chinook" with rotors fore and aft. With Lt. Col. C.H. Pitman at the controls, the big bird lands behind City Hall and loads aboard half-a-dozen police gunners armed with AR-15 automatic rifles. With the fog up, visibility is down, with the building's upper stories disappearing into a misty haze. And providing even more cover for the elusive killer. Despite the conditions, the big "Chinook" flies over. Guns blaze. Bullets rip. Chunks of concrete fly. And gun barrels get hot, too hot to touch. On the eight strafing run, the sniper pops out and takes a shot, tearing a hole below one rotor engine. But his attempted retreat to the bunker is cut off by bullets bouncing around its entrance. Now, zig-zagging like an infantryman, with the "Chinook" lighting him up, he is showered with bullets. And the sniper falls dead. The time, 8:50 p.m.

Up in surrounding buildings, squads of weary, grieving and too long mollified policemen, still wanting to put a piece of their lead in him, take aim and fire. And fire. And fire. Officer L.J. Delsa put it this way. "We had been waiting for hours to shoot him… so to tell the truth… we shot him for ten minutes after he was dead."

The sniper, the gunman, the killer, I want to tell all about him. His parents. His friends. His ambitions, even his life story. But "the pen" won't write it. Not even his name. And especially his name. Not to glorify him. For the history books, let's blot out his name. Let his own words scrawled on his apartment walls—My destiny lies in the bloody death of racist pigs—serve as his own legacy. Yea pen, as thy will, and let me add my plea… If there is no hell, please God, create one just for him, the one who fulfilled his life's ambition by serving up his special kind of hell up on earth for a day.

And remember, the loving honeymooners, the dutiful hotel executives, and the brave policemen, and in the history books, write their names… Robert and Elizabeth… Frank and Walter… Louis, Phil and Paul. Please God, let the Book of Life, remember them all.

For his pictures, Arnold is nominated for the Pulitzer, but it goes to another. But one thing is for certain, on the day of the sniper, he wasn't on the wrong side of the building.

On the home front, I continue my drinking while Carolyn continues her church going with the children. Occasionally, on an off Sunday, I park on a pew, usually, like Bill, when there's food in the offering. Carolyn is probably worrying that on those Sundays, the roof might fall without singling out just that sinner sitting to her right.

Next door, Bill and Billie are adopting boys, close to Candy and Jay's age, named Richey and Brian. The younger, Brian, still wears the scars from a foster home. Cigarette burns on his forearm. Later on blubber gut Bill goes on a crash diet and starts dripping pounds like hot butter. And perhaps, we should have suspected something. Perhaps, his motivation. After all, eating and drinking are his true loves. Or so we thought. Until a snooping wife opens his wallet and finds a love letter. In detail it describes her passion for "Big Bill" and the things she loves doing to him and for him. Things a Christian wife won't do. And making matters worse, she works under him at the office. Then after putting Bill on move-out notice, she calls me over and asks, "Jack! Did you know about this… about her?" "No Billie I didn't," I lied. And it was a whopper, because some recent Saturday night when "Big Bill" is supposed to be with me on the sidelines at LSU, writing caption information, he isn't. He's in New Orleans with her. Yes Billie, I knew because your husband was busting a gut to tell somebody about the young woman. About the way she pleases him. The way every man craves, unless he's still a young Army idiot as I was with Wally. But now, like Bill, my tastes have changed, and there's nothing better than the sight of one's sweet nectar dripping from beautiful lips.

Continuing my counseling, I plead, "Billie! Billie! Bill screwed up. Big time. He admitted to me… and you. He wants, he needs another chance." "Jack, I'm not sure I can ever forgive him." "But Billie, you are a Christian aren't you?" "Yes, yes, of course I am." "And isn't forgiveness the Christian way?" "Yes, yes, I know it is, but…" But, the "Big But" in Bill's favor is that Billie is a career housewife. Sure, Louisiana is a community property state. Sure, she can strip him of half the assets. But, with a daughter in college, another at home, and with the boys still to raise, the money can't last long. And with his paycheck split in half, she knows that her standard of living will diminish. And so, without a job resume, she makes a deal with "Devil" Bill. Get baptized. Join the church. Attend every service. And hallelujah brother you can sleep on here. But, remember brother, you're a brother, not a husband. When he's washed clean in that miracle water, isn't she supposed to "forgive" everything. All his errors. But, as sure as hell, according to Big Bill, she never lets him "forget" the error of his ways. Isn't that too… The Christian way?

With the clock watching Tunstall still the Chief of Bureau, a lot of catfish and a lot of beer go down without me. How I miss those Bozo's lunches. For the AP, it's a time for regionalization. A time from switching from teletypes to computers. And things are going badly. Breakdowns. Lost stories. Until finally, an upset Tunstall loses his temper with the New York bosses, the guys who already dislike him for demeaning himself by carrying a camera. He loves taking pictures and he loves for me to process and print 'em, whether for work or his pleasure. They advise him to cool down and accept the fact that computers are the future, meltdowns and all. But over every problem, he raves on and on… until the executives tire. Thus the ultimatum. Step down as Bureau Chief in New Orleans and go to Miami as sports editor. Tunstall refuses. Gets demoted to newsman and stays on.

Richard Daw, a man shorter than most, comes in as boss, my fourth, and finds the taller Tunstall towering over him, while obeying New York barking orders to assign Tunstall to work nights and weekends and perhaps, the bothersome bastard will get fed up and quit. Despite the humiliation, Tunstall, a good Catholic, hangs on, praying for a better day.

A few months later, on a Friday night, I get a call about a rumor circulating. The rumor is, the "demoted Tunstall" is being named "The editor" of the Times-Picayune, the AP's largest client in Louisiana and the place the AP hangs its hat and mans its computers. When I hear it, I can't believe it. My demoted, my disgraced boss, getting promoted to the most prestigious media post in the state? In the Army it's called "busted" and captains busted to privates never-never jump back to "an officer and a gentleman" status again. And unquestionably, never up to the rank of general. And the Associated Press considered the retiring George Healy a four-star general because, he's the guy who can order the AP out and the UPI in.

So, in order to put this ridiculous rumor to rest, but before doing so, I decide to have some fun and call Picayune chief photographer Guarisco at home. "Hey Phil, I hear you're getting a new boss." "Yea I know Healy is retiring, but we don't know who's replacing him yet." "I do." "Who?" "That prick, that asshole Ed Tunstall." "Jack, that's laughable. He's just a reporter now. Cut the crap and tell me why you're calling." "Phil, this crap is circulating in the form of a rumor." "That's bullshit." "To check it out, why not call your city desk, ask what they're hearing and call me back." "Okay, okay, but I'm telling you, it's bullshit… just bullshit."

Ten minutes later, Guarisco calls back, I answer and ask, "What did you hear?" "I heard Ed Tunstall." "What!" "Tunstall answered the phone." "At the city desk, out in the middle of the newsroom?" With my laughter erupting and continuing loudly and getting louder, finally I muster, "What did you ask him… is the rumor true?" Again, while laughter is consuming my every breath I hear, "Son-of-a-bitch! It's true. That that asshole is boss." Again, I'm overcome and howling at the top of my lungs until I can ask the crucial and cruel question. "Know what this means?" "Yea, I'm working for a prick." "And more." "What?" "It means you're on the clock. You're under the time stamp. So forget about leisurely lunches… and all that catfish and beer." And with my roaring growing louder and louder, and so loud, I can't hear him hang up the phone.

Down South, and in particular, down in Mississippi, things are a-changing. The State of Magnolias has a new governor. His name is William Waller. And the unusual news is that he's a liberal. And by Mississippi standards, very liberal. And that's because as a district attorney he put a "white man" on trial for killing a 'Nigger". And after the first ended with a hung—deadlocked—jury, he tried him again. And again, Byron De La Beckwith, charged with the murder of Medgar Evers, walks free after another mistrial is declared. But to reward a white man, who put another white man through such misery, with the governorship, well that's unheard of. And during past generations, even unthinkable.

And now in 1974, over in Alabama, there's a picture taken of George Wallace, still the sitting governor, shaking hands with the University of Alabama's new homecoming queen—Terry Points. And it's appearing on front pages across the land, and not just in Alabama. Why? What's so unusual to warrant such display? Well white folks, it's the color of the hand the "Segregation Forever" Wallace is holding. It's black.

In twenty years, since the Supreme Court in May 1954, ruled that the segregation of school children by race was unconstitutional, the Black race has come a long way. The justices, in a 9-0 decision that day, also laid down the principle that, "Separate but equal" was and is inherently unequal. And what of Linda Brown Smith? Remember, it was her father, who with attorney Thurgood Marshall petitioned the high court to end segregation. His reasoning, a practical one, was due to the sad fact that his children had to travel 30 blocks daily to get to their schooling, when, only three blocks away, a "for whites only" facility stood. And now, two decades later, how far do his grandchildren have to go for schooling in Topeka, Kansas? One block from home. At a formerly, "For whites only" school.

The "New" Mississippi now has 174 black elected officials, including four mayors. New York, Pennsylvania, and Massachusetts proudly sent to Washington four Negro Congressmen. In 1787, the new constitution of the United States, for the purpose of representation, only counted a black man as three-fifths of a white man. But now, across America, a black vote or a white vote, each counts as one.

Yea, from 1964 to 1974, the civil rights movement has come a long way baby. From fighting for the right of survival to fighting for the means of survival. And it took a lot of "We shall overcome" and a lot more of "burn baby burn". In Chicago, a cab driver turned his head and said to his passenger, "You look like a white liberal. I used to be a white liberal, but now, you're looking at a scared bigot. I take my life in my hands hacking at night."

"Makesense, your ears up?" "Up Cousin." "About this change of attitude, fear is definitely a factor." "Fear certainly motivates you Cousin… to do good… whether at riots or revolutions." "That is does Makesense." "Now Cousin, let Makesense ask a question." "Ask on." "How has this last decade changed you?" "From a conservative to a liberal." "How liberal?" "What is Makesense asking?" "If your Negro darkroom friend—Little Anthony—should visit New Orleans and call you on the phone, would you invite him to your home for dinner? Better yet, would you take him to Bozo's and fight for his right to dine at your—whites only—table?" "Geesums Makesense, you know me, really know me, and it appears, these 'raised by a bigot' roots are still down there, and awfully hard to pull up." "Keep on pulling Cousin… keep on pulling… and harder."

When I'm in New Orleans, and a story breaks around 4 p.m., I hate it, really hate it. And why? Because at 4:30 p.m. I get off and immediately, I'm off to Beau Louie's to quench that non-drinking problem. This afternoon and evening, I'm meeting AP technician Tex Scott and his boss, Chief of Communications Jerry Lupien. For a little pool, a lot'a laughs, and more than a few brews. And this night I can't get enough, but I tire of the Beau Louie's crowd, and convince Tex to walk over to the Cracker Barrel, just half-a-block away, for a few more. Despite the barman's warning, "Be careful boys, that's a bad place over there." After we enter, we see the joint is almost empty, but for two ugly goons -- pool hustlers I presumed after they challenged us to a game—a bartender, and a big bruiser sitting on a stool facing him. After spurning the hustler's offer to play for ten bucks a game, we take barstools, with mine being just one over from the big bruiser. With the evening growing late, with little business coming in, I find the bartender is becoming about as obnoxious as a body can. With the exception of me. Thus the battle of obnoxiety begins. And intensifies. Until the bartender orders me up and out. Like the civil rights chant goes, "I shall not be moved." Then, I play my trump card. "Man, don't you know that my boss is the editor of the mighty Times-Picayune?" So I lied a little. But only by a word… former. "I don't give a shit if you work for God Almighty, get the fuck out of my bar." Still, I won't be moved, but I did tell Tex, rather loudly, "Get up, call Editor Tunstall, tell him where we are and what's happening." As he moves to the phone, one of the pool hustlers, grabs it off the wall, and says, "Come and take it." "Tex forget it, walk back over to the

Beau Louie's and use their phone," I say. And that directive turns out to be the second mistake of the night, the first, not heeding the barmaid's advice, "About that bad place." With the door slamming shut behind Tex, unmistakably, there is a feeling of joy overcoming the two ugly goons behind me, the big bruiser beside me and the obnoxious bartender in front of me, when suddenly, everybody starts moving. And the barstool starts spinning and spinning me off and onto the floor, where now, over me, all four are fighting for the larger piece of my ass.

The next thing I can remember is that I'm standing just outside the door, dazed, bloodied and obviously beaten, when Tex returns with, "Christ! What happened to you?" Before I can answer, two deputies brush past me and go inside. From there, laughter is reaching out when Tex asks, "Aren't you going to tell the cops?" "Tell 'em what?" I'm so goddamn drunk, I can't remember who did what. And besides, can't you hear, them good ol'e boys are best buddies with the law.

When the door opens at home, instead of hearing the usual, "Where have you been?", I hear, "Oh my God! Look at you." After moving me into the lighted kitchen for a better look, she advises, "You need to get to the emergency room. Your ear, it's bleeding from deep inside. You're hurt bad… really bad." Unable to leave the kids, she rushes next door, awakens the Swarts at 2 a.m., and fetches Big Bill. When he sets eyes on me, he bursts into laughter and exclaims, "Jack! You really got the shit kicked out of you." And then, he drives the bruises, the busted lip, the black eyes, the gap from missing front teeth—actually crowns—and the damaged ear, apparently from a kick to the head from a pointed boot, to the hospital.

The next day, Dr. Charles Sicard finds me sitting in his dentist's chair. And instantly, turns inquisitor. "Goodness, what happened to you?" Embarrassed, I give him the standard answer. "I ran into a door." Laughing just like Bill did, he asks, "Where are the crowns? "I don't have 'em." "Why didn't you reach down and pick 'em up? I could have re-cemented them and saved you a lot of money." "Doc! Doc! I ain't got 'em, so could you please get on with it?" "Sure Jack sure… but that must have been some swinging door… and your head must have left one heck of a dent in that… that door," he concludes with even more laughter flowing as he forces that hot mold of wax into a tender and still throbbing mouth.

Sitting there, I allow my thoughts to distract me from my discomfort… if Mississippians, at least some of 'em, can change, then what about me? Especially my routine. Especially the part that can lead to a busted head at places like the Cracker Barrel Bar. And looking for a sympathetic ear to bounce my idea off, I summon and ask, "Does Makesense sense a change a-coming?" "A-coming Cousin. Makesense already feels the change, especially, that swelled head." "Come on Makesense, get OFF THAT SICARD KICK, this ain't funny. I'm not talking physical. I'm talking mental. I'm talking attitude. I'm talking responsibilities. I'm talking going home. Straight home. Right after work, without any stops in between. Beau Louie's and that Cracker Barrel, well, they're history, just b'aaad history." "Good and good luck Cousin, now make Makesense proud. Show Makesense you are indeed, a man of your word." "And my last word is not to Makesense, but to you Dylan… Put down that pot Bob… Clear the air… Splash some water in your face… Clear your head… and then… Lift those eyes and see… A-change a-coming."

When I walk in the door at 5 p.m., smile and ask Carolyn, "What's for dinner?" She can't believe her ears or her eyes. After an early dinner, I grab Candy and Jay, and neighborhood kids Richey and Brian, Chris and Keith, load 'em in the car and drive to a nearby playground for baseball lessons. After a few weeks of my new routine, a Friday night while playing hearts with the Swarts, Carolyn exclaims, "That beating that Jack took, it's the best thing that ever happened to him… and a blessing for me." And in the long run, a blessing for me, because when I get home and change clothes, I drop four of five dollars in a dresser cup, money I would have blown on beer. And when the cup fills up, I add it to the savings account down at Whitney. And with every dollar, my spirit, and my edge over at 503, is raised a little.

At home, a silenced piano brings more pain. Mine. And I sound off. Candy, now ten, is taking lessons. And a brand new Baldwin, costing a grand, sets untouched against a living room wall. I try imagining that beautiful instrument a-setting down at 503 where the only sounds comes from Mother's nasty-nasty mouth. And I can't. But I can imagine all that gooseliver the grand could have brought home during those hungry-hungry years. Back then, had I money, I would have purchased silence. Hours and hours of it. But now, with the piano lid down, silence is already mine, and yet I'm having to pay a piano note. And that keys me up. That sets me off. And that breaks the silence.

"Goddamn it Carolyn, all I ask is that when Candy gets home, let her eat her snack, take her rest, and then, make her practice for at least thirty minutes." "I try to do that. I really do." "Then, why are we having this fucking conversation? Try harder." A week later, as Candy is getting ready for bed, I ask, "Did you practice today?" "No Daddy, I didn't." And in the weeks ahead, I keep hearing, "No Daddy. I didn't." And I keep confronting Carolyn, and I even consult her piano teacher. Who reports, "Well Mr. Thornell, Candy always knows her lesson." And I think… and you always get paid.

A few weeks later, I get home and find Carolyn and Candy sitting on the sofa. Looking at Candy, I ask, "Did you practice today?" Candy looks at Carolyn. Carolyn looks at Candy. And then, both look back at me. And what do I get for an answer? Blank stares. Not one, but two blank stares. Oh how I hate those blank stares. At work, oh how I wish I could get by with one, just one of those fucking blank stares. And still have money to purchase enough goose liver to fill a belly, much less three more. While trying to contain the explosion I feel coming, I look over at one of those blank stares and ask, "Candy, do you want to continue with piano lessons?" "No Daddy, I don't." "Well, if you're not going to practice, you'll never be any good at it, and so, it's a waste of your time and my money." Now, putting my eyes on Carolyn, I direct, "Call her teacher, and cancel the lessons." And reluctantly, Carolyn does.

The next night, after we make love, Carolyn, undoubtedly figuring she now has me relaxed and reasonably agreeable, softly says, "I want to keep the piano." "Why? What for? A piece of furniture to collect dust. For kids to bang on. You're crazy. I'm selling it." And for $1200 and a nice profit, I do. Hell, it was like new, barely touched, except to wipe off the dust.

And now, when I get home I ask Carolyn, "Did you vacuum today? Did you mop today?" While searching her face and looking for any sign of that blank stare. And what Carolyn keeps forgetting and shouldn't, because she's seen it before… the monster living in me… the one filled with misery… dying to get out… dying to get drawn out with a "No I didn't"… and dying to share that misery with those the closest. And the morning after the monster is loosed, while I'm looking in the mirror shaving, my conscience asks… Why do you hurt the ones the closest… the ones you love the most on all of God's green earth? And from the

196

image looking back, all the question can evoke is… a blank stare. A fucking blank stare. The thing I hate the most.

At home the piano is missing. At the office it's Chief of Bureau Daw. The man New York directed to take the hatchet to Tunstall and try to cut him loose. But now, with Tunstall getting the feel of the editor's chair and flexing his muscles, New York feels that the AP would be better served with Daw gone. Even one of the AP's top execs flies down, to wine, to dine, and to smooth Tunstall's ruffled feathers. Spinning the story… that all that humiliation—those night shifts, those weekends of manning the lowly radio desk—was all the work of one man… Daw. The people that count in New York Ed, they love you. And admire you for coming so far. Yea Ed! They love you… I think… like they love standing me up in the line of fire. Whether bricks or bullets. And what does Tunstall's demotion and now, his promotion, mean to me? A new boss to prove myself to. A fifth in less than ten years. He's tall. He's balding. His name is Dorman Cordell. And he's from Texas. And when he introduces himself to me and reaches to shake my hand, I don't sense the sight of a happy-go-lucky carnival type begging for trinkets from passing floats and shouting, "Hey! Mister! Throw me something." No, no, from his firm and far too long grip, I sense another type, and someone shouting, "Hey! Show me something mister."

A few weeks after Cordell's arrival, with my pay, despite a Pulitzer, a mere twenty dollars above union scale, I sit down with a new boss for a heart-to-heart to say I feel that I am long past due for a "merit" raise based on performance. And his reply, "Gee Jack, I just got here. I can't put you in for a raise so soon… well… that is until you show me something."

"Makesense, your ears up?" "Up Cousin." "Did you hear that turndown?" "Heard every word." "Well, at least it looks like I found a back-up vocation." "Yea Cousin… Fortune teller."

Spring is in the air. Azaleas are blooming along the St. Charles street car tracks. In Audubon Park love birds are chirping. On Stonewall Jackson's statue pigeons are cooing. And in the bustling heart of the French Quarter, in front of famous St. Louis Cathedral, cops are kissing. What? Cops are kissing, real cops. Yep. Uniformed cops? Yep. On duty cops? Yep. Just a little smack? Nope. A locked-lips one. Yep. But, just one long one? Nope. How many then. As many as I asked for. Four or five. You just said kiss-kiss-kiss-kiss, and they delivered. Yep. From inside their parked patrol car and behind that screen? Nope. Where then? Straddling twin motorcycles tagged with sequential numbers. Seeing is believing and without seeing, no way. Well, open People Magazine and see it covering two pages with the cutie of a caption saying… A touching scene from a street car named Desire: "I love you 6103." "10-4, I love you too 6102." Gee! Gee! Geesums, are these gay cops out early. No! No! So relax cop lovers. They are husband, wife, and patrol cops Joseph and Anita Faucheux. And when Anita takes her helmet off, long brown locks drop almost to her waist. But, at first look, the picture crosses eyes across America, the Atlantic and the Pacific.

"Makesense!" "Yep Cousin." "Seeing that picture was worth a thousand chuckles, and more." "And Cousin, had you been paid per eye or per chuckle, you could have made your fortune." "Yep, and instead Makesense, it's lagniappe, and all the AP's."

Up in Monroe, not everybody is laughing. And certainly not brother Garnett. And that's because, with a nervous disorder, supposedly an offshoot of rheumatic fever he suffered in the

Navy, he is on total disability. And his sitting home all day is driving wife Nell crazy. And now, she wants him off the premises and half of his disability check. So with little money, his only prospect for a roof overhead, is certainly not with his children. Not in a million years. Hell's Bells! They can't or won't tolerate his presence either. Not even overnight. So what's left for Garnett? Only a leaky roof and a mother's mouth found down at 503.

After moving in, devastated beyond words, Brother Garnett and Mother come to Metairie for a visit. After welcoming them, and knowing he's a gun lover who always keeps one handy, I stop him at the door and whisper in his ear, "Where's your gun?" "It's in the car." "Come, let's get it. Let me have it... the kids, you know." And with a disturbed look on his face, he hands me his .38. "Thank you. It'll be secure with me," I say while I think... and we'll all be more secure without this in your possession. And perhaps now, I'll be able to find some sleep with just one eye open, instead of two.

Around polite, but limited conversation, we dine on catfish at Bozo's. After, Carolyn fixes his favorite dessert, pineapple upside down cake, which dumps out slightly lopsided. Imperfect like his life, he pretends not to notice. Although his eyes are made glassy by his nerve medicine, even that can't mask his pained expression. But, like with his lopsided cake, I pretend not to notice.

A few weeks after their visit, Mother calls. In hysterics, she screams, "Jack! Come and get me, Garnett done blowed out his brains." At the funeral, his children—Jimmy, George, Ronnie, and Judy—even wife Nell, all gather round the coffin, and cry over him. But those tears raining down, they don't bother him, not anymore, because he doesn't need a roof anymore, not even a leaky one. Because, after that one last look in the mirror, Garnett finds silence... beginning with a bang.

Down in New Orleans, another body is gone. Not from this life, but from a desk at the UPI office. The photographer, the good husband, the good provider for seven children and the naval reserve Chief Petty Officer sent in to sink my ship was fired today... August 26, 1974, just three days short of my 35th birthday. And the way he got the ax was cruel and inhumane, because his boss Craig Mailleoux flew in from Dallas unannounced to hand deliver a severance check of $11,000. UPI's management claimed that it was his "laxed paper work" that done him in. But, my conscience tells me it was his lose-lose-lose and my win-win-win. And it yells that it is you-you-you that takes food out of his children's—Patti, Chris, Bob, Theresa, Joe, Janet and David—mouths.

Bernie, I really liked, but Big Pete, his predecessor, I only tolerated. Frair, my third nemesis, was so short lived, I didn't get to know. And so, who is number four? His name is Mike Robinson, and when I greet him, I see that he is so young, so full of ambition and so full of ego. And his mission is the same as the past three. To knock Jack R. Thornell down off that high-high horse. One he's been riding too long... far too long.

So come on Mike Robinson, let's get on with it, but remember please, that sooner or later, one of us must depart... humiliated, with a broken spirit and without a livelihood. But, number four, you figure your youth, and your ambition are big advantages. But what you can't see is that black ace in the hole. Mine. And that young man is... fear. My fear of having to return to the poverty and pain found down at 503. And back there, be forced to find Brother Garnett's courage, and my silence.

Ten years have passed since I backed down those courthouse steps at Philadelphia, facing that knife wielding Redneck, and now, I'm going back, and, I'm hoping that things have changed. That's the purpose. That's why Crider is coming with me, to find and to report that change with words and pictures. If I can walk into that courthouse with a camera and without a threat of bodily harm, well, for me folks that'll be change enough. We arrive. We park in the same proximity that I parked that—one shot from the hip—day. And thankfully, there are no local Crackers waiting to greet us... or... engage us with conversation or knives. We take the steps. We walk right in, and despite the cameras showing, the Sheriff greets us with a handshake and a smile. So far so good. And then, things get better. I make a request. And the Sheriff obliges. By parking his Neshoba County car, so labeled on the door, in the same spot where the FBI put Sheriff Rainey in their car, and then, posing by it. And back on the sidewalk, instead of threatening Rednecks, two Negroes are calmly passing.

On the ride back, reflecting on our visit, I ask, "Bill, what brought about this change, especially the attitude of the local lawmen?" "It's simple Jack." "How so?" "Them Niggers can vote." "Yep. And their's counts the same as them Crackers." Now turning, taking his eyes off the highway ahead, putting 'em on me, until pulling mine over to his, then smiling broadly he says, "And Thornell, you know all about them Crackers. As many times as they tried cracking your head." "Like it was yesterday Bill."

After returning to New Orleans, reporter Mary Ganz and I are off to Angola, the state prison north of Baton Rouge, for a life on death row story. My picture of a scruffy and obviously, a stray dog finding the dilapidated and long out of use electric chair a comfortable place to curl up in, will undoubtedly be a shocking sight for dog lovers everywhere and even cause some curly hair to stand up. The chair, with its wide leather straps rotting and dangling, is found in a cluttered storeroom with its door opened wide, allowing the pooch to come and go to the outside.

Regardless of how thin I'm stretched, whether swamped in Louisiana, or smothered in Mississippi, New York feels there's enough of me left over to cover the news in places like Tennessee, Alabama, Arkansas, Texas, Georgia, Florida, Illinois, and Washington D.C., and any country in Central and South America. Surely Jack, you can fit these assignments into your life, apparently is their attitude. Vacations, days off, and time with the family, and such, perhaps, you can fit those into a next life Jack.

"Makesense! Ears up?" "Up Cousin." "For me to have a life, or any resemblance to a life, a normal life, what is the answer?" "Believe Cousin... believe." "Believe in what?" "Reincarnation Cousin... Reincarnation."

On this October morning of 1976, at 6:00 a.m., the air out is still damp and chilly. A steady breeze is blowing, and the fog is light, so light it's not a worry to the pilot or the passengers boarding the Destrehan Ferry. Ninety six of them. On their way to work at Luling, an industrial town, just a 10-minute shuttle across the wide and deep Mississippi River.

Loaded, the 120-foot George Prince pulls away, and starts its voyage across to the other side. Meanwhile, the 664-foot Norwegian tanker—Frosta—is pushing up river, at a steady clip, to dock and unload at Baton Rouge, just fifty miles north. On the ferry, George Lingo, steps out of his car, walks to the warm cabin, and joins the many walk-on commuters.

Minutes later, Lingo looks out and sees people out on the deck running in different directions. Some getting back in their cars, others getting out. "I didn't know what was happening," Lingo said. "But I reacted by heading for the door." The first out, with the ferry at mid-river, Lingo continues, "Next thing I knew, the ship was right on us. I mean it was just right there—huge—and I panicked. I just stopped dead." Seeing the ferry across his bow, the tanker pilot yanks the whistle cord. With its sounds blaring and blaring, he screams over the radio, "Luling Ferry! Luling Ferry! Look out." WHAM! Broadside, the giant Frosta hits the little George Prince. Flipping it over like a child flips a bathtub toy. Passenger Lingo hits the water. As do 35 cars, many with occupants still inside. For a few precious seconds, the cars bobble and float. Inside, terrified occupants frantically struggle to open doors held shut by the pressure of the mighty river. The occupants press out. The river presses in. And the river—polluted and poisoned for way too long by chemical plants along its shore—wins. And the cars and the occupants sink. Swallowed up. And finally, their cars as their coffins, come to rest 70-feet down on the river's muddy buttom.

Before the sun's first rays glint across the water, it was over for them, all 78, but for me, it's only beginning.

Ring! Ring! The phone sounds, pulling me out of the shower. "Jack, Bob Rowand. There's a ship collision." "Where?" "Up at Destrehan." "What happened?" "A ship hit a ferry...and the first report... there are many fatalities." "Okay! Okay Bob, I'll get going, but first tell me which side of the river." "What does it matter?" "Hell Bob, if I go to the wrong side, with the ferry out, it'll take me an extra hour to drive back and cross the Huey P." "Oh, I see what you mean. Let me call the Coast Guard back, and let you know." "Okay Bob, I'll be ready."

Ring! "Jack, the ferry sank closer to the west bank near Luling." "Thanks Bob." I say, while thinking... But for that second call, I would have gone to Destrehan on the east bank. And just like at the Rault Center fire, again, I would have been on the wrong side. Only this time, the river.

During the drive, while crossing the high Huey P., and looking down at that monster of a river, those fucking "what ifs" start rattling off in my head... What if the ferry sank to the bottom... What if the tanker steamed on... What's left to take a picture of... And if neither sink or sail, what if the weeping willows block the view from the levee, even prevent me from getting to the riverbank on foot... How the hell will I get pictures? "Geesums Makesense! Are your ears up?" "Up Cousin." "What if you help me out, cause these 'what ifs' are killing me." "What if you calm down Cousin... and wait and see." "Sure! Sure! But with New York screaming long and loud by now, and if I don't get pictures, then like those poor passengers, it could mean the deep six for me." "Nonsense Cousin, you're a Pulitzer prize winner now and since you got'cha your pit'cher on the cover of Rolling Stone, you're famous now. So, win or lose, you don't have to go down with the ship." "Nonsense, my pit'cher was on the cover of AP World and never Rolling Stone." "Oops!" "Oops is right, so Pulitzers be damned, because New York is always looking for a scapegoat to throw overboard. And the bigger the story, the bigger the beating, the better the chances of a once famous photographer becoming the fodder for alligators."

Nearing Luling, I see emergency vehicles and sheriff's cars parked along the levee. I see the dreaded willows, but I also see an opening to the river. I park, grab my camera bag, and start running, and like Grandpa Jones, when his prized Myrtis got stolen, not caring about the moccasins. Now, past the willows and nearing the water's edge, I see it. God! The bow, jutting up and out of the water at a 45 degree angle. Immediately, stopping, and raising my Nikon with a 105 on it, I see a would-be rescuer traversing the top of the flipped hull, while precariously extending his arms for balance like he was walking a tight rope. CLICK! CLICK! My Nikon sounds and then, apparently realizing the danger rushing below, he climbs down and gets back in his boat. And in the background hovering the whole time is a large Coast Guard helicopter. Jesus! It's my first picture, and God!, what a picture. Even the sun's cross lighting helped.

Just minutes later, as I'm turning to leave, to my left, about 75-feet up river, I see the States-Item's Jimmy Guillot and the Picayune's Arnold with their cameras raised. But, that doesn't worry me. Because, I know I had the angle, and not just by inches, but by feet. And Guillot's own paper proves it, spreading my picture across eight columns to fill the top half of their afternoon front page. Within minutes after "The Picture" is transmitted, a Florida photo editor calls and says, "Congratulations, you just won another Pulitzer."

A few weeks later, the "show me something" Mister Cordell calls me into his office and declares, "You're getting a merit raise... fifty bucks a week." "Thank you. That's great." "I put you in for fifty, thinking New York would cut it by twenty, but they approved the whole amount." "I like their way of figuring." "Good then, enjoy the extra money."

Enjoy it hell... I'm thinking... I'm saving every penny. So one day I can say good day and good night to the Associated Press. And possibly, just possibly, I can go out and find a life, a life with a lot of leisure. And towards that goal, my savings bonds, my certificates of deposits and my Whitney passbook account, the fruits of my labor from those 100 hour plus work weeks, just topped the $100,000 mark. And do I feel any more secure? No, not yet. And do I feel any further distanced from 503? Only by inches and not miles. And how does Carolyn feel about having all that money in the bank? Disappointed... disappointed she can't spend it. Every penny. In fact, she's been wanting to send her mother some every month. Just twenty-five dollars or so. And what did I say to that, "I'll consider it after I sit down with your three brothers and see how much they're willing to spend on your Mother's well being." "No! No! Forget it, I'm not obligating my brothers." "Then dear, if that's how you feel, you're not obligating me either."

And when we visit West Point, the mother, the brothers and Carolyn, go behind closed bedroom doors to discuss the family business, while I sit alone in the tiny living room, always the outsider. It's true, I don't care for Mrs. Wilson much. I admit I don't like her. But I love her cooking. And I collect a number of her recipes, including barbequed meatballs and chocolate pie. And her homemade biscuits, well, they'll just melt in your mouth, with or without the butter.

Bushed and baked, I'm done in. It's 10 p.m. Friday June 10th. The year, 1977. And though it's early, very early, for me to turn in, particularly when I'm on the road, but this night,

I'm more than ready, I'm eager, because this has been killer of a day. And what was supposed to be another routine, although back-breaking golf tournament turns into anything but. In fact, today turned out to be a history making day. The kind I prefer to avoid, always. But, I suppose I shouldn't have been surprised. I suppose I should have suspected something. Because, when I get assigned to Memphis, that routine, that insignificant, news shit usually explodes into something of significance. And when it hits the fan, it always comes flying my way. And without the courteous warning shout of, "Fore! Fore! Fore!", like that morning down on Beale, when it started raining bricks and bottles.

And today's history. Al Geiberger of Santa Barbara, California shoots the best round of golf ever in P.G.A. play. And how significant is it? Well, awed golf zealots first tried comparing it with Armstrong's walk on the moon. Shot down, they then, likened it to baseball's perfect games, and under four minute miles. It had been twenty years since Sam Snead carded a 60. One shot behind Geiberger's fabulous 59. And, am I in a state of awe after recording history making shots? No, after lugging heavy cameras for miles and miles, and after baking under a hot sun for hours and hours, I feel more like a victim of history. And ready to put it to bed. But, once under the covers, and not able to fall asleep, I think of the phenomenal pressure that I'll be under again tomorrow. But what I didn't think of, or even get a chance to dream of Mr. Geiberger, is that "pressure" won't be coming from following the "phenomenal" you. But, from one, I didn't expect to ever lay eyes on again. That is, anyplace short of a fiery-fiery hell.

ERRRR! ERRRR! ERRRR! The alarm sounds. "Man on the wall! Man on the wall!" shouts the guard from tower no. 3. Then, he fires two shots, and Jerry Wayne Ward—a 34-year-old bank robber doing a 40-year stretch—drops, wounded twice. But the six convicts ahead of him, have scaled the two-foot thick, 14-foot high stone barrier, have snaked under a high voltage line carrying 2300 volts and have disappeared in the rugged countryside surrounding Brushy Mountain State Prison in eastern Tennessee. And, one of the six is a confessed killer. One of the six is serving 99 years. One of the six killed Dr. Martin Luther King. One of the six is James Earl Ray.

After falling into a light and somewhat restless sleep, Ring! Ring!, Raises my head, and my hand picks up the phone to hear, "Gene Blythe here. Sorry to disturb you so late… But"…"But what?", I ask the Atlanta Photo Editor. "I need you to get over to Brushy Mountain." "Brushy what! Man! I'm in the middle of a golf tournament." "I know… I know. But James Earl Ray has escaped." "Gene, you're not shit'n me?" "No shit Jack, I'm not. In fact, New York said to send you." "Okay! Okay! What about all my darkroom stuff out at the country club?" "Leave it and get going. Because Kelly is on the way with a complete setup." "Okay Gene, let me hang-up and call the airport."

"Fuck! Fuck! Fuck!", I shout, "Fuck the sleeping beauties in the next room! Fuck the stiff neck! Fuck the aching back! And FUCK the sleep!" After getting that off my chest, I call the airport and book an early morning flight to Knoxville, and then, I call Commercial Appeal staff photographer Sheridian.

"Hello Jim, this is Thornell, sorry for disturbing you so late." "Forget it. What you need?" "Well Jim, instead of you helping me with the final two rounds, I need you to cover it alone." "Why? What's up?" "It's not up Jim, it's out. James Earl Ray has escaped." "Mother-Rue, that's a lollapalooza! I wish I was going with you." "Can you do it… cover the golf?"

"What about the darkroom setup?" "I'm leaving it for you to use." "Then I can do." "Thanks, I'll see you get a bonus." "Great, and good luck with the manhunt."

Escaping is nothing new for Ray, now age 49. When King is gunned down in 1968, Ray is a fugitive from a Missouri pen. And twice before he tried escaping from Brushy, once by leaving a dummy in his bunk and again by cutting a hole through the ceiling of his cell.

Early the next morning, I'm up, way up, and on a flight to Knoxville, when I summon Makesense. "This is going to be a big, big story… agreed?" "Cousin, like friend Jim said, a real lollapalooza." "Remember what else Jim said?" "About wanting to come with you?" "Yep. But instead of coming with me, I wish he was going instead of me. Because more pressure, pressure greater than yesterday's is coming my way, and I'm not so sure I can withstand it, not so soon." "Cousin, close your eyes. Rest your brain. Cause in a day or two, this story will be over." "Yeah, over until another pile of news shit hits the fan and comes a-flying. And I go a-running."

Twenty-two thousand feet below, the largest manhunt in Tennessee history, ensues. Road blocks are at every crossroad. Blood hounds are set loose. Over a 100 prison guards join with state police, with FBI agents and with deputies from six counties, to search the snake-filled hills surrounding Brushy Prison. They're looking for all six. But, the one who brings in James Earl will get promoted to "hero status" by the media.

After landing in Knoxville, I rent a car and start driving. Outside the prison gate, wall to wall press greets me. Among them is Charlie Kelly, the photog I love working—if I must—with because of his friendly and his never seems to get riled nature. "Hello Charlie, how are you?" "Good to see you Jack. As you can see I was bit lonesome out here, until the cavalry arrived," Kelly says as he reaches to shake my hand. Kelly and I, we've worked some stories together, mostly civil rights. Under his rotund frame is one calm character, and in every sense, a gentleman and a gentle man. Unless you're back pedaling for position and then, he will not be moved. His stories, his jokes are so precise, and he is so polite, and with that big friendly smile drawing you in, you can't help but like him, and like being around him. That is, unless you're with UPI and back pedaling for position alongside him.

"Charlie, where are we transmitting from?" "Back at the Oak Ridge paper. The D-76 is mixed and the transmitter is set up." "Okay, I shot a few pictures on the way here. Road blocks and such. What shall I do with them?" "Take 'em back to the paper, get familiar with the setup, and transmit something." "Will do. See you later."

"Hey! There he is… There! In the opening… crossing the field." The helicopter pilots radio below. "We see him… we got him," Anxious officers reply, before sweeping down on him, shackling him, and returning him to his cell. But unfortunately the "him" is not James Earl Ray. It's David Lee Powell, a 27-year-old, doing 100 years for murder. And the vigil of the media horde at the prison gate continues. With Kelly and I among 'em.

Sunday, just before midnight, after being up since early Saturday morning, I confer with Charlie. "We're both dead on our feet. Why don't you head to the motel and get a few hours shut-eye? This could go on and on for days." "You sure? You know UPI has three shooters here." "I'm sure, we got to sleep… sometime. And if things start popping, I'll call you back."

Less than an hour later, with Charlie finally pillowing his head, the call back comes. "Ray is still on the loose," I report, "But they just captured somebody else, so you'd better get back and pick up my film." "Alright. It'll take me about half an hour." "Fine, see you shortly."

Charlie returns, picks up my film, goes to the newspaper, processes, prints, transmits, and then, he returns to his bed. A few minutes later, I phone again. "Charlie! They got him... they got Ray, and I'm outgunned, UPI still has all three shooters here." "Okay I'm on my way."

While Ray is on his way back to Brushy, prison officials, trying to prevent a media stampede when he shows, rope off a walkway and announce, "Gentlemen, you must stay behind these ropes. Anyone crossing them will be arrested. So, gentlemen pick your place and stay there." Immediately I secure a spot, about halfway between the street and the building. UPI secures three. With media bodies to my left, to my right and behind, knowing that Charlie isn't going to get back in time, and knowing that I'll only get one crack at Ray while UPI gets three, my head starts spinning and searching for an equalizer. With my new 283 strobe set on "manual", when Ray is walked by, I will only be able to get off one shot. Because, by the time the flash recycles, Ray will be past me and showing his back. However, set on "automatic", it only uses enough charge to light the image and store the rest. But, the big dilemma, it's so new, I've never used it to set on "automatic" outdoors and in the dead of the night. Not yet. What to do? What to do? Manual or automatic... manual or automatic? On manual, I'll get one. On automatic, maybe more. And for sure, even on manual, UPI gets three shots from three positions. Shit! Shit! Shit! I mouth to myself. While accepting the probability that any minute now, just after UPI fires their three flashes, I'll become another dead man walking. Just waiting... and waiting for New York Photos to throw the switch. So, so, finally, I select automatic. Perhaps then, I won't get fried, or fired. And now, thinking that agonizing is over, I turn to Newsweek's Wally Macnamee on my left and ask, "What strobe setting are you using... manual or automatic?" "To be safe Jack... manual." And before I can mouth, Shit! Shit! Shit! Again, a car pulls up and parks. Seconds later, a haggard and a filthy James Earl Ray, flanked by prison guards, starts his walk towards me. Full length, click and the flash fires. Knees up, click, and the flash fires. Waist up, click, and the flash fires. And then, it's all back until he disappears inside. With the adrenaline still rushing to my head, I turn to Wally and ask, "How many shots did you get off?" "Just one. How about you?" "Three, I think, but with all those flashes going off, I'm not sure." Then, UPI's Sammy looks over, smiles, and waves as he sees Kelly arriving late. And I knew why friend Sammy was smiling. Knowing I was outgunned 3 to 1, he believes that his night of reckoning has come. And finally, he has stepped on me. He has hurt me. And perhaps, crushed me like I crushed him those two times before. And at this moment, I reckon... he's right. With the odds in his favor, 3 to 1.

After Charlie reaches me, I face him and say, "Come on, let's get to the darkroom." "Okay, but how did it go?" "Well Charlie, with UPI feeding from three places at the table, they probably just ate my breakfast, lunch and dinner. And it's only 3 a.m."

In D-76, it takes nine minutes to develop. Another two in the hypo. And one in the wash. Probably, the fourth longest twelve minutes of my life. Just behind the sheriff's arrest, the Meredith shooting and the Memphis riots. With the second and third being the two times I crushed friend competitor, Sammy, and now, his competitive spirit is dying to personally dish out a large plate of comeuppance, too, too long overdue. All for friend Jack.

Finally, I pick up the eyeball to take a look and I do. There! James Earl Ray head to toe. There! Knees up. There! Waist up. And all three negatives are perfectly exposed. "Thank God! And thank you Mr. Automatic," my raised voice bounces off the darkroom wall to reach Charlie's ears. "Jack, is the film okay?" "Charlie, it couldn't be better. Here, take a look. Then, go write captions while I print." "Man! These are going to be easy to print.," he replies as he rushes past me and toward the typewriter.

After transmitting all three pictures back to back on the network, I go back in the darkroom to look at earlier film. And then, I find it. The hero of the hour… Sandy… in the spotlight of television cameras. The bloodhound that sniffed out Ray. Hiding under a pile of leaves. And, looking and smelling like a pig just done wallowing in a sty.

"Charlie!" "Yes Jack?" "Come take a look." After he does, he laughs and says, "This picture is going to get played. Perhaps, as much as the capture." "Charlie, write a caption. Overline it 'newshound', while I print it." After the picture is transmitted, I turn to Charlie and say, "Let's get a bite, then, get to bed. It's 8 a.m."

At 10 a.m., with Charlie and I finally asleep in adjoining beds, the phone blares, sounding as loud as an escape alarm, startling me up, but leaving me still groggy and someplace less than half awake. Hesitantly, I pick up and the voice asks, "Thornell?" "Yes." "What are you doing?" "Sleeping. At least I was. Who the hell is this?" "This is Hal Buell." "Yes sir Mr. Buell, what do you need?", I reply to the big boss, Al Resch's replacement in New York. "I need for you and Kelly to get up and come up with something fresh. The bloody afternoon papers here, in different additions, used all three Ray pictures, leaving nothing for the morning papers." "But Mr. Buell, I only got three shots off. We were roped in. And I've exhausted them." "Well check the locals." "Sir, I already did, but, their one frame was so fuzzy I couldn't use it." "But Jack, that won't do. Get up, go back to your film, recrop, reprint, but do something. And do it within the hour."

After looking over at the other bed, I see Charlie with a pillow pulled over his head, and I start shouting, "Hey Charlie… Hey Charlie… Hey Charlie." When he finally lifts the pillow enough to respond with a pissed off sounding, "What?" I respond with, "Get up and OFF your ASS." "What!" "Buell's orders." "What?" "Yea, he wants more Ray pictures." "What does he want us to do… draw 'em?" "If we have to, because he wants 'em and he wants 'em bad." "For Christ sakes, didn't you tell him we just got to bed?" "Sure, but he don't care." HE thinks sleep is for pussies. Don't be a pussy, get up." "Well Jack, I never thought anyone would ever hear those words coming from me… in bed… forget the pussy, and just let me sleep." Laughing with him, I add, "Glad you got your wits back. Let's go work a miracle. We only got an hour."

Back in the darkroom we recrop two negatives. The knees up, we lower the enlarger and leave more in. The waist up, we raise the enlarger, and cut everybody out except Ray. This one really emphasizes his emaciated look, with his sweaty hair sticking to his forehead. When the transmitter finally stops spinning, I look to Charlie and say, "Come on big guy, let's get back to bed." Someplace, I hadn't been for the past 58 hours except for this morning, when boss Buell caught me cat-napping.

And when I awaken, do newspapers say it was indeed Sammy's day. And my day for come-uppance. Had I been stepped on? Had I been hurt? Had I been crushed? Hardly. My three pictures—make that five—of a cuffed James Earl Ray captured front pages everyplace. Including New York, Chicago, L.A. to name the large and the most competitive markets. Even bloodhound Sandy becomes famous… Newshound Sandy. And yet to come is a letter of commendation from A.P. president and general manager—Louis Boccadi—for our long, tireless and highly successful effort.

On the flight back to Memphis to pick up my darkroom gear, I keep asking myself… Why didn't I get crushed, or at least stepped on! And without coming up with a reasonable answer, I turn to Makesense, "Are your ears up?" "Up Cousin." "Was this success just luck… unexplainable luck?" "Perhaps Cousin. And perhaps, it is 'this success' that will lead you to your purpose." "Oh Makesense! Don't start up with that purpose nonsense. Not again… please." "But Cousin, everyone needs purpose." "Jesus. Put any more purpose—other than doing a job, getting paid, and feeding my family—on my plate, and it will push me over the edge." "Surely Cousin, there must be more to life than that." "If there is Makesense, I haven't found it. And the people that know me, think I'm damn lucky to have just 'that'."

Back home, the big news is that the Swarts are moving. General Motors is closing the warehouse here, and Bill is taking an early, and a most enviable retirement, and moving to Euless, Texas, a community just west of Dallas.

Meanwhile, our Jackson friends Sam and Betty are moving to LaPlace, just a 30-minute drive west of here. Sam misses the baseball diamond, the freedom, and the fresh air and hates sitting behind his desk at the stuffy Prudential Insurance office. But there's a golf course not far from his front door, and about that, he is most pleased.

Carolyn, Jay, and Candy, all belong to the Hickory Knoll Church of Christ where Billie led 'em. Although Jay hasn't been baptized yet, it won't be long, it was obvious to everyone after he recited the 23rd psalm. And recited it perfectly, loud, clear, and publicly before the whole congregation. And the unusual thing, he was only five, and hadn't learned to read. And topping that, little Jay was and is one of the shyest kids around. Perhaps, in the world. And when he got past… Thou anoinist my head with oil verse… I know he had nailed it. And how did he do it without being able to read? Well his Sunday school teacher Sarah Laguna realized his unusual ability and taught it to him. All six verses beginning with… The Lord is my shepherd. I shall not want. Although, an outsider and not a Christian, the sight of my son—a Thornell—performing that phenomenal fete brought tears to my eyes. But before showing them, I quickly brushed them away, knowing that if I ever show a soft side, my crumble will commence.

The Church of Christ is, to say the least, conservative. So conservative, it prevents the playing of instrumental music around here. No organs! No pianos! Not around here. Not even the plucking of those heavenly harps is to be heard. "And why," the elders, while holding the good book hard to their chest, shout, "When the Church was founded, those weren't even invented yet." They didn't use 'em and we don't fellowship them that do." And so how do they make a joyful noise unto the Lord? By raising their voices acapella style. And after hearing it, if I was the Lord, I'd shout tune it down, better yet, turn it off.

Carolyn and the kids seemed to have found something special there at Hickory Knoll, because it keeps bringing them back every Wednesday night and twice on Sunday. When I'm sitting there in that pew next to them, while tuning out that awful singing, I wonder… Just what is it that they have found here? Is it just an escape… like going to the movies? Or is it more? Such as… An escape from a demeaning husband and a demanding dad???

At work, there are changes too. The demoted, before he was promoted editor, Tunstall is kicking ass. And that ass is the AP's news staff. We got to go. According to Tunstall, it's all about space. He needs it to expand his news room, he says. But I say, it's about comeuppance long overdue. And we all, and in particular me, swallow hard because when something erupts like the Rault fire I won't be in their John to hear about. And when I want to get my hands on their film, I'll have to drive back over here. And compounding that, Bureau Chief Cordell is transferring to Dallas so Gary Clark takes his chair, shakes my hand, and implies, "Show me something too." Cause I want to get promoted to a hub city just like Cordell was. And the third compound thrown into the mix is the arrival of UPI photographer Pat Benic. What happened to Robinson, number four? Oh he's gone too. It was another paperwork glitch, and not me, that done him in, according to UPI's story. Fact or fiction, I can't say, but I can say that they have an extraordinary number of paper work glitches over there at the UPI. And the fact that those imperfect army clerks only make one paperwork glitch pertaining to me—the one that put me into photography instead of radios—truly was a most remarkable accomplishment. So come on fresh, strong, and hungry number five. Take your best shots. And maybe, just maybe, you'll be the guy that takes this one down, and with his back aching and his spirit breaking, perhaps, just perhaps, he'll stay down… down for the count.

With me fighting insomnia and with insomnia winning, on this hot July night, there is a most troubling thing I need to talk about. It's not the Tunstall boot. It's not the new boss. And it's not the new lensman searching for success at my expense. No, it's those church goings, Carolyn, Jay and Candy's. And so I turn to the only ears I can trust. "Makesense, Ears up?" "Up Cousin." "Why do they do it? Is it just to escape me and my authoritative ways? Or, is there more?" "Perhaps Cousin, there's more." "More what?" "Perhaps they're searching for purpose." "Geesums Makesense! Did you say purpose? Before, harping on my purpose and now, harping on theirs. It's the same old, and tiring song. Please write a second verse." "Perhaps Cousin, without purpose, there can be no second verse." "Goodnight Makesense!…….. I said goodnight Makesense!" "Oh, goodnight… And please dear Cousin, let Makesense wish Thee many purpose-filled dreams."

Today, August 16, 1977, the news is colossal, and a little personal… The King is dead. Not the King of great nations like England, Spain or Denmark, but the king of the world.

When the news found me, in a flash, my thoughts take me back to Germany and to the sounds of Little Anthony running into the room and shouting to the top of his lungs, "The King is coming… the King is coming." Well, Little Anthony, the King—Elvis "The Pelvis" Presley— is gone.

And he didn't go like brother Garnett with the flash of a .38. No, that was too quick, too painless, and too undeserved. Instead, he took the slow poison of excesses to kill himself. Among them, pills, pills, pills. Pills to get him up. Pills to let him down. Pills to escape his inner pain. And don't forget the wine, the women and the gluttony of too many peanut butter and banana sandwiches that led him to obesity, and forced him to appear as an over inflated caricature, just a distortion of his former beautiful to look at self. But, what was at the root of these excesses is the gnawing question. And let me shout it loud, loud enough for him to hear, even from the down side of the upset world that he left behind…

"Hey Elvis I know. It was shame that got you, like shame is trying to get me. You lost your war. I'm still fighting my battle. But dear Elvis, at least now, you're free. Free of shame's hold. It's still got me."

And to you physicians who say that it was simple heart failure that got him, I say it was a heavy and unhappy heart, tired, and too tired to keep on marching to the beat of shame's drums. And you physicians, challenging my unheard of diagnosis, might simply ask… How do you know? And my answer is… I saw it in his eyes. With one focused look, I saw something. The something I always felt from down deep inside… such emptiness… such inadequacy. And whatever degree of success comes our way, whether served on a platinum platter or embossed on a Pulitzer Commemorative Plate, it didn't matter, because the joy eater was always there, always gobbling away, until every last morsel is gobbled up. Leaving only the emptiness and the inadequacy remaining. In shame's hold dear doctors, one never feels that success was earned, and certainly, never deserved. After shooting up from such poor roots, how could one feeling so empty, so inadequate, ever feel worthy, even after becoming a king?

Now doctors, to support my diagnosis, let me share two case histories… He, born at Tupelo's Charity Hospital. Me, at Vicksburg. He, lived in a tiny two room house built with $180 of Daddy's borrowed money. Me, down at the decrepit 503, which only spirits of the dead could deem inhabitable. He, worked at Loew's State Theatre in Memphis as an usher. Me, at the Joy in Vicksburg as a ticket taker and usher. And it sickens me to wonder if he, as an impressionable and shy schoolboy, was humiliated too by the flashing of a free lunch card before his curious classmates' eyes. Perhaps, his parents, one-time share croppers like mine, didn't have a quarter to spare him that sickening shame.

Doctors, if shame wasn't the root cause for Elvis' willful demise, then, what was? When the idolizing world saw him as a man with every reason to live and to enjoy a long and most enviable life. He had fame. He had fortune. But, rich or poor, nothing changed. And when he looking into the mirror, he still saw what I saw looking back at me in Germany… those empty eyes. And he had what I'm praying for, early retirement, and to be able to sit back, count my money and finally, be able to seek a life. One that perhaps, I could learn to enjoy. But at this moment, the realization that Elvis couldn't, gives me cause to worry and, to wonder… Will my end come like his? Far, far too young! And with a helping hand.

Good doctors, as an expert on the inner workings of shame, I claim that Elvis' feeling of inadequacy was already instilled in him like mine was in me—innate—when he too was expelled from his mother's womb. From which his identical twin Jesse Garon failed to emerge alive. And perhaps in Elvis' eyes, after reaching the age of reason, he looked back and saw Jesse to be the lucky one. Stillborn.

Since all you PhD's claim that if one is born with a functional brain, behavior is learned. And if you all further claim that there is no such thing as innate shame, then, here's an egg-shaped conundrum for all to solve… When did Elvis learn how to feel inadequate, before or after, he learned how to become a king? And if your rebuttal question is… if truly in shame's hold, why did shame let Elvis climb to such heights? And my answer is… The higher the climb, the longer the fall, the louder the thud and the sweeter the splatter. And though Elvis was king, in his eyes, shame yet ruled.

And the climb to the top of the music world, really got off the ground in 1957 in Philadelphia when and where those gyrating hips of his caused quite a stir. "An instrument of the Devil", many church going and worried parents shouted. But their daughters, awe struck over the sexuality he generated, shouted back, "ELVIS THE PELVIS… We worship you." And thus, "Elvis the Pelvis", becomes the byword for a generation of adoring fans. Not only in America, but around the world.

From poor Mississippi soil, the throaty baritone sprang, going from truck driver in 1953 to riches in 1956 with the release of "Heartbreak Hotel". The first of 45 to sell over a million copies. From the bottom of his Blue Suede Shoes to the top of his long, slicked-back ducktails, this country boy, with long black sideburns bordering his sexy sneer, rocks his way into the hearts and homes of America, starting a sexual revolution. Bobby soxers go crazy, and chase after him for autographs and with offers to give up their precious virginity at this very minute. The boyfriends hated him, but like the girls, they just couldn't help themselves. Despite their jealousy, they craved to look like him. So, they grew ducktails and sideburns, put on black leather jackets—Elvis' favorite—and they imitated him. Undoubtedly thinking… If I look like Elvis, I too can easily score, and possibly, set some records of my own. What man on the face of the planet wouldn't die to step onto Elvis' shoes save one. And he wanted to step out of 'em. And did.

And dear doctors, despite his fame, his fortune, and his kingdom, all that the endeared Elvis could find at the top—like his first hit said—was a place on Lonely Street at the Heartbreak Hotel.

Simple heart failure. No! No! No! It was the failure of the heart to find joy in this life. And so learned men, in due time, it was shame that claimed "The King". Pill by pill.

And dear doctors, please forgive me for not signing my name under my findings as to "The King's" cause of death. But, I can't, I just can't. Because I cannot. I will not identify myself as a subject of shame. I must remain anonymous. That! Is shame's master plan. That! Is shame's hold.

Carolyn's in tears, not over my going to Memphis today, hell she's probably relieved, but over Elvis' going. "I can't believe it… I can't… I can't," cried the diehard fan. "Carolyn, he was just a man!" "Are you insane? Without Elvis, the world just won't be the same." "Can you imagine the world with two Elvis'es?" "Two?" "Didn't you know that he had a twin brother… well almost?" "What are you talking about?" "It's true, his name was Jesse Garon Presley, and he left his mother's womb just minutes before Elvis." "So he would have been the big brother." "Yep. And can you imagine two sets of pelvises on the stage gyrating in sync?" "I can't, and I'm not sure the world could have withstood that… I know I couldn't have."

With Carolyn attending her tears, my thoughts take me back… Oh Elvis, when I first saw you in Germany, oh how I envied you. So lean, and so good looking, even more so with the sideburns gone and your hair cut so short. Oh how I wanted to be you, or even less, be like a baby brother to you. To rescue me from my state of lonely, all you had to do was wiggle one finger and I would have come running to join your band. Maybe, we could have looked into each others eyes until we realized that we carried the same deep dark secret. And until we could have drawn close enough and comfortable enough to talk about it, and perhaps, draw it to the surface. And then, maybe, just maybe, together we could have put the joyeater on the run. Oh Elvis, maybe, we could have helped each other, maybe, saved each other. But now, look at you, look what you done gone and done. Just like you done in Germany when your army time was done. You stepped up on that big bird. You flew away. And you left me behind... far behind. But, this time Shame Brother, you left me far... far... far... behind.

My call came from Atlanta Photo editor Blythe. "Jack, Gene. I guess you heard about Elvis?" "Yeah. Carolyn's still wiping tears. What you need?" "For you to get up to Memphis." "When?" "Right away. The funeral's not till Saturday, but there'll be a lot of prelim stuff... Mourning fans and such outside Graceland." "Okay I'll pack up and get on the next flight." "Good, I'll see you there." "Oh, you're going?" "Yeah, and so are Kelly and Bourdier." "Looks like another big story." "The biggest... it's not every day a nation buries a king."

At the office where I'm loading up extra film and long lens, news editor Prince offers, "Jack, why don't you take your Elvis Army pictures up to Graceland and present them to the family. Perhaps, that'll get your foot in the door... for some inside coverage." "Kent, you must be kidding. Those frigging pictures wouldn't get me anywhere near the door. Hell, even the U.S. Army bowed a little before the King. Hell, when he arrived late for formation in his white BMW sports car, something the Germans called 'Der Elvis Wagon', you know what the company commander said or did?" "What?" "Nothing. Absolutely nothing, but keep looking the other way."

Outside, funeral wreaths, spreading around the mausoleum, are too numerous to count. Up and down Elvis Presley Boulevard, outside beautiful Graceland, long lines grow and grow, with mourners waiting and waiting for their turn to pause before his coffin, if only for a few, but precious seconds, to honor their king and idol. But perhaps, more consequential, to see with their own eyes that the unbelievable is true. The one they truly worshipped is dead... truly dead. At age 42.

In line just outside the gate, I see a young woman bleeding tears. I move close and capture her grief on film. Cameras on the grounds are forbidden and security guards are everywhere making sure. That picture takers adhere.

Thank God, the AP didn't coerce me into trying to slip a miniature camera inside like The National Inquirer did. Whether concealed in a pack of cigarettes, or sewn into a tie, I'm not sure. But, I'm sure they got a picture of Elvis laid out. Because, it appeared on the supermarket racks across America causing fresh tears to appear on faces in the checkout line.

I could have put my cameras away, got in line and waited my turn to pay my respects. And put my envy to rest. But by standing over him, what could I say or think... Dear Elvis, shame killed you, just like it's killing me. And perhaps, shame gave you a choice of how to escape. You didn't lift a .38 or fly off a bridge. That, would have been too quick and too easy. You chose the slow way. Perhaps, you needed time to feel something, anything real and lasting, even the pangs of death coming. Well dear Elvis, it's real, it's lasting, and you did it your way. And like Brother Garnett, you found your silence.

Our pictures are more that competitive, but none captured the essence of Elvis' passing. And what picture could. Not the essence of the one, the one still slim and stunning, the one who faced his faithful fans, the one who gyrated those precious pelvis'es, and not only shook the stage, but shook the world.

Back home and assuming that finally my envy of Elvis has ended, I soon discover that didn't come to pass. Because now dearly departed, I envy your rest. Because for me, there never seems to be time, or even space for it. When I'm working, I'm worrying. And when I'm not working, I'm worrying. Even if, I'm allowed a weekend off, my brain won't shut off. Always humming like my 283 Flash set on automatic, even when discharged, never fully emptying and always regenerating for another quick shot. Yea! Yea! I've heard, I've read that worry can kill. Although Elvis chose pills to shut his brain down, perhaps worry will become my choice… my .38.

After building and operating the Panama Canal for the past seventy four years, the U.S. is about to sign a treaty that will eventually turn control of the 533 square mile Canal Zone over to the Panamanian government. A government that has been demanding it during the 13 years of negotiations with four American presidents. The Panamanian people, many of them, see the Gringo presence as a "U.S. Colonial Enclave" in their country. But many Americans see the new treaty as a giant giveaway and possibly, a threat to the future security and operation of the Canal. For the September 7 signing, President Jimmy Carter will be there. As will Panama's leader Omar Torritos Herrera. As will Washington D.C. photo editor Toby Massey with photographer Charles Tasnadi and a darkroom Technician. As will I.

This should be another routine assignment, or so I thought until Toby and I returned to the hotel lobby after having dinner. It's around 10 p.m. when we find several television crews assembling. I approach ABC's Ferris and ask, "What's going on Chuck?" "Students are rioting at the university campus. And government troops are about to move in." "What's it about?" "About them demanding that all Gringos go home." Massy, a former Miami photographer and Atlanta photo editor before he got promoted to the capital, looks at me and says, "I guess you'd better get over there." "Yeah, I guess you're right. Want to come along, keep me company, I've got an extra camera?" "No, I think I'll stay back here," he said without hesitation… and I couldn't help thinking… since becoming a photo editor you think like those New York asses. Y'alls are far far too precious to put into harm's way. He'd been an excellent photographer, and as a photo editor he excelled. But as for accompanying me into the riot zone in the dead of the night, on that test, he didn't excel. In my eyes, he flunked. And flunked miserably.

The day is November 14, 1977 and the scoop belongs to Carolyn. A crazed gunman, on a downtown rampage, shoots ten people including a policeman. By the time we hear about it over in our vacuum at the Plaza Towers, the wounded have been picked up and the suspect Carlos Poree has been arrested. After rushing over to the Times-Picayune, picking up pictures from photographers Bill Haber, Jimmy Guillot and Robert Steiner, and returning to the office for transmitting, I go to police headquarters to await the parade of the suspect before the press. The usual custom after a big arrest. They parade him, and I shoot half a roll of film. I'm surprised to see that he is so clean-cut looking. Except a mustache, there isn't a mark on his face. Early that evening, while I am still at the office, I get a phone call. It's Carolyn. "Jack! I just heard a bulletin on the radio." "What is it?" "That gunman, he's been injured, They're taking him to Charity Hospital." "Thanks, I'm on my way." Only five minutes from the office I arrive before

Poree. Soon, I'm beginning to pick up vibes from the gathering police. They seem disturbed by my presence. And when he does arrive, they surround him and charge into the hospital like an offensive line protecting a prized quarterback by trying to shove me aside. But, before they do, I shove my pre-focused Nikon into that onslaught and manage to get off one, but just one shot. And I see why the cops are so angry and don't want any pictures taken. And that's because that clean and unmarked face isn't clean and unmarked any longer. And it's bloody, obvious that Poree has been beaten and beaten savagely. But, how could that have happened? He was in police custody all that time between picture number one and picture number two, wasn't he? So? "That boy" did shoot a white cop, didn't he? And he got less, a lot less than he deserved. In my eyes, the picture is a beauty. But to the world, it's ugly. Showing a bloodied face, and eyes already swelling shut. Like the face I presented Carolyn after it was beaten to a bloody pulp over at that baaad Cracker Barrel Bar. The before and the after combination are mine, and thanks to Carolyn, mine exclusively. And win, according to the AP log, lots and lots of front page play. And to be exact… smash play.

It's Christmas time and time for my vacation, which I schedule for then, trying to miss another Christmas Eve march or something worse. And as is the custom, it's time for Mother's annual visit. Still sitting down there at the bottom of that hill, she undoubtedly now feels, that she is sitting on top of the world. And why? Because, she's got security. Social security. And welfare security. Together the two monthly checks total just under $300. And she can live just fine on the under, and save the other $200. And mortgage free, she's never had it so good. Not in all her days. If I had to reveal one thing that I thought I had in common with the little woman, it would be the ability to save money. She proved with that allotment check from the Army. And she's proved it again. Had she married a man with two-bits worth of ambition for taking a paycheck home, I can only imagine how different those early—please somebody get me out of here—years might have been. Instead, she made the same mistake twice. Call them lollapaloosas, with the emphasis on "loosas". By marrying the Thornell brothers, who agreed that having to work for a living was twice as bad as catching leprosy.

Today, a week before Christmas 1977, before we can get to the top of the hill, she's pushing a roll of bills, one that would choke a goat, over the seat, into my face and asking, "Want to count it?" "Mother please, put that up, I'm trying to drive the car." And the next thing I hear, is the sounds of mother entertaining Candy and Jay with her counting. When she reaches $1150 and change, finally, she quits with the counting, but shut up, she don't. Because honeychild, to be alive is to talk. And believe me honeychild, whether flush or broke, that little woman is alive, incessantly alive, and I know because I've been there to count both. With her lap full of bills, she takes out her savings account passbook, opens it and starts passing it around with her grin spreading wider and wider. "Grandma, Jay and I have a little book like that. With our names on it too. Except ours is green, not gray." "That's good child. That's good." "Daddy put fifty dollars in it to start, and now he makes us put part of our allowance and our birthday money in it. So we can watch it grow." "Now, that's damn good child. Listen to your daddy."

And she was right, damn right about that, about listening to Daddy, because a propensity for saving money is not in Carolyn's blood, not even a smidgen's worth. Because Honey, there's just too many pairs of pretty shoes left out there to satisfy her hunger. That little green book, them savings bonds, those certificates of deposit don't do it for her, not a thing to satisfy her need. But that lovely dress still on the store mannequin, now that's a piece of heaven. That's worth showing. When it comes to money, particularly the saving of it, Carolyn's attitude is… What good is money if you can't spend it? While mine is… What good is it after you've spent it? And what does spending it mean. It means somebody's got to go out there and get some more. And Honey, that somebody is me.

If Mrs. Wilson has two cents in her purse or in the bank, I wouldn't know, because that's privileged information. But I do know that she's always shaking her head and telling her children that she's barely scrapping by. Perhaps, to become savers like Mother and me, it takes a real hunger. And a lot of those "scrapping by" days to appreciate the value of saved money. Apparently more than the Wilson Klan had experienced. They had choices. Whether or not to let their tomatoes ripen on the vine, while Thornell stomachs growled… otherwise. Vine ripen tomatoes now Carolyn, that's a luxury worth showing. Now, did I ever share a fried green tomato story with Carolyn? Most definitely not. Shame dictated otherwise. Those days, and the painful details of 'em, must forever remain… behind a door nailed shut.

So, between Carolyn and I, money is the source of a growing resentment. The more of it, in her eyes, the more the resentment. She's for spending more and saving less, while I dictate, sorry Dear, but we're going to save more and spend less. I'm not a Bible scholar Dear, but I do know, that God didn't wear a dress. So Dear, what's the use in your arguing about it? She even resents it when Mother pulls out all that money, counts it and carefully puts it away. "Why does your Mother do that?" she asks. "Because she can Carolyn, she's finally got money for a showing. Like when you put on a new dress to wear to church." If Mrs. Wilson's purse comes with a snap or a zipper, I'd have to guess, because I've never seen her open it. But when Mother opens hers at Bozo's to pick up the dinner check for five, Carolyn swallows her condemnation along with all that delicious, cornmeal battered, melt in your mouth, fried catfish.

In Mother's seventy odd years, she'd never voted. That was never high on her list of necessities like cleaning houses and sitting up with rich old ladies up there at that nursing home. If she was to ever get social security, she had to work for it herself. Because them Thornell men combined never worked long enough to qualify themselves or a wife for a dimes worth of benefits.

Carolyn never complains about that updated asset list, the one sitting up there on top of the bedroom dresser for her inspection. In case she gets lucky and I zig when I should have zagged and don't come home from the next riot, revolution or cyclone. Jesus! I wonder, how long would that money last if Carolyn ever gets her desirous hands on it, and is free to buy all them things for showing. And the one thing I wanted to shout in Carolyn's ear, is that my mother would never ask her boys for financial support. She'd rather starve first. And before asking, she would. Now that is high on her short list of necessities. I instead, I can take all my overtime money to the bank. A New Orleans bank. Which I do regularly.

Tonight, States-Item photographer Haber and his wife Chris, a writer, are stopping by for conversation and a few dinner drinks around 7:30. And since Mother goes to bed before 8 P.M. I calculate that her time with them will begin and end with a hello, a nice to meet y'all, and a goodnight. And her time for slipping out of one of her profanities will be limited. The couple arrives, Mother meets 'em, but instead of heading to bed, she heads for the den sofa, sits, and starts talking. And talking. And talking. Haber, who works for me on his weekends off covering Saints and LSU football, politely listens and listens. Chris, who has been the star of more than one of my fantasies, but not to worry, because sex with best friend's wives have been limited to just that—fantasies—since I tried it in Jackson and didn't like it—the guilt that is—politely listens and listens.

Mother finishes one story about the ruins of her life, and immediately, starts another even before we can begin a sentence. "Not quite 16 I was, living up there in Sataria in a little shack along the Yazoo, where Ben come for to rescue me. A good for nothing bastard, as he turned out to be, was a fully growed man over 40. I didn't know nothing, but I knowed I wanted to get free from Papa. Always preaching to me about right and wrong and keeping my precious virtue pure. Just like the Almighty intended. There weren't no TV back then, so what was a healthy young woman to do but…" My thoughts interrupt the story, oh my God, she's about to use the "F" word. Fuck! And embarrass Carolyn and me. Geesums! Somebody please! Shut her up, get her out of here. And then, somehow, perhaps miraculously, she skips the "F" word, at least for the moment. And continues. "…Meet up with Ben before daylight down there under the pecan and run off… what's that word when you run off and get married?" "Elope," the attentive Chris offered. "That's it. Elope. That's what we done. With Papa paddling down the river behind us, to grab me up and paddle me back after raising that shotgun he brung for blowing to kingdom come that child stealing Ben," she concludes, and with her laughter filling the room, I sink lower, trying to disappear into the sofa.

With that laughter pause, Bill stands up, looks at his watch and says, "Gees, it's 10:30. We got to get going." Then, Mother gets up, two and a half hours late, and says, "I'm going to bed."

At the door Chris pauses and says, "Jack, your mother is a wonderful story teller. Such tales. Such details. You should have recorded them." "Yeah, she's a talker all right. A real talker." After pillowing my head, I lay there thinking… Such tales, such details alright. Too many fucking details. Details I wanted to forget… to blot from history. Details that I never wanted another living soul to hear. And the worst of it, she resurrects, then introduces that good for nothing Ben. My father.

This visit, it's Mother's turn to sleep with Jay the ball player, baseball and basketball. And he's getting quite good at both over at Girard Playground. They are already in bed when I pass their closed door and hear Jay giggling. So I pause there for a moment to listen. Mother says something. Something I cannot hear. But after she speaks, I hear Jay's giggles again. Coming through the door loud and clear. It was then, I had to restrain myself. Because my reaction wanted me to burst through the door and scream, "Mother! Where were my giggles? My fucking giggles! During my entire childhood you never raised a single giggle from my hungry mouth."

Three days before Christmas, Carolyn has the television on, getting ready to watch her soap operas with Mother, when a news report catches my attention. "A huge explosion at a grain elevator has rocked the West Bank. Many fatalities are feared." As usual, that sets me to pacing and asking myself… What should I do? Seeing that I'm agitated over the news, Mother opens her mouth, "You still on vacation a'int ya?" "Yes Mother, I'm still on vacation. But this sounds like a big story. And bosses don't care about vacations when big stories break. And I got a new boss." After a few more strides across the room, I announce, "Carolyn, I'm going in."

214

A few months later, from Mother's mouth, comes bad news. "Son, you got to come." "Why Mother, what's going on?" "You know that mole on my chin. The one I had all my life. The one you said was starting to look suspicious." "Yes. The one I told you to get checked." "Well I did, and the doctor took it off and found cancer under there." "Jesus Mother, what kind?" "Here, I wrote it down. Let me spell it... M-E-L-A-N-O-M-A." "Melanoma Mother, melanoma." What I didn't spell out was that melanoma is the most deadly kind of skin cancer. And unless it's caught early it usually means curtains, in less than a year. "You want me to come up and get you?" "No, I want you to come up for my surgery." "I thought the doctor cut it out already." "He did. But after it heals up, he's gon'na operate again to look for more cancer down under there." "Okay, Mother, don't worry, I'll be there."

My telling Mother "not to worry" was like me telling me "not to worry", just a waste of words it would be. The difference being, she can never shut up about hers, and I can never open up about mine.

Three weeks later, I'm at the Vicksburg Hospital at Mother's side. As is Brother Marshall and his wife Jerry. As usual, Marshall doesn't have much to say. Like Mother, he's short, but thank goodness, that's all they have in common. And thank God, he's been spared her unceasing tongue. As soon as she awakens, she starts telling the nurse of the shot, of the anesthesia making her woozy, and of the nurses rolling her out. Thank goodness, I think, the shot put her out and she can't remember any more details to tell. And saving us from having to hear a longer version. Over and over again. Believe me when I say, if something happens to Mother, it's a big story. One that equates with that grain elevator explosion that claimed 34 lives just before Christmas. The one she told me not to get off the couch for.

After the biopsy report the surgeon advises, "The surrounding tissue is clean. The lymph nodes are clean. And there's not a sign of the cancer spreading."

A few weeks later, Mother is back in the yard, stooping, pulling weeds, pruning her roses and talking outloud to herself, to the sky, to the birds, to the trees. She's just happy to be alive. And that's a puzzlement to me. Elvis had everything and he wanted to die. Mother, in comparison, has nothing. Yet, she desires to keep on stretching that nothing out for as long as she can. She outlived Ben. She outlived John. She's even outlived a son. What is it that keeps her desire alive? It's not filet mignon, though she can afford it, but with just two teeth left she can't chew it, much less swallow the price of it. No, a slice of gooseliver with slices of a vine ripened tomato between two slices of bread go down just fine. And the fact she never tired of gooseliver is a puzzlement too. Perhaps though, it's because of those early years, when there was never enough of it. Mother, if you were here, you'd hear me say... to relax. Smell the roses, and enjoy your fill of precious gooseliver, because Mother dear you're going to live. And perhaps, long enough to bury another son.

Despite the fog, visibility is measured at four miles, and above standard, when the stewardess announces, "Please make sure your seatbelts are securely fastened, we are on our final approach at Pensacola." Seconds later, the National Airlines Boeing 727 with 58 passengers aboard, makes a perfect landing. But not on the runway, on Escambia Bay, skittering across the water like a thrown flat rock can. Blam! Blam! Blam! It sounds until stopping and settling into the mud about 10-feet below the surface, and about 500 yards short of the runway. Frightened and frantic passengers scramble out emergency doors and jump into the waters, darkened by the night, and covered by fog, much heavier at ground level. Down here visibility is zero. And now, they can feel and smell the leaking jet fuel collecting around them and somewhere in that darkness, Mrs. S. J. Fantauzzi is reaching for the precious hand of her 3-year-old daughter.

Ring! Ring! Ring! Carolyn turns over and says, "Jack, don't you hear the phone?" "I hear it just fine, but answering it at 1 A.M. usually means something else." On the next ring I pick up. "Hello." "Stan, New York Photos, a passenger plane crashed at Pensacola. We need you over there." "Crashed, where exactly?" "In Escambia Bay by the airport." "Okay Stan, I'll get going, but if the plane sank there won't be much to take pictures of… maybe divers." "Whatever, just get over there. Oh, Mark Foley out of Tallahassee is on his way. He'll be there to help you." "Okay then, since the airport is probably shut down, I'll start driving." "Fine."

After splashing water in my face, I pause, look into the mirror and say to myself what I wanted to say to Stan… Miami has three photographers, Florida is their fucking territory why not send one of them? So, I refuse this assignment on two grounds. One: Florida is not my responsibility. Second: I'm tired. Tired down to the marrow of my bones. And like everybody else, even ass sitting photo editors, sometimes I need to rest. This morning, Dear Elvis, I want to be you. Not as you were, but as you are… undisturbable.

During these three hours of driving, my mind is running at full throttle, as always, fueled by that awful anticipation, thinking… if that plane sank, I'm sunk. As are the picture possibilities.

"Makesense! Your ears up?" "Up Cousin. But at this hour, only droopingly so." "Will I get lucky today, like with the Luling Ferry, and find something worth photographing?" "If it depends on luck Cousin, Makesense must say, there's been no sign of you running out of it… not yet." "Oh Makesense, I hope so. But yet, that 'not yet' I find most troubling. Because luck, like everything else, sooner or later, comes to an end."

What's worse than that awful anticipation, it's arriving at a town, a town you don't know your way around and at 4 A.M. and have to find someone to ask directions. Like where will I find the newspaper? After I do, I have to talk my way through security, find the deserted darkroom, and start looking for their film of last night's events. After I find it and after figuring out the chemicals in the trays, I start printing. When, I'm ready to transmit, Foley arrives to help.

"Mark, it'll soon be daylight. One of us needs to get out in the Bay, and the other needs to go to the hospital for survivors." "Okay, since I know my way around, I'll go to the hospital. You go to the Bay." "Okay, just point me in the right direction."

When I emerge from the building, an unusually dark and cloud heavy sky releasing a slight drizzle, greets me. And like Mother can, I sense a storm brewing. Facing the Bay, I discover that I can't see a thing out there. Not a sign of wreckage. Nor a sign of rescue activity. That worries me. The question, how do I get out there? That worries me. The weather, with the wind picking up and the Bay waters getting choppier, obviously it's worsening. That worries me. With my worry worsening, a state trooper pulls up and starts putting his boat in the water, as I approach. "Officer, my name is Jack Thornell, I'm with the Associated Press. I desperately need to get out to the crash site. Can you take me?" "Now?" "Yes sir, now." "Look out there, the water is getting choppier and choppier. And look up, see that lightning, it's building and building… and getting closer and closer. Out there, in this small of a boat, we'd be sitting ducks." "I see your concerns officer, but newspapers are screaming. And I'd like to get a picture of you in the foreground with any wreckage in the background. It'll make front pages and I'll even mail you some 8X10 glossies." "It's risky, but if you want to chance it, I will." "I'm ready." "One more question." "Yes sir." "Can you swim?" "Like a Pisces," I lied. Swim? I can't even dogpaddle. Swim? I tried to learn once at the Y, but I sank like a rock, almost drowned and never returned for a second lesson because of pain, pain, from water getting into my lungs. Swim? That's why I joined the Army. Officer, that "Pisces" answer, that was just another fish tale. And a whopper. Officer, the truth is, water and I don't mix. Overboard, even in calm waters, you're looking at a drowned duck. And the other truth is, the fear of not getting "The Picture" always, always, trumps all others.

Out on the water, well away from shore, the wind whips harder, the waves lash higher, and our boat bounces harder and higher. And instead of lighter, the day is getting darker, while I'm thinking… Thank goodness I don't have to guess the exposure. The light meter on my little Nikormat ELW set on automatic makes perfect exposures… I know… because I've tested it over and over again. And it's reading 1/250 of a second at F2. Any less light and I can't stop the bounce of the boat and the pictures would be ruined by camera movement, like Lally's when he rested his camera on the window of that windblown aircraft.

"Look there! You see it?", the trooper shouts. "Yes! Yes! I do. " I see "The Picture!... I'm thinking… head on, the cockpit looking like a half submerged whale with its rear wings rising out of the water like fins. As soon as I raise my camera, the drizzle turns into a downpour, the lightning gets bolder, closer, and the thunder claps louder and longer. Then, the trooper shouts, "We need to go. Before that lightning singles us out." "Wait! Wait! Just make one pass, I haven't gotten your picture yet." "Okay, but if that lightning finds us, we won't be sitting ducks anymore. We'll be fried ones."

After we reach the shore, a pale and shaken him looks at a pale and shaken me, and I say, "Thanks for bringing your man in alive." With his laughter joining mine, we part company with rain dripping off our faces. On the way to my car I pass the arriving UPI photographer. I look back and see that he is approaching the trooper. Then, I laugh again. He'll pay hell, I'm thinking, of convincing that trooper to go back out there again. No matter how many pictures he promises.

After returning to the newspaper, I'm busy transmitting when Foley returns with news. "Jack, only three people died. One of them was a Mrs. Fantauzzi." "Why are you singling her out?" "Because she had a 3-year-old daughter who miraculously survived." "Gees, did you get her picture?" "No. They wouldn't permit it, but said she's resting comfortable."

On the drive back to New Orleans I summon Makesense and ask, "Was it the hand of God that reached down and plucked that child from that life threatening water?" "If it wasn't Cousin, it was God's hand guiding anothers." "And that was only one of the miracles." "And the other?" "Having the 'Little Mac' skipper Glenn McDonald there, lost in the fog, and yet, close enough to turn his barge into the prefect rescue platform, saving many lives."

The next week the AP log carries the picture titled "Water Wings" and reports that it won "smash front page play". Scoring another success, was that too a miracle? And the other questions still swimming around in my brain… How many more successes am I entitled to? Even the great Elvis was limited to 45—million sellers. So when will the end of my limit come crashing?

As kids come, Candy and Jay are good kids. Actually, better than good. Actually, they're great kids. But like the saying goes… Wouldn't take a million bucks for mine or give two cents for yours. Both are good students but Jay is slipping in Spanish. And falls to a "D". Daddy's not happy and darkens the T.V. Hey! There aren't any Spanish speaking programs on it. Cruel, perhaps, but the punishment promised for a semester is turned back on after a week. At the end of the next term, Jay's grade jumps to an "A" and at the end of the school term, he is called to the stage to be presented with a special citation as the "most improved" language student of the year. Daddy is there sitting patiently, just waiting to hear his own name called. Then, go up and get his award as the most "domineering dad" of the year. And but for my nagging, perhaps Candy could have been an accomplished pianist by now.

Sometimes in the dead of night, though laying next to a sleeping wife, I feel so alone, desperately alone. To the point, I keep asking myself… Why are you so hard on yourself and others? Why can't you be like other dads? Sharing a happy life with a happy wife and two happy kids. The kind of like Brother Garnett envisioned you had and envied. Yet at sad movies, in the dark, your face starts glistening with tears. Tears you fear someone might see, and see a caring side, a weakened side of you. But, the saddest picture you keep seeing over and over in your head is the one of a weakened you collapsing at the feet of number five or number six over at the UPI when your luck runs out. And then, be boxed and shipped fourth class back to 503 where the sounds of Mother's mouth are always beckoning… Son! Come home, back to where you belong… It's time. "Makesense! Makesense Talk to me." "Yes Cousin." "Is there any purpose in going on with this charade of a life, one that everybody but me thinks that I'm living?" "Cousin, you just said the magic word." "And what word is that?" "Purpose." "Oh Makesense, please, please, shut up about purpose. When my only purpose is to get through another day still in the upright position. Though wobbly at best."

While sitting at my desk, secretary Ellenor Kammler announces over the speakerphone, "Jack, pick up line two… Mr. Schwadel in New York. As I reach for the phone I feel the beat of my heart picking up because, when he calls, it's usually bad news, like put your wedding on hold and go cover that revolution. "Hello." "Hello Jack, have I got a trip for you." Hesitantly, I ask, "What is it?" "A week in Costa Rica… San Jose. You went there once before, didn't you?" "Yes sir I did. It's a beautiful country." "You'll be covering the annual meeting of the O.A.S., the Organization of American States." "But won't that be conducted in Spanish?" "Yes, that's right." "Well how will I know what's going on?" "Jack, you've always underestimated your own ability. You'll figure something out. And, as always, you'll do fine."

And have I learned any more Spanish to add to Si, Tequila, Siesta? What a stupid question. Of course I have. I've learned Senorita Quantas por Favor… How much please? Perhaps Jay, should order my T.V. darkened for the next six weeks.

And to you, Mr. Schwadel, I have every confidence in your ability to overestimate mine. Because you've tested and tested it again and again. Without regard to the pressure building and building with each of your new trial balloons. Like now, by sending me, rather than one of your Latin American photographers. What am I to do, sitting there and watching everything that's going on, turn to somebody and ask… "What's going on?" Now that is, stupid. And when I get there, I face UPI's Bruno Torres, an ace out of Chicago. And yes, he speaks Spanish. As well as he speaks English. Keep listening Mr. Schwadel, and one day soon, you'll hear a pop. The sound of a trial balloon. The one you overinflated… Until… Until… Until…

After returning from the usually restful and relaxing—with all its saunas—resort that San Jose is well noted for, rested, and relaxed, I'm not. Instead of feeling as fresh as a daisy, I feel like a long wilted sunflower, long overdue to get plowed under. Mentally: Draining, with my six words of Spanish, totally inadequate. Physically: Exhausting, with heavy cases to be carried through customs, back breaking. And mentally exhausting while straining to hear the snap. The one Dr. Phillips promised would put me under his knife. After lifting one heavy case too many and possibly, if not probably, put an end to my career. My only career. News photography. With the question begging to be asked and answered. Where will that leave me? Somewhere between 5236 and 503.

And as I sit down at a desk piled high, I know not to get comfortable like those New York Photo editors do, because I know that out there, news is waiting to happen. To get me off my ass, and to send me running. Just like WDSU cameraman Lala joked outside the federal courthouse… Thornell is here, so let the news begin.

News like… Train derailments, ship fires, airplane crashes, shootings, assassinations, riots, revolutions, rock concerts, shaking the nubs of lepers, celebrity funerals, chlorine gas escaping, jail breaks, inaugurations, presidents, governor, mayor, weddings, boxing, soccer, divorces, kissing cops, death row inmates, executions, civil rights marches, naked chickens, basketball, baseball, strikes, explosions, high rise fires, bridge jumpers, flying saucer witnesses, beauty pageants, fishing expeditions, gluttony, hunger, helicopter training, Blue Angels, alligator hunting, Nicklaus, Palmer, flash floods, regular floods, spillway openings, deer rescues, drownings, droughts, hurricanes, tornados, bus wrecks, ship wrecks, car wrecks, pile ups, Mardi Gras, fat asses, skinny penises, conventions, Republican and Democratic, press conferences, legislature, Mississippi's, Louisiana's, space shots, Lunar landings, big shots, little shots, good deeds, bad deeds, philanthropists, greedy evangelists, robbers, rapists, negro haters, sneaking preachers, tightrope walkers, track stars, movie stars, rising stars, falling stars, the good, the bad, the ugly, the pretty, the poor, the deserted, oil rig fires, coach hirings, coach firings, police brutality, my brutality, Candy's screams, and Carolyn's tears.

And the general consensus of those sitting New York bosses is… Forget that news, get down to Latin America, there's news there, bigger news, just waiting for your arrival. And forget those UPI photographers. Pat Benic down in Louisiana and Carey Womack up in Mississippi staying home. Snapping away and trying to beat, then perhaps, bury your ass while you're away with their pictures showing up everywhere. Everywhere but, Latin America. Sure, they'll make you look bad. And sure, even if you are away, Mis'Lou is still your first responsibility. But don't worry, because your reputation can withstand a good beating or two. And maybe more.

The thought of taking a good beating takes me back to a conversation I had with former UPI photographer, editor Gary Haynes, who is now the respected photo editor of the Philadelphia Inquirer, and who was in town for another Superbowl.

"Jack, there's one thing that you never have to worry about." "And what's that?" "Getting fired." "And why not?" "Your reputation won't permit it." "You think so Gary?" "Hell, I know so. From experience. You even crushed me a time or two." But what I couldn't relate to Gary then, or anyone now, about worry was that win or lose, worry—like shame—rules my life both day and night. Always keeping the joyeater close at my side.

The phone rings. It's 3 A.M. Calling is overnight editor Rowand. "Jack, a ship has crashed into an oil rig. There's a big fire. And men overboard." "Where Bob?" "Out in the gulf." It's a big Gulf Bob. I need coordinates, precise ones." "Okay, let me get back with the Coast Guard." With the coordinates in hand, I call Air Taxi at Lakefront airport and hire a charter. The pilot greets me with, "We'd better take off quickly, before they shut the sirport down. As you can see the fog is getting heavier by the second." "Let's go. I'm ready."

After the takeoff, we follow the river south until we hit a fog bank thinker than split pea soup left simmering far too long. Unable to fly out of it, the pilot, showing a troubled expression, looks over at me and says, "We got to get down." "Down, hell we can't even see where down is." "I know, I know, but I'm guessing we're still over the river… I'll try to set down there." "But even with pontoons, isn't that a little dangerous?" "Yes, but not as dangerous as flying blind." As he noses the single engine plane down, my thoughts rush me back to those two near death experiences. The first, when I landed in Germany with a gas tank on empty. The second, when I crash landed in that little bubble of a helicopter in Jackson. And what do they say about the third time? Is today the day for those shamebirds to be charmed by the sound and with the sight of my splatter?

With the answer still pending, suddenly, I see the muddy, but now beauteous waters of the Mississippi closing up fast under us. After bouncing to a stop, I turn to the pilot and ask, "How long can we bobble here?" "As long as it takes." "You mean hours?" "Could be, but with the sun coming up, it may not be that long." And with the wind picking up and joining the sun as our benefactors, our bobbling is limited to an hour. After clearing power lines, antennas and grain elevators, and rising to a safe altitude, I turn to the pilot and ask, "Was that luck or what?" "No, for a good pilot, just a piece of cake," he laughed, obviously releasing his tension and spreading it about the cockpit, like icing a cake.

The collision site is 100 miles out. Normally too far for a single engine plane to venture out. But, as the pilot advised, it was the only one available. And naturally, to get the picture, the risk is not a consideration. Now, even though the fog is no longer a problem, the haze is, limiting long range visibility. After flying to the approximate coordinates, the pilot says, "I don't see anything, do you?" "No, no smoke, no nothing. This haze is killing us." "All I can do, is start circling… and making wider sweeps." We circle and circle, and we see nothing. Finally, the pilot advises, "We got to start heading back. I'm down to less than half a tank." Geesums, thank goodness for those pontoons." Smiling, he says, "Out here, in those rough waters, we wouldn't stay afloat long. Even if we could make a safe landing." About to give a reluctant approval, I see smoke off in the distance. "See that!" Off the right wing?" "Yeah, I do, we'll head that way. But remember, fuel is a factor." After circling the crash site once, he announces,

"I'm heading back." Although I consider begging for another pass, with the thought of experiencing another empty tank, I put that notion down. And down immediately, with that saying… the third time is a charm… still echoing.

And when I return to the office, do I report the risk, the danger? Why would I? When to everyone there, getting the picture, is all that matters. Even to me.

ATTACK! ATTACK! I want to shout to those spooked pedestrians passing under my balcony perch. Reminiscent of that Japanese sneak attack on Pearl Harbor with those Zeroes diving down. But instead of raking ships and barracks, this attacker is raking heads. Male heads. Female heads. Never frontal attacks, but always from the rear. But, by the time the startled pedestrian looks back to see… What hit 'em, the attacker is already past there. And when they turn back, still not to be seen.

Birds! Birds! I wanted to warn. But that would be an exaggeration. That would ruin the surprise and those startled expressions. But more, that would have ruined a set of great pictures. Actually though, it isn't birds, plural, it's bird, singular. And it isn't a large and mean seagull. But feisty and fearless, this Mockingbird is, swooping down, and repeating attack after attack, when anyone walks near its precious nest situated in a small bushy tree just ten feet off the sidewalk outside the Plaza Towers on Loyola Avenue.

When secretary Kammler, calls me over to her desk and says, "Jack, you want to see something funny? Just look out there." As she pointed to the balcony just a few feet away, I look and I see. Then, I run for my camera, put a 500 mm lens on it, and run back to the balcony, look down, focus, and fire away. Catching the bird attacks, and the startled expressions of pedestrians breaking into a run while twisting their heads back to see… what the hell just hit 'em.

Reporter Crider, writes a short but funny story about it, likening the attacks to scenes from the Hitchcock classic… "The Birds"… where agitated sea gulls go on a rampage and start attacking people. Many newspapers give his story and my five pictures a full page in Sunday editions, and the best part, for these great pictures, I didn't have to leave the office. Merely step out onto our balcony.

Secretary Kammler's voice sounds, "Jack, pick up line one… Mr. Schwadel." "Shit! I'm thinking… what now? As I pick up the phone and answer, "Hello Jack, great pictures of the bird. And great play. Many front pages." Now thinking that his call is just to stroke my ego, I relax a little, and then he says, "Have I got a reward for you." A reward?" "How does seven days in beautiful Rio de Janeiro sound?" "That's in Brazil, isn't it?" "It is, and the view looking down on the harbor and Sugar Loaf Mountain is one of, if not the most spectacular sight you'll ever see." "Hey, that sounds great. Do I get to take my wife?" "Wife, no," he laughs, "Take your dark room equipment." Hearing that, I feel like I just dropped twin bowling balls, with one landing on each foot. Then, I ask, "What for?" "President Carter and wife Rosalyn are overnighting there. On their way to Europe." "When do you want me there?" "Early next month. When I get the White House itinerary, I'll fill you in." "Anything else I should know?" "Well, you won't have to shoot. I want you to play editor. And keep the pictures moving." "Who'll be the shooters?" "Bob Daugherty and Charles Tasnadi out of Washington. Gene Blythe out of Atlanta will be setting up a darkroom in Brasilia, the capital, where Carter is also going." "Anything else?" "Oh yeah, you'll need to take a second transmitter." "Can you ship me two of those new lightweight transmitters, the ones that I have been hearing about? The ones reported to be the size of a portable typewriter?" "No, not a chance. I don't have any to spare. You'll have to take two of the old ones."

As soon as he hangs up, my back starts indicating… it can't carry more weight. It'll never get through customs, coming and going, carrying those heavy cases without hearing that dreaded snap. The sound of a back breaking. Mine. Who knows about my fragile back? Everybody. Who cares? Nobody. Nobody but me. And when New York calls and says hop, I know I'd better skip and jump too. No matter how heavy the load I'm carrying.

After paying Varig Airlines an extra $500 for excess baggage, and returning from a successful outing as a photo editor, I make my move. It begins with an appointment with back doctor Phillips. After taking a new set of X-rays and scrutinizing them, he turns to me. "What can I say, but you've got the back of an old man. A very old man. One with too much wear and tear. Jack, you need to lighten your load." "If I don't… or can't, then surgery is on your horizon, and even that may not be successful." "Can you give me a letter to that effect?" "Sure, no problem."

Phillips' letter, dated May 25, 1981, the one I mail to Deputy Newphoto Editor Schwadel says… Mr. Thornell has a lumbar strain that is chronic. He should not lift weights over 25 pounds or bend and stoop repetitively. My accompanying letter says… my doctor advises me that X-rays reveal that my back is far older than the rest of me. And lifting those heavy transmitters is a "no no". So if there is ever going to be a new lightweight transmitter assigned to New Orleans, there would be no better time than now.

Ten days later, Chief of Bureau Clark approaches my desk looking red-faced, like his blood is nearing the boiling over point. "Jack! Step into my office." "Yes sir." Facing him, I see that he is holding up a copy of my letter… The Schwadel letter. "This is out of line… way out. If you have a problem… any problem… address it to me and not New York." "Sir, I carboned you in. See down there… at the bottom… C.C: Mr. Clark." "Yeah! I see it, but I was on vacation when you wrote it." Seeing his face getting even redder, I add, "Sorry but I didn't know that I couldn't communicate with New York without going through you. The next time they call me at 3 A.M., shall I tell them… Sorry but I can't talk to you without Mr. Clark's knowledge. Better call him. You don't mind taking those 3 A.M. calls do you?" Now, I can see that he is really pissed. Now, he's holding up the letter again and waving it vigorously, actually most vigorously. Back and forth, and looking like he'd rather be swatting me than swatting air. Suddenly, he stops, regains at atom of composure, and snaps, "Don't let this happen again… understand?" "Yes sir, I understand… perfectly."

Back in the darkroom, trying to reclaim a level head. I summon Makesense. "I learned something today, something new." "What Cousin?" "Well, I used to think that we photographers were only as good as our next picture." "And why is that?" "Because we are throw-a-ways. Like cheap cameras in a cardboard box. Use us up and then, throw us away."

Did Mr. Clark or Mr. Schwadel ever ask… Jack, how's your back? Hell no. Not once. And did New York start waking Mr. Clark at 3 A.M. Hell no. Not once. And did you ever get one of those light-weight transmitters? Hell yes. Immediately.

222

At home, why can't things work like things work at work? Where, when the boss barks orders, I salute, make an about face and march away. Not liking it, but always doing it. Certainly, by now, Carolyn knows how I like things. How I want things. How I demand things. And the kids, they know it too. So, why do they torment me? Why can't they obey orders, without me having to stand over them, swatting and shouting... Why haven't you vacuumed? Why haven't you mopped? Why haven't you taken the garbage out and straightened up your rooms? Can't anybody do things right? Can't I come home just once without having to raise my voice, like Clark raised that fucking letter? How I hate yelling the same things over and over when apparently, nobody living at 5236 Utica is listening. Perhaps, the day Daddy comes home vigorously waving a severance check and announces that Daddy just got fired. Perhaps then, somebody will be listening, and even ask... What does this mean Daddy? Well daughter, it means the end of filet mignon, thick juicy pork chops, boiled shrimp and those most desired sit downs over at Bozo's. Son, it means that when the savings runs out, we'll have to move in with Grandma down at 503. And share our meals in a kitchen where the stains of Garnett's shame still remain. Still nothing more than a stain on an old linoleum floor. See kids, what you haven't learned yet, is something Daddy learned today. And it is this. No matter how successful Daddy appears. No matter how many Pulitzers hang on the wall. No matter how many front pages his pictures fill. Daddy, your Daddy, can never be nothing more than a throw-away. Just like his daddy was. Living in a tent, and dying in a shed. Because his oldest son's wife wouldn't let that dirty, threadbare and decrepit old man set one foot in her nice clean house, though he lay laboring to draw a final breath. Sad, but sick to the stomach funny the story is kids, because, that was probably the only work he ever did consistently. Draw another breath. And now, he doesn't even have to do that. Not anymore. And kids, if you'd ever seen him, or seen your Daddy looking like him, you wouldn't have to wait long to feel worse about yourself, and your family roots. Because kids, any moment now someone who knows you, who sees you with him, someone like Madge, is going to shout across the concession stand, and pierce you with that observation... That! Was your father. And after that cruel but most correct of appraisals, the only place the value of one's self worth can go, is... down... down... down.

Today Vice President George Bush is making a three-state hop, trying to rally support for President Reagan's tax cut proposal. One of the stops is at Meridian. A town I'm most familiar with after spending weeks and weeks there covering the trial of the ones who violated the rights of those caring young men. Where, in any place, but down in Mississippi, it would have been called murder. Three counts.

After stepping down from the outdoor reviewing stand, Bush starts walking toward the armory. With me on his coattail, and with only the secret service between us. Suddenly, from behind us, a team of planes swoop down, cracking jet engines in unison, piercing the air, and the ears of an unexpectant vice president who is now, jerking his head around, shrinking his body in, looking up, and cringing. Just like I did sitting inside Bugeyes, with the passing roar of every giant semi. But today, I'm not there to cringe, but to react to the cringing of others. And I do, as the sounds of my Nikon's noisy motor drive can certify. As well as those front page pictures, appearing everywhere, can. And once again, UPI is impaled by me, and not me by them and their pictures.

Still serving under the command of the boss I crossed, good news reaches my ears. Mr. Clark is being promoted to Miami and being replaced by one Hank Ackerman, now working in

Argentina. He'll be number seven. Perhaps now, I'll get lucky and get promoted next. How does that saying go... Be careful what you wish for. And while I'm pondering that, the voice of Kammler announcing, "Jack, line three please, it's Mr. Cordell." "Hello Jack, how are you?" "Treading water, you might say." "I'm calling because I have an offer for you." "I'm listening." "How would you like to become the Dallas Photo Editor?" "What! What about Dave Taylor?" "He's retiring, bad ticker and all." "Yea, I noted that during those space shots he was eating a lot of cucumbers and tomatoes." "What about it? You interested?" "Would I have to shoot anyone?" "Only if you want to, only when you have time to. That'll be up to you." "That sounds sweet, but what about the money?" "Well, with your merit pay already peaking, I can't give you a raise, not right away." "What about overtime?" "No, no overtime when you move into management." "What about my company car?" "No, with you spending most of your time behind the desk, you won't have one." "Geesums Dorman, can I take a few days to think about this?" "Sure, take a week, and call me." "Will do, I'll get back to you within a week, if not sooner." "Fine, I'll talk to you then. Goodbye."

That night I tell Carolyn and ask, "What do you think?" "I like the idea of moving to Dallas and being close to Bill and Billie." "But how do you like the idea of a pay cut and the loss of a company car?" "What! What kind of promotion is that?" "That's what I keep asking myself. And you know what else?" "What?" "New York could keep calling, and keep me hop, skip, and jumping, until I drop. But, with one rather large difference." "And what's that?" "It wouldn't cost them a nickel's worth of overtime." "You think they'd do that?" "That Carolyn is a question worth thousands."

After calculating that it would cost me a minimum of $10,000 a year, I call Cordell and turn down "The Promotion". "Can you recommend anyone?" "I can." "Who?" "Harry Cabluck, out of Pittsburgh." "How do you know him?" "From covering a couple of superbowls, here and Miami." "But what specifically is it that you like about him?" "Like me, to some extent, he's a worrier and he's anxious too." "What's so great about those traits?" "Well it means he doesn't like sitting on his ass. He's anxious to get the job done and be free to start worrying about the next one." Laughing with my critique he says, "Hey I like that. Particularly about being one to get up and off his ass, without me having to order it. Just like I found you to be. Heck, you were there, many times before I even knew there was a story there." "Anything else?" "No Jack, except to say I'm sorry, real sorry, that we won't be joining up again. Goodbye and thanks." And would I be sorry at a later date for turning down that something less than a promotion? Yes. I would.

A few weeks later I'm offered another "promotion". This time from the States-Item. Their photo editor Wilfred D'Aquin is retiring. And they'd love me to fill his shoes and his desk. And even shoot some too. I considered it for a week, and then, I refused the offer. There, they couldn't even match what I was already making. Again the bottom line is the money. With me it's always the money! The money! Always the fucking money. And to have some to save. Titles and prestige, I can't take to the bank. And with interest rates soaring, every dollar saved puts me one step closer to retirement while inching me farther and farther away from 503. And from the possibility, the disturbing possibility, of my having to return. Flat and broke, like the day I was born, up there at Big Charity.

Today, more work related news comes. Not about me, but about Carolyn. She's taking a job. From nine till noon. With two lawyers over on Veterans Highway, only a five minute drive from our front door. Her motive? To send her momma something she thinks is, long overdue. Fifty bucks a month. She'll be making a hundred dollars a week, so she'll have plenty of money left over. For shoes and things. Or so, she thinks. And will she start paying me back for that Emporium debt, like she promised before we got married? Well, she didn't mention it. And I didn't mention it either, not and set off World War III. Her plan is to bank fifty dollars a month, write a check to momma and good golly, be free to spend the rest, but good golly dear you're forgetting the I.R.S. After a few months, the war comes anyway.

After opening the next few months of bank statements, I summon Carolyn for a sit-down. "Carolyn, I see you're sending Mrs. Wilson her check like clockwork." "So?" "But you're not putting the fifty in the checking account like clockwork." "So, sometimes I'm a little late." "Late hell, this month you skipped," I retorted, as I waved the statement, and say, "Come see." Reluctantly, she inches closer for a look-see. "Oh, apparently I missed that one." "Apparently so. Carolyn it's simple. You can't write checks before you put the money in the bank." "I'll take care of that," she snaps. "And one other thing." "What!" "How much are you saving for taxes?" "What!" "Let's see. You'll be making $5200 a year. In the 30 percent tax bracket that comes to $1560. F.I.C.A. figured at an even 10 percent, that comes to $520." "What! That's half of everything I earn." "Well, if you add your Mama's $600 actually a little more than half." "And it totals $2680 a year. So, let's see. $2680 divided by 12 comes to $223.33. That's what I expect to see deposited each and every month. Like clockwork." Shocked to tears, she gets up and starts walking away, when I stop her, and ask, "Carolyn! Do you understand?" "Yes!" "Good because I don't want to revisit this subject again. And as for having to pay all those taxes to Uncle Sam, you have my deepest sympathy. Because, it's enough to make anyone cry. Even a grown man. Even one with deep pockets."

Like Makesense tells me all too often… Life goes on, grass grows and needs attention. And these days, my attention is focusing on Candy. With blue eyes and dark black hair, she is turning into a beautiful young woman. But unfortunately, Daddy is not the only male noticing. And unfortunately, she is not interested in boys. Her only interest is boy. That's right, boy singular and not boys plural. His name is Kevin Ganucheau, and like Candy, he is not interested in college. And that bothers me, because it drastically limits one's career choices. But Candy doesn't see it, because she only sees a most handsome, blonde, blue-eyed man almost three years her senior. And one quite content learning the pipe fitting business from his father. But in the New Orleans area where the summer heat and the humidity don't start leveling off until nearing 100 degrees each. It's a dirty and sweat draining job, where in those closed attics and crawl spaces, that reading would merit smiles. After getting off, where do those drained working men deserve to go before going home? Places like Beau Louie's, and God forbid, the Cracker Barrel. And what happens when a pretty but poor young wife greets her drained, dirty and drunk working man with her endless bitching? Perhaps, something worse than a plate of flying spaghetti. Hell, I ain't got nothing against a working man. I'd a loved to have one for a daddy or a stepdaddy. Hell, flying spaghetti would have been a blessing. But the truth is, I don't want my daughter married to one. With her beauty, she deserves a doctor or a lawyer. SO that after having the privilege of ravishing her, he can lavish her with all them pretties that she and her momma so love, and feel they so deserve. Sorry young Mr. Ganucheau, but it is personal, very, and my short-term plan is to fire off my starter pistol and set you to running. But without my lovely daughter.

To accomplish this goal, I call for a family meeting, excluding Jay. And announce a new rule, a concerned father's rule. "Candy I like Kevin, but…" "I like him too daddy, I like him a lot." "But Candy, I think you're way too young to get serious. So, I'm setting a rule." "What rule Daddy," she asks while a nervous look of anticipation covers her face as if she has already read my mind. "Candy, you can continue dating Kevin. But not exclusively." With a look of disdain, she asks, "What does that mean… exactly?" "It means that between dates with Kevin, you have to date someone else." "But Daddy, I don't want to date anyone else." "That I know. That's why the rule. Because you need to broaden your field." "Daddy, I can't… I won't date anyone else." "That's up to you. But until you do, you sure as hell won't be dating Kevin, and that's final."

Unfortunately, my rule wasn't set in concrete, and after several weeks of watching a stubborn Candy sit home, like with Jay and his TV turnoff, I weaken, and then, succumb. And Candy and Kevin are back dating. Exclusively.

Meanwhile, Jay is occupied with sports. Starting at second base, and point guard at J.D. Meisler Junior High. Despite a lifelong struggle with allergies, he's grown quite strong. And in sports, quite good. In baseball, his coach nicknamed him "Electrolux" after the premier vacuum cleaner, because nothing, whether in the air, or on the ground, gets past his sweep. At 14, his game plan includes college. With his mind set on one and just one. Louisiana State University. Because, he loves those Tigers. With all his heart. And then some. Like his dad, Jay enjoys junk food. After supper and before bed he opens the pantry door time after time to pick and choose from a wide selection of salties. Seeing him standing there. Trying to make a decision, I try helping. "Son, there's ice cream in the fridge, that three flavor kind." Sounding frustrated, he replies, "I know, I know Dad. But I'm not ready for dessert… not yet." With him still leaning and looking, and with me still watching, I want to cry, "Son! You're seeing what I never saw as a boy. A pantry full of goodies. Or of anything else. But those childhood goodies, I'd never share with my kids. Or, with anyone else. That, shame cries, is the rule. One that never weakens.

"Jack, your Mother's on the phone." "Hello Mother." "Jack, I've been thinking. That big interest you've been drawing on your money down there." "What about it?" "I want to get some. So, here's what I want you to do. Take $10,000 out of my savings and put in one of those…" "C.D.'s… Certificates of Deposit Mother." "Yeah, one of those. Cause the bank here ain't paying shit." "Okay Mother, I'll be coming up to Jackson next week. I'll detour over and pick up the money. And here's what I'll do after. I'll put your $10,000 with my 10,000. That way, we'll get a higher interest rate. And then, we can watch it grow together." "That'll be fine… fine. Oh! One more thing." "What's that?" "Pick up some of that chicken." "Kentucky Fried." "Yes, but I want the soft kind." "You mean the original recipe." "Yeah… the original. I'll pay you for it." "Okay, you got it. See you next week."

Instead of driving straight up to Jackson, and then turning west, I take the Utica exit and the two-lane rural road. It's a break in the monotonous interstate, though made more dangerous by all the big trucks passing so close. I deliver the chicken, and after we eat, I pick up her passbook and drive to the First National without her. Thank goodness that my name is on the account and I won't have to be humiliated by her presence. It's troubling though, that I am more than willing to take her money, but most unwilling to be seen with the source of that money. Taking her money, Lord knows I done it before. I've even got comfortable doing it. As for being comfortable in public, in her presence, well that's entirely another matter. A matter I don't want to think about. Unless I want to start that feeling of a humiliation coming. And coming early.

At 17, Candy graduates from Grace King, an all-girls public high school. Shortly after, boyfriend Kevin asks for a sit-down. A man to man meeting, he calls it. I agree, and just after we take the couch, he reaches into his pocket. Pulls out a little box, and then, he opens it. A sparkling diamond sends me into shock, almost blinding me. "Mr. Jack, I'm asking your permission to give this to Candy." "Oh! Kevin, Kevin, Kevin, it's a beautiful ring and gesture, but Candy is too young, far too young to even consider marriage. She's only 17." "But Mr. Jack, we love each other." "I'm sure you do, but why not wait a bit? Keep dating, but please don't rush into marriage. You know how old Carolyn and I were when we married?" "No Mr. Jack, I don't." "She was 23 and I was 25. And I was secure with a good paying job." "Mr. Jack, my parents were only 18 when they got married. And I have a good job, a very good job." "But Candy doesn't. And to have a comfortable living these days, you'll need a second paycheck." "Mr. Jack, Candy already has a job at that insurance company." "Kevin, Kevin, that's a part-time job. An after school job. She, you, y'all will need a larger payday than that. So please, will you put that ring back on lay-a-way. At least for a while?" "Okay Mr. Jack I will, but Candy will be 18 soon… in just six months. After that, you'll probably be seeing it again." "Okay Kevin, we'll talk again then."

In June of 1982, I find that my support system—my attitude, my fortitude, my backbone, both mentally and physically has either collapsed, or, is in the state of collapsing. Night football is killing me, because my eyes can't follow focus like they used to. I'm getting like Arnold who quit working games with me because 33 of 36 of his frames were fuzzy. And after seeing his film again and again, I didn't try to change his mind. Because the morning papers want those pictures fast—like yesterday—and they want 'em crisp, clear and with the action peaking. And with long lens, whether in the Superdome or at Tiger Stadium where the lighting is poor, with the lens set on 2.8, the depth of field, and the margin for error in focusing is… zero. You're either right on, or you're off. And last season, I was more off than on. Except for my sweating, it was on, even in the winter. And making matters worse, UPI is still gunning for me, now with a fresh and young number six. His name is Jerry Lodriguss. And he's one hell of a sports shooter. I know because he used to help me cover Saints football. And when I edited his film, I saw 33 sharp frames and just 3 fuzzy ones. The reverse of Arnold's film. And now, mine.

In a state of tiredness, like never experienced before, I schedule a two-week vacation. And there's even a problem with that. That extra week. Because the longer I stay away from the job, the harder the comeback is. If I ever strung my four weeks of vacation together, only the Lord knows, if I'd show up after. And to make sure this vacation is not interrupted by a grain elevator explosion, a ship fire or a plane crash, I pen a letter: Dear Mr. Schwadel. I need two weeks of vacation without interruption. I'm sending my cameras off for cleaning and refurbishing. So, Mr. Schwadel, if anything blows up in Mississippi or Louisiana, take notice, I'm unavailable. Send someone else. Because… I'm on vacation.

In eighteen years with the Associated Press, sure, I've been bloodied before, even gone down before. But somehow, someway, I've always managed to pick myself up to get back out there and to score another round of successes before the bell sounded, the fight ended, and I was declared the winner. Time after time. But this time, there are two things missing. Energy and desire. And this time, I do not want to get back up. No smelling salts please. For the rest of this life, I just want to sleep…..

And did Mr. Schwadel respond with encouraging words? Like… Jack, don't worry about work. I've got you covered. Go. Relax. Enjoy. And rejuvenate yourself. So, tomorrow can bring a better day. No, I didn't hear or read a word. Not even, how dare you write to me directly. You know you're supposed to take your bellyaches straight to your Chief of Bureau. And never never to me. So, when I return from vacation, perhaps, there'll be a fresh ass chewing awaiting from New Orleans Boss Ackerman. Who is still waiting to see me show him something like all of his predecessors saw… great pictures. And what have I got left to show him? A gas tank sitting on empty. And a landing field not in the picture.

Today, I'm up in Jackson covering the State Legislature, where I find Editor Ward is back at work after his treatments for throat cancer. I walk over to his door and look in, just like that first day back in 1960 when I approached him for a job. Finally, he looks up, sees me and says in a very raspy voice, "Hey, come on in." "Hello Mr. Ward, How would you like lunch, compliments of the Associated Press?" "Sure that sounds good. And so finally, I'm getting paid off." "Paid off?" "Yep, for discovering you." And the fact that he hadn't fired me, when he should have, for that drunken night that I cursed him, I owed him. And a lot more than lunch. Perhaps, that Pulitzer.

Over lunch, we talk history. Mississippi's ole history. And it's clear that he prefers his old Mississippi readers over the new. Because his off-colored Negro jokes drew more laughs back then. Now, his conservative fans, when they read his column, because of the changes down in Mississippi, don't know whether to laugh or to cry. But, the one subject that doesn't come up is… Kay. My Kay. From what I hear, she has come full circle. Married. Divorced. Caring for a born handicapped child, and back living with Mother. There's little doubt, it was my attempt to possess Kay, body and soul, that ended our turbulent on-again, off-again relationship. And now, the irony is, that in the end, it was Kay that ended up possessing me. And, had she ever crooked her finger, what could I have done? The only thing I could. Come running.

This year, it's our turn to visit the Swarts. Last year, they spent a week here. This year we spend a week there. And afterwards I'll still have a week left to goof-off at home. And this year, I shouldn't have to worry about being disturbed. My Schwadel letter, and the sending off of my cameras should guarantee that. This year I promise myself. No pacing. No worrying. Let the news happen without me. And during that goof-off time, I can lift my spirits by counting my money and updating my financial statement. And how much is there to count? Over $150,000. And how did I do it? Such an amassing. Just like Mother, dollar by dollar. And with the help of Carolyn? Hell no. In spite of. Saving is not her thing. Spending is. And it's sad to see and say, the higher the pile of cash gets, the wider the distance between Carolyn and I grows. And my fear is, that if I don't return from an assignment one day, that stash will disappear faster than that fifth of Jack Daniels did down the toilet at the Monte Christo after I pushed the flush lever. And with the money spent Candy's choice to avoid college, will be a good one. And perhaps, Jay can join the Army, put in his time, get out, and then attend his beloved LSU on the G.I. Bill. And hopefully, from wherever my spirit is, I'll be oblivious to it. Because, seeing that, would be some kind of hell. And more than even I am is due.

Our hosts, the Swarts, are nice down home people. Every time I think of Bryan, an adopted son, and of his school escapes, I can't check my laughter. My favorite: Bryan is in the fifth grade and paying little attention. But his teacher is… and that's not because his grades are slipping. No. They've already dropped off the page. Pushed off by "F' after "F'. Not pleased, she gives him a note—asking for a call—for him to take home to his mom. But, after a week, no call. Another note. After another week, still no call. The teacher quizzes Bryan. And he swears he is making the deliveries. After the third note and still no reply, the teacher confronts her student and says, "I don't believe a word coming from your mouth." The student sits calmly and silent. "Well, I got news for you," she says as she holds up an envelope. "See this, I've written your mother, and I'm mailing it today." The next day, Bryan says he's sick and stays home. A week passes, another, and still no response. So one night from home, the teacher calls Bryan's mother and asks, Why not? What notes? What letter? His mom replies. After putting their heads together, they figured it out. The day Bryan feigned illness, was the day the mailman came. And that letter, just like Crider's Jack Daniels, got flushed. And despite that "F" in math, everyone had to agree that Bryan was pretty darn good at figuring things out. And a lot smarter than his grades indicated.

The week is flying by. We go to dinner, to church and we stay in playing hearts. Bill, Jay and I, take in the Texas Rangers while Billie and Carolyn go shopping. I've always found Billie attractive. And I've always felt it was and is reciprocal. Like the night Bill jokingly planted a good night kiss on the lips of Carolyn. So joking, on Billie's mouth, I planted back. I didn't hold back. Billie didn't hold back. And we let our tongues go. And unite if only for a brief but glorious, and most passionate moment. And between us, I felt the sparks. And seeing the wanton look in Billie's eyes, I was sure she felt it too, escaping like a passion pent up for far too long. Especially, with that fat again husband sleeping so close, and with the memory of his adulterous affair still between 'em, though never put to bed. Later while playing cards, we rub knees under the table. And but for that rule, my rule, to never again sleep with a good friend's wife, my rubbing may have reached higher. But, it never did. Because that unforgettable guilt of the first time, resounding and resounding, again and again, kept my zipper zipped. And odd is the thought, that I could do it with her, but I couldn't do it to him.

The drive home, the 500 miles, the ten hours, seems longer and is, more tiring. Just what I need, I'm thinking, returning home more exhausted than when I left it. But, I've still got a week to get my head screwed back on, and hopefully a lot straighter than it was just a week before. If I seem a little lopsided like Garnett's imperfect cake, nobody seems to be noticing. Not the Swarts. Not Carolyn. And certainly not New York. Can't they see that a lopsided cake can't float for long on another topsy-turvy Escambia Bay? Least not anytime soon. And certainly not until it's deck is leveled. At least though, there's money to be counted. And interest to be added. Thank God for Jimmy Carter, because under his rule, rates have been soaring. Twelve to fourteen percent on my money. That should be enough to lift a dead man's spirits, if he left money to invest. But when it comes to money, one attitude, unlike with young couples, isn't changing. My earnings is our money. Carolyn's and mine. But her earnings are her money, and hers alone. Because husband, providing for the family is your responsibility and yours alone. And compounding the problem of conflicting attitudes is more money. Carolyn has two part-time jobs now. In addition to her work at the lawyers office, she's taking in work at home. Typing for a court reporter, at odd hours. Late nights and weekends too. Making money, that seems to be her only interest, except for the joy of spending it. Every penny. Except for the

I.R.S.'s dues. Which I insist on every week, like clockwork. And in her eyes, that makes me a badder, a meaner, and a greedier penny-pinching blood sucking, till the last drop, vampirish villain. And, not her Uncle Sam, who every April is, everybody else's villain of the year.

At mid-afternoon, our first full day back, Carolyn walks to the door, looks out, and then, looks back. "Jack, your car is blocking mine. Want to come move it because I'm going shopping." "No, just take mine. I won't need it. I'm on vacation." And besides, I'm thinking, there's only one camera in the trunk because the rest are in New York being refurbished. And if something did blow, with only one camera, I couldn't be competitive. And these days, another disadvantage I don't need.

As I watch Carolyn back out in my silver Ford Ltd, I notice the sky is darkening like that morning in Escambia Bay. Still looking up, I see the clouds are in a disturbed state. Crashing together. Lightning flashes and a thunderstorm erupts. And down pours the rain. For weather news, I rush and turn on the T.V.

As the storm rages, Pan Am Flight 759, fully loaded with 146 passengers including the crew, is taking off from runway 10 at the New Orleans airport. Below, in Morningside Subdivision eleven-year old Jennifer Schultz, who has taken refuge under the carport of friendly neighbor E.V. Weems, is talking on the phone. Next door, sister Rachel, age 7, and her friend Lisa Baye, age 6, sit in the living room watching television. Above them, and above the Boeing 727, a phenomenon is occurring. The time is 4:11.

In my living room, a news bulletin flashes… A jetliner has crashed in a Kenner neighborhood… stay tuned for more details. And that crash detail alone, has me up pacing and thinking. Holy shit! That's ten… fifteen minutes from here. Jesus Christ! No Carolyn. No car. No camera. And the only thing I can do is, pace, worry and wait. And while I'm pacing, worrying and waiting, I hear a timer buzzing in my head and then, a recorded message sounding… Mr. Thornell, your time is up… your luck just ran out… so let the news begin… but… without you. And with every tick-tock of the clock, I knew the opportunity for getting "the picture" is vaporizing. And compounding my torture is that blasted ringing of the phone. Why answer? What could I say? I only have a sketch pad handy. Or I could take the offensive with… Hey! I'm on vacation. So, why are you bothering me? Hey! Didn't you read my letter? Why not call Mr. Schwadel and bother him. Oh! Forget that now I see the clock. It's 6 P.M. in New York. He's already home, having a Scotch and water, and waiting to preside over his family dinner. And you certainly wouldn't want to interrupt that. Because if you bother him like you bother me, on vacation or not, you just might be driving him to an early retirement. Or, off a cliff. Whichever comes first.

The phenomenon is called windshear, but unlike headwinds and tailwinds, it directs its powerful bursts straight down. And powerful enough to override an engine's thrust and push a 727 down like it is on an express elevator with no stopping until it reaches the ground. It hit the carport where Jennifer stood. Then, it strikes the house behind, sweeping it off its concrete slab and taking with it, Mrs. Sandra Giancontieri and her three sons before crashing through the brick home of Melanie Trahan, killing her and her four-year-old daughter Bridget. And leaving the 16-month old Melissa missing.

After damaging or destroying 15 homes with its fiery swatch, the plane comes to a stop on the house of Joseph Pace, who rushes home to find, "A 100 dead people in my yard." And finally, the third worse crash in aviation history, leaving 154 dead, is over. But my crashing is just beginning. And I fear, my crumbling.

Finally, almost two hours after the first bulletin, Carolyn is back with the car and my camera. She greets me with, "Boy was it nasty out there. I got stuck in the store." "And girl its been nasty in here." Noticing my pacing and my disturbed state, she asks, "What's the matter? What happened?" "A plane crashed, leaving the airport… and lots of people are dead." "Oh my God! Are you going now?" "No. It's too late. The good pictures are all taken." "Did your office call?" "I'm not sure, but the phone has been ringing off the wall." "You didn't answer?" "No. Without my cameras what's the use?" "What about now?" "Don't answer it, let it ring. Now, they will have to send somebody to fill my shoes to play catch up. Because, most likely, UPI will crush us. And besides, I'm on vacation and not to be disturbed." But of those three observations—about the good pictures, about the vacation and about not being disturbed—only one reverberates. Disturbed? Hell, I'm a walking, talking nervous wreck looking for a deep well to fall in. And have the guilt of not going in, cover me up. And all I ask of guilt is… do it fast. But unfortunately, guilt doesn't take requests, and besides, guilt never works that way. Guilt already prefers a slow and a deliberate pace to maximize its delight, just like shame does.

A half hour later comes guilt's coup'de tat. With live pictures showing up on my T.V. screen. "Jack, come look. Oh my God!", Carolyn yells as I'm splashing cold water in my face. After rushing back to the den, I see rescuers pulling a small child from under the still smoldering rubble. She's the missing Melissa. And she's alive. "It's a miracle! It's a miracle!" Carolyn shouts. As I resume my pacing, I resume my thinking… It's a miracle all right… and more… because all the good pictures hadn't been taken… because the picture I just saw was "the picture"… and it wasn't too late… I could have been there… I could have taken it… even with just one camera… with one hand tied behind my back. And with the rage over my decision roaring inside me, and trying to consume me, I direct my thoughts outward and upward by crying… God! Why are you doing this to me? God! You know I'm on vacation. You know I'm not to be disturbed. God! God! God! Why! Why! Why me!

Meanwhile, back at Morningside, young Jennifer who stood talking on the phone is gone. What of her baby sister Rachel, who was watching television next door with friend Lisa? Gone. And little Lisa? Gone. And what of the eight members of Baton Rouge's Donald E. Fitzgerald family who were flying to Las Vegas to attend a funeral? Gone. And before I can cry "Why me?" again, shame shouts… Why them? Hell man! You weren't even there. You were on vacation. And the grand slam: You're still here, still on vacation, and still feeling the pain of your shame. And yet, knowing this, I can't stop crying… Why me! With this added guilt nothing less than the perfect icing on shame's now perfect cake.

"Makesense, your ears up?" "Up Cousin." "Oh Makesense my shame is rearing, and still, I'm only focused on me. And how this tragedy affects me. Me! And not them, the real victims. What makes me so cold, so callus, so cruel?" "Actually Cousin, your condition is the result of a quite common malady." "And what malady is that?" "Well Cousin, it's called the human condition. Me first, and everybody else second. Even God."

The next five days of my vacation. I mow grass... as usual. I take the garbage out… as usual. I take Carolyn to the movie on Friday night… as usual. And yet, all the while, I'm thinking that nothing going on is really "as usual", because, come Monday morning I must face the most unusual. Coming in the form of humiliating and demoralizing questions. Call it a shellacking. One five days overdue. And sounding like this. Oh Jack! It's you, you're really here. Or, better late than never Jack. Or, why didn't you call in, or better yet, come in. You could have chalked up some points with new boss Ackerman like you did with Clark when you rushed in from vacation to cover that grain explosion even though your Mama told you not to. Or simply, Jack! Where the hell were you?

With my tank on near empty, and with my spirit sagging to a new low, how will I ever be able to straighten myself back up completely and continue to fake this perceived ability, now that luck has deserted me? Had luck been with me I would have been a passenger on that 727 that crashed and burned. And in a few seconds, I would have been over and done. And I wouldn't be here to endure a slow crumbling, like Elvis did with his pills.

I arrive early, and find friend and photographer Haber sitting at my desk. At my recommendation a few months back, he became an AP staffer in the Dallas office. Bill looks up, meets my eyes, and smiles. "Man! Am I glad to see you." "Hello Bill, it's good to see you too," I say, while forcing a smile. "Why are you here so early?" "There's a hospital press conference for that little Trahan girl." "The one they pulled out alive?" "That's the one." "When did you get here?" "Tuesday night, and boy did I put my foot in it." "How so?" "Well, when I heard about the crash, I picked up the phone, called New York, and volunteered to come help you. And when they told me that you were on vacation I said… AAAAH shit!" "And they sent you anyway." "Yep, and with you gone and UPI here, I knew I'd be playing catch-up. And would probably get killed." I laugh, trying to conceal the pain from the gnaw of guilt eating away at my gut, before I ask, "Did we get killed?" "No, we did okay. But that was because there weren't any great pictures taken." "Except by that lone TV cameraman." "Yea, and thank God UPI missed it."

While Bill continues talking, I'm thinking… no great pictures… no prize winners… no Pulitzers. And no lasting reminders to keep stimulating this gnawing. But, that's only the half of it. The other… shame. It's still alive, still thriving and still the best of reminders. And needs no props. "There was one fuck-up," Bill says, "It involved Joe Holloway." "What happened?" "Well, he flies in to help, gets off the plane, takes some night pictures of the crash scene, and then, he comes to the office and drops his film into the hypo, instead of the developer." "He didn't." "He did." "Doesn't he have any sense of smell? When even a whiff of hypo will take your breath away." With Bill laughing, he says, "Well I guess at that hour Joe just wasn't in the whiffing mood."

And after hearing that story, my thoughts take me back to Army photo school when Sgt. Dumbass made the Holloway error and erased the images on his film and the possibility of a photography career.

The first to arrive is news editor Prince. He takes one look at me, says, "Hello Jack," takes his desk and gives me his back. With his desk but a few feet from mine, I can feel the chill coming forth from a very cold shoulder.

The next greeting comes from chief of bureau Ackerman. To crush me, he keeps it simple. With the first words out of his mouth, not hello, but, "Where were you?" "On vacation, I thought," I replied. With that, he too, gave me his back and returned to his office. Coming off vacation has always been hard, but never this hard. Before, I've always managed to psych myself up, by saying over and over, "You can do it. You can do it. You can still be the best. How can you, when you can't even show up?"

Haber returns to Dallas. And the crash aftermath stories subside. Except for the one still crashing around inside my head. The one directed by shame. With me its star. Shame is shouting… Show more anguish. Here's your motivation… you didn't get off your lazy ass, even for a catastrophe. You didn't go in. You didn't do your job. A job you owe everything. A job that kept you out of poverty, and put you in Who's Who. And what did you do? You shit on it. Just like you were still a low-life, still sitting on one of those two-holers across Pearl, and still swatting lies with that coarse old newspaper, soon to be turned to a more useful purpose. Because, you couldn't even afford the price of a roll of cheap toilet paper to wipe your nasty ass with. That's it, you're getting it now. That anguish looks great. Roll cameras!

Despite all my win, win, wins, the vibes I'm receiving and the barbs I'm feeling, my co-workers seem to be confirming the obvious. They're looking at a lose, lose, loser. And to confirm that confirmation, I don't need a mirror. The welcome back let down is even worse than I expected. And a thousand times worse than the time Mrs. Bounds impaled me with, "Young man! Young man! A photographer you're not," after my first picture attempt turned out blank. Today, I wished that I had been passenger number 147 on Flight 759. Even more than when I was still on vacation. And now, there are two piercing questions to be answered. Can I accept not being up to being the best? And will the Associated Press accept anything less?

And the test comes sooner than expected, when bureau chief Ackerman calls me to his office. "Jack." "Yes sir." "New York wants you to pack up and get down to Argentina." "What for?" "They have invaded the Falklands, a British colony." "What?" "Argentines have long laid claim to the islands, and with economic chaos and civil unrest at home, the ruling dictator is trying to divert attention and unite his people with a war." Stunned, I stand there, while my face goes paler and paler, and while he continues. "Bourdier is already there and you'll be joining him." Finally, noticing my demeanor and my lack of a response, he asks, "Is there anything wrong?" "Yes sir, there is." "Then, what is it?" "I can't go." After showing a blank stare, he asks, "What did you say?" "I said I can't go." "And why not?" "Because I'm barely treading water." "What do you mean?" "It means that just coming to work, just putting one foot in front of the other, just doing the routine is almost unmanageable. And hardly the condition to cover a war in." "And what do you want me to tell New York… exactly?" "That, I can't go." "Okay, if you're sure." "I'm sure." Now with his shocked look joining mine, I retreat to the darkroom and close the door behind me. Just like I did that day in Germany, after Capt. Colville presented me with my degrading diploma before the whole company command after introducing me as the dropout of the year.

Never had I refused an assignment before. At least not directly. Some months back, I'd come close though. While I was battling a heavy depression, and with a national track meet coming to Baton Rouge, I call Mr. Schwadel in New York and make my plea. "I need two shooters to fly in to help me." "Sorry but you'll have to cover it alone." "Alone! That's impossible. When I covered it in Tennessee, we had three people. And that was a daytime event, and this one's at night. So deadline pressures will be enormous." "Sorry Jack, but the short answer is, we're not spending the money." "But Mr. Schuadel…" "And that's final." Floored by his decision, I'm thinking… This is impossible, just impossible. How can I be out on the track covering event after event and be in the darkroom transmitting picture after picture of the previous events? Needless to say, my heavy depression got heavier and heavier.

The day before the sound of the gun starts the races, I'm buried under the giant LSU stadium setting up a darkroom, with my back killing me and my mind working overtime. What to do? What to do? Call in, say you're ill. Make them send someone else in. And I do. And they do. Because, I remain on sick leave with something I diagnosed as walking pneumonia until the track cleared and the dust settled. And was it worth the enormous guilt I felt? With my eyes going, and my reaction time slowing, I'm not sure I could have survived the consequences. Fuzzy pictures. And most likely, an enormous beating.

With work days passing slowly, oh so slowly, and with the discouragement within me growing at breakneck speed, when I get off at 4:30, I just want to run from the office, get home, close the door, and shut out the world, which is pretty hard to do, and quite impossible for anyone wanting to continue in the communications business. I seem to have gone from wanting to hear about the news first to not wanting to hear about it at all. And the bad news. My livelihood depends on it. As does Carolyn's. And Candy's. And Jay's. And do they have a clue as to my dilemma or the turmoil I'm enduring? Naturally not. Those the closest. Shame shuts out first.

So, with my depression, and with my dilemma reaching new heights, and since I can't confide in my wife or a friend, what can I do except go see a psychiatrist. But after a few sessions of listening to relaxation tapes, I realize that he can't help me. How can he? When I can't open myself up and show him the emptiness and the inadequacy I feel. I never have, I never will. Remember! That's the rule. Shame's. So, why am I here? Perhaps, like Elvis, looking for a pill to fill that empty space. So, Dr. Palotta, forget about trying to look inside. Forget about coming up with a diagnosis. Just give me that goddamn pill. The Elvis pill. It sure ended his misery. And do I inform the grand Associated Press that I'm seeking help? That I'm seeing a shrink? And trying to turn the new me back into the old me? The go-getter, the one who don't want to come back alive without "the picture". Tell 'em? Hell no! Not when just the knowledge of someone seeing a shrink is enough to classify "that one" as crazy. Shrinking yes, but I'm still not crazy. Not yet. Even though it runs in the family. As demonstrated to perfection by crazy Uncle John who wouldn't consider sleeping without a pair of scissors tucked under his pillow, and kept handy. A necessity for his night prowling.

The pills, prescribed by Dr. Palotta, don't end the misery. And my days grow longer. My fatigue grows stronger. And my depression deepens. And next year, the World's Fair is coming to New Orleans. Already, there's letters on it. And to get to it, I still have to get through another fuzzy football season. There's Tulane, LSU, the Saints, the Sugar Bowl and the Super Bowl to survive. But, can I? After watching my work steadily decline, will I be able to get up to shave, look myself in the mirror like brother Garnett did, and still hold a razor steady? With this question still debilitating, self doubt asks the others about my Argentina refusal. What did Ackerman say to New York? And what did New York say to Ackerman? Ackerman never said. And I never asked. But, I bet the conversation ended with a question. One coming from the

New York end. One asking, if Thornell can't cut it anymore, then, what good is he to us, or to anyone?

What to do? What to do? The only thing there is to do. Write the letter. To: Hal Buell, Assistant General Manager for Newsphotos, New York. Dear Hal: I am suffering from tremendous mental and physical fatigue. I have reached a point where I feel that I no longer can handle the pressures of my job adequately. I have been battling this problem for some time and have finally decided that you should know about it. The nerve strain coupled with a blood sugar problem and a chronic back condition leaves me drained all of the time. I just recently returned from vacation hoping to be full of energy and vigor for a new beginning. However it's just the opposite. I can barely get through the day. I don't know what provisions can be made for someone with my condition, but at this point I am willing to consider anything. I will probably be taking some sick leave in the near future to undergo a complete physical and mental evaluation. I will advise you as to that outcome. Sincerely, Jack Thornell, New Orleans.

Immediately, I make three copies. One for Chief Ackerman, News editor Prince and me. And the original, I put into an envelope, address it to Mr. Buell, put a stamp on it, walk across the street to the main post office and drop it in the box. Yea! Yea! I know. Never mail this kind of letter right away. Instead, sleep on it, and in the morning re-read it and then, throw it away. But the fact is, I've been sleeping or trying to sleep on it for years. And now, no one can change my mind. Not Carolyn, not even me. The Ackerman and the Prince copies, I hold them until they leave for the day. Then, I slip them into their incoming mail tray. I wasn't up to facing any of their questions after they read the letter. Because, facing just one shocked face when I get home will be shock enough.

When I walk in, I find Carolyn, Candy and Jay sitting in our spacious den, where I present the letter. After reading it, Carolyn's eyes widen, her jaw drops, and her mouth opens just as shock directed. Then she cries, "Jack! I can't believe this… This letter… You never discussed this with me." "No! I didn't discuss a fucking thing with anyone. I did what I had to." "Have you mailed it?" With her now sitting on the edge of the sofa, I see fear replacing anticipation. "Yes I mailed it. I fucking mailed it." "Oh Jack! What will we do?" "I don't know, but I do know that I can't keep doing what I was. Can't you see that it's killing me? Fucking killing me." Then, the monster, the one dying to get out, the one Candy saw as a child, springs forth and kicks the coffee table over. The large ash tray falls and hits the floor with such force, it shatters and propels pieces of glass in all directions. As the glass collects around them, Candy and Jay jerk up their bare feet and fold them under their bodies. With their look of fear showing full and clear, the monster is satisfied, and I withdraw to the bedroom. Where I slam the door shut, go to bed, and try to force sleep to overpower my brain and stop it from injecting me with the painful question… How can you do such a stupid thing? Here, and at the office. Which leads me to thinking… For a hammer and nails, I would hock my soul, so that when I awake, I can look up and see that I am safe and secure… behind a door nailed shut. Just like those restless spirits down at 503.

When sleep won't come as ordered, and perhaps too late, I cry, "Makesense! Oh Makesense! I've really gone and done it, haven't I?" "Well Cousin, just let Makesense say, that when it comes to painting oneself into the corner, you've done one magnificent job." "And between the bad back and the crazies, I just realized, I left no room for a job. So where does that leave me, but trapped in that corner?" "Perhaps Cousin there's purpose in your being there."

"Purpose or not, Makesense, I'm there. And something else is gnawing at me." "What Cousin?" "The thought of having to spend my precious savings. And when that runs out… what? Does the number 503 ring a bell?" "Loudly Cousin, loudly."

Over the next few weeks, I spend most of the days and all of the nights behind a closed door, trying to sleep my life away. And that, I find to be a full-time and, an all consuming job. And undoubtedly, more difficult than covering that war in the Falklands could have ever been. Because, here I'm trapped in no-man's land, and taking fire from both sides. With my brain firing one shot. And shame firing back another. Of the two, shame is more persistent. Awakening me at regular intervals, like an alarm clock, and singing… Oh Jackie boy, the joy-the joy, the missing kind, the kind you've been seeking, is gone-is gone, along with your only source of pride, the job-the job. And soon, you, just like Daddy Ben, will be deserted by family and friends and left to die alone in an old tool shed. Unless, of course, you can look in that mirror and find Brother Garnett's courage before the deadline comes.

With every ring of the phone I cringe. And I cringe worse than I cringed when that ring could have meant my having to go out there and cover a war. But now, there's no need to go out there. Because, the war is going on in here behind this bloody door.

Three weeks after my crazy letter was mailed, a reply arrives at my home. It's from Buell. It says: Dear Jack, just a personal note to say, that we are sorry to hear that illness has sidelined you for a spell. But to also say that you should take the time to get your health back in good shape. We want you around for a long time to come, so get fixed up right proper. And we wish you a speedy recovery. Best, Hal.

Through reading the letter, I hand it to Carolyn, she reads it and says, "That's nice." "I think so, and coming from Buell, especially nice." "How so?" "Well, he's not a get close to kind of guy. In person or on the phone his voice sounds standoffish… Like, I'm Hal Buell, I'm the boss, so don't stand too close." "What are you going to do now?" "Take his advice. Take some time and work on my health. Next week, I'm having my third session with that new shrink. He thinks it would be good for your wife and his wife who is a therapist to sit in too." "When is it?" "Next Tuesday at 2:30." "I'm off at 1:00, so I can come." "Speaking of being off, with your job at the lawyers office and your job at home with that court reporter, you're never off. You're always typing, even Saturdays and Sundays." "So." "Wouldn't it be more practical to get one full-time job, work 40 hours and then, be done?" "No! No! I don't want to do that." "But, Carolyn you'd make more money, work less hours and have health coverage in case mine gets cut off." "No way. I like things as they are."

I wanted to reply, but didn't… Can't you see that keeping things the way "they are" is an impossibility. Because dear, my "they are" are not what "they were". And may never be, ever again.

And Buell's best of luck wishes remind me of a past conversation with news editor Prince just after I scored a big success. He looks down at my picture, and then, he looks up at me and says, "Thornell, you're one lucky son-of-a-bitch." If he was standing here, looking down at me, what could I say but… Well Kent, take a good look now. It looks like Lady Luck has left. What do you see? Snake eyes. Box cars. CRAPS. Loser.

The Buell letter was his first, and would be his last communication with me. He knew he'd better stand back. Because, if the ax falls, the blood flies. And standing too close could get nasty. So, my case is dealt to B. Eric Cooper, the head of the benefits department. His letter: Jack, you are entitled to 18 weeks and 3 days of sick pay. Long term disability, that's limited to two years unless you are totally disabled from any job for which you are reasonably fitted by training, education or experience. In that case, disability can continue until age 65. However, mental disorders are limited to two years, period.

This letter confirms my thinking… That just the knowledge of someone sitting on a shrink's couch draws discrimination. The company will only endure the crazies for two years, even if, it was the company that drove "that one" crazy by requiring his attendance at one too many riots or revolutions. After two years, the company's hands are washed of you. So, pack up your crazies and your woes and move to the funny farm located at Crazy land, U.S.A. The simple truth: Who cares? You shouldn't. You're crazy. And, if you weren't a throw-a-way before this dire episode, you certainly are now.

It's shrink time. Carolyn and I walk in, take separate chairs and face Mr. and Mrs. Shrink. The 45-minute session time is the same, but the cost is double. After all, now, two sensible people are having to listen to the nonsense of "that one". I try explaining my job. The long, never ending hours. The heavy lifting. The tremendous pressure to always come back with "the picture" at each and every outing. When he asks, "How much do you earn?" I tell him, "About $35,000 a year." His reaction is, "That's damn good money, you'd better hold on to that job. Considering your education and all." But my past, my poverty, my shame, those are not on the table for discussion. And I'm certainly not putting 'em there. Pay double to humiliate myself. Now, that is crazy.

After ten minutes into the session, Carolyn breaks in, and starts unloading. Anything and everything. About my drinking, my demands for perfection, my abuse, physical and mental. My! My! My! And on and on she goes until she ends up in hysterics. The crying kind, until Mr. Shrink looks over at Mrs. Shrink, and both look down at their watches, and Mr. Shrink says, "I'm sorry, but your time is done." But, Carolyn isn't done, her hysteria persists on, and she doesn't move. I look over at my collapsed wife and say, "Carolyn, our time is up. We have to go." With her uncontrollable crying worsening, she pleads, "But I don't want to go. I want to stay here." "Come on Carolyn, please get up." But instead, she threads and locks her arms around the chair like a drowning woman securing a life preserver tossed to her would. Then, Dr. Shrink stands up, interrupts our negotiations and interjects, "But you have to go. I have other patients waiting." His cold, calculating and comfortless voice lifts me up and takes me to Carolyn's side, where unassisted, I pry Carolyn loose from that arm chair, and then, in a collapsed state she screams, "But, I don't want to go home," over and over as Dr. Shrink directs me to take her out a back door. No sense upsetting stable patients and perhaps, risk setting off a chain reaction, may have been his concern. Or perhaps, he didn't want anyone to see one of his patients leaving a session in such a distressed state. After all, shouldn't a patient look better going than coming? Otherwise, what did he get paid for? Inside the car, getting ready to back up, I look over at a slumping Carolyn. She looks like she just buried her best friend, and then, been told that her lung cancer, from all that smoking, has reached the terminal stage. Then, I gaze at myself in the rearview mirror and think… Gee! And I thought I was the patient.

With shrinks I'm done. My depression, my anxiety, my crazies, don't seem to be shrinking, only my bank account. Perhaps it was Carolyn's treatment, or the lack of it, that triggered my resentment and then, my decision. Perhaps it was the sight of Dr. Shrink shrinking at the thought of all that paperwork necessary to support a claim of disability. Then again, perhaps it was my fear that he would reach back to my beginning and start digging. But those minutes, those hours, those days, those weeks, those months, those years, I can't, I won't talk about it. Not even to a paid listener. Not even one bound by the law and by ethics to keep my secrets secret. No! No! That bastardizing, that brutalizing history must not be uncovered. It must stay buried.

After reading Elvis' history, from beginning to end, I know he would have happily traded places with his stillborn brother. Let him have what I had, Elvis would have screamed, all that fame, all that fortune, thrust on me. But, never to be enjoyed. Not with shame's joyeater gobbling it up faster than he could pile it up. That's why Elvis was always running on a tank almost exhausted. If Elvis, or I, had a premonition of things to come, bring on Dr. Sampson if you must, but, even he wouldn't have the strength to pull us out and put us into a world filled with Oh! So many cold shoulders. And, that scenario would fit right in with what someone once said… It would have been better for him not to have been born. Sure. Elvis had some success. Sure he climbed high. But, his roots only stretched so far, until breaking like a rubber band and snapping his mind backward to where his life began. Even though he's moved to a mansion, shame ruined the experience by reminding him that he didn't deserve it. Not a moment's worth. It's all a huge mistake. Just like the Army's clerical error was for me. And, one soon to be corrected.

"Makesense, your ears up?" "Up Cousin." "Want to hear a life or death conundrum?" "Tell it Cousin." "The shrink told me to hold on to that good paying job at all costs." "And what's the other half?" "Even, if that job is killing me like Elvis' pills." "But perhaps, there's a third piece. Call it practical and personal… As long as you need a shrink, you need a job and a paycheck." "And after I'm dead?" "Then, you won't need any. The job. The paycheck, or the shrink." "But meanwhile, what do I need?" "What you've always needed." "And what is that?" "Your purpose Cousin, your purpose." "Goodnight Makesense." "Goodnight Cousin."

After advising Carolyn that shrink sessions are finished, mine and ours, she asks, "What now?" "Well, if there is disability in me, it lies in my back and not in my head. So, I'm going to Dr. Phillips." There's X-rays, physical exams, cat scans and thermograms taken by Dr. Phillips and the company's insurance doctor. I passed or I failed, depending on one's perspective. Anyhow, I qualified for disability, for up to two years, at 60 percent of my base pay. That comes to $1710 a month before taxes. A $12,000-a-year pay cut. Naturally, when I break that news to Carolyn, she shows disappointment, and with my next question I see it growing. "Don't you think it's time for a role reversal?" "What do you mean?" "I mean for you to trade in those two low paying jobs for one good paying one." "No! No! I'm not ready for that." "But Carolyn, our income is dropping and dropping drastically." "Maybe it is, but we've got money in the bank. A lot of it." "So that's your solution. Month by month, spend down the life savings until it's gone?" "Why else is that money there?" "For retirement Carolyn, for retirement. That money will take care of us when we get old. And perhaps, we won't end up living on poverty row like our mothers do." "And what will you be doing while I'm out working full-time?" "Becoming a Mr. Mom. That's honorable work isn't it?" With her look of disillusionment escalating to a look of resentment, she says, "I'm not changing jobs," before leaving the room and ending the discussion. And, had I asked one specific question, the one really gnawing at my gut, the session would have ended before I could have put the dot under the interrogatory mark. And it was this. Dear! After taxes and after your Mother's fifty bucks, where does the rest of "your money" go? Oh! I forgot. It falls through that "your money" crack.

With Carolyn at work in the mornings, I scan the newspaper want ads. Especially, those looking for legal secretaries. And, I find one that looks promising. When she gets home, undresses and is having a cup of coffee before starting in on her home typing, I approach her with the ad in hand. "Carolyn, take a look at this. With her eyes finding mine, she asks, "What are you up to?" "Oh nothing, except that I've found a job for you." "I told you, I'm not interested." "But, I am. And I'm goddamn tired of you pounding that typewriter days and nights and not having a goddamn thing to show for it. Now here, look at this goddamn ad." She looks, and quickly hands it back. "Bailey and Leininger, that sounds like a right proper firm, doesn't it?" She doesn't respond. "Here, I'm dialing the phone, take it and, ask about the job." And reluctantly, she does, and in less than a minute, she has an appointment. Partner Bailey conducts the interview, and after his questions, he hands Carolyn a pen and pad. And says, "Please take my dictation, go out in the office, type it, and, let me know as soon as you finish." "Yes sir," she replies, "Which typewriter?" "Oh, I'll show you." He does and she does, and when she's finished, he looks at a perfectly typed letter. Not able to contain himself, he walks back out into the office waving the letter in the faces of other secretaries and asks, "Why can't you all type letters like this?" And she takes shorthand. And that's perfect too." Needless to say, Carolyn lands the job and the title, "Miss Super Secretary".

Carolyn comes home happy and sad. With smiles she exclaims, "I got the job." And then, with tears she cries, "Now, I've got to start paying bills again." Undoubtedly, her thoughts are rushing back to those bills paying pressures in Jackson, when she charged her coffee at Turner's and her clothes at The Emporium. And as she remembers, those pressures add up, and how I know it.

Now, Carolyn works nine to five, and I work all hours. Cooking, cleaning, yard mowing, grocery shopping, taking Jay to this practice and then, that one, and I take over the check writing to pay the bills. And speaking of check writing, not only do I write one for Mrs. Wilson, but I also write one for my mother too. I explain to Carolyn, "I suspect that my mother draws less money than your mother, so, she deserves a fifty." Whether that is true or not, I didn't know because her mother's money matters are still top secret as far as I'm concerned. With the shaking of Carolyn's head, I could see that she resented it, because by that wad Mother was always flashing, it was obvious that she didn't need it. Not these days. And, since she didn't, I didn't mail her the money, instead, I just saved it for her in my Whitney passbook account. Just another way, I thought, to put away a buck. Or fifty. That's even better.

With her first paycheck in hand, Carolyn deposits it into our joint checking account. It was the first and the last deposit she would put in there. And, under my scrutiny, watching her money go for utilities, house payments, insurance, food, church contributions, car repairs and such, is upsetting. And before paycheck number two, she opens her own checking account. Sure, it is a joint account with my name on it, just like I have her name on all the other accounts. And I want to ask, why do we need two checking accounts, but I don't. Because, I know the answer. Her money is her money. Period. And when her monthly bank statement arrives, I place it on the kitchen counter unopened. And, when she gets home, it disappears with her into the bedroom. Just like I was at the Wilsons, and they were shut-up in the bedroom to discuss money matters, with me always the outsider. And so, what do I do when updating our asset list. For the balance of Carolyn's checking account, I put a great big question mark. Because, besides Carolyn, only "The Shadow" knows that bottom line. With all of my disability money going into our joint account, and her income going into her account, how do I get her to start paying bills? Call it apportionment. I force her to hand over half of our regular monthly bills. Her half, she gives, but, resentfully. But, only her half. And not a penny more for the unexpected like car repair and doctor bills. Nor, will she set aside a dime to fund her own I.R.A. retirement accounts. That $2000-a-year comes out of my disability pay. And that I resent, but, to not do it is more than resentment, it's irresponsible, and more, it's stupid! Stupid! Stupid! And I'm forced to accept one fact. Carolyn lives in the here and now, and to her, the future is just the future. And somebody else's worry.

And at that moment, and despite being on a reduced income, I'm dealing with that worry. Because, out of my disability pay, I'm saving $500-a-month. That adds up to $6000-a-year. From investment income comes $14,000 a year. So, I'm saving $20,000-a-year. With every dollar saved my resentment lessens while Carolyn's grows. With two things assured for two lifetimes. Things that will not change. I love saving as much as Carolyn loves spending. And, if we could have directed even half of that love towards each other, our marriage could have been secured, with money left over.

At church tonight, at age 14, Jay is making his debut. Actually though, it's not, because at age 5 he recited that 23rd Psalm. Debut or not, the young men of the church are speaking. And Jay is nervous, such so, he runs to the bathroom three times to go before we go. He's speaking on Job of the Old Testament. And of his suffering while being tested to satisfy a bet. God bet that good Job's faith would hold, even if Satan is allowed to shake it by taking away all the good things of life. His family, his friends, his fortune. And if that's not enough, torment him up to the point of death.

And when, Job's suffering ends he is exalted. As is Jay for his flawless performance. And as with his speaking voice, it's clear that Jay's ability as a communicator is well beyond his years, and tonight is only a beginning. Because, in the future, he'll speak again and again. But, not before running to the bathroom again and again. And, whether or not, I'll ever come to worship God or not remains unclear. But one thing is, and that's how I worship that son of mine. But, it's only clear to me, because, I can't say, I love you Son! Because that's not the Thornell way. Sure, I can say you played well, or you preached great. But, that "Love" word coming from a Thornell mouth, my mouth, well, that would clearly sound unnatural. And, when it comes to cursing, Jay has definitely broken the Thornell mold. If he has ever uttered one foul word, I never heard it, despite some fine examples coming from Mother and me. And whether one believes in God or not, one who knew the Thornells would certainly have to agree that with all those nasty words bouncing around him since birth, and for him to not have picked them up, well, that definitely required some kind of divine intervention.

After Jay's preaching debut, I become a regular pew setter over at Hickory Knoll. And with the family, I attend every Wednesday and twice on Sunday. Although, I haven't taken the plunge yet, I can't help but recall that time back at Bomar Baptist when I almost did. But, for those holey and humiliating socks, I would have become a Christian long ago. Even if now, a wayward one. I think the Baptist call it backsliding. When you stop practicing what's been preached to you. Until, they say, you slide so far away until the sounding of the word Christian doesn't mean a thing to you. Inside or out.

Finally, I force myself to return to the office to have a talk with boss Ackerman. "What are you doing about my vacancy?" "That's still up in the air, New York hasn't made a decision yet." "May I suggest something?" "Sure. GO ahead." "Why not bring in Haber from Dallas. This is home. So he knows his way around and he could hit the ground running. And, he's single now, so moving shouldn't be as big of a problem." "That sounds like a good idea. I'll pass it along to New York." Ackerman did, and soon, as I suggested, Haber is filling my chair. One that I never want to see again, much less, sit in. Going back there and facing them, and seeing my famous pictures hanging up there on the wall would just remind me of the painful past, of how high the climb, of how low the fall, of how loud the thud, and of how delicious the splatter.

Candy's boyfriend Kevin, the one and only, is a fixture at home. Both on the sofa and at the dinner table. Although raised a Catholic, he accompanies us to church regularly. Tonight, it's revival time. That's when the church brings in a special preacher, one noted for his motivating words. One like that fiery preacher that moved me out of my pew back at Bomar. His name is Maxie Boren, Preacher. Not reverend, because the Church of Christ don't put that word in front of any man's name, not even one of their own. And boring, he's not. I hung on his every word, until the power of the gospel lifts me out of my seat with the promise of turning the old me into a new me through a spiritual rebirth. Which everyone living with me would like to see, including me. This time, this chance for change will not be denied, not for a second time. It's been 33 years between chances, since Big Bertha tried and but for those holey and humiliating socks she would have succeeded. But, would that have changed me back then? Would I have grown into a sweet fuzzy peach, rather than a slick sour plum? Then, could my family have been spared from ever meeting the old me, and instead, only met the new and the born-again me. And, been spared the misery of sharing the hell generated by the old me? And to think that all that stood between them, me and that, was just perhaps, the price of a new pair of socks.

With those gospel sermons chipping away at my guilt week after week, and with the preacher's eyes zeroing in on me week after week, I felt this moment coming. So tonight, I'm prepared and humiliation can't prevent it. Because, tonight, I'm wearing a new pair of socks.

Why should I remain the lone target in the audience, or of Carolyn's eyes? Because, after I take the plunge, all my past sins are erased, like they never existed or ever took place. Even that slap, the one that Makesense said that a wife will never forget. But now, Carolyn will have to. Because the Bible says that the past is not only to be forgiven, it is to be forgotten too. So, that burden will be off me and now, on Carolyn.

So, how does the old me end and the new me begin? By drowning. Well, almost. And that's ironic, because, the only reason I didn't join the Navy was my fear of water. After standing in front of the church and confessing Jesus Christ as the son of God and after pledging to follow his mandates set forth in the Bible, I step down into the baptismal pool. In waist deep water, I bend backwards until I fall into the cradled arms of the preacher who lowers me into the water until every inch of my body is covered. Still bent backwards, with the weight of the water

241

pressing me down, I'm held helpless there… long enough to let the old me die. And, but for the lift of the preacher as directed by the Holy Spirit, I would have too. And as I spring forth out of the water, the congregation beholds the new me and shouts, "Praise the Lord!" Now, as clean and pure as a newborn after a first bathe, my new brothers and sisters in the Lord smother me with hugs and kisses. After my eyes find Carolyn's, Candy's and Jay's, eyes, the question is, are they beholding a new me? I'm not convinced. And, when I look in the mirror, neither am I. Change, I find, comes slow. Painfully slow. My drinking, even my beloved beer, and my cursing have to go. I let Kevin pick out the liquor that his dad likes from my well stocked bar. The rest I flush like Crider's Jack Daniels. Catholics, like Kevin's dad, are allowed their alcohol, but Church of Christers frown on it. Although Jesus, unmistakenably, was a partaker of the fruit of the vine, they teach that if you don't use it, you can't abuse it. And, as an abuser, I can certainly certify that teaching. Now my cursing, having been exposed to it by a professional, even in the womb, comes so natural it's impossible to just flush. It'll take work. And would be a daily battle. In addition to working on my weaknesses, I encourage Carolyn to work on one of hers. Smoking. There are articles, almost daily, appearing in the newspaper alarming readers to the hazard… lung cancer. Those, I clip and put on her dresser. Occasionally, I'll ask, "Did you see the article?" And Carolyn, resentfully will reply, "Yea! I saw it." And despite Jay's lifelong allergies, her smoke still fills the house, the car, even the ladies room at church when she slips out during services to sneak a puff or two.

At Hickory Knoll, there are only about 200 members so everybody gets to know everybody. And there, just like the Bible dictates, the men rule. Women are allowed to stand and teach children in Bible class, but only there. In the general assembly, only the men are allowed to stand and open their mouths. Men do all the preaching, the praying, the song leading, the baptizing, the money collection and make all of the business decisions, while wives hold their tongues. At least publicly. This is heaven here, I think, and if only it could be like this at home, where wives graciously submit to a single voice. Their husband's. Ruling the church are three elders, who are chosen by the congregation. They must have Bible knowledge. Be the husband of one wife, and have multiple children. Because the Bible says that an elder must first learn to rule his own house before he can rule God's. And they have the authority to add ordinances. Such as, girls those skirts are too short. Or ladies, don't wear those pant suits. Pants are for men. And, men only. And, we don't want any manly looking women around here confusing things.

After having withdrawn from my friends in the news profession, friends I no longer want to talk to, or to hear those "Get well soon and get back to work" cheers from, church life becomes my only life apart from being a prisoner of home. But, guilt, I find is inescapable. Even at church. Because, occasionally, a new couple will visit, sit behind me, and before church starts, reach across the pew and introduce themselves. And then, I start squirming, because I know what's coming next… the question. "What do you do?" Cringing, I quickly answer, "I'm retired." After heads spin, comes their blank stares. And, how I hate 'em. Then, comes the observation, "But you're too young to retire." With my smile my only response, the husband fires back, "But, how is that possible?" Praying for church to start before I'm forced to give an answer, but it doesn't, and shamefully I reply, "I'm retired on disability… a bad back." Then, more blank stares, and a final observation, "You don't look disabled. You look fine to me." And my thoughts fire back… Oh brother! Oh sister! If you only knew how disabled I feel, perhaps, you would have forgone the third degree and spared me those F_ _K_ _G blank stares.

Not yet 9 A.M. on a Sunday morning and already I'm guilt laden. Laid on me by other Christians, just trying to be friendly, just asking the first question that comes naturally after the introduction" What do you do? And if we are what we do, even as the daily obituaries—John Doe, a lawyer. Jane Smith, a teacher—seem to indicate, then, what the hell am I? A nothing? The nothing I was born to be. The one shame let climb that hill. To taste that success. And to realize, it was not for him, not with his roots back at 503. And with his inescapable return, the war is over. And, shame has won.

At home, I face a new guilt. One that tears at my very soul. And, it surfaces during a weekly get it off your chest session. Something I inaugurated after becoming a Christian. When, Carolyn, Candy, Jay, and I sit down together to air our gripes, Candy never says much, Carolyn does. Always complaining about the way I do things. But, when I ask what things? She's never specific. And I ask, "How can I work on that if you never can tell me what it is that I need to work on?" "Well, I just can't call it to mind right now," Carolyn responds. "Well Dear, for next week, write it down, and hit me with it."

Finally, I turn to Jay, who has been sitting quietly, and ask, "Do you have anything to say?" He doesn't respond, but, I sense he wants to, and so I encourage him. "Son, it's okay. Say anything you want to." Then, pulling his arms close to his body in a shrinking fashion, he says, "Dad, I'm afraid." "Afraid of what son?" "Afraid of making you mad." While absorbing that, I say, "Go ahead son, finish it." "Dad, that's it. That's all I have to say." Stunned, my mind starts deciphering his words. Jay's afraid… Afraid of making me mad. Geesums! Jay's afraid of me… Afraid of his dad. Geesums! Candy must have told him about seeing the monster come out… The one living in me. Geesums! A son that I love more than life is scared of his crazy dad. Scared! Not like crazy Uncle John scared me. Oh God! No! Not like that. Nobody should ever have to feel that. That kind of scared. And, never never never this angel of a son. And what was my reply? Without breaking down, the only words that would come are, "Son, I'm working on it… my temper." That ended the session, and left me sitting there in the living room alone and crushed. Like I feared being on a big story. To have avoided hearing Jay's words now, on the Meredith shooting, I would have gladly taking my crushing then, and let Sammy win that Pulitzer. That's how bad this hurt, hurt. And troubling too, from Jay's own mouth comes the painfully clear realization. He's not seeing a "new me". He only sees the "old me". The one he fears.

Christmas of 1983 is coming. And, so is Candy's 18th birthday. At our weekly sessions Candy is in the mood for talking, which is unusual. "Daddy, I want to buy a car." "You do. Why?" "I'm tired of driving your old car." "What's wrong with that Skylark?" "Daddy, you know what's wrong. The air conditioning is broke. The seats are split. And the ceiling, what you call that, droops." "Headliner, it's called." "Yea, headliner." "But, it runs great, doesn't it?" "Yea, so." "And it gets you there, doesn't it?" "Yes Daddy." "And it's free, isn't it?" "Yes Daddy… But" "Continue saving your money. How much you got now?" "About $3000." "And you want to blow it all on a car. You'll be 18 soon and you'll be free to do whatever you want without your dad's approval." In tears, as she's leaving the room she replies, "You got that right. I certainly will. I'll be free." And part of her freedom "to do" I fear is her ability to say "I do" to boyfriend Kevin without a daddy's signature.

A few days later Kevin drives up and catches me outside with my head under the hood of that Skylark. "Mr. Jack. Got a minute?" "Sure Kevin." "I'm keeping my word." "About what?" "About this," he says as he pulls out that ring for a second time. "I'm giving this to Candy for Christmas." This time, he's not asking for permission, he's telling. "Oh Kevin, can't you wait a bit longer. Save more money, date, and have fun without the responsibilities of marriage?" "No Mr. Jack, we can't, and we won't."

After telling Carolyn the big news, I decide to have a go at Kevin's parents. Hopefully, they'll agree that Candy is far too young for marriage. And, help me to persuade those kids to postpone, to postpone, to postpone until they grow weary of each other, decide marriage is a bad idea, and boyfriend Kevin disappears. But, naturally, the part of them growing weary and Kevin disappearing I plan to leave out of my presentation.

With the thick juicy ribeyes grilling, I face Lyle and Midge Ganucheau and make my pitch. "Kevin is a fine young man. And we really like him. But Candy, she's just too young to be getting married. Carolyn and I hope you will agree. And help us to convince them to wait." Lyle looks to Midge and catches her eyes turning to his, and as they shrug in unison, he says, "We can't help you." "Why not?" "We got married young. In our teens. And, it's been wonderful." "So, there's no sense in my talking postponement, is there?" "No, there's not." "Okay then, let me go check the steaks." Grilled to perfection, those ribeyes would be eaten and enjoyed by everybody, everybody but me, because, that bad taste already fermenting in my mouth, wouldn't allow it.

Two days after her 18th, Candy is wearing a ring, and the planning for a Spring wedding begins. Carolyn and Candy pick out a $500 dress. It's beautiful. But, for a one-time wear item, that price, I feel is steep. Like that hill leading away from 503. The fellowship hall at church is perfect for receptions, and it's free. But, Carolyn and Candy won't hear of it. They want it held elsewhere. And choose the expensive Sclafani's. Then, comes the demand for three long limousines. That's when I blow a head gasket, steam, then, I set Carolyn and Candy down and say, "Ladies! $3000 is the limit. That's it. No if, ands or buts, unless Carolyn, you want to put some of "your money" in the wedding pot." And, how does Carolyn respond? With a blank stare. That f—king blank stare. And what I wanted to scream, was…Ladies, if you haven't noticed, I'm on disability, and my career may be at an end. And when that insurance check stops coming, what then? Carolyn, you'll never yield a penny of "your money" to feed or clothe me. You know that. And, I know that too. That would be too distasteful to you. So, after the savings is spent, what am I to do? Go back to taking tickets at a Joy Theatre somewhere. But, somewhere, y'all won't be humiliated by the sight of me. No ladies, either y'all can't or don't care to see the big picture and its ramifications for me. Today, all y'all see is a sorry husband and a sorrier father. A tighter bastard, than ever seen before. Even, that Scrooge character. The most famous to y'all, till me. And all I can or care to see is, that $3000 could have kept me living up at 5236 Utica and not down at 503 Dabney, for three months longer.

Since the engagement, Kevin hasn't missed a service at Hickory Knoll and tonight he has invited his Catholic parents to join us, and surprisingly, they do. When the invitation for baptism is given, Kevin stands, and walks to the front of the church turning his back on his parents and his lifelong religion. As Kevin goes down in the water, his parents slide down in the pew, where again their eyes meet up, this time, in shocking disbelief that their beloved son could put his precious soul in such jeopardy. It's comeuppance time, I think. This is your due for letting your son get engaged to my non-Catholic daughter. I prayed for someone to shout Hallelujah to rub some salt in their wounds, but, that sounding didn't come. That's because the Church of

Christers don't want to be identified with the loud and lively Pentecostals who often stand and start speaking in tongues, a language unknown to anyone, even the one speaking it. I've heard it and I've identified it, and I call it what it is. Gibberish. Unintelligible. And, an unnecessary ear strain. Every now and then though, after the preacher hammers home a point, you'll hear a feeble Amen coming from the mouth of a Church of Christer. And if Lyle or Midge want to kneel and pray for their son to return to his senses, they can't do it here, because there are no prayer benches to let down. Here, there is no knee bending. Here, prayer is done either standing or sitting. The Bible says that on the Day of Reckoning that all knees will bend before the Lord. For many here, that will be a first time event. After Kevin pops up out of the water, he is not just a son-in-law to be, he is my brother in the Lord. He is a part of the church family. And now, I must accept his presence, like it or not.

At home, life goes on. Jay schools. Carolyn and Candy work. While, I wash clothes, cook, push mops, swing brooms, and cringe with every ring of the phone, just like I'm still on the Associated Press' phone first list. At 3 P.M. daily, I start cooking supper. Usually, it's a choice of chicken, pork chops, catfish, or shrimp, battered and fried. Sometimes, there's steak, shrimp-crabmeat supreme or my specialty, barbequed meat balls, a recipe I got from Mrs. Wilson and then, perfected. But, whatever's for the evening meal, it's freshly cooked, because Candy and Jay won't eat leftovers. Those, after a mere bite or two, they keep rearranging on their plates, until tiring and it's safe to ask to be excused, but, not before giving the cook that look. The one that says, those leftovers should have been part of yesterday's garbage. That, I supposed, could be hereditary. Because, down at 503, I didn't eat leftovers either. But, it wasn't a matter of choice. No, it was because there wasn't anything to make leftovers from. When, I think of my hungry-hungry youth, and when I see my kids frown at the sight of leftovers, I want to shake them and scream, "Wake up kids, that piece of cold chicken would have been a delight for me to even see." But, to fill their plates with those 503 leftovers, I can never do. When, just the thought of doing that sickens me, what would actually doing that do. To me, of how I see myself and to them, of how they would then see me. To serve up that, that hellish picture. The one I tried escaping from. The one they had already stolen several glimpses of during their short and infrequent but freaky visits. When, the first was one too many, and one more than I ever intended for them to see. Because, from those glimpses they might come to comprehend something I never wanted them to ever comprehend. Just how worthless I felt I was by having to live down there. And, live with them. My nauseating mother and my crazy Uncle John. Who, including my father, were in my eyes the three most worthless humans to have ever inhabited a body. And kids, in your defense, you're so right about something. Some leftovers do belong in yesterday's garbage. God! If only the garbage man could take away those leftover memories. And, all that shame left rotting.

Its May 1984, and it's wedding day. Candy looks beautiful in her $500 dress and Kevin handsome in his white tux. Me, I'm quite comfortable in my dark blue Sears and Roebuck suit, the one long hanging in my closet.

After walking Candy down the aisle, and as I'm raising her veil, I feel a cave-in coming. Seeing or sensing that, Candy whispers, "Daddy! Don't do it… Please." Somehow, I don't, and I manage to get to my seat, but feeling that my world is collapsing on top of me, and finding me without enough willpower to even contemplate moving an inch to the left or to the right to get out of the way.

Without a job for ten months, and now, with a daughter moving on with life, and after the ceremony, photographed by friend Arnold, comes to a conclusion, Candy and Kevin climb into that long white limousine, one of the two I rented, and head to Sclafani's for the reception. And, there's where the wrinkle lies. "What! No liquor. A New Orleans wedding without drinking. That's awful… just awful," are the words Kevin's dad reportedly said after hearing that disturbing news. If he thinks I'm cheap, he would be right. But, if he thinks that's the reason for this forced abstinence, he'd be wrong. It's because my fellow church members don't want to be seen associating with the drinking world. And, if that wrinkle just happens to save me some money, just call that what it is… a blessing. And if Daddy Lyle dares to whisper cheap in my ears in passing, I'll yell back, "Cheap is when you held the rehearsal dinner at your home and served cold finger food." But, before downing his last cup of fountain punch, he finds me and says, "Jack, it was a beautiful wedding and the food was terrific." Graciously, I smile and shake his hand, while thinking… Beautiful. Terrific, it was, and expensive.

After the wedding, I accept Kevin as the husband I wanted for Candy, and forget about her missed possibilities. Before, a doctor or a lawyer, or even a banker would have pleased me more. But, that was then, and this is the reality of now. And, now seems good, actually, better than good, because, our marriages are insured by one common denominator. Our religion. After wedlock, Jesus teaches that one man and one woman are bound for life with one exception. Adultery. Only then, is the innocent spouse free to divorce and to remarry. TO do otherwise, puts him or her into a constant state of adultery as well as the person they marry, innocent at the time or not. And, if a Church of Christer shrugs off Jesus' teaching as too narrow, even outdated, what happens next? The disfellowship ax falls. And, he or she, is cut off from the Church. And according to The Good Book, there's only one direction that an adulterer can go, and that is down… down… down… in that lake of fire come judgment day.

The Bible, the more I read it, the better I like it. Particularly its discipline on marriage. Now, if I keep my zipper zipped, Carolyn will never have cause to leave me. And, she'll be stuck with me for life. What about those past dalliances of mine? When I went to bed drunk and woke up to find a naked senorita sharing my bed? Doesn't that free Carolyn to divorce me and, to remarry? Then, it would have. But, she didn't know about it then, so now, if she finds out, it doesn't matter. Because, those past indiscretions were washed away by my baptism, and, can't be used against me. Not ever. Not by anyone still claiming Christian status. And now, knowing that it can't or it shouldn't hurt me to confess those past particulars to Carolyn, do I? Well, almost.

With Jay at baseball practice, several weeks later during one of our get it off your chest sessions, I turn to Carolyn and ask, "Do you ever think about your marriage paradox?" "What do you mean?" "Well, back when I was working at being Mr. Bad, you had good reason for leaving me, but, you chose not to. And now, with me working at becoming Mr. Good, you can't leave me, because the Church has us locked together for life." "What about it?" I asked, "Do you ever think about that?" "Yes, I think about it." Well, with that answer bothersome I make my decision about fessing up. Those past particulars, the ones that I had already put into God's hands, would remain in God's hands. And, God's hands alone. Why hurt her, and open the door for her hurting me back. Even, for good reason.

"Makesense, your ears up?" "Up Cousin." "Want to hear a Bible truth on marriage in the hereafter?" "Tell on Cousin." "Well, there ain't none." "What!" "Yep. I call it the

246

marriage misconception. Because, most good folks believe that after the resurrection, they'll be united with their spouses to live happily ever after." "And, that ain't so." "No, sir. Jesus, when asked whose wife will she be, this woman with seven dead husbands? You know what Jesus said?" "Say on." "Ye do err. For in the resurrection they neither marry, nor are given in marriage, but are as the angels of God." "Gee, that would be news to most married folks, even Christians." "And good news for some," I added with a laugh before offering, "I think there's a good reason for eliminating that." "And why?" "Because, if God did allow the husband-wife relationship to continue on, how long could Heaven be called Heaven? Not long Makesense, not long."

And, not long after Candy and Kevin say their I do's, there are signs of that relationship—the one they're tied to for life—unraveling. Candy has a new job. She works for a member of the Church—Harold Freeman—who is vice president of Radio Phone. It is there, she meets and works with an engineer named Mike Gros. He is older, never married, and drives a Porsche. Meanwhile, husband Kevin is getting hot and sweaty, working as a pipefitter. Until… he finds himself working alongside a "nigger with a smart mouth." And, what does Kevin do about it? He fills that black mouth with his white fist. And what does the white bossman do? These days, the only thing he can. Fire that racist white boy. And, he does. Now, while Candy is out working, Kevin is out playing golf. And, when Candy comes home, she comes home to a dirty house, and to go to work again. Making beds, washing dishes, vacuuming, mopping and laundering Kevin's sweaty golf attire. Because of a promise to her husband, Candy can't tell of his firing or of his refusal to help out with home work, until finally, the news leaks out.

"That's woman's work!" he snapped after I found out about his macho attitude, and set him down for a man-to-man talk. "My daddy never touched a broom, or washed a dish in his life. My mom does all that. That's not proper work. Not for a man." "Kevin, does your mother have a job?" "No Mr. Jack, she stays home." "And do you have a job?" "Well no, not right now." "And, you expect Candy to go off to work, make all the money and then, come home to a dirty house, while you're sitting on your ass or spending money playing golf, money that you don't have to spend?" With his eyes glued to the floor, my chastisement continues. "You can raise a fist at work to get fired, but, you can't lift a hand at home to help your wife. Kevin! Wake up. Look around you. Who cleans this house?" "You do, Mr. Jack." "Who cooks those big dinners you so enjoy?" "You do Mr. Jack." "And who washes the dishes after?" "You do Mr. Jack." "And Kevin, you can too. If, just to keep the peace. With Candy. And with me." "Mr. Jack, I'll try." With that manly posture of his drooping as he's walking out the door, I want to slam him with… if you and Candy had only listened to me, life could have still been fun, and you'd still be, just dating. And still anticipating the something that's missing. Marital bliss… but, the slam, I withhold, because it's clear that his illusion of marriage is clouded enough by just the thought of his macho hands having to sink into dishwater. Dirty or not.

The problem Kevin has with doing those "women things" isn't new to me. I had it, and, I have it. Doing them in front of family, I've gotten used to and it's no longer a problem. But, in front of company, while doing the dishes alone, I feel my manhood being questioned. By me, and by my guests. Especially, the macho men. So, Carolyn and I have an understanding. With company present, she does the dishes and I help with the periphery.

Kevin's resentment takes me back to the Swarts last visit, just after I started doing those "women things". After a big dinner, Bill is the first to leave the table. He takes a seat in the den, lights his cigar and picks up the paper, while Carolyn, Billie and I sit on. I keep waiting for Carolyn to make a move toward the sink so I can help with the periphery. But, she doesn't. And, we three sit on. Ten minutes pass. Fifteen, twenty, thirty. And the dirty dishes sit, as do we. Finally, with my anger about to explode, but without saying a word, I adjourn to the den to join that cigar smoking macho man who ain't going near any dishwater. And I decide, neither am I. Before I can take a seat, a voice from the kitchen reaches me. It's Billie's. "Jack! You're not doing the dishes?" Now, with my anger spilling out, I yell back, "No Billie I'm not. But, those delicious meat balls chock full of bell peppers and onions, I formed those. And, those potatoes, I peeled those. And, those peas, I put in a pot. And, those crisp corn bread muffins, I baked those. And, that fresh chocolate pie is homemade by me. And, I made the tea, and, I sliced the lemon. And now, you women want to sit your butts and watch me wash the dishes too. Keep sitting. Keep your sit-a-thon going. Sit there all night. I don't care, because ladies, I'm done." In a weakened voice, Billie replies, "Rather than cook, I'll do the dishes anytime… gladly." Gladly my ass, I thought, you just wanted to watch humiliation in progress. Mine.

On disability, I should be more at ease. But, I'm not. Not with this new pressure and that old fear following me home. And, not with the clock ticking, and two years closing in. And, what then? Watch that savings go, rather than grow. That thought is more debilitating than the thought of becoming like George Wallace. Paralyzed for life. At least then, my disability pay would be guaranteed. And, those what ifs I faced at work, I now face at home. What if Dr. Phillips, moves, retires, or dies? What happens to my disability status? What if the insurance company sends me to a new doctor who examines me and then says, get off your ass and get a job. Any job. Even one taking up tickets for which you're qualified for by experience. And then, there's the guilt weighing on me for not doing exactly that, but, how can I? And, is that wise? When, it was the job that delivered me to this place mentally and physically. Because, those New York executives never lifted a finger to lighten my load. Always pointing that finger at me and saying, go. Whether I was on vacation or not. When that war in the Falklands started, why didn't they point that finger at that New York photographer, the one who was supposed to help me cover that Chicago riot, but didn't? Why not give him another chance to conquer his fear before he retires? One war shouldn't kill him. Even if, he shows.

It's a good thing that Candy and Kevin's marriage vows said for better or for worse. Besides not getting comfortable doing those women things, and still being out of work, he agrees to move into the family home while his parents, for work reasons, temporarily settle in another city. Over dinner, they tell us about it. "That'll help, not having to pay rent for a while," I said. "Not rent Mr. Jack, we just have to pay the house note." "When are y'all moving in?" "Next week, my parents don't want to leave the house vacant for long." "Next week! What about your lease on your townhouse? Is it up next week?" Kevin and Candy's eyes connect, she shrugs, and he replies, "Mr. Jack, I'm not sure exactly when." "Well son, you'd better 'exactly when' find out, unless you can afford two rents." "Mr. Jack, it don't matter. I've given my dad my word, and we're moving in." A few months later, they find themselves in court facing an angry landlord demanding payment in full for the remaining six months of their lease. There went Candy's total nest egg, I assumed, the one she'd been building up since I presented her with that little green passbook while she was still a child. Needlessly, wasting that money now had to sicken her. But, not half as much as it sickened me. Because, in my view, there's no greater sacrilege than wasting money.

Wednesday night, Carolyn, Jay and I sit down for our session and Carolyn hits me with her demand. "I want a new car." "A new car now. With my disability about to run out." "I don't care. I want a new car… now. We can pay cash." "What! Dip into the savings for that kind of money with the AP's insurance company anxious to drop the ax on me? No way. No car. Not now." "If that's your answer, I'll go buy one on my own." "I can't stop you, but I don't recommend it. Not now."

After she storms out, leaving Jay and I sitting with our mouths open, but with nothing to say, I realize what's eating at her. It's those rich lawyer's wives. They drive up in their Jaguars, Cadillacs and Lincolns, park, and then, showing their fine garments and flashing those extra large diamonds, parade in front of those poor secretaries having to work for their husbands. And, if there's one thing that Carolyn loves, loves more than anything, even money, it's those show things. And, be able to show 'em.

After a few days and nights of feeling Carolyn's cold shoulder, I ask, "How's the car shopping coming?" With a look that could cut through glass without shattering it, she replies, "It ain't." "And why not?" "I can't get a loan." "Even with all that money in the bank?" "Nope. They say that money can be withdrawn at any time. But, I still want my car." I could see that she was pissed, really pissed. Pissed at those bankers who humiliated her. But, even more, pissed at me, because, that was all my doings, for putting her in that position in the first place. Now, realizing that her car demand isn't going to disappear, nor is her cold shoulder going to warm, even under the covers, I offer a compromise. "Carolyn, you really want this car?" "Yes. I'm ready for my car." "Are you ready to quit smoking?" "What!" "You want a car. And I want you to stop smoking. You've read those articles, when you're ready to stop, let me know and we'll talk about your car." Crushing her cigarette against the ashtray, she replies, "I'll think about that." Now, undoubtedly, she sees me as a manipulating bastard, but I don't care. Because, if she quits smoking everybody wins. Even her. And now, it comes down to a battle of hungers. Hers. Between the car and the cigarettes.

A week later, I ask Carolyn about her smoking. "I'm working on it." "Can I suggest something?" "Go ahead." "Forget cold turkey. Try tapering off. Instead of a pack-a-day, try getting by on half-a-pack. And so on, until, you stop." "That's what I'm doing." "Good, let me know when you're ready to talk car."

Two weeks later, Carolyn approaches me and says, "I'm ready for my car." "You've quit?" "Yes." "Good. Now, how much of a car note can you afford?" "What! I thought we were paying cash." "I never said that. I only said, we'd talk car. And, we are. But you're going to have to pay the note out of 'your money'. Money I never see." With her face reddening, and looking more pissed than before, I repeat the question. "Now! How much can you afford?" "$200-a-month. I can afford that." "Okay then, but before we go car shopping you have to promise me something." "What!" "If you start smoking again, you'll tell me. Agreed?" "Agreed." "And one more thing." "What!" "If you do start up again, we swap cars. I drive the new car, and you drive the old one. Agreed?" "Agreed."

Carolyn and I go banking, use a certificate of deposit for collateral, and secure a loan for $10,000. "Now Carolyn that's the way to buy a car." "What do you mean?" "Well, at the end of five years, the car is paid off and we get the $10,000 back plus interest minus 2 percent." "What's the minus 2 percent for?" "That's what they charge us for loaning us our money," I said smilingly, "A pretty good racket, isn't it?" But not as good as leaving all that money in the bank, rather than watch it drive away in that 1984 beige Buick Century. The car Carolyn picked out, I thought smilingly. And, if Carolyn only knew how much I feared the threat of poverty and so desperately needed the protection of its nemesis—money—then perhaps, she could form a new attitude. And, flush the old one: What good is money if you can't spend it. Oh Carolyn! If you only knew.

Today, it's my turn to go shopping. Carolyn needed a car. I need a gun. "What about that Baretta? I asked the clerk at Puglia's sporting goods. "It's a good one. A 25-calibre. With eight in a clip. But, it's only accurate at close range, very close." How's an inch from my right temple, is that close enough, I thought, not so smilingly. If my disability check stops. If the AP drops the ax. I need to be prepared just as I was for Rap Brown's crack of dawn arrival. Just in case I wake up late and find the house emptied. Jay in school. Carolyn at work. And, me alone. Except, with Garnett's courage. "How much is it?", I asked. "$215-plus tax." "I'll take it. With a box of ammo."

Carolyn's got her car. I've got my gun. Perhaps now, there'll be peace at home. At least for a couple of months, until my short term disability ends with a February 1986 check, or so I thought. Supper's over, when the doorbell rings. It's Candy. She's alone. Except for her tears. Those are streaming. And she is screaming, "Daddy! I want to come home." "Why? What's wrong?" "I just can't live with Kevin. Not any longer." "Why not. He's your husband." "But Daddy, I don't love him anymore." "Oh Candy, you're just upset. You'll get over it." With anger now trumping her tears, she snaps, "Can I come home or not?" After looking over to Carolyn and getting her nod of approval, I reluctantly reply, "Sure you can. Until you get your head straight, And, until you and Kevin work things out. Maybe all y'all need is a little space." Perhaps, I should have paid more attention to her quote, "I don't love him anymore." But I didn't. I just blew it off. Hell, I've fell out of love with many a woman, until I got good and horny, and then, I fell right back in love, and in bed with them. Candy will stay a week, maybe two, and then, tired of the sound of my voice, she'll run back to Kevin. Or, so I thought. So, I hoped.

Before a week passes, over supper, Candy makes a request. "I want to bring somebody by. For y'all to meet." "Who is it?" "A friend from work." "What's her name?" "It's not a her. It's a him. His name is Mike Gros. He's an engineer." Shocked by such a shameful request, particularly coming from my fine, or so I thought, Christian daughter, I shout back, "What! Are you crazy? You're married! You're not entitled to any men friends. And, you certainly aren't bringing any here to this house. Not ever." In tears, like when she arrived, she runs to her bedroom and shuts the door. "Jesus!", I exclaim before turning to Jay with instructions. "You're the preacher in the family. Better put some of that preaching on your sister. Maybe, she'll listen to you. And, try to mend her fences. She doesn't have another choice. Kevin's her husband for life."

With Candy moved to her own apartment, with Jay in school, and Carolyn at work, I'm home vacuuming when the doorbell rings. It's Kevin. "Mr. Jack! Mr. Jack! I need to talk to you." "Come on in, calm down, take a seat and let me shut this racket off." He does and I do, but his calm is short-lived. "Mr. Jack. What is Candy doing?" "What do you mean?" "I keep seeing this Porsche parked outside of her apartment." "Oh, her friend Mike at work drives one. He's probably just stopping by… checking on her." "At 3 A.M." "What!" "That's right. At that hour there's no TV to watch. So, what are they doing?" "God Kevin, I don't know," I replied to the out of work pipe fitter, now moon lighting as a self-employed detective. "Mr. Jack! She's my wife. She can't do this to me." And, before I could console him, I see the macho man dissolving. He quickly turns away. But, he cannot hide his tears or his sense of loss. And, not only of Candy. "Mr. Jack! My other girlfriend, the one I dropped to date Candy, she never would have done me this. She worshiped me. I should have married her." And, what could I add to his conclusion. Not a word. But, what did I think? Oh Kevin, you're so right. Because, there's nothing worse than having to watch another grown man cry, unless of course dear boy, you are the grown man crying.

Soon, Kevin is not the only one playing detective. The church elders are. And, the three, make a house call. Unannounced. When, Candy opens the door, they march in and find who else? Her man friend from work. The engineer with a Porsche. After he excuses himself, the elders confront Candy about her irreverent, intolerable, and most important, her unwifely behavior. After chastising her, they warn her to stop seeing this "man friend".

If she doesn't, she will face public disgrace. It's called disfellowship. If, and after that is announced, church members are forbidden from socializing with Candy until she repents and begs forgiveness for her behavior. Until then, she is an outcast. And, her soul belongs to Satan.

After the elders advise me as to the seriousness of Candy's situation, I sit down with Carolyn and Jay, and, tell them of our conversation. "IF Candy is disfellowshipped, how will that affect us?", I asked. "We're church members too." Jay shrugs and says, "Dad, I'm not sure." Sternly Carolyn says, "I don't care what anybody says or does, I'll never turn my back on Candy." "But if we don't practice tough love as the scripture says, and Candy continues with this, what then?" Carolyn and Jay both hunch their shoulders, and keep silent. "Wouldn't we be aiding and abetting," I continued, "Wouldn't we be saying, "Candy, do whatever makes you happy. It's okay with us. And, with God. Wouldn't that be the devil in us talking?"

How does that old saying go… if things are going bad don't complain, because things can certainly get worse. And, things do in the form of a letter. It's from Connecticut General, the A.P.'s insurance company. It says that my disability checks will stop coming at the end of February. Just a month away. There's another old saying… time flies when you're having fun. Well, with this news, I've thought of a new one… when you're miserable time can fly too, especially if you're anticipating a greater misery to come. And, the thought of having to stand by and watch my savings dwindle away day by day just to buy the necessities of life, to me, there is no greater misery. What to do? What to do? That question bombards me. And, the answer. The only thing I can.

After supper, I find Carolyn in the bedroom putting on her night face and, I tell her of the letter. "What are you going to do?", she asked. "The only thing I can," I answered. "And, what is that?" "Go back to work." "Oh, that's great news. Just think of the extra money we'll have," she exclaimed with a look of glee now spreading across her face. But, her reaction sinks my spirits to a new low. With me, it's about the money. And now, with Carolyn, it's about the money. From Carolyn, I didn't expect glee, I expected concern. And, questions. Are you sure you're up to it? Wasn't that work killing you? Remember how you shut yourself away when you left it? My anger over her reaction explodes into a question. "Why is everything about the money?" With me. With you. With the whole fucking world… it's always about the money."

After I visit back doctor Phillips and convince him to okay me for a return to "light duty", on March 3, 1986, I mail a copy of his report to bureau chief Ackerman in New Orleans and benefits manager Cooper in New York. My letter is dated February 17. And then, I wait and I pace, while questioning my actions. Do I want to return to work? No… Hell no. Then, why am I trying? Because, if I don't, when that last disability check comes, I'll get my own letter. And, what will that letter say? My benefits have been exhausted, and my employment, terminated.

Two weeks later, I get a reply. It's not from Cooper. It's not from Ackerman. It's not from Buell. It's not from Schwadel. It's from a Bruce E. Richardson, manager of labor relations. It's not a familiar name. But, I know who he is. The hatchet man. My hatchet man. That's why Buell and the other photo executives took ten giant steps backwards after my disability began. It is just as I thought earlier. To avoid the splatter. Mine. And, what does Mr. Richardson say? In short, I can't return to work unless I can hit the ground running at full speed. "We can't establish special jobs and create staff additions in bureaus." And then, he did something he shouldn't have. He attached a list of the job requirements. A job that I had performed so well for 20 years that my personnel file is filled with letters of commendation. Where was your list when I took this job? I never saw anything in writing about me having to be a pack mule first and a photographer second. Hell, I didn't even get a chance to see a job application until after I worked for the A.P. for several months.

Alone, sitting in my living room, with my Mr. Mom duties still to be performed, my thoughts rampage on… Oh Bruce! That reply. What that did to me. To my self-doubts. It's nothing personal, you think, it's only personnel and business. But Bruce! The risk of life and limb, isn't that personal? How about a broken back and a broken mind, isn't that personal too? And Bruce, let me ask something. How many pairs of eyes peered over your shoulder for dotting every 'i' and crossing every 't' while you were composing this letter? And, how many pairs of hands patted you on the back and said, "Good job Bruce." He's drained. And, ready for disposal. Oh Bruce! Just light duty, that's all I asked, just for a chance to see if perhaps, I could cut it anymore. Even for a day. But, you said loud and clear, be forewarned! BE ready to lift 300 pounds. Be ready for riots and revolutions. Face it! There's no light duty for you. Not a day. Not an hour. Not even a minute. Forget it! Get that out of your head. OOPS! Sorry, but you got the crazies too. Well Bruce, perhaps you're right. But now, I'm not just crazy, I'm mad too.

My reply:

Dear Mr. Richardson. Thank you for your letter of February 24, 1986, explaining the cold bare facts regarding my request to return to work for a period of "light duty". These things, however, I never asked of you. One: I never asked you to report to Gulfport, Miss. At 5 A.M. on your first day of employment to cover the first school desegregation in the state's history without the benefit of a newsman. The result was an exclusive page one picture in the New York Times that I sneaked from the back of a taxi. Two: I never asked you on the second day of the job to go 275 miles farther north for the second school desegregation. Three: I never asked you on December 4, 1964 to be the only photographer crazy enough to go into Philadelphia, Mississippi with a camera the day the FBI arrested the sheriff in the civil rights slayings. Even after I was threatened by a knife-wielding redneck accompanied by a pack of good buddies, I still managed to sneak one frame from the hip and escape with my skin and a world-wide exclusive. Four: I never asked you to go to the Dominican Republic to cover a "shooting" revolution just two weeks before my wedding with a promise that I would be out in plenty of time to take my marriage vows. I was left there and had to delay my wedding without notice. The AP said they forgot. Five: I never asked you to climb out of bed at 2:00 A.M. over a period of years and walk and run thousands of miles carrying heavy equipment and risk personal safety during the civil rights era, much of it without pay. Six: I never asked you to leave the state on Christmas Eve on a civil rights story the day after your wife gave birth to your first child, without the benefit of family and friends in town to be with her. Seven: I never asked you to walk 259 miles from Memphis to Jackson without the benefit of a single newsman to cover the James Meredith march. Eight: I never asked you and your wife to skip an all-expenses paid trip to Columbia University to accept your Pulitzer Prize so you could cover another civil rights story for hopefully 30 cents on the dollar. I received my Pulitzer in the mail after someone from New York AP took the bows and ate my dinner. Nine: I never asked you to stay in Gulfport, Mississippi when the hurricane of the century with 200-plus miles per hour blew the place away. Ten: I never asked you to work 100-hour weeks over a period of years in Mississippi-Louisiana without proper compensation and be paid only with the promise that I was one of the company's most respected photographers and that the Associated Press would be there for me in my time of need. Eleven: I never asked you to be on call 24-hours-a-day, 7-days-a-week, vacation or not, while other news staffers worked their eight hours and went home to enjoy a normal life with their families.

And, the "I never asked you" list goes on and on and on and on. No, Mr. Richardson, I only asked that after a very lengthy job-related illness, that I be offered a chance to rehabilitate myself and try to return to a productive life in my profession.

I accept your answer of "No", but I hope and pray that you never need rehabilitation from an illness and be told the company offers nothing. That, Mr. Richardson, is sad, not only for you and I, but for all the dedicated journalists who take that extra step and often risk life and limb to be able to say, "I did my very best."

Yes, Mr. Richardson, that is sad indeed. Sincerely, Jack R. Thornell.

While waiting for a pissed off Richardson to drop the ax with a second letter, I contemplate how future job interviews would likely go. "Mr. Thornell, tell us about your education." "High school dropout." "Uh-huh. And what have you been doing the past two years?" "Nothing." "Uh-huh. And, why not?" "I've been on disability." "Uh-huh. Mental or physical?" "Both." "Uh-huh. That'll be all. We've got your number. We'll keep it on file." Uh-huh, I thought, the dead file.

Ten days after I mailed my reply, the phone rings. I pick it up. It's Ackerman. "Hello Jack. How're you doing?" "Okay, I guess." "Look, next week Assistant General Manager Ron Thompson will be in town. And, he'd like to have a sit-down with you... over lunch." "Fine. When and where?" "How about next Thursday at Delmonico's on St. Charles. About 1 P.M.?" "I know where it is. I'll be there." Perhaps, my reply pricked some New York consciences, I think, but probably, it was the insertion of those three words in paragraph fifteen that drew executive attention. "Job-related illness". At least though, Thompson I know. When he was a science writer, we worked together in Houston on space shots. And later, we worked even closer when he was appointed News Editor in New Orleans.

Delmonico's, with its red-checked table cloths is reported to be a fine restaurant. But for validation, don't ask me. Because, these days everything tastes the same. Flat, and tasteless. After Ron and I recall a few stories that we worked together, and after he empties his plate and puts down his fork, finally he gets to the point. "Jack, there's nothing we'd like better than having you back," he said. Then realizing his error, corrected it and said, "Than having the Old Jack Thornell back. He never missed. He always came back with 'the picture'. But, for now, in your present condition your best bet is to try staying on disability." And, why is that I ask and answer myself. Because you Ron, and those photo executives in New York know, the "Old Jack Thornell" is dead. And, all that's left is the burying. And that "best bet" you suggested, I think I might lose, because, disability beyond two years is most difficult to qualify for. Even Dr. Phillips has told me of wheelchair patients he can't get approved.

After I get home, finding myself alone, I collapse on the couch to examine my dilemma, when the crazies take over. Flipping cartwheels and singing… Jack Thornell! Come out! Come out! From wherever you're hiding. Old you? New you? Which will it be?

Unwilling to gamble on getting more disability, I start trying to resurrect a new old me. With back exercises, and daily jogging. Feeling better after a few weeks, I go see Dr. Phillips and ask for his approval for my return to work without limitations. "Are you sure?", he asks. "I'm sure. I'm feeling great." "Okay, then you got it."

With Dr. Phillips release, I write Ron in New York, advising him that I am fit for work and most eager to return. How about June 2? Now, management starts doing cartwheels. They, I heard, even consulted their nemesis—the union—about my rights. The union ruled in my favor. I was entitled to my old job back. But, the fact that the company consulted them sent me a message. It said, management doesn't want Jack Thornell back. Old or new. Instead of a job, give him a shovel. And, the great feeling, that I was trying to keep pumped up, went flat before I took my first step through the office door.

If going back to work after a two-week vacation was torturous, what kind of torture will it be after a two-year absence? I can't imagine. What's imagined, I know from experience, is usually worse than the reality I find myself in later. But now, how can that be, when I can't even imagine something worse. And from experience I know that after Flight 759 crashed in my backyard and I didn't show, the reception I got a week later was as cold as I could bare. With the guilt they spread topping mine.

My first day back I arrive at 7:30, a good half-hour before the staff starts trickling in. Facing them one by one seems easier. But, I didn't have to wait for anyone to arrive to get my first letdown. It is already there just waiting to be delivered. He's young, new, and I don't know him, so I walk over to his desk and I introduce myself. Rather than marveling at meeting his first Pulitzer Prize winner, He strikes back with a look sharp enough to cut through glass and says, "Oh! You're him… The guy replacing my buddy Bill." But before I could tell him that Bill Haber was my buddy long before becoming his, he turns away and buries his attention on the computer screen. So, I walk over to my old desk, now Bill's, and I sit down thinking… So far, so bad, and, not to have awakened this morning, so good, so worry free, so wonderful, so dead.

Thank God that Bill is the next to arrive, and as always, he greets me warmly before we move into the dark room and close the door. "Bill, I'm sorry, really sorry about this mess and putting you in the middle. But, my two years of disability are up and I didn't know, what else to do, but to try a comeback." "Jack, don't worry about it. Do what you have to do." "Thanks Bill. And by the way, you've got a good buddy out there. From his look, he was entertaining the thought of murdering me so I couldn't take your job away." Smiling, he says, "Oh, don't worry about him, he just don't want to lose his beer drinking buddy." "And, he may not." "Oh, what do you mean?" "Well, if that was a taste of the official welcome back, I'm not sure how long I'll be here… how long I can stand being here."

Seeming puzzled by my response, Bill replies, "Like I said, do what you have to, whatever is best for you and your family."

The next to arrive is Austin Wilson, the sports writer, but more importantly to me, he is the local union representative. Immediately, he corners and confronts me with the controversy, the job controversy. Whose is it? Is it mine? Is it Bill's? And then comes the official reply. "Jack, the union ruled that the job is still yours… that is… if you can still do it." Then I feel a chill as he walks away without uttering an encouraging word, such as… welcome back Jack, it's good to see you back on your feet.

Next, boss Ackerman arrives, finds me and says, "Let's go talk in my office." Once there, he continues, "I've got some big plans for the photo operation. We'll be discussing them over the next few weeks." "What about Haber?" I ask. "Oh, he'll be returning to Dallas." "May I ask when?" "Right away." "Can I suggest something?" "Sure." "That you keep him here for a coupla weeks until I get grounded." "Say, that's a good idea. I'll do that."

After breaking that bit of news to Haber, I suggest that I do most of the shooting to see how it goes. He agrees and meanwhile, I sit by the phone waiting for it to ring. Waiting to hear a New York voice. Any New York voice. Perhaps, a voice that had once dispatched me to cover riots and revolutions. A voice to say…"Jack, it's so good to have you back, back from the dead." But, the phone doesn't ring and those New York voices don't sound. Not Hal Buell's. Not Schwadel's. Nor any other. Photo executive. The ones that once dictated, "Send Thornell! He'd rather come back dead, than come back without the picture and alive."

Thank goodness for two voices that did sound. Those of photo editors Toby Massey of Washington and Gene Blythe of Atlanta. They welcomed me back and wished me well. They were veterans like me. They paid their dues. They didn't start off behind a desk, but on the street ducking bottles and bullets, like me. But, those New York photo executives, the closest they ever got to that reality was by the watching of it on TV. Get real! The only thing they ever ducked was a bar bill after a three-martini lunch.

Cold is the only way to describe my first day back. Colder than that blizzard at Fort Monmouth in 1958. Colder than the frozen ground I shared with Elvis' buns back in Germany. Even colder than the day I walked into the office after my vacation crashed and burned with flight 759 in 1983. If this is the icy equivalent of hell, then God, I promise to be good. I promise! I promise! But then, what good are promises, even to God, I thought, while remembering such a promise. The one I made as a boy. A life or death one. The night the scissors stood. The night I cried out into the darkness screaming, "Please God, take away these blades, let me live, and I'll be a preacherman… your preacherman." And, did I live? Yes. And, did I keep the promise? No. Be a preacher man, hell, I didn't even attend church until I was in my forties.

"Oh Makesense, if a man doesn't stand behind his word, where can he stand? And, how could I have any standing with God now? Now, has God turned down the thermostat too, cause I'm freezing?" "Sorry cousin, only God knows all the answers."

Somehow, I get through the day, only to go home and to contemplate the pressure of a second day. And, contemplate alone. Sure, my family was there, but I couldn't share my thoughts with them. Pour out my guts. No, never. That's a no-no. Besides, they're spilling out on their own, a little at a time. Surely, they must see that. Watching me dissolve must be devastating to them too, knowing that their life of plenty is in peril too. Knowing that if Daddy's paycheck stops, eventually there will be less and less of everything until there's nothing left to see. And, the big question pending is… If that happens, how long will Carolyn hang around before she takes her paycheck and run, run, runs?

Day two back at work is no better. Nor is day three. Though there is one noticeable change: The camera bag seems to be getting heavier and heavier. Even after I put it down, I can't seem to escape the weight of it. Finally, on day four there is a New York voice on the phone. Not a heavyweight like Buell or Schwadel, but an underling, with a member request that required a call. And, then comes the slip. "Jesus Jack, I would have liked to call you earlier to welcome you back, but…" And then, realizing his slip, stops short of revealing any more information, as to why there weren't any such calls, even from underlings. And, when he hung up, one thing ran clear, the absence of calls from New York wasn't a coincidence. No! It was a conspiracy… the "Cold Shoulder Conspiracy." And, it was working.

Tick-tock! Tick-tock! Uneventfully, week two is wearing to an end. Till now, my assignments have been routine. But, how long can this last? How long before a big story breaks, I collapse, fail and tons of humiliation rain down to bury me? Jesus! Why couldn't I have been at the Saenger Theatre the day the tornado spun down and took them away. For me, what better way to go than at the movies. Because, the movies were always my escape from the realities down at 503.

The return and the attempt to resurrect my career is not working. With each passing day, showing up for another is getting harder and harder. But meanwhile, shame is working overtime. It's whispering… They don't want you… They know that you're used up… you know it too… it's obvious… you're finished… kaput… done… only waiting to be done in by God or man. Or, by the acquisition of brother Garnett's courage.

Haber is in the darkroom packing for his return to Dallas tomorrow when I join him. "Leave it Bill, you're not going anywhere… I am." "Jack! What do you mean?" "I mean that New York's cold shoulder worked. I can't take any more." "But Jack! Are you sure? What will you do?" "Something… nothing… I don't know… But, I do know that I can't do this… not anymore."

Minutes later, Chief of Bureau Ackerman shows surprise when I walk into his office and tender my resignation. "The only thing I ask in return is severance pay," I said. "Even the worst employees are entitled to that." "Jack, you've only been back two weeks. Don't you need more time to think about this?" "Hank, that's all I've done... Think about this. Geesums! Look at my pants. They're wet. I can't even hold my water anymore. There was a time when I could stand outside a courthouse all day without going. And now, with the bathroom but 30-feet away and I can't make it there without pissing on myself." "Jack, are you sure about this?" "Absolutely." "Okay then, I'll advise New York."

Instead of severance pay, New York executive Thompson calls and offers the possibility of a return disability. "If your doctor approves, your disability pay will resume and all your benefits—healthcare, life insurance, retirement—will continue." "For how long?" I ask. "Indefinitely," he says, "Up to age 65." So, my short-lived resurrection ends with my return to disability, nearly brain dead and without an occupation.

"Makesense, your ears up?" "Up Cousin." "Is a man what he does? Is that his sum total? Like Elvis. Like Astaire. Just a song and a dance? Scales and steps, do they equal identity? Newspaper obituaries seem to say so. Always following the name of the dearly departed comes the occupation. A doctor. A lawyer. A school teacher. A nurse. So, if a man does nothing in life, does he end up a nothing in death? Like my father Ben. At least that's how I saw him, the little that I did see him. A nothing. Now, the question is, am I working at being "a nothing" too? No need to say Makesense because I already know how the saying goes." "How Cousin?" "Like father. Like son."

Now, I'm back to cooking and cleaning while Carolyn is at work and Jay is at school, but I'm not alone. I'm never alone. Guilt is here, always here, keeping me company. Directing my thoughts. Always casting me as "the coward". Always running away. Like dropping out of high school and fleeing from 503. And now, running away from my career. One that had elevated me above others in the eyes of many. But unfortunately, not in my eyes. When I look into the mirror, I can only see someone doomed to be unworthy, especially of success. Now, in view of my crumbling, others are seeing it too. My unworthiness. And, my birthright.

These days, Candy isn't getting any closer to getting back with husband Kevin. But, the elders at Hickory Knoll are getting closer to taking action against her for her wayward behavior. The vote is three to zero to disfellowship her from the congregation. But, emergency hospitalization saves her from their immediate judgment. "At least for the moment," Elder John Rawdon explains, "But it's coming because we made a surprise visit to her apartment one night and she wasn't alone. She was entertaining a man there. Mike from work she said. Just a friend she said. But, I didn't believe her. We collectively didn't believe her. After Mike fled, we read her the riot act about her behavior. And, on our way to the car, we agreed that our chastisement was to no avail, just falling on deaf ears."

With the threat of disfellowship hanging over Candy, I sit down with Carolyn and Jay to discuss its ramifications on us as a Christian family. "We all know what the scripture says, don't we," I offer. "Refresh my memory," Carolyn asks. "Jay, you tell your mother what the Bible demands." "That we're not to eat, drink, or otherwise socialize with errant church members." "That's right son. That's exactly what the scripture says. And that declaration puts us into a precarious predicament. Do we obey God or do we listen to our hearts?" With her face reddening, and with anger tempering her tone, Carolyn responds, "Turn my back on Candy. Shun Candy. Never! Never! Never!" "But Carolyn, the elders aren't doing this out of spite. They're just trying to wake her up for her own sake. Her soul's sake. It's the church's form of tough love." "I don't care, I repeat, I'll never turn my back on Candy," Carolyn concludes as she exits the living room.

For Jay and I, the question of shun or not to shun is more difficult to answer, "If we support her in this, where will it lead," I ask, "To divorce? To re-marriage? To a state of adultery? To hell?" After pointing out those hazards, I ask Jay, "What do we do?" "Let me talk to her alone. Maybe she'll listen." "I hope so son. I really hope so."

A few days after "the talk" with Jay, Candy invites us over to her apartment for dinner. But guess who the guest of honor is? It's none of us. It's the driver of that pretty Porsche. The friend from work. After a most uncomfortable visit, I leave with more than indigestion on my mind. Once home, I speak, "That was a mistake. We should have walked out. It's obvious as to what she's up to." "And what is that?" Carolyn inquires." "Hell, she's trying to ram friend Mike down our throats. And get us to accept friend Mike as boyfriend Mike. And, I can't do that and practice this religion too. What would be the point of it? Am I supposed to say it's okay daughter, trade in your husband for a boyfriend. And, throw in your soul too. It's a bargain."

Meanwhile, my mind asks… wouldn't I, wouldn't she be taking on the role of God. In essence, overruling God, just like Adam and Eve did in the Garden of Eden. God said don't eat of the forbidden fruit. Both decided otherwise, did eat, making themselves God for the day. But, their God complex was short-lived by their getting booted out of paradise and into the cold world of sin and suffering. And now, having to taste of death for their comeuppance. "Gees daughter!" I want to shout, there are consequences for our actions, even deadly ones, but, before I can close my mind on the subject, it races away with alternative thinking, peppered with stinging questions.

Without a God to be, would man be free?

Freed from shame, freed from imperfection?

Without a God to be, would man be free?

Freed from immortality, freed for life?

But, that train of thought doesn't take me far. How can I buy that? Not when, I'm already buying into religion for $40-a-week in contributions. And money, I hate wasting. That, surely would be an abomination. Finally, I conclude that it is best if we let God be God and not any of us bad actors.

Six months later, Candy asks if she can move back home to save money so she can buy a car. But, without a yes or a no, I suggest she come over for dinner and a talk. About such a possibility. After dinner, we four gather in the living room and I take the floor. "Moving back home, it's a good idea, and it's okay. But, there are conditions." Nervously, she responds, "What conditions?" "This friend Mike, this Michael Gros, he ain't welcome here." "And why not?" "Jesus Candy, you're married. You got a husband." "Would it be different if I divorced Kevin?" "Even if you did dear, you're not entitled to another man. Not short of the death of, or the act of adultery having been committed by Kevin. And, since Kevin is still breathing and you haven't charged him with adultery, you're stuck with the man you chose to marry." As I pause, Candy goes silent and her body goes rigid. "So daughter, you can move back in, but friend Mike is out. He's not welcome. What do you say?" With tears gathering, she stands and says, "Well then, I'm not moving back."

Later that night, lying in bed, I'm thinking… Candy's game plan was the same. Get her foot back in the door and slowly wiggle friend Mike's toe in too, get us to know and like him and to accept their relationship while turning a blind eye to God's decree. And, if we do, look out brother because here comes the snowball effect. Now, over the actions of one, seven souls are in jeopardy. Candy and Mike's. Kevin and new mate. Carolyn, Jack and Jay. All for embracing adultery. And now, call it… Satan's Delight. No daughter dear, deal me out of that game for there's not a snowball's chance in hell of my playing.

Time creeps on, Candy continues on with Mike, Kevin continues his crying on my couch and the elders drag their feet on. It seems they forgot to enact their secret vote. The one to disfellowship Candy. And, before they remember, Candy flees to Memphis, moves in with her Uncle Stephen and gets a job there. Her decision for a fresh start away from friend Mike pleases me, until, I learn who drove the moving van. Yep! Friend Mike. Finally, husband Kevin abandons the church he gave up his Catholic faith for. The conservative church. The stand behind the scripture church. Except of course, the discourse on divorce. So now, with the elders not having to face Kevin every Sunday and Wednesday, and now, with Candy no longer a part of the Hickory Knoll Fellowship, the elders never announce their secret vote to the congregation. And Candy, dodges the disfellowship bullet, while leaving the "snowball effect" in play. Seven souls for the price of one.

Time continues on, my disability check continues on, the worry of my disability check not continuing on, continues on. The savings continues on. Climbing up to a quarter of a million dollars. When Carolyn sneaks a look at the asset list, it probably makes her sick. Knowing that she can't spend it. Remember honey, none of your paycheck gets credited there. It all goes into your own bank account or on your back, or on your hair or on your feet. All for show and tell.

Money is always an issue between us. Not the lack of it, but the abundance of it. And now, Carolyn wants to tap into that abundance to update the house with new carpet, cabinets and such. But naturally, I have a better idea, so I present it. "Carolyn, we don't have to dig into our savings to remodel the house." "Then, how else can it be done?" "Well, with your paycheck, my disability check and two interest checks, our income is over $50,000-a-year." "So?" "We can use some of that, especially the extra income of yours that I never see. Put that into a house fund with my leftover disability pay. And, presto, there's the money for your projects without touching the savings. What do you say?" "I say, you'll never change… I say… I'm going shopping." Naturally, the mere mentioning of "her money" makes for anger and makes for flight. With the sound of the front door slamming, a funny thought surfaces… If heaven doesn't come with a giant shopping center, Carolyn will conclude… this place is hell.

Jay hit his first home run today. A real home run. Not an error assisted home run, but, a knock it over the left centerfield fence home run. A 320-footer plus. And, I saw it. Since he was six, he has hit a lot of baseballs, but none so majestic as this day at Bonnabel Stadium. And, it came none too soon, as he is finishing his senior year at Grace King High School where he owned second base. Carolyn, coming directly from work, just missed it. And boy, she's sick. Together, we've attended a lot of games, and we've watched Jay get beaned, get spiked, get ejected for slinging the bat, purely accidental, and get his head down to lead the team in prayer. In my observation and opinion, if there is a better kid on the planet mister, please show me.

Today though, Jay hurt me, really hurt me. My ears, he doesn't need 'em, not anymore, not for his practice preaching sessions. Usually, with me sitting in the den and listening, Jay stands behind the kitchen counter, delivers his prepared sermon and then after, I offer my critique. But now, with his talent blossoming, he has decided to practice behind closed doors. And, I'll hear it on Sunday, just like everyone else. His plans include attending Louisiana State in the fall to study communications. Hell, at 18, he's already a fine communicator with the perfect voice for it. And, if he has ever uttered one word of profanity, I've never heard it, despite all those fine examples expressed by Mother and me.

But this Spring, something changes Jay's plans. It's called a revival. It's when the elders call in a motivational speaker to arouse a sleepy congregation. His name is Goebel Music. And his message is "few". "Brothers and sisters, hear me when I tell you that "few" will enter the kingdom of heaven. And you think I'm talking about the lost souls out there, outside the church, but you'd be wrong. Because, I'm talking about those inside the church and sitting here right now. That's right, only a few of us will see glory." Over the next several nights, with a chalk board behind him and a Bible before him, he proves his point with mathematics. The mathematics of the scriptures. And, when Goebel Music was done, and the congregation was done squirming, most of us, including Jay and I, were on our feet to re-dedicate ourselves to serving the Lord.

Later that night, Jay asks, "Dad, have you mailed in the room deposit for LSU?" "No son, I plan on mailing it tomorrow." "Don't." "Why?" "Because I won't be going to LSU." "Are you kidding? Not going to your dream school. Why not?" "Because tonight, I decided to become a preacherman. And that profession requires a different kind of school." "Jesus Jay, are you sure, completely sure?" "Completely Dad, completely." "Okay, that's it then."

Moments later, alone in the quiet of the den, my mind travels back in time. Back to my youth. Back to the promise. My promise to become a preacherman. A promise I never kept. And, a secret best kept between God and me.

So now, with Jay majoring in Bible, LSU is out and Freed-Hardeman University way up in Henderson, Tennessee, is in. Jay's decision to switch majors, according to my calculations, will double the cost of his education. But then, Hickory Knoll with the revival blood still stirring, announces its first scholarship. And it's awarded to Jay. The church will pay one-half the cost.

With Jay gone, with Candy gone, and with Carolyn gone to work, the house is filled with me and my emptiness. When Carolyn gets home, we eat the dinner I prepared. After I wash the dishes, we sit and watch TV with indifference filling the space between us. It's obvious that Carolyn is smoking again. The aroma of air freshener in the bathroom is thick enough to choke me when I follow her in. Then, I find the water-filled ashtray stationed under the bed in the spare bedroom. Now, with proof, do I confront Carolyn and remind her of the new car deal? The when and if she starts smoking again, she'll give me the new car and she'll take an old one for daily driving. But confront, I don't. The thought of haggling over cars or cigarettes is painful enough without experiencing the reality. SO, Carolyn keeps her car and her cigarettes.

At church, we befriend a new couple. Huey and Sammy Mayfield. He works for the I.R.S., and she, like me, clips grocery coupons at home. The fifty cent ones, doubled, are a real find. They love my homemade chocolate pie—a Mrs. Wilson recipe. It's easy, cheap, and delicious.

Meanwhile, brother Marshall is married again. Wife number three is Margie. She owns a fine home in Clinton. Apparently, even though she married one, she doesn't think too highly of many other Thornells. In fact, she has barred her door to Marshall's three children—Debra Jean, Diane, and Kenny—and his granddaughter Tasha. And especially to his nasty-mouth mother. At least, unlike Hickory Knoll, the daughter of a Baptist preacher, knows how to disfellowship people and does. And, where does Marshall stand in all of this? Just behind her coattails. However, her disfellowship doesn't extend to us. In fact, she loves visiting us, loves my cooking, especially my desserts. When I ask, "What would you like, my homemade chocolate pie or the cherry cheesecake?" "Oh, I can't decide, better give me a little slice of each," she responds.

Mother hasn't seen son Marshall for two years now, and she is tore up about it. "God! What did I do! Besides, giving him a free place to live, giving him money and cleaning up after him. This ain't my boy doing this, it's that fucking miss Margie. This is all her doings. Her shit." Then, Mother gets a notion, and when she gets a notion, she won't shut up about it. And, that notion is to change her will. "Are you sure Mother?" I ask. "My mind's made. That Margie ain't getting one cent, not one goddamn cent of my money. If Marshall gets it, she gets it. And, you know about Marshall and his women. How weak he is. How they control him."

So, Mother hires a lawyer, writes a will and leaves me her entire savings, which has miraculously grown to $20,000. But, that's not all she left me, she left me the house at the bottom of the hill. She left me 503. The place I'd spent a lifetime trying to escape from. Now, I owned it.

Still spry for 81, Mother is still picking up leaves, still sweeping and mopping, and still carrying on a loud conversation with herself, whether inside the house or out. Still carrying on with life despite the departing husband Ben and Crazy Uncle John. Even sister Maddie has passed. But to talk of dying, that gets her ear. That talk scares her. Even commands her silence like the time the crows paid us a visit in my youth, and she drew close to me, closer than ever before, while we were sitting on the edge of the porch. And, over the years, have we grown any closer? Not noticeably. However, on the phone, on long distance, we might exchange an I love you. But in person, it's a reach. It's impossible.

Today, Mother calls. She's scared. She needs me to come, right away. Her doctor discovered something. It's under her chin. A lump, back where that melanoma was years ago. Together in the doctor's office we hear the prognosis. "Mrs. Thornell, it's metastasized melanoma. There's really no treatment. At least not one that works. Radiation or chemotherapy, in my opinion, would be a waste." Conferring with the doctor in private, I explain, "I don't think she understood. Got the picture. Your terminal picture." So, he tries again, but still comes up short of saying, "Mrs. Thornell, you're terminal. You'll be dead in less than a year." On the drive back to New Orleans, I turn to Mother trying to explain the cold hard facts of it. "Mother, do you understand what the doctor told you? About how bad this is? About the outcome?" Swallowing hard and touching the lump on her throat, angrily, she snaps back,

"Shut up! Just shut up about it. I don't want to hear any more." So, like a good son, I obeyed, knowing that she had in fact, heard enough.

After a week of visiting and figuring, Mother returns to Vicksburg, looking for a miracle and enlisting for radiation therapy. "Medicare will pay for it," she argues, "And, if I can get ten more years, then, that'll do me." "Geesums!" I'm thinking… Ten more years, plus the ten she already got since the melanoma was first discovered. Mother amazes me. Her hold onto life attitude is incomprehensible. Especially, the life down at 503.

Bad news travels fast, and when Marshall and Margie hear it, they decide to start visiting Mother again. But, if they knew of Mother's notion to disfellowship them from her will, would they keep coming? "Mother, there's time to change your will back, to put Marshall in." "No! I ain't changing nothing. And let's keep that our secret," Mother snickers, let 'em keep coming." "Are you sure?" "You're goddamn right I am. Miss Margie's fine home is just a 30-minute drive, and I ain't ever set one foot in it. Not ever."

Mother did see the house though. Back when Marshall was scarce, she got his Clinton address from the phone book, paid her boarder, and my cousin Harold Davis, to drive her there for a look-see. As Harold would circle the block, Mother would gawk for a glimpse of her boy. "There he is, getting into his pickup truck," Mother exclaims, "That'll do. He's alive. He's got a good roof. That'll keep me. We can go now." Often, Mother recanted her drive-bys to me, reliving those stolen glimpses of her missing boy. The boy who shared her roof longer than any other.

Even I tried to get Mother's foot through Margie's door. And, I got close. Mother is visiting and Marshall and Margie are visiting. Mother isn't doing well, with the cancer having spread to her bones. Complicating matters, Carolyn and I have to drive up to Memphis to put Jay on a plane for the Philippines where he is going to do some summer mission work. So, after dinner, I turn to Marshall and Margie with my suggestion. "Next Saturday, we'll be driving by Clinton, on our way to Memphis, what if we drop Mother off. Let her stay with you Saturday and Sunday night, and we'll pick her up Monday on our way back?" They agree, return home and then, Margie phones back. "You know Jack, dropping Mrs. Thornell off here may not be such a good idea." "Why not," I ask. "Well, you know that my mother is in a nursing home and I could get called away on a moment's notice. Then, what could we do with your mother?" Margie explains before adding, "But you, Carolyn and Jay can stop, stay over, whatever." "Okay Margie, I understand, really understand." "Well then, will you be stopping by?" "No Margie, we won't be stopping by." So, Mother, I've never set one foot in Margie's house either. And after her ridiculous alibiing and with your dying, I never wanted to.

With Mother dying up in Vicksburg, and with my disability situation killing me in Metairie, I reach for Carolyn for some physical relief. While pushing my hand away, she says, "No! Sex doesn't interest me." "Do you mean now, just now, or do you mean never?" "Never! I mean never." "Okay then, I won't press you. But, if you change your mind, let me be the first to know. Meanwhile, I handle it myself. Just to keep things working. Possibly, for later use."

So, with disinterest ruling the bedroom, I make my move and suggest, "Since you go to bed early, and me, late, why don't you move into the spare bedroom so we won't disturb each other." She moves and I sense her resentment adding to those cigarette fumes still lingering in her new bedroom. So, our little separate-beds life continues on, revolving around Carolyn's career, my being Mr. Mom, and church activities, where I am excelling. I head a visitation team, and I'm often called on to do the public scripture reading on Sunday morning. After one such reading, a member stops Carolyn and I and says, "Jack, you read beautifully. You and Jay sound just alike. It's obvious where he gets his talent." Hearing such compliments seem to annoy Carolyn. You'd think that she'd be pleased with my progress. With my walking the straight and narrow. And, be very pleased with the absence of flying spaghetti. Meanwhile, I remain patient and hopeful. Sooner or later, I figure, she'll get horny and return to my bed. What other choice does she have, when our precious religion keeps us locked together as man and wife for as long as we live.

Fridays are yard days. Fridays are excused from cooking days. Fridays are hot dog and chili days. After perfecting the lawn, this Friday, October 6th, 1989, a brother in Christ, Don Wilson, and I are driving to Laplace to visit a hospitalized sister. Don is a real talker and a sometimes preacher who loves to take the pulpit and stir people up with his booming voice. His rhetoric is force-fed. He's the ram it down your throats, now choke on it, kind of preacher. Today, Don is smiling. He's a newlywed. He married a good Catholic lady. And that was odd, I thought, considering how Don hates Catholics. And hates 'em with a passion. Perhaps, he has hopes of converting her like Candy converted Kevin.

Don considers Jay at 19, a gifted preacher as does the congregation, always singing his praises after he speaks. At college the head of the Bible department noted, "It's been at least ten years since anyone with Jay's God given ability has passed through these doors." So, it's obvious that this young man has a gift.

After dropping Don off, I drive home to make the hot dogs and chili for supper. It's 4:30 and still an hour before Carolyn is due. When I arrive, I find Carolyn already there, pacing the floor. Facing me, she says, "Sit down. I need to tell you something." "Oh God! Is it Mother… Candy… Jay… what?" "No, no, it's not that. Everybody is okay." "What then?" "It's that I'm leaving." "Leaving! What do you mean?" "Jack, I'm leaving you. I'm not happy. And, I don't need you anymore." "Carolyn! You can't do this. It's not right. And besides, the church won't allow it." "Let's leave the church out of it. If it's okay with us, then it's none of their business." "But! But! It's not okay with me. You're my wife. And, as far as happy goes. Well, I'm not happy either. Hell, I've never been happy either, but I'm not blaming you." "Jack! It's too late to change my mind. I've decided." Then, the doorbell sounds and in walks her brother Stephen from Memphis. "Stephen's here to help me move," Carolyn announces before disappearing into the bathroom to collect her things. Stephen joins me in the den and says, "This can be easy, or, it can be difficult." "Stephen, you've never been married," I reply, sitting in shock with tears welling in my eyes. "There's nothing easy about this."

Moments later, Carolyn returns to the room, hands me a slip of paper and says, "That's my phone number at my new apartment. Stephen and I will be back tomorrow with a moving van." My voice follows them to the door. "Take whatever you want. This stuff, you can have it all. I'll stay away while you move."

With their departure, the facts hit me. She already has an apartment, already has a phone, and has brother Stephen in place here. It's obvious that she's been planning this move for weeks, even months. God! What about the money? The savings. The CD's. The bonds. Shit, and it's Friday. And banks are closed until Monday. No, Monday is Columbus Day so it'll be Tuesday before I can take a look in the safety deposit box, the one that Carolyn has access to and sees what's there. Oh, but there's the passbook savings account. There's $20,000 in there. With my heart jumping out of my chest, I run to the bedroom, retrieve the little green book, and open it. There's the bottom line. There's a deduction. There's $10,000 missing. The transaction is dated today. Oh Carolyn! What are you doing to me? Taking my money. Don't you know, that's the only thing separating me from 503 and the misery found there.

Tonight, I take the Beretta to bed with me, laying it under the covers within hands reach. Perhaps, during my dreams, I'll find Garnett's courage and this nightmare will end.

Jay's at college, Candy's at Memphis. And according to Carolyn, they don't know of her decision. John Rawdon, the church elder to whom I am the closest, is in Argentina attending a wedding. But, I need someone to talk to. Finally, I decide to dump my misery on the Mileys, our friends for twenty-five years. It was news to them. And then, I told them of my past sins, of our sleeping apart, and of the missing money. After unloading my burden and my tears, they said, "We're sorry." What else could they say? In fact, that's all they ever said. After that visit, I never saw or heard from Bette or Sam again. And, a friendship of twenty-five years quietly dissolves and disappears.

Sunday at Church, I take my regular seat in front of the Mayfields. Seeing me alone, Sammy leans forward and jokes, "Where's Carolyn, did she finally leave you?" "As a matter of fact, she did." Then, Carolyn arrives, sits next to me and Sammy thinks that I too am joking. Later during services, Carolyn leans over and whispers, "We need to meet. To talk business. How about 2 p.m. at the house?" "Okay" is all that I can say and still withhold my tears. Just as the last hymn ends, Carolyn exits and enters the restroom, probably to sneak a cigarette before Bible class.

When the services end, I turn back to Sammy and say, "You were right. Carolyn left me." Half laughing, she responds, "And the Pope's not Catholic. You're kidding." "I wish I was. But I'm not. It's true." With my tears confirming my truth, Sammy replies, "Oh Jack, I'm sorry. Sorry for saying such an awful thing." "That's alright. You didn't know. Nobody knew, except her brother." "Well, that explains it." "Explains what?" "Why Carolyn turned down our dinner invitation for Friday night. She said you had other plans." "You mean, she had other plans. I would have preferred dinner with you and Huey."

Carolyn arrives, takes a seat in the living room and begins, "I'm here to divide up the assets." "You're what! Are you out of your skull? You just took $10,000 on Friday, and you're back for more? What else did you take?" "Nothing, that's all." "Do you know how long it takes to save ten grand? Some people never do. And now, poof, it's gone." "I'm sorry, but with the savings, you never let me feel like a partner. And the law says different. It entitles me to half." "A partner you weren't. You couldn't spare a dime of your money for saving. When it came to saving, you were my greatest hindrance. You even resented my saving." "I helped. I helped pay bills." "Carolyn, everybody pays bills. That's got nothing to do with saving. Saving is a discipline." "Jack! I'm not here to argue about money. Not anymore. I'm here for my share." "Am I missing something here? You haven't mentioned divorce." "I don't want a divorce." "What! No divorce but you want half of the assets. Wait! Let me see. Have I got this right?" After splitting the loot, you live at point A and I live at Point B. And we live happily ever after?" "Yes, that's right." "No way honey. No divorce. No more money. Meanwhile, you've got a $25,000-a-year- job and a $10,000 cushion. Support yourself. I'll live on my disability pay and the rest of my money stays put." "We'll see about that," Carolyn shouts as she exits the house upset that her business meeting didn't yield any more fruit.

About the leaving, Carolyn tells Candy and I agree to tell Jay, but not over the phone, so I drive up to Henderson, for a face to face with my preacher son. He knows the scriptures. He knows separation leads to divorce, leads to adultery and finally, leads to perdition for both Carolyn and I. There, after telling Jay, I expected to see a face full of disbelief. I expected to hear a preacher's outrage. Instead, blank stares filled his face. Only those awful blank stares that I hate so much. So a comfort to me he wasn't. In fact, he looked downright uncomfortable just being in my presence. So, it's clear, my attempt to enlist an ally is fruitless.

Elder Rawdon is back. Thank God! Because the church must get involved before Carolyn—like Candy—goes too far. For me, ten thousand dollars is far enough. We get together, and I bring him up to date. I even confess my past behavior, detailing the abuse Carolyn suffered at my hand. "But that's not happening now is it?" "No John, that ended long ago, even before I became a Christian." "Then, what's her beef?" "John, she simply said that she wasn't happy and left. But she didn't leave empty handed." "What do you mean?" "I mean that she took ten grand with her." "Okay, I'll update the other elders and we'll go talk to her." "Okay John. Thank you." As he is leaving, I'm hoping that "the talk" includes the scripture in Genesis when God tells Eve, "Thy desire shall be to thy husband and he shall rule over you." And, in my eyes, Carolyn has already broken my golden rule. The savings honey, it stays in the bank. It's not for spending.

The elders, like Rawdon, John Hutchens and Al Laguna, are the caretakers of the congregation. Like good shepherds they are responsible for watching over the flock, knowing that one day they must give an accounting. So an elder's soul is locked in with the souls of others. With what others do or don't do. And what the elders do or don't do about it.

After meeting with Carolyn, Rawdon reports back to me. "We didn't make any progress, but we'll be talking to her again." "John, this sure looks like a replay of the Candy-Kevin situation, doesn't it?" Frowning now, Rawdon shakes his head in disapproval, as I continue, "You know Carolyn is a legal secretary familiar with precedents, figuring that she can do what Candy did and get away with it without the church retaliating." Seeming uncomfortable, as if twinged by pain, he replies, "That's too bad about Candy. We were ready to disfellowship her, then she got sick, we delayed and never got back to it." "And now, you know where Candy is headed... for divorce... for re-marriage... and for a permanent state of adultery." "Yea! Yea! I know." "But don't you see, you've taught Carolyn that this is okay. That you can get away with it and keep your good standing in the church." "Okay! Okay! You've made your point. I'll be having another go at Carolyn soon, real soon."

Meanwhile, Carolyn calls her own meeting. With me. And she isn't brandishing a Bible, but an asset saw. And, she still wants her cut and she wants it now. And as always her figuring unnerves me. Her money is her money. All hers. And, my money is half hers. After I refuse to divide the money for a second time, she says, "I want you to pay my car off out of the savings." "Carolyn, that's not what we agreed. You said you'd make monthly payments." "Well, I'm not any more. Just pay it off," she orders. Pay it off, I didn't, but I started making the $200-a-month payment out of my disability pay.

By now, the elders, by talking with Carolyn and by talking with me, have uncovered my flaw. My savings flaw and the size of it. "$250,000, that's a lot of money," Elder Laguna observes. "Money is to be used, not hoarded," Elder Hutchens offers. "Perhaps brother Hutchens that's why you have seven cars parked in front of your house in your upscale neighborhood. It's obvious you use your money on thyself, on creature comforts," my thoughts are processing, but my voice speaks, "It's true, I'm a saver, but you can see that my family isn't lacking. And remember, my career is over. I'm on disability. A fixed income that could end at anytime. So, I'd better be good with money."

Sensing confrontation, Rawdon turns the conversation to a more agreeable subject. "How is Jay? How's he doing?" "Fine, just fine. Other than wrestling with Greek." As they stood to leave, I offer my resignation as captain of a visitation team. Laguna insists, "That's not necessary." But, I insist, "In view of this mess, it is."

Carolyn wants another sit-down. This time at the doughnut shop. The subject? What else? The dough. But today, I bring the sword of the spirit—the Bible—with me and place it on the table between us. Wide-eyed, she asks, "What's that for?" "To show you that what you're doing is wrong. That God disapproves." "You've got your nerve. Preaching to me. I'm not here for that." "Then why are you here?" "For my money. Either give it to me or I'm taking you to court." "What about divorce? Are you taking me to court for that too?" "I don't want a divorce. I want my money." "Well, I'm sorry honey. No divorce. No money."

After contemplating Carolyn's court threat, I decide to call and to plead my case. "Please wait. Don't file any lawsuits, not yet. The holidays are approaching and you know how depressed I get then." Without a reply, I continue, "Take your time. Make sure that you're never coming back. Because, if you take the money you can never come back. Not to me. Not in this lifetime." Her reply, "I'll think about it," it didn't give me much comfort. Because, all she's been thinking about and talking about is the money.

The doorbell rings. It's Don Wilson. "Man! I just heard. Your wife left you. Is that true?" "It's true." "But why?" "In the pursuit of happiness." "She can't do that. Not a Christian wife. Not in the church. That's not scriptural." "I agree. But, she's doing it. Just like Candy." "What are the elders doing about it?" "Just talking, just like with Candy, talk, talk, talk." "You might not like what I have to say, but, your daughter should have been disfellowshipped. Leaving her husband like that." "I agree Don, I agree."

Today, I'm raking leaves, thinking about Mother and the fact that she still doesn't know about Carolyn's leaving. Why, I figure, trouble a dying woman with my living troubles. Then, my thoughts are interrupted when a car pulls up, a man gets out, approaches me and asks, "Are you Jack R. Thornell?" "Yes, I am." "Then, these are for you," the stranger says while handing me an envelope. Inside it are court papers. A petition for the partitioning of community property. Oh shit! She is putting the money in the court's hands, claiming that I am a threat to the assets. That I might abscond with the money. Me, a threat, that's hilarious. A safeguard, a watchdog, a guardian, for sure. But a threat? Hell, you're the absconder. You grabbed $10,000 and run off with it. And, now you've turned your office law dogs loose on me. Oh Carolyn!

Why couldn't you have waited? At least until after Christmas? Mother will be down. She'll find out. And, she's got money mixed in with ours. Oh Carolyn, this worry, this just might finish Mother, and me.

Who is this law dog, this Morgan J. Wells from her office who signed off on the petition? Then, something floors me. Something my neighbor—Mr. Conner—said about her leaving. "This don't figure. You keep the house, the yard, do the cooking, the dishes, and save a lot of money. This woman, any woman would be crazy to leave you, unless." "Unless what?" "Unless, there is someone else in the picture." "You mean another man?" His shrugging off my question has me thinking. Well, Mr. Wells, are you in the picture? Let's see, here's your name in Carolyn's office directory. Here's your home address. Holy shit! It's the same complex. At The Creeks. Son-of-a-bitch! You live next door to my wife. Coincidence, or something more I write in the blank box on my calendar.

After Wednesday night services, I face elder Rawdon, and inform him of the impending lawsuit and ask, "Doesn't I Corinthians, chapter six, forbid this. Church members going to court among the non-believers?" "Jack, you know it does. We'll sit down with Carolyn again, and talk to her again."

Later that night, Candy calls with her own news. "Dad! I'm coming home. I miss everybody." "That's good. Are you moving in with me, with Mother, what?" "No, I'm getting my own place." Another coincidence, I wonder. Carolyn moves out. Candy moves back. Now, Carolyn with her own place can entertain Candy and her friend Mike and make him feel welcome without me standing in the way. Coincidence or conspiracy? Time, perhaps, wedding bells will tell.

Sunday morning after the closing song and the preacher invites anyone with special needs to come forward and make it known, I find myself up front, facing the congregation and saying, "I'm here asking for your prayers and asking for my wife to forgive me and to please come home." With my tears flowing, I retake my seat while my thinking continues on. Isn't this the way of it? This Christianity, this forgiveness business. Doesn't Carolyn have to drop whatever it is that she's holding against me, bury it and return home to a repentant husband while rejoicing and praising God for the grace of it? Well, not exactly.

While members of the congregation supply me with hugs, Carolyn's embrace doesn't reach me. Only her cutting look and her condemning words, "Why are you doing this? Embarrassing yourself, and me." And, that I find is the forgiveness business. Sometimes, I hear, "I forgive you but." But God doesn't put any "buts" in the way of his forgiveness. So Christians, you can't either. Put your "but" in the way and you put your butt in jeopardy. Because God's forgiveness is conditional on us forgiving each other, and no "buts" about it. So Christians, if you're not willing to forgive, get out of the forgiveness business, and put your money, your time, and your faith into a new corporation and why not call it… The get even business. Now, that makes sense, and no "buts" about it.

With it just a week before Christmas, another ordeal awaits. Facing Mother. Telling Mother. Having survived radiation, she's ready for me to come and get her for a visit. Geesums! Do I hate telling her that Carolyn is gone, because afterwards she'll never shut up about it. Because, when Mother gets stirred, there's no last word on it, even in her dying mode.

Vicksburg is an hour behind us and Mother is done counting her money, having pushed two twenties on me for "gas money". And now, done detailing every bit of her treatment. The x-marks on her neck. The burning sensation. The hard swallowing. Finally, she goes quiet, catching her breath and touching her throat. It's on a lonely stretch of Highway 18 between Utica and Interstate 55, when I decide it's time. "Mother, when we get to Metairie, you won't find Carolyn there. She's moved out. She left me. She's gone." With her eyes widening, she replies, "Jack! You're putting me on, pulling my leg, aren't you?" "No Mother, I'm not. It's true. She left over two months ago." "For Heaven's sake, why didn't you tell me?" I didn't want to worry you, and I thought she'd come back." "What about the money, the bank money?" "So far, she took ten thousand, but, she's after the rest. She's taking me to court next month." "Lord, I never would have thought this, not this."

During the holidays, Mother blasts me with suggestions. "Grab the money, and run. Go to Canada, Mexico, or back to Germany." "Mother, I can't. I'm tied to the house, to my doctor and to my disability." "But what about my money in that CD of yours?" "Don't worry, Carolyn won't get one cent of your money. Not a penny. Not a peso. Not a mark. Not while I'm still breathing."

It's Sunday, four days before D-Day, before Carolyn's show me the money court day, and the elders are seemingly content with their occasional fiddling and twiddling, just like before, just like with Candy, when they did nothing. So, with the elders appearing to have dozed off on the path to a doctrinal unsound lawsuit, I decide a wake-up call is in order. It comes in the form of a note, hand printed, just three paragraphs long, and tucked inside the cover of my King James Bible. A gift from Carolyn. The Bible inscribed with my name. The name cleared and cleansed by the Baptismal waters. The waters that washed away all my sins. The sins that are now resurfacing, that Carolyn, the elders and even I are rehashing and finding disgusting. The sins identifying me with the former me, the supposed to be erased me. But instead, I'm seeing the old me being resurrected again and again. Like those old sins are for collecting, and to be used again. Just like spent bullets, let's collect 'em, dip 'em in guilt, reload 'em, and fire 'em again. Yea! Great ammunition those old sins are. Great for justification.

After the final hymn concludes, preacher Gray offers the invitation for any in distress to come forward and make their needs known. Hey, I'm in distress, I think, and it's time to move. But, I can't. I seem to be glued to the pew. I can't go forward. I can't humiliate myself again. But then, the thought of disappearing dollars flashes across my mind, lifts me up and takes me front and center, where I can feel the eyes of the church focusing on my back as they wait to hear my request.

Preacher Gray moves to me, bends down and whispers, "Jack, how may I assist you?" "Just read this," I say, while handing him my note. It says… I need the prayers and the assistance of the church. My wife is taking me to court this Thursday. An act that will ultimately lead to an unscriptural divorce. While reading on his way, Gray gets halfway back to the pulpit before making a u-turn and returning to me. "Are you sure you want me to read this? To embarrass your wife like this?" "Yes, I'm positive." But, instead of returning to the stage, Gray finds elder Laguna, approaches him and shows him the note. Now, returning to me, Gray says, "Brother Al doesn't want me to read the whole note. The prayer part is okay, but not the other, the court thing." "And why not? Doesn't the book of Mathew say that when a brother or sister won't listen, to take the matter before the whole church? Carolyn isn't listening and I don't want this kept secret. I need the help of the church. Again Gray huddles with Laguna and again Gray returns to me and says, "I can read the prayer part, but that's all." While taking the note from his hand, I reply, "In that case, forget it. It's all or nothing."

Now, after a ten minute delay, a flustered Gray returns to the pulpit with nothing to say to a more than curious church no doubt wondering… what was that all about? With services ended, I approach elder John Hutcheons and expose my unread note. After reading it, with his face reddening, he says, "After Bible class, come to the office. We need to discuss this."

Inside the cramped office, it's warm with the temperature, along with my voice rising. "The church isn't a secret society is it? Perhaps, someone in the church can help. Influence Carolyn. Help change her mind. Besides aren't lawsuits among members forbidden? Well, aren't they Al?" With his usually fixed grin dismissed, he says, "Yes, they are." "Well then, why am I due in court this Thursday?" With his eyes spilling anger and with his voice quaking, Hutcheons retorts, "Okay! Okay! We'll talk to Carolyn. But, I'm concerned about the congregation. About their questions about this. So tonight, can we read your prayer request? Can we do that?" "You mean just that part? No court stuff?" "Yes, just that." "Well, John if you think it's that important, then go ahead. Read that. Just that."

The next day, the I-wonder-if-you're-more-than-just-my-wife's-attorney calls and wants to talk money. "But first," I ask, "Just what is your relationship with my wife, Mr. Wells?" "We work together. I'm helping her out. That's all." "What about living next door?" Now laughing, Wells replies, "That's true, I do, but I live there with my wife." "Is that so?" "I assure you, it is. I'm happily married. You can call my wife and ask her." After laying my suspicions to rest, I agree to a sit-down with Mr. Wells and my wife.

"Mr. Thornell, we don't have to go to court. All Carolyn wants is her half of the assets. That's all." "But Mr. Wells, she doesn't want a divorce, only the dough, and that's not happening. File for divorce, then we can talk dollars." "But, Carolyn is worried that you might take the money and run." "Hell, I could have absconded already, but I haven't, have I?" "Yea, but that don't mean you won't." "I'll tell you what, Carolyn can come to the bank, check out the safety deposit box, see everything is secure, and then, entrust the key to Carolyn's boss, Dan Picou, for safe keeping. Will that do it?" Carolyn nods in agreement, but her face is showing disappointment. And, I know why. She's broke. The ten thousand, according to Jay, is already spent for furnishing her luxury apartment. "Now Miss Hollywood—the name my sister-in-law dubbed her—is having trouble trying to live off your income," my thoughts suggest.

So, with the assets secured and with Carolyn feeling church pressure, the court date is dropped. The next evening, Elder Rawdon stops by to chat and suggests that I give my nine hundred-a-month of interest income to the church. "Now, you don't really need it, do you?" "John, I do need it. Carolyn deserted, not only me, but all the bills. The house. The cars. The insurance. Everything. Besides, I already give sixty dollars-a-week. That's over three thousand-a-year. Isn't that enough for a guy on a fixed income?" Sensing my outrage at his suggestion, he cuts the visit short by saying, "We want to see you and Carolyn tomorrow night after Bible study." With his departure, a new guilt rushes over me and reduces my pride in giving to a paltry sum.

Carolyn, sitting and stiffened like an upright mummy, is silent, when Elder Rawdon begins. "We're not happy about your situation. But for now, things can remain as they are." And then, turning and fixing his gaze on Carolyn, he warns, "But no more lawsuits, is that clear?" Still silent, Carolyn nods, but Elder Hutchens, apparently still hot over my note passing in church, can't hold his tongue, "I don't see why Carolyn didn't leave you long ago!" Knowing that he is privy to my past, having heard my confessions and Carolyn's accountings, I explode back, "You mean before… before the blood of your Jesus cleansed me of all my sins? Is that what you mean Mr. Elder?" Rawdon stands, steps in between us, and says, "That's enough. The meeting is over."

Now, with Rawdon's threat hanging, it appears that Carolyn is boxed in. If she can't sue, she can't get to the money. The money is safe. Or is it, I wonder? Her boss has the key. He could break the agreement and hand it over to her. Ha! Then, she'll find out where that leads. To a new box with a new number. The one with her name eliminated from the signature card. The little something she failed to notice the day we visited the bank. So Carolyn, boxed in, perhaps not. But boxed out, most definitely.

During a visit to Vicksburg, I find everything about Mother is weakening. Everything but her mouth. It's still lively. Still biting. Still constant. Hoisting her blouse, she greets me with, "Jack, look at this." Between her breasts, above her heart, a large firm mass arises. The size of an orange. "I see Mother, I see! Now cover yourself." "Mother, it's time for you to come and live with me," weren't the easiest of words to say knowing that a steady diet of Mother's mouth can eat on you. But who else will take her? Certainly not Marshall or Margie. So Mother, I'm stuck with you. Come share my misery down in Metairie, I'm thinking, how much worse can things be? But, after a week of her harping on and on, about Carolyn, about the money, and about what I should do about it, finally I scream, "Mother! Please! Please! Shut up about it, because you're driving me crazy, even past crazy, if there is such a place." After an hour of her sitting silently, probably a record, she orders, "Take me back home. I can take care of myself." "Gladly Mother, is tomorrow morning soon enough?"

Ten days later, the phone rings. It's Mother. "Jack, I can't manage it any more. Not alone. Please come get me." "Yes Mother, I'll be there in the morning."

During the long drive there, the car is filled with talking and preaching. My talking, my preaching, to myself. A kind of self-hypnosis. Remember Jack, Mother is dying! Let her rave on. Mother is dying! Don't let her upset you. Mother is dying! Just nod your head. Mother is dying! Just tune her out.

There, we go to the doctor's office and secure her medical records, next to the bank for her financial records, and then, to the courthouse. There, the steps are steep and many, and almost impossible for Mother to negotiate. But like someone said, money is a great motivator. And, that's what this exhausting climb is about. Money. Her money. Money mixed with my money. Down in the Metairie banks. The notary asks, "Mrs. Myrtice Thornell, do you solemnly swear that this affidavit is true, so help you God?" "Yes sir, I do, every word." It states: The accumulation of my money that is being managed by my son. Jack R. Thornell, is $22,780.00. I am 82 years old and suffering from cancer. I respectively request that Jack R. Thornell, my designated executor, be allowed to remove and to manage these monies apart and separate from his community property with Carolyn W. Thornell.

While returning to the car, I'm thinking, Geesums! Putting your mother through that, was it necessary? Wasn't that likened to witnessing one's own death certificate? Yes, it was, I answer, because, after totaling up the amount of Mother's money mixed in with ours, and explaining it to Carolyn, all I got in reply was, "I don't remember that. Not any of it," accompanied with a blank stare. So, with Carolyn's amnesia, a dying, declaration is more than necessary, it's downright mandatory.

The doorbell rings, and immediately comes the banging. Behind the noise stands newlywed Don Wilson. He's anxious, anxious to drop his bomb. It seems that Catholicism and the church of Christ, isn't mixing, not since emphysema forced him on disability. "Mary is afraid," he announces, "Of catching something. And, she wants me to move out." "But Don, emphysema isn't contagious. There must be something else." "Yea! You betcha. It's my missing paycheck. Without it, she doesn't want me." It's said that misery loves company. And so, my misery marries brother Don's misery, and when we're not attending church or visiting the sick and the shut-ins, we sit commiserating over our misfortune, always coming up with the same common denominator for the why of it. Money!

Elder Rawdon calls, admitting, "We're getting nowhere in our discussions with Carolyn," and suggests professional help. "This Dr. Macklyn Hubbell is supposed to be good. Elder Hutchens recommends him. But, he's expensive, like sixty dollars an hour." "John, if you think this can help, I'll go, I'll pay, but unless Carolyn is interested in a reconciliation, it's a waste of time and money." "Okay then, you'll go?" "Yes sir, I'll call and set it up." "Good then, by the way, how's your mother?" "Hanging on John, just barely."

Dr. Macklyn Hubbell has a PhD certificate on the wall, has a copy of his book in plain sight, and soon I learn, has a missing ex-wife. That news slipping out with his talk of the advantages of keeping assets together, even after a divorce. Startled by that news, I wonder, what am I doing here, paying for expertise on keeping it together to an expert on not keeping it together. But Carolyn is here and my word is my word. Resting on my lap is Carolyn's gift, my thick King James Bible. "Oh I see you brought the sword of the spirit with you," Hubbell remarks while smiling and making me aware of his Bible knowledge. "Yes sir. Carolyn, me our family, our lives revolve around this book and what it teaches."

During our second session, Carolyn, apparently tiring of my Bible rhetoric, declares, "I'm not sitting here and listening to this. Not any longer." "But Carolyn, these aren't my words, they're God's." Then, Dr. Hubbell, trying to calm Carolyn, declares, "From now on, we'll leave the Bible out of this." Naturally, his tossing out the Good Book and all my references to it, not only surprises, but also, disturbs me. But, to keep my word to Elder Rawdon, I sit still for it. So now, the smarter than God mediator, turns to a now settled-down Carolyn and asks, "What's the worst thing that Jack ever did to you?" Geesums! I'm thinking, look out. Here it comes... the spaghetti... the sauce... the slap... the straddle... what? Carolyn, now pausing, then fixating her gaze on the wall, replies, "It was when I was six months pregnant, carrying Candy, and feeling amorous, when I turned my affection towards Jack." "And, what happened then?" Hubbell asks. "He refused. He turned away. And he said, "Forget it honey, you're too damn fat.""

Now, Dr. Hubbell turns to me and asks, "Is that true? Do you remember that?" "Jesus! That was twenty years ago and I was most probably drunk. But, remember, no, I don't remember it. But, I don't deny it. Because, I remember doing worse things than that, a lot worse." And, after discussing many of those worse things, I ask, "Are we here to study history, or to discuss the present and to decide the future?" Hubbell replies, "All of the above. It's all tied together."

"Makesense, are your ears up?" "Up Cousin." "Is this fair?" "What Cousin?" "Keeping my past sins alive and using them to crucify me over and over again?" "No Cousin, it's not. It's like double jeopardy, since Jesus already acquitted you." "Why can't Carolyn see the change, recognize it, and credit me for it?" "It's hard to see change when you keep looking backwards, and only backwards."

While each day, the mountain on Mother's chest, now about the size of a grapefruit, keeps rising, I notice a change for the better. Her mouth, she's cleaning it up. Noticeably, fewer and fewer of her sentences start with Goddamn. Perhaps, it's just common sense kicking in, knowing it's just not courteous to insult your host at the door. Now, she can't get up from the bathtub and with my back, I can't lift her, so now, I stand her in my shower and let the water run over her. It's awkward, handling a naked Mother. Candy bathed her once, but only once. And Carolyn, never offered. Dr. Hubbell, when he learned of my tending to a dying mother alone remarks, "That during crisis, many couples forget their differences, unite, and pull together." Only silence follows his suggestion.

Mother's appetite has left her. Tonight, after forcing down a few mouthfuls of asparagus and a little ice cream, she stands, starts holding her private area, and rushes towards the bathroom dripping. Warm urine behind her while I'm shouting, "Please Mother! Put on some panties to help catch some of that." Afterwards, angry over the mess, she comes back snapping, "I can't wear those, they're too damned uncomfortable." "But Mother, if you don't, the whole damn house will be stinking."

Late Sunday afternoon, after a little more asparagus and ice cream, Mother collapses in the hall. "Jack! Jack! Come help me." With my arms locked around her waist, half-lifting and half-dragging, I maneuver Mother into bed. But this time, more than urine is trailing. Oh shit! Without underwear, it's everywhere. Undigested asparagus. While I'm holding my breath and wiping, Mother digs a set of hateful eyes into me while shouting, "Get every speck of that... Every goddamn speck." With morning, and with Mother unable to get up, she manages to raise her head and snap, "Get me out of here. Get me to a hospital."

From Utica Street, it's a short ambulance ride to East Jefferson Hospital. There, Mother is wheeled up to the fifth floor and into a special wing, a very special wing. It's where the living are dedicated to the dying. Here, death is an undertaking understood.

Inside the wing, clinging to stands on rollers, the walking dead push their hopes with them, hooked to bottled chemicals dangling and dripping slow poison into their faltering souls, with some stopping, bracing and battling for breath, for enough to continue, for the moment, still clinging to life, still choosing to suffer the sickening consequences of a hopeless treatment. Thank goodness, these hopes, these consequences are beyond Mother's grasp, and she'll be spared that.

A good patient, Mother is not. Neither is patience a virtue. After two days, she's screaming, "Get me out of here. Take me back to your house. I'll be alright there." "But

Mother, I can't. You can't get up. Get to the bathroom. And, I can't lift you." So how does Mother react? With a blame campaign. Against the hospital? No. Against me. It's me keeping her here. It's me torturing her. It's all my fault. Ironically, when a visitor enters the room, she smiles and greets them warmly. With their exit, it's back to business. Back to blaming Jack.

"Your treatment by your Mother, that's normal," the hospital counselor advises. "Dying is difficult. Some get real angry and strike at those closest. Those they care for the most. That's you Jack. So, consider it all a compliment." My reaction, if verbalized, would have been… Spare me the compliments. Please!

Spring break is here and Jay is coming home with a guest. Mother worships him, and perhaps, his presence will lift her spirits and she will let up on me and her compliments. God knows that I could use a break. His guest is Diana Thompson of Culleoka, Tennessee, his fiancée, who graduates this Spring. They're getting married in August. If asked about their plans, my advice would have been to wait, at least until Jay graduates next year. But unasked, and standing between me and my advice was a promise. The culmination of a father-son talk. Actually, a son-father talk. Actually, a lecture. Jay's. "Dad, I know you're a smart man. You know things that I don't. But, it's time for me to start making my own decisions. Sure, I'll make some mistakes. But, from them, I'll learn. So, let me learn." Geesums! I thought… Mother's dying. Carolyn's gone. My career's dead. My money's in jeopardy. And now, my only son is fed up. Fed up with his dad. Fed up with his advice. And how did I react? Surprisingly, coolly and calmly, I replied, "Alright Jay, no more advice. If you want any, you'll have to ask. And, ask me twice." So now, since that conversation, what happens to all of my precious advice? I choke on it.

With Jay home and with Candy recently divorced, the marriage counselor suggests, then schedules a family sit-down. With it my turn to talk, and with only a few words uttered, Dr. Hubbell interrupts, "Jack! Look at your children." To my right, side by side, sit Candy and Jay, clutching the arms of their chairs and cringing as if feeling the first volts of their immediate electrocution. I respond, "But doctor! I haven't said anything of consequence, not yet." "That doesn't matter, a voice can be a weapon, a powerful weapon. Yours is so strong. Just your tone is enough, sufficient to shatter." With his costly observation noted, my thoughts rush me back to Mother and her mouth, one freely observed by me as the most despised mouth ever created on man or beast. Her tone too, sufficient enough to shatter. Has this egghead revealed a truth, a horrible truth, a truth that I have refused to recognize… That my voice and Mother's voice are two of a kind? Twins. That thought too, is sufficient enough to shatter.

With the session ending, Hubbell asks, "When can you return?" "Doctor, you know my mother is dying. I slipped away from the hospital today, but…" "Okay, I understand, just call me when you're ready." After dropping the sixty dollar check on his desk, I catch up with Carolyn outside. "It doesn't appear to me that you're interested in getting back together. Are you?" While moving her head left to right, she says, "No. No, I'm not." "Well then, the five sessions, the three hundred dollars, is enough wasted." Nodding in agreement, she walks to her car, actually to my car, the big two-door Ford LTD, the car Carolyn took when she left, now showing a damaged rear fender. The last of the line. The car I loved. The car Carolyn wrecked.

Sunday afternoon, Candy comes to the hospital, visits with Mother, then asks me to join her in the cafeteria for a conversation. Before she can begin, I begin. "If you're going to ask me

273

to accept your boyfriend, to accept this relationship. Don't. I can't. Not before pitching out my religion first. I'm sorry, but I won't." Apparently startled by my statement Candy stands and says, "Daddy, I'll see you later. I'm going." Later, when I relay the one-sided conversation to Jay, he says, "Gees you must have blown Candy away." "What do you mean?" "She was going to tell you of her engagement to Mike. They're getting married."

Marshall and Margie come to the hospital, learn of my separation, discover that I'm caring for Mother alone, visit for less than an hour, then go. On the drive back, could they be wondering, even estimating an expected windfall coming their way? Over their miscalculation, Mother could have had the last laugh, but for that nasty thick mucus creeping up from her chest and filling her mouth. Above the coughing and the choking with a suction tube I stand, coughing and choking at the mere sight of that nasty stuff coming up.

With morning light come words never uttered before, not to me, not by Mother. Awakened from her daze, the surprising, even startling, words rise up to reach my ears. "Jack, Jack, please let me die. I just want to die." Then, I begin asking myself… Why? Why? Why must you work overtime, feeding her, clearing her throat, and trying to keep her alive, a someone you've always wanted to hide? In this final hour, is your shame showing? Finally, are you ashamed of being ashamed of your mother? The someone who gave you life, gave you milk, then bread. The only person on the planet who would give you her last penny and proved it by doing it. Now, even her last will and testament is dedicated to you. All of it. And you know how much you love and respect money. But, before I can render a verdict, a doctor enters the room, looks Mother over, directs me into the hallway and suggests, "You know if you quit coming in and feeding your mother, this would go a little quicker." "No! I can't. She's only eating a few bites as it is. No! No! I can't do that, starve Mother, she's had enough of that for two lifetimes." So now, near the end, it appears that Mother and I are still at odds. She wants to die. And, I won't let her.

Today is the start of the seventeenth day at East Jefferson Hospital. It's the day for going home, not a heavenly home, but instead, home with me. "Sorry, but your Mother can't stay any longer," the hospital liaison explains, "But we can't do any more and Medicare won't pay to just keep her here." So, even in the dying wing, I find time is limited. Having already searched out several nursing homes, having found the rooms full of too many deserted and lifeless bodies, with the stench of stale urine filling the air and finding my nostrils, and having decided that Mother's last days, last hours, won't be spent there, I put a hospital bed and an oxygen making machine in Candy's old room.

With everything ready at home, I stand by Mother's bed and whisper, "I wish you could hear me, because today, you're getting your wish, today you're coming home with me. Just like you wanted." Moments later, Dr. Marcus Black arrives, looks Mother over, notes the labored breathing, then turns to me and says, "I'm not releasing your mother. Not today. Is that okay?" "Whatever you say, but you know that the hospital wants us out. And, they've been nice, exceptionally nice. But, you're the doctor."

Outside at the nurses station near Mother's room, I hear raised voices with Dr. Black's overriding the objection of the hospital liaison. "I don't care what you worked out. I'm not releasing Mrs. Thornell. Not today."

For Mother, nothing ever came easy, not a roof overhead, not her daily bread. Despite her life-long living conditions, her staying power has always amazed me. If she had had any notion of how life would go, would she have gone to meet old Ben under the big pecan or would she have stayed in her warm bed on that chilly morn remaining dirt poor but virtue rich. Choices, even at sixteen, change things. That's a certainty. Had she chose to stay, then I wouldn't be me or Jay Jay, nor Candy Candy. Simply, we wouldn't be. But Mother, because of your choice, we are here and you are lying here in this helpless and hopeless condition awaiting eviction without a voice in the matter.

It's late afternoon, still day seventeen, and except for the sounds of Mother's gaspings, the room is quiet. Suddenly, the gasping sound lessens, startling and moving me over to Mother's side. There, my eyes find and fix onto the oxygen line feeding into her nostrils. "God! What's happening," I ask. Then, I see. Mother's face, it's, it's changing. Around her nose, the pink of her skin, it's fading. The new found pallor, it's spreading, now reaching her cheeks. God! It's dividing, creeping upward and creeping downward, towards her forehead and towards her chin. Now, outside in the hall, I can hear the voice of Dr. Black, but I can't summon him, because the transformation of Mother's face traps and holds me close, with my face now only about 12-inches above her face. Paralyzed there, my voice can't call, my legs can't move, and my eyes can't blink. Then suddenly, the changing and creeping ends. The picture is painted. Pink is pallor. And Mother's death mask is complete. And so, while holding me close, Mother's spirit passes. Passes before my eyes. Passes from life to death. And, leaving me alone.

Now is the time for me to consider the "no funeral" excuses: Bury Mother down here? Never! Take her body back to Vicksburg? Too far! Besides, on the verge of collapse, I'm not up to it. What then? Cremation. Cremation! But, wouldn't your mother cringe, even at the thought of that? Only if she knew. But, she won't know, will she? Cremation, certainly is the easiest and most certainly, the cheapest way to go. So, easy and cheap, with the emphasis on cheap, are my choices.

Thus, for a thousand of Mother's dollars, I pay for her body to be picked up and to be pushed into a fiery furnace. Then, I call relatives and tell them about the memorial service scheduled up at Vicksburg next month. But, about the cremation, that ending, I leave out of the story. But, J.C. Kettleman, my first cousin, pins me down. "But Jack, what happened to Aunt Mert's body?" Reluctantly I answer, "I had her cremated." "You what! How could you? How could you do that to your mother?"

For an extra fifty dollars, Mother's remains are boxed extra special. When I pick them up, they seem heavy, heavier than ashes. What else could it contain, I wonder? That thought causes concern. But, after leaving the funeral home, the possibility of another question causes greater concern. Someone passing and asking, "Hey Jack, what's in the box?" Shall I answer, "Just parts. Just a few indestructible parts." Now, on a closet shelf in Candy's old room, a new guilt is secretly stored. A guilt heavier than ashes.

After Mother's death, Don drops by and proposes a trip to Phoenix. Since his wife put him out, and with his emphysema worsening, he's considering a move to a dryer climate. Agreeing, I suggest stopping off in Euless, Texas, and visiting my best friends, the Swarts. "Perhaps, we can spend Saturday night with them, and go to church Sunday morning before moving on westward. Besides, Billie and I need to talk. If anyone can persuade Carolyn to end this craziness and come home, it's Billie."

After the hospital confinement, getting on the open road and getting away from all the pain stored up back there, feels good. But, when the Swarts open the door, that feeling leaves me. There's something different. I sense it. There's a chill. I feel it. And it's uncomfortable.

At dinner, before we cut into her specialty, brisket of beef, Billie takes charge, asks us to bow our heads, and proceeds to lead us in prayer. Knowing this might not sit well with the by the book Don, I steal a peek. Don's face is reddening. God! He's steaming, ready to explode. But somehow, he holds his tongue, and when prayer is done, instead of attacking Billie, he stabs the brisket. Later, after cornering me alone, Don lets loose. "What did she mean, leading the prayer like that? A woman ain't supposed to do that, not with men at the table." "I know, I know, but hold your voice down. Remember, we're guests here." "Okay, okay, but I almost got up and walked out, but for that brisket. It looked so dang good and I was so dang hungry."

Finally, Don and Bill turn in, leaving me alone with Billie, my last hope, my wing and a prayer. If anyone can change Carolyn's mind and can convince her to come home, it's Billie. Didn't she lead Carolyn to the church? Didn't Candy, didn't Jay, and didn't I, follow her into the baptismal waters? Weren't we all equally cleansed by it? And that question, I find troubling, particularly now with Carolyn putting me through hell, while trying to hold onto her religion with both hands. And that, according to the scriptures won't wash, because letting go of me, means letting go of God too. And that's because the church is in the forgiveness, and not the get even business.

"Billie please! You've got to help me. Help me persuade Carolyn that this is wrong. That it places both of our souls in jeopardy, unless I'm willing to remain a eunuch forever. Will you talk to her? Intervene." Coolly, Billie looks me squarely in the eyes, and replies, "No, I won't do that." "But Billie, for God's sake, why not?" "I remember the things you put her through. Your abuse. Your control." "But Billie, those things happened before I became a Christian. Years and years ago. That's behind us." "Sorry, but I don't see it that way." "Billie please! This is me. The guy you played hearts with, went to the movies with, vacationed with, even trusted your house keys with. The guy who did everything he could to save your marriage to Bill, after you found that love letter. Remember?" "Carolyn's suffering, I remember. Her feelings of worthlessness, I shared. Her pain, I felt. And all of it, caused by your control, your complete domination." "But Billie please!" "No Jack, I can't, I won't tell Carolyn she can't leave you, because she can. And she has." After she excused herself for bed, one thing became perfectly clear, no matter how hard I try, I can never erase the old image of myself, not even in a best friend's eyes.

Mother's memorial service is set for 1:30 p.m. on May 19th, at Glenwood Funeral Home on North Clay, just blocks from Vicksburg's historic battlefield. Everybody has been called, but Brother Marshal is non-committal. He has a conflict of interest. His step-daughter is graduating from Mississippi College that day, and he feels that he needs to be there for her. But, he knows and I know that's not the reason for his hedging. The real reason is wife Margie and her fear of hubby-dear running into his estranged children and possibly reconnecting after all these years. And, Margie has made it perfectly clear that his offspring are not welcome under her roof under any circumstances, any more than his mother was.

Jay officiates at the service and does well, even managing his tears until the very end. Marshal's children, Marcie, Debra Jean and Kenny are disappointed by his absence. And it shows. Outside in tears, Marcie whispers in my ear, "I only wanted to see my dad, just see him, just for a moment, nothing more." Cousin J.C., apparently still upset over the cremation, is a no-show too. Missing too is the little box of Mother, left unseen in the trunk of my car. Without bearing her, my guilt is heavy enough.

Back home, two days later, Marshall calls with his regrets, while announcing that the graduation went well. In the background, I can hear Margie asking him to ask me if his kids were there? After my affirmative, he cuts right to the meat of his call. "About Mother's money, my portion, when will I get it?" Rather than breaking the news—Jack gets it all—I decide on a more humane method, and inform, "Mother's will, a copy of it, will be in the mail today." Seemingly satisfied, with the usual absence of brotherly small-talk, he hangs up.

Three days later, Marshall calls back and I hear, "I can't believe it, not this, Mother promised that she would take care of me." While wanting to scream, "Like you took care of her on her death bed." Instead, I counter, "This will, it's Mother's dictation. Near the end, I even asked her about changing it. About putting you in it. And her last word was no. The will stands." Then, the voice of Margie bursts in. "Why this, this will isn't valid. It's not even witnessed." Explaining, I say, "Look at the letterhead and find the attorney who drew it up." And then, further explaining, "The witness signatures are on page two, and since that was the only thing on page two, to save a quarter, I didn't copy it. But, I will now, and I'll get it in the mail for your verification." The only response was the sound of the phone crashing down.

Two days later, attorney Way calls me about a call. "Man! Your sister-in-law, was she mad, about your mother's will. She claimed it was invalid since Marshall didn't get anything. To be legal, she said, "Marshall had to inherit—at least a dollar." After breaking for laughter, he continues, "I told her that she'd been watching too much Perry Mason. I could understand your brother calling with some questions, but his wife, man! Has she got some balls." "Well, is there cause for concern?" "No! Hell no! Don't worry. The will is solid. The little woman knew what she was doing, precisely and decisively."

A week later, Carolyn summons me for a meeting at her office. Besides my signature on her pension liquidation form, what does she want? What she always wants. Money. Her entitlement. Her half. Again my answer is "No." And again, I remind her of the co-mingled money, the $22,783 of Mother's money, which is now, my money. Again, she just shrugs as if still suffering with amnesia. And again, I find her reaction bothersome, figuring that Mother's money plus her memory loss equals big trouble in little Metairie.

At home the phone rings and I hear the voice of Elder Rawdon. "How are you?" "Okay I guess." "Jack, I've got an idea I want to run by you." "Okay, what?" "Are you willing to offer Carolyn some money, and I mean real money, to come home?" Exploding, I answer, "You mean a bribe? You mean pay her for services rendered? Isn't that prostitution?" "No! No! You know that's not what I mean. But, nothing else has worked. Our words haven't moved her. She hasn't budged, not even an inch." After cooling down, and warming up to his most zealous, but less than scriptural approach, I ask, "Have you got a dollar amount?" "No, but it must be substantial." "Let me think on it tonight John and I'll get back with you tomorrow, okay?" "Sure, that's fine. We'll talk tomorrow."

While being nauseated by the idea—buy back your wife—in bed, I toss and turn. Wrestling with the thought until finally concluding… It's clear, the elder's pressure, my tears, and even God's hate of divorce, isn't enough, even collectively they're worthless. This calls for, as elder Rawdon put it, "real money".

With daylight common sense comes and convinces me that "real money" although substantial, is substantially less than a divorce split. Under Louisiana's community property laws, I know, Carolyn can claim and probably take half of everything. And that end, at all costs, I must try to avoid.

"Hello John, this is Jack, can you talk?" "Sure go ahead." "Here's my offer. $10,000 for a new car… $10,000 to fix up the house… And another $10,000 to spend next year. Plus, I forgive the $10,000 she already took." "Dang Jack, that's a lot of money. She'll be shocked… I am. She won't believe it. This is great… This might work." After hanging up and collapsing on the couch, I'm thinking… Yea great, down with God's word, and up with money. Because money talks, even louder than God.

Unfortunately though, money didn't talk loud enough and Carolyn refuses the offer. Rawdon reports, "She said she's entitled to half and she wants it. All of it."

On top of the offer, Carolyn could refuse, reality comes crashing down. It's announcing… Carolyn isn't coming home, not today, not tomorrow, not ever. Now, a question stirs my thoughts. How long before she unleashes her law dogs again? This time not calling them off. This time, leaving them until she is satisfied, and I am devoured in court.

My next and perhaps my last move to save the marriage comes in the form of a letter to the elders of Hickory Knoll stating…Surely, you will agree that the clock is ticking down on my marriage. During the past ten months, you've asked me to do two things—set up counseling and offer Carolyn a great deal of money. I did both. Now, I'm asking something of you. Along with your wives, sit down with Carolyn and I, and expound the scriptures regarding marriage, divorce, adultery, lawsuits, and forgiveness. During our separation, this hasn't been done. If the word of God can't convict Christians of wrong doing, then what can?

With me cramped behind the wheel, and with my thoughts of impending Armageddon torturing me, the nine hour drive is nearing an end as the Culleoka, Tennessee town limits sign greets me. Tomorrow, my handsome son Jay will wed pretty Diana. Although Jay can't see it, but in my eyes, he has, with the exception of a less than dream dad, lived a dream life in a dream house with bills paid and a refrigerator filled. The smell of goose liver, now called liver cheese, Jay can't stand or even bring himself to taste, even at my request. And that brings up a question, perhaps born of envy, of my childhood versus his. It asks… Son, want to trade histories, flash back to my time and to my place, stand in that kid's sandals and stare into that empty pantry without even a slice of smelly goose liver to spare? Just the thought of asking that question sickens me, but not to worry, because my shame of that time, of that place, won't allow it. That history, my history isn't for sharing. Not now. Not ever.

The in-laws to be, the Thompsons, I find are very nice, very down to earth people given they own hundreds of acres along Culleoka Highway. Jimmy, a deacon in the church of Christ, and his brother run the family business, a dairy. It's work. It's a handful. It's twice a day milkings, seven days a week. Jay, I can't imagine sitting on a stool and pulling on multi-tits. His just touching a tit would register with me as an achievement.

The old country home belonging to Jimmy's mother and the setting for the wedding I find, is beautiful. It's something out of a magazine. A carpet of grass, rich and green, covers the yard. Around the high porch, flowers in full bloom reach up with their beauty compelling a soul to sigh, even a troubled soul such as mine. And, in the foreground, framing it, two large oak trees stand making it picture perfect.

Tonight in these beautiful surroundings, before God, before family and before friends, handsome Jay and pretty Diana pledge to unite for life, regardless of life's consequences. Amidst all that beauty, I find it most unpleasant sitting there next to my wife in those lovely white chairs pretending that those words, those vows, really meant something. Really dear, then where to hell has our regardless gone?

Early in our separation, Deacon Jim Keaton suggests, "Send her flowers, buy her candy, take her out, court her. If it was my wife, I would." While remaining silent, I thought… If your wife left you Jim, you wouldn't be a deacon full of advice. Without a faithful wife in subjection, you'd be forced to resign. No Jim, ten thousand dollars is enough to cover the cost of hearts and flowers. More than enough.

While driving home, my thoughts turn to Jay and a life just beginning. It's obvious the Thompsons love Jay and love his preaching even more, recognizing a talent far ahead of any schooling. Surely, having Jay for a son-in-law, they must feel blessed.

"Makesense! Your ears up?" "Up Cousin." "This talent, this speaking ability of Jay's, where does it come from?" "Perhaps, talent, when untaught of man, is a gift of God, and when freely shared, is a gift indeed." "Geesums Makesense, where did that poetic ability come from?" "Perhaps Cousin, from the same place as Jay's." "Yep, it's obvious to anyone with ears, that Jay's got the gift."

Back home, an uneasiness heavier than usual, settles on me, knowing that Carolyn and her law dogs are poised to pounce. It's Monday evening, about 7:30, when the door bell rings. It's elder John Rawdon, who'd been scarce lately. "Hello Jack, just thought I'd stop by and spend a little time with you. If it's okay." "Sure John, come on in." As usual, I'm alone. While making our way back to the den, I offer refreshments, but he declines, so we take a seat on opposite ends of the couch. After a little small talk, the conversation turns serious. "Jack, I, we, the other elders and I, have decided to back away from your situation." "What! Back away! What the hell does that mean?" "It means we're going to stay out of it. The trouble between you and Carolyn." "Oooh John! And you're telling Carolyn this too, that you're withdrawing the disfellowship threat?" "Yes, that's right." "Jesus John! How can you do that with souls at stake, mine, Carolyn's?" With his face reddening, he holds his tongue, but I don't. "And what about my letter, my request for a sit-down to discuss the scriptures. What about that?" Shrugging he says, "We just never got around to it." "Oh John! Back away. Wash your hands of us. Oh John! What about Mathew 5:32… But I say unto you that whosoever shall put away his wife saving for the cause of fornication causeth her to commit adultery. Doesn't that scripture worry you? Doesn't it say that sooner or later, Jack or Carolyn or both will turn into adulterers. And, don't adulterers pass go, go straight to and monopolize Hell? Although his face

279

tightens, he remains silent but I don't. "Damn it John! You're turning Carolyn loose. She'll sue. I'll divorce her. All while the eldership sits on its hands, withholding disfellowship, all contrary to the scriptures. Well, I won't. Somebody is getting disfellowshipped! In fact, right now, I disfellowship you, Carolyn and the whole damn church. Now, with his face reddening, past saturation, he stands and says, "I don't have to sit here and listen to this." Starting toward the door and with me trailing, I shout, "Well, you'll have to listen to it some Sunday morning when I go before the whole congregation and announce it and say why." That threat stops John, who turns and says, "Will you give us some warning, about when you plan to do this?" "No, I'll just surprise you. It'll be fascinating. Especially, exposing the big bribe offer to Carolyn to come home. The idea you came up with. What scripture was that John?" With an upset Rawdon slamming the door, it is clear that my worries are no longer his worries. His only worry, now hinges on a big mouth, one capable of disgracing him before the church. And, if and when I deliver on my threat, someone will be disfellowshipped. Officially so! And, that someone will be me.

Five days later, while looking out the front window, I see the mailman approaching, and I open the door. Greeting me he says, "I have a certified letter for you. You need to sign." With my heart racing and my eyes fixing and fixating on the return address, I see it says Leininger, Larzelere and Picou, attorneys at law. After quickly signing the receipt, on wobbly legs, I back up to the living room sofa, collapse there, and continue staring at the envelope. Suspecting, but dreading to confirm its contents, finally I do and I see the heading: Carolyn W. Thornell Vs. Jack R. Thornell. Petition for partition of community property. Quickly, I see that there's no mention of divorce. Paragraph four states: Petitioner and defendant have not reconciled since physically separating and have no intention of doing so at any time in the future. In my head, "At any time in the future," echoes again and again. On page five is a list of assets—CD's, bonds, IRA's, house, cars—with a net worth of $333,503.50. The bottom line: distribution to Carolyn W. Thornell, $166,751.75. Distribution to Jack R. Thornell, $166,751.75. Jesus! I thinking, you're asking for court approval of your addition and your division. But here, on this document, your subtraction stinks. Here you failed. Mother's money, the $22,783.00, rather than subtract it, you added it in, and then, you divided it. Geesums! If Mother had a grave to turn over in, she'd be rotating at record RPMs. Now, my eyes fix on the date the petition was filed. It's September 17. That was Monday. That was the night Rawson showed. "Son-of-a-bitch," I scream out loud, "Rawdon, you snake, you already knew about the lawsuit when you slithered over here with your backing away revelation. And, Carolyn knew, that despite your admonition, that she wouldn't reap any church discipline. Because, you told her. Jesus John! It was you that loosed the law dogs."

While knowing that I had burned my bridge to Rawdon, I write a note, attach it to a copy of the lawsuit, and deliver it to the mail slot at the home of elder Al Laguna. The note is actually a request… Please God, take me home. That would be best. Best for Carolyn. Best for me. She would be free to re-marry and I would be free of this life. Please God! Take me now. Right now.

A few hours later, the phone rings and it's elder Al. "Jaaaack, are you okay?" "No, but I'm still alive. You got the papers?" "Yes, I got 'em. Okay then, I just wanted to check on you. I'll talk to you later." But, later never comes, because that was my last conversation with little elder Al. And later, the intent of his call seems clear, because between the lines of my note he read suicide, he was merely checking to establish my state… dead or still worrisome.

Now, with Mother gone, with Carolyn gone, with the church gone, and now, with the money going, there doesn't seem to be any point to going on. That is, until a meeting with Carolyn and lawdog Wells. Until they get me pissed. "In regard to your mother's money," Wells argues, "You co-mingled it. That's too bad. Now, it's community property." I fire back, "Mr. Wells! You're telling me that if you gave me $10,000 to manage and if I co-mingled it with $10,000 of my money for both of us to gain a higher rate, and then, if Carolyn and I split, you lose your $10,000? Is that right?" Instead of a reply, all I get back is one of those fucking blank stares. "And what about a divorce?" I inquire, "The petition doesn't mention one. Give me a divorce and you'll get your split." "Mr. Thornell, Carolyn doesn't have to divorce you to dissolve community property." "Without a divorce, and without credit for Mother's money, we've got nothing to talk about," I snap back. Without having settled anything, only having my anger stretched to the limit, while walking out, I'm thinking… Greed can backfire and wake up a befuddled person. It did me. Just now. Kill myself and let Carolyn take it all? Not on your fucking blank stare Mr. Wells. That pissed me off, really pissed me off, enough to put my death wish on hold until after the split. Perhaps, I'll kill myself then. That'll cost her. Exactly $166,751.75. Enough to piss her off. Enough to keep her pissed off till her dying day. Okay now! Let me see that fucking blank stare, once more please, for the road.

"Makesense, your ears up?" "Up Cousin." "For the future, it's lucky I realized that anger can be channeled, even be used to form a kind of life preserver." "Lucky indeed. And make that two." "Two what?" "Two life preservers."

Today, after that meeting, I realized that I needed something and needed it bad. For protection, I needed a law dog of my own. Preferably, one that, on command, could bite back and bite hard. And one that specializes in divorce. Over coffee, a friend and a former UPI competitor, hands me a card. On it is the name Sandra S. Salley, Attorney at Law. "Gee Bernie, her address is 5020 Utica Street. That's only two blocks from my house." "That's convenient." "And my wife Laura says that she's good and she's cheap. Look at the back of the card." I do and I see, there, handwritten, $85 per hour.

Attorney Salley is attractive, in her 40's, with dark hair and long, white legs, the kind that attract and hold men's eyes. But sexy legs, even crossed, uncrossed, and re-crossed, even after 18 months of eunuch-hood, aren't crossing my mind. Only legal questions are. After reading the petition, she looks up and I ask, "Can she do that, take the assets, without a divorce?" "She can, and she will, by default if you don't answer this within…" Then hesitating, while checking her calendar, adds, "Within the next seven days." "Mrs. Salley, I've never heard of such a thing." "Well, usually a divorce is in the offering, but not here. It looks as though Mrs. Thornell wants to take the money and keep you as her husband too. So, tell me about your marriage."

About my drinking, about my abuse, both verbal and physical, about my perfectionism, and my demand for it, and finally, about my baptism, I told of, and observed, "Carolyn's got enough history to crucify me before any judge anywhere." "Mr. Thornell, how long since you hit your wife, slapped her, or touched her, or anything like that?" "Gee, let me think. Fifteen years, maybe longer. I quit the bars. After work, I started hitting baseballs in the park to my son Jay." Seeing the tears accompanying my story, she says, "Mr. Thornell, Mr. Thornell, don't dwell on the past. Don't worry about it." "Why not," I ask. "Because, she can't use it against you." "You mean that she can't beat me up with it in court?" "No, she can't. Every marriage has ups and downs, even ugly ones. The court won't sit still and listen to it. If you stayed together, the past is considered forgiven." "Jesus! Did you say forgiven? You mean, the court, without even being asked, forgives me my sins. Forgives what my Christian wife won't, even I won't?" "That's right, the judge is only interested in current events. That's all. Now, tell me about your wife. Why she left." "For the pursuit of happiness, she implied." "Explain that, what did she say... exactly?" "She said, 'I'm not happy and I'm leaving.'" "That's it, no fussing, no fighting, preceded the event?" "No, nothing. But after she left, every time we talked, the conversation never touched on her state of happiness." "What did it touch on?" "The money, always the money. She wanted her split. Even the church elders investigated her motive." "And, what did they come up with, the root of it?" "They concluded too, it's all about the green stuff... the money."

For the next hour, Ms. Salley sits patiently, listening and hearing about my disability, my being Mr. Mom, my being a saver and her a spender, her taking the $10,000 and her larger paycheck and leaving all the bills behind. After learning of the elders solution—bribe her—she laughs heartily and says, "Well Mr. Thornell, how do you want to answer the petition?" "Answer! I don't want to answer, I want to attack. Hell, sue her for desertion, for alimony and most importantly, for a divorce. And, if I could, I'd throw the book at her too." "What book?" "The one she totes to church twice on Sunday and once on Wednesday... her Bible." "Okay, but seeing your assets, alimony is unlikely. For that requires both fault and need. You've got fault, but need is questionable. But, we'll ask. It's a good bargaining chip." "Okay, is that it then?" "Yes, just stop by tomorrow, and sign the documents."

"Makesense, are your ears up?" "Up Cousin." "Is this revelation a miracle or what?" "What revelation Cousin?" "That a civil court can grant what a Christian wife won't." "And, what is that?" "Forgiveness Makesense... Forgiveness for my badass years."

The next day, after signing the petition, Ms. Salley suggests, "Mr. Thornell, we can send this by certified mail and save the $35 service fee." "No! I want her served. I want the deputy to push the papers in her face, just like she did me the first time." "Okay." "Oh, and one more thing." "What?" "Don't talk, don't negotiate anything until they let go of my mother's money. Until then, tell 'em, there's nothing to talk about."

Later in the week, Candy stops in, and while walking back to the den and nearing the dining room table, her eyes find the divorce papers laying there. "Can I see these?" she asks. "I guess you have the right. So, sure," I answer without thinking. Seconds into the reading, she stops, and starts crying. Then, comes a muffled, "Oh Daddy... no." "Candy, what is it? What's wrong?" With me at her side, she points to article II. Petitioner and defendant were married on the 12th day of June 1965. My eyes froze there. That June date, that uncelebrated date jumps up and hits me. Now, I know what Candy knows. What she calculated. June till December, her birth date, is just six months. She knows she was conceived out of wedlock. "Oh Candy, I'm sorry you found out. I, we, never intended for you to know. Believe me, if that date had registered, I wouldn't have let you read those papers." "Daddy, now I understand." "Understand what?" "Why you and Mom never celebrated your wedding anniversary. It was because of me." "This is a shock, I know, but keep in mind, your mother and I dated for two years. That's a long time." "I know, but now a lot of things are beginning to make sense." Before I can ask, "What things?" Candy, with her tears still streaming, says, "Daddy! I gotta go." "Okay, but will you promise me something?" "What?" "Will you keep this our secret, at least, for now. Your mother will think that I did this on purpose. To hurt, to disparage her in your eyes. I've done some rotten things. Some that really stink. But this, on purpose, I did not do." While following Candy to the door, I'm hoping and listening to hear a promise, but one isn't heard. Silently, Candy gets in her car and drives away until disappearing in the darkness about her. Did Candy discuss her news with Carolyn? She never said, and I never asked.

These days, having divorced myself from the Hickory Knoll congregation, I find myself alone, except for my thoughts of a quick escape, but standing in the way, keeping me here, isolated, is my promise to myself to piss Carolyn off, and piss her off at a premium, before I go with a bang. With a splash. Or, with a thud. With the shamebirds desiring the latter and my splatter. Then, my get-a-way thoughts are interrupted by the sound of the phone. "Hello Dad, how are you?" Jay asked. "Kinda lonesome Son. And, I haven't seen Candy for a while." "You don't know why?" "Should I?" "It's because she's busy planning her wedding." "Seriously?" "It's serious alright. Big time serious, with a church, a band, a white wedding gown, the works." "Just like the first time?" "Yep." "Jesus! I warned the elders that at Candy's age, it would come to this." "To what Dad?" "To re-marriage, to adultery." "Well, Candy invited Diana and me, but I declined." "You think she has the stomach to invite me?" "I doubt it Dad." Jay is right, the invitation never comes. And it was a wise decision. Because, how in God's name could I sit there, hold my peace, and celebrate the act of adultery with champagne.

Today, I'm meeting with Attorney Salley and delivering the paper trail of Mother's money, following it from the First National Bank of Vicksburg to Pelican Homestead in Metairie where it is co-mingled with my money. "Jack, I'm impressed, if we go to court, these records will help." "Have you heard from the other side yet?" "Yes. Wells called, wanted to schedule a sit-down to work out a settlement." "And how did you reply?" "Well, when I asked about your Mother's money, about the status of it, he went silent." "What then?" "So I said, then, there's nothing more to talk about and I hung up the phone as you instructed."

After several more attempts by lawdog Wells for a sit-down, after Salley's steady refusals and with the court date looming in just four days, my phone rings. It's Salley. "Mr. Thornell, Mr. Wells just called and he is anxious, most anxious for a get together." "What about Mother's money?" "They calculate it at $22,000." "That's close enough. I'll take it."

With the issue of Mother's money resolved, we sit down in the plush conference room of Leninger, Larzelere and Picou where the sawing starts. Carolyn, you take the $60,000 CD. Jack, you take the $80,000. Carolyn, you take your IRA. Jack, you, yours. Carolyn, you take the LTD. Jack, the thunderbird. And, in my ears, those buzzing sounds continue, Carolyn you, Jack you, until everything is sawed in half. Except for the house. And that, instead of alimony, I can live in for the next five years as long as I pay the note. By then, the house is to be sold, and the money split. After considering the house proposal and the sixty months before my removal, I agree, while thinking… By then, hell, what by then? The chances of a "by then" ever arriving would amount to a miracle. Before then, either by God's hand or with Garnett's courage, I shall be removed.

Carolyn, wearing gray, arrives in the lobby of the Joseph Yenni Building, sees Salley in a sexy white suit, and me in my dark blue Sears and Roebuck, approaches us and asks, "Have you seen my attorney yet?" "No, we haven't," Salley replies, adding, "And it's almost court time. We'd better get upstairs. We're first on the docket." On the elevator, thinking ahead, I ask, "If Wells doesn't show, do we go ahead without him?" Carolyn asks, "Can we?" And Salley answers, "We can. Everything is settled and signed. It's just a formality." And leaving me to think, she means finality… just a finality."

With the judge taking his seat, and then, with the clerk sounding, "Jack R. Thornell versus Carolyn W. Thornell," A flustered and sheepish Wells arrives and squeezes in on the bench beside us. After moving forward, Salley introduces herself and calls me to the stand. After I'm sworn in, the judge interrupts and asks, if Carolyn is represented by counsel. Wells, still sitting in the audience, pops up and answers, "Yes your honor, I'm here." "Well, come on down and introduce yourself." Wells obeys and the questioning begins. At first, just routine stuff. The length of the marriage. The number of children. And then, she zeroes in on the assets and the agreed split thereof. After less than five minutes, I step down, Carolyn steps up and Salley asks, "Mrs. Thornell, did you hear the questions I asked?" "Yes." "And, the answers Mr. Thornell gave?" "Yes." "To these same questions would your answers be the same?" "Yes, they would." "Your honor, I'm finished." "Mr. Wells, have you anything to add?" The judge inquires. "No your honor." "Then, the divorce is granted."

With the rap of the gavel, a 25-year marriage ends and Carolyn's dream of getting her hands on the untouchable—the money—is only four miles away. We meet at the Whitney National Bank, empty the safe deposit box and take the contents to the house just a few blocks away. At the kitchen table we sit, shoulder to shoulder, where I remove the wide rubber band securing the stack of U.S. Savings Bonds, now the thickness of a deck of cards, and where I begin dealing and saying, "One for you, one for me."

With the dealing done, and with that pile in front of her, I'm thinking… There goes $44,000. The discipline of twenty years of payroll deductions, my payroll, my deductions. How many of those babies came out of your pay? And, the answer dear, is not a fucking one. But dear, with your mouth watering, you must be thinking… this is payday. A day she deserves. A day I deserve. Her back pay. My payback for those years of abuse. This is justice owed. And besides, it's legal and there ain't a fucking thing you can do about it dear.

Today, Carolyn got her money. In dollars. In pounds. One hundred and twenty thousand of dollars. And, twenty five pounds of flesh. My flesh. From my face. From my frame. Leaving me taut and gaunt and looking like brother Garnett must have looked, when he looked into Mother's mirror that one last time. But, if Carolyn knew what she didn't, just how close she came to raking in the whole pot, she might, somehow, feel cheated. All, but for that fucking blank stare, would have been her's.

With her split stuffed into a large shopping bag and with her mind, undoubtedly set on the search for happiness, Carolyn is off, with my thoughts in pursuit. If Carolyn realized the cost, really grasped it, and knew how close the split came to pushing me over the edge, would she, could she, have pursued it, particularly with my life looking to be hanging but by a thread? Then again, she might have rationalized… what life dear? You haven't got a life. And with my security blanket—the money—half gone, and while feeling the return trip to Vicksburg being shortened by a 100 miles, and the poverty found down at 503 creeping closer and closer, Carolyn would be right. I don't have a life. I only have the past, with it's constant gnawing towards the present. To find me. And, to take me home. Back to the shamehold.

Besides leaving me for the poorer, Carolyn leaves me in a state of urgency. Underneath my ill-fitting clothes, two urges, one high and one low, engage. One cries… Go! Get laid to rest. The other… Go! Get laid. But today, the "other" need is being re-enforced, and growing. Understandably so, because it's going on two long years since Carolyn and I connected. And so, for the moment, I choose, "Go! Get laid." That choice takes me to the St. Clement of Rome's singles dances, where I hear the women are plentiful… and plenty needy.

There, I see her. Her red hair flowing. Her body, erect. Her face, wholesome, and flourishing with a proud look. And seeming more than comfortable in her shoes. She isn't slim. She isn't fat. Hearty and strong is my conclusion. Easily, a good decade younger than me. Women in their forties, having suffered through a divorce, I hear, are ready to be appreciated again. And appreciate, I'm ready, willing, and able to do. Yes, she's the one, I thought, but already, there's a problem. No, make that two. First, I can't approach her and ask her to dance. And, why not? Because, I can't dance. Not a step's worth. And second, if I just engage her in small talk, what will the second question out of her mouth be? After, "How do you do?" Of course, it will be, "What do you do?" And, I'm not ready to be humiliated by that question. Not from her. Not from my urge's choice. Not with the shame assuring me that the answer, "Retired on disability" would garner the response—if not said, but thought—"Get lost" or worse, "Drop dead". Consequently, I choose to wait and to watch as she dances the night away, never rejecting a single invitation. That night, thinking of her, of pressing her body against mine, garners a more than pleasant response. One that I handle.

Several Saturdays later, back at the St. Clement dance, my eyes search the large ball room until finding her, "the choice". Suddenly unquestioned, my desire overcomes my fear of humiliation, and I approach her. "Hello, my name is Jack." "Hello, I'm Linda, how do you do?" "Oh, fine, except for…" "For what?" "Well, I'd like to ask you to dance, but…" "But what?" "I can't dance. I don't know how." "Oh, don't worry about that," she says while smiling and pulling me onto the dance floor, before adding, "Most of the guys out here can't dance either. Only they don't know it." While hearing a song for slow dancing, I say a little prayer of thanks, as I shuffle my feet ever so slightly, while rotating in a small circle and while pulling her close and holding her hard against me. "Now, just pick up the beat and move your feet accordingly," she encourages, while not choosing to back away from the firm erection pressing against her. After one dance, it's clear that Linda isn't the backing away kind of girl, and hopefully is, the looking to be appreciated kind. And, to the redhead, hopefully it's clear, perhaps even fulfilling, is the realization that… impotent, I'm not.

The fact that I am on disability doesn't seem to faze her. As proof, the next night she's having dinner with me at Impastato's, an upscale Italian restaurant. As we're pushing our plates away, I ask, "Would you like to stop by my house for a drink?" "Yes, yes I would," she responds with an overly generous smile.

Once inside, after admiring my plaques and particularly, my Pulitzer, covering the wall behind the bar, she moves close and then closer until our bodies, and then, our mouths come together. Her lips are full, soft and delicious. And apparently, she finds mine tasteful as her words indicate. "Oh Jack! You're a good kisser… kiss me again." Naturally, again and again I oblige, while pressing my constant erection harder and harder against her. "Oh Linda, I want to make love to you. Here. Now." "You do?" "Oh yes, and please don't say no. It's been two long years since I touched a woman." "Who's saying no?" With enough said, without wasting time to move to the bedroom, we collapse to and come together on the braided rug covering the den floor. And make love. And make love. And make love. And, all the while, I feel as though I'm experiencing a miracle… longevity. Mine. And, allowing Linda time for multiple orgasms, before allowing myself one. "that was, was, was wonderful, all three," a sighing Linda responds. Pleased that she is pleased, I inquire, "How long has it been, you know, since you had sex?" "Not since the day I kicked my husband out." "Come again?" "Well, right after we had sex that morning, I told him it was time to go. To move out." "What! Isn't that a bit unusual? In my case, the sex stopped six months before the move out." "Unusual, maybe. But not knowing how long before another opportunity might arise, I had it. Kinda a going away present. For him, and for me." "After sex, you kicked him out of bed, out of the house, the works?" "Yes, that's right." "Oh Linda, I'm so glad." "Glad of what?" "Glad that you like sex. Like it so much. Knowing that when and if you give me the boot, at least, I'll leave satisfied, and wearing a smile." My laughter, joining with hers, is soon interrupted by pain. Looking down, I find the source. Both knees, they're bloody. Victims of rug burn.

The next day, after joining the boys—all senior citizens—for coffee at the Tastee's Doughnuts shop, the tell-tale scars forming on my knees, come up for review. "Man! Who is she?" Kober asks, while grinning and pointing to my exposed knees. "You must have given her quite a ride." "Oh Kober, what are you talking about?" I said, while trying to cover up the origin of my wounds. "Rug burns, I'm talking about rug burns, from fucking. Son, you should have taken her to bed then, or worn long pants now, to avoid that, to cover up that." Now, the boys, share Kober's discovery and with it, his delight. Now, everybody in the small coffee shop knows that I got laid last night. Although I don't admit it, and despite the pain, I'm proud to bear those scars and to keep 'em bleeding in the nights ahead.

With the bleeding continuing for the longevity, I feel a new miracle in the works, and if not a miracle, at the very least, a record. Because, sex with anyone, even with a wife of 25 years, never, never, never, happened, not for 17 consecutive nights. And, it's more than obvious, Linda loves sex. With each climax, I could feel the heat emitting from her body, like a steam iron sizzling. And it's obvious, what's said about redheads is true. Because Linda, in bed, or on the rug, is hot! Hot! Hot! Now, instead of night 18, Linda's scheduled trip to St. Louis breaks the chain, and, not a lessening of desire, her's or mine. Hopefully now though, my knees can begin to heal.

Several weeks later, once in bed, and after a round of passionate kissing, Linda slips her head under the covers, moves down until finding her goal, upright and throbbing with anticipation. With her next moves, it comes… The score. And, surprisingly, passionate Linda has rewarded me with "a wally". "Oh Linda, that, that was special." "Oh Jack, my desire is to please you, as you please me, with your lips and with your tongue. That too is special." And, before I can contain myself, out pops the same stupid question, that popped out all those years ago with Wally, "That, that maneuver, where did you learn it?" "I didn't. I didn't learn it." "Huh, what do you mean?" "I mean that this is the first time I ever did that." "Not even with your husband?" "No. Not with him or anyone before him. Not ever." "Well Linda, I feel honored." "I'm pleased you liked it." "Actually, I loved it. So, feel free to honor me again and again, anytime you so desire."

Laying there quietly, but thinking it interesting to note... how taste evolves over time. The first "wally" comes with hard admonition. The last, with high praise. But, more than "a wally", I needed to be needed again, to be desired again, by Linda, or by any attractive woman, because since Carolyn disposed of me, I felt like garbage. Unworthy to be picked up at the curb. Unworthy to be properly disposed of. Unworthy, even to be recycled. Now, I find this sexy, attractive redhead to be delivering a two-fer, stirring not only my passion, but raising my self-esteem, and confirming that old saying... Somebody's garbage is somebody else's treasure. And how, O how, I needed to be treasured again, if only for a night or two... or for a record seventeen.

Under that red head of hair, I discover a brain, one operating a busy C.P.A. (Certified Public Account) office out of her rather large home that she shares with a daughter and two sons, all students at the University of New Orleans. And this brain I like, actually love, for not disparaging me for not having a job or any intention of finding one, even though it directed the exiting of her longtime husband, an electrician, for the lack of steady employment.

During our first year together, while enjoying dine outs, the movies, playing pool in her large den, and engaging in sex, scheduled and unscheduled, the only thing causing us to cross words, is that old ghost from the past. The one that hounded and haunted Carolyn and Kay. The green-eyed one called jealousy. Mine. Surprisingly, despite my age, still as vigorous and vigilant as ever. Particularly at St. Clement dances, where she still refuses to turn anyone away empty handed. And, in particular, the hands of a handsome Hispanic named Carlos, a member of Linda's support group for spouses, family and friends of alcoholics, who are always present at the dances in large numbers. And, amid that group, there is a lot of hugging going on. And, in my view, an excessive amount. Even a female friend noted, "Jack, isn't that your Linda hugging that man over there?" "Oh, that's nothing to worry about, just a friend," I lie, while catching glimpses of him looking at Linda the way I looked at Linda the first time, with eyes full of hunger for more then a look or a hug. So naturally, I can't stand him touching her or drawing her close on the dance floor, and leaving me to wonder... is there something else coming up between them, like it was for me during our first embrace. So, after they disengage, I watch for tell-tale signs. And, what do I see? The immediate planting of his hands in his pockets as though he's hiding something, just like I hid that "something else" after our first dance. So, I conclude... there's no doubt about it, handsome Carlos has a hard on for Linda, my Linda. Just like sports editor Baker had for my Kay.

Over the next year, over Carlos and his closeness, we argue. "Just dance with me. Refuse his request. And for damn sure, tell him to quit stopping by your office-home for chit-chat, I'm tired of seeing him standing there with his fucking hands in his pockets." But, Linda won't yield. "Sorry, but I'm not giving up my friends for anyone, not even you." So finally, I give up the war. To Linda's superior will, I surrender. Accepting the conclusion that Carlos is not going anywhere and neither am I. So, I inaugurate the test, actually more of a challenge, to never argue over Carlos again. Or even mention his name. And, after each day of success, I make a check mark in a square on a calendar, until the check marks extend for a year. On that anniversary, with Linda lying close, I say, "Do you realize something?" "No. What?" "That we haven't argued over anything for a whole year... not even over him." "That long, I didn't realize," she declares before continuing, "But, what him? Whoever could you mean?" Without answering, without mentioning his name again, I only allow my manufactured laughter to join hers. Then, while slipping her head under the covers, she whispers, "Now, let Mama reward you for being a good boy, a very good boy. Oh! For so long." While feeling honored, so honored, my thoughts explode with appreciation… Thank God! Thank God for Wallys.

Soon after our two year anniversary, just like the typing lesson spells out—now is the time for all good things to come to an end—our relationship, our good thing does. Is it over another man? Is it over another woman? No, neither. Then, who? What? God! It is God that comes between us. More specifically, it's God's words labeling me "fornicator" and "adulterer" just like it does my daughter Candy. After I condemned a daughter by using those very same ugly words, my guilt is causing me to coin a new phrase… Like daughter, like father.

Despite being a Catholic and a regular at Sunday mass, Linda is not well versed on scripture, and specifically the ones condemning us and our relationship. And, she doesn't care to be. Because, if something feels right and good to Linda, her judgment is… it is right and good. In short, Linda's rules trump God's rules. And, if confronted, she doesn't deny it, and adds, "God gave me a brain didn't he? To use. To make decisions." And, make 'em she does. And despite this conflict of rules, does she continue receiving holy communion? Only every Sunday. And, on Holy days, at weddings, even at funerals.

With me though, it's another story, knowing that the Good Book forbids the taking of The Host until one sets his house in order. Thus, it has been over two years since I received communion. Doing so, I felt, would be like slapping God in the face. And that, I'm not willing to do. Not to a God I'm most anxious to meet.

So, I ask Linda to sit down with me and to explore my current feelings. "Linda, I think, now I know, that what we're doing is wrong. And, it's troubling me more and more." "And now, you're troubling me." "How so?" "Well personally, I'm fine with our relationship but…" "But what?" "But, I can't keep enjoying sex with you if all you feel is guilt." "No, I guess not. Cause that wouldn't be the Linda I know and love." "Well then, this is the end, the end of us." "Apparently so. But, is there any reason we can't remain friends?" "No, no reason." "Friends then." "Friends." Thus, on a friendly note, my nights with Linda end, with guilt and God winning the day. With a new chapter beginning, I hear an old and redundant life lesson playing on and on in my head, and reminding me that… life isn't a bowl of cherries, nor is life a box of chocolates. No! Life is ajar with jawbreakers. And now this—giving up the pleasure—is going to be hard to swallow. Very hard.

While attempting to fill the void left by the absence of Linda, I become a Monday night regular at St. Clement's Bible Study. There, I feel like a Bible scholar, and that's because most Catholics, like Linda, have never read the Good Book. Most rely on their priests for guidance. Some attending are interested in study, while others, particularly the ladies, are interested in hooking up with a Godly man to marry. But, that won't, can't be me. Because, I'm not free to marry again until after Carolyn gives up the ghost. And, that's because, Carolyn's explanation, "I'm not happy" is not justification for divorce. Not in God's eyes. Only adultery is. And even then, only the innocent party is free to tie the knot again. So, to borrow a Catholic term, Carolyn and I are stuck in a state of "limbo", a prolonged uncertainty for the rest of our lives. But, being stuck there, I feel, is better than being stuck here in a state of sin, while I'm still in bed with glorious Linda. With any attempt at repentance futile. Nothing more than wasted lip service. Such as… Please God! Forgive me for doing Linda while I'm still doing Linda. That too, is slapping God in the face. Even uneducated Momma knew that. Even her prayer, often bursting outloud, confirmed that. Clearly it said… Please God! Let me outlive my bastard husband, so I can repent of my adultery, and go to heaven. When it comes to getting to Heaven, Momma weren't no fool. Since she had so little peace in this life, she was praying for a little piece of it in the next. Even Momma knew… you can't fool your way into heaven. And, I knew it too. Her, from the ravings of her daddy—the deacon—and me, from diligent study of the Bible, the book that preachers and priests hold high on Sundays proclaiming it as "The word of the Lord".

The singles ministry at St. Clement is designed to busy the body and the mind. And by utilizing a kind of misdirection strategy, fills your nights with dances, dineouts, games, movies and Bible classes. So, if you're in the middle of a nasty divorce, or if you just lost a loved one, there's precious little time to dwell on it. For that, there's one night a week set aside for share and support.

At Bible class, I meet and make new friends. Like Wilma, George, Johnny, J.W., Leo, Patsy and Patricia. Immediately, Johnny and I bond. He'd worked as a sound man at WDSU-TV before going into the rental business, so we share mutual friends. Soon, he is a regular at the afternoon coffee sessions with Kober and the boys. And soon, he is my best friend, until the night he doesn't show up for Bible class where he usually is a steadfast regular. After closing prayer and after failing to connect with him by telephone, I rush over to his home. Once there, I find yesterday's paper, still in the yard, still uncollected. After my bangings on the front door go unanswered, I rush to the back, peer through the glass and see the television is playing in his den. I can see his recliner, but, it's black, and with only the glow of the television, I can't tell if there is anybody in it. To my hammerings on the door, and to my shoutings, there's no response. After finding his car still in the garage, I call his daughter, with whom I was well acquainted. "Hello Angella, this is Jack, Jack Thornell." "Oh, hello Mr. Jack, what can I do for you?" "Well, I'm worried about your dad. I'm at his house, his car is here, but, there's no answer at the door. Did he go anywhere?" "No, not that I know." Hearing the concern in her voice, I ask, "What should I do?" "Can you wait there? I'm on my way over." "Sure, Angella, sure." After rushing over, she unlocks the door, and we find that the recliner isn't empty. There's Johnny. Fully reclined. Ankles crossed with his feet comfortably in place on the foot rest, his head, comfortably lying back on the head rest. His eyes, closed. His mouth, closed. His face, showing no signs of discomfort or distress, or, of offering even the slightest resistance to death. As if, choosing to nod off, and to sleep on… willingly… oh, so willingly.

Later that evening, I summon Makesense, and say, "Know what we witnessed tonight?" "Tell me Cousin." "The good death. One you don't see coming, or even know when it arrived." "Like Johnny's?" "Yes, Makesense, just like Johnny's." After seeing the apparent ease with which my friend left this life, if I had any departing words, they would be these… Way to go Johnny, way to go.

On Wednesday night, I attend a second Bible class, this one conducted by Ron Ritter. Although, he is not Catholic, he is president of the St. Clement singles. And, he persists in calling on me to lead prayer, and I persistently refuse. At Hickory Knoll, I read the scriptures aloud during worship services, but only after practice reading the verses multiple times. Because, one never knows when one might stumble into a word like sepulcher (tomb). And slaughter it's pronunciation. His calling and my declining goes on for weeks, until finally, I acquiesce. The prayer is short, and to my ears, awful. Thank God, I thought, this will be the end of that, my public praying. And, it was, until the next Wednesday night, when Ron called my name again. "Jack, will you please lead us in prayer?"

Months later J.W., a regular at Ritters class, approaches me with an idea, his big idea. "Jack, I want to start off the Saturday night dances with a prayer." "You do?" "Yep. And, I want you to lead it." "What! Are you kidding? Most people there aren't in the mood for prayer. They're in the mood to get laid. Prayer would be a turnoff." "I don't care." "And, what about those of the Jewish persuasion, want to offend them with… In Jesus name we pray." With his face reddening, and with his voice raising, he responds, "Jack! I ain't worried about offending anyone, except Jesus Christ. So, will you do it?" "Okay! Okay! I'll have a go at it, but…" "But what?" "Well, it won't be spontaneous, I'll write it beforehand." "Fine, fine, any way you want."

"Makesense! Your ears up?" "Up Cousin." "Then, give a listen to my prayer for Saturday night… Almighty God! Dear Father. We humble our heads and our hearts tonight giving thanks that you are our God. Giving thanks that you are a forgiving God. And, asking that you help us to forgive as you forgive, unconditionally. While reminding us, that forgiveness is at the heart of your nature, that forgiveness is at the heart of our sanctification, and while reminding us that when we forgive, we let go, and when we let go, we not only free another, but we free ourselves. And now Father, after acknowledging our responsibility, let your peace find and fill us, and then… let our spirits dance. In Jesus name we pray. Amen… Well Makesense?" "They prayer's fine, mighty fine. That's not the problem." "Problem! What problem?" "Getting 400 people to shut up long enough for anyone to hear it."

Makesense has a point. The crowd won't shut up for the president's opening remarks, leaving them for the most part, to go unheard. So, why will they shut up for me?

After Saturday night comes, and after J.W.'s welcoming remarks, he announces the prayer, introduces me, and asks the crowd to quiet down. They don't. Most never even hear his request. Again, J.W. asks. Again, they don't. Finally, with the loud chattering continuing, J.W. ends his appealing, hands me the microphone after saying, "Here's Jack." And then, I beign. "Almighty God!" But the noise sounds on. I stop, and begin again, but louder. "Almighty God!" But the noise sounds on. I stop and I begin again, even louder. "Almighty God!" Still, the noise sounds on. Until finally, I summon Mother's voice, her powerful weapon, the one you couldn't turn off or tune out, even with the covering of ears. And, with that final "Almighty God" blasting, bouncing off the walls, and reverberating throughout the giant hall, the sounds of silence prevail, and, I prayed on.

In the weeks and months ahead, I become known as the "prayer man". Not exactly the moniker you want to wear at the dances, not if you're looking to undress one of those lovely ladies later. But then again, I'm not looking to score. Not now. Not when I'm finally back on the straight and narrow, and denying myself the pleasure. And perhaps, that "prayer man" moniker might serve as a buffer, with the ladies backing away if I weaken, rise to the occasion, and begin pulling them too close on the dance floor, like I did with Linda.

Unfortunately though, I find that the ladies aren't backing away, and I find that my urge is growing, along with my dilemma. Without a woman, all I got is God. And on Saturday nights, I find, God is not enough. Not with the scent of a woman filling my nostrils, not with her body pressing against mine, and mine aching for more… More than God allows.

After going six months without the pleasure. And with God's choice for me—celibacy—gradually sliding back into second place, I narrow my choice between Delphine and Wilma. Delphine is choice one. She's tall, thin, stands on glorious looking legs, and her skin is like silk to the touch. And she is even younger than Linda, perhaps, in her late thirties. But, she has two drawbacks, no, three. Two school age kids, and she lives in Slidell, a good hour drive from Metairie.

After a few dates of going out to eat and having to feed four, and after the kids are sent to bed, I discover Delphine's major drawback. She's not interested in a serious relationship. And, by serious, she means sexual. So, my needs dictate that I withdraw my attentions from Delphine and direct them towards choice number two.

Wilma is sweet, caring, raising three children without a husband, who directed his attention towards his secretary before divorcing Wilma and marrying his "girl Friday". She is short, a bit overweight, but not enough to discourage me or my desire. A regular at both my weekly Bible classes, she's educated, and teaches the fifth grade at a Catholic school.

After having dinner out on our first date, we end up in the den at my place. She's sitting on a foot stool. I'm standing nearby. She urges me to move closer. I do. Now, towering over her, she commands, "Now close your eyes." And I do. Then, I feel a tug on my zipper. I feel her reaching in. Drawing me in. And, with her full, soft and velvet-like lips, pleasuring me, until I come to Wallydom. Immediately I discover, that this sweet, caring, mother of three, who appears shy, hardly opening her mouth during Bible classes, is full of surprises. Wonderful, wonderful surprises.

During the days ahead, Wilma surprises me with many trips to Wallydom, until I decide to surprise her. And pleasure her the way she pleasures me. And although, it's not one of my favorite things to do, I face up to the task, and after I do, and after my head rejoins her's on the pillow, she softly asks, "What was that for?" "Oh that… that was your reward." "Reward for what?" "For being a good girl, a very good girl, again and again."

In the months ahead, we busy ourselves with the usual, movies, dineouts, Bible classes, dances, and now, with school functions. But Friday nights, we reserve for our together time. A time Wilma described as "my favorite part of the week". When we unite solely and purposely to pleasure ourselves, and each other. It is there in the dark, lying next to caring Wilma, we me fully relieved and relaxed, and still quite naked, I surprise myself by exposing more. Those parts, always kept hidden. Of my youth. Of my poverty. Of my parents. Of my shame. Parts never revealed to another living soul, not even to a wife I bedded for near twenty-five years. And caring Wilma, with her head lying on my shoulder, listens, just listens. Never pressing for more than I am willing to reveal. Never revealing her thoughts, or her feelings. The only inkling comes in the form of tears. Hers. The ones I feel dropping onto my chest. The other inkling comes a few weeks later.

Christmas Eve 1993, I leave the house, pick up Wilma, and we attend the early mass at St. Clement of Rome. Afterwards, we return to my house to exchange gifts. After entering the den through the back door, I note something odd. A wad of paper ahead, lying on the living room floor. "Huh," I thought, before saying, "Wilma, wait here, while I check out the house." After reaching Jay's room, I find nothing askew. The same in Candy's. Then, I enter my bedroom. There, I see the top two drawers of the dresser are opened. I look in and everything appears to be in place. Even a sixteen ounce cup of change, full of nickels, dimes and quarters remains. Nothing's missing, I thought, as I turned away to leave the room and to rejoin Wilma in the den. Then I stopped, deciding to check one more thing. Quickly, I bend and pull back the cloth covering the nightstand next to the bed, where my eyes find and fixate on the lower shelf. It's empty, I see, it's gone, my gun, my Beretta, it's gone.

While returning to the den, by way of the kitchen, I see the small window over the sink is broken. "The thief must have been some kind of skinny to squeeze through there," I observe, and report to Wilma who moves to my side. "Awfully skinny," she says before asking, "Was anything taken?" "Only my gun… my Beretta."

Later that night, lying quiet in bed after having appreciated each other, the other inkling surfaces. The one concerning her thoughts. "Jack, I'm glad, so glad." "Glad about what?" "Glad your gun was stolen." "Oh, and why?" "I just am… that's all… I just am." As Wilma hadn't pressed me for more details the night I brought those snippets of my shame to life, I didn't press her for more now. Perhaps, when looking deep into my eyes, she sees or senses the same darkness I discovered in Elvis that day deep in those German woods. A darkness, even our successes in life, couldn't lighten. So press, I don't, because I didn't want to possibly hear the words… Jack dear, I fear you are near, so near to, beginning silence with a bang, just like your poor brother did.

Later, after taking Wilma home, I summon and quiz Makesense. "Think Wilma senses something, something worrisome in me?" "Well Cousin, she's a caring soul, both sensitive and sensible, so, how could she not? Especially, with your constant state of depression covering you like a cloud, and more often than not, still showing through." "Well, one thing is clear." "And, what is that?" "I've been robbed of an option, haven't I?" When Makesense doesn't respond, I do, "Makesense! Makesense! Are you there, hearing me?" "Yes Cousin, loud and clear. In fact, too loudly, and too clearly."

These days I begin at 7 a.m. at Lafreniere Park where I meet up with new friends, and new friends, because after my separation, all my old friends took flight. Such as Fern and Kenneth, who like Betty and Sam, were close for 25 years. After Fern stopped by, and found out that Carolyn had flown the coop, she and Kenneth flew my coop too. Never to be seen or heard from again, at least, not by me. Perhaps they thought that what Carolyn and I caught was contagious, like the salmonella carried by our feathered friends. So, when I needed support the most, those closest married couples weren't going, going, gone as would be expected over time, they were gone, gone, gone, as soon as they heard the word separation drop.

So today, I join new friends Leo, Anna, Judy, Patricia, Cheryl and Dick, to navigate the two-mile walking track before we head off for our morning coffee together. Also accompanying me is my depression and today, it's carrying heavier than usual, so I'm not talking, only listening to talk, talk, talk. Cross talk, colliding talk, and constant talk, with everyone needing to be heard, and to be heard at once without order, and translating into noise, annoying noise, and useless noise, except for collectively managing to raise my level of depression.

Geesums Makesense! If they could only hear what I'm thinking… How I don't want to be here, hearing their endless trivial dribble containing even the minutest detail of their little daily lives. Details, when collected, piled together, and exchanged for manure wouldn't be of quality or quantity enough, when applied, to encourage a single stalk of corn from the ground. And thinking… How I'd rather be lying back down, face up, on the bottom of the adjacent canal, and be able to drown out the sounds of their useless dribble, and only be able to hear the faint swishes of the fishes, or see the occasional duck bottom, passing over me. Oh Makesense! How many times have I thought of laying my thoughts to rest, and with them, my shame. And if Makesense's ears were up, the answer would most certainly be… too many cousin. Too many.

Saturday morning, with the walkers narrowed down to just Patricia and me, I see him coming, head-on and towards me. "Oh my God!" I exclaim. "What is it?" Patricia asks. "It's him." "Him who?" "It's John Rawdon, the elder from church. The one I chastised for just talking the talk, but not walking the walk, when it comes to divorce." "Well honey, he's walking the walk now. What you gonna do?" "Just face him, just like I did the night I accused him of hypocrisy."

In passing, Rawdon doesn't utter a word. Not a good morning. Not a hello. Not even a hi. His only acknowledgement comes in the form of a weak wave, managing to lift his hand only about waist high. And, probably praying that our encounter won't trigger my old threat to expose his hypocrisy up at the microphone, where he is always preaching purity. Always demanding that the church must be kept pure and apart from the world where divorce is rampant and going unchecked. Pure bologna, I thought, but is my bologna any better? Don't I wear the title "prayer man", and begin the dances by praising God before hundreds. And then afterwards, don't I retire to satisfy a greater desire—my lust—with a woman that according to God, I'm not entitled to. "Yep Makesense! Both the elder and the prayer man are guilty. Guilty as charged. Hypocrisy in the first degree." And, I found no reason to poll Makesense, because in my heart of hearts, I knew the verdict to be… unanimous.

In the days and the nights ahead, is it guilt, is it God, or, is it too much of a good thing that comes between Wilma, me, and the pleasure. No, it's none of those. It's the splendidly skinned Delphine, the one whose body is often seen in my mind while I'm making love with Wilma. The "come between" begins innocently enough, with a phone call. "Hello Jack, this is Delphine, how are you?" "I'm okay, doing my walking, my dances and such. Haven't seen you there lately." "No, my dancing has been put on hold, I've been staying home, parenting." "Well, you need more, to get out. To meet someone." "Oh I know, and I was wondering if you might want to come over. I miss your company." "Gee, I don't know. You know I'm seeing Wilma. And, she's a wonderful lady." "Yes, I know, but I only need a friend. You can even sleep over." "Sleep over?" "Alone!" She laughs, "On the couch." "Okay Delphine, I'll think about it and let you know."

And think about it I did, until it was all I was thinking about, until I tired of just thinking about it, and just visualizing those long glorious legs wrapping around me in the throws of passion.

A week later, with Wilma's Sunday otherwise occupied, I call for and accept Delphine's invitation to visit. After taking Delphine and her kids out to dinner, we watch a movie before going to bed. Them, to their separate bedrooms, and me, to the couch.

After stretching out, alone in the dark, I find my guilt to be keeping me awake and prompting me to ask... How would this visit sit with Wilma if she found out about it? But, no foul, no harm, I thought... I'm just visiting a friend, and sleeping on the couch. Alone.

Well, alone lasts until about 5:30 a.m., when I feel a warm body squeezing up against me. And she feels as glorious as imagined. Soon, I'm on her and in her, but only for minutes, when she begins to withdraw by saying, I need to shower. Get ready for work... before the kids get up." Now, just laying there alone, yearning for more of her, I thought... She reminds me of me. Actually, the old me. Get on. Get off. And, get gone.

Besides the guilt accompanying me on the ride home is my desire to hold on to Wilma and our relationship. Again, I ask myself... what happens if she does find out? And find out, she does. But how? Who told her? I did. At least, my stupid conscience did. It wouldn't let me two-time a wonderful caring woman like Wilma. So, after Monday night Bible class, I hit her with it... the truth. "Wilma, I've got something to confess." "Oh Jack, what?" "Well, the long and the short of it is... I screwed up... with Delphine." "Screwed up! You mean you fucked Delphine?" "Yes, I'm afraid so." "When?" "Last night, well actually, this morning. But, only briefly." With tears welling, but with anger soon overriding her anguish, she roars back, "Oh Jack! How could you... do this... do this to me... to us?" "It was stupidity I guess, mine." "Oh Jack! I would have done anything for you... anything." "And you did Wilma, time and time again. Not only did you give me pleasure, but you listened to me... to my darkest thoughts... just listened, never passing judgment." "But, no more... No more." "What do you mean... exactly?" "It means I can't trust you. I married one man like you, and believe me, one is enough... Enough for two lifetimes."

After a six-month relationship, and after our first and our last argument, Wilma and I call it quits. Actually, she did the calling. It was her first and last judgment concerning me.

What now? Stupidity. And, more of it. It keeps taking me back to Delphine's couch where I anxiously await for my sleep to be interrupted by one of her irregular visits and get lucky, if only for a few minutes. Before with Wilma, it was too much of a good thing, and now with Delphine, it's too little. To say I couldn't get my fill of her would be a gross understatement. That is, until I get the call... The wake-up call. "Jack, I'm worried." "Worried... about what?" "My period, I've missed it." "How long now?" "Two weeks, just over two weeks." "Geesums! Why haven't you said anything... before now?" "Well, I didn't want to worry you, unnecessarily."

Well, worry me she did, with my thoughts worrying me back to Wally, and worrying me on to Carolyn and my predicaments then, and possibly, my predicament now... Daddydom. Back to now, trying to console Delphine, I offer, "Try not to worry too much. Rest assured, I'll do the right thing by you." "Oh! I know... I know." "Look, I'll come over Friday, stay over, and we can talk... okay." "Okay, I'll see you Friday."

Doing the right thing, I quickly concluded, would be doing the wrong thing in God's eyes. It would land me in the permanent state of adultery, one that I couldn't retreat from or repent of. Marry and I would be rolling the dice just like Mother did. And after the relationship wears thin, would I, like Mother, be hoping and praying for Delphine to die first, leaving me with enough time to restore my fellowship with God. But those odds are against me. She is 15 years younger, and I'll soon be 55, the age brother Garnett looked into the mirror to find his courage. But, even if the dice favors me, and she died first with her sins still intact, how could I stand there looking at myself in that fucking mirror knowing that my reward, my eternity in heaven, has cost Delphine hers.

After that scare ended with the arrival of her period, with neither of us ever being completely satisfied physically or otherwise, our relationship wanes and dies. During those few return trips to the couch, when Delphine joins me for those quick and irregular encounters, she finds something of value added… a condom.

God works in mysterious ways, it's said, and perhaps that explains the phone call that will prevent the possibility of me backsliding—returning to a state of sin—into the arms of Wilma once again. "Hello Jack, George here." "Hello, what can I do for you?" "Well my good man, would you mind if I call Wilma… ask her out?" "Mind George, hell, I don't have a say in that. Call her. She's a wonderful gal." "Okay then, I will. I'll see you Saturday at the dance. And hopefully, you'll see Wilma on my arm."

Once again, it's Saturday night and once again, I'm back in the big hall, assuming my role as "prayer man" and trying to escape from reality even for a few hours. The reality of a miserable and empty life that's mine. And now, with the sighting of my Wilma being held ever so snugly and so securely in George's warming arms, I'm made even more miserable. Even the loud sounds of Jake and the nifty 50's, coupling with the crowd noise, aren't enough to deafen that reality. That when the music stops, I'm going home alone, again without the pleasure, while good friend George may well be on his way to Wallydom.

While the band is taking a breather, I engage George, a bank examiner for the state and undoubtedly the most positive sounding person that I've ever met, in conversation. And immediately, I attack his positivity with my latest negative-ism. "George, don't you know that… happy, the adjective is, but happiness, the noun, the state of isn't, because happy is the now, period." "Jack! Jack! Jack! You never have a positive thought do you, that's a shame." "George, you just said the secret word." "Yea, what word?" "Shame George, you said shame." "Well, what about it?" "Well, I'm going to write a book about it… well, at least try." "A book about shame… what shame?" "Mine, my shame, the kind that rules and ruins my life from within." "Jesus! If you're talking about the guilt you carry for all the bad stuff you've done, unload it with your pastor, your priest or your shrink, and be done with it. But, write a book?" "But George, I'm not just talking about guilt and the shame attached to it, I'm talking about root shame, innate shame, unearned shame. The born with kind. Like, shame of mother, of father, of home, and the shame of poverty endured there with them." Now, with his face contorting, perhaps out of disbelief or of disgust, or possibly, of both, George fires back. "Come on man! You're not responsible for that. Who your parents were or were not. Man! You're a smart guy, you know that." "And, on the surface I try buying that, believing that, but deep down, down at my roots, I don't. I can't overcome the dread of others knowing what's hidden there. That's the hell of it. And, that's shame's hold over me." "Sorry Jack, but I don't buy that, the kind of shame stuff you're selling and you shouldn't either. Just bury it. And leave it buried." "I've done that. I've kept it buried for over fifty years. But, it ain't dead. It's still very much alive. Still gnawing. Still smothering. Still gobbling up any emergence of joy. Perhaps, now is the time to dig it up, expose it, and see if that will put an end to this joy eater." "If that's your book, I'm not buying it, but I would buy a book about your news exploits, winning the Pulitzer and such. Now, that would be worth while reading." "Well then, you should be pleased, at least, half pleased." "Why?" "Because, it's about both exploits… mine and shame's." "And, do you have a title for this… this book?" "I do George, I do." "Well then, tell me, what is it?" "THE SHAMEHOLD George… THE SHAMEHOLD."

The next day, Sunday afternoon, with Makesense prodding me on, I pick up the pen, impale the beast, and on the purity of white, I begin exposing my shame. Both of 'em. Earned, and unearned. The gnaw and the smother.

The writing begins… The afternoon of August 29th, 1939, Dr. Nathan B. Lewis lumbered down the long corridor of the charity hospital at Vicksburg to take a peek at a black-haired baby boy, one Jack R. Thornell, delivered earlier that day. According to the staff, that was a most unusual occurrence because Dr. Lewis never, never, visited the nursery or so they told the infant's mother. Myrtice Jones Thornell had just had her third son, the first to be born in a hospital, even a charity hospital. She checked into the facility with 50 cents which she quickly put under her pillow. Later that evening she willingly gave it up to her eldest Garnett, who had a yearning to visit a local honeytonk. Some 37 years later, at the age of 55, Garnett took a pistol and blew his brains out. Seems his wife had left him.

It is there, after discovering a fact now in evidence, and before putting the pen down, I sign off with that fact… I can't write. With the sound of the pen dropping, Makesense butts in with, "Write on Cousin, write on, you've just begun." "But why, when my writing ability stinks, really stinks. Who'd read it. Even I can't." "Hold your nose for now, and perhaps with each try, your ability will improve." "And how you figure that?" "Perhaps Cousin, shame weakened is intellect strengthened." "You're suggesting that the more I weaken shame by exposure, the more my writing can improve?" "Yea! That's the ticket. And remember, you don't have to be a great writer, only a good story teller like your mother was. So, pick up the pen, give it another stab, and write on."

Following Makesense's lead, I write on, using the pen to attack and to draw out shame, but shame proves to be a worthy adversary, often counter-attacking by blinding me with tears and drowning me with depression, its most potent weapon. Unearthing those pieces of my past and having to view them again—like the cold corpse of a father finally at peace, whether earned or unearned—I find to be nothing short of torture, and worse now, a self-imposed torture. The time between my attacks and shame's counter stretch on for weeks… for months… for years, without a single word finding the page. And, when I am asked by others, like friend George, "How's the book coming?" More often than not, I reply, "Right now, it's not!" "Oh, you're pausing, just collecting your thoughts?" they add. "No, actually, I'm trying to turn them off." When I do return to the writing, it rules my days and ruins my nights. Awaken by a thought at 2 a.m., it forces me up to write it down, and after I return to bed and before I can get back to sleep another thought pops into my head, with these ups and downs leaving me drained and exhausted. Mentally and physically. Also disturbing and distracting me from the task of trying to write-off shame are other thoughts, negative thoughts, thoughts demanding to be written down.

Thoughts like... the trouble with life is, you never get done with it, until finally, unequivocally, and hopefully suddenly, life gets done with you.

Like... Death! Just the beginning of a new experience, or, the end of all experience?

Like... LIFE AND DEATH put into just three words... UNNENDING EXPECTATIONS ENDED. Explanation: LIFE you argue isn't unending because everyone dies. Yes, but that is called death, not life. So life, while it's called life, is unending. AND are the expectations that come after birth. Expecting to be fed. Expecting to grow up. Expecting to continue on and on with life. DEATH is those expectations coming to an end. Thus the equation: LIFE AND DEATH equals UNENDING EXPECTATIONS ENDED.

Like... Everybody needs a body to lord over, besides their own, naturally.

Negativisms one, negativisms all, my positive friend George would freely point out. And about that, he would be right. "Makesense, your ears up?" "Up Cousin." "These distractions, these negativisms that I'm being bombarded with, could it be a shame tactic to redirect the pen and point it elsewhere?" "Could be Cousin, shame is sly." "So, what'll I do?" "Write on Cousin. Write both if you must. But write on. And, note, not all your isms are negative..."

Like... Happenstance after "the big bang" was all it took to create the universe, science first concluded. But for the universe to emerge and to expand, for life to emerge and to evolve and for everything else—the sun, the moon, the stars, the seasons—to fall into place so perfectly, science later concluded... that in the beginning, it took more than Happenstance, it took Perfect Happenstance.

Like... Oh no! Can you imagine Sundays without our football heroes being idolized down on the field and up on the screen. Starstruck Sundays! Idols idoled! Oh God! Can you imagine who then worthy to draw our praises? Who? God. Who? God. Oh, God. OH GOD! OH YES!

Like...so you want to be God, that's good, that's "a beginning". Say what! Your need to be more, more than you are, isn't unique with you, you know. It's innate and it's God proof too. Say what! Wanting to be God means acknowledging that there is a God to be, means acknowledging that someone like you saw God and wanted to be God too. That's Godproof too. Say what! Well, you know what's written about Adam and about Eve, our God parents in the way back when. You know about their taste for Godhood, you know about their trying for it, and you know about their dying for it. That's Godprrof. And so, if there is a God, and if you believe there is, then, why not act as if there is. Simply said, God is God and Man, you're not. Now, acknowledge that! Oh God! There's something missing here. Now, that's Godsense. That's very good. And that's "The Beginning"... Amen Cousin, and good night." "Night Makesense."

Months into the writing, Jay arrives home from school in Tennessee where he is seeking his Master's degree. The culmination of a promise that if he finishes college in four years, I'd help with the cost of graduate school. He did, with honors. And I honored the contract. And perhaps, prompting the promise more than the love of a father, is shame. The same shame that prevented me from picking up my Pulitzer in person, from being pressed into the same awards hall at Columbia with the highly educated, while all the while, feeling unworthy, totally unworthy, to be partaking of the same air there. So now, when it comes to the question of education, when asked, I want my son's head to be held high, and above most.

Jay knows that I'm writing a book, or at least, trying to, but as yet, he hasn't been exposed to a word of it. He assumes that it is strictly about my news exploits. About shame's, he hasn't a clue.

After dining at Bozo's on his favorite catfish and French fries, we return home, collect ourselves in the den. When the conversation turns to my writing, I ask, "Would you care to read some?" "Sure Dad, let me see it." After delivering a notebook with the first hundred pages, all hand printed in big black letters and not wanting to see his first reaction, I retreat to the back bedroom, stretch out and wait. An hour later, I return to the den and find Jay still reading until he notes my presence, pauses, then asks, "Dad, who's going to publish your book?" Without hesitation, I reply, "Doubleday." "Gee that's great. Who'd you talk to there?" "No one. Not a solitary soul." "Dad you're losing me. Why did you say 'Doubleday' when you haven't contacted them?" "Because of a dream. A long ago dream. Not a daydream, but a lay down and go to sleep dream. And, in that dream, I could see a book, at least, a portion of a book. And, on the cover, I could read by Jack R. Thornell. And, at the bottom of the binder I could read Doubleday. But, as hard as I tried, I couldn't see the title." "And why do you think that was?" "I don't think Jay, I know." "Know what?" "I couldn't recognize my shame then, not even in my own dreams." "Wow!" Jay exclaimed before returning to his reading.

A few weeks later, Candy calls and that's unusual, because since she married Mike we rarely talk on the phone, and in person, even less. "Hell Dad, I've got some news for you." "Good or bad?" "It's bad, real bad." "Well, let's hear it." "Bill Crider is dying… over at Cannon Hospice." "Jesus! I'm sorry, so sorry to hear that. Cancer I presume?" "Yes. You know he talked about you. About your exploits together. He laughed about the constable carroll episode up at Grenda." "And, about my pouring out of his only bottle of Jack Daniels in a dry county." "Yea, that too. And, you know what else he said about you… about my dad?" "No, tell me." "He said, you were one of the best news photographers he'd ever worked with. Then hesitating, and correcting himself, he said no Candy, your dad was the best, the absolute best." "That was nice of him to say, real nice." "Yes it was, and he'd like to see you. But, you'd better not wait too long to go." "Okay Candy, thanks for calling." But, wait I did. I couldn't bring myself to face the best friend I'd ever made in the news business, and relive those experiences. Not in person. Not when just writing about those was already weighing on me, exacting its toll. A heavy toll. Too heavy to bear, I felt, for much longer.

"Makesense, are your ears up?" "Up Cousin." "Can you fathom anything, anything more humiliating than being remembered as the best… the best of the has beens?" "Perhaps Cousin." "Perhaps what?" "Not being remembered at all. You know what Ben Franklin said on the subject?" "No, what did ole Ben say?" "He said, "If you would not be forgotten, as soon as you are dead and rotten, either write things worth reading, or do things worth the writing." "Well, I sure hope one thing." "And, what is that?" "That ole Ben's writing came easier than mine."

While examining pieces of my past, while experiencing the emptiness of my present and while finding that my depression is seeking new highs and my self-esteem new lows, I look into the mirror for a solution, a permanent solution. But, I know I can't find it there. Not with my

Beretta gone. Not even if Garnett's courage was to suddenly appear. Since beginning silence with a bang is off the table, I must look elsewhere. And I do. In the kitchen cabinet, I find a trash bag. The heavy duty kind. And, I take it to bed. There, I put it over my head. I gather it in. I tie it tightly. I lie back. I cross my ankles just like my friend Johnny had done while experiencing the good death. And instinctively, I fold my arms to form a cross over my chest, just as I have done since my youth, since the night Crazy Uncle John came calling. And, had it not been for that stupid prayer, that promise, that plea—Please God, take away these blades, let me live and I will become a preacher man, your preacher man—back then, I wouldn't be here now to face this end, emptied and alone. Now, all that is left for me to do is for me to nod off before the air is gone, and sleep on. Laying there in the dark, my only wish is to be free, free of this thing called… life. Suddenly, flashing in my head like a neon sign is a negativism that I had written recently. Redundant! Redundant! Redundant! Life is, until facing the alternative, and contemplating the eternal redundancy of it. Despite those words, I'm convinced that if peaceful, dream-free sleep without the threat of a rude awakening to face more of the same is all there is, then, I'm ready, more than ready, to share in that eternal redundancy. But, before I can begin, "Butt-Butt" sounds, "Cousin! Get a grip. Examine the irony here. All your life, shame has been smothering you, and now, you chose this way, shame's way, to end it." "Makesense please! Let me go." "But Cousin, remember, whether thou goest Makesense goest too." "Makesense, please, please, butt out." "No! And besides you haven't paid for the right." "Right? Right for what?" "To be a baghead. Only the Saints fans have. To show their disgust for having to watch their beloved team lose another game. And, since you never bought a ticket, you can't be a baghead too. So, take it off." "Okay! Okay! If you'll cut the comedy, I will, I will, I'll take the stupid bag off." "Enough said Cousin, enough said." "Except for something Mrs. Bounds of my Joy Theatre days would add." "And, what is that?" "Makesense! Makesense! A comedian, you're not."

The new millennium is arriving and I'm still here, stuck in redundancy, and preparing to make my last appearance as the prayer man at St. Clement's Christmas dance. It's time, I decided, for a new face to take my place and for a new voice to override the crowd noise. Or, at least, try. So now, I seek a second opinion of the words I have written. "Makesense, care to listen?" Listening Cousin, read on." "Almighty God! Dear Father. This Christmas Day as we gather around the tree to share gifts with family and with friends, let us all take pause to remember the greatest gift of all, by remembering… the birth of The Christmas Child. By remembering… the life of The Prince of Peace. By remembering the death of The King of Kings. And by remembering… the resurrection of The Savior, your gift to us Father, your son, our hope, and the greatest gift of all… Jesus Christ The Lord. Well, Makesense, what do you say?" "Well Cousin, Makesense says… Amen and amen."

Three years have passed since Makesense butted in, denying me the right to become a baghead, a serious baghead. As always, managing to win out over any of my rebuttals. Always managing to keep me in the present tense, in the here and now.

Now, with my brain drained and my pen dry, now is the time to summon Makesense for a showdown over this unending Shame War. And I do. "Makesense! You said, pick up the pen, and I did, again and again. And I, not shame, felt pain, and bled tears, again and again." "True Cousin, but with each re-stabbing, with each re-writing, with each re-telling to friends and lovers, wasn't your lagniappe less pain and fewer tears. And couldn't you feel the shamehold weakening?" "True, but now, I'm left here emptied and without the strength to even pick up a pen again." "And that's because, there's no need to." "And, why not?" "Because your war with shame is over." "Over! For Christ's sake then, tell me please, who won?" "You Cousin, you won. You found and fulfilled your purpose, without even knowing it." "Hell! And I still don't know it. This purpose, what was it?" "To live this life… to survive the Shame War… to live to write about it… and finally, to put it in a book as a guide for others at war with shame to follow. Expelling and exposing their shame as you have done, until "the gnaw" and "the smother" are made impotent. And powerless over you." "Jesus! If that's true, where do I find my happy ending for this life, for this book?" "By looking within. What did positive George tell you about this elusive happiness?" "He said, if I wasn't happy, it was my own damn fault, because happiness comes from within." "True, but then, you didn't have room for happiness because shame held that space. But now you do. With shame evicted, in that empty space, you can plant the seeds of happiness, nourish them and watch them sprout and how. For all to see, even you. Look, look at you. You've been successful as a ticket taker, a student, a soldier, a photographer, a Mr. Mom, and a saver. And, you've got twice the money you had before the divorce split. So, you should be doubly happy about that." "I know! I know! But still, I don't feel worthy, truly worthy to be happy. So what do I do, what can I do, to find, to recognize this happiness?" "Well Cousin, you got to look within again, but before you do, you must embrace a truth, a truth you've ignored for all of your life. And then, you must embrace thyself." "And pray tell, where do I find this truth?" "In the book you hold so near and so dear. The one you tote to Bible Class twice a week." "Pray tell, what is it, this truth?" "Actually, it's more than a truth, it's a commandment, Christ's second." "And…" "It's… Love thy neighbor as thyself. And, it's the love of thyself that you have ignored, have failed to recognize." "Love myself. Jesus! I don't even like myself. Let alone, love. Hell! I've never felt worthy enough to own either." "But now, with shame gone, expelled, exposed, and trapped on the purity of white, you can be happy. You can, you can, you can. At least, try." "Oh Makesense, you've got me teetering. Seesawing between worthy and unworthy. But, it won't end, won't let me fall one way or the other. Perhaps, you can settle it, can put an end to it, this teetering." "How Cousin, just tell Makesense how?" "By picking up the pen, well, at least, by directing my hand to write a story, fact, fiction or fantasy, even a combination of all three, I don't care, but in the writing reveal a truth so powerful that it will finally shake me loose, completely loose, from shame's hold and end all lingering doubts of my worthiness, doubts when magnified by shame become my reality. Then perhaps, I can plant the precious seeds of happiness." "As you wish Cousin. Fact, fiction or fantasy, it will be, or perhaps, the sum of all three." "Well then Makesense, my pen and my hand are yours. Write on."

Once upon a sunny bright Sunday, while enroute to the mile high city for a convention of higher-ups, Gabrielle looks down, sees the blue grass that's Kentucky and says, "Michael, let's stop here, spell our wings and absorb all this great beauty." In agreement, Michael directs, "There, that yellow brick church, let's alight there and find rest on its steps." The pair with the uncanny ability to take on any shape or form, are usually unseen, unless deemed otherwise by The Most High, to deliver a particular message to humankind. Today is just a travel day, so unseen, is the agenda.

Once grounded, Michael notes, "It's hot today, particularly hot for humankind, hot enough to encourage any hesitant, but sensible soul, particularly the lovers of air conditioning, to be good and do better, wouldn't you say Gabrielle?" Smiling, but knowing full well that judgment isn't in the realm of her expertise, doesn't say, but after looking up at the three storied building, does say, "The church structure seems a bit oversized for the rather small town of Paris. Perhaps, it was overbuilt in the beginning to remedy aforetime the growing pains to hopefully come later. But unfortunately, sometimes, even in the fields of our Lord, growth is slow, tryingly slow."

But inside, before a mere crowd of sixty, the preacher is trying, trying to please God, and praying in his heart that his message today is God's message too.

Soon, the sounding of his voice, "Almighty God, dear Father, we humble our heads and hearts today praising you as our beloved Creator, while thanking you for your mercy and your grace," is heard. The voice, not sounding spurious or counterfeit, is strong and clear and blessed with a maturity beyond its years, and is now, reverberating through the auditorium before escaping outside and capturing Gabrielle's ear. An expert on judgment, she is not, but an expert on voices she is, remembering them and connecting them to the time and the place she first heard them, even if she only heard them once. But so is Michael, and much to her dismay, she has never stumped him, when putting him to the test of identifying voices. Until perhaps, today. And let's say, when it comes to competition, she is no angel. After turning his way, she says, Michael, listen to that voice leaking out around the door, and tell me if it's familiar?" Seconds pass, the preacher's voice strengthens, Michael listens, but withholds his answer. Now, filling with excitement, and thinking she has finally stumped the unstumpable, the quizzing begins.

"Remember the terrible thunderstorm. Remember the old house, the attic, we took refuge in. Remember the peephole we shared with Esnesekam, our charge, who we were escorting to the city of brotherly love to be fitted with his crowning glory... The Golden Wings. Before taking up the position as "His Guardianship" and be stationed at the left hand of "The Most High". And in rank and privilege there, a status second only to "The Son". And after a thousand years, finally done with the daily grind of dealing with humankind and their frailties. And now for "His Guardianship", where frailties are no more, only ease and glory awaits."

With Michael still silent, Gabrielle continues, "Remember the crazed man... remember the raised hand. Remember the scissors in them. Remember the lad lying innocently below like a kid set for slaughter. Remember how Esnesekam shot through the peephole like a bullet, landing on the lad's chest and folding up there like a blanket before the thrust struck. Remember the lad opening his eyes and thinking the scissors stood on him and not on Esnesekam. Remember the plea and the promise... to live and to be a preacher man. Remember how we arrived at our destination without our charge because Esnesekam chose to stay on with the lad, and how we expected to catch hell for our failure. There, while facing only the backside of The Most High, with our voices breaking and our bodies shaking, we explained just how we lost Esneskam. With the reporting done, remember how The Most High turned to face us, but instead of anger, we felt the brightness of glory reaching out, consoling us, comforting us, and erasing all concerns. Seemingly, not in the least surprised by Esnesekam's choice, with a soft and soothing voice The Most High spoke. "Michael, Gabrielle, with your report I Am well pleased. Go. Join the others in the great hall. Refresh yourselves and tell all of Esnesekam's choice. Then, shout his name and sing his praises. For indeed, he is worthy. Truly worthy."

Finished with the remembering, while thinking that a mere cherub has finally topped one of the highest of seraphim at any contest, and unable to contain her excitement over her conclusion any longer, reaches down, pulls up the still silent Michael and says, "Come, let's go inside. Let's see the lad grown up."

Once there her eyes race to the front of the church, up to the pulpit, then focus and fasten on the face behind it. There, disappointment sets in. "Oh oooh, it's not him," she relates to Michael, "It can't be. He's too young, far too young. Only in his 20's. The lad by now, would be 50-ish. Oh oooh, but I can't get over it, the voices, the lad's and the preacher's, they are identical."

Now, touched by her sighs, Michael breaks his silence. "True, it's not him, but, it is the son fulfilling the promise of the father. The one, because of shame, even the son was unaware of." "Oh oooh Michael, the story, the story we shared a part in, is so marvelous to hear. Oh oooh, listen to the young preacher's voice, so powerful, and yet, so loving, so clear. And listen to his message, it's music to my ears. Clearly, it's God's message too. And so marvelous, even we take pause to hear. Come, let's sit awhile. Let's fill ourselves with the fruits of labor."

With Makesense's story ringing loudly in my ears, I butt in. "Oh Makesense! Oh Esnesekam! Oh your guardianship! Oh your worthiness! Whom ever. Whichever. Oh! Oh! Oh! You're my guardian angel come late, but one with impeccable timing. You gave up your all for me, even your golden wings. The son of The Most High gave up his all for the whole wide world to share, but you, you gave up yours for me, just me, just an undernourished kid unschooled on life or in religion."

"Fact, fiction, or fantasy, Makesense will never tell, but the undeniable truth, Makesense will." "And what is it, this truth, I need to hear?" "Cousin it's… Makesense loves you. And loved you, even before our first hello." "Oh Makesense! And, I love you. You are the best part of me. The better half. The worthy half." "So then, if Makesense loves you and you love Makesense, and now, with love flowing inward and outward, do you know what the sum of all this means?" "Oh Makesense, you know I'm good at math." "And…?" "And, it means two halves make a whole." "And…?" "It means…" "Say it Cousin, say it." "It means…I…I…I…I love me too." "Touché! Touché Cousin. And thus, let the love of thyself begin today."

With Makesense's mindboggling story still stirring me, particularly of Esnesekam's choice, proving that all life is precious, even mine, suddenly, the pen drops, and by instinct, I pick it up again, restore it to the writing position and squeeze. And then, a zealous tingling sensation at my fingertips begins, and continues, radiating into the hand, up the arm, over the shoulder, through the neck and exploding into the SHAMEHOLD. There, allowing the marvelous rays of enlightenment to flood in and to flush out any remains of shame, the stored-up kind. The kind held down deep, deep at the root.

Now, my mind's eye flashes back to 503, sees a seal door kicked wide, and hears the rousing sighs of relief from those troubled souls long trapped up there above the sawed-off stairs. And, in their midst, I see a face, a familiar face, oh oooh, I see the face of me being set free… From Behind A Door Nailed Shut.

Now smiling, with the feel of Makesense easing over and making room for Makepeace to ease in, and with all doubts of my worthiness to live, to love, and to be happy, now ended, I know! I know! From my head to my hand that… THE SHAMEHOLD IS BROKEN. Broken for today. Broken for all of my tomorrows.

And now, in my book, I count shame—the gnaw, the smother, the joyeater—as dead. And, just as dead as that blood sucking Dracula is when exposed to the light of day.

With my spirit soaring, I want to cry… Attention! Attention! All grounded Shamebirds, look up and gawk, gawk one last time, for this shame-free son of Myrtis and Ben is gonna step off the page, gonna fly, gonna soar to new heights not imagined.

Suddenly a voice rains down. It's a familiar voice, so familiar. It's, it's, it's saying, "Young man! Young man! A writer you're not." Now, with a joy, a joy like I've never felt before, erupting from the depths of my being, welling upward and exploding into laughter, a laughter growing louder and louder, there's only breath enough for managing a whisper… Amen Mrs. Bounds… Amen.

THE END.

www.ingramcontent.com/pod-product-compliance
Lightning Source LLC
Chambersburg PA
CBHW081433170526
45166CB00008B/2195